IMPROVING COMMUNICATION—

A skills-oriented text for teaching students what they need to become competent communication senders and receivers

Clear and effective pedagogy focuses on improving communication skills.

ENCODING

Getting back to our example, once Jack decides (consciously or not) to send a message to Jill, the next step in our slow-motion description is for Jack to *encode* a message. **Encoding** is the cognitive process of transforming a thought (idea, concept, feelings, opinion, etc.) into a message (oral, written, or otherwise). In simple terms, encoding is everything that goes on inside Jack's head from the moment he decides to address Jill to the moment his message is produced.

The encoding process is so complex that psycholinguists who have studied it for decades still don't completely understand how encoding happens. At the very least, Jack has to select appropriate words from a vast mental storehouse of possibilities; then he has to decide which of several viable grammatical constructions to employ; and then he has to coordinate his lungs, vocal cords, jaw, tongue, and lips to speak the constructed phrase. And all of this happens within a matter of milliseconds!

This book will not deal with the psycholinguistic details of how encoding occurs. We will, however, emphasize the importance of planning and encoding messages *carefully*—that is, the importance of thinking before speaking. For public-speaking situations, planning the message takes many hours; for interpersonal situations, many common

● T R Y   T H I S

To get an idea of how quickly the mind makes encoding decisions, try to think of all the different ways in which Jack could have said essentially the same thing. Try this for each of the possible goals you can imagine he might have had for the French-fries message. See Figure 1.3, for example.

Try This exercises ask students to stop, think, and respond actively to text material in a practical, nonthreatening way.

MODES—VERBAL AND NONVERBAL

Jack's "These French fries are bland" message is his attempt to represent his thoughts and/or to accomplish his goal via symbols—**verbal** symbols, or *words*, in this case. If he had wanted to, he could have attempted to communicate the same meaning with **nonverbal** (nonword) symbols. To simply express his displeasure with the French fries, he could have pushed them away with contemptuous flair; if he wanted Jill to pass the salt, he could have pointed back and forth to the salt shaker and to himself; and so on for other communicative goals.

We have said that meaning is carried by symbols and symptoms, and we have said that messages may be verbal or nonverbal. As for how these concepts combine, *words* are *symbols*, not symptoms. (There may be rare exceptions. Some would say, for example, that the oath you utter when you accidentally hit your thumb with a hammer is a symptom rather than a symbol, but many would disagree. In any case, words are usually symbols.) Nonverbal behaviors, however, are split. Some are symbols, and others are symptoms. More specifically, behaviors instigated by communicative intention are symbols. Behaviors *without* communicative intention may carry meaning as symptoms. An obscene gesture is clearly a symbol; a stomach growl is clearly a symptom. An intentional frown—say, to get a child to stop doing something displeasing—is a symbol; a natural frown, especially when we don't even know anyone is watching, is usually a symptom. And so forth. This means that people

Note Card feature provides checklist summaries of the key aspects of communication skills discussed in the surrounding section of the text.

The Message (in a typical communication situation)

- ✓ Consists of symbols
- ✓ Is either verbal or nonverbal
- ✓ Is transmitted vocally or nonvocally
- ✓ Will be interpreted

Unparalleled sections from one of the most respected authors in public speaking include sample speeches.

Sample Informative SPEECH

WARMING OUR WORLD AND CHILLING OUR FUTURE

When Mark Twain was in London in 1897, a rumor reached the editor of the *New York Journal*, who immediately wired his London correspondent: "HEAR MARK TWAIN DIED, SEND 1000 WORDS." The correspondent showed the telegram to Twain, who sent back this message: "REPORT OF MY DEATH GREATLY EXAGGERATED." This response applies to my speech topic today. Despite the efforts of some to write its obituary, and to erase it from the public's agenda, the greenhouse effect is a growing, not a declining, problem. The reports of its death have been greatly exaggerated.

Almost twenty years ago, environmentalists urged scientists to look to Antarctica for signs of what they called the "greenhouse effect"—the gradual warming of the earth because of human activity. During the winter of 1995, *Time* magazine reported that a gigantic iceberg—23 miles wide and 48 miles long, almost as large as the state of Rhode Island—broke off the Larsen Ice Shelf in the Antarctic Peninsula. During the winter of 1997, new large crevasses were found in the shelf. These suggest that the rest of the shelf is ready to break loose. Do these things signal the arrival of full-scale global warming? It may be. And because of the greenhouse effect catching up with us? It may be. And because of

Note how source citations become oral footnotes woven into the text of the message. These oral footnotes make the speech authoritative and strengthen the speaker's credibility.

Five appendices—including one on *interviewing skills*, by Suzanne Osborn, and another on *overcoming anxiety*, by Michael T. Motley—reflect the widely respected work of the text authors, who are both researchers and practitioners.

Our strong and diverse ancillary package includes:

- *Instructor's Resource Manual with Test Items*
- Speech Preparation Workbook
- *Multicultural Activities for the Speech Communication Classroom*
- *Overcoming Your Fear of Public Speaking*
- Computerized Test Bank for Windows or Mac
- Speech Designer Software for Windows or Mac
- *Contemporary Great Speeches Video Volume XI*
- *PowerPoint* Slides on the Houghton Mifflin web site
- *ESL Teaching Guide* on the Houghton Mifflin web site
- Student Speeches Video

Improving Communication

Improving Communication

Suzanne Osborn

University of Memphis

Michael T. Motley

University of California, Davis

Houghton Mifflin Company   **Boston**   **New York**

Senior Sponsoring Editor: **George Hoffman**

Assistant Editor: **Jennifer Wall**

Project Editor: **Rachel D'Angelo Wimberly**

Senior Production/Design Coordinator: **Jennifer Waddell**

Senior Manufacturing Coordinator: **Marie Barnes**

Marketing Manager: **Pamela J. Laskey**

Marketing Associate: **Jean Zielinski DeMayo**

Cover design: **Nina Wishnok**

Cover image: **Nola Lopez/Graphistock**

Printed in the U.S.A.

Library of Congress Catalog Card Number: 96-76944

ISBN: 0-395-63206-4

1 2 3 4 5 6 7 8 9—DOC—02 01 00 99 98

The Improvement of Communication

S. O.   M. M.

FUNDAMENTALS

3 NONVERBAL BEHAVIOR — 48

4 DEvElOPING YOUR LiSTENING SkILLS _____ 70

PART

TWO

INTERPERSONAL AND SMALL- GROUP SETTINGS

5 THE SELF—PeRSONAL AND InTERPERsONAL PERCePTIONS _____ 88

PART

THREE

PUBLIC SETTINGS

9 PRINCIPLES OF PUBLIC COMMUNICATION _____ 176

10 MESSAGE PREPARATION _____ 199

11 SUPPORTING MATERIALS   224

12 ORGANIZING AND OUTLINING YOUR SPEECH _____ 249

13 PRESENTING YOUR SPEECH _____ 274

PReFaCE

Sharing our thoughts, feelings, opinions, and knowledge is crucial to our relationships and interactions—whether we are communicating with friends, family, lovers, colleagues, clients, acquaintances, or even strangers. This in itself does not necessarily justify a course or a book on improving communication, however. The vast majority of our day-to-day communication with friends, loved ones, acquaintances, and so forth is, after all, neither difficult nor particularly in need of serious improvement. Most of us do a decent job with most of our communication.

There are those occasions, however, when communication is problematic. Sometimes we realize after a communication episode (or series of them) that misunderstanding, ill will, or some other unanticipated and unwanted outcome has occurred. Sometimes we realize in advance that an impending communication encounter may be difficult. Certainly this is the case for most public-speaking engagements. It applies also to various interpersonal dilemmas in which we find ourselves wondering whether and how to tell someone something that will be difficult for us to say and/or difficult for the other person to hear. And there are also those times when we are thrown into a difficult communication situation with no advance warning—as when we are unexpectedly asked to deliver a speech, when we experience an unexpected conflict, when we are asked by a friend how we like her new hair style (when we think it looks awful), and many more.

Problematic communication situations constitute a relatively small fraction of our total communication experience. But they are common enough to concern most of us. And very often they are crucial when they occur. Virtually all of us find ourselves wishing from time to time that we had handled a certain situation better than we did, or wishing we knew how to best handle one that we anticipate. Obviously, it is within these problematic communication situations—both public and interpersonal—that we have the most room for improvement.

Thus we have oriented this book toward improving communication in situations that many communicators find to be difficult. Virtually all of the information we present is aimed at increasing the potential for our communication encounters to have mutually satisfying and successful outcomes. Sometimes the information applies across the board to most any communication situation. Other times the information is more situation-specific. We have especially tried to highlight communication situations that most young adults find to be particularly problematic.

No doubt, both the instructor and students will personally identify with the difficulty found in some of these situations but not in others. For example, whereas most adults need advice on how to effectively prepare and deliver a speech, some readers will be among the very few who do not. While most communicators welcome advice on dealing with conflict, some readers will be among those rare individuals who already handle conflict to the complete mutual satisfaction of all parties. While most young adults fret over sharing feelings about a relationship during its early stages, some students will be among the few for whom this is not a problem. And so on. In other words, it may well be that a few of the communication dilemmas we discuss are not dilemmas for all individual readers. (The information should be valuable to one's understanding of other people, nevertheless.) But most likely there will be plenty of situations we discuss for which virtually any reader can recognize his or her own "room for improvement." Recognizing the areas in which there is room for improvement is an important key to getting the most out of this book. In those areas where our readers recognize their room for improvement, it is our hope and our belief that the information we have provided will be of considerable practical value.

PLAN OF THE BOOK

The book is both logical and flexible. While there is a natural progression to the organization we have provided, there is little to preclude assigning or reading the chapters in a different sequence. We begin with an overview of the fundamentals of communication, then move to communication in interpersonal and small-group settings, and then move to public communication.

Part One, "Fundamentals," provides basic information that students need in order to understand the communication process. Chapter One highlights the basic communication components and characteristics such as meaning, feedback, encoding, context, and others. The chapter also previews ways in which misunderstanding and other communication difficulties can occur. Chapter Two provides a brief introduction to language components and characteristics. It emphasizes message-related communication barriers such as ambiguity, indirect messages, emotional loading, classification, stereotyping, prediction, and closure. This chapter also contains a section on the most common language (grammatical) errors. Chapter Three focuses on nonverbal behavior with a slant toward dispelling myths. Topics covered include kinesics, proxemics, vocalics, chronemics, haptics, physical appearance, and intercultural variations. Chapter Four, on critical and constructive listening, identifies common listening problems and explores ways to overcome these problems, helping students to sharpen their critical listening skills.

Part Two, "Interpersonal and Small-Group Settings," begins with consideration of the self. Chapter Five focuses on self-perceptions and others' perceptions of us. It includes discussions of emotional maturity, self-concept, and self-esteem, and focuses especially on self-acceptance and self-awareness via an expanded section on personality. Discussion also includes communication avoidance and nonavoidance in interpersonal contexts. Chapter Six focuses on interpersonal relationships such as those we engage in with friends and "significant others." It covers relationship stages, common relationship problems, relationship repair, and relationship maintenance. Chapter Seven highlights interpersonal communication dilemmas such as those arising from cultural differences, gender differences, conflict, deception, tactlessness, and problems with assertiveness. Chapter Eight discusses group communication processes, introducing students to group problem-solving processes and the responsibilities of group members. It provides guidelines for managing informal and formal meetings and introduces students to the basic concepts of parliamentary procedure.

Part Three, "Public Settings," begins with an introduction to some of the basic tenets of public communication. Chapter Nine covers the various types and functions of public communication as well as the influence of mass media on public communication. Chapter Ten provides a guide to topic selection, information on audience analysis, and information on acquiring responsible knowledge from libraries, the Internet, and interviews. Chapter Eleven covers the use of supporting materials such as facts and figures, testimony, examples, narratives and visual aids. Chapter Twelve provides guidelines for determining and arranging the main points of a speech, preparing introductions and conclusions, and outlining a message. In Chapter

Thirteen we cover oral language, types of presentations, handling questions and answers, making video presentations, and using the voice and body to communicate more effectively. Chapter Fourteen discusses the functions of informative presentations, the basics of audience motivation and attention, types of informative speeches and their designs. Chapter Fifteen covers the functions of persuasive speaking, the process of persuasion, the challenges to effective persuasion (including an extensive section on the ethics of persuasion), the development of good rationales and sound reasoning, the types of persuasive speeches, and their designs.

The text also contains five appendices. The first, on library and Internet resources for research, provides a rich array of print and web site sources. An appendix on interviewing concentrates on how to best prepare and participate in job interviews. An appendix of MBTI (Meyers-Briggs) personality profiles is provided as an accompaniment to Chapter Five. An appendix on public-speaking anxiety goes well beyond mere description of the phenomenon to provide pragmatic information designed to be of value in reducing students' anxiety. Finally we have included an appendix of four student speeches, two informative and two persuasive, for further study and analysis.

LEARNING TOOLS

We believe the best pedagogical tools for learning are often the simplest; that is, they do not get in the way of meaning. We have tried to do this in our writing and in our features. Integrated throughout the text where appropriate are "Try This" exercises that ask the student to stop and think and to sometimes respond to what we have just covered in the text. Our aim is to engage the student in a critical-thinking exercise that serves to make the reading and learning experience more interactive. We also include throughout the text a "Note Card" feature that provides internal-summary checklists of the key concepts discussed in the previous section of text. Finally, every chapter contains chapter objectives, In Summary, and Terms to Know sections.

SUPPLEMENTAL MATERIALS

The publisher has made available a large assortment of ancillaries that should prove helpful to both the instructor and student. Please contact your Houghton Mifflin sales representative for information on the following:

For the Professor:

Instructor's Resource Manual with Test Items
Computerized Test Bank (Windows and Macintosh)
PowerPoint slides on the Houghton Mifflin web site
ESL Teaching Guide on the Houghton Mifflin web site
Contemporary Great Speeches Video Volume XI
Student Speeches Video

For the Student:

Overcoming Your Fear of Public Speaking
Multicultural Activities for the Speech Communication Classroom
Speech Preparation Workbook
Speech Designer Software

ACKNOWLEDGMENTS

The authors and publisher are indebted to a number of people who have helped in one way or another during the production of this book.

Suzanne Osborn wishes to thank her public speaking students at the University of Memphis, University of California at Davis, Indiana University, Vanderbilt University, and the University of New Mexico for providing a laboratory for her ideas and techniques. Michael Motley wishes in particular to thank the management and staff of Mocha Joe's (Davis, California) for allowing him, for endless hours, to use their wonderful establishment and perfect work environment as a "second office" to write and write and write. Together, the authors wish to thank the team at Houghton Mifflin, especially those who assisted us most directly: George Hoffman, Jennifer Wall, Rachel D'Angelo Wimberly, Elisa Adams, Tezeta Tulloch, Jennifer Waddell, and Marie Barnes.

We also wish to thank the following reviewers for their many helpful suggestions: Joel C. Passey, Weber State University; Roynda Bowen Storey, Richland College; Kristi Schaller, George State University; Thomas E. Ruddick, Edison Community College; Sarah S. King, Central Connecticut State University; Virginia Chapman, Anderson University; Theo Ross, Northwest Missouri State University; Rob B. Vogel, Spokane Community College; Robert Dixon, St. Louis Community College at Meramec; Patti Cutspec, Western Carolina University, Carol Lynn Thompson, University of Arkansas at Little Rock; Marilyn J. Hoffs, Glendale Community College; Carolyn Lee Karmon, Washburn University.

Suzanne Osborn
Michael T. Motley

Improving Communication

ONE

FUNDAMENTALS

CHAPTER ONE

COMMUNICATION—
BACKGROUND
CONCEPTS

THIS CHAPTER

will help you

- Appreciate the reasons to study communication

- See how communication difficulties can occur

- Begin to understand communicators' responsibilities

- Understand the objectives of this book

YOU'RE TELLIN' ME YOU **MEANT**
WHAT YOU **SAID**, but I'm tellin' you
YOU MEANT WHAT I **HEARD**.

—F. Richards

I t is almost a cliché to say that we live in a "world of communication," that this is an "age of communication," that we are in the midst of a "communication revolution," and the like. It is fairly obvious that communication is central to our lives, our relationships, and our culture. Nevertheless, some students, perhaps yourself included, will look at the topics covered in this book and wonder why it is necessary to *study* this information. "After all," you may say, "I've been communicating my whole life, and I never needed lessons before, so why do I need to learn about communication now?"

WHY STUDY COMMUNICATION?

It is true that we all have many years' experience as communicators, and that each of us communicates successfully every day, using common sense that we have acquired without formal instruction in communication. But it is also true that we all experience occasional communication breakdowns, dilemmas, frustrations, and difficulties. And these communication difficulties often occur within situations and relationships that are terribly important to us. For example, you can probably think of at least one or two communication dilemmas that you are experiencing now or have experienced recently. And perhaps there are a few that you experience over and over. Despite our experience and common sense, we sometimes find ourselves wondering *whether* to tell someone what is on our mind, or *how* to say something without causing problems, or *what* to say in delicate, unique, or otherwise problematic communication situations. These may represent only a small fraction of our total communication encounters, but they can be of major consequence in our lives.

There are three common answers to the question, "Why study communication?" One is simply that it is interesting. Many of us find it fascinating to take a behind-the-scenes look at how we humans operate, and at what "makes us tick" in even the most ordinary communication situations. Another answer is that gaining formal knowledge about communication is simply part of becoming an educated adult. Communication is all around us, and there is much more to it than meets the eye, so at least a basic understanding of communication is an essential part of knowing about our world. The third answer, and perhaps the most important one, is that the study of communication can help us to deal with the crucial communication dilemmas that we occasionally face in our everyday lives.

This book will target all three objectives of studying communication. But where it is possible to do so, we will focus especially on the third goal by offering information designed to help you in problematic situations. We will examine some of the problems encountered when communicating with large groups (as in public speeches), small groups (as in committees and business meetings), and individuals (friends, roommates, significant others, family members, and so forth). It is important that you realize from the beginning that these situations are not as different as they may appear, since most of the principles for effective communication apply to both public-speaking and interpersonal (small-group and one-on-one) contexts.

Sometimes we know what we want to say, but have difficulty finding the best way to say it. And a wrong decision can have consequences. For example, how should the woman pictured here tell her fiancé that she wants to break up their relationship?

COMMUNICATION DEFINITIONS AND CONDITIONS

It makes sense to begin the study of communication with "the big picture," and it makes sense to introduce the big picture by defining communication. It is easy to produce a definition of communication. It is practically impossible, however, to produce one with which everyone will agree.

Communication scholars have suggested dozens of definitions for communication.[1] Most of the various definitions agree at least that *communication is a process in which meaning is assigned to a "message" behavior or event.* Unfortunately, this common-denominator definition, by itself, doesn't really tell us very much. It is so broad that it includes all kinds of elements that some scholars would prefer to include and others would prefer to exclude.

Many definitions of communication add specific conditions to this common denominator. The tremendous variation among definitions comes from differences of opinion as to what these conditions should be. In other words, we could summarize most of the various definitions of communication as something like this: "Communication is a process in which meaning is attributed to a message, where conditions required of the sender include [*conditions vary*], conditions required of the receiver include [*conditions vary*], and conditions required of the message include [*conditions vary*]."

This may seem overly picky. However, although you probably don't realize it, you already have your *own* list of conditions that form your *own* definition of communication. Do the accompanying Try This exercise for example.

TRY THIS

You can see the conditions within your own definition of communication by answering questions such as those in Figure 1.1, comparing your answers with those of classmates, and then discussing your answers to discover what conditions are being required by some people but not by others.[2] Figure 1.2 gives a summary of how these discussions usually work out.

COMPONENTS IN A TYPICAL COMMUNICATION SITUATION

For an introductory discussion such as this one, it is not necessary to determine which conditions must be present in *all* communication situations. But we do want to introduce some of the conditions that are present in *typical* communication situations. Let's take an event that almost anyone would agree is an example of communication, and go through it in slow motion: Imagine that Jack and Jill are having lunch and Jack says, "Gosh, these French fries are bland."

THE SENDER—COMMUNICATIVE INTENTION

Even a simple statement like "These French fries are bland" can be more complex than it seems. Can you think of other simple statements that would be natural in this setting, yet subject to misinterpretation regarding meaning or motives?

First, a thought (opinion, idea, concept, impression, etc.) occurs to Jack. He may or may not decide to express it or share it, but in our example he does. The decision to express one's thoughts—that is, the decision to produce a message for someone else to interpret—is called a **communicative intention.** The reason or motive for the decision to communicate—what it is that one is trying to accomplish—is called the **communication goal.** Sometimes we are very conscious of our communicative intentions and goals; other times we are not.[3]

Whether intention is required of *all* communication is a fairly controversial issue among communication scholars. Imagine, for example, that Jill's stomach growls, that Jack hears it, and that he correctly concludes that she is hungry. Obviously, there is no communicative intention here, because the stomach growl was not a behavior that Jill decided to perform for a receiver. Many would claim that since there is no communicative intention, this is not communication.[4]

You Classmates   Answer Yes or No

___ ___   1. If you read and understand something written several centuries ago, is this communication?

___ ___   2. Can an inanimate object (clouds, an ocean, etc.) communicate to a person?

___ ___   3. If you send a letter to someone who receives it, but misunderstands what you meant by it, is this communication?

___ ___   4. If you send a letter to someone who never receives it, but someone else reads and understands it, is that communication?

___ ___   5. If you send a letter to someone, but it gets lost and no one ever reads it, is that communication (not counting "communicating" with yourself when writing the letter)?

___ ___   6. Does a person have to be conscious of his or her goals in order for there to be communication?

___ ___   7. When a trained dog obeys the master's command, is that communication?

___ ___   8. If you put your foot in front of an ordinary cockroach to "tell it" to change direction, and it does, is that communication?

___ ___   9. Can two nonhuman animals of the same species communicate with one another?

___ ___ 10. Can a person communicate to an inanimate object such as a wall or clouds or the ocean?

___ ___ 11. Is blushing a form of communication?

___ ___ 12. Is a spontaneous yawn a form of communication?

___ ___ 13. Is a fake yawn communication?

___ ___ 14. Could two people be talking and yet *not* be communicating?

___ ___ 15. Can a person communicate with himself or herself?

FIGURE 1.1
Defining Communication

There are no right or wrong answers to these questions. Answer them according to your own opinions. Then review your classmates' answers. When there are differences, let each side explain and debate its position. Notice the various features and required conditions of communication assumed by different individuals.

Source: Adapted from J. H. Powers, "Human Communication Theory: A Tier-Based Introduction" (unpublished manuscript, Hong Kong Baptist University, 1995).

Many others would claim that since meaning was inferred by a receiver, this is communication—in other words, that intention is not required for communication.[5]

Whether or not we define communication as requiring intention, certainly goals and intentions are present in the large majority of situations with which this book and this course are concerned. As we shall see, an important feature of effective communication in most problematic contexts is to recognize our true goals, for this can guide the construction of our messages.

ENCODING

Getting back to our example, once Jack decides (consciously or not) to send a message to Jill, the next step in our slow-motion description is for Jack to *encode* a message. **Encoding** is the cognitive process of transforming a thought (idea, concept, feelings, opinion, etc.) into a message (oral, written, or otherwise). In simple terms, encoding is everything that goes on inside Jack's head from the moment he decides to address Jill to the moment his message is produced.

Motley	Osborn	Your Instructor	You	
Y	Y	__	__	**1.** If you read and understand something written several centuries ago, is this communication? **No.** There is no receiver-to-sender feedback, and feedback is required for communication. **Yes.** There is no feedback, but feedback is not required.
N	Y	__	__	**2.** Can an inanimate object (clouds, an ocean, etc.) communicate to a person? **Yes.** A person may derive various kinds of meanings, feelings, ideas, etc. from inanimate objects. **No.** We may derive meaning, but this is not communication because communication requires encoding, symbols, and/or intention by the sender.
Y	Y	__	__	**3.** If you send a letter to someone who receives it, but misunderstands what you meant by it, is this communication? **No.** Communication requires a match between the sender's and receiver's meanings. **Yes.** Communication does not require complete understanding of the message.(Complete understanding is in fact very rare. Misunderstanding may exemplify *poor* communication, but it is still communication.)
Y	Y	__	__	**4.** If you send a letter to someone who never receives it, but someone else reads and understands it, is that communication? **No.** Communication requires reception by the target receiver(s). **Yes.** If communication requires reception of the message, the requirement is reception by a receiver, not necessarily the original target receiver(s).
N	N	__	__	**5.** If you send a letter to someone, but it gets lost and no one ever reads it, is that communication (not counting "communicating" with yourself when writing the letter)? **No.** Communication requires the message to be at least received. **Yes.** Communication does not require reception of the message.
N	N	__	__	**6.** Does a person have to be conscious of his or her goals in order for there to be communication? **Yes.** Communication requires a conscious and deliberate goal, purpose, or objective. **No.** Communication does not require that goals be conscious goals. Or **No.** Communication does not even require goals, much less conscious goals.
Y	N	__	__	**7.** When a trained dog obeys the master's command, is that communication? **No.** Communication takes place only among humans. **Yes.** The dog has learned to decode the encoded symbols.
N	N	__	__	**8.** If you put your foot in front of an ordinary cockroach to "tell it" to change direction, and it does, is that communication? **Yes.** The cockroach interpreted the message as intended. **No.** The cockroach acted instinctively without decoding learned symbols.
Y	Y	__	__	**9.** Can two nonhuman animals of the same species communicate with one another? **No.** Communication takes place only among humans. **Yes.** Example: The dance of honeybees—in which the direction, intensity, and duration of the dance by one bee indicates the direction, amount, and distance of newly found nectar to the other bees—is intentional behavior performed only when nectar is found and when other bees are present as receivers. Moreover, the code is learned and decoded by the receivers (i.e., is not purely instinctive), since different hives have different dance "dialects," and since bees transplanted from one hive to another will learn the new dialect.

(continued)

FIGURE **1.2**

Defining Communication

Here are some (not all) of the common rationales in defense of both positions for the questions of Figure 1.1. Notice the communication features at issue within each yes/no pair. On the left part of the figure, notice the relative positions taken by the authors, your instructor (if he/she supplies it), and yourself.

Motley	Osborn	Your Instructor	You		
N	N	__	__	10.	Can a person communicate to an inanimate object such as a wall or clouds or the ocean?

Yes. A person may express anger by kicking a wall, may experience catharsis emoting to the clouds, may experience a sense of communion with the ocean, etc.

No. Inanimate objects cannot perceive (much less decode) these kinds of messages and meanings. Perception, or perception and decoding, are required of receivers.

N	Y	__	__	11.	Is blushing a form of communication?

Yes. Blushing communicates embarrassment, stress, etc.

No. Blushing indicates embarrassment, etc., but without intention, encoding, symbols, etc., which are required of communication.

N	Y	__	__	12.	Is a spontaneous yawn a form of communication?

Yes. [Same as blushing above, but communicating fatigue, boredom, etc.]

No. [Same as blushing above.]

Y	Y	__	__	13.	Is a fake yawn communication?

Yes. It is a nonverbal behavior intentionally performed (encoded) to indicate (symbolize) boredom, etc.

No. Communication requires spoken or written messages.

N	Y	__	__	14.	Could two people be talking and yet *not* be communicating?

Yes. They could be talking without understanding (e.g., using completely different languages), and communication requires understanding. [This is similar to "No" in question 3.]

No. [At least, it's highly unlikely.] They may not be communicating well, but they would be communicating *something,* even if only communicating a desire to communicate. [This is similar to "Yes" in question 3.]

(N)	(Y)	__	__	15.	Can a person communicate with himself or herself?

Yes and **No.** Virtually everyone agrees that we can silently tell ourselves things—"Did I remember to turn off the stove," "I wish I'd said such and such instead of what I actually said," etc. But virtually everyone agrees that this is a very *different* process than any of the above situations one may consider to be communication. The commonly accepted compromise is to give this situation a special name—*intra*personal communication.

FIGURE 1.2 (continued)

The encoding process is so complex that psycholinguists who have studied it for decades still don't completely understand how encoding happens. At the very least, Jack has to select appropriate words from a vast mental storehouse of possibilities; then he has to decide which of several viable grammatical constructions to employ; and then he has to coordinate his lungs, vocal cords, jaw, tongue, and lips to speak the constructed phrase. And all of this happens within a matter of milliseconds!

This book will not deal with the psycholinguistic details of how encoding occurs. We will, however, emphasize the importance of planning and encoding messages *carefully*—that is, the importance of thinking before speaking. For public-speaking situations, planning the message takes many hours; for interpersonal situations, many common

● TRY THIS

To get an idea of how quickly the mind makes encoding decisions, try to think of all the different ways in which Jack could have said essentially the same thing. Try this for each of the possible goals you can imagine he might have had for the French-fries message. See Figure 1.3, for example.

Give me	some	salt and pepper
Pass	the	salt shaker
Pass me	that	salt
Hand me		
Get me		
I want		(please)

. . . ETC. . . .

These	potatoes (are)	yucky	
The	fries	lousy	
Those	French fries	bland	ETC. . . .
My	French-fried potatoes	need salt	
		tasteless	

. . . ETC. . . .

"These French fries are bland."

What does that mean?
    He thinks those things he's eating need additional seasoning—most likely salt, and/or pepper, and/or catsup.
So what? Why is he telling me this?
    He wants me to know he doesn't like the French fries.
    or He wants me to know he doesn't like this restaurant.
    or He wants to make sure I don't snitch any of his fries.
    or He wants me to pass him the salt.
    or He wants me to pass him the catsup.
    or He's hoping I'll say that I like mine.
    or He's just griping because he's had a bad day.
    etc.

FIGURE **1.3**
Encoding and Decoding Messages

Here are just a few encoding (and decoding) options for Jack and Jill's message. Can you think of others?

difficulties can be avoided if we take at least a moment, and sometimes several moments, to plan our message before we deliver it. Later chapters will discuss some of the factors that should go into planning messages in both public-speaking and interpersonal situations.

THE MESSAGE—SYMBOLS

Jack's encoding produced, "Gosh, these French fries are bland." In this slow-motion example, Jill will almost certainly be able to derive some sort of meaning from the message. But whether she will derive the correct meaning (from Jack's point of view) is much less certain, for meaning is very slippery.

We can begin to understand how meaning operates by considering how it is that something can *mean* something. For example, how is it that dark clouds mean rain, a flag at half-mast means that someone is being mourned, lightning means that thunder will be heard, a red traffic light means stop, one's face turning red means that one is embarrassed, a frown means that someone is upset, *baloney* means a kind of luncheon meat, *baloney* means that one does not believe what another has just said, and on and on? Part of the answer comes from noticing that all of these "meanings" fall into two categories: those in which the meaning comes from *natural relationships* (dark clouds and rain, lightning and thunder, blushing and embarrassment, etc.) and those in which the meaning comes from *relationships made up by other people* (red lights and stopping, half-mast flags and mourning, the word *baloney* and debunking, etc.).

When something has meaning because of an inherent natural (truly by nature) relationship, we say that it carries meaning as a **symptom.**[6] Thus, blushing is a symptom of embarrassment, dark clouds are a symptom of rain, and so forth. When something has meaning because of an arbitrary relationship created by people, we say that it carries meaning as a **symbol.** Thus, half-mast flags symbolize mourning, red traffic lights symbolize the appropriateness of stopping, utterances are symbols of the speaker's thoughts (or goals, feelings, desires, etc.), a fake yawn is a symbol for boredom, and so forth.

The Sender (in a typical communication situation)

✓   Has something in mind that could be expressed

✓   Has a reason to express it (the goal)

✓   Decides whether or not to express it (the intention)

✓   Encodes, deciding on words and grammatical form

✓   Transmits the message(s), spoken or otherwise

You may have noticed in the earlier list of meaning examples that for each meaning given (from dark clouds to *baloney*), you could reply, "Not necessarily." Lightning does not *always* mean that you will hear thunder, a flag at half-mast does not *necessarily* mean mourning (maybe it got stuck halfway up or down), facial flushing does not *always* mean embarrassment, and so forth. Indeed, meaning is often uncertain. This will be a major theme later in this book, along with things we can do to clarify the meanings within our messages.

MODES—VERBAL AND NONVERBAL

Jack's "These French fries are bland" message is his attempt to represent his thoughts and/or to accomplish his goal via symbols—**verbal** symbols, or *words,* in this case. If he had wanted to, he could have attempted to communicate the same meaning with **nonverbal** (nonword) symbols. To simply express his displeasure with the French fries, he could have pushed them away with contemptuous flair; if he wanted Jill to pass the salt, he could have pointed back and forth to the salt shaker and to himself; and so on for other communicative goals.

We have said that meaning is carried by symbols and symptoms, and we have said that messages may be verbal or nonverbal. As for how these concepts combine, *words* are *symbols,* not symptoms. (There may be rare exceptions. Some would say, for example, that the oath you utter when you accidentally hit your thumb with a hammer is a symptom rather than a symbol, but many would disagree. In any case, words are usually sym-bols.) Nonverbal behaviors, however, are split. Some are symbols, and others are symptoms. More specifically, behaviors instigated by communicative intention are symbols. Behaviors *without* communicative intention may carry meaning as symptoms. An obscene gesture is clearly a symbol; a stomach growl is clearly a symptom. An intentional frown—say, to get a child to stop doing something displeasing—is a symbol; a natural frown, especially when we don't even know anyone is watching, is usually a symptom. And so forth. This means that people may interpret our nonverbal behaviors (as symptoms) even when we do not intend those behaviors as messages, and even when we do not realize they are being interpreted. In Chapter 3 we will see how this and other elements of nonverbal behavior may lead to difficulties in common interaction situations.

> The Message (in a typical communication situation)
> ✓ Consists of symbols
> ✓ Is either verbal or nonverbal
> ✓ Is transmitted vocally or nonvocally
> ✓ Will be interpreted

MODES—VOCAL AND NONVOCAL

Notice that when we define *verbal* to mean "with words," we are defining it differently from what is often meant in everyday usage. In everyday language, we will hear statements such as, "We didn't get it in writing, but we agreed verbally," or "Even though it was only a verbal contract, I assumed it was binding." In these examples, *verbal* means "spoken, not written." But this is *not* what it means in communication courses.

It is more accurate for *verbal* to mean "with words." When we wish to identify whether or not a message is spoken, we can use the terms *vocal* and *nonvocal* (some prefer *oral* and *nonoral*). **Vocal** behaviors are those that use the vocal tract (lungs, larynx, tongue, lips, etc.), and **nonvocal** behaviors are those that do not.

In these terms, *verbal* has nothing to do with whether a message is spoken. Verbal messages may be vocal (as in speech) or nonvocal (as in writing or sign language). And nonverbal behaviors may be vocal (screams, laughs, groans, etc.) or nonvocal (gestures, facial expressions, and so forth). Thus, for example, if Jill were talking to Jack about her roommate and said, "We had a verbal agreement," Jack's reply might well be, "Aren't they all?" It would be more informative for her to say, "We had a *vocal* agreement" (or *oral,* or *spoken*—assuming that this is what she meant).

We are introducing the primary modes of communication (verbal/nonverbal and vocal/nonvocal) mostly to preview the range of options for communication messages. But these modes of communication serve also to clarify terminology that we will use throughout our discussions.

THE RECEIVER—DECODING AND MEANING

Jill *receives* Jack's message when she hears (and/or sees) it. Technically, what she actually receives is an acoustic (and/or visual) signal, which she then *decodes* into a message. **Decoding** is the process of transforming a perceived stimulus into a psychological meaning (thought, feeling, etc.) according to a learned language or code. In simple terms, decoding is everything that goes on in Jill's brain that gets her from the vibrations of her eardrum to the meaning she assigns to Jack's message.

As Jill begins to assign meaning, she will do so on several unconscious levels. First, there is the **semantic meaning**—a level of meaning akin to a literal translation. Jill has to determine what the sentence, "Gosh, these French fries are bland" means in the general, linguistic sense: What are "French fries?" what does *bland* mean? etc. While the French fries message is fairly straightforward at the semantic level, some messages are not. (As a simple example, "I'm going to the bank" could mean *bank* as in "edge of the river" or *bank* as in "financial institution.")

Next comes the **personal history meaning.**[7] Here, meaning is influenced by our personal knowledge and opinions concerning matters related to the message. This comes in part from other relevant messages we have heard in the past from this sender and from other senders. Jill will base part of her interpretation on a subconscious summary of her own experiences, plus messages from Jack and others about French fries (e.g., Do most people like them bland?), about food in this particular restaurant (e.g., Is it surprising that the French fries are subpar?), about blandness (In the case of French fries, what ingredient is probably missing?), and so forth.

Next is a level called **pragmatic meaning.** This is the phase at which Jill consciously or subconsciously wonders, "So what?" "Why is he telling me this?" "What am I supposed to do with this information?" and so forth. She may interpret the French fries message as an instance of Jack's chronic complaining, as a simple comment to make small talk, as a device by Jack to discourage her from taking his French fries, as an offer to give her the French fries since he doesn't like them, as a request to pass the salt, or as any of a number of other possibilities.

At each level of meaning, the receiver is making guesses and reading between the lines. Each of these guesses may be correct or incorrect from the sender's point of view, so each involves the potential for misunderstanding. A crucial step toward improving communication is to recognize these and other sources of misunderstanding.

> **● T R Y   T H I S**
>
> The text mentions several ways that Jill could have interpreted Jack's message. As an exercise, try to imagine other possible interpretations. Then do the same (with semantic, personal history, and pragmatic meanings) for other hypothetical messages. For example, (1) Jill: "Our electricity bill sure was high this month," or (2) Jack: "I've got a big exam tomorrow," or (3) Jill: "I hate that iron my mother gave me." Make up your own potential interpretations and compare them with a classmate's or friend's.

RECEIVER RESPONSE—FEEDBACK

Once Jill has formulated her various levels of meaning, she responds to the message. At the very least, she will develop a mental, or cognitive, response. She may or may not display an overt behavioral response as well. That is, after decoding, "Gosh, these French fries are bland," Jill may disagree but say nothing, or have a sort of in-one-ear-out-the-other ostensibly neutral response, or reach over and grab one of Jack's French fries to see for herself, or say, "That's strange, mine are fine," or say, "Yeah, mine too," or pass the salt to Jack, and so on.

Jill's behavioral response is called **feedback.** Feedback is the process by which the receiver's (Jill's) response to the message is indicated to the sender (Jack). With most feedback, the original receiver is now taking a turn as sender, with the original sender becoming a receiver. (Jack sends, Jill sends, Jack sends, Jill sends, and so on, with each turn representing a feedback response to the preceding message.) Sometimes the receiver's feedback gives a clear indication of how the message was interpreted. (For example, Jack: "These fries are bland." Jill: "Tough. You always whine about your fries, anyway.") Other times, the receiver's reaction is less clear. (For example, Jack: "These fries are bland." Jill: "Hey, did I tell you I aced my chemistry exam?") And sometimes the absence of an overt response constitutes feedback. (For example, if Jack tells a joke, and Jill laughs, the laughter is feedback. But if she doesn't laugh, that's feedback, too.)

Clear feedback—clear indications by the receiver as to his or her response to the sender's messages—can be extremely helpful in both ordinary and problematic communication situations. For example, feedback is one of the primary ways in which ambiguities and other uncertainties within messages are acknowledged (e.g., "Hold it; are you saying X or saying Y?"). But receivers sometimes fail to provide enough feedback, even in informal situations where they have plenty of opportunity to do so. And in public-speaking situations, the built-in delay in verbal feedback is the primary factor that makes the situation challenging. The audience cannot interrupt when the speaker is unclear (as receivers can in most interpersonal situations), and the audience doesn't get a turn as sender until the end of the speech. Thus, the speaker must carefully plan the speech content, making wise guesses about the audience's probable interpretations of the message segments, and must adapt to very sketchy and relatively superficial nonverbal feedback during the speech. In simple terms, in both interpersonal and public communication situations, the absence of feedback forces senders to read receivers' minds with respect to understanding, agreement, emotional response, and so forth. Thus, it is usually advantageous to optimize feedback in communication situations.

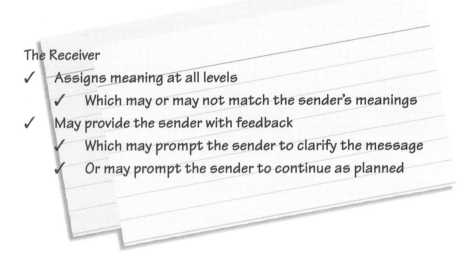

The Receiver
✓　Assigns meaning at all levels
　　✓　Which may or may not match the sender's meanings
✓　May provide the sender with feedback
　　✓　Which may prompt the sender to clarify the message
　　✓　Or may prompt the sender to continue as planned

SENDER-RECEIVER MATCH OR MISMATCH

Suppose Jack wants Jill to pass the salt, but when he says, "Gosh, these French fries are bland," Jill replies (without passing the salt), "Yeah, mine too. You know, I saw the most incredible accident on the way over here. Two cars were on fire and . . . [on and on]." In this case, Jill's pragmatic understanding and response to Jack's message did not match Jack's meaning and the purpose of his message.

The degree to which the receiver's understanding and response match the sender's meaning and purpose is perhaps the most common criterion for evaluating the *quality* or success of communication. Certainly, in public-speaking situations, the primary criterion (some would say the *only* criterion) for determining whether a speech is a good speech is whether the speech achieves the speaker's communicative goals (assuming that these were appropriate goals). In interpersonal communication also, we may consider the **sender-receiver match** or **sender-receiver mismatch** to be a primary criterion for evaluating a communication experience. In simple terms, this criterion suggests that communication is *good* communication when things turn out as planned or desired from the participants' separate or combined points of view. (Notice that for definitions of communication that do not require intention, this approach to evaluating communication will not work.[8]) In many ways, the primary objective of this book is to help you find ways to ensure a sender-receiver match, or sender-receiver satisfaction, in various communication situations.

THE RELATIONSHIP DIMENSION

Another feature of communication is that it often has both content and **relationship dimensions.**[9] That is to say, messages obviously carry *content* information about their apparent topic (the French fries in our ongoing example). But much more subtly, messages often carry between-the-lines information about how the sender views the *relationship*. Suppose, for example, that after Jill's "Yeah, mine too . . ." response, Jack were to say, "I guess you don't realize it, but I told you to pass the salt." If it is not apparent to you that Jill might be offended by this comment, compare it with, "I guess you don't realize it, but I asked you to pass the salt." Notice that "*told* you to" and "*asked* you to" carry very different relationship-dimension meanings, since "told you to" indicates that the sender views the receiver as subordinate rather than equal.

A second example comes from my (Motley's) son. One day when he was about nine years old or so, he told me, "Dad, my friends think you're a grouch." Not wanting to be seen as a grouch, and not wanting him to feel I was seen as a grouch, I was eager to correct my ways. But he couldn't explain what I was doing that conveyed this impression. After a couple of weeks of conscious effort on my part, I checked with him about my improvement, only to be told that I hadn't improved! We agreed that the next time I was a grouch, he would let me know, since I had no idea what I was doing wrong.

A couple of days later, he and a friend were in the back yard on the trampoline, jumping over and through a stream of water from the water hose—no problem as long as they remembered to turn off the water, which was collecting in a garden area. So, being as nice and as ungrouchy as possible (or so I thought), I said, "That looks like fun. Make sure you turn off the water when you're finished, buddy, so you don't flood the garden." My son replied—also quite nicely, by the way—"Dad, *there's* one." I finally realized that the problem had never been about how nicely I made requests; it was about making requests, period, since any request or order from me served as a reminder to him and his friends of his (and their) subordinate status. From that day on, I began calling him over privately, making my requests and "giving my orders" beyond earshot of his friends. He let me know a couple of weeks later, "Dad, now you've got the hang of it!"

The relational dimension is present in public speaking as well. Surely you have seen speakers whose attitude—style, message choices, vocal characteristics, and so forth—seemed to show that they did not sincerely respect the audience, or were intimidated by the audience, or did not really care what the audience thought or believed about their message, and so forth.

THE FAR SIDE

"So. Andre! . . . The king wants to know how you're coming with 'St.George and the Dragon.' "

As these examples are intended to demonstrate, the relationship dimension of communication is often very subtle. Through the particular words we use, the context within which the message is delivered, the nonverbal behaviors that accompany the message, and so forth, we may signal relative status, respect or disrespect, affection or disaffection, selfishness or selflessness, empathy or coldness, and so on. Sometimes we deliberately reveal these relational impressions, of course. But serious communication problems can arise when we accidentally reveal our true relational impressions, or when we accidentally imply a relational impression we don't have.

NOISE

We have already seen a few factors that can jeopardize communication efforts, and these are only the tip of the iceberg. Indeed, there are so many of these factors that a single overall label has come to be used for them: **noise.** Noise is anything that impairs or impedes a particular communication episode. Its opposite, a **catalyst,** is anything that facilitates, improves, or enhances communication.[10]

Sometimes the interference or enhancement is *external,* coming from an alteration of the actual physical signal (usually light waves and/or sound waves) by which the message is carried. For example, too much light in a room where a public speaker is trying to use a slide projector for visual aids would be external noise. More difficult to recognize, however, are the various sources of *internal* noise and catalysts—the psychological and sociological factors that may affect the production or interpretation of our messages. For example, suppose Jill's mind is so preoccupied with having just failed an exam that she barely registers Jack's comment. Her anguish would be a source of noise. Or, suppose she had just tasted her own French fries and noticed that they needed salt. Her experience would be a catalyst when she interprets Jack's comment.

We introduce these concepts only briefly here, for in a sense this entire book is about sources of noise and catalysts. For now, simply note that the factors affecting public-speaking and interpersonal communication go far beyond messages and meanings. They include similarities and differences in sender and receiver attitudes, personalities, styles, emotional maturity, background knowledge, culture, gender, world-view, and much more. And as we shall see, minimizing noise and optimizing catalysts is often much easier said than done.

CONTEXT

Another feature of communication is that it is contextual. That is, our communication behaviors tend to vary according to the environment or context within which they take place. Communication patterns adapt according to **physical context**—for example, we will talk differently at a loud night club than on a quiet picnic, even if we are talking with the same person about the same topic. Communication varies according to **social context**—we will probably talk differently with our best friend than with our boss, for instance. And communication varies according to **psychological context**—we will usually talk differently when we are pleased with our communication partners than when we are upset with them, for example.

These cases of contextual adaptation are fairly obvious. Let us return to Jack and Jill for a more subtle example: Suppose the salt shaker is much closer to Jack than to Jill (physical context). Jack can still comment that the French fries are bland, of course. But in this context, it is less likely that Jill will interpret his comment to mean "Pass the salt," since it would be impolite for Jack to ask her to do this unless the salt shaker were closer to her than to him.

It is rare that communication breakdowns are caused by a failure to adapt to contexts. Still, later chapters will discuss a few communication situations in which it is especially helpful to consider context.

Meaning
- ✓ Depends upon semantic interpretation, personal history, and pragmatic interpretation
- ✓ Has content and relationship dimensions
- ✓ May be affected by various forms of noise and catalysts
- ✓ May be affected by context

GOALS AND SUBGOALS

As we have indicated, communication is instigated by *goals* (according to some definitions, at least) and may be evaluated on the basis of whether the goals were achieved. Often, therefore, it is useful to consciously examine our goals before we develop our communication messages.

Close examination of communication goals frequently reveals one or two primary goals, each containing several identifiable **subgoals**.[11] Rather than charging blindly into a communication episode, hoping or assuming that our general goals will be accomplished, it is usually better to organize a strategy for dealing with goals and subgoals systematically. Certainly, this is the case with public speaking. For example, a Kiwanis Club speech with a primary goal of, say, pointing out how to recognize warning signs of eating disorders would no doubt have a long list of subgoals (establishing the relevance of the topic, dismissing misconceptions about the issue, establishing the speaker's credibility on the topic, and many more), each of which would deserve attention in planning the speech.

Less obviously, the same is often true in interpersonal communication. A favorite example of dealing with subgoals systematically is one I witnessed a couple of years ago. My wife and I had agreed to get our son his first car, and he had picked out a tiny two-seater convertible that was old and inexpensive but still definitely "cool." Dad was in favor, but Mom was against it. She was concerned that it was so old that there would be a problem with repair bills, and so small that there was a problem with safety. Over a period of about five weeks, our son's campaign unfolded. First came a blatant "what a bargain" phase, in which he showed her innumerable used-car prices from the newspaper. He was able to make the point that this was indeed a bargain, but she held her ground based on safety and repair bills. Then came a subtle "what's fair for one is fair for all" phase in which he capitalized on her equestrian hobby: He found out the average frequency and cost of her veterinary and blacksmith's bills, and made the point—politely and effectively—that even with the worst predictions, the car's repair bills would probably be less than her horse's veterinary bills. The size/safety issue remained, however, so he tried a sort of "let's make her see small as a *good* thing" strategy. He casually announced one day, "You know, Mom, maybe that car *is* too small. Not because it's dangerous, though. I've been thinking—I'll be dating soon, and a big car would have some definite advantages." That did the trick; he got the car!

On the one hand, in most interpersonal situations, we cannot deal with subgoals over a period of weeks, as in the above example, or spend weeks planning a single extended message, as with some public-speaking situations. But on the other hand, in many of our more difficult interpersonal communication situations, we have plenty of time to analyze goals and subgoals—if we remember the importance of doing so.

FRAME OF MIND AND EMOTIONAL MATURITY

Achieving our communication goals and subgoals often requires an appropriate "frame of mind," or social attitude. For example, it is advisable in public speaking to be *sincere* (about a number of matters); it is often advisable when dealing with conflict to be *willing to compromise;* it is often advisable in avoiding conflict to *recognize our own idiosyncrasies* and hang-ups; it is often advisable in relationship maintenance to *accept others' "faults"* as mere differences; and so forth. But while these frame-of-mind catalysts may make perfect sense when studying communication rationally, they are not always easy to put into practice within actual communication situations. This is partly because *emotion* is a powerful source of noise in most problematic communication situations. And emotion can make it difficult to adopt an advisable frame of mind.

As an example, consider the following Dear-Abby-type letter written as a class assignment by a student in a course similar to yours. Go ahead and imagine what advice you would give if you were playing "Abby." Then imagine how you would expect the letter writer to react to your advice.

> *Dear Doc,*
> *I am writing to you about a problem I have with one of my housemates. She is a very overbearing and manipulative person who is known for getting her way. A couple of weeks ago she asked to use my computer to type a paper, and I said that it was fine. Ever since then she asks to use it all the time, and after saying yes a few times I feel obligated to let her use it, especially since I do not need to use it much. If I do say no, she takes it very personally and acts hurt. Now it has come to the point where she does not ask anymore. I come home from class to see her on my computer and her boyfriend lounging on my bed. This really bothers me because I feel like my room is my own space and I am really regretting that I ever let her use it in the first place. Should I tell her to stop using my computer or is this selfish and rude? If I do tell her to stop, how do I do it without causing tension because I still have to live with her until the lease runs out.*
>
> *—Desperate Housemate*

When the above letter was discussed (anonymously) in class, with the instructor and classmates playing "Abby," by far the most popular suggestion was an obvious compromise: Move the computer out of her room and into the living room, dining room, or some other common area, so that the housemate can continue to use the computer but without invading Desperate's space. Now, we can imagine Desperate hearing this advice and thinking to herself, "What a great idea; why didn't I think of that?" But we also can imagine her thinking, "No way! I'm not about to do anything that makes it *easier* for my housemate to use my computer." That is to say, the negative emotions present may make it difficult for Desperate to see compromise as a solution on her own, and they may make it difficult to adopt a compromise frame of mind even when it is advised by others.

To put it another way, in some situations the advisable frame of mind requires a certain degree of *psychological maturity,* or **emotional maturity.** ("Emotional intelligence" is what this is called in popular psychology these days.[12]) Among other things,

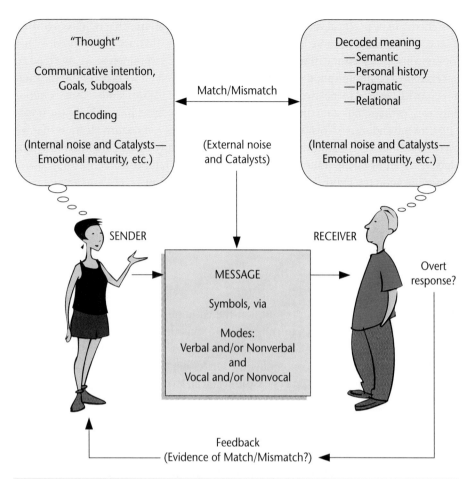

FIGURE 1.4
Components of a Typical Communication Situation

This figure illustrates some of the concepts we have introduced in this chapter. Note that some situations you or your instructor consider to be communication (see Figure 1.1 for examples) will not have all of these components present.

emotional maturity is the ability to suppress emotion-based noise in our interactions with others. As we will see throughout our discussion of communication, unless we can manage our emotions, much of the advice for handling difficult situations will remain easier said than done.

AND MORE

We began this discussion by acknowledging that skeptical students may imagine the study of communication to be little more than common sense. But while we have only scratched the surface in this introductory chapter, certainly you can see already that there is more to communication than meets the eye—even in a simple message about French fries, let alone more crucial messages.

There can be practical value just in that simple observation—that is, in recognizing that communication is more involved, or more complex, than we had realized. When we subconsciously assume that communication is simple common sense, we tend to take our own communication episodes for granted. And when we take communication for granted, we tend to make communication mistakes of various kinds—usually minor mistakes, perhaps, but sometimes irreparable errors. Of course, if we went to the opposite extreme and were so overwhelmed by the complexity of communication that we were reluctant to communicate for fear of failure, certainly that would be counterproductive. To err by taking communication too seriously is rare, however. To err by taking communication too lightly is, unfortunately, rather common.

The discussion thus far has identified several specific ways in which complications may arise during communication, and later chapters will discuss many, many more. Whether they are common sense is debatable, perhaps. Whether effective communicators take them for granted is not.

IN SUMMARY   We have analyzed in slow motion the basic steps and components involved when one person tries to communicate something to another. And we have seen that things can go wrong, and sometimes do, at virtually every step along the way. Part of the blame for this falls on neither the sender nor the receiver, but rather on the nature of the communication process. Meaning (at all levels) is sometimes elusive, noise (in various forms) may be present, encoding and decoding may provide competing message and interpretation options, and so forth. However, the responsibility for overcoming these obstacles lies with us as participants, and there are things that we can do to optimize our communication efforts: encode carefully (with respect to all levels of meaning, both content and relational), solicit and provide feedback, analyze goals and subgoals, be aware of contexts, maintain emotional maturity, and so forth.

While later chapters will provide helpful details for a variety of communication situations, it is useful to recognize communication problems and responsibilities at a general level. As we begin to recognize the complexity of communication, we are less likely to take it for granted, more likely to exercise care in our communication efforts, and thus less likely to experience difficulties.

TERMS TO KNOW

communicative intention	pragmatic meaning
communication goal	feedback
encoding	sender-receiver match
symptom	sender-receiver mismatch
symbol	relationship dimensions
verbal	noise
nonverbal	catalyst
vocal	physical context
nonvocal	social context
decoding	psychological context
semantic meaning	subgoals
personal history meaning	emotional maturity

NOTES

1. For example, G. R. Miller, "On Defining Communication: Another Stab," *Journal of Communication* 16 (1966): 88–98.

2. This exercise is adapted from J. H. Powers, "Human Communication Theory: A Tier-Based Introduction" (unpublished manuscript, Hong Kong Baptist University, 1995).

3. M. T. Motley, "Consciousness and Intentionality in Communication: A Preliminary Model and Methodological Approaches," *Western Journal of Speech Communication* 50 (1986): 3–23.

4. For example, M. T. Motley, "Communication as Interaction: A Reply to Beach and Bavelas," *Western Journal of Speech Communication* 54 (1990): 613–623; and M. T. Motley, "How One May Not Communicate: A Reply to Andersen," *Communication Studies* 42 (1991): 326–339.

5. P. A. Andersen, "When One Cannot Not Communicate: A Challenge to Motley's Traditional Communication Postulates," *Communication Studies* 42 (1991): 309–325; J. B. Bavelas, "Behaving and Communicating: A Reply to Motley," *Western Journal of Speech Communication* 54 (1990): 593–602.

6. G. Cronkhite, "On the Focus, Scope, and Coherence of the Study of Human Symbolic Activity," *Quarterly Journal of Speech* 72 (1986): 231–246.

7. Based on S. L. Becker, "What Rhetoric (Communication Theory) Is Relevant for Contemporary Speech Communication?" (unpublished paper, University of Minnesota, 1968).

8. M. T. Motley, "On Whether One Can(not) Not Communicate: An Examination via Traditional Communication Postulates," *Western Journal of Speech Communication* 54 (1990): 1–20.

9. P. Watzlawick, J. H. Beavin, and D. D. Jackson, *Pragmatics of Human Communication* (New York: W. W. Norton, 1967).

10. M. T. Motley, *Orientations to Language and Communication* (Palo Alto, Calif.: Science Research Associates, 1978).

11. G. A. Miller, E. Galanter, and K. H. Pribram, *Plans and the Structure of Behavior* (New York: Holt & Co., 1960).

12. D. Goleman, *Emotional Intelligence* (New York: Bantam Books, 1995).

LANGUAGE—THE BASIS OF VERBAL MESSAGES

THIS CHAPTER will help you

- Recognize how language affects meaning

- Recognize sources of ambiguity in communication

- Discover how language distorts thoughts

- Recognize language-based barriers to communication

- Recognize receivers' expectations for "proper" language

LANGUAGE WAS GOD'S ULTIMATE GIFT.

—N. Webster

mproving our communication efforts involves both refining the messages we produce and refining our interpretations of others' messages. To make these refinements, we need a basic understanding of how language operates to both facilitate and impede communication efforts.

LANGUAGE BASICS

Language is the basis of verbal messages. We define **language** as *a structured system of arbitrary symbols used for communication messages*. It is a *system* because it contains components of different kinds (sounds, syllables, words, etc.), all of which depend upon and interact with one another. And it is *structured* in that it is governed by *rules* that allow certain arrangements of the components while disallowing others.

When we refer to **language rules,** we do not mean the guidelines for "proper" language that parents and teachers have taught us. "Don't end a sentence with a preposition," "Don't use double negatives," and other such admonitions are guidelines that some of us follow and some of us don't. (Ending a sentence with a preposition, for example, is easy to get away with!) Rather, a language is rule-governed in the sense that it contains conventions that are followed by virtually everyone who speaks it. Most of these conventions have never been consciously pointed out to us, but we still follow them.

As an example of a language rule, we're going to invent a new word. I have in mind a certain object for which there is no name (as far as I know), and I've decided to call it a *kwug*. Now, suppose you and I are talking, and I wish to refer to *several* of these objects. What sound will I add to *kwug* to make it plural? (Try saying it aloud.) You probably knew that adding a *z* sound will make *kwug* plural. But unless you've studied this sort of thing somewhere else, you probably were not consciously aware of this knowledge. Our spoken language has a "rule" by which nouns ending with certain consonant sounds (*p, t, k, f*) are made plural by adding an *s* sound. Nouns ending with certain other consonant sounds (*b, d, g, v, m, n, ng, l, r*) are made plural by adding a *z* sound. And most nouns ending with other consonants (*s, z,* etc.) require adding an *iz* syllable.

Chances are, you "know" these rules in the sense that you follow them subconsciously and automatically, but not in the sense that you consciously studied them in order to learn them. Likewise for the many other structural rules by which language is governed.

● TRY THIS

To see that refinements to our messages might be worthwhile, you may wish to try the exercise in Figure 2.1 on the next page.

COMPONENTS

We have said that language is a system of components that depend upon and interact with one another. Several of these components are directly responsible for affecting the meanings within our messages.

PHONEMES

Since every known language emerged first in spoken form rather than written form, the study of language tends to focus on language as it is spoken. Accordingly, the smallest element in a language—at least, the smallest element that can affect meaning—is the **phoneme,** or speech sound. In American English, there are about forty phonemes (for

(a)

(b)

(c)

(d)

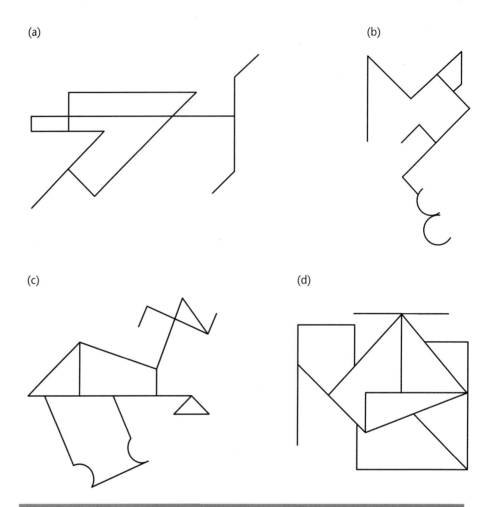

FIGURE **2.1**
Practice Your Communication Skills

Try to instruct one or more of your friends to reproduce these diagrams; or watch two friends as one tries to instruct the other. The sender's job is to give instructions so the receiver(s) can draw a near-perfect copy of the diagram. The sender may not draw the diagram in the air, allow the receiver to look at the target diagram, or look at the receiver's effort until it is completed. When the drawing is finished, the sender and receiver should compare the target images to the receiver's final drawing. People are often surprised at how poorly they do on this exercise. If communication is this difficult when referring to simple, two-dimensional, objective figures, imagine how much miscommunication must be taking place when we discuss more abstract and subjective matters.

example, the *f* sound in "phone" and "fun," the *th* sound in "then," a different *th* sound in "thin," the *ee* sound in "beat," the *ah* sound in "father" and "bother," the *uh* sound in "mother" and "mugger," and so forth). And, as we saw when we made *kwug* plural, the phoneme level of language is rule-governed. As another example, my hypothetical *kwug* is allowable, but *kdug* is not (because English has a rule by which the *k* phoneme at the beginning of a word must be followed by a vowel or an *l, w*, or *r* sound).

MORPHEMES AND WORDS

Phonemes combine to form units called **morphemes**, and morphemes combine to form **words.** For our purposes, we may think of morphemes as word roots, prefixes, and suffixes (although technically this is an oversimplification). For example, consider the words *cat* and *cats*. These words have slightly different meanings, of course. With *cats* there is one word, but there are two morphemes, *cat* and *s*, where *cat* means (among other things) a feline animal, and *s* means more than one. Many other words combine morphemes in a similar way (for example, *un + like, doubt + ed, sing + ing,* and *other + z*). And again, there are rules. For example, many morphemes may occur only in designated prefix or suffix positions (*-s, -ed, un-, re-,* etc.).

SYNTAX

Phonemes combine to form morphemes and words, and words combine to make up the phrases and sentences of typical communication messages. The structure of a language at its phrase or sentence level is called **syntax.** At the syntax level, rules are more obvious. In English, we can say, "The dog chased the man," and we can say, "The man chased the dog." Although the words are the same, rules regarding subject-verb-object sequencing change the two meanings drastically. And while the words are the same in "Chased man dog the the," rules of syntax disallow this "phrase" as virtually meaningless.

SUPRASEGMENTALS

Vocal inflections, or **suprasegmentals**, are yet another component of language. There are three kinds of suprasegmentals: stress, juncture, and pitch. **Stress** is a vocal cue involving the amount of emphasis or intensity given to word syllables. For example, consider the sentence "I'm going to the store." If this sentence were a response to the question, "Who's going to the store?" then the word-syllable *I* probably would be stressed. If it were a response to, "Where are you going?" the stressed syllable should be *store.* In response to, "I've told you twice to go to the store," the stress probably would be on the *go* syllable of *going*. And so forth. Stress can affect the meaning of individual words as well. Notice the differences between *abstract* and *abstract, contrast* and *contrast, increase* and *increase, digest* and *digest,* to give just a few examples. (And here we see another rule, by the way. On words like these, the noun form gets stress on the first syllable, and the verb form gets stress on the second syllable.)

Another vocal cue of language is **juncture,** the degree of pause between phonemes of adjacent syllables. Juncture can affect meaning at the phrase level, as with *a name* versus *an aim, first I'm* versus *first time, right eye* versus *right tie,* and so forth. Juncture can carry meaning at the sentence level, as well. Compare the subtle pause differences in these utterances, for example: (1) "I'll go jump-start the car; then go to the store." (2) "I'll go jump-start the car, then. Go to the store." (3) "I'll go. Jump-start the car; then go to the store." The various meanings are differentiated primarily by juncture.

Pitch is a vocal cue involving tonal changes over portions of a phrase. The most familiar usage of pitch is the one that occurs in some of our interrogative statements. Sometimes syntax will indicate that a phrase is a question, as in "Is Dave here?"

THE FAR SIDE By GARY LARSON

"Ha ha ha, Biff. Guess what? After we go to the drugstore and the post office, I'm going to the vet's to get tutored."

Source: THE FAR SIDE © FARWORKS, INC. Used by permission. All rights reserved.

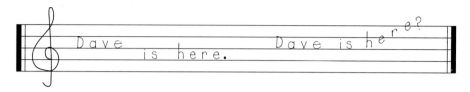

FIGURE **2.2**
Pitch as a Vocal Cue

(Beginning a sentence with *Is* usually indicates a question.) In such cases, there is no particular pitch rule to indicate a question, because a question is already indicated. Other times, however, a question is indicated not by syntax but by pitch alone. For example, the statement "Dave is here" may be turned into the question "Dave is here?" by raising the pitch (tone frequency) toward the end of the phrase.

Suprasegmentals are not the same as the vocal inflections used to communicate mood—talking louder when angry, softer for romance, and so forth. The latter are inflections applied to large sections of an utterance to indicate general emotion. Suprasegmentals are applied to small language segments to indicate meaning.

PAYING ATTENTION TO LANGUAGE COMPONENTS

There are several reasons to become aware of the basic components of language. First, each of the components we have discussed affects the *meaning* of utterances. Recognizing the features that affect meaning can make us more careful with our own utterances at all levels. Just a few days ago, for example, I (Motley) overheard a minor altercation in which a coffee shop patron complained that she had received a regular latte, although she had ordered "an ice latte." The waiter apologized, saying that he thought the order was for "a nice latte." It is easy to see that ambiguous juncture caused the error, and it is not too far-fetched to imagine that greater sensitivity to juncture might have prevented it.

A second reason to examine the basic components of language is to become more aware of our personal language idiosyncrasies. By paying attention to others' language

Language Components Affecting Meaning Include

✓   Phonemes (*fun versus pun, beet versus bit, etc.*)

✓   Morphemes (*cat versus cats, redo versus undo, fade versus faded, etc.*)

✓   Syntax ("The dog bit the boy" versus "The boy bit the dog," etc.)

✓   Pitch ("That horse is a thoroughbred" versus "That horse is a thoroughbred?")

✓   Stress (*contrast versus contrast, etc.*)

✓   Juncture (*as aim versus a name, I scream versus ice cream, etc.*)

at the component level, it becomes easier to adapt to norms and to eliminate our own quirks. Those of us who unnecessarily raise the pitch at the end of utterances (so that everything we say sounds like a question?), rush words together with unclear or confusing juncture, have unique pronunciations for common words, and so forth, may confuse or annoy our listeners without realizing it.

A third reason for paying attention to language components has to do with the differences between language modes. It will be crucial to your effectiveness as a public speaker that you talk the way people talk, not the way people write, read aloud, or recite from memory. We have already seen a few of the ways in which spoken language is different from written language. And you know from experience—from public speakers you have heard, and telephone solicitors you have tolerated—that subtle differences in language features may betray messages that are being read aloud or recited from memory. A basic familiarity with the various components of spoken language can help you establish a conversational style in your public-speaking efforts.

MEANING

In Chapter 1 we introduced the concept that words are symbols, not symptoms. Recall that symptoms (increased heart rate, thunderclouds, etc.) carry meaning because of relationships established by nature, whereas symbols (a trophy, an alarm bell, words, and so forth) carry meaning because of relationships established by humans. Let's take a closer look at how meaning operates for symbols—words in particular—to see how it becomes slippery in communication.

ARBITRARINESS OF SYMBOLS

When humans establish a word/meaning relationship, that relationship is arbitrary. That is, there is no inherent connection between the word and the thing or concept it is supposed to represent. Almost any other word would have worked just as well. One way to demonstrate this **arbitrariness** is to notice the difference in the words that different languages use for the same concept. For example, think of the animal that cowboys ride in Western movies. It becomes clear that there is nothing natural about calling this animal a *horse* when we notice that what it is called in other languages is nothing like *horse*: in Turkish it is *at;* in French, *cheval;* in German, *Pferd;* in Spanish, *caballo.* (The only words that tend toward natural meanings are onomatopoeic words—words that imitate sounds. But even these are more arbitrary than you would think. For example, the French version of *splash* is pronounced *plouf,* the German for *bang* is *paff,* the Turkish for *ring* is pronounced *chan,* and so forth.)

Another way to demonstrate that word/ meaning relationships are arbitrary is to create such a relationship. For example, a few pages ago I invented the word *kwug.* But I never told you what it means. Suppose I said that a kwug is one of those little holes in the mouthpiece of a telephone. Once we agree on this word/concept relationship, we can use this word just like any other word in the language. A few seconds ago it would have made no sense to say, "The man disguised his voice by covering the kwugs with a handkerchief." Now it does.

maison
house
casa

房子 /fæŋtzɰ/

FIGURE **2.3**
The Arbitrariness of Symbols

To prove that we are not always in agreement about meaning, ask a few classmates to write down their meanings for given words. You will almost certainly see differences in meaning, especially for abstract concepts—*freedom, friendship, justice,* and the like.

FIGURE **2.4**
Personal Connotations Vary

Here is an exercise to demonstrate that meanings are not shared as easily as we may think: Pair up with a classmate or friend, pick a topic of conversation (a controversial topic works best), and decide who will start the conversation. (We will call this person She, and the partner He.) She begins the conversation in an ordinary fashion, saying whatever she wishes about the topic. Before He gives his natural reply, however, he must first translate her comment *to her complete satisfaction.* He says, "I think what you meant by that is . . ." If She is not satisfied that He has been *completely accurate,* she says, "No," and he tries again (and again and again, if necessary). When he has, in her opinion, captured exactly what she meant, he says whatever he wishes in reply. She must then translate this to his complete satisfaction before she is allowed to reply. And so on for several turns.

CONNOTATIVE AND DENOTATIVE MEANING

Thus, we can see that the meaning of a word depends upon agreement among users of the word. And sometimes individuals are not in agreement.

A common reaction to disagreement about the meaning of a word is, "Look it up in the dictionary." Here is what a dictionary says for the word *snake,* for example: "Any of numerous scaly, legless, sometimes venomous reptiles of the suborder Serpentes or Ophidia (order Squamata), having a long, tapering, cylindrical body and found in most tropical and temperate regions."[1] But what happens if we ask an ordinary language user for his or her meaning of *snake?* Here is what an acquaintance said when I asked: "You know, it's a long, wiggly slimy thing. Well, I know they're not really slimy, but to me it's a slimy thing that scares the [daylights] out of me."

Which meaning is correct? *Both* are. The dictionary provides a **denotative meaning.** This is a *hypothetical standard* meaning. It tries to represent the common denominator among different individuals' personal meanings when they have used the word. An individual's *personal* meaning for a word is its **connotative meaning.** While denotative meaning makes convenient reference material, everyday communication between people is based on their connotative meanings. And since connotations may vary among individuals, two or more people will at times attach slightly different, or even drastically different, meanings to the same word.

A popular version of this concept is the saying *"Meanings are not in words; meanings are in people."* Few principles of communication are as important as the fact that others' meanings for messages may not match our own. As a very simple example, consider how many questions, confusions, and false hopes have been generated when a letter or greeting card has closed unexpectedly with "Love, . . ."

As we begin to become aware of how easily meanings vary among individuals, we become more careful to anticipate others' connotations, and to adjust our messages accordingly. You may have noticed this as you tried the exercise in Figure 2.1.

Another exercise is described in the accompanying *Try This* panel. The typical experience in this exercise is that early in the conversation, receivers' understanding of their partners' comments is very poor—surprisingly so to both partners. As in ordinary conversation, participants make casual comments expecting (but not necessarily obtaining) understanding by their receiver. However, the accuracy improves significantly as senders begin to recognize that their messages are not being understood as intended, and as they begin to increase their efforts toward clarity. Apparently, a major step toward reducing misunderstanding is to recognize the *potential* for misunderstanding. Differences in connotative meaning are one source of misunderstanding; we will see many more.

LANGUAGE AND THOUGHT

Even though meaning is fuzzy, language is powerful. Our use of language affects our communication partners' thoughts and emotions, and theirs affects ours. Indeed, many scholars have found it intriguing to consider the ways in which our own language affects our own thoughts.

LANGUAGE AND PERCEPTION

The best-known view of language and thought is the Whorf-Sapir hypothesis.[2] This hypothesis says that language has a major role in determining thought—so much so that speakers of different languages actually *perceive reality* differently. The classic example is that the Eskimo language has a dozen or so different words for snow—snow in the air, windblown snow, gently falling snow, and so forth. According to the Whorf-Sapir hypothesis, this variety allows (or even compels) Eskimos to perceive snow and its variations differently than speakers of languages like English, to whom snow is snow, more or less. Similarly, the hypothesis assumes that speakers of languages that have no past,

If your language had different words for the kinds of snow falling in these pictures (as the Eskimo language does, for example), it would not cause you to perceive the pictures differently than you do. But it would cause you to remember them differently tomorrow. And it would make it easier to describe the pictures to someone else.

present, and future tenses are unable to grasp these concepts as well as speakers of languages like ours.

While this idea remains popular in some circles, it has been repeatedly disproved by psycholinguists.[3] It turns out that language does *not* determine the way we perceive things. The person whose language has fifteen color words (*blue, red, yellow,* etc.) can perceive or discriminate differences in color no better than the person whose language has only three color words, for example. Current thinking is that neither the Eskimo with a dozen words for snow nor the skier with seven or so words for snow perceives snow any differently than someone whose language has one word for snow. It's just that those seven or dozen variations have been important enough to the other cultures to justify the additional vocabulary.

Current views of language and perception focus on two relationships. The first is **memorability.**[4] Having accessible language symbols for particular concepts makes the corresponding perceptions easier to remember. Persons whose language does not have different words to distinguish our *red* and *orange,* for example, will have more trouble remembering which flower they saw on the table yesterday (the "red" one or the "orange" one) than we will (although they will agree that the two flowers are not the same color).

The second accepted relationship between language and perception is **communicability.** When two persons share the same language code, it is easier for them to communicate about perceptions. Two skiers of the Sierras can communicate relatively easily about a certain kind of snow by using the word *ice,* but they will have more difficulty communicating the concept to a skier of the Catskills, to whom *ice* means a different kind of snow, and will have even more difficulty communicating it to a nonskier, for whom *ice* has relatively little connection to snow.

LANGUAGE AND DISTORTION OF THOUGHT

While language does not determine the way we perceive reality, it can influence the way we organize and think about the reality we perceive. There are several disparities between reality as it is and reality as it is represented by language. It is worthwhile to examine some of these.

Exaggerated Similarities. We've all heard that no two snowflakes are alike. But even though each of a zillion snowflakes is unique, it would be inefficient to use a different word to refer to each of them. Instead, we focus on the features they have in common—crystallization, precipitation, etc.—lump them all into the same category, and call them all by the label for that category: *snowflake.*

Certainly it is convenient that languages have nouns to represent categories of objects and events that the culture considers to be important. But there is an unfortunate byproduct of this classification function of language: Using the same word for two or more objects or events exaggerates their similarities and obscures their differences. No matter how often we've been told that no two snowflakes are alike, whenever we use the same category label—*snowflake*—for more than one of them, our natural tendency is to think of them as being essentially alike, and not to think about all the ways in which each is unique and different.

In the case of snowflakes or elm leaves or aardvarks, individual uniqueness is perhaps a mere technicality. But in the case of people, it can be particularly unfortunate when language obscures our differences. Here, the classification function of language can make us prone to a more serious form of stereotyping and prejudice.

Suppose, for example, that you personally know two people who fit the category *jazz musician,* and suppose that both of them happen to be, in your opinion, irresponsible individuals. (Or, worse yet, suppose you've never met a jazz musician, but you've heard others say that the ones they know are irresponsible.) Now you make a new acquaintance and discover that this person is a jazz musician. If you let the *jazz musician* label trick you into believing that this person must also be irresponsible, you have allowed language to seriously distort reality. The reality, of course, is that all jazz musicians *are* alike, but in only *one* respect: They all perform a certain kind of music. The common label should not imply other similarities. The same thing is true, of course, of other labels—*athlete, sorority member, attorney, engineering major, professor, nursing student,* and so forth.

A group of scholars in the 1940s contrived a hypothetical solution to the problem we have been discussing.[5] The suggestion was that nouns should carry an index number to remind language users that no two members of a category are identical. If, for example, you were to label a new acquaintance not as simply another *Texan,* but rather as, say, Texan^{241}, the indexing would remind you that this Texan is not the same as the others you know—*Texan^{103}, Texan^{002},* etc. The same would apply for *physician^{076}, professor^{017}, athlete^{112},* and so forth.

Indexing was never meant to be a serious suggestion for changing the language. Rather, the concept was introduced to highlight the fact that the absence of indexing in ordinary language tends to hide differences that exist in reality. In other words, hypothetically, indexing could emphasize the differences within categories. But the fact that language operates instead with what we may call **absent indexing** obscures those differences. This places a greater burden on us to recognize that these differences are in fact present.

A similar distortion of reality via language comes from the fact that things change over time even if the words referring to them remain static. When a changing object carries the same word across time, this again exaggerates similarities and obscures differences. To put it another way, we have just said that *attorney^{003}* is not the same as *attorney^{024}*. But *attorney^{024}* is not the same person in 1999 as in 1997. If it were practical, we could both index and date our nouns—*attorney $^{024}_{1990}$, dog $^{416}_{1998}$,* and so forth. But since language operates with **absent dating**, the burden of assuming change across time is again on us. Sometimes the differences will be clear despite absent dating, of course. Most of us have had or will have the shock of discovering that our *hometown*$_{year\ Y}$ is not our *hometown*$_{year\ X}$, for example. But there will be times when we need to remind ourselves that dating exists in reality despite its absence in language. Otherwise, people and things for which we have formed negative impressions in the past may have an unfair strike against them in the present. Just as *sauerkraut* $_{age\ 5}$ (or whatever food you used to hate) is not *sauerkraut* $_{age\ 19}$, *Joe Smith* $_{1999}$ is not *Joe Smith* $_{1989}$.

Exaggerated Differences. Thus, there are ways in which nouns carry too little information to represent certain aspects of reality. There is also a sense in which adjectives tend to distort reality. In particular, our language tends to organize attributes into **dichotomies**—either/or extremes such as *tall–short, fast–slow, hard–soft, easy–difficult,* and so on. In reality, of course, these attributes are not either/or dichotomies, but rather points on a continuum. This continuum includes the entire range, from one extreme (for example, the tallest *ever*) to the other (the shortest *ever*); so the majority of our reality falls somewhere in the middle.

The problem we are getting at is sometimes called **polarized thinking**—that is, thinking of things and people in "either/or," "black and white," "all or nothing" terms. As an example, consider a hiring decision made by a certain university a few years ago. The department advertised the job opening and got more than three hundred applications. A committee narrowed these down to the top twenty, and another committee narrowed those down to the top ten. Then the whole department agreed on the top two young scholars, both of whom were invited to the campus for an interview. The department voted, then offered the job to its first-choice candidate, and he accepted. Several weeks later, when a few members of the faculty were chatting about articles and authors in a recent journal, one colleague interrupted with, "Hold it; that name rings a bell, but I can't place it. Oh yeah, that's the loser we interviewed for the new position." The second best of more than three hundred candidates was now labeled a loser! That's polarized thinking.

Chances are, you know one or two people who are so blatantly polarized in their views that the problem seems more a matter of personality than of language. Maybe it's a bit of both. In any case, we have the responsibility for ensuring that our own personality or world-view recognizes the very many shades of gray between the black-and-white extremes of our language's dichotomies.

Bias from Word Labels.   Read the following list of words slowly and silently: *tree, lake, mother, snake, sex, chair, spider, money.* It is not likely that you were conscious of emotional reactions to these words, but it is almost certain that you did in fact experience emotional responses. When hooked up to a polygraph ("lie detector"), for example, people clearly exhibit emotional responses to certain words, even though they are not aware of having done so. You can see this in Figure 2.5.

In some cases, our mental and emotional responses to words combine to distort our view of reality. In particular, our view of something can sometimes be manipulated by the word chosen to label the thing. For example, the same thing may be viewed positively when it is referred to by one word, and negatively when it is referred to by another word. "*The word is not the thing*" became a popular maxim decades ago to remind us that we should not allow words to determine the character of things.[6]

I admit that I never fully understood this "*word is not the thing*" admonition until one day one of my instructors began class by passing out some odd little crackers he said were left over from a faculty party. Almost everyone in the class took a small handful and munched on them during class. Toward the end of the class period, the instructor asked if anyone wanted more, got a few enthusiastic nods, and with a flourish refilled the bowl from a box of Hartz (the flea-collar company) "Dog Treats." We had been eating dog food! A giant "yuch" arose practically in unison from about half the class, several of us started noticing a "bad aftertaste," a couple of us asked permission to go to the water fountain, and nobody wanted seconds from the refilled bowl!

The point was that the *thing*—what we had been putting in our mouths—hadn't changed. Only the label had changed—from *cracker* or some such label to *dog food*. With one label, the reality was seen as satisfactorily edible, if not pretty darned good; with the other label, the reality was seen as inedible, if not pretty darned disgusting. We were reacting to the word as if the word determined the nature of the thing it arbitrarily represented.

You've seen similar cases, no doubt. *Escargots* sounds more appetizing than *snails*. *Sweetbreads* sounds more appetizing than *thymus glands*. Lest we think that these mat-

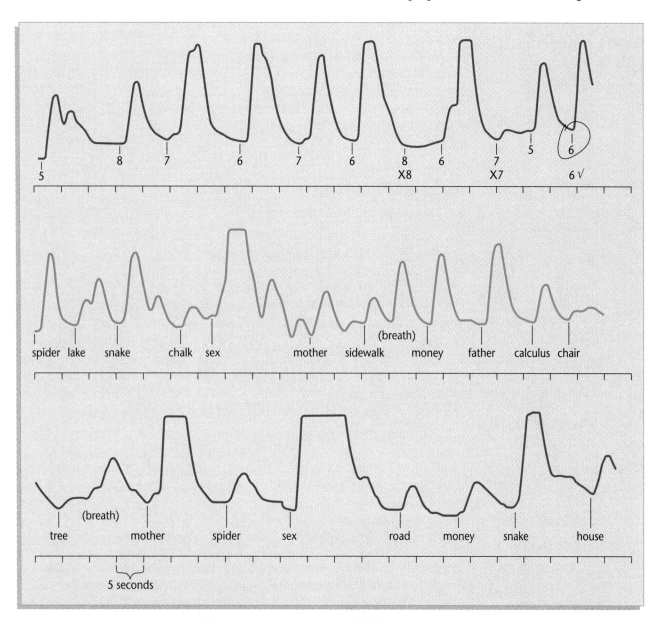

FIGURE 2.5
Emotional Responses to Words

Galvanic Skin Resistance (GSR) measures emotion. The higher the inflection, the greater the emotional response. The top record demonstrates GSR sensitivity with a lie-detection game. The subject picked a number, and then answered "No" when asked, "Is it three?" "Is it five?" etc. (On the selected number, "No" is a lie, of course.) After finally getting a flat line on 8 and 7, the operator correctly guessed 6. The middle and bottom records are from two different subjects and show their reactions as they listened to words being read aloud. Certain words clearly activate strong emotional responses for each individual.

ters are trivial, or apply only to food, here is a more serious example—a letter to the well-known newspaper advice columnist: "Dear Abby, I need to know if I am a virgin. My boyfriend and I have never actually had intercourse, but we have done everything else, and I do mean everything. Does this mean I am still a virgin? This is very important to me."[7] Here is a woman who, for whatever reasons, apparently hopes desperately that she can "warrant" a certain word label: *virgin*. It seems as if she may be devastated if she is told that she can no longer label herself with this word. But the reality is not found in the word. What she and her boyfriend have or haven't done is the reality. Whether their behavior matters is a subjective opinion. But certainly a mere *word* should not be the most powerful element in the equation.

Our Language Interacts with Our Thoughts By
✓   Making concepts easier or harder to remember
✓   Making concepts easier or harder to express
✓   Obscuring differences among members of the same noun category
✓   Obscuring changes that occur across time
✓   Obscuring "shades of gray" in attributes
✓   Allowing particular words to bias our view of particular things

The true difference between a thing when it is called by one name and the same thing when it is called by another is, of course, zero. The fact that we sometimes act as if there is a difference provides additional evidence of the power of language to distort our organization of reality. And it underscores the importance of remembering that, indeed, the word is not the same as the thing, and that the word is not (or at least should not be) what matters in determining our view of reality.

COMMUNICATION BARRIERS IN LANGUAGE

Polarized thinking, absent indexing, and so forth are ways in which language can distort our organization of reality. When language is used as a tool to communicate our thoughts to others, there are additional problems.

AMBIGUITY

All of us have had the frustrating experience of asking for directions in a strange town and then not being able to follow them. Perhaps we were told to turn left at the third traffic light, but we don't know whether to count the flashing yellow light we encounter. Or whether this railroad overpass is what the directions meant by "the bridge." Or whether the nursery school we see is the one meant by, "If you pass the school, you've gone too far." And so on. Or consider the case (supposedly true) in which a department store clerk was taking a phone order for personalized stationery, and asked the customer, "Do you want your name at the upper left or the upper right?" The customer replied, "Put it in the middle," and later received her new stationery with her name and address printed not in the upper middle, where she wanted it, but right in the center of the page!

Clearly it is possible for a message to have one meaning for the sender but an entirely different meaning for the receiver. That is to say, messages may contain **ambigu-**

ity, the possibility of more than one distinct meaning. Ambiguity may occur when a particular word in the message can have more than one meaning, as in "The sentence was too long" (message sentence or prison sentence?). Ambiguity may arise from an unclear pronoun reference, as in, "I dropped my computer on the table and broke it" (broke the computer or broke the table?). Ambiguity may come from unclear grammatical constructions, as in "He saw that gasoline can explode." (Is *can* part of the noun *gasoline can* or part of the verb *can explode?*) And ambiguity may operate in a number of other ways, as well.

We have all experienced situations in which we have heard an ambiguous utterance, spotted the ambiguity immediately, asked the sender for clarification, obtained it, and continued on our merry way, so to speak. Unfortunately, this is not the way ambiguity detection typically operates. And this fact exacerbates the problem of ambiguity in communication.

When we hear an ambiguous utterance, we typically interpret only *one* meaning.[8] Subconsciously, we select one meaning, disregard the other possibilities, and assume that our interpretation is correct. Sometimes when we select incorrectly, there will be other cues in the message to help us make a correction. But sometimes there will not be.

Consider the following message: "Speaking of former boxing champions, many men used to brag that they could handle Mike Tyson's powerful punch. But in reality few people could withstand that much alcohol." Almost certainly you immediately assigned one particular meaning to *punch*—the wrong meaning, as it turns out. In this case, information that showed the error was provided a few words later, so the error was easy to correct. But suppose the speaker of that utterance had ended with, ". . . but in reality few people could," or even with, ". . . but I'm the only one who could." It is possible that the receiver would never recognize the sender's intended meaning.

This tendency to notice only one meaning in ambiguous utterances is a strong one. To demonstrate this, I will warn you in advance that the following sentences are ambiguous, and ask you to notice both meanings. Probably, you will indeed spot both meanings. But notice that there is a lag. Most likely, you will notice one meaning immediately, have to search consciously for a second or so to find the other meaning, and then find it with a sort of "Aha!" reaction:

1. They sent the requisition over a week ago.
2. The chickens are ready to eat.
3. Visiting relatives can be a nuisance.
4. I just read a three-year-old infant behavior study.

In case you are still looking for the other meaning on one or more of these:

1a. They sent over the requisition a week ago.
 b. They sent the requisition more than a week ago.
2a. The chickens are ready to be eaten.
 b. The chickens are anxious to eat.
3a. Visiting relatives is a nuisance.
 b. Visiting relatives are a nuisance.
4a. . . . a three-year-old study on infant behavior.
 b. . . . a study on three-year-old infants' behavior.

Taking that second or so that to search for the other meaning does not usually happen in natural communication. Rather, receivers of ambiguous messages usually jump on a single meaning and ride with it. Ambiguity would not be a serious barrier if receivers always noticed it and could seek clarification. But since that is not what happens, we need to be especially careful to avoid sending ambiguous messages in both interpersonal and public-speaking situations.

CONTEXT

Of course, in real conversations and speeches, utterances are not as isolated as in our examples. Rather, they are usually produced within a larger **context**—the situation at hand, or the particular topic or issue being addressed. Discussions of context often treat it as a sort of protective shield against ambiguity, correctly pointing out that context often *disambiguates*, or clarifies, ambiguous messages. For example, it seems obvious that one meaning goes with "I need a new driver" when it is spoken in the motor pool of a taxi company and that another meaning would be applied if the same sentence were spoken on a golf course. Likewise, "The sentence is too long" seems naturally to mean one thing if we're talking about someone's writing style, and something else entirely if we're talking about the penalty phase of a trial.

It is true that context *can* disambiguate. But it is unwise to assume that context will always eliminate ambiguity, because two problems remain. First, context is not always sufficient to disambiguate. If on a golf course Chris says, "Where can I get a new driver?" and Pat says, "I have no idea," Chris may have been talking about a new club for tee shots, or a new chauffeur, or a new caddy to drive the cart. It is easy to imagine that some of the preceding examples—"three-year-old infant behavior study," "sent the requisitions over a week ago," etc.—might remain ambiguous in any number of natural contexts.

A second problem is that communicators sometimes do a poor job of *establishing* contexts for their messages. Most of us, for example, have had the experience of getting far into a conversation, only to discover that whereas we were talking about Joe, our conversation partner had been talking the whole time about Jim. I (Motley) experienced a version of this not long ago when my father visited me in California. While driving on the freeway, we had the following strange conversation:

Dad:	"Did you see those 'turbunz'?"
Me:	"Just over those hills there are acres of them."
Dad *(confused)*:	"You mean like a village?"
Me *(confused)*:	"Well, more like an orchard, maybe."
Dad *(frustrated)*:	"Orchard? They don't grow them!"
Me:	"No, but they're lined up in rows as far as you can see."
Dad:	"You mean they're for sale at a market of some sort?"
Me:	"What are we talking about?"
Dad:	"Yeah, what *are* we talking about?"

As it turns out, he was commenting on some men who had driven by wearing *turbans*. I hadn't seen them. But it happens that this part of the state has several square miles of high-tech wind *turbines* for generating electricity. I had caught a glimpse of these, but he hadn't. No wonder we were confused:

"Did you see those turbans?"

"[Yes, I saw the turbines.] Just over these hills there are acres of them."

"[Acres of turbans!?] You mean like a village [of people who wear turbans]?"

"[Village of turbines!?] No, more like an orchard [with lots of even rows]."

Etc.

Granted, in this rather comical exchange, the misunderstood contexts had no serious consequences. But there are times when a mismatch in assumed context—especially if it goes undetected—can indeed cause serious problems.

In public-speaking situations, establishing context—at every point in the message—is especially crucial. If the audience is confused, a polite audience is not able to interrupt the speaker with, "What the heck are you talking about?" but rather must try to figure out the meaning on its own. Even if the members of the audience do figure it out eventually, the effort has distracted them from what was being said. Of course, the consequences are even more serious if they never figure it out. Imagine the following excerpt from a speech, for example: "So, when they go up, we're happy; when they go down, we're not. Of course, if we knew when they were going down, that would be OK, because then we could bail out." This makes virtually no sense unless the speaker has established the context, as in: "Having said that, let's return to the matter of buying stocks. When they go up, we're happy; when they go down, we're not. Of course, if we knew when they were going to go down, that would be OK, because then we could bail out."

The confusion that can arise from an unclear context is a primary reason that public speakers are encouraged to use clear transitions between their various points and subpoints, to restate key themes, and otherwise to clarify and highlight the organization of their ideas for the audience. And again, the same problem of unclear contexts exists in interpersonal communication.

FIGURE **2.6**
Conversing within Different Contexts

DIRECT AND INDIRECT MESSAGES

We have seen that two individuals may give entirely different meanings to the same message. Now, to make matters worse, we need to notice that while the sender of a message often wants the receiver to accept the literal meaning, there are times when the receiver is supposed to *ignore* the literal meaning. Suppose you are sitting in class and the instructor interrupts the lecture or discussion by saying, "George, please close the door." This would be a **direct message** (assuming that the instructor wants the door closed). A direct message is one in which the literal translation is meant to match the intended meaning. But suppose instead the instructor had said, "Gosh, that noise out in the hall is unbearable." If the instructor simply meant to state an opinion about the noise, then this is another direct utterance. If, however, the instructor wanted someone to close the door because of the noise, then we have an **indirect message**—a message in which the intended meaning ("close the door") is not meant to match the literal translation ("it's noisy in the hall").

It seems odd that we would use language to communicate meanings that are radically different from what the literal message implies. But we use indirect messages all the time. When we ask, "Do you know what time it is?" we don't want a literal, "Yes, I do" response. When we ask, "Can you reach the salt shaker?" we want the salt, not just "Yep." And so on.

Language philosophers have devoted considerable attention to the mystery of how humans correctly attach intended but nonliteral meanings to indirect messages. And it is indeed an intriguing question. Somehow we know that when a stranger stops us on the street with, "Do you know what time it is?" this is an indirect version of, "Please tell me what time it is." And we also know that when we are running late for an engagement and a parent or spouse asks, "Do you know what time it is?" this is probably an indirect version of, "If you don't hurry, you'll be late." Although the mystery of how we *accurately* decode indirect messages is intriguing, we should not let it obscure a more important point, for our purposes at least—namely, that we often decipher indirect messages *inaccurately*.

In a sense, indirect messages are *hints* of a sort. There is plenty of room for misinterpretation. I remember, for example, a close call I experienced in my first job after graduate school. A few days before the Christmas break, I found a gift on my desk and opened it to find several very fine neckties. But there was no card to tell me who had given me the gift. I checked with two or three people I thought it might have been, but to no avail. Many months later, I discovered completely by chance that the ties were from my boss, and that he had intended the gift as a hint that I should start wearing a tie to work! (Indirect message: "Here are some ties" = "Please start wearing one.") All that time, not only had I committed the faux pas of not thanking my boss for the gift, but from his point of view, I also had been "refusing" to wear a tie even after he had "told me to!" Luckily, this was fairly easy to patch up once the situation became clear, but it is easy to imagine irreparable tension if I had not discovered the meaning of this indirect message.

Misunderstood indirect messages are much more common than we realize. I recently spoke with a student, for example, who was frustrated and angry because her roommate continued to leave a mess in their kitchen after being "told repeatedly that it bothers me" and after having been "asked repeatedly" to please clean up. When pressed to recall and quote *exactly how* she had told and asked her roommate these things, the only specific example she could give was, "Well, I always clean up after her, and when I do, I always say, 'Don't you just love it when the kitchen is clean?' so she obviously *knows* I'm asking her to do it herself." Does she?

We can hardly do away with indirect messages, for they function positively in a number of ways. As a simple case in point, indirectness is expected in certain forms of politeness. But while we need the indirect-message option, we must be careful when we exercise it, and we need to be on guard so that we notice when our indirect messages have been missed by our receivers.

CLOSURE AND PREDICTION

A convenient feature of perception is that the mind attempts to fill in the gaps if part of a message is missing. If a cough in a classroom makes you miss a couple of words, if a momentary distraction makes you miss a sentence or two, if confusion causes you to miss an even larger segment, your mind attempts to perform **closure**—that is, to fill in the missing segments. Sometimes we will look for confirmation that closure was performed correctly; other times we will simply assume that it was correct. Obviously, miscommunication is bound to occur in many of the cases in which we simply assume correct closure.

To make matters worse, closure is not always a conscious process, so seeking confirmation is not always an option. Consider the following messages, which were part of a long-running television advertising campaign: (1) "The best coffee is mountain-grown." (2) "Folgers is mountain-grown." (3) Therefore, Folgers is the best coffee. Actually, the commercial never stated the conclusion—part 3. Viewers were supposed to come up with it on their own. Laboratory studies found that not only did viewers indeed come to this unstated conclusion, but most were emphatic in claiming—incorrectly—that they *heard* this conclusion statement in the commercial![9]

There is an even more subtle closure demonstrated here, however. Notice that the implied conclusion is not valid unless the second premise is that *only* Folgers is mountain-grown. (In fact, virtually *all* coffee is mountain-grown, so the conclusion actually is not valid.) As you might guess—and as the advertisers most assuredly did—viewers' closure filled in the word *only* as being intended in the second premise (did you?), and many viewers swore that the commercial actually said "*Only* Folgers is mountain-grown" until they were allowed to view the commercial again.

A process called **prediction** is likewise concerned with filling in parts of messages. With closure, we fill in part of a message after the fact—that is, after it is received. With prediction, we fill in by anticipating and guessing about part of a message *before* it is received. You've almost certainly performed predictions yourself—for example, when you "know" the first word on the next page of a book as you are turning to it, or when your conversation partner gets stuck trying to think of a word and you supply it, and so forth. Whether prediction operates as noise or as catalyst depends upon which of two prediction modes we adopt.

When we predict part of an incoming message in advance of receiving it, we may do so with an attitude of *cautious* prediction (I *think* I know what's coming, but I'm not absolutely positive) or with an attitude of *overactive* prediction (I *know* what's coming). When we make incorrect predictions in the cautious mode, we tend to notice our mistakes as we process the actual message. But when we make incorrect predictions in the overactive, I-*know*-what-they're-going-to-say mode, we tend not to notice mistakes, and to stick by our incorrect predictions even after we receive the actual message. It is as if we have decided, "Why listen to the actual message since I *know* what it's going to be?"

The lesson for senders is to try to avoid leading receivers' predictions astray. A common mistake of beginning public speakers, for example, is to intentionally lead the audience to expect a bogus issue, topic, subtopic, or conclusion, and then surprise the audience with the real point. This is almost always an unwise strategy. The fact that inaccurate predictions are not always noticed and corrected is one of the reasons that speakers are advised to always make clear exactly where the message is and isn't going. The same is true for serious conversation, of course. The lesson for receivers is to practice prediction in the cautious mode, not the overactive mode.

As a sort of closure/prediction blend, consider the following questions of the type you might encounter in a game of Trivial Pursuit or on a TV quiz show. If you can, answer them as you read them:

1. What feature of Helen of Troy is said to have "launched 1,000 ships"?
2. How many animals of each kind did Moses take on the ark?

3. Was John Wilkes Booth prosecuted after he shot Abraham Lincoln?

4. What psychological condition caused Renoir to cut off his own ear?

A couple of these are trick questions. Most people answer the second question with, "*Two* animals of each kind," even though they know full well that it was Noah, not Moses, who supposedly took animals on an ark.[10] (Read the question again if you fell for it. If you didn't, try it on a friend or roommate—preferably aloud—to see that it almost always works.) And on question 4, the most common answer is, "Depression," even by people who know that it was Van Gogh, not Renoir, who cut off his ear. Psycholinguists have yet to come up with a satisfactory explanation for this so-called Moses effect, but it has become an effective device for demonstrating a variation of what we saw with closure and prediction: Receivers of messages tend to listen (and, to a lesser extent, to read) at the forest level of messages. Receivers tend to sacrifice details at the "trees" level if the details are not necessary for the "forest" (or big picture, or gestalt) they are constructing in their minds. This is important to remember, since the differences between the sender's and the receiver's trees will sometimes create entirely different forests.

SUBJECTIVE INFERENCE

Even when our communication has not been impeded by the barriers discussed thus far, we still may not be in the clear. With communication messages, meaning is subjective, and differences in subjective interpretation will sometimes go beyond closure, emotional responses, direct versus indirect messages, and the like.

As an example, a recent lawsuit was filed by a man who had been seriously injured while using a chin-up exercise bar designed to fit into doorways. Although the device came with support brackets that could be screwed into the doorway, he had relied on the bar's suction cups. The manufacturer denied liability, claiming that the brackets should have been used. Believe it or not, a major issue in the case was whether the words "PORTABLE AND CONVENIENT FOR USE AT HOME OR OFFICE"—which were prominently displayed on the bar's package—"mean" that one is expected to screw "permanent" brackets into the doorway. One side said yes; the other side said no. Even in a courtroom, there was no acceptable answer, because what a message *infers* is a subjective matter. Notice that in this particular example, there is very little ambiguity from connotations, context, indirectness, or other barriers we have discussed. The disagreement was at the inference level—the general, "so what?" level of the message.

Inference is not limited to the assignment of meaning, per se. It also applies to guesses about the sender's motives, character, sincerity, personality traits, and so forth, as well. As a simple example, the hostess at a reception I attended a while ago offered a glass of wine to a guest, who responded simply, "No, thank you." Four witnesses to the exchange had four entirely different interpretations. (1) The hostess assumed that the guest preferred the other wine she was serving, and offered it. (2) I assumed that the guest didn't drink wine, or perhaps didn't drink alcohol. (3) Another guest popped in with, "Oh, you must be supporting the Gallo boycott." (4) And the original guest explained that he already had a full glass that he had put down so that he could manage his hors d'oeuvres. These alternative interpretations of motives and reasons were of little consequence, but I like the example because the message is so simple and so apparently unambiguous. We all know what "no, thank you" *means* in the linguistic sense. But language in actual use involves meanings and inferences at additional subjective levels.

Language-Based Barriers to Communication Include

✓   Variations in individuals' connotations

✓   Ambiguity in messages

✓   Potential confusions of context

✓   Indirectness

✓   Incorrect closure

✓   Overactive prediction

✓   Subjective interpretations

A FINAL NOTE ON LANGUAGE BARRIERS

We began our discussion of language-related communication barriers to show that communicating well is not so easy as we might think. But learning to guard against certain traps, rather than taking language for granted, is not something that we can accomplish overnight. The good news, however, is that the effect is cumulative. As we start noticing, correcting, and avoiding any of these potential sources of miscommunication we usually become more aware of the others, and begin to become better communicators on several levels.

"CORRECT" LANGUAGE

So far in this chapter, we have been concerned with ways in which language may be responsible for distortions of thought and breakdowns in communication. We should add a reminder that language may be judged to be "correct" or "incorrect," "proper" or "improper," regardless of whether communication has been accurate in the sense we have discussed thus far. If you ask someone for directions and the reply is, "I don't know; I ain't never been here before," the message will be *understood,* but will it be *correct?*

There are two distinct points of view on the matter of "correct" or "proper" language in the present sense. One point of view is that there is a set of rulebook-type conventions for what constitutes correct language use, that these conventions are based on the language patterns of our most educated speakers and writers, and that when these conventions are not followed, the language is being used incorrectly. Thus, we are taught these conventions in school—don't use double negatives, don't end a sentence with a preposition, don't say "ain't," and so forth.

The other point of view is that our language patterns should match those of our receivers. And since most of our receivers do not follow all of the rulebook conventions, we would sound strange if we were to follow them. From this point of view, for example, if you were responding to "Who's there?" it would be more correct to say "It's me" than to say "It is I," despite the rulebook's preference for the latter. To put it another way, this approach would advise that the safer course is to ignore the rulebook and use the language patterns favored by the majority of users.

In practice, the wise approach falls between these extremes. Most of us have adopted some of the rulebook conventions we were taught and have abandoned others. It doesn't bother us much when we hear people violate conventions that we have abandoned also. But it does bother us when we hear our own pet conventions violated. More importantly, our receivers respond to *our* language in the same way. They forgive some of our technically "incorrect" language habits, but not others. Thus, the wise course of action is to adapt to our receivers and avoid at least the errors that they are likely to notice and find troublesome. Would you consider any of the following to be bothersome, for example?

1. The jury was present.
2. If I was the boss, I'd make some changes around here.
3. She took the news badly.
4. The people that came to my party were nice.
5. Both movies are acceptable choices.
6. The number of burglaries are increasing.

Each of the odd-numbered sentences is acceptable, or correct, both according to formal conventions and according to popular usage. Each of the even-numbered sentences is incorrect, however, both according to formal conventions and according to "typical" individuals' lists of most bothersome language errors.[11] In case you didn't catch the errors, compare the version above with the correct version here:

2. *If* I *were* the boss . . .
4. The *people who* came to my party . . .
6. The *number* of burglaries *is* increasing . . .

If this seems like just one more lesson in how to avoid instructors' corrections on your essays, you may be surprised to know that the second most serious complaint that business executives make about young new employees is that they "write and speak with poor grammar."[12] (The first complaint is poor training; the third is improper manners and etiquette.) And many job interviewers report that they routinely accept and reject applicants on the basis of their spoken grammar when the competition is otherwise roughly equal. Therefore, the rulebook conventions—at least those still followed by a significant number of receivers—are worth learning and following.

So here is a *partial* list of the most bothersome and **common language-usage errors** of today.[13] (We have omitted a few that are more common in writing than in typical interpersonal communication or public speaking. For a more extensive list and discussion, see a *contemporary* handbook.[14])

I. SEXIST LANGUAGE

About twenty years ago, sexist language was discussed along with dichotomous language, absent indexing, and so forth as a way in which language distorts our view of reality. If, for example, the gender of a hypothetical police officer is unknown, *policeman* distorts reality by implying that the officer is male when this may or may not be the case. Unlike the situation with other sources of distortion, however, a determined effort has been made to *change* common usage of sexist language. The effort has been so successful that these days sexist language is viewed not as a mere technical inaccuracy, but as improper language usage. Moreover, some receivers will regard sexist language not only as a blatant language-usage error, but also as an insult to an entire gender.

The three most common forms of sexist language are these:

A. The generic *he, his, him,* or *himself,* when referring to a noun of unknown gender, is generally regarded as a mistake. For example:

X = Wrong   √ = Correct

X **1**a. A bank manager is in a position to know the financial state of *his* community.

X   b. . . . *her* community.

√   c. . . . *his* or *her* community.

√   d. . . . *the* community.

X **2**a. A journalist must protect *his* sources.

√   b. . . . *his* or *her* sources.

√   c. . . . protect *all* sources.

X **3**a. We have no idea who committed the robbery, but we'll catch *him*.

√   b. . . . catch *him* or *her*.

√   c. . . . catch *whoever* did it.

X **4**a. I suggest you visit a physician and see whether he can help.

√   b. . . . see whether *he or she* can help,

√   c. . . . see whether *a doctor* can help.

B. Avoid suffixes (*-man, -ess, -er,* etc.) indicating gender in a *job* or *position* when the gender is unknown.

X **1**a. Who will be the *spokesman* for the group.

√   b. Who will speak for the group?

√   c. George will be the *spokesman* for the group.

X   d. Elizabeth will be the *spokesman* for the group.

√   e. Elizabeth will be the *spokeswoman* for the group.

√*   f. [George, Elizabeth, Who] will be the *spokesperson* for the group.

X **2**a. Why can't the restaurants in this city hire good *waitresses?*

X   b. . . . *waiters?*

√   c. . . . *waiters and waitresses?*

√   d. . . . *servers?*

X*   e. . . . *waitpersons?*

*Note: The *-person* suffix sometimes works well as a replacement for the *-man* or *-woman* suffix, but it creates contrived constructions in many other contexts.

C. Avoid nonparallel or unequal treatment when describing both genders. Use consistent and parallel treatment.

X **1**a. The senatorial candidates are Harold Jones, a Wall Street lawyer, and Amanda Smith, a pert, blue-eyed grandmother of three.

√   b. . . . and Amanda Smith, a retired economics professor.

√   c. . . . Harold Jones, a tan, athletic, grandfather of two, and Amanda Smith, a pert, blue-eyed . . .

X 2a. The men's basketball team posted its third straight victory, while the ladies hung their ponytails in defeat.

√   b. . . . while the women's team posted a loss.

√   c. The players on the gentlemen's team flexed their tattoos in victory while those on the ladies' team hung their ponytails in defeat.

II. *GOOD* VERSUS *WELL*

Good is an adjective. It modifies *nouns*. *Well* is an adverb. It modifies *verbs*. It is rare is for *well* to be incorrectly substituted for *good*, but *good* is often incorrectly substituted for *well*.

X 1a. I did *good* on my exam.

√   b. I did *well* on my exam.

√   c. I got a *good* grade on my exam.

X 2a. He played *good*.

√   b. He played *well*.

√   c. He played a *good* game.

X 3a. If I build it, I'll build it *good*.

√   b. . . . I'll build it *well*.

III. LATIN-BASED PLURALS

In general, native English speakers rarely err when distinguishing between singular and plural nouns. There are a few nouns from Latin, however, that are troublesome in this regard, and errors on these are especially annoying to some receivers.

1. *Media* is plural; *medium* is singular.

X   a. The *media is* responsible for much of today's violence.

√   b. The *media are* responsible . . .

X   c. Television is the most popular *media* these days.

√   d. Television is the most popular *medium* . . .

2. *Data* is plural; *datum* is singular.

X   a. *This data indicates* that you are correct.

√   b. *These data indicate* that . . .

√   c. *This datum indicates* that . . .

√   d. This *piece of data indicates* that . . .

3. *Criteria* is plural; *criterion* is singular.

X   a. She never gave me *a single criteria* for my grade.

√   b. . . . *a single criterion . . .*

√   c. . . . *any* of the *criteria . . .*

4. *Phenomena* is plural; *phenomenon* is singular.

X   a. True love is a fascinating *phenomena.*

√   b. . . . *a* fascinating *phenomenon.*

√   c. Love and friendship *are* fascinating *phenomena.*

IV. *WHO* VERSUS *THAT*

Here is a case where the convention is very simple, yet the error is very common—so common, in fact, that the convention may soon be passé. In the meantime, it is wiser to follow the convention: *that* is never used in reference to humans; use *who* instead.

X   1a. She's the one *that* played the piano at the party.

√   b. She's the one *who* played the piano at the party.

√   c. She's the one *that* gave birth to these kittens.

X   2a. And now, here is someone *that* needs no introduction . . .

√   b. . . . someone *who ...*

X   3a. Where is the valet *that* parked my car?

√   b. . . . valet *who . . .*

V. SUBJUNCTIVE MOOD

The subjunctive mood expresses a nonexistent hypothetical condition as in *I wish . . . , If only . . . , What if . . . ,* and so forth. The convention is that *was* becomes *were.*

X   1a. *If I was* president, I'd . . . .

√   b. *If I were* president . . .

X   2a. I *wish she was* the boss.

√   b. I *wish she were* the boss.

X   3a. *Suppose he was* to ask you for a date.

√   b. *Suppose he were* to . . .

X   4a. *What if I was* to tell you what I really think?

√   b. *What if I were* to tell you . . .

VI. PREPOSITIONS AT THE END OF A SENTENCE

Here is a convention that is definitely changing. The rule that a sentence must never be ended with a preposition was considered rather inflexible not too many years ago. Today, the convention is more sub-

---

Common Language-Usage "Errors" Include

✓ Sexist language

✓ Good for well

✓ That for who

✓ Singular/plural confusion with Latin-based nouns

✓ Inappropriate preposition placement

✓ Subject-verb agreement

jective: avoid a preposition at the end of a sentence unless the alternative is awkward. In other words, if doing otherwise results in an awkward sentence, then go ahead and end the sentence with a preposition. But avoid a redundant or unnecessary preposition at the end of a sentence.

Redundant Prepositions

> X **1**a. I told him where I would be *at*.
>
> √   b. I told him where I would be.
>
> X **2**a. Tell me where you're going *to*.
>
> √   b. . . . where you're going.

Note: *At* is virtually always inappropriate at the end of a sentence.

Convenient Alternatives

> X **1**a. I couldn't believe what I saw when I turned the TV *on*.
>
> √   b. . . . when I turned *on* the TV.
>
> X **2**a. After dinner, she turned the lights *down*.
>
> √   b. . . . turned *down* the lights.
>
> √   c. . . . *dimmed* the lights.

Awkward Alternatives

> √ **1**a. Ending a sentence with a preposition is easy to *get away with*.
>
> X   b. . . . is *something with which* it is easy to *get away*.
>
> √ **2**a. I got lost because I forgot which street *to turn onto*.
>
> X   b. . . . because I forgot the street *onto which* I was *supposed to turn*.

VII. SUBJECT-VERB AGREEMENT

You may or may not have been aware of the conventions mentioned thus far. The next one is almost certainly familiar, however. If you are a native speaker of English, you know of the convention whereby a singular subject requires a singular verb, and a plural subject requires a plural verb. Indeed, we rarely make errors when the subject and its number (singular or plural) are obvious. The following would be practically unheard of among educated speakers, for example:

> X **1.** My *father are* here.
>
> X **2.** *Both dogs is* sick.
>
> X **3.** If there's one thing I hate, *it are* broccoli.

On the other hand, when sentence constructions get more complex, we sometimes lose track of which noun is functioning as the subject of the sentence. In these cases, errors are more common. For example.

> X **1**a. The *rate* of homicides *are* climbing.
>
> √   b. The *rate* of homicides *is* climbing.
>
> X **2**a. The *grocery,* along with the barber shop, *were* destroyed.

√   b. The *grocery,* along with the barber shop, *was* destroyed.

√   c. The *grocery and the barber shop were* destroyed.

√   **3.** *Writing* jazz tunes *is* among John's hobbies.

√   **4.** *Each* of the wines *has* its own special character.

Note: Always use a *singular* verb when the subject is one of the following: *each, either, anyone, everyone, much, no one, someone.*

A QUICK SELF-ASSESSMENT

If you already follow these language-usage conventions, there should have been no surprises in the "X" and "√" examples above. If you found several surprises, however— things you say every day that are "wrong" according to our list of most bothersome errors—then it may be worthwhile for you to learn the more accepted conventions. You may or may not wish to switch over to these forms in your everyday interpersonal communication. But it is valuable to be able to adapt to standard language conventions when the situation demands it.

Following standard language conventions in one's interpersonal communication pays off on the job, in making a favorable first impression with new acquaintances, in minimizing mental distractions for receivers who expect standard language, and so forth. Moreover, correct language in one's ordinary interpersonal communication is crucial to effective public speaking before educated audiences. Since correct language is expected of public speakers, and since a spontaneous, conversational (nonscripted) style also is expected of public speakers, speakers who are not comfortable with standard language are at a disadvantage: If they are truly spontaneous, they make errors, and if they script the speech in order to avoid errors, they sacrifice spontaneity and directness.

Granted, both formal audiences and interpersonal communication partners will forgive an *occasional* error such as, "Take a look at *this* data" or "It was our governor *that* made this possible." But when our communication repeatedly shows us to be unfamiliar with standard language conventions, we put ourselves a disadvantage in certain interpersonal and public-speaking situations.

IN SUMMARY

We have highlighted some of the ways in which language can interfere with communication. The underlying theme has been (1) that our messages often do not achieve their desired effect, (2) that sometimes this is because language usage allows meaning to be imprecise, and (3) that part of the solution is to become more alert to the many interactions among language, thought, and emotion.

We began at the microscopic level, examining the components of language. Carelessness with these components can distort meaning and can lead to idiosyncrasies and styles that make us sound strange to others.

We then explored the more macroscopic level of language and thought, seeing that the relationship between language and meaning is imprecise, and noticing that language can operate to shape (sometimes inaccurately) the individual user's organization and view of reality.

Our discussion focused next on several specific barriers to the effective transmission of messages via language. In some cases, the problem boils down to imprecision in the message itself (as with ambiguity, failure to establish context, and indirect messages). Other barriers are related more to the way in which receivers process messages (as with closure and prediction), and still others are related to what the receiver's mind may do with the message after its meaning is processed (as with subjective inferences).

We ended by noticing that the correctness of our messages may affect receivers' impressions of us as educated individuals and competent users of the language. We highlighted common errors that create negative impressions in some receivers.

With language-based difficulties, it is impossible to suggest solutions in the form of a list of specific messages or specific language behaviors. There are simply too many potential-misunderstanding situations (via imprecise juncture, ambiguity, confused context, and so forth) for us to anticipate them all and prescribe the ideal messages. Thus it is necessary for us to take a more general, consciousness-raising approach to language-based barriers. The burden is on the individual communicator to *become aware* of the potential problems, to more *closely monitor* his or her own communication so as to notice when these barriers may be operating, and to *adjust* and *adapt* the communication accordingly.

TERMS TO KNOW

language	memorability
language rules	communicability
phoneme	absent indexing
morphemes	absent dating
words	dichotomies
syntax	polarized thinking
suprasegmentals	ambiguity
stress	context
juncture	direct message
pitch	indirect message
arbitrariness (of symbols)	(inaccurate) closure
denotative meaning	(overactive) prediction
connotative meaning	common language-usage errors

NOTES

1. *The American Heritage Dictionary of the English Language,* 3d ed. (Boston: Houghton Mifflin, 1996, p. 1705).

2. B. L. Whorf, *Language, Thought, and Reality* (Cambridge, Mass.: MIT Press, 1956).

3. R. W. Brown, "Reference: In Memorial Tribute to Eric Lenneberg," *Cognition* 4 (1954): 125–153; R. W. Brown and E. H. Lenneberg, "A Study in Language and Cognition," *Journal of Abnormal Psychology* 49 (1954): 454–462.

4. E. R. Heider, "Universals in Color Naming and Memory," *Journal of Experimental Psychology* 93 (1972): 10–20.

5. For example, S. I. Hayakawa, *Language in Thought and Action* (New York: Harcourt Brace Jovanovich, 1972).

6. Hayakawa, *Language in Thought and Action.*

7. As seen in a "Dear Abby" column by Abigail Van Buren. Copyright ©1989 by Universal Press Syndicate. Reprinted with permission. All rights reserved.

8. For example, D. J. Foss and C. M. Jenkins, "Some Effects of Context on the Comprehension of Ambiguous Sentences," *Journal of Verbal Learning and Verbal Behavior* 12 (1973): 577–589.

9. C. P. Wrighter, *I Can Sell You Anything* (New York: Ballantine Books, 1972).

10. T. D. Erickson and M. E. Mattson, "From Words to Meaning: A Semantic Illusion," *Journal of Verbal Learning and Verbal Behavior* 20 (1981): 540–551.

11. L. Kessler and D. McDonald's, *When Words Collide*, 4/e, (New York: Wadsworth, 1996).

12. M. T. Motley and students, "Cumulative Pilot Studies, 1989–1997: RCM 105 & RCM 134" (unpublished paper, University of California at Davis).

13. L. Kessler and D. McDonald's, *When Words Collide*, 4/e, Wadsworth Publishing, ©1996. Reprinted by permission of Wadsworth Publishing.

14. For example, L. Kessler and D. McDonald, *When Words Collide*.

NONVERBAL BEHAVIOR

THIS CHAPTER
will help you

- Look for nonverbal idiosyncrasies you may have

- Become aware of the latitude in meaning of nonverbal behaviors

- Recognize that nonverbal behavior is guided by cultural norms

- Recognize that interpretations of nonverbal behavior may take place without intentional "messages" by "senders"

- Notice nonverbal norms in order to make your delivery of speeches more "conversational"

EVERY LITTLE MOVEMENT HAS A MEANING all its OWN.

—C. Porter

As we begin this chapter on nonverbal behavior, I (Motley) am reminded of an occasion on which my son, when he was about twelve years old or so, passed by a pile of my books, surveyed the titles, and asked, "'Nonverbal behavior'— what's that?" Eager to acquaint him with a part of the communication field, I explained that nonverbal behavior included such things as the meaning of facial expressions, the function of gestures, the distance we stand from one another in conversation, the norms of eye contact, and so on. He soon interrupted, rather unimpressed, with, "In other words, a bunch of common sense."

In some ways he was right; in some ways he was wrong. On the one hand, it would indeed be silly to discuss facial expressions, gestures, and certain other forms of nonverbal behavior for the purpose of learning how to do them correctly. For the most part, we already follow the nonverbal norms of our culture "correctly," and we do so with little conscious effort. Knowing how far apart to stand during a conversation, knowing that we should smile instead of frown when we are happy (or wish to appear so), and so forth, is indeed common sense.

But on the other hand, there are subtleties of nonverbal behavior that go beyond common sense. For example, without realizing it, many of us will have one or two quirks or idiosyncrasies that violate nonverbal norms. Also, for some nonverbal behaviors the norms are flexible, so that our common-sense expectations may not match those of our partners. Moreover, when it comes to common-sense interpretations of others' nonverbal behaviors (and their interpretations of ours), there is more room for error than one might think.

As suggested in Chapter 1, **nonverbal behavior** is behavior that *does not use words*. That covers a lot of territory! This chapter is especially interested in nonverbal behaviors that affect our interactions. Before we examine these behaviors, there are a few background considerations to keep in mind.

NONVERBAL BEHAVIOR— A FEW BASICS

VERBAL/NONVERBAL BOUNDARIES ARE FUZZY

Here is an interesting contradiction: Suppose you were to ask a group of communication scholars whether American Sign Language (ASL), as used by deaf and hard-of-hearing communicators, is verbal or nonverbal. Most would answer that it is verbal. The hand signs stand for words. Indeed, the signs *are* words, so ASL is a verbal system (verbal-nonvocal, in terms of the categories introduced in Chapter 1). Now suppose you were to ask the same scholars whether the hand sign we all make by raising a forefinger to our lips to mean "quiet, please" is verbal or nonverbal. Most would answer that it is nonverbal. What's the difference between these two kinds of signs? None, actually.

The distinction between verbal and nonverbal behavior in this case and a few others comes more from research traditions than from strict definitions. Be prepared, as we discuss nonverbal behaviors, to take the nonverbal designation with a grain of salt. Some of these behaviors are indeed clearly nonverbal (e.g., hair styles, body shape, etc.), some are quite verbal (e.g., signed substitutes for words, as in obscene gestures or our "quiet, please" example), and some are in a gray area, neither completely verbal nor completely nonverbal (such as the vocal inflections that accompany speech).

SOME NONVERBAL BEHAVIOR IS COMMUNICATIVELY INTENTIONAL AND SOME IS NOT

With verbal behavior, it is obvious that there is communicative intention. People generally do not speak (or write, or sign) *words* unless they are trying to tell somebody something. With nonverbal behavior, however, it is not so simple. Sometimes intention is clearly present, as when you perform a fake yawn to tell a friend across the room that you are bored. Sometimes communicative intention is clearly absent, as when one's face involuntarily turns red with embarrassment. And in some cases, it is difficult to determine whether nonverbal behaviors represent an intentional message. In all these cases, however, nonverbal behaviors are subject to interpretation. Thus, when we interpret others' nonverbal behavior, sometimes they will indeed be trying to "tell us something." And other times we will be interpreting behaviors even though there is no "message" as far as the sender is concerned.[1]

As for how we know which is which, often we don't. We make assumptions, and sometimes we are wrong. As an example, a recent newspaper article told of an incident in Los Angeles where a former professional basketball star beat up a man for driving by and making an obscene gesture. According to the victim, he was simply flicking a cigarette out his car window.

As we discuss the "meaning" of certain nonverbal behaviors, it is important to remember that sometimes there is no encoding by the "sender," and no "message" except the one imagined by the receiver. (This is one reason that our discussion will be in terms of nonverbal *behavior* rather than nonverbal *communication*.) And it is important also to recognize that people sometimes are interpreting our own behaviors whether we mean for them to or not.

MEANING IS UNCERTAIN FOR NONVERBAL BEHAVIORS

While there are a few nonverbal behaviors that operate as symbols, most nonverbal behaviors are interpreted as symptoms. When we introduced symptoms in Chapter 1, our examples were of relationships that exist by nature—dark clouds meaning impending rain, stomach growls meaning hunger, and so forth. In the case of nonverbal behaviors, people often *infer* symptoms on the basis of "human nature." For example, (1) she's sitting closer to me than normal; (2) that means she's attracted to me, because (3) it is "natural" to sit closer than normal when there is attraction. But one person's view of what is natural, in the human-nature sense, will often differ from another's view. Moreover, almost any nonverbal behavior may be symptomatic of more than a single given condition. Maybe she's sitting closer than normal because she wants to say something that is confidential, for example.

In other words, meanings and interpretations of nonverbal behaviors often are on very shaky ground. When an acquaintance is repeatedly late for your dates, is that symptomatic of his or her relative disrespect or disinterest in you? When a roommate becomes unusually quiet and sullen, does that mean that anger is being directed toward you? When a new acquaintance to whom you are attracted exhibits a greater-than-normal level of eye contact, does it mean that the attraction is mutual? In all these cases, the answer is, "Maybe yes, maybe no." Our understanding of "human nature"—within our own culture, at least—tells us that these inferred meanings are possibilities. But a closer look at nonverbal behavior reminds us that they are not at all the *only* possibilities. In short, the "meanings" of nonverbal behaviors are often less certain than we may think.

Even when our inferences are based on a *composite* of several nonverbal behaviors, they may not be accurate. As an example, let me describe a hypothetical individual: Person A is relatively quiet. He or she doesn't say much; he or she will speak if spoken to, but usually doesn't initiate the conversation. This person is also relatively plain in appearance. Based on attire, Person A seems not particularly well-to-do; and in terms of physical attractiveness, Person A is what most would consider to be average or below average. Now, what personality trait would you assign to Person A? In other words, how would you fill in the blank if you were asked, "Person A seems like a(n) _____ individual?" Most people fill in the blank with *shy.* Let's look now at Person B. Person B is quiet—he or she doesn't say much, will speak if spoken to, but usually doesn't initiate the conversation. Person B is relatively sharp in appearance. Based on attire, for example, Person B seems relatively well-to-do. And in terms of physical attractiveness, Person B is what most people would consider to be far above average. Now fill in the blank again. Person B seems like a(n) _____ individual. Most people fill in this blank with *arrogant* or *stuck-up.*

Notice first that you probably used the entire composite for your impressions of Persons A and B. Given any single characteristic, you probably would not have made the same inference. And, of course, an inference based upon a composite of nonverbal cues should be more valid than one based on a single behavior. But more importantly, notice how tenuous these inferences are, even though we are using a composite. Isn't it possible that Person B is a nicely dressed, good-looking, *humble,* and *shy* individual, for example?

BOTH VERBAL AND NONVERBAL BEHAVIORS ARE IMPORTANT

In popularized discussions of nonverbal behavior, it is common to read that nonverbal behaviors carry most of the meaning in ordinary messages. Some extreme versions claim that 70 percent or more of the meaning in a message is carried nonverbally, with only 30 percent or less carried verbally. It takes only a moment's reflection to see that this is absurd. There are many situations in which the large majority of the message clearly is verbal (for example, listening to news on the radio, having an unemotional telephone conversation, or reading this book), and there are rare situations in which the majority of the message clearly is nonverbal (for example, when someone's sobbing makes his or her words unintelligible). In ordinary conversation, the majority of the information usually is verbal, although there will be special situations—certain romantic episodes, for example—in which the majority is nonverbal.

The question of which mode—verbal or nonverbal—dominates meaning is somewhat moot, because the answer will vary from one situation to the next. Moreover, arguing the question is a bit silly, since both modes are extremely important. On the one hand, popular claims about the nonverbal mode superseding the verbal mode simply are not true for ordinary interpersonal and public-speaking situations. On the other hand, the role played by nonverbal behavior in these encounters can be very important nevertheless—crucial, in fact. In short, in most situations, effective communication depends upon both verbal and nonverbal elements.

KINESICS

Our discussion of nonverbal elements will be organized according to broad categories of nonverbal behavior. The first category we will explore is **kinesics**, or *body movement*. In particular, we will see how certain communicative functions are carried out, at least in part, by eye contact, facial expressions, gestures, and body position.

EYE BEHAVIOR

During conversation, we are expected to look at our conversation partners. But why, and how much?

As for *why*, eye contact serves a variety of functions. The most obvious of these is that it signals interest in the conversation and in the individuals. More subtly, perhaps, eye contact is also one of the cues indicating a conversational turn. For example, if the person who is talking pauses for a moment while looking away from the listener, it usually indicates that the speaker is going to continue after the pause. But if the speaker stops talking and looks directly at the listener, this is often a signal for the listener to take a turn as speaker. Eye contact also functions to receive feedback with which to gauge the listener's response to the message.

As for how much eye contact takes place, it is less than you might think. During conversation, the listener typically will be looking at the speaker about 60 percent of the time.[2] (Some listeners look at speakers' eyes, some look at the mouth and chin, and some look in between, around the nose area.) The speaker, on the other hand, will look at the listener only about 40 percent of the time. There are situations in which these percentages may be much higher (when there is romantic interest, for example) and situations in which they may be lower (when there is anxiety or other emotional discomfort, for example).

It is rare to find people deviating from these norms enough to create discomfort for their partners. However, it does happen. The most common criticism of *others'* eye contact is that some people make *too much* eye contact. Their "stare" is bothersome for their conversation partners. When we evaluate our *own* eye contact, our most common concern is that we may habitually make *too little* eye contact. Most often, however, those who are concerned that they make too little eye contact are in fact operating completely within the nonverbal behavioral norms. That is, in most cases their eye contact is satisfactory to their conversation partners.

In the public-speaking context, eye contact represents a bit of a paradox. With most nonverbal behaviors, public speakers should behave just as in conversation—using natural and "conversational" gestures, facial expression, vocal inflection, and so forth. But public speakers need to maintain a much higher level of eye contact than the 40 percent common for speakers in conversation. Eye contact should be maintained about 80 percent of the time in public speaking, being distributed among various members of the audience. Effective public speakers typically look at one audience member for a short while, then another, then another.

How long would you want to look into these eyes without breaking off if you were in a normal conversation?

Even when we are not talking, eye behavior can carry information. Between strangers in a bar, for example, repeated eye contact and/or slightly longer than normal eye contact is a primary sign of attraction (especially if accompanied by a smile). On the other hand, blatant stares from several people in the same bar are probably a hostile sign that we are not welcome there.

FACIAL EXPRESSION

The area of kinesics that has been studied most extensively is facial behavior. Facial movement and expression serve two main communication functions. One is to *accent* and emphasize parts of our messages as we speak. As we talk, we will often wrinkle our forehead, raise or lower our eyebrows, squint our eyes, and so forth, in concert with words and phrases we wish to emphasize. As we will see later in our discussion, this accent function of facial expression is also performed by certain kinds of hand gestures and head movements. The speaker's head, hands, and face move with the rhythm of the spoken message to accent, punctuate, and emphasize what is being said. Indeed, some prefer to call this kind of facial expression **facial gesture.**

The second primary function of facial movement is that of **affect display**, or more simply *display of emotion*. Facial displays of emotion function to inform one another of emotional states, to provide feedback to one another's messages (via expressions of confusion, surprise, amusement, and so forth), to show interest or lack of interest in the interaction, and to show the intensity and sincerity of our involvement in the communication episode.

Facial expression is not always a reliable indicator of emotion, but it is often a very strong cue. As a simple demonstration of how powerful the relationship between emotion and facial expression can be, look at the following diagrams and match them with these emotions: *angry, happy, embarrassed, vengeful, sad:*

(a)   (b)   (c)   (d)   (e)

By changing just the mouth and eyebrow lines on these cartoon-type faces, we are able to represent very different emotions. Real-life facial expression includes a much richer array of movement, of course, as more than a hundred facial muscles operate upon the lips, forehead, eyes and eyebrows, and so forth. This makes facial affect displays easier to read in some situations, and harder to read in others.

Affect displays via facial expression are especially accurate when the facial expression is intentional, as when we intentionally put on an angry expression (whether we are truly angry or not) to signal a child to stop doing something, for example. Research studies in which actors are photographed while posing facial expressions for various emotions find that people match the photographs and the emotions with very high accuracy, as you probably did with the cartoon faces here. (The answers, by the way:

A = *happy,* B = *sad,* C = *angry,* D = *embarrassed,* E = *vengeful.*) In fact, people from virtually all cultures, even those who have had no media or other contact with our culture, match most of the posed expressions with their corresponding emotions very reliably. Apparently, many of our prototypic, or posed, facial expressions are universal.[3]

It is a very different story with spontaneous facial expression, however, at least in conversation. Here, facial expressions tend to represent the *presence* of an emotional reaction, but not the *type* of emotion (sad, angry, happy, etc.). We determine the particular emotion *from the verbal context.*[4] For example, researchers have secretly videotaped facial expressions during natural conversations in which one of the partners is a confederate working with the researcher. The confederate manipulates the conversation in order to insert certain comments designed to elicit emotional responses from the partner. For example, *sadness* was elicited by a true story about the confederate's being at her boyfriend's bedside when he died from a motorcycle accident; *confusion* was elicited by an impossible-to-understand explanation of forthcoming changes in course registration; and so forth for various other emotions. Then people were shown the videotaped facial expressions and asked to match facial expressions and emotions. With facial expressions only—no audio—people were not at all accurate in their matches.

When audio was added, so that the facial expressions were shown along with the corresponding conversation, people were very accurate in matching the correct emotion to the facial expressions. But the most interesting results came when expressions and conversation segments were spliced together in random combinations—when the part of the *conversation* that had elicited emotion X (the dying-boyfriend story, let's say) was dubbed onto the *facial expression* for emotion Y (confusion, let's say), people identified the facial expression according to the emotion that fit the *verbal* (audio) context. (The original *confusion* expression was interpreted as *sadness* in the sadness context, as *anger* in the anger context, and as *confusion* in the confusion context, for example!)[5]

Thus, it appears that in conversation, spontaneous facial expressions function as **nonverbal interjections.** An ordinary verbal interjection is an expression such as *gosh, golly, geez, wow, my goodness,* and so forth. Whatever your favorite verbal interjection happens to be, you may say it when someone has told you something saddening, something surprising, something maddening, and so forth. In other words, the interjection signals the *presence* of an emotional response, but not the *type* of emotion. The type of emotion is deduced from the verbal context. Apparently, the same is true for much of the spontaneous facial expression in conversation.

There is another way in which facial affect displays do not directly correspond to the emotions present. In many typical everyday situations, social conventions of politeness and proper conduct discourage us from revealing our emotions as clearly as we do in posed or exaggerated displays. These conventions are called **display rules.**[6] In a few situations, these display rules suggest that we *exaggerate* our affect displays, as when we open a gift in the presence of the one who gave it to us. But many of these display rules dictate that we *subdue* or even *disguise* our affect displays. We are not "supposed to" display our full glee when we are presented with a coveted award in public, we are not "supposed to" display our full amusement when someone who is "asking for it" slips and falls on an icy sidewalk, we are not "supposed to" display our full anger when a coworker has ticked us off, and so forth. We follow these rules, in part, by subduing or disguising facial expression.

People control facial expression in accordance with self-imposed display rules, as well—they exaggerate, downplay, or disguise their true emotions for one reason or another. Granted, we can have genuine and sincere conversations in which we make no effort to hide our emotions, positive or negative. But there are also situations in which we are very much on guard with respect to our own affect displays. Our conversation partners have the same facial control, of course. Thus, it is wise to be cautious when inferring others' emotions from their facial expressions. As a case in point, research has shown that even though we think we can tell, from facial expressions and other nonverbal behaviors, when someone is lying to us, we are in fact very poor at detecting deception.[7]

We have mentioned two primary functions of facial expression—the accent, or gesture, function and the affect-display function. Our discussion has focused more on affect display. This is not because the gesture function is unimportant, but rather because facial gestures are similar to other gestures, and we are going to discuss gestures at some length.

GESTURES

Especially during conversation, but also at other times, we signal one another with **gestures**—movements of our head, our face, and especially our hands. You have doubtless noticed that some people gesture either far less or far more than you. Chances are that you've never met anyone who routinely gestures inappropriately, however.

Communication difficulties are rarely the fault of anyone's gesturing skills. We all know how and when to gesture. There are two main reasons for us to take a look at gestures, however. First, it is interesting to notice the various communicative functions served by gestures. Gestures are not as pointless as one might think. Second, while gestures rarely cause problems in conversation, they are sometimes problematic in public speaking. Because of admonitions we have heard from teachers during our oral reports in grade school—don't do this or that with your hands—some public speakers are self-conscious about gesturing. Ironically, however, thinking about one's gestures is a mistake, because gestures operate naturally on a sort of unconscious "automatic pilot." Better advice for public speakers, therefore, is to not think about gestures and simply gesture naturally. And this may be easier to do if we understand the functions served by gestures in natural communication.[8]

Emblems are gestured symbols that function as *direct substitutes for specific words or phrases*. As such, they are at least as much verbal as nonverbal. We nod our head up and down to say *yes,* and move it from side to side to say *no*. We put our hand palm-forward behind our ear to say "louder, please," and we put our index finger to our lips to say "quiet, please." We have hand gestures to say "A-OK" (either the thumbs-up gesture or the circle made with the thumb and forefinger), and another to say "no good" (thumbs down). Each of these is an emblem, and there are dozens of other examples.

While there are a few exceptions, emblems generally do not operate within conversation or in public speaking. Rather, they usually operate when it is impractical to speak the message. For example, we often use emblems when there is too much noise, too much distance, or insufficient privacy to allow the message to be sent vocally.

Illustrators, on the other hand, usually operate in concert with spoken language. These are gestures that provide a sort of visual aid by showing or demonstrating what is being talked about. Pointing at the thing you are talking about is a simple example of an

● TRY THIS

To prove that gestures are—and should be—on "automatic pilot," you can teasingly irritate friendly conversation partners by simply staring at their hands while they are talking. As soon as they notice that you are watching their gestures, they usually stop gesturing altogether!

Soviet premier Nikita Khrushchev was known to pound his shoe on the table for emphasis during political discussions. Some would say that this is taking the concept of accent gestures too far!

illustrator. Holding your hands apart with the palms toward each other while saying, "I caught a seven-pound bass," is an illustrator. These illustrators are not absolutely necessary in order for the corresponding message to be understood. But they do add to the overall message, and they can help the receiver to understand the message. Moreover, they are to some extent expected. Imagine being in a strange city and receiving directions from someone who used no illustrators, for example.

Accent gestures are head, hand, and facial movements that operate in concert with spoken language to add emphasis to specific segments of an utterance. Suppose you were watching two people in conversation, but you were too far away to hear what they were saying. You might see an occasional illustrator that you could decode, perhaps even a rare conversational emblem. But no doubt you would see many more accent gestures—head bobbing, seemingly random hand movements, and facial gestures—that make no sense without hearing what is being said.

It is common for several accent gestures to operate simultaneously. That is, a single accent might include a combination of head, facial, and hand movements. And it is especially common for kinesic accents to operate simultaneously with vocal-inflection accents or emphases. Indeed, kinesic accents and vocal accents serve very much the same function. (This is why some public speakers can be very engaging despite minimal hand gesturing when their facial gestures and vocal inflections are expressive.)

Regulators are gestures (and certain other behaviors) used to control conversational turns. Listeners use regulators, in the form of head nods, facial expressions, eye contact, and hand gestures, to indicate that the speaker should slow down, speed up, get to the point, keep going, repeat, stop and give the listener a turn, and so forth. Speakers use regulators to indicate that they are almost finished with their turn, to indicate that they are indeed finished, to indicate that although they know the listener wants to speak, he or she will have to wait, and so forth.

In conversation, a person who consistently fails to heed others' regulators is likely to be considered rude or socially inept. In public speaking, turn-taking regulators do not operate so overtly, of course (except, perhaps, when someone raises a hand to interrupt the speaker's turn with a question). Most audience members will consider it rude to signal "slow down," "get on with it," "I understand this point; let's have the next one," and so forth. But there usually will be one or two individuals in the audience who, consciously or not, are providing regulation cues. The speaker needs to be alert to these.

Adaptors are not really gestures in the usual sense. Adaptors are movements—usually with the hands—to *satisfy some physical or psychological need.* Typical examples include scratching an itch, brushing hair out of the face, licking dry lips, rubbing hands together when one is cold, and the like. In these examples, the need being satisfied is fairly clear. With other adaptors, the need being satisfied is less clear, but we can make a good guess. For example, some adaptive movements appear to signal anxiety—rapidly swinging the free foot when one's legs are crossed, fidgeting with one's necklace while talking, and so forth. Still other adaptors seem to be performed for no apparent reason, such as casually clicking a ballpoint pen while talking, fondling a piece of chalk when lecturing, and so forth.

While adaptors may satisfy a need for the "sender," they usually serve no practical communicative function. (If we actually want to communicate a need, we usually do not do so via adaptors. For example, there would be better ways of telling someone that we are nervous than by swinging our foot.) Accordingly, the impact of adaptors on communication usually is neutral—neither positive nor negative. For example, we are talking, we itch, we scratch, nobody particularly notices, the itch is satisfied, and the communication event continues on its merry way relatively unaffected.

Adaptors can have a negative effect on communication episodes when the behaviors are excessive, however. If, for example, we scratch *too* much, click our ballpoint pen *too* constantly, swing our foot *too* vigorously, and so forth, then the adaptors will distract from our messages. Overdoing adaptors to the point of distraction occurs only rarely in conversation, but it is common among beginning public speakers.

BODY POSITION

The kinesic behaviors we have discussed so far are movements of fairly specific parts of the body—the head, hands, eyes, and face. Our more general **body position** or *posture* also plays a role in communication, especially in interpersonal communication. Perhaps the most common case is that body position seems to correspond to our interest in the conversation and our impression of our conversation partner. Often (but certainly not always) we tend to lean toward our conversation partners—slightly when standing, considerably when seated—when we like them and are interested in what they are saying. We also tend to face a person more directly—that is, with our body more squared up in the partner's direction—when our feelings about the interaction are positive. Dislike or disinterest, on the other hand, is sometimes accompanied by leaning back and/or placing ourselves at more of an angle to the partner. Crossing our arms in front of us is believed to sometimes indicate negative feelings toward the person or situation, as well.

Body position will sometimes correspond also to one's overall anxiety or nervousness, with rigid, straight-up postures accompanying anxiety and "loose" postures accompanying comfort. For example, males who were uptight about job interviews used to be advised to "sit relaxed"—that is, to sit with legs crossed ankle-on-thigh style, to lean back in the chair, and to drape one arm over the back of the chair. And nervous public speakers used to be advised to intentionally assume a relaxed body position, at least toward the beginning of the speech—for example, to stand with one foot on a chair seat, lean forward, and rest a forearm on the knee. The idea in both situations was that if you aren't relaxed, at least you can fake it. (These days, the approach is to help the communicator to actually become more relaxed. See Appendix D on reducing public-speaking anxiety, for example.)

As in other areas of nonverbal behavior, we need to be careful about reading meaning into others' body posture. For any of the body positions we have mentioned, there are other good explanations. Crossed arms may be due to feeling physically cold rather than to negative feelings about the partner, standing at an angle may not be due to dislike but rather to the need to terminate a completely pleasant conversation with a completely likable partner, slouching back in one's chair during conversation may come from feeling very relaxed and comfortable with the partner rather than from being disinterested, and so forth. The relationship between body position and internal states and attitudes does exist, but it is not reliable or consistent.

As for our own behaviors, it is worthwhile for us to be generally aware of impressions we may be making via body position. But as with other behaviors that operate fine on automatic pilot, monitoring ourselves too vigilantly can be counterproductive. As an extreme example, I know of a colleague who read that when sitting and talking with a group, the way one's legs are crossed means that one is being "open" to some people (those on the side of the bottom leg) and "closed" to others (those on the side of the top leg). Given this information (which for most situations is not even true, by the way), he developed the annoying practice of constantly crossing and recrossing his legs—first one way, then the other—so as to give everybody "equal time" to his supposed openness!

PROXEMICS

Proxemics is the area of nonverbal behavior that describes our *use of space.* There are two primary categories of proxemic behavior. One involves norms governing the distance we maintain from one another during our communication interactions. The other involves ways in which we signal and protect areas and territories that we consider to be ours.

PERSONAL SPACE AND INTERACTION DISTANCES

The distance we try to maintain between ourselves and those with whom we are interacting depends largely upon the social situation. The appropriate distance is different for a romantic seduction, a casual conversation, and a meeting in the dean's office, for example. One popular categorization system identifies four primary **interaction distances.**[9]

1. *Intimate distance* ranges from actual contact to a distance of about eighteen inches. As the label implies, this distance is common in more intimate situations—comforting a friend at a funeral, having a romantic conversation, and so forth. To put it another way, most people in our culture will feel uncomfortable being closer to another individual than eighteen inches or so if the situation is not one of intimacy. This would be too close for comfort in casual conversation, for example.

2. *Personal distance* ranges from about eighteen inches to about four feet. This is the typical distance for casual conversation. According to certain theorists, it is not coincidental that this range roughly corresponds to two partners' individual and combined arm length. Apparently, personal space begins at about eighteen inches because this is the space that one partner can physically protect, and ends at about four feet because this is the distance at which two people can no longer push each other away. (Other theorists reject this explanation, since it implies that cultures whose members are generally taller—and therefore longer-armed—would have larger personal distances than shorter cultures, and this is not the case.) In any event, the eighteen inches to four feet range is the accepted norm for casual personal conversation within our culture.

3. *Social distance* ranges from about four feet to about twelve feet. It is the distance appropriate to more formal or more impersonal one-on-one or small-group interactions—business meetings, job interviews, and so forth. This is the distance you would probably maintain when going to the office of a professor, for example (except that most professors' offices are not big enough to place the chairs that far apart).

4. *Public distance* ranges from about twelve feet to the threshold for vision. This is the distance found in relatively formal situations with large audiences—large-scale public speeches, concerts, and so forth.

There are exceptions to each of these distance norms, of course. We may have a quick casual conversation with a friend we see on the other side of a street, we may conduct a personal conversation in an elevator so crowded that the distance becomes intimate by the gauge presented above, our public-speaking classroom may be too small to place twelve feet between the speaker and the audience, and so forth. (Notice, by the way, that in large-enrollment courses, if the front row is twelve feet or so from the professor's lectern, it fills up fairly early on the first day of class, but if the front row is much closer, it fills up last!) Generally, however, we will feel awkward when others violate these distance norms. And we will make others feel uncomfortable if we violate them.

Why isn't the front row filled? Do you think it would still be empty if it were farther from the speaker?

TERRITORIALITY

There is a sense in which the above interaction distances represent imaginary boundaries of each person's territory in interaction. Indeed, the eighteen-inch threshold for personal distance is sometimes referred to as an imaginary "space bubble" that outlines each individual's "own" space or territory during casual interaction. This bubble is not fixed to a specific area, but rather floats along with us and goes where we go. A second dimension of proxemics, **territoriality**, demonstrates that we also have sensitivity about *fixed and specific areas that we consider to be ours*.

Some areas or territories are indeed legally ours. Whether we own the area outright (our car, for example) or conditionally (a leased apartment), we tend to be protective of our own territory, and we are expected to be respectful of others'. We are not supposed to enter someone else's house without an invitation, for example.

More curiously, though, we sometimes treat areas that are not truly ours as if they were. For example, a certain seat in a classroom may be "your seat" (at least in your mind), even though it has never been assigned to you. Similarly, if you are studying at a table in the library and there are lots of empty tables available, then the next student who enters is not expected to sit down at "your table."

As for what territoriality has to do with communication, there are two primary connections. First, territoriality is another dimension of nonverbal behavior because there are nonverbal cues by which we mark our real or imagined territory. These **territorial markers** are intended to communicate to others that the territory has been claimed. We put fences around our yards and doors on our rooms, for example, to say, in effect, "by invitation only." But we will also put a coat on a seat at a theater to say "saved," or leave a drink at the bar to say "This area is taken" when we go to the dance floor. Sometimes these markers will be fairly elaborate, as when we stake out an entire table in a crowded library by putting our backpack on the chair to one side of us, our coat on the chair to the other side, and our books, notebooks, laptop computer, etc., in a large semicircle to dominate the table.

The second connection to communication may be seen when territoriality assumptions are violated. As we discussed earlier, violations of the norms for interaction distances (personal distance, social distance, etc.) often make people uncomfortable. But in the case of territoriality, violations are more serious. Major conflicts between individuals (not to mention between nations or groups) can occur when one person enters or occupies another's territory without being welcome, or when one person contaminates another's territory.

This happens to be a primary source of conflict among roommates, in fact. Notice that territoriality is a common denominator among the following common causes for roommate conflicts:[10]

1.   One roommate becomes upset because another roommate's boyfriend or girlfriend spends too much time in the apartment or house.

2.   A roommate's boyfriend or girlfriend is perceived as using an unfair share of the utilities, groceries, etc.

3.   One roommate takes or borrows another's clothes, food, etc., without permission.

4.   One roommate brings a pet into the apartment or house, and the pet gets in the way or contaminates the space.

5.   One roommate makes a mess of another's room, bathroom, closet, etc.

6.   One roommate makes a mess of a "common" area such as the kitchen, dining room, den, etc.

This list omits a few sources of roommate conflict that have nothing to do with territory. But it may surprise you that so many sources of roommate conflict are territorial. All the more reason to be sensitive to proxemics.

VOCALICS

The lyrics of a once-popular song suggest, "It ain't what you say, it's the way that you say it." The *way* we talk—that is, the nonverbal-vocal characteristics of an utterance—is known as **vocalics**, or **paralanguage.** This includes "tone of voice," manner, style, and other such accompaniments to spoken messages.

As we saw in Chapter 2, speech is almost always accompanied by suprasegmental cues—inflections of pitch, stress, and juncture. These vocal cues, as you may recall, are attached to very small segments of an utterance in order to clarify its content meaning—for example, the rising pitch inflection on "You're a skydiver?" to indicate that the sentence is a question instead of a statement. Suprasegmental cues are usually considered to be part of the verbal language.

Paralinguistic cues, on the other hand, are inflections that operate over larger sections of an utterance to indicate overall *mood,* such as talking louder and faster in a heated argument with an equal, or talking louder and slower when angrily laying down the law to a subordinate. Since these cues are optional, and since they convey meaning that goes beyond the content of the message, inflections of paralanguage are usually considered to be nonverbal.

In addition to paralinguistic indicators of mood, certain types of *vocal nonfluencies* are sometimes treated as nonverbal behavior. These nonfluencies are self-interruptions in the flow of speech. They include the minor stutters, corrections, slips of the tongue, and so forth that sneak into virtually everybody's spoken messages from time to time. Nonfluencies also include *vocalized pauses,* such as ". . . umm . . . ," ". . . uh . . . ," and the like. They can also take the form of verbal *fillers,* as in, "I was going to say that, *well,* my only complaint about our relationship is, *you know,* the fact that, *like,* you always, *like,* seem to get upset when . . ."

Research suggests that in our speech, both during conversation and in public speaking, we need to strike a happy medium between too few and too many nonfluencies. Too few nonfluencies in conversation causes us to be perceived as too "slick." If there are too many, we seem to lack conviction or confidence in what we are saying. Too few nonfluencies in a speech causes us to be perceived as mechanical, artificial, and insincere. Too many tends to indicate a lack of knowledge of the topic, or excessive anxiety.

Nonfluencies and paralinguistic inflections will vary according to the message, the mood, and the situation. But listeners are also influenced by certain vocal features that happen to be more static, or fixed, within individual speakers. Stereotypes will sometimes be attached to our *regional dialect,* for example. A Boston accent, New York accent, Southern accent, or Texas accent, to name a few, may evoke a particular positive or negative reaction, depending upon the regional dialect of the listener and the gender of the speaker. Similarly, certain *voice qualities*—nasal, resonant, strident, breathy—evoke stereotyped reactions, some positive and some negative.[11] In milder cases, problematic vocal features will subside with minimal effort. For example, when we move to a geographical area in which our dialect is uncommon, we usually adapt to the local speech patterns and lose a good bit of our "accent" fairly quickly. In extreme cases, however, changing a negative vocal quality can require professional therapy and/or long periods of training.

> **Nonverbal Behaviors with Relatively Standardized Norms of Appropriateness Include**
> ✓ Kinesics (eye contact, facial expression, gesture, body position)
> ✓ Proxemics (personal space, territoriality)
> ✓ Vocalics

CHRONEMICS

Unless special circumstances supersede the norms of kinesics, proxemics, and vocalics we have discussed so far, we are expected to follow these norms most of the time. With the remaining areas of nonverbal behavior, however, the norms are not so well agreed upon. Some communication partners will have one set of expectations and interpretations, and some will have another.

Chronemics, for example, is our *treatment of time.* It is relevant to our discussion because there are situations in which our view of time may produce behaviors that are subject to others' interpretations. Probably the clearest example occurs when we do things that may be judged by others as being "on time," "too early," or "too late."

The message that is "communicated" when one person is late by another person's standards is almost always a negative one. If we are late with our assigned portion of a group project, we are likely to be judged as selfish and irresponsible; if we are late for a task-oriented meeting, we are likely to be considered self-absorbed and disrespectful; if we are late for a social engagement, a likely interpretation will be that we do not value the other person (or his or her time); and so forth. How late is "late" in these situations? It depends on the *other* person's standards, and those standards may well be more precise or more conservative than yours.

Differences in the way we view time can lead to other difficulties, as well. If, for example, Joe takes a more conservative view of being on time, and Pat takes a more liberal view, then we can forecast at least mild conflict when the two of them go together to, say, a dinner party. Joe is likely to get upset with Pat's dawdling (from Joe's point of view) making them late.

Similarly, people view time differently with respect to scheduling their activities. Some of us are dedicated to a preplanned list of things to do, for both work and play activities. Others of us put together our itineraries more spontaneously. While each type has something to learn from the other, either is likely to have difficulty understanding the other's mode from time to time. If Sam is of the first type and Chris is of the second type, for example, then Sam may become upset with Chris for springing ideas for things to do (movies, dinner out, etc.) unannounced and "always at the last minute," while Chris may become upset with Sam's lack of spontaneity and his need to have all their activities planned far in advance.

Use of time matters in public-speaking situations, as well. The speaker who is not ready to go at the appointed time—because the visual aids are not set up, or the microphone doesn't work, or the videotape is not yet cued, and so forth—is likely to be viewed as amateurish and ill prepared, and is likely to be resented for wasting the audience's time. Worse yet, perhaps, is the speaker who talks longer than scheduled or expected. This is a sure way to lose favor with the audience, even for an otherwise well-received speech. Even if feedback tells us that our audience is enthralled, we should conclude the speech on time. An acceptable variation is to conclude on time and announce that those who wish may stay to continue the discussion informally. In any case, the speaker needs to recognize that the audience's time is valuable to them.

TOUCHING (HAPTICS)

We noted earlier that our personal space bubble generally precludes physical contact with others except in intimate situations. But it is obvious that we do sometimes initiate contact in nonintimate situations—a handshake, a pat on the back, a quick hug, and so forth. Touching, or **haptics**, is less common than the other nonverbal behaviors we have discussed, but its positive and negative consequences can be important.

Haptic behaviors may serve a variety of functions and be open to a number of interpretations.[12] Some of these are *ritualistic*, as in handshakes or hugs for hellos or goodbyes. Another haptic function, of course, is to *express positive emotions* for one another, either as in physical arousal between intimates or as in "I care for you" messages between friends. Touching can also indicate *playfulness*, as when a light slap on the arm or mock punch to the shoulder seems to say, "I'm only kidding." Sometimes touching gives pragmatic *assistance*, as when we brush something off someone's shoulder as a favor or take someone's arm to help in crossing the street. Sometimes touching is to actually *control* or manipulate the behavior of another, as when we lightly push down on someone's arm to say, "Stay here," or gently push the small of someone's back to say, "Let's go." And sometimes touching operates to *accent* or emphasize our enthusiasm or involvement in a part of the conversation, like those touches that some people add to expressions like "Oh, my goodness," "You don't say!" and so forth.

Like other nonverbal behaviors, touching varies according to certain features of the situation.[13] It varies according to status, for example. In situations in which a clear status or power difference is recognized, the higher-status or dominant person is usually the one who initiates touching (if there *is* any touching). Where status and power are not clearly defined, the person who initiates touching often will be perceived as having greater status.

Touching varies according to gender, as well. Same-sex touching—during conversation, for example—is more common and accepted among women than among men.

Opposite-sex touching during conversation is more acceptable to men than same-sex touching. Some studies say that the same is true for women, but other studies disagree.

More important than status and gender, however, is the variable of individual preference. At the extreme, some people simply do not like to be touched, period—even in situations for which most of us would consider touching to be completely acceptable. And even within the normal range of preference, it is likely that our partners in many communication situations will have haptic tendencies and preferences that differ from our own. There will be times when people innocently and unknowingly touch us more than we like to be touched. And if we are not careful, there will be times when our touching makes someone else uncomfortable.

Especially in encounters with relatively new acquaintances whose haptic behaviors we have not yet determined, it is wise to be a bit on the cautious side with respect to initiating touching. And if we do initiate touching, it is important that we monitor the partner's reactions carefully, lest our haptics rub our partner the wrong way— literally!

PHYSICAL APPEARANCE

No matter how often we hear the familiar admonition "you can't judge a book by its cover"—indeed, no matter how often we find it to be true—we persist in forming first impressions of one another based on little more than **physical appearance.** Knowing that our snap-judgment first impressions are unfair and often false, we tend to deny their power. We may pat ourselves on the back for the times our negative first impression of someone has turned positive. And we may downplay the importance of the kind of first impression we make ourselves, figuring that those whose opinions matter to us will soon know what we are "really" like.

Denying the power of first impressions can be naive, however. Once we have formed a first impression (and once other people have formed a first impression of us), we interpret the subsequent information we gather—upon meeting and talking with the person, for example—*in ways that support the first impression.* It is as if the first impression is a hypothesis that we are much more eager to support than to dismiss. In those relatively rare cases when we do change our first impressions, the change usually requires both a considerable period of time and an overwhelming contradiction of the initial impression. In other words, first impressions often are permanent, or at least slow to change. Thus, they can put us at a significant advantage or disadvantage in various communication situations. Very often, first impressions are based primarily on what we see when we first view one another. And there is a lot to see.

BODY SHAPE

You would not expect Hollywood to cast someone built like John Goodman as James Bond, and you would not expect someone with Mia Farrow's **body shape** to play the role of Wonder Woman. Unfortunately, perhaps, certain stereotypes tend to be attached to certain body shapes.[14] In particular, *endomorphs,* those whose bodies are large, round, and soft (the classic Santa Claus shape), are often judged positively as kind, jolly, warm, and sympathetic, but negatively as lazy and dependent. *Ectomorphs,* those whose bodies are thin and frail-looking (the classic Ichabod Crane shape), are

● TRY THIS

You should be able to think of exceptions to each of the stereotypes for each of the body shapes. Think of endomorphs you know who are *not* lazy, dependent, and so forth. Think of ectomorphs you know who are *not* withdrawn, awkward, etc. And think of mesomorphs you know who are *not* dominant, self-absorbed, and so forth.

often judged positively as considerate, thoughtful, and precise, but negatively as withdrawn, tense, and awkward. *Mesomorphs, those* whose bodies are muscular and well proportioned, are often judged positively as confident, energetic, and enthusiastic; but negatively as dominant, overly competitive, and self-absorbed.

With respect to our own bodies, these various attributes are important as insights into how we may be perceived by others—at least at first, if not later. With respect to others' bodies, it is most important that we remember that our stereotypes are just that—stereotypes—and will be inaccurate as often as not.

CLOTHING, ARTIFACTS, AND GROOMING

Part of the image we portray to others is expressed by our *clothing*—its type, style, neatness, newness, and so forth. Another part is expressed by the accessories and **artifacts** we wear and carry—jewelry, glasses, watches, backpacks, and the like. And still another part is formed by our *grooming*—cleanliness, neatness, hairstyle, hair color, etc.

Together, clothing, artifacts, and grooming produce impressions concerning social and economic background, education level, professional success, status within business organizations, and more. Sometimes these are intentional, almost to the point of affectation. For example, optometrists in college towns report that students finishing Ph.D. degrees often insist on glasses even after being told that their vision is perfect (presumably because glasses will make them appear more scholarly)! At other times, our clothing and other adornments are an adaptation to group norms. For example, it may seem that you can identify the sorority members in your classes just by their clothing. At still other times, these adornments are more subtle and subjective. For example, chances are that the last time you shopped for clothes, you rejected certain items not because they were unattractive or not affordable, but because, in some inexplicable, subjective way, they "just weren't you."

It seems hard to imagine that someone would be unaware of the image produced by his or her own appearance. We tend to assume that our clothing, grooming, and artifacts jibe fairly well with the way we see ourselves and the way we want to be seen by others. We may or may not be correct, however. For example, I can recall a former student who was shocked when friends told her that her attire, hairstyle, and makeup led people to think that she was sexually promiscuous (she wasn't); a colleague who was surprised to hear his clothing and adornments described by others as "nerdy" (unfairly, in his opinion); and another acquaintance whose "preppie" attire was partially responsible for his being perceived as stuck-up (although he wasn't). Apparently each of us should at least consider the possibility that our clothing, grooming, and artifacts may create unwanted impressions.

> **Nonverbal Behaviors with More Individual Variation in Norms of Appropriateness Include**
> ✓ Chronemics
> ✓ Haptics
> ✓ Physical appearance (body shape, clothing, artifacts, grooming)

MISCELLANEOUS OTHERS

While the areas of nonverbal behavior introduced thus far are the most frequently discussed and most extensively researched areas, there are many others. For starters, in case you noticed that the behaviors discussed thus far have involved only three of the five senses (vision, hearing, and touch), let us recognize that the remaining senses—taste and smell—are sometimes involved as well. As a simple example, the use of perfume and our various reactions to it demonstrate nonverbal behavior via *smell*. And in a chili cook-off or other culinary contest, one attempts to influence others (the judges) via *taste*. Other areas of nonverbal behavior include the influence of *color* (especially in that different colors can initiate different moods), *pupil dilation* (our pupils tend to enlarge when we like what we see, including the appearance of our conversation partner), and *silence* (as when we think we are being given the "cold shoulder" or silent treatment by an acquaintance).

And there are still others. As we said initially, "behavior without words" covers a lot of territory. The nonverbal behaviors that seem most influential in day-to-day interactions, however, are those we have examined in more detail: kinesics, proxemics, vocalics, chronemics, haptics, and physical appearance.

CULTURAL DIFFERENCES

When we interact with someone from a different culture and experience difficulties with verbal communication, it usually doesn't surprise us. We are well aware that different cultures use different languages and dialects, and that differences in language are likely to make communication more difficult. But for some reason, we often expect nonverbal behaviors to be the same across cultures. Probably, this is because we think of nonverbal behaviors as being "natural" in ways that they are not, as we discussed at the beginning of this chapter. In any case, to expect the nonverbal behaviors of other cultures to match ours is unrealistic. Norms and interpretations of nonverbal behavior vary tremendously from culture to culture.

A complete discussion of intercultural nonverbal differences could fill a book. Let's look at only a very few general areas to highlight the fact that nonverbal behaviors and interpretations that we take for granted may need to be modified when we interact with members of other cultures.

For example, is it "natural" to nod the head up and down to indicate *Yes,* and to shake it from side to side for *No?* Apparently not, since in the Turkish nonverbal system an up-and-down head nod means *No.* Likewise, many of our other kinesic behaviors are interpreted differently in other cultures. *Eye-contact* rules vary from culture to culture, for example, with some cultures considering our norms to be excessive and impolite, and other cultures considering our eye-contact levels to be inadequate and evasive. *Facial expression,* while relatively universal in some regards, nevertheless varies between cultures, as well. For example, some cultures stick out the tongue for common expressions in ways that would seem somewhat repulsive or obscene in our culture. And people from some cultures find it very odd and disquieting that we smile at strangers in school hallways and on the street. In the case of *gestures—emblems,* in particular—the list of differences is very long. As a classic example, our A-OK hand gesture is an obscene gesture in some cultures and a reference to money in others.

Proxemic cultural differences are perhaps most noticeable when we converse with someone whose culture has a much smaller personal space bubble than our eighteen-inch threshold for casual situations. In these cases, the partner may encroach on our space, which we view as being impolite or improper, so we back up or retreat, which our partner views as being impolite. Then he or she advances and closes in again, we retreat, the other advances, and so forth. I once witnessed one of these exchanges in which a male from a Middle Eastern culture backed a female from a North American culture down the entire ninety-foot length of a hallway! Chances are, each considered the other's behavior to be inappropriate. But chances are, either could have adapted to the other's norms with a little understanding and a little effort.

Chronemic differences between cultures have accounted for many a social error and many a ruined business transaction. Our ten-minute "fashionably late" norm for social functions is much too early in some cultures, and our expectation that business-related deliveries will arrive within a day or so of when they are promised is unrealistic in others.

The list goes on and on. There are dramatic cultural differences in the associations and interpretations attached to clothing, territorial markers, paralanguage, touch, silence, grooming, and indeed every area of nonverbal behavior.

It would be naive to think that these intercultural differences are unimportant to us. The odds of our doing business in a foreign country, having neighbors or other friends from another culture, having coworkers from other cultures, and so forth, are fairly high. While it is impossible to prepare for these interactions by learning the nonverbal nuances of every culture in advance, it is important to be alert to cultural differences.

In the case of business meetings abroad, or even vacation travel, it is becoming easier to adapt to cultural differences. Brochures and pamphlets covering particularly important nonverbal norms for almost any culture are available from travel agents and from many employers. In the case of friends and acquaintances from other cultures, one may do the same sort of research, or may seek information directly from the individual. For example, most people welcome well-intentioned questions like, "Are there things you've noticed Americans doing that are considered impolite or odd in your culture?" or "I've noticed that you sometimes do such-and-such. Is that common in your culture? What does it signify?" "Would you prefer that I try to follow suit, or do you prefer that I follow my own culture's norms?" And so forth.

In any case, when we interact with those from other cultures, we need to be especially aware that our own nonverbal norms are not universal. We need to be especially observant, patient, and empathetic toward the ways in which a given behavior may elicit completely different interpretations in intercultural interactions. (This brief discussion is barely the tip of the iceberg. We will return to the topic of communication between cultures in Chapter 7.)

A PRACTICAL NOTE

As we conclude our discussion of nonverbal behavior (until it is revisited in our discussion of public-speaking delivery), consider the following Dear Abby–type letter written as an assignment by a female communication student:

Dear Doc,

I have a problem whenever I encounter new people. I always seem to give them a negative first impression. I can't understand it. I try my hardest to be friendly during my first encounters with other people, but no matter how I try to be friendly as a sender, my receivers always receive negative messages.

My good friends tell me the reason may be because of my physical appearance, a certain look that I have that easily intimidates others. My friends tell me that it is something I do unconsciously without thinking about it. I do not think it is fair that people judge me by their first impression. When I think I am being friendly, others may not, just because of the way I look.

Most of the time, it is hard for me to make friends because their first impression of me is already negative. I usually have to earn their respect and win their friendship.

I am told that most guys are easily intimidated by me. Somehow, they receive messages that I am "stuck up." I just do not understand how these guys could think that, because they do not even know me.

It's just not fair! Why do people make judgments about a person before they even get to know them? Will this change?

—Unfairly Judged

Several things about this letter make it a fitting conclusion to this chapter, I think. First, for what it's worth, I happen to concur with this student's friends. Her attire, heavy makeup, and perpetual frown gave her a hard, almost mean, look. The impression I always got as she sat in class was that she was either mad at the world in general or upset with me personally. At the least, she seemed to be "not a happy camper." As it turned out, these impressions were wrong. She was in fact a very kind, rather vulnerable, reasonably happy, and quite friendly young woman. But she was one whose naturally relaxed, "neutral" facial expression happened to be closer to most people's frown than to most people's neutral, and she happened to be copying a much older sister with respect to attire, makeup, hair style, and so forth.

As we said at the outset of the chapter, each of us, without realizing it, may have personal quirks that violate nonverbal norms. Maybe we have noticed our idiosyncrasies simply by reflecting upon the discussion in this chapter, but maybe not. Since our personal nonverbal behaviors have become second nature to us by now, we may need to have a close friend or two point out our quirks to us, as the writer of the above letter was fortunate enough to have. However, our reaction should not be that of the letter writer. We get nowhere by protesting repeatedly that "it's just not fair" when our violations of nonverbal norms have negative consequences. Usually it is wiser to be aware of the norms and to adjust our own nonverbal behavior accordingly.

Thus, the approach we have taken in this chapter has been to discuss a wide array of nonverbal norms. In some cases we have explicitly indicated that violations of the norms can create problems for communicators. For example, we have mentioned some of the consequences of violating proxemic norms, overdoing adaptors, violating others' territorial assumptions, and so forth. In other cases, the idea of consequences has been implicit. It stands to reason, for example, that we will make our communication partners uncomfortable if our eye contact is excessive, if we use emblems or other sign-language gestures during ordinary conversation, if we use inappropriate facial interjections during conversation, and so forth, since these would constitute quite odd behaviors.

In short, habitual violators of nonverbal norms are rare, and since they are rare, they stand out as deviants. For example, it is probably only one in a thousand or more conversation partners who violates the eighteen-inch threshold for ordinary conversation. But while it is extremely rare (or because it is rare), this "in your face" style is so irritating to conversation partners that it is parodied in TV comedies, privately criticized by acquaintances, and so forth. This is also true of other habitual violations of nonverbal norms.

Thus, in matters of kinesics, proxemics, and vocalics, it is especially worthwhile for us to privately check ourselves against the norms for nonverbal behavior discussed in this chapter, and to ensure that we are not frequent violators of these norms. And in matters of chronemics, haptics, and physical appearance, it is worthwhile to check our behaviors against the expectations of our individual communication partners.

On the other side of the communication equation, there is an important lesson for us as receivers and interpreters of others' nonverbal behaviors, also—namely, that the "meanings" of these behaviors are unreliable. Defensiveness is not the only reason our partners may cross their arms over their chests, their facial expressions may or may not be sincere, their appearance may or may not be an indicator of their personality, and so forth for almost any nonverbal behavior. We need to exercise caution when we assign meaning to nonverbal behaviors. Granted, they can be indicators of others' attributes and states, but they are tentative and often unreliable indicators.

IN SUMMARY   We have explored six major categories of nonverbal behavior: kinesics, proxemics, vocalics, chronemics, haptics, and physical appearance. In every case, we have seen that certain behaviors tend to correspond to certain moods, states, and situations. But we have seen also that these relationships are not without plenty of exceptions. To put it another way, while the temptation to "read" other people by their nonverbal behaviors is sometimes overwhelming, it is virtually inevitable that we will sometimes, if not often, read them incorrectly. It will be wise, therefore, to treat our interpretations as mere hypotheses, and to gather more information before forming a conclusion. The additional information may come from interpreting additional nonverbal behaviors. But it may come also from verbal verification. In other words, we may simply ask whether our interpretations are correct. Generally, there is nothing wrong with making inquiries like, "You seem preoccupied; would you rather talk about this later?" or, "You seem upset; is it something I said?" or, "You're almost always late; can we discuss how that makes me feel?" And so forth.

As for our own nonverbal behaviors, we have seen that monitoring ourselves too self-consciously can be counterproductive. But this applies only if our "automatic pilot" behaviors are not problematic. It is advisable for us to first be aware of our culture's norms—and sometimes a partner's personal norms—and to ensure that our own nonverbal behaviors are consistent with them. This can begin with a self-check according to the discussion in this chapter. We should ask whether we are one of those few who consistently stands too close in casual conversation, or touches our conversational partners on practically every utterance, or uses a consistently whiny voice to make requests, and so forth. This can be followed by inquiries to trusted friends who may be willing to give us their impressions of our nonverbal behaviors.

TERMS TO KNOW

nonverbal behavior	body position
kinesics	proxemics
facial gesture	interaction distances
affect display	territoriality
nonverbal interjections	territorial markers
display rules	vocalics
gestures	paralanguage
emblems	chronemics
illustrators	haptics
accent gestures	physical appearance
regulators	body shape
adaptors	artifacts

NOTES

1. M. T. Motley, "On Whether One Can(not) Not Communicate: An Examination via Traditional Communication Postulates," *Western Journal of Speech Communication* 54 (1990): 1–20.

2. M. L. Knapp, *Nonverbal Behavior in Human Interaction* (New York: Holt, Rinehart and Winston, 1978).

3. P. Ekman, W. V. Friesen, and P. Ellsworth, *Emotion in the Human Face: Guidelines for Research and the Integration of Findings* (New York: Pergamon Press, 1972).

4. M. T. Motley, "Facial Affect and Verbal Context in Conversation: Facial Expression as Interjection," *Human Communication Research* 20 (1993): 3–40; M. T. Motley and C. T. Camden, "Facial Expression of Emotion: A Comparison of Posed Expressions Versus Spontaneous Expressions in an Interpersonal Communication Setting," *Western Journal of Speech Communication* 52 (1988): 1–22.

5. Motley, "Facial Affect and Verbal Context."

6. P. Ekman and W. V. Friesen, "The Repertoire of Nonverbal Behavior: Categories, Origins, and Coding," *Semiotica* 1 (1969): 49–98.

7. Ekman, Friesen, and Ellsworth, *Emotion in the Human Face.*

8. M. Argyle, *Bodily Communication* (New York: Methuen, 1988); R. L. Birdwhistell, "Background to Kinesics," *ETC.* 13 (1955): 10–18.

9. E. T. Hall, *The Hidden Dimension* (Garden City, N.Y.: Doubleday, 1966).

10. M. T. Motley, "Mindfulness in Solving Communication Dilemmas," *Communication Monographs* 59 (1992): 306–314 (raw data).

11. D. W. Addington, "The Relationship of Selected Vocal Characteristics to Personality Perception," *Speech Monographs* 55 (1968): 492–503.

12. P. A. Andersen and K. Leibowitz, "The Development and Nature of the Construct Touch Avoidance," *Environmental Psychology and Nonverbal Behavior* 3 (1978): 89–106.

13. N. M. Henley, *Body Politics: Power, Sex, and Nonverbal Communication* (Englewood Cliffs, N.J.: Prentice-Hall, 1977); S. Jones and E. A. Yarbrough, "A Naturalistic Study of the Meaning of Touch," *Communication Monographs* 52 (1985): 19–56.

14. W. H. Sheldon, *Atlas of Man: A Guide to Somatyping the Adult Male at All Ages* (New York: Harper & Row, 1954).

CHAPTER FOUR

DEVELOPING YOUR LISTENING SKILLS

THIS CHAPTER
will help you

- Understand the importance of effective listening

- Overcome barriers to effective listening

- Improve your critical listening skills

- Understand your ethical responsibilities as a listener

THE MOST **BASIC** of all **HUMAN** NEEDS
IS THE **NEED** TO UNDERSTAND
and be UNDERSTOOD.

—R. Nichols

There are a number of misconceptions about listening that contribute to the problems many of us have with it. To begin with, listening is an integral part of the communication process. Second, listening is not the same as hearing. And finally, listening can be improved through training.

Most people are not good listeners. Former president Franklin Delano Roosevelt once decided to see how well people listened to what he said in a social situation. He greeted his guests in a White House receiving line with, "I murdered my grandmother this morning." Typical responses included, "Thank you," "How kind of you," and other polite platitudes. It was a long time before he met someone who really listened and replied, "I'm sure she had it coming to her."[1]

Poor listening has its costs. If you don't listen well to a classroom lecture, you may miss important information. If you don't attend carefully to things you are told at work, you may make costly mistakes. When people in a group don't listen, the group may make poor decisions. When juries don't listen critically to the evidence presented, they cannot render a sound verdict. When people who care for each other don't listen to each other, their relationship may suffer.

At the very least, poor listening skills can create an impression of incompetence. I (Osborn) recall talking to customer service representatives on the phone when I was single. After seeming to listen to a problem, the representative almost invariably said, "Would you please spell that last name for me." I invariably replied, "S-M-I-T-H," but always wondered, "If they can't remember the name or can't spell 'Smith,' how can they help with my problem?"

In this chapter, we explore the nature of effective listening. We also discuss the external and internal sources of interference that impede effective listening and suggest ways to cope with these problems.

● TRY THIS

As an exercise, think of a time when not listening well put you in a difficult situation. What problems did not listening well cause you? How did you feel? How do you think the other person in the communication interaction felt? What could you have done differently? Share your insights with a classmate and discuss the similarities and differences in your experiences.

THE NATURE AND IMPORTANCE OF EFFECTIVE LISTENING

Although we spend most of our communication time listening to others speak, we receive far less formal training in listening than we do in speaking, writing, or reading.[2] Perhaps educators assume that we are born knowing how to listen, despite much evidence to the contrary. Listening may be undervalued in the dominant U.S. culture because it is associated with following rather than with leading. Leadership is typically more admired than "followership." In a world that values being "on the move," we may think that listening is a passive activity. In reality, effective listening is a dynamic activity in which the listener seeks out the intended meaning in messages.

Other cultures place a higher premium on good listening behaviors. Some Native American tribes, for example, have a far better appreciation of the importance of these behaviors. The Lakota recognize the value of listening. In their culture:

> *Conversation was never begun at once, nor in a hurried manner. No one was quick with a question, no matter how important, and no one was pressed for an answer. A pause giving time for thought was the truly courteous way of beginning and conducting a conversation. Silence was meaningful with the Lakota, and his granting a space of silence to the speech-maker and his own moment of silence before talking*

was done in the practice of true politeness and regard for the rule that, "thought comes before speech."[3]

We will try to apply the lessons of the Lakotas to help you improve your listening skills.

WHAT IS EFFECTIVE LISTENING?

The Chinese symbol for the word *listen* has four basic elements: attention, ears, eyes, and heart.[4] This symbol illustrates some of the differences between hearing and listening. *Hearing* is an automatic process in which sound waves stimulate nerve impulses to the brain. *Listening* is a voluntary process that goes beyond physical reactions to sounds. At the very least, listening involves hearing, paying attention, understanding, and interpreting:

* You must be able to hear a message, even though you don't necessarily listen to everything you hear.
* You must attend to a message, blocking out other distractions that may compete for your attention.
* You must understand both the words and the point of view of the speaker.
* You must interpret meaning in terms of your own knowledge and experiences.

Scholars of the listening process generally suggest that there are five different types of listening. **Discriminative listening** uses the ability to distinguish and identify the auditory and visual stimuli that make up messages. It includes learning to identify changes in pitch, inflection, stress, loudness, and rate that can affect meaning. In **comprehensive listening**, a message is interpreted, so that the listener understands what the speaker meant to say. The listener's attention span, ability to concentrate, memory skills, and adequacy of vocabulary are used. In **critical listening**, evaluation and judgment are added to comprehensive listening. It allows listeners to detect problems in messages and adds a fifth element, mind, to the Chinese symbol. **Empathic listening** entails providing a sympathetic, comforting, and reassuring reception of messages. It encompasses the human and humane aspects of communication. **Appreciative listening** emphasizes the personal enjoyment you get from hearing certain messages. It comes into play when you hear the beautiful language of literature or respond to the sounds of enjoyable music.

Because listening is an interactive communication process, we believe that truly effective listening is **constructive listening**—a concept that combines comprehensive, critical, and empathic listening. Constructive listeners *add* to a message by finding its special applications to their lives. As they listen to someone talk about the importance of air bags in cars, they may balance the amount of money they can spend for a car against the advantages of air bags. They may question whether there are differences in the quality of air bags from one automobile to another. If they don't hear the answers directly, they may question the speaker, creating a dialogue that extends the meaning of what was said. Such dialogues can produce discoveries, better realizations of common values, and better answers to questions of soci-

The type of listening skills used depends on the context of the situation. These people at a concert would be practicing appreciative listening.

etal concern. In short, constructive listeners join with the speaker in **participative communication**, a process in which both share responsibility for the development of meaning.[5]

Constructive listeners also look beyond the words they hear for the motives and feelings that underlie them. They are able to empathize and identify with someone, even when they disagree with that person's position. They "listen" with their hearts as well as with their ears. Constructive listening makes possible the transformative effect of successful communication, in which both the speaker and the listener grow because of the communication experience.

BENEFITS OF EFFECTIVE LISTENING

Effective listening has many benefits that we can see and experience in our daily lives, in school, and at work.

Good listening skills can help protect you from questionable persuasion. Effective listeners are less vulnerable to snake-oil salesmen[6] who hide a lack of substance behind a glib presentation or irrelevant appeals. How many times have you seen attractive, scantily clad young people appear in ads for everything from sodas to automatic transmission repair services? Such ads try to connect their products with unrelated basic needs. Or, consider ads based on celebrity endorsements. What are these ads really selling—the products, or the lifestyles and values of the celebrities?[7] Other ads may ask you to buy what "doctors" recommend without telling you anything about the credentials of these doctors—Ph.D.'s in history may know very little about health foods! Political hucksters may substitute assertions for evidence, or appeals to prejudice for reasoning. Effective critical listening skills may help you guard against such deceptions.

Listening skills also have many applications in your academic and professional life. Students who listen effectively earn better grades and achieve beyond expectations.[8] Effective listeners concentrate on what is being said and focus on what is important. They explore the value of what they hear for their lives. Effective student listeners read assignments ahead of time to familiarize themselves with new words that may be used in the lectures and to provide a foundation for understanding the material.

At work, improved listening skills may mean the difference between success and failure—both for individuals and for companies. The Department of Labor recently reported that listening was one of the basic competencies that young people need for the world of work.[9] A survey of over 400 top-level personnel directors suggested that for graduates the two factors that were most important in finding jobs were speaking ability and listening ability.[10] Another survey of major American corporations reported that poor listening is "one of the [company's] most important problems" and that "ineffective listening leads to ineffective performance."[11] If you listen effectively on the job, you will make fewer mistakes, and you will improve your chances for advancement.[12] This is especially true in organizations that provide services rather than goods because they are dependent on communication skills.[13] Listening skills are also vitally important in occupations in which employee and customer safety is a major concern.[14]

Companies that encourage people to develop effective listening skills receive many dividends. They suffer less from costly misunderstandings. Employees are more innovative and productive when they sense that management will listen to new ideas. Morale improves, and the work environment becomes more pleasant. The late Sam Walton, founder of Wal-Mart Stores, saw the business benefits of listening and noted, "The key to success is to get out into the store and listen to what the associates have to say. It's terribly important for everyone to get involved. Our best ideas come from clerks and stockboys."[15] For these reasons, many *Fortune* 500 corporations provide listening training programs for their employees.[16]

Effective listening skills are also important to the development and maintenance of interpersonal relationships and for personal growth and development. As the noted psychiatrist Karl Menninger suggested, "The friends who listen to us are the ones we move toward. When we are listened to, it creates us, makes us unfold and expand."[17] Not listening to significant others places a strain on relationships.

Having an audience that listens effectively will also benefit you as you move into the public speaking component of this course. When audiences do not listen well, they do not give speakers useful feedback. Without such feedback, speakers cannot adapt their messages so that audiences understand them better. In addition to helping you present more effective messages, by creating a supportive classroom environment a good audience can help alleviate some of the communication anxiety that you may experience.[18] Speakers need to realize that you, as a listener, want them to succeed. You can convey your support by being pleasant and responsive rather than dour and inattentive.[19] Smile at speakers before they begin. Stop talking, clear your desk of everything except a notebook and pen, sit up, and give them your undivided attention. Show them that you are listening to their ideas rather than counting how many times they say "er." When appropriate, nod in agreement with what they say. Show respect for speakers as people, even if you disagree with their ideas. Try not to overreact when you disagree; if you do, you may miss something of value in what they say.

An audience of effective listeners also can boost a speaker's self-esteem. How many times have you had people *really listen* to you? How frequently have your ideas and advice been taken seriously? If your answer to these questions is "seldom" or "never," then you may be in for a pleasant surprise when you make your presentations. You will soon discover that there are few things quite as rewarding as having people really listen to you and respect what you say.

DEVELOPING EFFECTIVE LISTENING SKILLS

The first step in developing effective listening skills is to become aware of the things that keep us from being good listeners. Some barriers to good listening arise from external sources of interference, such as a noisy room. But the most formidable barriers to effective listening are internal, based in the listener's own attitudes. At best, these barriers present a challenge; at worst, they may completely block communication. They must be overcome before we can engage in participative communication.

TRY THIS

Once we understand what our listening problems are, we can begin to correct them. Read our description of the major listening problems, then use the Listening Problems Checklist in Figure 4.1 to help you identify areas that may be giving you problems. Look through the list and place a check mark next to items that describe your listening attitudes and behaviors. *Be honest!* Compare your listening problems with those of a classmate and discuss what you might do to correct them.

EXTERNAL SOURCES OF INTERFERENCE

External sources of interference are those that arise from the environment, the message, or the presentation. Most of the time, these sources of interference are relatively minor contributors to poor listening.

_____ 1. I believe listening is automatic, not learned.

_____ 2. I think about something else when a message is not interesting.

_____ 3. I find it hard to listen to topics about which I feel strongly.

_____ 4. I react emotionally to certain words.

_____ 5. I am easily distracted by noises.

_____ 6. I don't like to listen to people who are not experts.

_____ 7. I am often taken in by people who have the "gift of gab."

_____ 8. I don't like to listen to people whose values are different from mine.

_____ 9. I argue mentally when I disagree with what someone says.

_____ 10. I know so much on some topics that I can't learn from most speakers.

_____ 11. I believe speakers are responsible for effective communication.

_____ 12. I find it hard to listen when I have a lot on my mind.

_____ 13. I stop listening when a subject is difficult.

_____ 14. I can look like I'm listening when I am not.

_____ 15. I listen only for facts and ignore the rest of a message.

_____ 16. I try to write down everything a lecturer says.

_____ 17. I let the way someone looks determine how well I listen.

_____ 18. I jump to conclusions before I listen to all someone has to say.

FIGURE **4.1**
Listening Problems Checklist

The most obvious source of external interference is noise that makes it difficult for you to hear what someone is saying. If the general noise level is high, you need to be sure you can hear the other person. External interference can also arise when messages are full of jargon or unfamiliar words or are poorly organized. As a listener, you must work to overcome such problems. For example, if you know that some of the words in a lecture may be unfamiliar, read about the topic in advance and look up the difficult words. If a speaker is poorly organized, taking notes can help. Try to identify the main points the speaker makes. Differentiate these from supporting material such as examples or narratives. Figure 4.2 on the next page provides some helpful suggestions for taking notes during lectures.[20]

People who talk too fast may be difficult to follow. On the other hand, people who talk too slowly or too softly may lull you to sleep. People may also have habits that are

When the noise level is high or when two or more people try to talk at the same time, it is difficult to listen effectively.

distracting. They may sway to and fro or fiddle with their hair while they are talking. Occasionally, you may even encounter people whose dress or hair style is so unusual that you find yourself concentrating more on them than on what they are saying. As a listener, sometimes just being aware that you are responding to such cues may be enough to help you listen more attentively.

1. Familiarize yourself with the material ahead of time.
2. Leave a large margin on the left.
3. Take notes in outline form and leave spaces between main points.
4. Omit nonessential words.
5. Be alert for signal words such as:
    A. for example suggests supporting material will follow
    B. the three causes suggests a list you should number
    C. before or after suggests that the time sequence is important
    D. therefore or consequently suggests a causal relationship
    E. similarly or on the other hand suggests a comparison or contrast will follow
    F. above all or keep in mind suggests this is an important idea
6. Review your notes as soon as possible.
7. Use the left-hand margin to paraphrase, summarize, or write questions on the material.

FIGURE 4.2
Guidelines for Taking Notes

INTERNAL SOURCES OF INTERFERENCE

Our most serious listening problems stem from interference that is within us. These problems may be caused by reactions to words, personal concerns, attitudes, cultural differences, or bad listening habits. As Figure 4.3 shows, good and poor listeners respond differently to such problems.

One of the most common barriers to effective listening is simply not paying attention. Do you ever find yourself daydreaming when you know you should be listening? Our minds can process information faster than people speak. Most people speak at about 125 words per minute, but we can process information at about 500 words per minute.[21] This speed gap gives listeners an opportunity to drift away to more delightful or more troublesome personal concerns. Often daydreamers will smile and nod encouragingly even though they haven't heard a thing the speaker has said. This deceptive feedback is one cause of failed communication. Both personal reactions to words and personal distractions can set off such reactions.

Reactions to Words. As you listen to someone, you react to more than just the objective meanings of words. You respond to the emotional meanings as well. Some **trigger words** may set off emotional reactions so powerful that they dominate communication interactions. Obscene language and racial, ethnic, or sexist epithets are examples of negative trigger words.

For example, the use of the term *girls* to refer to adult females may really set you off. You see this as demeaning and disrespectful. Now suppose a recruiter visiting your campus is describing opportunities for advancement in his company. As an example, he tells you about "one of the girls from the office" who was recently promoted to a management position. His use of the term *girls* makes you think that he is a sexist person, and therefore this must be a sexist organization. As you sit there stewing over his insensitiv-

Good Listeners	Poor Listeners
1. focus on the message	1. let their minds wander
2. control emotional reactions	2. respond emotionally
3. set aside personal problems	3. let personal problems interfere
4. listen despite distractions	4. succumb to distractions
5. don't let biases interfere	5. let biases interfere
6. don't let mannerisms interfere	6. let mannerisms interfere
7. find something they can use	7. tune out dry topics
8. think listening is important	8. think speaking is important
9. listen actively	9. listen passively
10. reserve judgment	10. jump to conclusions
11. pay attention	11. feign attention
12. give honest feedback	12. give false feedback
13. listen for ideas and feelings	13. listen only for facts
14. don't demand to be entertained	14. want to be entertained

FIGURE 4.3
Differences Between Good and Poor Listeners

ity, you miss his saying that over the past three years, two-thirds of all promotions into management have gone to women.

While some words are certainly offensive, you should try to control your reactions to words and not let words control you. Do not let trigger words prevent you from hearing and evaluating the entire message within its total context. How can you manage your reactions to such language? Try to look at the total message and analyze the particular case. For example, would it be different if the recruiter were a woman rather than a man? Ask yourself: Why is this person using such language? Is he personally insensitive, or is he testing me? Is his attitude one that is widespread within the company?

By concentrating on such questions, you can defuse trigger words of some of their power and distance yourself from your emotions. You can then decide whether you wish to confront the person to clarify the situation. For example, you might *tactfully* say, "I'm extremely impressed by what you've told me about your company. But I'm troubled by your use of the word *girls*. Sometimes that word is a sign that women are not really respected in a company. Can you help me with this?" There is a risk in such a strategy: you might offend the recruiter and not get the job you want. But there is also risk in committing to a job that might be wrong for you.

Trigger words can be positive as well as negative. Positive trigger words can blind you to dangerous messages. How many times have people been deceived by such trigger words as *freedom, democracy,* or *progress?*[22] This technique is often used in ads: products or services are associated with words like *American* and *Mom* or tied to traditional cultural

● T R Y　T H I S

One way to improve your concentration is to keep a listening log in one of your lecture classes. As you take class notes, put an X in the margin each time you notice your attention wandering. By each X, jot down a few words pinpointing the cause—for example, "used *girls* for women." After class, count the number of times your mind drifted and note the causes. Can you identify a pattern of reactions? This exercise will help you identify the conditions that bring on inattention and make you more aware of your tendency to daydream. Once you realize how often and why you are drifting away, you can more easily guard against this.

heroes. For example, Chevrolet trucks sound the "heartbeat of America," Qantas is the airline "your mother would prefer you to fly," and the Franklin/Templeton mutual fund uses a picture of Ben Franklin as its logo.

Your attention also can be waylaid by chance associations with words. Suppose the person you are listening to mentions the word *desk,* which reminds you that you need a better place to study in your room, which reminds you that you have to buy a new lamp, which starts you thinking about where you should shop for the lamp, which gets you thinking about the good fried mushrooms at Friday's in the mall, which reminds you that you didn't eat breakfast and you're hungry. By the time your attention drifts back, you have lost track of what is being talked about.

Personal Concerns. If you are tired, hungry, angry, worried, or pressed for time, you may find it difficult to listen effectively to others. Your personal problems may take precedence. With a friend, you can simply confess that you are distracted by personal problems. In the classroom or other formal lecture situations, however, you must work to control such interference. Come to your classes well rested and well fed. Remind yourself that you really cannot do your homework for another class when someone is talking. Leave your troubles at the door, even if it means scheduling a time to worry later in the day. Clear your mind and your desk of everything except paper on which to take notes. Sit erect, establish eye contact with the speaker, and get ready to listen!

Attitudes. You may have strong positive or negative attitudes toward people or topics that diminish your listening ability. All of us have biases of one kind or another. Listening problems arise when our biases prevent us from receiving messages accurately. Some of the ways in which bias can distort messages are filtering, assimilation, and contrast effects.[23]

Filtering means that you don't process all incoming information. You hear what you want to hear. You unconsciously screen the speaker's words so that only some of them reach your brain. Listeners who filter will hear only one side of "good news, bad news" messages—the side that confirms their preconceived ideas. **Assimilation** means that you see positions similar to your own as being closer to it than they actually are. Assimilation most often occurs when listeners have a strong positive attitude toward a speaker or a topic. For example, if you believe that the president can do no wrong, you may be tempted to assimilate everything he says so that it seems consistent with all your beliefs. A **contrast effect** occurs when you see positions that differ from yours as being more distant than they actually are. For example, if you are a staunch Republican, you may think that anything Democrats say will be different from what you believe. Biases can make you put words in a speaker's mouth, take them away, or distort them.

The more competent, interesting, and attractive you believe a person is, the more attentive you will be and the more likely you will be to accept what she or he has to say. If your positive feelings toward a person are extremely strong, you may accept anything you hear from that person without considering the merits of his or her words. But if you think a person is incompetent, uninteresting, or unattractive, you may be less attentive and less likely to accept his or her ideas. You may dislike people because of positions they have previously espoused or groups with which they are associated. Such biases may impair your listening ability.

Your attitudes toward certain topics also can affect how well you listen. If you believe that a topic is relevant to your life, you may listen more carefully than you would if you were indifferent to the topic. You may listen more attentively, although less critically, to messages that support positions you already hold. If you feel strongly about a subject and you oppose a person's position, you may find yourself thinking up counterarguments instead of listening. For example, if you have strong feelings against gun control, you may find yourself silently reciting the Second Amendment to the U.S. Constitution instead of listening to someone's arguments in favor of gun control. When you engage in such behaviors, you may miss much of what the person actually has to say.

Attitudes are not easy to control. The first step in overcoming biases is to admit that you have them. Next, decide that you will listen as objectively as you can, and that you will delay judgment until you have heard the entire message. Being objective does not mean that you must agree with everything a person says—it only means that you believe that what the person is saying deserves to be heard on its own terms. What you hear may help you see clearly the faults or the virtues of an opposing position. As a result, you may feel confirmed in what you already believe, or you may decide to reevaluate your position.

Habits. Many listening problems are simply the result of bad habits. This is especially true when listening to lectures or speeches. You may have watched so much television that you expect all messages to be fast-moving and entertaining. You may have learned how to pretend you are listening when you really are not. In classes, you may have trained yourself to listen only for facts. You may jump to conclusions before hearing a complete message. Such habits can interfere with effective listening.

Television messages are characterized by fast action and short bits of information. Habitual television viewing may lead us to want all messages to follow this format. William F. Buckley Jr. has commented that "the television audience . . . is not trained to listen . . . to 15 uninterrupted minutes."[24] Television watching may also lead you into "the entertainment syndrome," in which you demand that presentations be lively, interesting, funny, and charismatic in order to hold your attention.[25] Unfortunately, not all subjects lend themselves to such treatment, and you can miss much if you listen attentively only to those who put on a "dog and pony show."

You probably also know how to look as if you are paying attention—even when you are not. You may sit erect, gaze at a speaker, nod or smile from time to time (although not always at the most appropriate times), and not hear one word that is said! You are most likely to pretend you are paying attention when a message is difficult to understand. If you are asked, "Do you understand?" you may nod brightly to seem polite or to avoid looking dumb.

Your fear of failure may cause you to avoid listening to difficult material. If you are asked questions later, you can always say, "I wasn't really listening," instead of, "I didn't understand." You may believe that asking questions would make you look less than intelligent—that your questions may be "dumb." (In fact, the truly dumb question is the one that is not asked.) Your desire to have things simplified so that they are easily understandable leaves you susceptible to oversimplified remedies for everything from fallen arches to failing government policies.

Your experiences as a student may contribute to another bad habit: listening only for facts. If you do this, you may miss the forest because you are so busy counting the leaves

Poor listening in the classroom can come from a fear of failure or listening only for facts.

on the trees. Placing too much emphasis on facts can keep you from attending to the nonverbal aspects of a message. Effective listening includes integrating what you hear and what you see. Gestures, facial expressions, and tone of voice communicate nuances that are vital to a message.

Overcoming bad habits requires effort. When you find yourself feigning attention, stop and ask yourself what this is doing to you. Don't try to remember everything or write down all that you hear. Instead, try to identify the main ideas. Paraphrase what you hear so that it makes sense to you. Build an overall picture of the message in your mind. Attend to nonverbal cues. Does a person's tone of voice change the meaning of what she or he said? Are the gestures and facial expressions consistent with the words? If not, what does this tell you?

Practice extending your attention span. If your listening log shows that you drifted away from a lecturer twenty times in one class session, see whether you can reduce this to fifteen, then to ten, then to five. The Note Card on "Improving Your Listening Skills" summarizes how you might listen more effectively to messages.

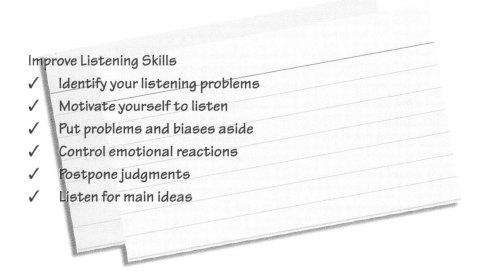

Improve Listening Skills
✓   Identify your listening problems
✓   Motivate yourself to listen
✓   Put problems and biases aside
✓   Control emotional reactions
✓   Postpone judgments
✓   Listen for main ideas

DEVELOPING CRITICAL THINKING AND LISTENING SKILLS

Developing your critical thinking and listening skills will further increase your effectiveness as a listener. **Critical thinking and listening** is an integrated process of examining information, ideas, and proposals. It calls upon a variety of skills:

- It involves questioning what you hear.
- It involves examining competing ideas.
- It involves being open to new perspectives.
- It involves evaluating evidence and reasoning.
- It involves discussing with others the meanings of events.[26]

Use the following questions to guide your critical listening.

- *Are ideas or claims supported by facts and figures, testimony, examples, or narratives?* Whenever someone asserts, "This is beyond dispute!" it is a good time to start a dispute. Listen for what is *not* said, as well as what is said. No support equals no proof. No proof should equal no acceptance. Do not hesitate to ask challenging questions.

- *Are supporting materials relevant, representative, recent, and reliable?* Information, testimony, examples, and narratives should relate directly to the issue in question. They should be representative of the situation rather than exceptions to the rule. The person who announces, "Television is destroying family values!" and then offers statistics that show a rising divorce rate has not demonstrated a causal relationship between television and family values. Facts and figures also should be the most recent ones available. This is particularly important when knowledge about a topic is changing rapidly. Supporting materials should come from sources that are trustworthy and competent in the subject area. Controversial material should be backed up by more than one source, and the sources should represent different perspectives on the issue.

- *Does the person cite credible sources?* When a source's credentials are not given or are described in vague terms, the testimony may be questionable. We recently saw an advertisement for a health-food product that contained "statements by doctors." A quick check of the current directory of the American Medical Association revealed that only one of the six "doctors" cited was a member of the AMA and that his credentials were misrepresented. Always ask yourself, "Where does this information come from?" and "Are these sources qualified to speak on the topic?"

- *Does the person distinguish among facts, inferences, and opinions?* Facts are verifiable units of information that can be confirmed by independent observations. Inferences are projections based on facts. Opinions add personal interpretations or judgments to facts: they tell us what someone thinks about a subject. For example, "Mary was late for class today" is a fact. "Mary will probably be late for class again tomorrow" is an inference. "Mary is an irresponsible student" is an opinion. Making these distinctions among facts, inferences, and opinions may sound easy, but you must be constantly alert to detect confusions of them in the messages you hear. Facts, opinions, and inferences all have a legitimate place in discourse, but all can be misused.

- *Does the person use language that is concrete and understandable or purposely vague?* When people have something to hide, they often use incomprehensible or vague language. Introducing people who are not physicians as "doctors" to enhance their testimony on health subjects is one form of such vagueness. Another trick is to use pseudoscientific jargon such as "This supplement contains a gonadotropic hormone similar to pituitary extract in terms of its complex B vitamin–methionine ratio." If it sounds impressive but you don't know what it means, be careful.

- *Does the person ask you to ignore reason?* Vivid examples and stories often express a person's deep passion for a subject and invite listeners to share such feelings. However, people should also provide sound information and reasons to justify their strong feelings. Politicians who try to inflame feelings to promote their own agendas, without regard to the accuracy or adequacy of their claims, are called **demagogues.** We should always ask, "What are these speakers asking us to forget?" In the face of conflicting emotional claims, the critical listener will exercise skepticism and investigate the claims carefully before coming to a conclusion.

- *Does the person rely too much on facts and figures?* Although we have just cautioned you to be wary of people who rely solely on emotional appeals, you also should be wary of people who exclude any emotionality. You can never fully understand an issue unless you understand how it affects others, how it makes them feel, how it colors the way they view the world. Suppose you were listening to a speech on environmental pollution that contained the following information: "The United States has 5 percent of the world's population but produces 22 percent of the world's carbon dioxide emissions, releases 26 percent of the world's nitrogen oxides, and disposes of 290 million tons of toxic waste."[27] These numbers are impressive, but what do they really tell you about the human problem of pollution? Consider how much more meaningful this material might be if it were accompanied by the story of Colette Chuda, a five-year-old California girl who died recently from cancer that many feel resulted from exposure to a polluted environment.[28]

- *Does the person reason logically?* When reasoning is logical, conclusions follow from the points and supporting materials that are presented. In other words, they make good sense. The basic assumptions that support arguments should be those on which most rational people agree. Whenever reasoning does not seem logical, ask yourself why, and then question the speaker or consult with other authorities before you make decisions or commit yourself.

- *Does the message promise too much?* If an offer sounds too good to be true, it probably is. The health-food advertisement previously described contained the following claims: "The healing, rejuvenating and disease-fighting effects of this total nutrient are hard to believe, yet are fully documented. Aging, digestive upsets, prostrate [sic] diseases, sore throats, acne, fatigue, sexual problems, allergies, and a host of other problems have been successfully treated. . . . [It] is the only super perfect food on this earth. This statement has been proven so many times in the laboratories around the world by a chemical analyst that it is not subject to debate nor challenge." Maybe the product is also useful as a paint remover and gasoline additive.

- *Does this message fit with what I already know?* Although it is important that you be open to new knowledge, inconsistent information should set off an alarm in your mind. You should always evaluate information that is inconsistent with your

Guides for Critical Listening

✓   Require that claims be supported with information

✓   Evaluate support for claims

✓   Evaluate credentials of sources

✓   Separate facts, inferences, and opinions

✓   Be wary of language that is vague or incomprehensible

✓   Look for a balance between rational and emotional appeals

✓   Question claims that promise too much

✓   Check what you hear against what you know

✓   Consider alternates

✓   Ask questions

beliefs very carefully before you accept it. Yet, keep in mind that what you think you know may not necessarily be so. Apply your critical thinking skills. Ask tough questions of the material as suggested by the note card "Guides for Critical Listening." Use the library to further verify information.

● *What other perspectives are there on this issue?* How would someone from a different cultural background see the problem? Someone older? Someone of the other gender? Why might they see it differently from the way you see it? Would their solutions or suggestions be different? Whenever a topic is important, try to examine it from several points of view. New and better ideas often emerge when you look at the world from a different angle.

These questions provide a framework for critical listening. When we add these skills to the improved listening behavior that comes when we solve our listening problems, we are on the way to becoming effective listeners.

YOUR ETHICAL RESPONSIBILITIES AS A LISTENER

Listeners have ethical responsibilities. Ethical listeners do not prejudge messages; they keep an open mind. It is irresponsible to think, "My mind is made up on that issue. Don't try to persuade me." John Milton, a seventeenth-century English poet and intellectual, noted in his treatise on freedom of speech, *Areopagitica,* that listening to opponents can be beneficial. We may learn something from them and gain a new and better perspective on an issue. Or, as we question them and argue with them, we may discover *why* we believe as we do. When we protect ourselves from ideas we disagree with, we deprive ourselves of the chance to exercise and strengthen our own convictions.

Just as we should be open to ideas, we should also be receptive to the lifestyles and cultural backgrounds of others. Prejudice can prevent us from realizing that people should be judged as individuals, not as members of races, classes, or cultural groups. Moreover, we may have misguided ideas about different races or cultures that keep us from appreciating their unique contributions. While we may *hear* others, we may not *listen* to them. When this happens, we are deprived not only of the chance to explore other worlds, but also of the opportunity to understand our own more clearly. In comparing and contrasting our way of life with those of others, we learn more about ourselves.

While as an ethical listener you should remain open to ideas that may at first seem strange or hostile, you should not lower your interference barriers to all messages. When given fair consideration, some ideas will prove to be faulty, risky, or even evil. Not every person has our interests at heart. Perhaps the best advice is to be an open but cautious listener, combining the best traits of ethical and critical listening.

IN SUMMARY

Listening is as important to communication as speaking. Listening involves hearing, paying attention, comprehending, and interpreting a message. The major types of listening are *discriminative listening, comprehensive listening, critical listening, empathic listening,* and *appreciative listening. Constructive listening* suggests the additional vital role of the listener in the creation of meaning.

Effective listeners are less vulnerable to unethical advertising or dishonest political communication. Improved listening skills will help your performance as a student and may mean the difference between success and failure at work. Effective listening also benefits interpersonal relationships. An audience that listens effectively can help improve public speaking skills. A supportive audience can help relieve some of the communication apprehension that speakers experience and boost a speaker's self-esteem.

Listening problems may arise from external sources, such as a noisy environment. They may also be a function of the use of language that the audience does not understand or of a speaker whose presentation skills are distracting. However, most serious listening problems arise from factors within the listener, such as personal reactions to words, worries, attitudes, or bad listening habits. Personal reactions to trigger words may set off strong emotions that block effective listening. Biases can interfere with listening. Bad habits, such as pretending we are listening when we are not or listening only for facts, can also interfere with listening.

Effective listening skills can be developed. The first step is to identify your listening problems. Strive for objectivity, withholding value judgments until you are certain you understand the message.

Critical listening skills help you analyze and evaluate messages more effectively. Critical listeners question what they hear, require support for assertions and claims, and evaluate the credentials of sources. Critical listeners differentiate among facts, inferences, and opinions. They become wary when language seems overly vague or incomprehensible, when inflammatory speech takes the place of cool reason, or when a message promises too much. When what they hear does not fit with what they know, critical listeners consider the message very carefully and ask questions.

Listeners have ethical responsibilities. Ethical listeners do not prejudge a speech, but remain open to ideas and receptive to different perspectives. They test what they hear and are sensitive to the impact of ideas on others.

TERMS TO KNOW

discriminative listening	trigger words
comprehensive listening	filtering
critical listening	assimilation
empathic listening	contrast effect
appreciative listening	critical thinking and listening
constructive listening	demagogues
participative communication	

NOTES

1. Cited in Clifton Fadiman, ed. *The Little, Brown Book of Anecdotes* (Boston: Little, Brown, 1985), 475–476.

2. L. Barker et al., "An Investigation of Proportional Time Spent in Various Communication Activities by College Students," *Journal of Applied Communication Research* (1981): 101–109; Walter Pauk, *How to Study in College* (Boston: Houghton Mifflin, 1989), 121–133; and Larry L. Barker, *Listening Behavior* (Englewood Cliffs, N.J.: Prentice-Hall, 1971), 3–9.

3. Luther Standing Bear, Oglala Sioux chief, cited in *Native American Wisdom: Photographs by Edward S. Curtis* (Philadelphia: Running Press, 1993), 58–59.

4. Ronald B. Adler and George Rodman, *Understanding Human Communi-cation,* 5th ed. (Fort Worth, Tex.: Harcourt Brace, 1994), 130.

5. We describe this concept further in Michael and Suzanne Osborn, *Alliance for a Better Public Voice: The Communication Discipline and the National Issues Forums* (Dayton, Ohio: National Issues Forums Institute, 1991).

6. Waldo Braden, "The Available Means of Persuasion: What Shall We Do About the Demand for Snake Oil?" in *The Rhetoric of Our Times,* ed. J. Jeffery Auer (New York: Appleton-Century-Crofts, 1969), 178–184.

7. Jeffrey A. Trachtenberg, "Beyond the Hidden Persuaders: Psychological Aspects of Marketing," *Forbes,* March 23, 1987, 134–137; and "Michael Jordan's Magical Powers," *The Economist,* June 1, 1991, A28.

8. W. B. Legge, "Listening, Intelligence, and School Achievement," in *Listening: Readings,* ed. S. Duker (Metuchen, N.J.: Scarecrow Press, 1971), 121–133.

9. U.S. Department of Labor, "What Work Requires of Schools" (Washington, D.C.: U.S. Government Printing Office, 1991).

10. Dan B. Curtis, Jerry L. Winsor, and Ronald D. Stephens, "National Preferences in Business and Communication Education," *Communication Education,* (January 1989): 7–14.

11. Gary T. Hunt and Louis P. Cusella, "A Field Study of Listening Needs in Organizations," *Communication Education* (October 1983): 399.

12. B. D. Sypher, R. N. Bostrom, and J. H. Seibert, "Listening Communication Abilities and Success at Work," *Journal of Business Communication* (Fall 1989): 293–303.

13. B. E. Ashworth and R. H. Humphrey, "Emotional Labor in Service Roles: The Influence of Identity," *Academy of Management Review* (Winter 1993): 88–115.

14. Patricia Senecal and Ellen Burke, "Learning to Listen," *Occupational Hazards* (December 1992): 37–39; Heather Harrison, "Attention Please, Are You Listening?" *Healthcare: Trends and Transitions* (March 1990): 12–15, 26.

15. International Listening Association, "Quotes on Listening," http://www.listen.org/pages/quotes.html. Updated September 13, 1997; downloaded February 7, 1998.

16. Andrew D. Wolvin and Carolyn Gwynn Coakley, "A Survey of the Status of Listening Training in Some Fortune 500 Corporations," *Communication Education* (April 1991), 152–164.

17. International Listening Association, "Quotes on Listening."

18. Lou Davidson Tillson, "Building Community and Reducing Communication Apprehension: A Case Study Approach," *The Speech Communication Teacher* (Summer 1995): 4–5.

19. Some material for this section was synthesized from William B. Gudykunst et al., *Building Bridges: Interpersonal Skills for a Changing World* (Boston: Houghton Mifflin, 1995), 228–229.

20. Adapted from Walter Pauk, *How to Study in College,* 4th ed. (Boston: Houghton Mifflin, 1997), 201–223, and Dave Ellis, *Becoming a Master Student,* 7th ed. (Boston: Houghton Mifflin, 1994), 136–150.

21. Andrew D. Wolvin and Carolyn Gwynn Coakley, *Listening,* 2nd ed. (Dubuque, Iowa: William C. Brown, 1985), 177.

22.   Richard M. Weaver, "Ultimate Terms in Contemporary Rhetoric," in *Language Is Sermonic: Richard M. Weaver on the Nature of Rhetoric,* ed. Richard L. Johannesen, Rennard Strickland, and Ralph T. Eubanks (Baton Rouge: Louisiana State University Press, 1970), 95.

23.   J. J. Makay and W. R. Brown, *The Rhetorical Dialogue: Contemporary Concepts and Cases* (Dubuque, Iowa: William C. Brown, 1972), 125–145.

24.   William F. Buckley Jr., "Has TV Killed Off Great Oratory?" *TV Guide,* February 12, 1983, 38.

25.   James J. Floyd, *Listening: A Practical Approach* (Glencoe, Ill.: Scott, Foresman, 1985), 23–25.

26.   John Chaffee, *Thinking Critically*, 2nd ed. (Boston: Houghton Mifflin, 1988), 59.

27.   *Time,* December 18, 1989, cover.

28.   Jim Motavalli, "In Memory of Colette," *E: The Environmental Magazine,* (May/June 1994): 30–31.

PART TWO

INTERPERSONAL AND SMALL-GROUP SETTINGS

THE SELF—PERSONAL AND INTERPERSONAL PERCEPTIONS

THIS CHAPTER
will help you

- Recognize personal characteristics to foster self-awareness

- Recognize personal characteristics to foster self-acceptance

- Recognize others' characteristics to foster mutual acceptance

- Recognize features of emotional maturity

- Consider your level of communication avoidance

UNDERSTAND thyself.

—A. Pope

UNDERSTAND other PEOPLE.

—Menander

t takes two to tango," the old song says. It's the same with interpersonal communication: It takes two (at least). So it may seem a bit strange that we begin our section on interpersonal communication with an entire chapter about the self. Our personal psychological makeup is crucial to our interpersonal interactions, however. This is partly because of psychological tendencies that are generalizable across most individuals. For example, there are certain irrational thought processes that most of us are guilty of from time to time, and being able to recognize these, in ourselves or in others, can be helpful in difficult communication situations. Psychological makeup is important also because of features of the self that are more individualized. Recognizing our idiosyncrasies—ways in which we are *not* like most other people, and they are *not* like us—can be of enormous help in understanding others and in being understood. This chapter will focus especially on some of these personal idiosyncrasies.

COMMUNICATION AND SELF— GENERAL APPROACHES

There are various approaches to examining the influence of the self upon communication. Virtually all of them focus on one of three basic aspects of the self: self-evaluation, self-acceptance, and self-awareness.

SELF-EVALUATION

A very common approach to communication and the self focuses on **self-evaluation.** Each of us has a *self-concept*—the way in which we would describe our self if asked to do so. This self-description tends to be evaluative, and this evaluation constitutes our *self-esteem.* For example, if one's self-concept includes the description "I am a quiet person . . . ," the self-esteem evaluation may be ". . . and that is good," or it may be " . . . and that is not good." Or, if one's self-concept and self-esteem include the description and evaluation "I am a friendly person, and that is good," further evaluation may include " . . . so I am satisfied" or " . . . but I ought to be still friendlier." And so forth. In addition to an evaluation of our individual traits, our self-esteem also includes feelings and evaluations having to do with a more general sense of our importance and value to other people.

Self-concept and self-esteem begin to form at an early age. They are determined in part by compliments and criticisms we receive from those whose opinions we value, and by conscious and unconscious comparisons we make between ourselves and others in terms of various traits and abilities. For most of us, the subsequent connection between self-esteem and communication has to do with the simple notion that our self-evaluations in specific areas will give us relatively more confidence or anxiety, assertiveness or passivity, eagerness or reluctance, etc., in specific communication situations. For example, our self-evaluation in the relevant areas may affect our eagerness or reluctance to approach an attractive member of the opposite sex, raise our hand in classes generally, raise our hand in chemistry (or some other) class in particular, voice our opinion when discussing a topic on which we evaluate our self as knowledgeable, voice an opinion when discussing a topic on which we consider our self to be relatively ignorant, and so forth.

SELF-ACCEPTANCE

Another approach to self and communication focuses on accepting features of our self-concept *without* evaluation. It is psychologically healthy to reach a point at which our overall self-evaluation is relatively neutral. This involves a balance in which we maintain a positive self-evaluation in certain areas, accept those shortcomings over which we have little control and those that are of relatively little consequence, and work to improve in those areas that concern us most. The idea is to have a generally satisfied, "doing the best I can with what I've got but always improving" level of **self-acceptance.**

Self-acceptance is considered to be important to communication because of its role in influencing our more important relationships. Individuals with lower levels of genuine self-acceptance are more likely to put up *façades* in their interactions with others. **Façades,** or false fronts, are ways in which we hide or disguise our true self in interactions with others—acting more or less competent than we really feel, more or less hurt than we really feel, more or less happy or upset than we really feel, and so forth. Façades make for phony relationships because the partner relates to the façade rather than to the "true" individual. Higher self-acceptance leads to fewer façades, which leads to more genuine, less superficial relationships.

SELF-AWARENESS

Yet another approach to self and communication focuses on the importance of *introspection*—the process of looking inward to analyze and understand oneself. The resulting **self-awareness** is a first step in the self-acceptance we discussed a moment ago. But self-awareness is important in other ways, also.

Ideally, self-awareness can make us more accepting of others. As we come to understand "what makes us tick" as an individual, we come to recognize that others don't tick the same way in certain respects. And as we come to accept that there is nothing wrong with certain of our idiosyncrasies, it becomes easier to accept that there is nothing wrong with certain of others' idiosyncrasies either.

Moreover, as we come to understand the ways in which our self ticks differently from others', we take more responsibility for our reactions to others' behaviors. For example, rather than being upset when the kitchen is messy and blaming it on our roommate's being a slob, we may mediate the blame by recognizing that we happen to be the type of individual who doesn't like messes (or doesn't like others' messes, or whatever). By recognizing that not everybody would be as upset as we are with the messy kitchen, we may recognize that our feelings are more a byproduct of our individual self than a "natural" reaction to a messy kitchen. This recognition helps us to take a less accusatory stance when we approach our roommate about the mess.

This approach can be used throughout much of this chapter. As we discuss the nature of individual preferences and styles, you are bound to recognize yourself in some of the descriptions. And when the discussion doesn't fit you, you may use it to improve your understanding of others.

PERSONALITY, PREFERENCES, AND STYLES

Intuitively, we know that different people have different personalities or styles—traits that seem to correspond to particular ways of thinking or behaving. We can point to certain of our friends and acquaintances and say, with varying degrees of confidence, "This person is a [*whatever*] type." They can fill in the blank for us as well, of course; and we can fill it in for ourselves (perhaps the same way they do, but perhaps not).

A list of all imaginable personality traits would be a very long one, of course. It should not be surprising, therefore, that many theories concerning the concept of personality have been developed. While the various theories have their differences, most of them seem to take one of two general approaches: some assume that we are all basically alike, whereas others assume that we are all basically different from one another. There is truth in both perspectives.

WE ARE ALL BASICALLY ALIKE

Most early personality theories took the view that all humans (within a given culture, at least) are essentially the same, and that personality types represent deviations.[1] That is to say, in terms of the more important traits, most of us are "normal" and a relatively few individuals possess far more or far less of the trait than normal. To exhibit much more (or much less, depending upon the trait) than what is normal will often be viewed as undesirable. This is the approach most of us use when we attribute personality traits to acquaintances. When we identify someone as an "opinionated type" or a "competitive type" or an "overachiever type" or an "argumentative type," we usually mean that they have much more of the trait than is normal.

As an example, consider the following data from questionnaires asking college students to name the trait or personality style that describes the type of individual they most *dislike:*[2]

43%	*Arrogant (arrogant, vain, egotistical, snobbish, conceited)*
25%	*Overbearing (loud, obnoxious, overly aggressive, boisterous, overbearing)*
15%	*Dogmatic (dogmatic, opinionated, close-minded, judgmental)*
12%	*Pretentious (phony, fake, pretentious)*
5%	*Quiet (too humble, quiet)*

There are several interesting points about these data. First of all, notice that these traits represent the "deviation from the norm" approach to personality. The idea in the third category, for example, is not that having an opinion is undesirable, but rather that being *too* opinionated is undesirable. Notice also that virtually all of these traits are *manifested via communication.* More than anything else, it is one's communication style that makes one appear arrogant, overbearing, dogmatic, and so forth. Finally, notice an irony: Of those who have any of the five traits listed, the arrogant individual is the least likely to see his or her own trait as a problem, yet this trait is very undesirable in the eyes of many others. The quiet or self-labeled shy individual, on the other hand, is the one most likely to see the trait as a problem, yet this trait is not so often viewed by others as undesirable.

Cautions When Attributing Traits to Others. Once we assess others' "deviant" traits, we often apply our own **implicit personality theory**[3]—our own hunches about which personality traits tend to be *associated* with one another according to our view of "human nature." If, for example, you meet someone and determine from what you have seen that he or she is both loud and egotistical, you may make guesses about other traits the person has, even though you haven't yet seen direct evidence of these other traits. But one person's implicit personality theory will not be the same as another's. One of us may assume that someone who is loud and egotistical is probably insecure, insincere, and shallow as well, whereas another of us may assume that someone who is loud and egotistical is probably confident, adventuresome, and ambitious as well. In any case, we are making guesses about multiple traits based on only a few traits that we have actually observed. And we are bound to be wrong from time to time. It is wiser, of course, not to make the assumptions about a trait until we have seen good evidence of it—evidence beyond mere association via our implicit personality theory.

There is another reason we should be cautious when attributing traits to others. The process is subject to various kinds of bias. As a simple example, we are prone to exaggerate in others certain negative traits or faults that we sense within ourselves. This process, called **projection**, operates especially for negative traits that we sense vaguely within ourselves, but have not yet consciously acknowledged or admitted to ourselves. To put it another way, we are especially likely to project onto others negative traits that we sense within ourselves, but have not yet made a serious effort to fix or change. (Thus, increased self-awareness should decrease instances of projection.)

Attribution theory suggests another way in which we may be biased when attributing traits to others:[4] When someone else does or says something that is unusually positive (kind, considerate, appropriate, intelligent, etc.) or unusually negative (unkind, inconsiderate, inappropriate, dumb, etc.), we tend to formulate *explanations* and *reasons* for the behavior. Our explanations tend to attribute the unusual behavior either to the person's *traits* (e.g., he or she did that because that's just the kind of person he or she is) or to extenuating *circumstances* (e.g., the person wouldn't ordinarily do something like that, but under the circumstances he or she had little choice).

Thus, if we wanted to give everyone the benefit of the doubt, we would attribute their unusually *positive* behaviors to their *traits* (e.g., that's the way they are) and attribute their unusually *negative* behavior to the *circumstances* (e.g., they aren't normally that way, but the circumstances forced them to act so in this instance). This *altruistic* approach is in fact the one most of us take with people we like.

With people we dislike, however, most of us become more *cynical*. We attribute their unusually *negative* behaviors to *traits* (e.g., that proves it; that's the kind of person he or she is) and attribute their unusually *positive* behaviors to *circumstances* (e.g., the only reason he or she is being so nice is because he or she wants something; or he or she is being diligent only because the boss is here today).

With new or neutral acquaintances—those whom we neither particularly like nor dislike—some of us tend toward the more **altruistic mode**, whereas others tend toward the more **cynical mode**. There are a couple of lessons in this. For one, if others' behaviors, positive or negative, may be due to either traits or circumstances, we are being very presumptuous amateur psychologists whenever we assume that they are due to traits (or

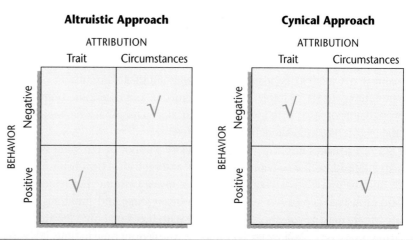

FIGURE **5.1**
Approaches to Trait/Circumstance Attributions

circumstances) without plenty of evidence. Our assumptions are bound to be incorrect some of the time. For another, to the extent that we do analyze others' traits, certainly the more altruistic, benefit-of-the-doubt approach (even for those we dislike, if possible) will get our interpersonal interactions off to a better start than the more cynical approach.

WE ARE ALL BASICALLY DIFFERENT

Although it is common to think of personality in terms of deviations from norms, we are going to place more emphasis on another perspective, one that has been growing in popularity over the past few years. This perspective does not deny that there is value in recognizing norms and deviations, but it stresses that there is more value in recognizing certain essential ways in which we tend to be naturally different from one another.[5]

This approach originated with Carl Jung and has become popular over the past decade with the additional work of Isabel Myers and Katheryn Briggs.[6] The Myers-Briggs approach focuses on four specific *dimensions* of personality. Each of these dimensions has two somewhat opposite *styles,* and each of us tends to favor one style over the other. In effect, each of us "naturally" tends either more toward style X or more toward style Y on each of the four dimensions. That is to say, it is quite normal for human beings to be *different* from one another in these four ways.

As we lay out some of the details of this approach, keep in mind its relevance to interpersonal communication. First, learning more about personality should be helpful to our self-awareness. It should help us to understand our own reactions to interpersonal situations, and to recognize ways in which our reactions are somewhat unique. Second, the "we're all different" approach should help us to see that various styles and preferences that are somewhat foreign to us personally are nevertheless quite common to others. This should help us to become more tolerant of certain differences we notice in others. Third, by recognizing not only the strong points of our particular styles, but also the strong points of "opposing" styles, we may become more adaptable to a variety of interpersonal situations.

Tendencies of Which to Beware Include
- ✓ Applying our implicit personality theories
- ✓ Projection
- ✓ Cynical trait/circumstance attributions
- ✓ Displacement

Introversion/Extraversion (I/E).[7] The first dimension in the Myers-Briggs system distinguishes between the *Introvert* and *Extravert* styles. You should recognize from the outset that within this system, neither of these terms means what it often means in everyday language. By "introvert" we do *not* mean a nonsocial hermit, and by "extravert" we do *not* mean a gregarious, back-slapping, "politician" or "used car salesman" type. (It will be helpful to ignore common connotations for the remaining Myers-Briggs dimensions, as well.)

The introversion/extraversion dimension has to do with the extent to which we find it to be either draining or energizing to be in either social or solitary situations. Introverts (*Is*) enjoy solitary activities—working quietly alone, participating in activities that involve few or no

An extreme *F* (*Feeling*) type like Dr. McCoy and an extreme *T* (*Thinking*) type like Mr. Spock of the *Star Trek* television series, have quite different personalities. But both personality styles are natural and each has its advantages.

Most everyone likes either of these settings from time to time. But in settings like the one on the left, an *I* usually will begin to feel "antsy" much sooner than an *E*, and in settings like the one on the right, an *E* usually will begin to feel "antsy" much sooner than an *I*.

other people, and dealing with the "inner world" of concepts and ideas. Extraverts (*E*s) enjoy social activities—working actively with others, participating in activities involving several or many other people, and dealing with the "outer world" of people and things. *I*s are energized by having time alone by themselves, are rarely bothered by having to be alone, but are sometimes drained or agitated by spending too much time with groups of other people. *E*s are energized by spending time with groups of other people, are rarely bothered by having to be with groups, but are sometimes drained or agitated by spending too much time alone.

Which are you, an *I* or an *E*? You may be inclined to answer, "It depends." Most of us have our *I*-ish moments and our *E*-ish moments, and can function competently in either kind of situation. But which mode, *I* or *E*, do you *usually* take, and which mode do you *usually* prefer, if given a choice? When the question is put that way, most of us can identify ourselves as more (a little or a lot more) *I* than *E*, or more *E* than *I*.

There will be several connections to communication as you combine your **introversion** preference or **extraversion** preference with your preferences on the remaining dimensions. But a few connections can be made already. For example, *I*s have more trouble remembering names and faces, whereas *E*s have little trouble greeting people by name. Also, *I*s will more often "think before they speak" to the point that the message becomes too complex for the receiver; whereas *E*s will more often "speak before they think," so that the message is too superficial to adequately convey their complete meaning.

Sensing/Intuiting (S/N). A second dimension concerns a difference in ways of solving, analyzing, and finding out about problems and situations. Some people prefer what is called a **Sensing** mode *(S)*, whereas others prefer an **Intuiting** mode *(N)*. *S*s pride themselves on being practical and solving problems in traditional, tested, tried-and-true

FIGURE **5.2**
Sensing versus Intuiting

An *S* and an *N* may assimilate information differently.

ways. *N*s pride themselves on being innovative, solving problems by creative, novel means. For *S*s, successes are usually the result of their perspiration. For *N*s, successes are usually the result of their inspiration. While everybody has hunches, *S*s tend to be skeptical of their hunches and usually do not act on them. *N*s tend to trust their hunches and act on them more frequently.

*S*s and *N*s differ especially in their relative attention to facts versus principles. Almost everybody makes decisions by gathering facts, putting two and two together to derive principles from the facts, and then making the decision. But *S*s emphasize facts for the sake of facts. They spend more time gathering and analyzing the facts, and less time deriving and analyzing the principles. *N*s emphasize facts for the sake of deriving principles. They spend more time deriving or considering the principles, and less time gathering or analyzing the facts.

So, which are you usually? In communication, one of the primary effects of your preference probably will involve the fact that *S*s prefer operating at the "trees" level of information, whereas *N*s prefer operating at the "forest" level. Thus, when an *S* and an *N* communicate with each other, they tend to treat the information differently. This can make interactions frustrating. The *N* will tend to forget the details, which may lead the *S* to think that the *N* was not listening. On the other hand, the *S* will sometimes miss the *N*'s true point—the "obvious" (to the *N*) and more important "big picture." Research has shown that for this reason, *S* students do better in classes with *S* instructors, and *N* students do better in classes with *N* instructors. Preliminary research indicates that the same effect on understanding operates in interpersonal communication.[8]

Thinking/Feeling (T/F).   The next dimension distinguishes between the **Thinking** type *(T)* and the **Feeling** type *(F)*. In the simplest terms, *T*s tend to make decisions based upon what their head tells them, and *F*s tend to make decisions based upon what their heart tells them. That is, *T*s tend to decide on the basis of thinking. They use thinking to predict the logical result of their actions, and make their decisions impersonally—usually on the basis of cause-and-effect reasoning. *F*s, on the other hand, tend to decide on the basis of feeling. They use their feelings to take into account what is important to them or to other people (without requiring that it be logical) and make their decisions empathetically—usually on the basis of personal values. *T*s rarely complain that others are too hard-hearted, remote, or impersonal; but they do sometimes complain that others are too soft-hearted, illogical, or overly emotional. *F*s rarely complain that others are too soft-hearted, illogical, or emotional; but they do sometimes complain that others are too hard-hearted, remote, or impersonal. Which are you usually?

Several *T/F* differences are specific to communication. One of the most noticeable is in situations requiring tact or diplomacy, where the truth about something is likely to hurt someone's feelings or cause embarrassment. *T*s tend to lean toward telling the truth in these situations, even if it hurts (to tell it or to hear it), whereas *F*s lean toward sparing others' feelings, even if it means bending the truth. In a *T/F* pairing, therefore, the *T* will be likely to sometimes consider the partner to be evasive or too soft, and the *F* is likely to sometimes consider the partner to be insensitive and too blunt. Moreover, *T*s are more likely to question the claims and conclusions of other people, whereas *F*s are less likely to challenge others. Thus, *F*s will sometimes view *T*s as too argumentative, and *T*s will sometimes view *F*s as too passive. Another difference is that *F*s find it difficult to be brief and businesslike, whereas *T*s are somewhat "naturally" brief and businesslike. Thus, *T*s will sometimes seem (to *F*s) to lack friendliness and sociability, whereas *F*s will sometimes seem (to *T*s) to be rambling and unable to get to the point.

Judging/Perceiving (J/P).   The fourth and final dimension of the Myers-Briggs system is best explained in terms of differences in our preference for order versus spontaneity. The two styles are the **Judging** mode *(J)* and the **Perceiving** mode *(P)*.

*J*s like to have both their work and their leisure activities scheduled and planned in advance. They are dedicated to their list of things to do, and are bothered when their schedules and plans are interrupted. *P*s like to have their work and leisure activities unscheduled, flexible, and spontaneous. They may carry a daily planner or other written schedule for their activities, but they are quite willing to ignore or change their plans. *J*s are more work-oriented and tend to feel that the work, errands, and duty items on the list should be completed before rest or play is allowed. *P*s are more play-oriented and feel that rest or play can come first as long as the work gets done later. *J*s regard deadlines as absolutes, whereas *P*s regard deadlines as guidelines. In short, *J*s like their lives to be organized, methodical, and planned; whereas *P*s like their lives to be flexible, adaptable, and spontaneous.

*J*s and *P*s also approach decisions differently. *J*s usually like to have decisions made and settled as promptly as possible. They are often *uncomfortable before* a decision, but *comfortable after* a decision. *P*s usually like to keep decisions open as long as possible. They are more often *comfortable before* a decision, but *uncomfortable after* a decision. Thus, there can be difficulties when a *J* and a *P* are working together on the same decision. The *P* may see the *J* as rushing into decisions with inadequate forethought, whereas the *J* may view the *P* as indecisive.

As for other interpersonal J/P difficulties, the organized Js sometimes view the spontaneous Ps as aimless drifters, whereas Ps sometimes view Js as dull and only half alive. When a J and P live together, the J—who feels that everything has its proper place and doesn't like wasting time finding his or her things—will sometimes regard the P as a hopelessly disorganized "slob." The P, on the other hand, will sometimes regard the J as compulsively "anal-retentive."

MUTUAL USEFULNESS OF OPPOSITE TYPES

As we have seen, the Myers-Briggs system is helpful to our self-awareness and self-acceptance. Since each of the preferences (I or E, S or N, etc.) has its own strengths, we can be an I or E and "proud of it," so to speak, and likewise for the other preferences.

But just as our preferences have their special strengths, the opposite preferences have theirs. Thus, there will be certain situations in which those with opposite preferences can benefit from our perspective. And it is perhaps more important that we realize that there will be situations in which we can benefit from their perspective.

In other words, *opposite types are mutually useful* to each other.[9] When we recognize that there are situations in which, because of our nature, we may need an opposing viewpoint, it becomes easier for us to seek, understand, and consider our communication partners' perspectives.

For example, Ss are usually stronger than Ns in the following areas: remembering and highlighting important facts, applying past experience (of what has and has not worked) to problems, identifying what aspects of a problem need attention now, and focusing on the joys of the present. Thus Ns may find themselves needing an S's perspective in these areas. On the other hand, Ns are usually stronger than Ss in the following areas: bringing up realistic new possibilities, applying workable ingenuity to problems, identifying how to prepare for the future, and showing how future joys or successes are worth working toward. Thus Ss may find themselves needing an N's perspective in these areas.

The situation is similar for the other opposites. An F may want a T's advice on how to fire someone, whereas a T may need an F's advice on patching up a conflict, for example. Is may find themselves needing an E to help them understand problems between individuals, and Es may find themselves needing an I to help them understand problems involving concepts and ideas. Js often need a P to help them put more spontaneity and freedom into their lives, whereas Ps often need a J to help them put more organization and structure into their lives.

And so forth. This is just a partial list of ways in which we may benefit from others' opposing perspectives, either to help round out our overall view of what is important to people generally, or to help us in specific situations in which others' perspectives may provide useful tools. In either case, our openness to others' perspectives will be fundamental to improving our communication with other people.

Combining the Dimensions. The Myers-Briggs approach has become quite popular in the past few years, especially in business, career counseling, and premarital counseling. In these contexts, the focus has been on an application we have not yet discussed.

The four preferences we have discussed *(E/I, S/N, T/F, and J/P)* allow sixteen combinations *(ESTJ, ISTJ, ENTJ, INTJ,* etc.), each of which represents a distinctly different overall personality type. Each of the sixteen personality types has its own elaborate profile or description, and each has a number of special strengths. You will probably find it interesting to examine the profile for your personality type—at least for the fun of it, if not also to increase your self-awareness. Thus, we have provided profiles in Appendix C at the end of the book. Take the profiles with a grain of salt, however! You may or may not be able to determine your type just from the descriptions given in our discussion. Ordinarily, a fairly elaborate questionnaire would be used to determine your preference on each of the dimensions. The agreement between types when determined by questionnaire and types when determined by asking people to simply identify themselves from general descriptions (as in our "which are you usually" questions earlier) is about 87 percent. In other words, there is a 13 percent or so chance that you are not yet able to accurately determine which of the sixteen personality types is yours.

Dimensions of Self that Should Be Accepted

✓ Our style preferences
    ✓ Introversion/Extraversion
    ✓ Sensing/Intuiting
    ✓ Thinking/Feeling
    ✓ Judging/Perceiving
✓ Others' style preferences
✓ Our communication avoidance (unless we are dissatisfied)

EMOTIONAL MATURITY

Regardless of the preferences and strengths of our particular personality type, each of us operates by balancing rational thoughts on the one hand, and emotions on the other hand. Ideally, emotion and rationality work in harmony. This balance is crucial in interpersonal interactions of virtually all kinds. But for most of us, there will be occasions when emotions take over and interfere with (or perhaps even wipe out) rational thought. Our ability to minimize the frequency and duration of these emotional takeovers is referred to as **emotional maturity** (or, in some circles, *emotional intelligence*).

Emotional maturity is crucial to interpersonal communication at the general, frame-of-mind level. For example, solving conflicts often requires compromise. But seeking compromise requires emotional maturity. The emotionally mature individual holds emotions in check during conflict, and goes easily into a compromise-seeking frame of mind. The emotionally immature individual, on the other hand, lets emotions override rationality and stays in an emotional and competitive, "I want to *win* this" mode. In Chapters 6 and 7 we will see several kinds of situations, in addition to conflict, in which the advisable frame of mind requires emotional maturity.

The concept of emotional maturity is a fairly new one in psychology and communication. Research to provide more information about its features, ways to identify it (in ourselves and others), and ways to achieve it will continue over the next decade. At present, we can at least identify a few of its features as being important goals of interpersonal interaction.[10]

CONTROL OF ANGER

For most people, anger is the emotion that is controlled least successfully and is the most common emotion to override rational thought processes. In communication, anger can interfere regardless of whether the object of the anger is our communication partner. That is, it can interfere in our communication with Sam, let's say, whether we are angry at Sam or at someone or something else.

No doubt, you know some people who "fly off the handle" at the slightest provocation, and others who "keep their cool" in even the most heated situations. Emotional maturity plays a role in both reducing the incidence of anger in the first place and dealing with it when it occurs. Emotionally mature individuals experience fewer instances of anger to begin with, partly because of their "don't sweat the small stuff" attitude. They operate with the basic premise that few things are worth becoming angry about. Similarly, emotionally mature individuals experience less anger because they have an "agree-to-disagree" attitude. Where the immature individual allows disagreements to escalate into anger-laden conflicts, the emotionally mature individual reasons, "We still don't agree, but we don't *have* to agree. We know we don't agree; now we know why; and that's fine."

Moreover, emotionally mature individuals are less likely to displace their anger. **Displacement** is the tendency to substitute a less formidable false obstacle for the true one. In the case of anger, displacement operates when we are unable to take out our anger on the person with whom we are angry (because of her or his superior status, for example) and, without recognizing the displacement, take out our anger on someone more convenient instead (because of his or her lower status or availability, for example).

The classic case is becoming angry with a spouse or a child when we are in fact angry with our boss. Variations include displacing anger with a boyfriend or girlfriend to anger with a roommate, displacing anger with a coach to anger with a friend, and so forth. In any case, communication with the person on whom the anger is displaced is unnecessarily ruined, at least temporarily. Emotionally mature individuals, since they are better able to prevent their anger from overriding rational thought, are less prone to displacement.

As for the role of emotional maturity in controlling anger when it does occur, the most effective approach requires the most maturity. Contrary to popular opinion, dealing with anger by simply taking time to cool off is often ineffective. So is the opposite: venting one's anger for the sake of catharsis. "Cooling off" time is often spent inventing new reasons to justify the anger or coming up with ways to retaliate. And venting one's anger can ruin relationships, temporarily if not permanently. The most effective means of dealing with anger is through *cognitive reframing*—examining the anger-inducing situation from alternative points of view. The idea is to see and understand alternative viewpoints, even if we do not agree with them. But this requires rational thought to override the anger, and that requires emotional maturity.

OPTIMISM

Another feature of emotional maturity is **optimism**—having a positive, "things will turn out well" view of the future. Its opposite, pessimism, is a negative view of the future. The emotionally mature and more optimistic person views failures and disappointments as resulting from things that can be changed, so that success or satisfaction will occur the next time around. Pessimistic individuals blame failures and disappointments on circumstances they consider difficult or impossible to change. This might be some supposed feature of themselves ("I got a bad grade on my paper because I'm just not good at writing essays") or of someone else ("I got a bad grade on my paper because the professor is biased against me").

In short, if we are emotionally mature, we handle failures and disappointments better, and this prevents the emotional frustration of failure from disrupting our rational interactions with others. Optimism allows us to motivate ourselves to persist in the face of failures and disappointments.

"OWNING" THE PROBLEM

A key feature of emotional maturity is the ability to recognize that our reactions to situations, especially our negative reactions, are not simply the result of the situation but also the result of our personal makeup. This kind of awareness is sometimes called **owning the problem.** For example, one may think, "I'm upset because my date keeps flirting with other men . . . or looking at other women . . . or not being on time . . . or not calling often enough . . . or forgetting my birthday . . . [and so forth]." But it is in some ways more accurate to own the problem by recognizing, "I'm upset because I happen to be the *type* of person who becomes upset when my date flirts with other men . . . looks at other women . . . is not on time . . . [and so forth]."

Owning the problem can be extremely valuable in interpersonal communication. When we recognize that our own makeup is part of the situation, and that not everyone would be equally upset by what is upsetting us, then we can reduce the defensiveness of the other person(s) involved by acknowledging this when we discuss the situation with them. As an example, I am reminded of an acquaintance who used an owning strategy for dealing with a coworker whose "crude" behaviors had bothered her. She waited until the next incident and then calmly explained to him that she realized that many people would not be offended by the behaviors, realized that she was a bit on the conservative side in such matters, realized that he had no way of knowing of her reaction, and just thought he might want to know that she was the type who was offended by these kinds of behaviors. She reports that he apologized, that he has never since repeated the behaviors in her presence, and that their working relationship and mutual respect have grown continually more positive. Owning the problem helped her to see the situation as more than a simple matter of an insensitive coworker. And because she presented the problem in a way that did not blame him completely, it was not necessary for him to become defensive.

Owning the problem can be similarly helpful in a wide variety of potential conflict situations—when you are bothered by the brother or sister who borrows your clothes, the roommate who messes up "your" kitchen, the friend who criticizes your new boyfriend, and on and on. But it requires emotional maturity to recognize that when we

---

TRY THIS ●

Think of the last few times you have become very upset because of something someone else has said or done. Now ask yourself whether *everybody* would have become so upset in the identical situation. The answer is almost bound to be that yes, some people would have become upset, but no, not everybody would have—not by a long shot. It follows logically that if not everyone becomes upset by the things that upset us, then one of the reasons we are upset is that *we happen to be the kind of person* who is upset by such things.

are upset, it is due as much (if not more) to our own psychological makeup as to any fault on the part of another.

CONTROL OF IMPULSES

A fourth feature of emotional maturity is the ability to control our impulses. Exercising patience and delaying (or even forgoing) gratification—as opposed to taking, doing, or insisting on everything we want when we want it—is something we are supposed to learn as children, of course. Some adults, however, remain emotionally immature and do or say whatever they want to do or say, immediately and impulsively. Emotional maturity includes recognizing impulses and taking time to reflect upon the wise course of action. In communication, this applies especially to controlling the impulse to speak our thoughts and feelings without reflection. The emotionally mature individual *considers* what he or she is about to say, then approves it and says it, or edits and revises it, or perhaps even censors it entirely—in other words, thinks before he or she speaks.

Most of Us Can Use Improvement In
- ✓ Self-awareness
- ✓ Self-acceptance
- ✓ Emotional maturity
  - ✓ Controlling anger
  - ✓ Optimism
  - ✓ Learning to "own the problem"
  - ✓ Controlling impulses

COMMUNICATION ANXIETY

Just as we may sometimes be overly eager to say what is on our mind, we also may be overly reluctant to express ourselves. Reluctance to communicate is referred to as **communication anxiety** or **communication apprehension**. Typically, it occurs when we are concerned that there may be negative consequences to *us* if we say what we want to say. Communication anxiety can be a positive force in helping us to avoid communication blunders. But if we yield to communication anxiety too often, we will miss opportunities to achieve our goals. This anxiety can operate at both a situation-by-situation level and a more general, across-the-board level.

SITUATIONAL COMMUNICATION ANXIETY

Many of us experience communication anxiety in certain situations, such as admitting to a touchy roommate that we forgot to mail the letters he or she asked us to mail, telling a spouse about a shopping spree, alerting a boss to a major mistake we have made, and so forth. In fact, some of us tend to experience communication anxiety fairly consistently in certain recurring situations—asking someone for a date, being called on in class, being interviewed for a job, and so forth.

Situational communication anxiety (anxiety tied to the situation) occurs because of certain features of the situation, of course.[11] For example, we are especially likely to experience communication anxiety in *novel* situations—situations we are not used to. If you have never before been called as a witness in a court case, for example, it would not be unusual for you to experience at least some anxiety when you are called.

Anxiety is also tied to situations that seem to involve *scrutiny* and *evaluation*. Most of us don't like the feeling of being put under a microscope by others, and most of us become anxious at the idea of being evaluated by others. Being called on to work a physics problem on the blackboard and then explain it to the class would induce at least some anxiety in most of us, for example.

Anxiety is also common in situations that allow for only *complete success or failure*. Perhaps this is why asking someone for a date is anxiety-inducing for some people. It may also explain the anxiety sometimes experienced during those door-to-door sales you may have had to do to raise money for school organizations. There is a clear success/failure indicator in these and similar situations, and the outcome is uncertain.

Situations of excessive *formality* are often anxiety-inducing as well, partly because we have a sense that we are supposed to play by rules of which we are not fully aware. This is one reason that job interviews are anxiety-inducing, for example (not to mention the scrutiny and success/failure dimensions). There is a sense that the interview is supposed to proceed according to the interviewer's unstated rules rather than according to the familiar rules of ordinary conversation.

A sense of *incompetence* in a given situation will also induce anxiety in some individuals. For example, some people will experience communication anxiety if a conversation about movies turns to the topic of foreign films and they know nothing about foreign films, or a conversation about sports turns to cricket and they know nothing about cricket.

Thus, because of certain features of specific situations, most of us will experience at least a bit of communication anxiety from time to time. Whether this is a good thing or a bad thing depends upon how the anxiety affects the communication event. Suppose, for example, that Al has so much anxiety about a job interview that he decides not to go; Beth has considerable anxiety, handles it badly, and blows the interview; Chris has just as much anxiety but handles it well and lands the job; Dale has almost no anxiety but respects the situation and lands the job; and Earl, with no anxiety whatsoever, is so oblivious to the demands of the situation that he blows the interview. Assuming that all were equally qualified, anxiety had costs for Al and Beth but not for Chris. And the absence of anxiety had costs for Earl but not for Dale.

In short, situational communication anxiety is common. It is not necessarily a bad thing, and in fact may be a good thing, as long as it does not severely disrupt our communication efforts. For those who consider their situational anxiety to be so frequent or so severe that they want to do something about it, the most direct solution is usually to identify the situational *feature* responsible for the anxiety, and then deal with the feature. For novel situations, gain experience so that the situation is no longer novel; for formal situations, become familiar with the new rules; for success/failure situations, come to accept and learn from an occasional failure; for incompetence situations, either develop competence or learn to deemphasize the ego; and for scrutiny and evaluation situations, learn how the sense of scrutiny and evaluation is often exaggerated.[12] For an expanded case of acting on anxiety in supposed scrutiny and evaluation situations, you may wish to consult Appendix D on anxiety in public speaking.

GENERAL COMMUNICATION APPREHENSION

Some people seem to have across-the-board apprehension about communication.[13] They are cautious in almost all communication situations. In contrast, some people seem to have virtually no apprehension in any communication situation. Those with much too much **general communication apprehension** are often ineffective because their extreme apprehension leads them to avoid communication in situations where their input would be beneficial to themselves or others. Those with much too little general apprehension are often ineffective because their lack of self-censorship makes them appear boorish and low in credibility.

To put it another way, there are relative advantages to both high and low communication apprehension. With too little communication apprehension, we run the risk of speaking before we think, giving uninformed opinions, talking when we don't really know what we're talking about, coming across as too loud or boisterous or overbearing, and being too aggressive. With too much communication apprehension, we run the risk of being insufficiently assertive, thus missing opportunities and possibly being taken advantage of, and risk coming off as too quiet or shy.

How much communication apprehension is too much? Perhaps the best answer lies in your own evaluation of whether your level of avoidance (or nonavoidance) is satisfactory. Consider an informal questionnaire, for example, where the issue is, "How often, in situations where you *don't* say what you could say, or want to say, do you have the following reactions afterward?"

Answer with "very often," "sometimes," or "rarely."

1. Afterward, I wish I'd said what I was going to say, and I regret that I didn't.
2. Afterward, I think of the perfect thing I could have said, and I wish I'd thought of it at the time.
3. Afterward, I'm sort of glad I didn't say what I was going to say.
4. I don't have these "afterward" reflections about not speaking up.

Now, how often, in situations where you *do* say something, do you have these reactions afterward?

5. Afterward, I'm glad I said what I said.
6. Afterward, I'm sorry I said what I said.
7. Afterward, other people think I shouldn't have said what I said.
8. I don't have these "afterward" reflections about things I've said.

These questions put the focus on whether you are *satisfied* with your communication avoidance, or lack of it. If, for example, you are the type who often avoids communication, but you answered "very often" for 3 and "rarely" or "sometimes" for 1, then there should be no reason for you to view communication avoidance as a problem. Answering "very often" to 1, however, may indicate that the avoidance exceeds your own preferred threshold.

If, on the other hand, you are the type who rarely avoids communication, and you answered "very often" to 6 or 7, then your communication probably needs at least more self-censoring and editing, if not also a bit more apprehension and avoidance. And if you answered "very often" on 8 but not 7, you may wish to check with a few acquaintances to see if they agree with your perceptions on 7. (Answers of "very often" on 2, 3, 4, 5, and 8 are not particularly problematic, nor are answers of "sometimes" or "rarely" on 1, 6, and 7.)

Very few of us need to change our behavior with respect to our communication apprehension. The problems arise, generally, only at the two very extreme ends of the avoidance continuum. Much more research attention has been given to the high-apprehension end of the continuum. If you happen to believe that your general communication apprehension is so excessive that you want to change it, much has been written elsewhere that may help.[14]

Researchers have been slower to recognize extreme low avoidance as a problem. But those concerned about excessively low communication avoidance can perhaps get at least some help from the many cautionary notes throughout this book concerning ways to be careful in both interpersonal and public communication.

IN SUMMARY   It is worth noting in closing that communication apprehension and avoidance, as a topic, provides a nice example of how some of the various issues of this chapter can be linked together. On the one hand, communication apprehension has been studied using the deviation-from-norms perspective (we are all basically alike). On the other hand, an examination of the profiles for the Myers-Briggs types (we are all basically different) will show that certain types seem "naturally" inclined toward one side or the other of the communication-avoidance continuum. This implies that various levels of communication avoidance are equally natural, with differences corresponding to normal personality types rather than to unnatural deviations. Further research is likely to show that this is the case not only for communication avoidance or nonavoidance, but for other psychological states and traits relevant to communication as well.

To discover that certain traits are natural for our given personality type, however, does not mean that we need not view the traits as problematic. On the contrary, it suggests that each of us has inclinations that represent communication strengths, and each of us also has inclinations that represent communication weaknesses. These strengths and weaknesses may apply to our communication encounters generally, or may apply especially to communication with individuals of particular types. Self-awareness is crucial in recognizing these inclinations. And our emotional maturity is crucial both in preventing us from taking unfair advantage of others through our communicative strengths and in helping us get past natural but sometimes counterproductive tendencies toward certain communication weaknesses.

TERMS TO KNOW

self-evaluation	intuiting (mode)
self-concept	thinking (type)
self-esteem	feeling (type)
self-acceptance	judging (mode)
façades	perceiving (mode)
self-awareness	emotional maturity
implicit personality theory	displacement
projection	optimism
attribution theory	owning the problem
altruistic mode	communication anxiety
cynical mode	communication apprehension
introversion	situational communication anxiety
extraversion	general communication apprehension
sensing (mode)	

NOTES

1. For example, S. Freud, *Introductory Lectures to Psychoanalysis* (New York: World Publishing Co., 1920).

2. M. T. Motley and N. L. Smith, "Effects of Temperament upon Hiring Decisions: A Preliminary Examination of Global Personality Traits and Communicator Compatibility," *Communication Reports* 2 (1989): 22–29.

3. D. M. Wegner and R. R. Vallacher, *Implicit Psychology: An Introduction to Social Cognition* (New York: Oxford University Press, 1977).

4. G. A. Kelly, *The Psychology of Personal Constructs* (New York: Norton, 1955).

5. C. Jung, *Psychological Types* (New York: Harcourt Brace, 1923).

6. I. Myers and P. B. Myers, *Gifts Differing* (Palo Alto, Calif.: Consulting Psychologists Press, 1980).

7. The preference descriptions are based on I. B. Myers, *Introduction to Type* (Gainesville, Fla.: Center for Applications of Psychological Type, 1976); I. Myers, *Manual: The Myers-Briggs Type Indicator* (Palo Alto, Calif.: Consulting Psychologists Press, 1962); and D. Keirsey and M. Bates, *Please Understand Me* (Del Mar, Calif.: Prometheus Nemesis, 1984).

8. Keirsey and Bates, *Please Understand Me.*

9. Myers and Myers, *Gifts Differing.*

10. Based mostly on D. Goleman, *Emotional Intelligence* (New York: Bantam, 1995).

11. J. A. Daly and J. C. McCroskey, *Avoiding Communication: Shyness, Reticence, and Communication Apprehension* (Beverly Hills, Calif.: Sage Publications, 1984).

12. M. T. Motley, *Overcoming Your Fear of Public Speaking: A Proven Method* (Boston: Houghton Mifflin, 1997).

13. For example, see V. P. Richmond and J. C. McCroskey, *Communication: Apprehension, Avoidance, and Effectiveness* (Scottsdale, Ariz.: Gorsach Scarisbrick, 1985).

14. For example, P. G. Zimbardo, *Shyness: What It Is, What to Do About It* (Reading, Mass.: Addison-Wesley, 1977).

RELATIONSHIPS

THIS CHAPTER will help you

- Understand the role of communication in friendships

- Repair problems within friendships

- Understand the development of emotionally intimate relationships

- Avoid common communication problems within intimate relationships

EVERY PERSONAL RELATIONSHIP [is like] a pair of
INTERSECTING CIRCLES...
PERFECTION is reached when the area of the two
OUTER CRESCENTS, added together,
is exactly equal to that of the LEAF-SHAPED
PIECE IN THE MIDDLE.

—J. Struther

Judging by TV talk shows, best-selling self-help books, and popular magazine articles, people are especially concerned these days about their relationships. It probably is not coincidental that this increased attention to relationships comes during a period in our culture in which divorce rates, single-parent families, domestic violence, and other signs of the delicate nature of relationships seem to have reached an all-time high. Along with the knowledge that our relationships are fragile comes an increasing recognition that they are terribly important to us.

It should not be surprising that advice about relationships often focuses on communication. After all, it is through communication that we form relationships, maintain them, repair problems in them, and destroy them. It would be an exaggeration to say that *everything* that goes well or goes badly within a relationship does so because of communication, but communication is certainly one of the most important factors in determining the nature of relationships and their fate.

This chapter provides information that you should find useful in maintaining your own present and future relationships. We describe common communication problems and difficulties in relationships, and outline some general guidelines for avoiding difficulties. In some cases, we can offer specific prescriptive do's and don'ts for communication within relationships. In other cases, we discuss communication norms that will allow you to perform "reality checks" within your own relationships.

Relationship is a vague term, of course. For example, do you have a relationship with the grocery-store checker whose line you've been through a dozen or so times? The last time you rode with a talkative cab driver, was that a relationship? If so, does that relationship still exist? Some would answer "yes" and some "no" to questions such as these. Theoretically, every communication episode and encounter may be viewed as a relationship, if only a temporary one. Whenever we are communicating, we are "relating," so all communication can be said to form relationships. For the purposes of this chapter, however, we are going to focus on more clear-cut relationships of the type that most people report to be especially important to them. We will take a close look at relationships with *friends* and at relationships with *intimates* ("significant others").

FRIENDS

While many of us do not consider communication with our close friends to be a problem, it is worthwhile to take a brief look at communication within friendships. We can see that communication plays a major role in distinguishing between true friendships and more casual acquaintances, in causing most friendship breakups, and in repairing and restoring threatened or damaged friendships.

INDICATORS OF FRIENDSHIP

Occasional surprises and disappointments notwithstanding, we know who our "real friends" are. But *how* do we know? What is it about our relationships with especially good friends that differs from our relationships with people whom we consider more casual friends or acquaintances? Research on these questions suggests that in virtually every case, the difference shows itself in communication.[1]

1. Friends *communicate easily.* That is, friends enjoy each other's company, find each other easy to talk with, communicate on a greater range of topics, and communi-

It can be enlightening to review these friendship indicators with specific acquaintances in mind. In the case of close friends, a review of the indicators usually will provide reassurance of the friendship. For other relationships, the list can point out what is missing that prevents a closer friendship.

cate in more depth than do more casual acquaintances. Friends know each other's preferences, interests, tastes, values, and so forth, because they enjoy sharing such information. They also share their feelings about events that affect them—positively or negatively.

Of course, these features might also fit conversations you have had on a bus or plane with a total stranger. With good friends, however, *all* of the **friendship indicators** listed here tend to be present.

2. Friends *have spent significant time together.* This is not so much a matter of how long people have known each other as it is a matter of having shared significant periods of "quality time" or "critical time." For females, it is important that *communication* with friends be ongoing, whereas for males, this is less critical. When females are asked to name their best friend, for example, they usually name another female with whom they currently communicate frequently. In some cases, this best friend is a fairly recent acquaintance. When males are asked to name their best friend, they usually name their wife first (if married), and then name another male with whom they have shared special times (in military service, as college roommates, on athletic teams, etc.)—often in the distant past. In many cases, males will not actually have spoken or communicated with their best friend for months or even years!

3. Friends *confide* in each other. Trust and disclosure are cyclical in friendships and other close relationships. As trust develops, we disclose things about ourselves that it would seem too risky to disclose otherwise. This amplifies our partner's trust, and she or he in turn confides in us. This increases our trust, and so on. Casual acquaintances talk about many things, but with discretion and self-censorship, whereas special friends discuss practically everything. This is especially true for female-female and female-male friendships.

4. Friends are *conflict-tolerant.* Although friends have much in common, their increased communication, increased time together, and increased disclosure often reveal differences of opinion. Yet, while differences in tastes, values, politics, expectations, and so forth ordinarily fuel conflicts, friendships seem to be relatively conflict-free. Two principles operate to account for this. First, for issues on which we have not yet formed an opinion, we are more likely to simply agree with a friend's position—giving the issue less thought, doubt, or mental challenge—than we would if the identical position were offered by someone else. And second, when we do in fact disagree with a friend, we are more likely to simply write it off or to discuss it in a cooperative "agree-to-disagree" mode than when we disagree with others. In short, conflicts are common among friends, but they don't seem like conflicts, because with friends we are more tolerant on conflict issues.

5. Friends *stand up for each other* to outsiders. In general, our friends are highly regarded by others with whom we associate. But on the rare occasions when we hear someone criticize one of our good friends, we usually come to our friend's defense. We may justify a criticized behavior, dispute a criticized trait, point out positive traits, and so forth.

6. Friends *help each other* when needed. We offer both tangible assistance and emotional support to our friends when they need it. Perhaps more importantly, we do

it gladly. Behaviors that might otherwise seem to be sacrifices do not feel like sacrifices when we do them for friends in need.

This list of friendship indicators demonstrates a few ways in which communication is different between close friends than between others.

HOW FRIENDSHIPS ARE DAMAGED OR DESTROYED

Just as communication is central to most of the behaviors that indicate friendship, it also is central to the most common causes of friendship deterioration. Indeed, some of the causes of broken friendships are simply the converse of friendship indicators.[2]

We noted above that all the listed indicators tend to be present in friendships. However, it takes only one of the following to seriously damage a good friendship.

1. Friendships may be damaged when *confidences are broken*. Most of the risky disclosures we make to trusted friends are made confidentially. Sometimes a friend will leak confidential information knowingly. Other times, he or she will do so innocently, as when one leaks information without realizing that it was supposed to be confidential. In either case, the friendship is likely to be seriously damaged.

2. Friendships may be damaged when one partner *expresses or endorses public criticism* of the other. As we have seen, close friends usually defend each other against criticism by outsiders. Thus, when we implicitly endorse such criticism by not defending our friend, or explicitly endorse it by agreeing with the criticism, or instigate it by offering the criticism ourselves, the friendship is threatened. Friends who hear of such criticism (and they always do, it seems) are likely to question the friendship (since one of the indicators has been contradicted) and, of course, are likely to feel hurt and/or angry as well.

3. Friendships may be damaged by excessive *nonconstructive personal criticism*. On the one hand, we can be more honest with a good friend than with most others when it comes to giving criticism. In solid male-male friendships, a comment like, "You're getting quite a belly there, pal," would not be unheard of. And in solid female-female friendships, a question such as, "How do you like my new dress?" is more likely to elicit a response such as, "It really doesn't do anything for you," than in more casual acquaintanceships. This kind of honesty is one of the benefits of friendship. But on the other hand, many friendships have been damaged when one partner has viewed the other's criticism as excessive or as motivated by a desire to nag rather than to be constructive.

4. Friendships may be damaged when one partner *takes advantage* of the other. True friends gladly make sacrifices for each other, but friends are not expected to be slaves to unnecessary or unreasonable demands. It is natural to bend over backwards to help our friends, but an underlying assumption is that the help is truly needed. When the requested sacrifices are felt to be excessive, the friendship may be threatened.

5. Friends *should not be asked to violate personal moral principles*. It makes sense that friends will enjoy their mutual conflict tolerance. Discussing opposing viewpoints in a noncompetitive, agree-to-disagree mode is one of the more stimulating and enlightening forms of communication. The expectation of conflict tolerance can go too far, however, when one partner expects or insists that the other sacrifice

his or her personal values. In one study, for example, college students reported the following reasons (among others) for terminating friendships: having been asked or expected to cheat on an exam or paper, lie to a boyfriend or girlfriend, lie to a roommate, betray another friend, betray a parent, or participate in or endorse an illegal or improper activity to which they were opposed. It is not unusual for friends to be "partners in crime" in violating certain social or moral taboos, but when one partner feels required to do so unwillingly, it jeopardizes the friendship.[3]

6. Friends *should not restrict each other's freedom.* Although not so clearly communication-related, an especially common reason for friendships to deteriorate among college-age individuals is excessive demands by one friend upon the other's time, freedom, and individuality. In the most common variation, one friend feels that the other is spending too much time with a new boyfriend or girlfriend, a job, schoolwork, or a hobby. While one indicator of friendship is spending lots of time together, problems may arise if one friend becomes overly dependent on having this time. And it is especially troublesome when one friend *demands* that the other take time away from important activities, obligations, and engagements.

Friendship Indicators and Friendship Problems Are Linked. Friendship Is Indicated by (A); Threatened by (B)

✓ (A) Confiding; (B) breaking a confidence
✓ (A) Standing up for each other in public; (B) endorsing criticism of the partner
✓ (A) Being conflict-tolerant; (B) giving excessive criticism
✓ (A) Helping each other; (B) taking advantage of the other
✓ (A) Spending time together; (B) restricting the other's freedom
✓ (A) Going along with the partner's views; (B) prostituting one's own values

REPAIRING DAMAGED FRIENDSHIPS—UNREQUITED ROMANTIC ATTRACTION AS AN EXTENDED EXAMPLE

The behaviors we have just listed may destroy friendships entirely and permanently. Sometimes when friendships are damaged, however, the damage can be repaired. Although the steps involved in the repair will vary according to the situation, we are going to examine one particular friendship-repair situation in detail. We have chosen it partly because it is increasingly common, and partly because research has provided an elaborate description of communication behaviors that are critical to repairing the friendship.[4]

The situation to which we refer is the male-female friendship in which one partner begins to develop romantic feelings for the other. This creates a dilemma. If the romantic feelings are not disclosed, then the friendship is robbed of its openness. Moreover, of course, the partner's feelings and responses remain unknown. If the romantic feelings are disclosed and are mutual, then the opportunity for a romantic relationship presents itself. But if the romantic feelings are disclosed and are *not* mutual, then the friendship may be damaged. About 94 percent of us will find ourselves in this situation at least once.

As one student wrote when trying to decide whether and how to tell a long-time friend of his romantic feelings for her,

> *I don't know how she feels about me, but I know how I feel toward her. We flirt a lot, but I don't know if she's being friendly or giving me a hint . . . If I cross the line of friendship, I might lose a friend. The truth is, if she wants to be friends, that's fine. But I keep asking myself, "What if she feels the same way?" How can I tell her how I feel and not lose the comfortable relationship we have as friends if she doesn't feel it too?[5]*

The fact is that when romantic inclinations are disclosed but not reciprocated within solid friendships, the friendship is indeed disrupted. At the least, both individuals will feel awkward. Many friendships do not survive the disruption, of course. But some do. Research has looked into what factors determine whether the friendship will last or dissolve. The findings provide advice for repairing and maintaining our friendships in unrequited romantic disclosure situations. And some of the advice almost certainly would apply to other situations in which a friendship is damaged or threatened for virtually *any* reason.

Do's and Don'ts for the Romantically Inclined Partner.

Suppose you are the one with the *romantic* feelings, you disclose them, and your partner's response is some variation of, "I care for you, but as a friend, not as a romantic partner." Most likely, you will feel embarrassed and perhaps hurt, and your partner will feel awkward. But suppose that you want to restore and maintain the friendship.

In these situations, the following is advised[6]:

1. *Do discuss the situation* with your partner, assuring him or her that you are able to accept his or her absence of romantic inclinations. This helps to offset your partner's guilt over having hurt you via the rejection. It also offsets your partner's assumption that your disappointment or embarrassment may be overwhelming.

2. *Do reaffirm the friendship* by telling your partner that the friendship is important and takes priority—priority over the hopes that had accompanied the disclosure, and priority over the discomfort of the rejection.

3. *Do drop the matter* with respect to efforts to pursue romance and/or hopes that the partner will eventually "come around" to reciprocate the romantic feelings. Granted, you cannot simply flip an emotional switch to instantly extinguish your romantic feelings. But it is crucial that your partner not feel pressured to act or feel differently than the way he or she did before the disclosure.

4. *Do cut back on flirtations* and sexual innuendo. Resume the friendship at a reduced level of overt attraction, leaving it to the partner to restore the earlier levels if he or she wishes. Behaviors that did not seem overly suggestive to the partner before your disclosure are likely to feel too suggestive or pressuring for a while afterward.

5. *Don't complain* about your partner's lack of romantic feelings, probe for the reasons (e.g., "What's wrong with me?" "Why don't you love me too?" etc.), push for a

future romantic interest ("Do you think you might fall for me someday?" etc.), or otherwise pressure your partner. If you can't be sincere in accepting the friendship the way it is, then it probably is doomed.

6. *Don't change your earlier patterns of contact and activities.* If you used to meet after class each Friday for coffee, or go out with the gang on Saturday nights, or phone once a week, keep doing so. Reduced contact can be interpreted in too many negative ways (e.g., that you are too embarrassed, can't handle the situation, are angry, no longer want the friendship, etc.).

7. *Do accept your partner's subsequent romantic interest in others* and *do disclose your own romantic interests as they develop.* Openness about the targets of one's romantic interest is a sign of innocent, platonic friendship. We tend to hide this kind of information only from those with whom we imagine romantic or otherwise intimate potential. As one student put it when discussing her repaired friendship after an unrequited romantic disclosure, "I knew we were friends again when he asked if he could double-date with me and my new boyfriend."

Do's and Don'ts for the Platonically Inclined Partner. Now, suppose that you are the one with *platonic* feelings. Your friend discloses his or her romantic feelings for you, you don't feel the same way, but you would hate to see rejection and awkwardness destroy the friendship.

Many of the do's and don'ts are the same as for the romantically inclined partner:

1. *Do discuss the situation,* assuring the partner that it is acceptable for him or her to have had and disclosed the romantic feelings.

2. *Do reaffirm the friendship,* its importance, and its priority.

3. *Do maintain earlier patterns of contact and activities.*

4. *Do cut back on flirtations* and sexual innuendo. It is likely that the romantically inclined partner will have felt "led on" by flirtatious behaviors before his or her disclosure. After the rejection, these behaviors will fuel futile hopes of your "coming around" to similar intimate feelings. Repaired friendships of this sort may *eventually* resume their earlier levels of flirtation, innuendo, and signs of innocent attraction, but it is advisable for this to be a slow process.

5. *Do show understanding* (as opposed to complete shock or surprise) at the romantic disclosure. It reduces the partner's tendency to feel foolish about the disclosure when you acknowledge ways in which you may have led him or her to believe the feelings were mutual.

6. *Don't hint that romantic feelings may develop in the future.* It may seem kind to reject your partner with a "not now, but maybe later" message, but the effect of this message is only to maintain the partner's romantic mode and further disrupt the friendship.

7. *Don't give your attraction for someone else as an explanation* for the unreciprocated feelings. To reject with, "because I'm falling for [or have recently fallen for] someone else" will, more often than not, end the friendship entirely. The partner will wonder why this was not disclosed earlier, and is likely to question the sincerity of the friendship. Revealing attraction to others is helpful in establishing a friendship mode, but this should wait until the friendship is repaired.

Generalizability to Other Friendship-Repair Situations.
We have provided this extended example of friendship repair both because unrequited romantic attraction is a common threat to friendships and because it is a situation for
which an extensive list of communication do's and don'ts is
available. The next time we are agonizing about whether to
make such a disclosure, we may at least take comfort in
knowing that there are steps we can take to maintain the
friendship, if we wish, in case the romantic feelings are not
mutual. The same is true, the next time we are on the receiving end of such a disclosure.

But another reason we provided these do's and don'ts is
that some of them may generalize to other friendship-
repair situations. For example, in almost any friendship-
repair situation, it probably would be advisable to discuss
the situation, to reaffirm the friendship, and to maintain
or reestablish earlier contact patterns—and for very much
the same reasons as in unrequited-romance situations.
Similarly, in many friendship-repair situations, it would
seem advisable to drop the matter that originally threatened
the friendship (once it has been discussed), to show understanding of the friend's position, to avoid complaining
about the situation, and to avoid the impression that we are
pressuring the friend to "come around" to our position.

> ● **TRY THIS**
>
> As an exercise, take a few moments to see what we mean
> about applying this list of do's and don'ts to other friend-
> ship-repair situations. Think of a specific situation in which a
> good friendship has been damaged (one of yours or an
> acquaintance's), review the lists of do's and don'ts for repair
> in unrequited-romance situations, and extrapolate parallels
> for your scenario. If you know whether the parallel do's and
> don'ts were followed, reflect on how that affected the re-
> pair. If you don't know, then speculate. It is interesting also
> to do this for the unrequited-romance situation. If you have
> experienced disclosures of unrequited romance within a
> solid friendship (as either the romantically or the platonically
> inclined partner), reflect on whether the friendship lasted or
> dissolved, and then review the do's and don'ts above to see
> which ones, in your opinion, affected the fate of the friend-
> ship by their presence or absence.

INTIMATE RELATIONSHIPS— PHASE I

While friendships are extremely important to us, people tend to list their *emotionally intimate* relationships—those with a "soul mate," "significant other,"
boyfriend/girlfriend, or spouse—as their most important relationships. And
while our culture promotes the notion that each of us eventually will find a
permanent intimate relationship, it is obvious that these are outnumbered by temporary ones. We needn't view these as failed relationships since what we learn from them
can be applied to our subsequent relationships. And, of course, usually they are very satisfying while they last.

We will discuss intimate relationships by examining what is typical in four sequential relationship *phases*.[7] In actual relationships, the boundaries between the end of one
phase and the beginning of the next can be fuzzy. The phases themselves are usually
easy to identify, however.

Phase I involves the initial meeting of the individuals and their finding out about
each other. Behaviorally, it is little different than any other getting-acquainted situation. But psychologically and emotionally, there usually is a definite attraction, and a
sense that *maybe* this person would be worth getting to know beyond mere acquaintance. (The amount of time each of the relational phases takes varies from case to case.
For example, what we have described for **Relationship Phase I** could take place within
a thirty-minute conversation, or could be spread across months of after-class conversations, or could take even longer.)

During Phase I, we are more curious about this other person—what is he or she *really* like?—than we are with more casual new acquaintances. Yet our disclosures in this

phase are minimal. We don't reveal too much that is negative about ourselves, lest we turn off the potential partner; and we don't reveal too much that is positive, lest we appear arrogant or pompous. Often, therefore, we will try to find out more about our new acquaintance by asking mutual acquaintances.

INITIATING AND EXPERIMENTING

Some researchers prefer to think of Phase I as consisting of two steps: **initiating**, which is simply the initial exchange ("Hi. That was a tough exam, wasn't it?" "Wanna dance?" "So, how do you know Mary?"), and **experimenting**, which is finding out about each other and feeling out the possibility of continued or future interaction ("Do you like jazz?" "Do you ski?" "How did you become interested in meteorology?").

Initiating is relatively easy when someone else introduces the other person to us, and it is relatively easy when the felt attraction takes place *after* the initiation. But when we sense an attraction to someone *before* having met the person, initiating contact is difficult for some people. It is, in fact, one of the dozen or so most troubling interpersonal communication problems identified by college students.[8] As one student puts it,

> *I find it incredibly difficult to introduce myself to women I find attractive unless we are introduced by some third party, or she introduces herself. I do not have a problem talking after we meet. [But I can't initiate a meeting.] What are some ways that I can introduce myself to women I find attractive?*

Research on initiating statements, or "opening lines," provides advice for those who have trouble initiating contact.[9] Opening lines tend to take one of three forms. One form, called the **cute-flippant** approach, involves a feeble attempt at humor, along with a clear suggestion of continued interaction or contact, usually with sexual overtones. Examples include: "It's cold. Let's make some body heat." "Do you fool around?" "I've got an offer you can't refuse." And so forth. (If your reaction to these examples was "Yuck," you're not alone! "Cheesy" is how most of my students describe the cute-flippant lines.) A second form of opening line is called the **direct** approach. These messages involve a clear invitation to initiate contact or continue interaction, but without an attempt at humor and without overt sexual overtones. Examples include: "Hi! You look like somebody I'd like to get to know." "It's hot in here. Would you like to go outside for a while?" "Since we're both eating alone, would you like to join me?" A third form is called the **innocuous** approach. These initiating lines do no more than invite conversation. They are the same sort of friendly conversation-starter that we might use even if we were *not* attracted to the receiver. For example, at a bar: "What do you think of the band?" At a grocery store: "Aren't these tabloid headlines incredible?" At a laundromat: "Do you know how long these machines take?" At the beach: "What radio station is that?" And so forth.

Studies indicate that as receivers of initiating statements, females most prefer to hear innocuous messages, and least prefer cute-flippant lines. Males respond conversationally to innocuous lines, but have a preference for the clear signs of interest found in the direct approach.[10]

It is ironic, then, that cute-flippant lines are fairly common (especially among males, but increasingly among females). One explanation is that in

THE FAR SIDE   By GARY LARSON

case of rejection, cute-flippant lines provide deniability. One can claim, "Well, obviously I wasn't really *serious* about meeting that person." Another explanation is that in targeting someone with whom one is interested in initiating contact, some people tend to assume a one-shot, all-or-nothing strategy. There seems to be a sense of needing to grab the target individual's total attention and interest right from the opening line, as if he or she is supposed to make a yes/no decision about us on the spot.

With this attitude, it is no wonder that some people feel very anxious about initiating contact with someone in whom they may be interested. (You may recall from Chapter 5 that success/failure situations increase anxiety.) The fact of the matter, however, is that intimate relationships usually grow from a very *ordinary* initiation, followed by increasingly interested experimentation and exploration. Although some people have a hard time imagining that initiation with an intriguing potential partner should take place in the same way that we initiate casual conversation with anyone else, this happens to be the case. In simple terms, since Phase I includes *experimentation,* and since experimentation requires conversation, *initiation* can take place with a single, low-key, innocuous utterance.

INTIMATE RELATIONSHIPS— PHASE II

Phase II of emotionally intimate relationships begins when the pair recognizes that some sort of nonordinary relationship is beginning—maybe a special friendship, maybe a physical relationship, and/or maybe a romance. As a case in point, I (Motley) recently heard a friend say of himself and a fairly new acquaintance, "We have a relationship of a yet-to-be-determined nature." This sounds like early Phase II.

If a relationship moves into later stages, Phase II *ends* at roughly the point at which the pair makes a commitment to maintain a bond as a couple. By this point, their love for each other has been expressed, they consider themselves a committed couple ("significant others," long-term girlfriend/boyfriend, eventual marital partners, etc.), and they present themselves to friends and others as a couple. As you would imagine, a lot goes on in **Relationship Phase II.**

PHYSICAL INTIMACY: THRESHOLDS AND COMMITMENT

While there are exceptions, it is usually during Phase II that couples initiate physical intimacy. How far and how quickly the intimacy escalates varies from couple to couple, of course. There are two communication-related problems associated with initial physical intimacy that are both common enough and sufficiently researched to warrant discussion.

One problem has to do with what *meaning* is attached to the physical intimacy. Does sexual activity mean that you are making a commitment (of any kind) to your partner? Does it mean that he or she is making a commitment (of any kind) to you? Does it mean that the relationship is headed for emotional intimacy rather than simple physical intimacy? Does it mean that at least for now, you are "more than friends?" Does it mean that the relationship is bound to endure for at least a short while, and probably much longer? And will your partner answer these questions the same way as you do? Quite possibly not.

There is a reasonable chance that any two partners may have different interpretations of what their physical intimacy means with respect to their relationship. It is not uncommon for people to report being hurt by having gone further than usual with a particular partner, assuming that the behavior signaled emotional commitment, only to discover that for the partner it was merely physical. The problem, in simple terms, is that there is no way to know for certain what our sexual behavior signals to our partner, nor to know what our partner's behavior should signal to us. Our subsequent discussion of Phase II will provide some indicators of emotional intimacy that are much more reliable than sex, per se.

A related situation that is worth mentioning is that during early stages of physical intimacy, one partner's threshold for how far to go is often lower than the other's. This can become especially troublesome when the one with the lower threshold feels pressured to "put out" more than he or she wishes at that point in the relationship.

There are many variations on the theme, but the most common occurs when, during physical intimacy, a woman indicates that she wants to go no further, yet the male partner tries to take it further anyway. Most women have had this experience more than once by age twenty-three or so. Women consider it to be unpleasant, often extremely so, whether it happens at relatively early stages of petting or at more advanced levels of physical intimacy. Often, therefore, the male's attempt to escalate intimacy beyond the partner's threshold will damage the relationship and preclude its advancement. (And even if advancement of the relationship is not a concern, the situation is socially undesirable.)

If she indicates that she wants to go no further, then why does he try to take it further anyway? Traditionally, the answer has been that he knows she wants to stop, but he ignores her wishes because—due to hormones and/or social conditioning—that's just the way men are. Not only does this answer—"boys will be boys," in effect—provide no solution to the problem, but it also is not completely accurate, according to recent research. It appears that often (not always, but often) males in fact do not realize that they are being asked to go no further.[11]

Women's **sexual resistance messages**—what is said to indicate that one wishes to go no further—vary. Some of these are **direct resistance messages**—for example, "Please don't do that," "Let's stop," "Let's not do this," and "I don't want to do this." With these direct messages, she usually means "stop." And with these direct messages, he usually *understands* that she means "stop."

But women's resistance messages, especially with relatively new partners, are more often *indirect* statements. Typical examples include "I'm not sure we're ready for this," "I'm confused about this," "I'm seeing someone else," "It's getting late," "I'm having my period," "I can't do this unless you're committed to me," "I don't have protection," "I'm saving that [activity] for marriage," "That's against my religion [or principles]," and others. When a woman says any of these things during physical intimacy, she *almost always means "stop."* When males hear these statements, however, they often *think* it means to *proceed!*[12]

For example, when she says, "I'm seeing someone else" (and, remember, to her this means "stop"), he is likely to think she means, "It's OK to do this as long as the other guy doesn't find out." When she says, "It's getting late" (meaning "Let's stop"), he is likely to think she means, "Let's step up the pace, we're running short of time." And so on for other **indirect resistance messages**. Research has shown that the most common male interpretation of virtually every *indirect* resistance message is something *other than* "stop." See Figure 6.1, for examples.

When, during physical intimacy at any stage, she says . . .

1. **"I'm not sure we're ready for this,"** she almost always means **"Stop,"** yet He often *thinks* she means: a) "Let's continue, but you're special because usually I only do this with guys I've known longer." Or, b) "Let's continue, but first you have to reassure me that the relationship has reached the point where this is appropriate or expected."

2. **"I'm seeing someone else,"** she almost always means **"Stop,"** yet He often *thinks* she means: a) "Let's continue, but please don't let the other guy find out." Or, b) "Let's continue, but don't interpret this as a commitment."

3. **"I'm having my period,"** she almost always means **"Stop,"** yet He often *thinks* she means: "Let's continue if you want. I'm telling you this in case it matters to you."

4. **"I can't do this unless you're committed to me,"** she almost always means **"Stop,"** yet He often *thinks* she means: a) "Let's continue, but I'm going to interpret it to be a commitment." Or, b) "Let's continue, but first tell me that you're committed to me."

5. **"It's getting late,"** she almost always means **"Stop,"** yet He often *thinks* she means: a) "Let's step up the pace; there's no time to waste." Or, b) "Let's continue, but only if you don't mind how late it will be if we do."

6. **"I'm confused about this,"** she almost always means **"Stop,"** yet He often *thinks* she means: a) "Let's continue, but I want you to reassure me that it isn't purely physical." Or, b) "Let's continue, but I wish I knew what it implies about our relationship."

7. **"I don't have protection,"** she almost always means **"Stop,"** yet He often *thinks* she means: a) "Let's continue if you have protection." Or, b) "Let's continue, including anything except conventional intercourse."

8. **"I'm saving that [activity] for marriage,"** she almost always means **"Stop,"** yet He often *thinks* she means: a) "We can do anything else, but not that."

9. **"That's against my [religion/principles/morals],"** she almost always means **"Stop,"** yet He often *thinks* she means: a) "Let's continue, but I want you to know that I'm a 'nice girl' who doesn't usually do this."

10. **"I don't think I know you well enough for this,"** she almost always means **"Stop,"** yet He often *thinks* she means: "Let's continue, but I want you to know that I usually do this only with guys I've known longer."

11. **"Let's stop,"** she almost always means **"Stop,"** and He usually knows she means "Stop."

12. **"Please don't do that,"** she almost always means **"Stop,"** and He usually knows she means "Stop."

13. **"I don't want do this,"** she almost always means **"Stop,"** and He usually knows she means "Stop."

FIGURE **6.1**

Common Misinterpretations of Resistance Messages During Physical Intimacy

Source: M. T. Motley and H. M. Reeder, "Unwanted Escalation of Sexual Intimacy: Male and Female Perceptions of Connotations and Relational Consequences of Resistance Messages," Communication Monographs *62 (1995): 355–382.*

Women use indirect resistance messages for two reasons. First, they fully expect the message to be understood to mean "stop." As we have seen, this is not always a safe assumption. Second, many women feel that a direct resistance message is too harsh—that it will make him think she is mean, will offend or anger him, will make her appear prudish, will reduce the chances that he will want to date her again, and so forth. As it turns out, this is not true either.[13] Males, although often hoping otherwise, expect that their female partners will probably draw the line at some point. They may be disappointed, but typically males are not hurt, offended, angered, etc., by resistance messages—including direct messages.

There probably will always be some males who persist despite understood resistance. But this discussion suggests a way to at least reduce the number of situations in which resistance to physical intimacy is ignored. The implication for women is to *use direct messages*. These are the messages he is sure to understand, and there is no social or relational advantage to the more polite or indirect forms. The implication for men is to *be aware of the range of resistance messages* that women use to say "stop." Review all of the common resistance messages listed above and in Figure 6.1, and recognize that they almost always mean "stop."

FINDING OUT ABOUT FEELINGS WITHIN THE RELATIONSHIP

Ordinarily, Phase II of intimate relationships is by far the most dynamic period with respect to developing and discovering each other's feelings. During the early and middle stages of Phase II, it is not unusual for people to be a bit uncertain even about their own feelings—whether the emotional attraction is "the real thing," whether they want to commit to this relationship for at least a while, and so forth.

One of the great ironies about emotionally intimate relationships is that while there is a strong—sometimes almost overwhelming—need to know what one's partner thinks and feels about the relationship, and often a strong desire to express one's own thoughts and feelings, the relationship itself is a topic most couples avoid. For some reason, couples tend not to discuss openly their feelings about the relationship itself except during a relatively brief transition period between Phase II and Phase III.

If we are dying to know how our Phase II partner feels about the relationship, yet discussing the relationship is practically taboo, then how do we find out? One approach is by **secret tests**.[14] Secret tests are tricks and gimmicks designed by one partner to elicit a sign of commitment from the other. They may work, but they may also backfire and ruin the relationship.

For example, one secret-test device is what has been called the *endurance test*. This involves posing unreasonable demands to make the relationship costly to the partner. For example, Pat may demand that Chris sacrifice a business, family, or other engagement or commitment in order to do something that Pat wants instead. The idea is that if the partner is willing to make such a sacrifice, it is a sign of his or her devotion. The downside, of course, is that the partner may refuse to make the sacrifice despite his or her devotion to the relationship, or may agree to the sacrifice, but resent it to a degree that prevents subsequent relational development. Another secret test is the *separation test*. This involves "cooling it" for a while—separating or seeing much less of each other for a trial period, often with permission to date others. The idea is that if the partners wish to resume the relationship after the separation, this must be a sign that the relationship is solid. (Summer break is a common time for college students to try this.) Problems occur when there is no set time for the end of the trial separation period (e.g., each waits so long for the partner to reinitiate the relationship that the relationship fades), and especially when the ground rules for the separation are not explicitly agreed upon (e.g., "Well yeah, we agreed that it was OK to date others, but I didn't think you'd actually *do* it; *I* didn't"). Another device is the *triangle test,* in which a real or hypothetical potential target for one's affection is intentionally revealed to the partner. The idea is that if the partner displays jealousy, then that is a sign of his or her genuine affection. The test backfires, however, when the introduction of a rival makes one's partner vanish. The partner may feel that he or she has been "led on" to believe in a deeper level of commitment than one that allows rivals. Another secret test is the *third-party query.* Instead of initiating discussion about the relationship with our partner, we may ask a mutual acquaintance to find out from our partner how he or she feels about us and the relationship. Junior high schoolers ask others to "find out if he or she likes me," and so do adults. The primary danger is simply that the test isn't reliable. The third-party query is likely to get a noncommittal but slightly positive response no matter whether the partner is lukewarm or head over heels.

SIGNS OF RELATIONSHIP DEVELOPMENT

So far, it may seem that we have painted a bleak picture of Phase II in intimate relationships. Each of the partners is working out his or her own feelings and trying to discover the other's, yet the relationship is a taboo topic, physical intimacy is not a reliable indicator, and secret tests may backfire.

What's a couple to do? They could simply discuss the relationship openly, but, as we have said, most Phase II couples find this difficult. Most commonly, couples just "let nature take its course." Thus, it is helpful to see how emotionally intimate relationships normally evolve. That is, we can get an idea about the state of our own Phase II relationship by comparing it with norms.

Early in Phase II, a number of intensifying behaviors begin to occur. **Intensifying** is simply the process of becoming emotionally and psychologically closer. While increased closeness also occurs in other kinds of relationships and in other phases of intimate relationships, "intensifying" usually refers to moving from mere friendship into the early stages of a real or potential intimate relationship. Many intensifying signs and behaviors are the same for adults on the verge of "the real thing" as for junior high schoolers' infatuations:

1. We try to find ways to increase the frequency and duration of contacts. Rather than leaving the next interaction more or less to chance or whim, as we sometimes do with friends, we go out of our way to ensure interaction through acknowledged planned encounters, or sometimes ostensibly "accidental" planned encounters.

2. As the frequency of interaction increases, we tend to miss the partner when interactions do not take place.

3. The frequency and/or depth of our disclosures increases.

4. We may feel jealousy of, or threatened by, others to whom the partner seems to be attached.

5. Friendly teasing begins or increases.

6. Private slang and idioms develop. These may include pet names for each other, special names for mutual acquaintances, private names for intimate behaviors, pet names for partners' physical features, and so forth.

7. Physical intimacy increases, at least beyond the partners' thresholds for mere friendship.

8. Expressions of affection and closeness begin to be verbalized. Early on, this may or may not involve "the L word." Some people are extremely reticent about saying "I love you" until very late in Phase II, whereas others say it freely even in close but nonintimate friendships. But L word or not, intensifying usually includes at least subtle verbal declarations of emotional closeness (e.g., "I missed you," "Seeing you means a lot to me," "You mean a lot to me," "You're more than just a friend, you know").

Another part of the evolution of intimate relationships is integration. **Integrating** is the process of becoming psychologically unified or fused. The partners develop a sense of "we" or "us" in which the sum (or couple) is indeed greater than the parts (or autonomous individuals). Integrating signs vary, but the following are typical:

1. The couple thinks of itself as a couple. The partner is consulted, included, or taken into account on what once had been routine independent decisions—where to spend the holidays, whether to go skiing this weekend, etc.

2. Verbal declarations of affection become more explicit, more frequent, and less inhibited.

3. The couple presents itself publicly as a couple (this is my boyfriend, girlfriend, significant other, etc.).

4. The possibility of a long-term or permanent commitment is recognized and may be discussed openly or hinted at.

5. Physical intimacy increases to at least the level reached in the more conservative partner's prior relationships.

6. The ability to predict the other's responses to various situations increases at least a bit, and sometimes to an uncanny, "ESP-like" degree.

7. Differences of opinion, even on important issues, tend to be ignored, glossed over, or casually resolved. This is similar to the conflict tolerance of close friendships that we discussed earlier.

8. In some but not all couples, the relationship itself is openly discussed. As we have suggested, open discussion of the relationship is rare except during the transition from Phase II to Phase III of the relationship.

Communication Problems in Early Relationship Stages Include

✓ Initiating contact with a potential partner (Phase I)

✓ Interpreting physical intimacy (Phase II)

✓ Establishing thresholds for physical intimacy (Phase II)

✓ Discovering each other's feelings about the relationship (Phase II)

INTIMATE RELATIONSHIPS— PHASE III

Phase III of intimate relationships is the period that follows **bonding**—the couple's explicit commitment to a presumably permanent union, usually via marriage vows or a similar contract. This is supposed to be the happily-ever-after phase. And often it is—more or less. There is no easy formula for ensuring that the relationship will be a permanent one or a happy one, but a few common communication-related problems are worth looking out for.

REAFFIRMING THE RELATIONSHIP

When an intimate relationship gets all the way to Phase III, there usually has been at least a brief period during which the partners have openly expressed their affection for each other and discussed the value they place on the relationship. For many couples in **Relationship Phase III**, however, these expressions and discussions taper off and sometimes end entirely. Often this is not because the partners' feelings have changed, but rather because they consider the expression of their feelings to be unnecessary. "He or she *knows* how I feel; I don't have to actually *say* it" seems to be the assumption operating here. Partners will say to themselves (or to counselors), "Well, of course I still love him or her. I shouldn't have to *say* it. It should be *obvious,* because I [work all week for us / spend the holidays with his or her family even though I'd rather not / go to the opera when asked, even though I hate the opera / take him or her out to dinner once a week / am still with him or her / etc.]." This kind of reasoning can be dangerous. Its flaw, of course, is that these routine behaviors are not necessarily signs of love, and even if they are, they are very indirect compared to verbal expression. It is important that couples who are fortunate enough to reach Phase III remain open about their feelings for each other, and for the relationship itself.[15]

WHY DO I LOVE THEE, OR NOT?

Here is yet another irony about intimate relationships: characteristics of one's partner that at first were seen as *positive* features, largely responsible for the attraction, sometimes come to be viewed *negatively* and become a target for criticism.[16] For example, if, in Phase II, she was attracted to him because he was diligent and ambitious, she may complain in Phase III that he is a workaholic. Or, if he was attracted to her because she was intelligent and confident, he may later complain that she is domineering and egotistical. For more examples of these **attraction-criticism reversals,** see Figure 6.2 on the following page.

The good news is that not all couples experience these reversals—at least not to such a degree that the relationship is threatened. The bad news is that they are sufficiently common to paint a fairly bleak picture in which it seems that we can't win. Apparently, there is a good chance that whatever our mate finds attractive about us will come back to haunt us later in the relationship! Knowledge of these reversals should serve as a warning to Phase II couples: Be aware that some people experience reversals and complaints of the sort given in Figure 6.2, and consider carefully whether you are likely to do so with your partner. And knowledge of these reversals provides a corrective strategy for Phase III partners who find themselves inclined toward these complaints: Recognize that you once viewed the criticized feature positively—indeed, you once considered it particularly attractive—and temper your present criticisms with reflections on the positive views you held in the past.

PLAIN OL' CONVERSATION

It is common to hear dissatisfied couples blame their troubles on "communication problems." Exactly what that means depends on the couple, of course. But one very common problem in Phase III relationships is the demise of simple casual conversation.

In Phase II, casual conversation usually is abundant. It is fun, it manifests interest in the partner, it increases intimacy, and it affirms the relationship bond. In Phase III, casual conversation is *needed* for the same reasons. Unfortunately, however, casual conversation usually becomes less frequent in Phase III. For some couples it becomes

Some **women** who are at first attracted to a man because he is . . .	will later *complain* that he is . . .
Fun, entertaining	Immature, incapable of taking the relationship (and/or other things) seriously
Nice, kind	Not assertive enough
Laid-back, easy-going	Unfocused, unambitious
Persistent, assertive	Domineering
Successful, ambitious	A workaholic

Some **men** who are at first attracted to a woman because she is . . .	will later *complain* that she is . . .
Intelligent, confident	Domineering, egotistical
Caring, compassionate	Smothering
Innocent, pure	Naive, inhibited, prudish
Sexy	Slutty, cheap
Gorgeous	Vain

FIGURE **6.2**
Examples of Reversals (from Positive to Negative) of Impressions of Partners' Traits

practically nonexistent. Usually, the demise of couples' conversation may be attributed to demands on the partners' time. With stress, fatigue, domestic responsibilities, job responsibilities, and so forth, couples sometimes relegate casual conversation to the back burner in favor of time for their individual interests, rest, and responsibilities.

To make matters worse, as couples take less time for casual conversation—small talk, shooting the breeze, catching up—they may substitute *quasi-conversation*—that is, half-baked, abbreviated conversation usually motivated by some purpose other than simple socializing. And with these abbreviated dialogues, several **conversational bad habits** sometimes emerge.[17]

One of these conversational bad habits is **polyphasing**—devoting only a small part of one's attention to what one's partner is saying, and directing most of one's attention elsewhere (the TV, fixing a meal, straightening up the room, and so forth). Another conversational bad habit is **fragmenting.** This is the habit of following the partner's remark with an irrelevant, off-the-wall, comment from left field (for example, A: "I'm worried about the dog; he's showing signs of old age." B: "So is your mother. What she said last week really burns me up"). Sometimes the fragmented remarks will be on a repetitious, one-track-mind theme; sometimes not. In any case, they derail the conversation. The habit of persistent **challenging** does the same thing. It seems that some Phase III partners love to stir up controversy by taking an opposing position on practically anything the partner says. Sometimes these are honest differences of opinion (e.g., A: "I've decided to vote 'yes' on Measure H tomorrow." B: "Big mistake! It'll cost us in taxes, and we'll never see any benefits."). Other times the challenge seems fairly pointless (e.g., A: "Wow, they say it's going to be a wet winter this year." B: "I'm sick of hearing about the weather forecast. Why do you believe that crap, anyway? Have you ever known the weather people to be right about anything?"). In either case, this kind of challenge can shut down the conversation, especially when it reaches the point where one partner "knows" in advance that practically anything he or she says will be met with a challenge or rebuttal. Other conversational bad habits sometimes found in Phase III include **monopolizing** the conversation, **chronic complaining** about one's problems (regarding work, home, health, finances, etc.), and excessive **negativity**, or putting a negative, pessimistic spin on practically every conversation topic.

Looking at this list of ill-advised conversational devices, it is easy to hypothesize that each is derived in part from a sort of conversation starvation—a need to get one's two cents' worth in quickly or emphatically, because full-blown casual conversation has become a thing of the past. While it may not be a cure-all for every case, couples are repeatedly advised by counselors to occasionally take time out for casual conversation of the sort engaged in by most couples back in Phase II. Whether it is by going out to dinner (*without* other couples), having morning coffee on the patio (*without* the newspaper), relaxing together after dinner (*without* the TV), or taking occasional weekend getaways (*without* the kids), it is crucial that Phase III partners make time for casual conversation despite the various pressures that compete for their attention.

Communication Problems in Later Relationship Stages Include

✓ Knowing each other's ongoing feelings about the relationship (Phase III)

✓ Relating via conversation (Phase III)

✓ Discussing concerns about the relationship (Phase III*)

✓ Terminating the relationship (Phase IV)

*This should take place in Phase III but often is delayed until Phase IV.

INTIMATE RELATIONSHIPS— PHASE IV

Relationship Phase IV is the dissolution or breaking up of the relationship. Not all relationships break up, of course. When they do, it may be during Phase II or Phase III.

REASONS FOR BREAKUPS

When relationships break up during Phase *II*, it is often for one or more of the following reasons:[18]

1.   One or both partners simply did not feel inclined to make a commitment: For example, "Although I cared for him, I wanted to start dating other people," "I was primarily interested in having a good time rather than in maintaining a relationship," "While the relationship was a good one, I was getting bored·with it," and so forth.

2. Faults with the partner or other incompatibilities emerged: "His or her personality was not compatible with mine," "He or she was too demanding," "He or she was too weird," and the like.

3. Logistic problems (usually distance) interfered: "One of us moved away, and we couldn't see each other as much."

4. The relationship interfered with other relationships: "Most of my friends didn't like him or her," "My parents didn't approve," and so forth.

When relationships break up during Phase *III*, the blame usually is placed on one or more of the following:

1. Specific faults of the partner (e.g., "He or she was just too _____ ").

2. Failure of the relationship to match one's image of an ideal relationship (e.g., "There wasn't enough_____ in the relationship").

3. Perceived incompatibility between the self and the relationship (e.g., "I've personally outgrown the relationship, in the sense that_____ " or "I can't be the 'real me' in this relationship in the sense that _____ ").

4. Supposed irreconcilable differences (e.g., "We just never could agree about _____ ").

Sometimes dissatisfied partners can fill in the specifics; sometimes they can't. More surprising, perhaps, sometimes a dissatisfied individual has *never discussed* the situation with the partner. And many who do discuss it have waited until they are ready to give up on the relationship. We should, of course, communicate with our partner about concerns of the type listed here (or virtually anything else)—not just nag or complain, but actually discuss the situation in depth—as soon as they begin to arise.

SIGNS OF RELATIONSHIP DETERIORATION

Whatever the real or imagined cause of a breakup, certain signs of deterioration seem fairly consistent across intimate relationships in distress:[19]

1. Conflict tolerance is replaced with *conflict seeking.* In troubled relationships, gone are the days when almost anything the partner proposes is acceptable and differences of opinion seem insignificant. Not only is there less conflict tolerance, but in deteriorating relationships one or both partners may appear to *seek* conflict by nagging, criticizing, complaining about the partner, and so forth. Moreover, the conflicts become more competitive (more win-lose oriented) than cooperative (win-win).

2. *Defensiveness* increases. As the partners become more conflict-prone, they become more defensive. They are looking for ways to justify their own behaviors and positions, and are less interested in the other's point of view, per se.

3. *Deception* increases. As partners become less conflict-tolerant, they become more easily upset with each other. And as one partner becomes more easily upset, the other may begin to deceive, lie, or shade the truth on issues that he or she fears may be upsetting.

4. *Trust* decreases. As partners discover or sense that they are being deceived, trust erodes.

5. *Favors and sacrifices are less appreciated.* It is common for partners to do little (or big) favors for each other. Ideally, either partner does favors—gladly and with pleasure—and the other expresses appreciation. Problems arise when the favors come to be expected and are no longer appreciated (e.g., when "Thanks for fixing breakfast; you didn't have to do that" becomes, "Where's my breakfast?"), especially when one partner perceives himself or herself to be on the short end of the stick with respect to favors, sacrifices, and the appreciation of them.

Some of these changes are to be expected to a *slight* degree. For example, it may be normal even in healthy relationships for conflict tolerance to subside just a bit. And minor deception is found in most normal relationships. As a case in point, a study of four *satisfied* couples found twenty-seven different ways in which the partners tried to deceive each other to conceal or justify their spending—"It was marked down 40 percent" [truth: 20 percent], "We needed this" [truth: I wanted this], "Here is the check stub for the groceries" [truth: including cash for $40 over the amount], and so forth.[20] Thus, a mere hint of these difficulties does not mean that a relationship is doomed. But they are warning signs, especially when they manifest erosion of the partners' feelings for each other or for the relationship.

BREAKING UP IS HARD TO DO—OR IS IT?

One of the dozen or so most common communication dilemmas cited by college students is the decision of whether and how to break up an existing unsatisfactory relationship.[21] "I just don't know how to tell him or her that I want out" is not only a common situation but, for some, an especially agonizing one.

The fact of the matter, most likely, is that we already know *how* to break up. I am reminded, for example, of a student who had been agonizing over how to break up with his girlfriend of a year or so. One day a mutual acquaintance told him that his girlfriend had been overheard saying that she intended to manipulate him into marriage. He broke up with her that evening! Obviously, his earlier agonizing had not been about not knowing *how* to break up.

There are, after all, a few fairly well-known ways of breaking up.[22] The most direct way, of course, is to simply *tell the partner* that you no longer wish to continue the relationship at all (i.e., that it is over) or no longer wish to continue it at its present level (e.g., "Let's go back to being friends"). A less direct way is to *drop hints* of various kinds—decreasing the amount of contact, cutting back on romantic behaviors, and so forth—so that the partner will sense that the relationship is deteriorating. The idea behind the hints, apparently, is to soften the blow when we announce the breakup, or to get the partner to bring up the topic. Yet another strategy is to *make oneself undesirable or intolerable* to the partner—for example, by cruel or mean-spirited acts or comments—hoping that he or she will do the dirty work of terminating the relationship.

If most breakups follow one of these three strategies, then the matter of *how* to break up would appear to be fairly simple. However, people do agonize about breaking up. Often, there is reluctance based on hope that the relationship can be repaired. And sometimes there is a feeling that so much has been invested in the relationship that to leave it would be to give up too easily. It is perhaps easier to understand this kind of reluctance in, say, a couple married for ten years, nine of them happily, than in, say, a boyfriend-girlfriend relationship of ten months, the last six of which have been unsatisfactory. But the "I hate to just give up" reluctance may be found in either case.

Dear Prof. M:

My problem is kind of complicated. I have had a boyfriend for almost three years. A few months ago, he was accepted at [another university, about four hours away] and decided to go there. At this point we decided that we should start dating other people. This put uncertainty into the relationship. We both dated other people, and started lying to each other to save hurting the other's feelings. This led to a lack of trust between us. Then, a month ago, my boyfriend was arrested for attempted rape. I honestly did not know what to believe. Because of the breakdown of trust, and the lying, I didn't know if what he was telling me about the situation was true or if once again he was trying to save my feelings. Although I have told him that I believe him, I'm not sure if I do, and he doubts me. The relationship has broken down so far that I don't know whether I should just "get out while I can," or whether I should stick around and try to work it out. It seems a waste to have spent three years in this relationship and just bail out, but it seems like there is no hope. *Is* there hope?

Sincerely,
Confused

FIGURE 6.3
Should They Break Up?

As an example, consider a Dear-Abby-type letter written as an assignment by a student in a course similar to yours. You'll find it in Figure 6.3. Read it now, and decide what your advice would be.

Over 99 percent of those who read this letter say that they would advise the letter writer to terminate the relationship. Even if we take an innocent-until-proven-otherwise approach to the boyfriend's arrest, it is clear that trust between them has eroded to a level below what is needed and deserved in a satisfactory relationship. As obvious as this seems to most of *us,* notice that the writer is focused on "hope" and on the notion that a breakup means having "wasted" three years. While some of the specifics in this example are atypical, the reluctance to break up even an obviously unsatisfactory relationship is typical indeed.

Another source of reluctance in potential breakup situations is a *concern about hurting the partner.* In fact, this is the most common reason given by college students for delaying breakups of Phase II and early Phase III relationships. Some would claim that this is a poor excuse for delaying a breakup, however, for two reasons. First, while it is true that one's partner is sometimes hurt when one initiates a breakup, sometimes the partner isn't hurt because he or she has also been wanting to get out of the relationship. Moreover, even when it does hurt, it usually hurts for only a little while. For example, when surveys ask adults to think back to all their past relationships that were broken off by the partner, and then to report how badly they were hurt by the breakup, less than 1 percent of the breakups are reported to have been devastating for four months or more. The very large majority (over 90 percent) of partner-initiated breakups hurt "a little" for about a week.[23] Not to be cruel, but even if your partner's degree of hurt were double this norm, that's not much hurt in the overall scheme of things, some would argue.

There is a second reason that not wanting to hurt the partner may be a poor reason to delay a breakup. When we say, "I want to break it off, but I don't want to *hurt* him or her," this is a bit arrogant. It suggests, "After all, how will he or she possibly be able to live without wonderful me?" Moreover, the rationale ("I don't want to hurt him or her") is altruistically misguided. That is, if you want to be *kind* to a partner with whom you wish to

Dear Doc,

I have a problem with my boyfriend. We've been seeing each other for almost seven months now. He is very serious about us and we talk about getting married some day.

When we first met, he fell in love with me first and eventually I fell for him too. However, I don't think I love him as much as he loves me. Sometimes I need to be apart from him, and when I am, I don't miss him much. But I still tell him I do miss him. I hate lying to him but I don't want to hurt him and I feel it's unnecessary to tell him the truth when I don't know how I really feel.

He is the sweetest guy in the world and all our friends think we are perfect together. We seem to have the perfect relationship.

This is my first serious relationship. I haven't seen very many other guys before him, however he has been with many other girls.

Here's the problem. I feel that I haven't had a chance to really meet other guys, and now I want to. I miss going out with the girls on weekends and picking up on guys at parties. I've pretty much decided that I'm going to do this. I don't want to tell him, but I'm afraid he may find out from his friends if they see me.

There's another problem too. He's not really sure what he wants to do with his future. His major doesn't offer many promising career opportunities. I know this sounds shallow, but I'd like to be fairly well off when I'm older. At least as well off as my family is now. I'm also being pressured by my parents to meet someone with a stable future.

I guess I'm being a bit selfish, but I'm thinking of my future. I really do love him and I don't want to hurt him. I know I have to find the answer to my problems myself, but any suggestions would be helpful.

Thanks,
In Love But Wanting More

FIGURE **6.4**
Sometimes Breaking Up Is a Kindness

break off a relationship, then which of the following is the kinder act: (1) disguising your desire to end the relationship lest he or she be hurt, thereby holding him or her in a relationship with a partner (you) who does not feel emotionally close or committed, or, (2) releasing him or her from a bogus intimate relationship so that he or she may be free to find a partner with whom to form a more genuine intimate relationship?

That was supposed to be a rhetorical question, with the answer apparent. But to emphasize the point, read another student's Dear-Abby-assignment letter in Figure 6.4. Don't you agree that releasing the letter writer's partner from the relationship is the kinder option? Now ask yourself if the same wouldn't apply to virtually *any* "I want out" situation.

So, perhaps it's not that "breaking up is hard to do," as the maxim says, but rather that breaking up is easy to do, but *deciding* to break up is hard to do. No doubt, part of our reluctance to break up sometimes lies in our disappointment that things didn't turn out as we had imagined, and in our not wanting to admit to being a "failure" at maintaining the relationship. As we said at the outset, however, only a tiny fraction of initially satisfactory Phase II relationships evolve into permanent Phase III relationships. Dissolved relationships are the norm; permanent relationships are the exception. But dissolved relationships are valuable preludes to subsequent permanent relationships, and they are important to us while they last. For example, when surveys ask adults to recall all of their past, once-serious relationships and to answer whether, in retrospect, they are both (1) glad the *breakup* happened and (2) glad the *relationship* happened, virtually everyone answers yes to both questions for virtually all past relationships.[24] Thus, dissolved relationships may be viewed as a sign of becoming relationally experienced—older and wiser, so to speak—rather than as a sign of failure.

By no means are we saying that relationships are made to be dissolved, or that playing the field is superior to forming a lasting relationship, or anything of that sort. We happen to agree (although some would not) that a permanent and satisfied Phase III relationship is the ultimate intimate relationship. But this suggests that if one is *dissatisfied* with a present relationship, there are essentially three options: (1) Dissolve the unsatisfactory relationship, (2) Do nothing and continue, as is, in an unsatisfactory and unsatisfying relationship, (3) Fix or repair the problems in the existing relationship. This chapter has suggested a few ways in which couples may avoid and/or repair certain problems, and there are other tips in other chapters.

IN SUMMARY

Several times in this chapter we have discussed dilemmas that rank among the most common communication difficulties identified by college students and other adults. It may seem surprising that we experience major problems with people who are among those we most value—our close friends and our partners in emotionally intimate relationships. Most likely, of course, the fact that these relationships are so highly valued is what makes these communication problems so critical to us.

For both friendships and emotionally intimate relationships, we have discussed two levels of information: We have discussed the *general* conditions and features of the relationships, and we have discussed *specific* communication dilemmas that many relationship partners find to be especially problematic.

The more general conditions—indicators of friendship, signs of relationship deterioration, causes of damage to friendships, norms in the development of intimate relationships, and so forth—may be used as a checklist for our own relationships. They can help us to understand which features of our relationships are normal and which are abnormal, they can alert us to difficulties that perhaps can be prevented in advance, and they can indicate difficulties in progress. In most cases, communication will be at the heart of the matter.

The specific communication problems we have discussed—initiating contact with someone in whom we are interested, disclosing romantic attraction within an ostensible friendship, discovering each other's feelings, trying to deter unwanted attempts to escalate intimacy, initiating a breakup, and so forth—will seem more critical to some than to others. But most of us will face these situations more than once. In virtually every case there are specific communication guidelines that can help—sometimes considerably—to make the situation less difficult.

We began the discussion by suggesting that it is through communication that important relationships are formed, damaged, maintained, and terminated. And we have seen many ways in which this is the case.

TERMS TO KNOW

friendship indicators	direct (opening lines)
Relationship Phase I	innocuous (opening lines)
initiating	Relationship Phase II
experimenting	sexual resistance messages
cute-flippant (opening lines)	direct resistance messages

indirect resistance messages
secret tests
intensifying
integrating
bonding
Relationship Phase III
attraction-criticism reversals
conversational bad habits

polyphasing
fragmenting
challenging
monopolizing
chronic complaining
negativity
Relationship Phase IV

NOTES

1. P. H. Wright, "Self Referent Motivation and the Intrinsic Quality of Friendship," *Journal of Social and Personal Relationships* 1 (1984): 114–130; M. Lea, "Factors Underlying Friendship: An Analysis of Responses on the Acquaintance Description Form in Relation to Wright's Friendship Model," *Journal of Social and Personal Relationships* 6 (1989): 275–292; M. T. Motley, H. M. Reeder, and L. J. Faulkner, "Influences upon the Fate of Friendships After Unrequited Romantic Disclosures" (paper, Speech Communication Association, San Diego, 1996).

2. P. H. Wright, "Self Referent Motivation and the Intrinsic Quality of Friendship"; M. Lea, "Factors Underlying Friendship"; Motley, Reeder, and Faulkner, "Influences upon the Fate of Friendships."

3. Motley, Reeder, and Faulkner, "Influences upon the Fate of Friendships."

4. Ibid.

5. Ibid.

6. Ibid.

7. Based liberally on M. L. Knapp, *Interpersonal Communication and Human Relationships* (Boston: Allyn & Bacon, 1984); and L. A. Baxter, "Dialectical Contradictions in Relationship Development," *Journal of Social and Personal Relationships* 7 (1990): 68–88.

8. M. T. Motley, "Mindfulness in Solving Communication Dilemmas," *Communication Monographs* 59 (1992): 306–314.

9. C. L. Klienke, F. B. Meeker, and R. A. Staneski, "Preference for Opening Lines: Comparing Ratings by Men and Women," *Sex Roles* 15 (1986): 585–600.

10. Ibid.

11. M. T. Motley and H. M. Reeder, "Unwanted Escalation of Sexual Intimacy: Male and Female Perceptions of Connotations and Relational Consequences of Resistances Messages," *Communication Monographs* 62 (1995): 355–382.

12. Ibid.

13. Ibid.

14. L. A. Baxter and W. Wilmot, "Secret Tests: Social Strategies for Acquiring Information About the State of the Relationship," *Human Communication Research* 11 (1984): 171–201.

15. J. Browne, *Why They Don't Call When They Say They Will and Other Mixed Signals* (New York: Simon & Schuster, 1990).

16. D. H. Felmlee, "Fatal Attractions: Affection and Disaffection in Intimate Relationships," *Journal of Social and Personal Relationships* 12 (1995): 295–311.

17. B. A. Baldwin, "Couples in Conversation" (paper, Direction Dynamics, Wilmington, N.C., 1991).

18. Based on M. J. Cody, "A Typology of Disengagement Strategies and an Examination of the Role Intimacy Reactions to Inequity and Relational Problems Play in Strategy Selection," *Communication Monographs* 49 (1982): 148–170.

19. D. Goleman, *Emotional Intelligence* (New York: Bantam, 1995); Cody, "A Typology of Disengagement Strategies"; P. D. Kramer, "Relationships: Should You Leave?" *Psychology Today* 30 (1997): 38–45.

20. M. T. Motley and students, "Cumulative Pilot Studies, 1989–1997: RCM 105 & RCM 134" (unpublished paper, University of California at Davis, 1997).

21. M. T. Motley, "Mindfulness in Solving Communication Dilemmas," *Communication Monographs* 59 (1992): 306–314.

22. M. J. Cody, "A Typology of Disengagement Strategies and an Examination of the Role Intimacy Reactions to Inequity and Relational Problems Play in Strategy Selection," *Communication Monographs* 49 (1982): 148–170.

23. Motley and students, "Cumulative Pilot Studies, 1989–1997"

24. Ibid.

CHAPTER SEVEN

INTERPERSONAL COMMUNICATION DILEMMAS

THIS CHAPTER

will help you

○ Recognize barriers and partial solutions to intercultural communication

○ Recognize barriers and partial solutions to male-female communication

○ Develop ways of viewing and dealing with conflict

○ Recognize common deception situations and their alternatives

○ Develop approaches to situations demanding tact and diplomacy

THINK BEFORE THOU **SPEAKEST.**

—Cervantes

n trying to discover the various communication dilemmas that are common in our everyday lives, communication researchers have classified thousands of individual cases into dozens of communication-dilemma categories. This chapter will provide a brief overview of just a few broad categories of common communication difficulties. In particular, we will discuss the challenge of recognizing and adjusting to others' *cultural perspectives*, with *male-female communication* as a particular example—difficulties presented by *conflict*, the dilemma of *truth versus deception*, and guidelines for *assertiveness* and *tactfulness*.

RECOGNIZING CULTURAL PERSPECTIVES

In Chapter 5 we noted that individual personality differences cause people to see the world from different perspectives—through different "common-sense" lenses. An appreciation of these differences can help us to understand people whose preferences and styles are different from our own, and thus can help us to communicate with them more effectively. Personality is by no means the only factor accounting for different perspectives, however.

Various cultural influences shape our perspectives as well. Individuals with different cultural influences are likely to have different perspectives, different norms, different ways of communicating, different meanings for similar messages, and so forth. An appreciation of these differences can assist mutual understanding.

Culture refers to any kind of societal grouping in which members of one category or group tend toward beliefs or behaviors that differ from those of other groups. Thus, we may find certain cultural differences among people raised in different countries (France, United States, Japan, etc.), people of different ethnicities (American Black, Asian, White, etc.), and people with different religions (Jewish, Catholic, Baptist, Lutheran, etc.). We might also find cultural differences among those with different education levels, those of different socioeconomic levels, those from areas with different population densities, and so on. Even gender differences may be viewed as cultural differences.

MALE-FEMALE COMMUNICATION AS INTERCULTURAL COMMUNICATION

It may seem strange to treat male-female differences as cultural differences. The parallels between male-female communication difficulties and other **intercultural** (i.e., between-culture) communication difficulties are abundant, however. We experience male-female communication problems regularly, sometimes without consciously recognizing that there is a problem. And when we do recognize a difficulty, we usually do not attribute it to differences between male and female cultures. Thus, male-female communication can serve as an enlightening example of how virtually all intercultural barriers operate. Moreover, it is an interesting topic in its own right.

Prejudices and Stereotypes. We may not like to admit it, but each gender has certain negative stereotypes of the other. Suppose your instructor were to ask the women in your class to complete the sentence, "One of the problems with men is that they _____," and then ask the men to complete, "One of the problems with women is that they _____ ." If your class is typical, both groups would have no trouble coming up with a half-dozen or more responses. For example, it is very common for women to complain that men are emotionally blank, are insensitive (undiplomatic and nonempathic), have an attitude of superiority, try to settle discussion issues too quickly, and don't listen. And it is very common for men to complain that women are moody, are too emotional, play mind games, talk too much, and read too much between the lines.

As for the source of these stereotypes, one possibility is that they are true. Perhaps most men really are more insensitive (in certain ways) than most women, and perhaps most women really are more talkative (in certain contexts) than most men, for example. If this is the case, then an understanding of the cultural norms responsible for the stereotypic behaviors can help us to accept and adjust to them. But another possibility, and the one we wish to emphasize, is that differences in the behavior norms of two cultures can create *false* stereotypes. That is, maybe there are cultural differences that make men *appear* to women to be poor listeners when this isn't true, differences that make women *appear* to men to be overly emotional when this isn't true, and so forth.

Male-Female Differences in Communicative Function. Different cultures develop different communication norms. The same gesture or utterance may have different meanings in different cultures, for example. Furthermore, at a more general level, different cultures may view communication itself as serving different social *functions*.

Males and females, for example, tend to have somewhat different views of what communication is for and what purpose(s) it serves. In a nutshell, women tend to view communication as serving the purpose of *communing*, or *bonding*, whereas men tend to view the purpose of communication as *making points* and *providing facts or opinions*. As one sage has put it, women view communication as *rapport*, men as *report*.[1] This difference in how people view the social function of communication is at the heart of many male-female communication difficulties, as we will see.

It is useful to understand the *source* of male-female communication differences. Apparently, males and females develop different approaches to communication because of differences in the ways in which we interact and play with others of our own gender as children. Some of the contrasts between girls' and boys' play patterns from age four to thirteen or so carry over into adulthood.

Girls, for example, usually play together in small groups, most often pairs, with others of approximately the same age. The play is usually private, with participation requiring invitation. (A girl who passes by when two other girls are playing in a front yard is not supposed to just join in uninvited, for example.) Girls' play is usually cooperative and noncompetitive, with the object being to establish closeness. Even in ostensibly competitive situations like board games and card games, the play is as much for the enjoyment of being together as for ensuring victory. Equality is assumed and maintained in girls' play, and conflicts are resolved through compromise and voluntary submission rather than by power or superiority.

And conversation is a key ingredient. Girls' play usually includes extended conversation to establish and maintain friendship and closeness. With communication at the center of the play, the conversation is relaxed and unrushed. Each playmate will get her turn to talk, will have plenty of time to say what she wants, and will be listened to. Because conversation and closeness are all-important, girls learn to support one another, acknowledge what others are saying, and criticize or question one another diplomatically.

Boys' play is quite different. Boys often play together in larger groups in which ages vary. Competition is common, and rather than seeking equality, boys' play groups tend to establish hierarchies, or pecking orders. A given boy will see his relative status fluctuate, depending on the activity being engaged in and the relative age and ability of the other boys. He may be "king of the hill" in today's game and group, and "low man on the totem pole" tomorrow with a different activity and group.

Talk becomes a vehicle for asserting position, status, and dominance. The boy who strikes out each time he is at bat partially redeems himself by telling the funniest joke, coming up with the best insult, correcting someone else's misinformation, and so forth. Even talk itself becomes a competition sometimes, with boys making sure—via interruptions, putdowns, and challenges—that no one in the group gets too much control of the audience. This usually is not a mean-spirited sort of competition, but rather a friendly and probably unconscious jockeying for position. As a somewhat typical example of boys' competitive talk, I (Motley) recall a post-ski-trip conversation between three boys about ten years old. Each had taken turns recalling a jump he had made that surpassed the jump just mentioned by one of the others, until the boy who had certainly made the longest jump of the day said, "Yeah, but when I went off that ledge on Razorback, it seemed like I was in the air forever." To which the very next comment, by one of the other boys, was, "Yeah, that was neat. And remember that time you *crashed* on Ax Handle? That was so funny!"

As adults, our approach to conversation contains holdovers from these childhood play patterns. Women, when talking with other women, use talk to negotiate relationships. Getting the floor is not a problem, for each will get her turn. The art of conversation is to keep the partner engaged. Men, when talking with other men, jockey for position via jokes, storytelling, interruptions, challenges, debates over minor issues, and so forth. The purpose of talk is to accomplish a practical goal, such as making a point, giving information, or getting information that may be "useful" in later conversations or in other situations.

Some of the differences in girls' and boys' forms of play are evident in these photographs. Could these early styles of play be the beginning of differences and difficulties in adult male and female communication patterns?

We do not mean to imply that women *never* approach communication from the point of view described as typical of men, or that men *never* approach communication from the perspective described as typical of women. The point is that in the United States there are gender differences in *general tendencies* regarding the function of communication.

Male-Female Differences in Specific Behaviors. In addition to the difference in the ways in which men and women tend to view the general function of communication, there are differences in their approaches to several specific communication behaviors. Some of these differences can lead somewhat directly to misunderstandings and misperceptions.

Men and women tend to have entirely different meanings for **positive minimal responses**, for example. Positive minimal responses are behaviors such as head nods, "um-hmm," and "I see" made by listeners during conversation. When women make positive minimal responses, they usually mean, "I'm listening, please go on." When men make positive minimal responses, they usually mean, "I agree (or I understand); you can stop now, and we can discuss a different point." These meanings could hardly be more opposite! Consider the implications: When Jill gives head nods while Jack is talking, she means that she's listening, and he should continue. But he thinks she is agreeing with his point and telling him to stop pursuing it. Or when Jack gives no head nods while Jill is talking, it is because he doesn't yet understand or agree, yet she thinks it's because he isn't interested or isn't listening. And when he does give positive minimal responses, he means that they can switch topics because she's made her point, yet she thinks it means to continue. No wonder women sometimes complain that "he doesn't talk to me, even when I ask him to," and men sometimes complain that women "agree with everything, so you never know what they really think."

Men and women also have different meanings for the *function of questions*. Women often ask questions simply to engage the conversation partner. In these cases, the answer to the question is not particularly important; what is important is that the partner keep talking so that the conversation is maintained. When men ask a question, usually it is a request for information—period. Thus, Jill asks a question of Jack, hoping that he will converse, but he answers it and stops talking. Jack asks Jill a question, hoping that she has an answer, but she takes it as an invitation to just talk. No wonder men sometimes complain that women don't get to the point, and women complain that men think they know the answer to everything! (Obviously, women *sometimes* ask questions because they want an answer, and men *sometimes* ask questions just to stimulate conversation. The differences we have described are differences in general *tendencies*, for which there are exceptions. The same is true of the other male-female differences we discuss.)

Along the same lines, men and women have different assumptions about **topic shifts** in conversation. Women often are less concerned about having a specific topic of conversation. The topic develops and emerges gradually, in somewhat vague terms, and it shifts gradually. The topic is less important than the communion. Men have a greater tendency to focus on one narrow topic at a time, finish with it, then shift clearly to the next specific topic or issue. Usually their talk must be *about* something. Thus, when a male and a female converse, he will sometimes perceive her as unable to "see the point" or unable to "get to the point." And as he keeps trying to return to "the point," she will sometimes perceive him as selfishly dominating the direction of the conversation.

Men and women also have different conventions for beginning a **conversational turn**. Women tend to follow a rule by which one explicitly acknowledges what the partner has just said, sometimes by making a transitional connection to it, when beginning one's turn in a conversation. Men have no such rule. It is acceptable for a male turn to begin with no reference to the preceding comments. In male-female conversation, her linking her comments back to what he has just said is not a particular problem, although her token links will sometimes seem illogical to him. His failure to link back to what she has said may be more of a problem, however. She will often interpret this to mean that he wasn't listening to her. When researchers interrupt conversations at random points, and quiz participants on what their partner has said during the conversation, it turns out that males and females listen equally well, regardless of the gender of their conversation partner.[2] But to the women, male partners do not *appear* to be listening as well as female partners.

Another male-female difference involves *verbal aggressiveness* of various kinds—friendly insults, teasing, challenges, interruptions, and so forth. With males, verbal aggressiveness indicates closeness and bonding, since these messages are acceptable only between males who have become fairly close and comfortable with one another. A male can say, "Shut up, baldy" to a close friend, for example, but cannot do so with a male he has just met. Thus, as a male becomes more comfortable with a particular female, he sometimes uses these familiar "friendly" **verbal aggression** devices. Very often the woman may be insulted or offended, or may think of the man as rude, since women's norms for friendly conversation do not include these verbal aggression devices.

A particularly critical difference in male and female norms comes from assumptions about **problem sharing**. When a male tells someone about a problem he is experiencing, he is usually looking for suggested solutions. When a female tells someone about a problem she is experiencing, she is often expecting empathy and affirmation of her feelings. For the male, empathy is unnecessary; for the female, a solution often is secondary.

Deborah Tannen gives a nice example of this difference with a story of a woman who, while recovering from a breast lumpectomy, was concerned about the cosmetic effects of the surgery and also about feelings of having been "invaded" by the procedure.[3] When she mentioned this to her husband, his response was to assure her that the scarring was minor, that it certainly did not affect his attraction to her, and that it was cosmetically insignificant. He also assured her that if the scarring really mattered to her, he would be glad to get her whatever cosmetic surgery was necessary to eliminate it. Her sister, on the other hand, assured the woman that her feelings were quite natural and justifiable, and that she understood and could identify with these feelings based on a similar experience.

Male and female readers tend to have quite different reactions to this story. Men tend to view the husband's response as close to perfect and the sister's response as fairly lame. Women, on the other hand, tend to view the husband's response as missing the mark by a mile and the sister's response as right on target!

It should be easy to see how these different approaches can cause difficulties when males and females mention their problems to each other. Suppose that he mentions a problem he is experiencing, hoping that she has a solution. And suppose she responds by acknowledging that the situation is common, that his dilemma is understandable, and that she is sympathetic to his situation, but does not offer any insights to solving the problem. Might he feel, despite her good intentions, that his mentioning the problem to her was a frustrating waste of valuable time? Now, suppose that she mentions a problem she is experiencing, hoping to generate a conversation that will allow a discussion and reaffirmation of her feelings, yet he responds with a simple statement of his best idea for a solution. Might she feel that he is closed and just doesn't care?

Males and Females Tend to Have Different Expectations For

✓ The general function of communication

✓ Positive minimal responses

✓ Replies to questions

✓ Topic shifting

✓ Turn-taking transitions

✓ Verbal aggressiveness

✓ Responses to problem sharing

Adjusting to the other gender's approach to problem sharing is especially difficult for males. It is counterintuitive for him to stop what he is doing and discuss her feelings when she mentions a problem for which, to him, the solution is "obvious." But empathic conversation is appreciated by her and may be surprisingly enriching for him. By the same token, despite her best intentions when she reacts to his problems with empathy, suggested solutions will sometimes be more appreciated.

Reflecting on Stereotypes. For most of these differences in male-female communication behaviors, we can see the influence of the patterns that begin to develop in childhood. Some of the stereotypes mentioned at the beginning of this section can now be seen in a new light. Our discussion has pointed out the source of some of these stereotypes, and it is wise to reflect upon others that may be similarly unfair.

GENERAL INTERCULTURAL DIFFICULTIES[4]

As we said earlier, this discussion of male-female communication serves to identify not only some of the cross-gender difficulties we face regularly, but also common barriers to communication in other intercultural situations. One common intercultural barrier, for example, is that we often *do not anticipate* intercultural differences. We tend to assume that our way of doing and viewing things is human nature, and thus we overestimate the universality of our norms. Just as males often assume incorrectly that females want answers when they ask questions, or females sometimes assume incorrectly that males' positive minimal responses are encouraging them to keep talking, the assumption that other people are like ourselves is normal but naive when we are communicating across different cultures.

● **TRY THIS**

Take a look at the typical female complaints about males, then use a template such as "Maybe men only *seem* this way to women, because _____" and fill in the blank with speculations about how differences in the genders' communication norms could give a false impression. Then do the same with the male stereotypes of women—"Maybe women only *seem* this way to men, because _____."

Do the same for additional opposite-sex stereotypes that you and/or your classmates generate. (To explain some of the stereotypes of both genders, it may be useful to look back at information in earlier chapters.)

Another common intercultural barrier is *language*. Errors can occur even when we try to adjust to obvious language differences. For example, a male professor on my campus, wanting to make a new female student from Japan feel welcome, learned to say "Pleased to meet you" in Japanese and greeted her with the phrase when they met. Unbeknownst to him, however, there are several variations of this greeting in Japanese, and the one he used is reserved for situations with blatant sexual overtones! In this case, a well-intentioned effort to overcome an obvious language barrier failed. Moreover, sometimes the language barrier isn't even obvious. As we saw with the male-female examples, even when we appear to be speaking the same language, cultural norms can distort the interpretation of our messages.

Yet another intercultural barrier is *stereotyped preconception*. One problem with stereotyping is that it denies our partner his or her individual uniqueness. As we discussed in an earlier chapter, stereotyping overemphasizes the assumed similarities among members of a group and hides their individuality. And as we saw with the male-female discussion, many stereotypes may be false to begin with.

Yet another difficulty with stereotypes is that they may, through a sort of self-fulfilling prophecy, *slant interactions in the direction of expectancies* established by the stereotype, and thus reinforce the stereotype. If Jill believes, for example, that men don't listen, she may avoid important issues in her conversations with Jack (and other males), saving those conversations for her female friends. If she never gives Jack a chance to listen on important matters, the stereotype is reinforced. Likewise, if Jack believes that women can't help to solve problems, never shares problems with Jill (or other women), and never gets to see her problem-solving competence, the stereotype is reinforced. Cultural stereotypes of a communication partner can lead our interaction in a direction that does not allow the partner to disprove the stereotype.

As for how we can avoid intercultural communication difficulties, there are no easy answers, for there are so many intercultural differences, and so many of them are subtle and unexpected. When we know of an intercultural encounter in advance, study and preparation are often possible, however. The U.S. traveler about to depart on a business trip to Istanbul can study differences in politeness norms, nonverbal behaviors, chronemic (time) assumptions, verbal expressions, and so forth in advance. So can the person from a rural Southern background who is about to take a new job on Wall Street. Advance study probably will not cover everything, but it can help. When friends, neighbors, colleagues, and others with whom we interact frequently have different cultural backgrounds, we need to be observant and tolerant of misunderstandings and social blunders, and to inquire about the possibility that cultural differences are responsible.

CONFLICT

One of the most disturbing of the communication dilemmas we will discuss is **hostile conflict**. For most of us, arguments and conflicts are unpleasant, especially when they are accompanied by anger or frustration, and especially when the conflicts are with friends, loved ones, colleagues, or others with whom we wish to have continued interaction. Yet it seems impossible to avoid conflict, even with those we most care for. This simple, common-sense observation—that conflict seems unavoidable, even with those we love—will be useful to keep in mind as we discuss conflict. We will see that conflict is indeed unavoidable. Thus the interpersonal-communication "objective" with respect to conflict is not so much to prevent conflict as to handle it in ways that do not damage our relationships.

BASIC ASSUMPTIONS (AND MISCONCEPTIONS) ABOUT CONFLICT

A useful way to get insights into communication and conflict is to contrast some of the assumptions of ordinary communicators with the assumptions made by conflict theorists. From the theorists' perspective, the lay public holds several misconceptions.[5]

Defining Conflict. Most of us think of conflict as tension-filled confrontations in which people square off against one another. Conflict theorists, however, would define conflict to include *any* expressed difference in beliefs or preferences, even the tamest and most friendly disagreements. With this definition, conflict may be thought of as a continuum. At one end of the continuum is a zone called **cooperative conflict**. Cooperative conflict is characterized by a mutual desire to see that all parties are satisfied. This "win/win" attitude usually leads to compromise, cooperation, and quick, tension-free resolution of the issue. In cases where the difference of opinion still exists, cooperative conflict often involves an "agree-to-disagree" approach, in which neither party has been persuaded, yet the difference in positions is simply understood and accepted. A middle zone of the conflict continuum is called **competitive conflict**, and the zone at the remaining end of the continuum is called **warfare**. Competitive conflict is characterized by a "win/may-lose" orientation, in which the object is one's own satisfaction, regardless of whether the other is satisfied. Warfare is characterized by a "win/must-lose" orientation, in which the object is to ensure both our own satisfaction and the other's dissatisfaction. Warfare sometimes includes a "no holds barred" or "winning at all costs" orientation, in which the participants use deception, dirty tricks, and unfair tactics to ensure their victory and/or the other's defeat. In short, the conflict continuum looks something like this:

LEVELS OF CONFLICT

COOPERATIVE CONFLICT	COMPETITIVE CONFLICT	WARFARE

There is an important moral to this interpretation of conflict—namely, that *conflict levels are attitudinal.* In large measure, what makes one conflict mean, nasty, and destructive, while another conflict is tame and inconsequential, is our *attitude* toward conflict in general, and toward each conflict in particular. The win/win and win/lose attitudes are *voluntary.*

Conflict Is Inevitable. Although some people prefer to believe that harmony is the natural state for human beings, conflict theorists emphasize that conflict is natural and inevitable. Since we are all different from one another, with different opinions, different tastes, different preferences, and so forth, it is only natural that any two individuals will experience conflicts on a regular basis. This is not necessarily bad news, however, since these conflicts can, if we wish, be handled at the cooperative level. To assume that conflict is natural and inevitable is not being cynical, just realistic. Rather than being alarmed at conflict ("This is terrible; my best friend and I are having a disagreement; there must be something wrong with me / him or her / the friendship"), it can be helpful to view conflict as something to be expected.

Communication Is a Dimension of Conflict. Contrary to popular belief, not all conflict arises from misunderstandings or poor communication. Sometimes we understand one another completely but simply disagree. However, communication certainly plays a crucial role in conflict. Some conflicts do arise from misunderstandings. Moreover, all conflicts are manifested by communication. That is to say, it is through what is said—or, as in the case of the "silent treatment," what is not said—that we know that a conflict exists in the first place. And it is through communication that conflicts are negotiated.

Conflicts May Be Destructive or Constructive.   It is no surprise that conflict can be destructive to relationships. After all, a perceived threat to the relationship is one of the reasons that competitive conflicts with friends and loved ones are so disturbing. Conflict theorists point out, however, that conflicts may be *constructive* also. With respect to the conflict *issue*, conflict is constructive when it leads to new solutions or compromises. A couple's conflicts over finances may lead to the discovery of new budgeting approaches, or investment approaches, or income sources, for example. And with respect to the *relationship*, conflict can be constructive in that working things out often brings people closer together. Research has shown, for example, that families are stronger when conflicts are discussed openly, and weaker when they are suppressed or ignored. The same is almost certainly true for other kinds of relationships.

The Object Is Not to Eliminate the Conflict.   It is perhaps natural, when we face a difficult conflict, to wish it would just go away and to look for ways to make it go away. Once in a while this approach will be effective, but usually it is naive. Conflict scholars suggest that we approach conflicts with the objective of *moving the conflict toward the cooperative-conflict end of the continuum*, rather than trying to eliminate the conflict entirely. In most cases, this is more realistic and more productive. Usually, it is OK for the difference in opinions, preferences, and so forth to remain if mutually satisfactory ways to manage these differences have been found. The assumption is that *any* movement toward the cooperative level of conflict is progress, but the more the better.

CAUSES OF ESCALATED CONFLICT

Usually, conflicts occur because of individual differences in opinion, preference, and taste. One person believes that the Democrats have the right answer, while another supports the Republicans' approach (opinion); one roommate wants to keep the new dog, while another wants to get rid of it (preference); Sue hates Joe's jazz tapes, and Joe hates Sue's Broadway show tunes (taste); and so on. However, when we ask not simply what causes conflict, but rather what causes people to *escalate* their differences to the competitive or warfare level (rather than operating at the cooperative level), the answers are less clear. A few common **causes of escalated conflict** have been identified, however.

Internal Conflict.   There are times when we become upset with ourselves. This may occur when we fail to live up to our own standards of competence or integrity, for example. People handle these situations in different ways, of course, but some have a tendency to displace their **internal conflict** onto others (somewhat as we discussed in Chapter 5). When a participant is experiencing internal conflict, an interpersonal conflict may escalate beyond its ordinary level.

Perceptions of Roles.   In relational units—colleagues, family members, lovers, friends, etc.—participants expect themselves and others to act according to **roles**. Roles are guidelines for how one is "supposed to act" within a relational unit. Often the role expectations are simply assumed rather than explicitly agreed upon, however. Problems can arise when people have different expectations for one another. For example, a long-running feud between two professors at a certain university began several years ago because of a misunderstanding regarding roles. Professor A invited Professor B to a graduate seminar one evening when the topic was to be one on which Professor B is an internationally recognized scholar. Professor B assumed that his role was to share his knowledge on the topic. Instead, he sat through the seminar listening to the students discuss their research on the topic. Professor A had assumed that Professor B might enjoy learning what the students (who were now in the role of instructor, with Professor B in the role of student) had to say. Professor B was insulted because his ego and/or time commitment could accept one role but not the other.

A variation on this theme may be seen in some of the conflicts between college students and their parents. Typically, the student is becoming more and more independent of his or her parents in certain ways, yet still is dependent upon them in certain other ways. The student tends to recognize and amplify the signs of independence, but to downplay the contradictory signs of dependence (bringing the laundry home to Mom, borrowing the "good car" from Dad, etc.). The parents tend to amplify the signs of dependence (they are, after all, in no hurry to "let go") and downplay the signs of independence (all the various ways in which the student is managing his or her own affairs). Clashes often arise over whether the parents have "the right" to "make demands" (e.g., "You have to be here for dinner with Aunt Hilda on Friday; after all, you're only going to be home for a few days and that'll be the only chance for her to see you"). From the independence point of view, the parents don't have the right to make demands; from the dependence point of view, they do.

Differences in Values. Role expectations are difficult to compromise on, because violations in this area upset our basic view of "the way things are supposed to be." The same is true of conflicts arising from differences in **values**. Values are nonfactual beliefs and opinions about what is normal and proper. Often, however, our values are so deeply ingrained that we tend to see our own opinion as the only reasonable opinion, or even as fact.

Suppose, for example that in a typical suburban neighborhood with well-manicured lawns, there is one neighbor who never waters, never mows, and just lets nature take its course. And suppose that this "natural look" is what the neighbor truly prefers. We can imagine that the large majority of the neighborhood will consider this approach to be "wrong." But as with all differences in values, that is a matter of opinion, not of fact. The same is true of more typical conflicts over such things as whether it is mandatory to clean up the dishes immediately, whether and how soon borrowed items must be returned to their "proper" place, whether it is appropriate for roommates to have guests stay over unannounced, and so forth. If we view our values as fact, then agreeing to disagree, compromising, and other elements of cooperative conflict become elusive.

Emotional Immaturity. We mentioned earlier that the difference between cooperative, competitive, and warfare levels of conflict is largely attitudinal. And we mentioned in Chapter 5 that adopting the proper attitude in dealing with communication dilemmas is sometimes a matter of emotional maturity. Certainly this is true when attempting to manage conflict.

It is important that we keep our emotions in check when we experience conflict. Some people are better at this than others. Those who become defensive too easily, who are prone to believe that others are always against them, who believe that they are always right, who must always have their way, and so forth, have a couple of strikes against them when trying to manage conflict. As we go through a list of conflict-management suggestions, notice that getting one's ego out of the way and controlling emotions are basic requirements in several cases. Indeed, it takes a bit of emotional maturity even to decide that one *wants* to employ these conflict-management devices.

CONFLICT-MANAGEMENT SUGGESTIONS

Depending on the particular conflict situation, one or more of the following suggestions may be helpful.

Understand the Conflict Phenomenon. Identifying the cause(s) of escalated conflict and recalling the basic assumptions and misconceptions about conflict can be helpful in some situations. Perhaps most important is to remember that the objective of conflict is to keep it at, or to move it toward, the cooperative level.

Anticipate Conflict Situations in Advance. Common sources of conflict in most kinds of relationships are well known. In marriages, for example, these include finances, household duties, how often to visit each spouse's parents, and so forth. Among roommates, common sources of conflict include visits by boyfriends/girlfriends or other guests, new pets, fair division of rent and utility bills, late payment of bills, cleaning up, borrowing clothes and other items, and so on. Rather than waiting until the conflict situation actually arises, which sometimes will put one person in an implicitly defensive position (the one who spent "too much," the one whose boyfriend stayed over last night, etc.), it can be helpful to discuss these situations in advance. We are not suggesting a written contract, or a list of demands, or a discussion of all imaginable situations. But it can be helpful to have an occasional conversation along the lines of, "How do you think we ought to handle it if and when . . .," or an occasional conversation of the type, "How would you feel if . . . " in anticipation of conflict situations.

Consider Timing. There are relatively good and relatively poor times to discuss conflicts. One guideline is to allow *sufficient* time for discussion. Beginning a conflict discussion when one partner is late for a class or an appointment is almost certain be unproductive, for example. A second guideline is to pick a time when emotions are cooled down, so that rational discussion can occur. It is sometimes advisable, for example, to mention a conflict issue the first or second time it comes up, when it is "no big deal"—yet. We are not suggesting that you become a nag by mentioning everything that you find bothersome. Rather, we are advising against your staying silent while growing increasingly irritated as a conflict-causing situation is repeated. Putting off discussion of the problem often allows the emotional interference to grow out of proportion.

On the other hand, when intense emotions accompany a conflict situation, whether it is an initial or a repeated occurrence, it is often advisable to delay discussion until the emotions have subsided. This is the familiar "count-to-ten" recommendation. When emotions are high, it is sometimes

If this person wants to resolve conflict, then what is wrong with this picture?

better to wait a few seconds, or even a few hours, before addressing the issue (so long as the time is not spent plotting to escalate the conflict). The essence of **timing** in interpersonal conflict management is to discuss the conflict at a time when emotions are not running high, and when there is sufficient time for a complete rational discussion.

Attack the Problem, Not the Person. When dealing with conflict, it is wise to deal with only one or two issues at a time. It is important that we be specific about the behavior, attitude, or other issue involved, and it is especially important that we make this the target of our remarks rather than targeting the partner personally. For example, "I'd like to talk about some problems I'm having with your new dog," *not*, "You were really inconsiderate to bring that stupid dog here." Or, "About that mess in the kitchen last night . . . ," *not*, "You're such a disgusting slob. . . ." And so forth.

● **TRY THIS**

For a nice example of the need to recognize our own role in our conflicts, see Figure 7.1 (on the following page). In this student's description of a particular conflict, it is apparent that she does not recognize her own part in creating the problem. Imagine how the conflict might have played out differently had she acknowledged her own errors much earlier.

Take Part of the Blame. One of the general goals in effective conflict management is to reduce the defensiveness of the conflict partner. And one of the most effective ways to reduce the partner's defensiveness is to acknowledge ways in which we are partially to blame for the conflict situation. Did we lead our partner to believe that the behavior we are protesting was acceptable? Are we being hypocritical by protesting something of which we are sometimes guilty ourselves? Did we encourage the behavior we are protesting by not mentioning our concern the first few times it happened? Are we simply hypersensitive with respect to the particular issue at hand?

In Chapter 5 we discussed the notion of owning the problem. The idea was that when other people's behaviors bother us, our reaction is due as much to the kind of person we are (the kind who is especially bothered by that particular behavior) as it is to the behavior itself. Owning the problem—chalking it up to our own quirks rather than to the partner's faults—can be very helpful in taking the partner out of a defensive position, and thus very helpful in managing conflict.

Seek and Accept Compromise. If the primary objective in conflict management is to ensure that conflict operates at the cooperative level, then it should be obvious that seeking compromise is crucial. There are a few counterproductive approaches to compromise, however. One of these is insincere compromise. For example, conflict management is not likely to be effective if one's version of "agree to disagree" is, "I'll *pretend* that he or she is entitled to that opinion, but anyone with that opinion is an idiot," or some such. Likewise insincere is "compromise" in which the attitude is, "I'll give a little if they give a lot," "I'll pretend to compromise, but I don't really mean it," and the like.

Another counterproductive approach to compromise is to single-handedly decide in advance on the compromise conditions. Often with good intentions, one conflict partner may work out an acceptable arrangement alone, then present it to the other partner as a solution to the conflict issue. Even if the arrangement is reasonable, the receiving partner may feel as if he or she is being pressured or controlled. It is usually more productive for conflict partners to discover workable compromises together through discussion.

Conflict Management Depends in Part Upon

✓ Understanding the nature of conflict

✓ Anticipating conflict situations

✓ The timing of conflict discussions

✓ Owning the problem

✓ Seeking compromise

Dear Doc,

1   In February I became good friends with Jan. We really started
2   spending a lot of time together. I always found it odd that she would try to
3   pay for everything, and I tried to keep it pretty even by paying for things also.
4   On a Thursday (last month) she had asked me if I wanted to go to a concert
5   that Sunday. I said "I don't know, but it sounds good. I need to know what
6   time it is so I can see if I can make it." Jan said "No problem. I'll look it up
7   in the Calendar." She mentioned it one more time the next day and I said the
8   same thing to her. I didn't hear anything else from her and I also lost
9   interest in going and had made plans for all of Sunday afternoon and
10   evening. Sunday morning I was talking to her and she said, "Oh, I need to
11   get the tickets for the concert, I'll talk to you later." At that point, since I had
12   never said, "yes, I'll go," I assumed that she was not planning on me
13   attending. She calls back and says "I bought the tickets. We got great seats
14   for only $35." At that point I was too shocked to say anything and I got the
15   information on the tickets.
16   I called her back to say I wasn't going, and she basically got super irate
17   and hung up on me. She then proceeded to call my ex-boyfriend and told him
18   how I flaked on her and I had definitely said, "yes I'll go." Also, she
19   complained to him that I never had any money and she felt she always had to
20   pay for everything. This is simply not the case. I always had the money, but
21   she would always pay before I had the chance to interject. The only time I
22   wouldn't have enough money is when I thought we wouldn't be going out,
23   and I would ask if we could stop at an ATM, and she would always say no. I
24   don't really understand how she could have gotten the money thing
25   confused.
26   Also she had a bunch of my things. I gave her a couple of weeks to cool
27   down, and then I asked for their return. When I got the stuff, two compact
28   discs and two books were missing. In their place was a ticket to the concert.
29   Maybe she just forgot those particular CD's, although I doubt it because she
30   loved both of them. I want my things back. I understand that she's out $35,
31   but I don't feel I should have to pay for her mistake.
32   Basically I want these problems addressed:
33   (1) Should I tell her how hurt and angry I am that she would say those
34   things to my ex? Or is that just water under the bridge since we aren't
35   friends?
36   (2) How do I go about getting my belongings back? CD's aren't cheap
37   and the two novels were my favorites and one of them is out of print.
38   This is a major crisis for me right now and I would like to have this read
39   in class ASAP!

FIGURE 7.1
Is the Letter-Writer Partly to Blame?

Did the letter-writer play a role in creating this conflict? Once the conflict began, might she have controlled it better by recognizing and acknowledging her errors? For her role in the concert misunderstanding, see lines 5, 7–8, 8–10, 11–13, and 14. For her role in the frugality issue, see lines 3, 21, and 23.

It is sometimes helpful also to recognize that compromise does not always require a perfectly even 50/50 sacrifice by the partners. Often compromise can be completely acceptable—and certainly preferable to competitive conflict—even if we give a bit more than our partner does.

Compared to conflict and intercultural communication difficulties, telling the truth may not seem to present a serious dilemma. After all, most of us consider ourselves to be generally truthful with little effort. Research has shown repeatedly, however, that people lie much more than they realize. This suggests that telling the truth is often problematic. For example, one study determined that 61.5 percent of the statements made by college students during their important conversations were not completely true.[6] According to another study, most people exaggerate, bend the truth, distort the truth by omitting relevant information, or simply lie more than thirty times per day.[7]

DECEPTION—AN INDICATOR OF COMMUNICATIVE AWKWARDNESS

Communication scholars have responded to the high frequency of interpersonal deceptions in various ways. One approach—the one we prefer and will pursue in the following discussion—reasons that most lies are attempts to avoid a difficulty that is anticipated as a consequence of telling the truth. That is, lies provide an easy way out of certain awkward communication situations. Thus, one goal of improving communication is to find effective ways of telling the *truth* while avoiding the potential consequences. Lying, after all, requires very little communicative skill. In our discussion of **deception**, we will highlight a few of the common situations in which people tend to lie. In most cases, we will see that there are alternative messages that are more truthful but at the same time avoid the problems that lies are designed to avoid.

● TRY THIS

As an exercise, you may wish to keep a log of the lies that you tell in a one- or two-day period. Most students approach this task believing that they will find few examples, and then are amazed at the number of lies, especially "little ones," they utter per day.

As for what constitutes a lie, two features are commonly agreed upon:[8] (1) The message distorts what the sender believes to be the truth. Whether the message is actually true is secondary. For example, if I say, "Let's cancel the picnic plans; it's going to rain," it is a lie if I heard and believed a forecast for sunshine. Whether it in fact rains is beside the point. (2) The sender assumes that the receiver will not easily discover the sender's version of the truth. Although this is debatable, some people will not consider a false message to be a lie if the sender knows or plans that the receiver will soon discover the truth. For example, suppose that as you arrive at your chemistry class, the classmate sitting next to you says, "There's going to be a pop quiz at the beginning of the period today." Then about five minutes after class begins, the same student passes you a note saying, "Ha, ha. Just kidding!" Since the sender knew that you would soon discover the truth, we might consider this to be a practical joke rather than a lie.

While these objective criteria may be used to decide what constitutes a lie, the question of what constitutes a little lie or a big lie is much more subjective. As a general rule, people rate lies as being more serious when there is a *tangible* gain for the sender and/or loss for the receiver. But there are gray areas. Almost everyone agrees that B and C below are "bigger" lies than A, for example, but there is disagreement about B versus C. Some people consider B worse than C, and others consider them to be equal.

A. "My friend asked me how I liked his new car. I thought it was a piece of junk, but I told him I thought it was really nice."

B. "I told this guy his car needed a valve job when it only needed a tune-up. I got $350 for a $50 job [and pocketed the extra $300]."

C. "I told the insurance company that all the estimates on my car were around $1,500. Actually, I found one place that would do it for $1,200. I got the check for $1,500 and took it to the less expensive place [pocketing the extra $300]."

The deception we will be discussing is of the more innocent variety—so-called white lies. While most of us agree that lies such as B and C above are unethical, many would consider "little" lies such as A to be completely acceptable. Our approach will be to concede that there will be times when small lies may seem socially appropriate, but that there are preferred alternatives in most cases.

COMMON DECEPTION SITUATION 1: AVOIDING CONFLICT[9]

One of the most common rationales for lies is to *avoid conflict* that we anticipate if we were to tell the truth instead. Examples A and B below are fairly typical.

A. "I told my mother I paid less for a new dress than I actually paid. The truth would have started an argument."

B. "I told my neighbor that I remembered to feed her cats while she was away. Actually, I forgot to feed the cats. I lied because I didn't want her to get mad."

Lies to avoid conflict are prime examples of the concept that *lying is* **mutually negotiated.** This means that although the sender of a deceptive message is guilty of lying, the receiver—because of his or her anticipated reaction to the truth—is partially responsible for the lie. Thus, if the mother in example A above or the neighbor in example B has a history of losing her temper over transgressions like the ones that were lied about, we could say that she was partially responsible for "forcing" the sender to lie.

The notion that lying is mutually negotiated is important to remember—not because it gives us an excuse when we are the sender of a lie, but because it adds an additional perspective when we are the *receiver* of a lie, especially a "white lie." It suggests that if we wish to be the kind of parent who is not lied to, the kind of boss who is not lied to, the kind of friend who is not lied to, and so forth, then we need to be the kind of parent, boss, or friend who handles the unpleasant truth in ways that do not make people regret telling it to us.

The fact that lies to avoid conflict are very common emphasizes that people feel discomfort in conflict situations. The suggestions we made earlier for dealing with conflict situations will, in some cases, provide viable alternatives to deception.

COMMON DECEPTION SITUATION 2: SAVING FACE FOR THE SENDER

Another common lie situation occurs when the sender fears that the truth will make him or her "lose face," or appear less competent or desirable to others. Examples A to C below are typical.

A. "I'm doing really well in French class. I told my French teacher that I haven't had much French. Actually, I had two years of French in high school and lived in France for two years after that. But this way she thinks I'm really smart."

B. "I was telling someone about this white-lie project. I said that I would have serious problems collecting white lies because I don't lie that much. Actually, I knew that I already had plenty of examples, but I wanted to keep a positive image."

C. "I told some friends that I couldn't go with them to San Francisco for the weekend because my parents were coming up for a visit. The truth is that I didn't have the money to go [but didn't want them to know that]."

Lies of this sort are variations of the masks and façades we discussed in Chapter 5. Façades are devices for hiding aspects of our true selves—acting more competent than we really are, more composed than we really are, and so forth. On the one hand, we could argue that the façades in examples A to C are harmless. But on the other hand, it is easy to argue that they are unnecessary. After all, it is doubtful that the truth would have had practical or social consequences in any of these cases. (Review examples A to C and see for yourself.) As we discussed in Chapter 5, façades become less frequent as we develop, and become more accepting of, our self.

COMMON DECEPTION SITUATION 3: AVOIDING REQUESTS AND DEMANDS

A common situation in which lying occurs is when others make requests or demands with which we do not wish to comply. Where the truth is "I don't want to," the response is a lie taking some form of "I can't." Examples like A and B below are familiar to most of us. Chances are that the desired state of affairs could have been negotiated simply by telling the truth.

A. "I told my manager I could work only two hours that day because of exams. Actually I wanted to be at an election party in two hours."

B. "I told my mother that I didn't have time to clean my room. The truth was, I just didn't want to."

In one study of white lies by college students, one of the most common types of lie was told by women in turning down requests for dates.[10] For example:

C. "I told him I couldn't go out that weekend because my sister was visiting. Actually, I don't have a sister; I just didn't want to go out with him."

D. "I told him that I had to study, but the truth was that I didn't want to go anywhere with him."

Lies such as these are curious in light of research on male and female preferences concerning the truth.[11] College students were asked, via questionnaire: "Imagine that you ask someone for a date. The truth is that he or she doesn't want to go on this, or any other, date with you. Would you rather: A. *He or she tells you the truth* (e.g., 'I really appreciate you asking me, but no, I don't really want to go with you.'); or, B. *He or she lies by implying that he or she would like to go on the date but is unable to* (e.g., 'I can't go this weekend, because [false excuse]')." Of the male participants, 90 percent said that they would prefer the truth, and only 10 percent preferred the lie. Of female participants, however, 80 percent said that they would prefer the lie, and only 20 percent preferred the truth. Thus, when women tell lies to get out of dates, they are doing so partially because that is what they would prefer if the circumstances were reversed; not realizing that the lie is unnecessary because most males prefer the truth. The male preference for the unpleasant truth is probably a combination of having learned to accept being turned down for dates and a desire to simplify the list of prospective dates. (In other words, if Ruth says, "I'd love to, but I can't," and then Betty says, "I'd love to; pick me up at 7:00," he feels an obligation to get back to both Betty and Ruth next week. That's fine if Ruth meant it, but a waste if she didn't.)

COMMON DECEPTION SITUATION 4: SAVING FACE FOR THE RECEIVER

The final deception situation we will discuss (although there are a few others) is that in which the purpose of the lie is to save face for the receiver. The rationale for the lie is concern that the truth would hurt the receiver's feelings. The following are typical:

A. "My roommate introduced me to her boyfriend and asked me if I thought he was cute. I told her I thought he was real good-looking. He wasn't good-looking, but it made her happy."

B. "I told my roommate that her haircut looked great. Actually, it was much too short and made her look like a rodent, but it would've hurt her feelings to say so."

C. "I told my friend, 'That dress looks really good on you.' The dress didn't look that good. I didn't want to hurt her feelings."

> **Common Reasons for Telling "Small" Lies Include**
> ✓ Avoiding conflict with the receiver
> ✓ Saving face for the sender
> ✓ Avoiding tasks and demands
> ✓ Saving face for the receiver

Often lies such as these are told as an act of kindness. But it is worthwhile to reflect on whether the lie actually is kinder than the truth. Notice that in some of these situations, the "problem" (in the sender's view) that would be revealed by the truth is not easily fixed. In these cases, lies to save face for the receiver are more clearly kind. For example, in B above, giving a more honest opinion about the roommate's haircut would accomplish very little, since hardly anything can be done about it until the hair grows back. Some communication scholars would argue that in **repairable situations**, however, telling the truth may be kinder than telling a lie. For example, in C above, the problem is easily fixed, since the roommate can change into a different dress. Assuming that the sender's opinion of the dress is a reasonably typical opinion, it might actually be kinder to tell the truth about the dress so that the receiver could at least consider wearing a different one.

Research suggests that as *receivers,* most people would rather hear the truth in a situation where an acquaintance wishes to offer constructive criticism or other information that is unpleasant to hear.[12] Yet as senders, people are reluctant to offer such information and often opt for a deceptive message instead of the truth. If receivers indeed prefer the truth, however, then the lie is not necessarily kinder.

ASSERTIVENESS VIA TACTFULNESS

The lie situations discussed above occur when people are likely to feel awkward about saying what they would like to say—something that might initiate a conflict, hurt the receiver's feelings, and so forth. And elsewhere in the book we have discussed other situations in which people are reluctant to say what they wish—initiating contact with others, self-disclosure situations, and so forth.

Indeed, there are many situations in which we may hesitate to say what is on our mind. But Americans tend to believe that we are entitled to express our thoughts and feelings. Thus, communication scholars stress the importance of **assertiveness** in communication. Assertiveness is the expression of (as opposed to the suppression of) one's wants, needs, thoughts, and feelings.

One approach to instruction in assertiveness is to treat the absence of assertiveness as a personality trait, and to simply encourage nonassertive types to be more forthright.

This approach emphasizes that it is important to ensure that assertiveness stops short of **aggressiveness,** which is the expression of one's wants, needs, thoughts, and feelings *without regard for others'.* A second approach to assertiveness is the one we have taken in this and other chapters. We have examined specific situations in which everyday communicators often feel awkward. We have tried to alleviate the awkwardness by correcting counterproductive misconceptions about the situation, or by providing effective communication options, or both. The assumption is that communicators become more appropriately assertive when they understand the situation and have a repertoire of effective communication strategies for dealing with it.

While we have assumed this approach to assertiveness throughout the book, we wish to use the topic of **tactfulness** as an explicit example of the point that reluctance to express oneself in particular situations may disappear as one becomes more facile with effective communication strategies for the situation.

TACTFULNESS AND TACTLESSNESS[13]

Tact refers to consideration of others' "face" and feelings when forming communication messages. Tactless messages have negative effects on receivers' face and/or feelings, and tactful messages avoid these negative effects.

Tactless messages are those which cause accidental or unintended loss of face, hurt feelings, embarrassment, etc., to the receiver. (Messages designed to intentionally hurt others are simply mean, not tactless.) Typically, **tactlessness** occurs when the sender has a negative thought regarding the receiver and says something that accidentally leaks that thought. For example:

A. "That's a brilliant observation for someone with your image."

B. "What? You mean that *you* can wear a *small?*"

Sometimes the sender does not realize that his or her prejudicial stereotypes or other negative thoughts apply to the receiver, as in C to E.

C. Sender: "Yeah, but jocks are so dumb" [not realizing that the receiver was on the football team].

D. Sender: "Anyone who gets married before age twenty-one is really stupid." [Receiver: "Well, I got married at seventeen and I've been married twenty-two years."]

E. Sender [to a parent at a youth-league soccer game]: "The problem isn't the kids, it's the coaching." [Unbeknownst to the sender, the receiver was the coach.]

A less frequent but still troublesome form of tactlessness occurs when the sender does *not* have a negative thought regarding the receiver, yet a negative thought is inferred by the receiver. For example:

F. "Wow, you look great tonight!" [Receiver interpreted this to mean that her looking good was unusual.]

G. [After class in late October, on a campus where a Haunted House was the major campus event] Him: "Where ya going?" Her: "To the Haunted House." Him: "It figures." [He was trying to be friendly, and simply meant that practically everybody was going there. She thought he meant that she *belonged* in a haunted house.]

We all stick our foot in our mouth via tactless remarks from time to time. Since tactlessness is accidental, there is little to offer in the way of advice beyond the general admonition to think before you speak. A micro-moment's reflection might have changed comment F above to, "Wow, you look even better than usual," or G to, "Isn't everyone? May I join you?" A split second of reflection might have realized the absurdity of the prejudice in C and D, might have edited A into simply, "That's a brilliant observation," and so forth.

For *tactfulness,* more specific strategies are available. Tactfulness is an intentional effort to edit a message so as to avoid negative feelings on the part of the receiver. There is something we want to say—a criticism or other information—that is likely to be unwelcome to the receiver, and we make a conscious effort to construct a diplomatic version of the message. One approach to tactfulness highlights four levels.

Level 1 Tactfulness. We have already seen situations in which attempts at tactfulness are common, namely the situations in which people tell lies to *save face for the receiver.* Indeed, the lie is a common tact strategy. It is tactful, since it avoids hurt. But it is nonassertive because it denies our own point of view. That is to say, it does nothing to change the "problem" that would have been addressed by the truth. This characterizes simple Level 1 tact: *hurt is avoided,* but the problem is not manipulated. This version of tactfulness is done via white lies (A below), via intentional ambiguity (B and C), and by deflecting the focus of attention (D).

A. Thought: "That dress is bad." —> Message: *"It's nice."*
B. Thought: "My roommate's term paper is awful." —> Message: *"Your paper is interesting."*
C. Thought: "That hat is awful." —> Message: *"That's quite a hat."*
D. Thought: "That dress is out of style and doesn't fit." —> Message: *"I like the color."*

Level 2 Tactfulness. The next level of tactfulness still tries to avoid hurt (as in Level 1), but it also tries to *manipulate the problem.* It differs from the subsequent levels in that it tries to manipulate the problem without revealing the problem. However, since the problem is not actually revealed, it is likely to resurface in the future. Thus, while Level 2 is more assertive than Level 1 (which did not even attempt to manipulate the problem), it is less assertive than the subsequent levels. For example:

A. [Committee Chair] Thought: "Speak up, George, you haven't contributed anything." —> Message: *"George, we'd be interested in your opinion."*
B. [Instructor, during group-discussion project] Thought: "Eve, everything you've said has been irrelevant." —> Message: *"Eve, you've made some interesting comments about evolution and creationism, but we don't know how you feel about euthanasia."*
C. [Dinner host, when dessert menus arrive, hoping guest will not order one] Thought: "My dinner partner should be dieting instead of eating these desserts." —> Message: *"My gosh, these desserts are terribly overpriced."*

Level 3 Tactfulness. At the next level of tactfulness, the sender attempts to avoid hurt (as in Levels 1 and 2) and manipulate the problem (as in Level 2), but now *the problem is revealed.* What is *not* revealed is that the problem exists between the sender and the receiver. There are two common approaches. One is to deny that the *sender* views the situation as a problem. Usually this is done by attributing the perception that this is a problem to some other authority, as in A and B below. The other approach is to deny that the *receiver* has the problem. Usually this is done by referring to a real or hypothetical person with the same problem (or solution), as in C and D below.

A. Thought: "Your smoke is bothering me and I wish you'd put out the cigarette" —> Message: *"Excuse me, but they don't allow smoking in here."*

B. Thought: "I hate it when you come into my store trying to sell me insurance" —> Message: *"There's a company policy against soliciting,* so I can't talk about it."

C. Thought: "I wish he'd be more romantic" —> Message: *"I love it when guys send flowers and write poems and stuff like that."*

D. [Jazz quartet leader to substitute drummer] Thought: "You play much too loudly." —> Message: *"The guy you're filling in for has a big-band style that was way too loud for a combo."*

At Level 3, assertiveness has increased, but only slightly. When the sender denies that he or she views the situation as a problem, the receiver may assume that the sender accepts the behavior even if others do not (A and B), and when the sender denies that the receiver has the problem, the receiver may not take the hint (C and D).

Level 4 Tactfulness. In the final level of tactfulness, Level 4, the sender attempts to avoid hurt, manipulate the problem, reveal the problem, and *place it within the context of the sender and receiver.* (Figure 7.2 summarizes the dimensions added at each level of tactfulness.) Level 4 comes very close to "telling it like it is," yet still employs devices to soften the blow and avoid hurting the receiver.

Telling it like it is is what we are shying away from when we use lies and other lower levels of tactfulness to present unpleasant information to others. Part of the reason we avoid this kind of assertiveness is that we are not quick enough on our feet to see ways to present the truth in a diplomatic way. We will explore some good ways momentarily. But another part of it has to do with basic assumptions about potentially hurtful remarks. It will be helpful to an understanding of Level 4 tactfulness—and perhaps assertiveness more generally—to examine these assumptions.

A common but questionable assumption is that there are only two options in situations requiring tact: either say something false but kind, or say something true but hurt-

	Avoid hurt	Manipulate problem	Reveal problem	Acknowledge sender/receiver context
LEVEL 1	√			
LEVEL 2	√	√		
LEVEL 3	√	√	√	
LEVEL 4	√	√	√	√

FIGURE 7.2
Cumulative Features at Four Levels of Tactfulness

ful. Notice that neither of these options requires very much communication skill. Perhaps that is why they are often the only options that come to mind. As you can probably guess, we are suggesting that there is a third, and preferable, option—namely, saying something true *and* kind. Independent of the specific strategies and examples we will be discussing, it is useful to recognize this third option as a basic choice in tact situations. After all, part of coming up with true but nonhurtful messages on the spot is knowing that the option exists and looking for ways to satisfy it.

A second assumption that is crucial to Level 4 tactfulness is that often the unpleasant truth helps more than it hurts. Consider the following scenario, for example: You are leaving your communication class after a round of speeches, and one of your classmates asks, "What did you think of my speech?" You thought the speech was awful, you are fairly certain that most of the class would agree, and you suspect that the instructor agrees. Which of the following should be your reply?

A.1 "You did great. I really liked it."
A.2 "It took guts to give a speech like that."
A.3 "It wasn't very good, but don't feel bad about it."
A.4 "It was terrible. You really did a bad job."

Options A.1 and A.2 avoid hurt with Level 1 tactfulness, but they are not really helpful. They encourage the classmate to make the same mistakes in future speeches, to oppose the instructor's grade and suggestions, and so forth. Options A.3 and A.4 are truthful and are probably hurtful, but at least they point out the presence of a problem. Consider one more option, however:

A.5 "To tell you the truth, it was really hard to follow. I can show you what I mean, if you like; or maybe I could help you organize your next one."

This response is truthful, and it attempts to help. Moreover the response is not likely to be hurtful (compared to A.3 and A.4) *because* it tries to be helpful. Combining honesty with a constructive attitude is critical to Level 4 tactfulness, and it requires an assumption that the unpleasant truth sometimes helps.

A third assumption concerns the role of criticism in established relationships. While comments that are merely hurtful devalue the relationship, helpful criticism can affirm the strength of the relationship. I once witnessed the following dialogue between a father and daughter, for example:

Daughter: *"Dad, you need to start going to the gym again."*
Father: *"Why, am I getting fat?"*
Daughter: *"Yep."*
Father: *"Maybe I shouldn't wear this shirt."*
Daughter: *"Dad, it's not the shirt!"*

Within solid relationships, constructive criticism does not imply that one is finding fault because the relationship is shaky. Rather, the freedom to offer constructive criticism proves the strength of the relationship.

Given these assumptions, Level 4 tactfulness becomes easier. A Level 4 strategy coming directly from these assumptions, for example, is the strategy of *emphasizing the constructive intent* of a negative message, as in example B.

B. Thought: "That's a horrible way to dress for a job interview." —> Message: "*I know this interview is important to you; I really think you'd make a better first impression if* you wore something a little more conservative."

Another convenient and simple Level 4 strategy is to *add several positive and complimentary points* to the negative "problem," as in example C. When we add positive comments, the effect is to say, "I'm not criticizing you in order to be negative, mean, or hurtful, because if I wanted to be hurtful, I wouldn't be laying on the positives." (It is better if the positives are sincere, of course.)

C. [To friend and director of a play, when asked for an opinion] Thought: "The acting was terrible." —> Message: "The acting was weak, *but the staging and lighting were fantastic.*"

Other Level 4 strategies may be seen in examples D to G. In D and E, the idea is to soften the blow by *acknowledging that the problem is a common one.* This approach can reduce the impression that the sender is blaming the receiver. In F and G, the idea is to anticipate the excuse the receiver is likely to offer and show understanding by *acknowledging the excuse* in the message.

D. [Boss to new secretary] Thought: "You're messing up the filing system." —> Message: "*Everyone who comes here gets this wrong at first, so I should have mentioned it,* but we file discipline cases by date, instead of by name."

E. [Professional jazz musician to amateur] Thought: "Your solos have no texture." —> Message: "You play too many notes, man. *All beginners do that, though. Heck, I did that myself at first.* Play fewer notes, and use more spaces; it'll give your solos more texture."

F. [Boss to employee] Thought: "He's late with the Jones account." —> Message: "*I realize how much other work I've given you lately,* but we really do need to finish the Jones account ASAP."

G. [Restaurant business partner] Thought: "Ordering these napkins was a mistake." —> Message: "*I know you were trying to save on expenses, and I'm all for that,* but let's not order these napkins any more. They're too small and they fade too easily."

TACT AND ASSERTIVENESS

In situations in which our version of truth would threaten the receiver with loss of face, there are three *easy* but often *unsatisfactory* solutions: we can keep our mouth shut, which is not at all assertive (though still advisable in some circumstances); we can lie, which likewise is not assertive (though perhaps sometimes appropriate); and we can speak the blunt version of the truth, which may be aggressive to the point of doing more harm than good. Obviously, these easy solutions have their shortcomings. Tactfulness often requires more skill, but the extra effort brings rewards. Usually it is possible to be assertive enough to ensure that we are true to ourselves, yet sufficiently diplomatic that the receiver's face and feelings are not sacrificed. Several approaches have been suggested above for reducing awkwardness, increasing assertiveness, and respecting the receiver in these situations.

> **● TRY THIS**
>
> As an enlightening exercise, you might wish to explore various message options with a few friends or classmates: Come up with situations in which the receiver could potentially lose face. Take turns as hypothetical senders and receivers. Discuss message options, and discuss how the receiver would probably feel, and subsequently behave, when hearing each of the messages in a real-life situation. For those instances in which silence or a lie seems to be preferred, try to identify the common factors—whether the situation is irreparable, repairable but trivial, and so forth.

IN SUMMARY

As we said at the outset, there are many different kinds of interpersonal communication dilemmas. This chapter has covered a few of the most common and problematic interpersonal communication difficulties.

In some communication dilemmas, we do not realize the problem until *after* the communication episode has occurred. These are the situations in which we find ourselves asking, "What went wrong?" Many intercultural communication difficulties, including male-female difficulties, manifest themselves after the fact, for example. In other cases, we realize *in advance* that we are having trouble constructing a message that will accomplish all of our communication goals. These are the situations in which we find ourselves asking, "How can I say what I want to say without making things worse?" The general conflict condition and the various white-lie and tact situations are examples of these premessage dilemmas.

TRY THIS

A worthwhile exercise, both for improving your own communication skill and for grasping the concepts in this chapter, is to write two "Dear Abby" letters. Write one letter about a recent situation you have experienced in which something went wrong communicatively, yet you are not certain exactly what caused the problem. End the letter by asking, "What went wrong?" Write a second letter about a current situation in which there is something you wish to say to someone, yet you have been avoiding saying it. End the letter with, "Should I tell him/her/them, and if so how should I say it?" If your letters are not too personal, ask classmates to play the Abby role with your letters while you play Abby with theirs. Otherwise, play Abby with your own. As for solutions to these dilemmas, look over the ideas suggested throughout this chapter. (In some cases, you may wish to consult earlier chapters, as well.)

TERMS TO KNOW

culture	internal conflict
intercultural	roles
positive minimal responses	values
topic shifts	timing
conversational turn	deception
verbal aggression	mutually negotiated (deception)
problem sharing	repairable situations
hostile conflict	assertiveness
cooperative conflict	aggressiveness
competitive conflict	tactfulness
warfare	tact
causes of escalated conflict	tactlessness

NOTES

1. Most of the discussion on male-female communication is based on D. Tannen, *You Just Don't Understand* (New York: Ballantine Books, 1990).

2. M. T. Motley and students. "Cumulative Pilot Studies, 1989–1997: RCM 105 and RCM 134" (unpublished paper, University of California at Davis, 1997).

3. Tannen, *You Just Don't Understand.*

4. This discussion of intercultural barriers is based loosely on L. Barna, "Intercultural Communication Stumbling Blocks," *Intercultural Communication: A Reader,* 2nd ed., eds. Larry Samovar and R. Porter (Belmont, Calif.: Wadsworth, 1976).

5. R. J. Doolittle, *Orientations to Communication and Conflict* (Palo Alto, Calif.: Science Research Associates, 1978).

6. R. E. Turner, C. Edgely, and G. Olmstead, "Information Control in Conversation: Honesty Is Not Always the Best Policy," *Kansas Journal of Sociology* 11 (1975): 69–89.

7. C. T. Camden, M. T. Motley, and A. Wilson, "White Lies in Interpersonal Communication: A Taxonomy and Preliminary Investigation of Social Motivations," *Western Journal of Speech Communication* 48 (1984): 309–325.

8. M. L. Knapp and M. D. Comadena, "Telling It Like It Isn't: A Review of Theory and Research on Deceptive Communication," *Human Communication Research* 5 (1979): 270–285.

9. Deception categories are from Camden, Motley, and Wilson, "White Lies in Interpersonal Communication."

10. Ibid.

11. Motley and students, "Cumulative Pilot Studies, 1989–1997."

12. Ibid.

13. This section is based mostly on M. T. Motley, "Mindfulness in Solving Communicator's Dilemmas," *Communication Monographs* 59 (1992): 304–314. Acknowledgments are due also to H. Weiginger, *The Critical Edge* (New York: Harper & Row, 1992), and to J. B. Bavelas, A. Black, N. Chovil, and J. Mullett, *Equivocal Communication* (Newbury Park, Calif.: Sage, 1990).

IMpRoVING CoMMUNICATION in SmALL GRoUPS

THIS CHAPTER will help you

- Understand the basic principles of group communication

- Develop some basic group problem-solving skills

- Understand your role and responsibilities as a group member

- Understand your role and responsibilities as a group leader

- Plan and conduct effective meetings

- Use parliamentary procedure for running formal meetings

NEVER DOUBT THAT A SMALL group of THOUGHTFUL, CONCERNED CITIZENS CAN Change the world. INDEED, IT'S THE ONLY THING THAT ever has.

—M. Mead

Many of the important communication interactions of your lives are conducted in small-group settings. In classes, you may be assigned to a project team to develop a presentation on some particular problem or area relevant to the class. At work, you may be assigned to a committee that is involved in planning for the future of the company. In your community, a problem may arise that can be solved only by the concerted efforts of people working together. In social organizations, you may be involved with others in planning activities that will affect all the members of the organization. The communication interactions in such settings involve both interpersonal and public communication skills.

In order to understand how group communication functions, we need to consider the nature of a group. Is any accumulation of people a group? Not necessarily. For example, an accumulation of people waiting for a bus would not be considered a group. To be considered a *group,* an accumulation of people must actively interact with one another over a period of time in order to reach a goal or goals. Let's suppose that the same people have been meeting at the bus stop every workday for several months. They may chat with one another while waiting for the bus, but this interaction is not enough to turn them into a group. Now, suppose that the Metropolitan Transit Organization (MTO) announces in the morning paper that it wants to raise fares from $1.00 to $2.50 each way for the trip from the bus stop to downtown. That morning, when the people get together, they begin to discuss with considerable outrage the problem of the increase in fares. One of the people at the bus stop suggests that they all get together at her apartment that evening at 7:00 to come up with a plan to try to get the MTO to reconsider its proposal. When these same people get together that evening, they will be interacting as a group. The remainder of this chapter will discuss how such groups function and how you can be a better participant or leader in such groups.

THE ADVANTAGES AND DISADVANTAGES OF GROUP PROBLEM SOLVING

If we listen to someone present information or make recommendations, we generally hear only one interpretation of a situation or problem. That perspective may be biased or based on self-interest, or it may simply be wrong. When vital issues are involved, we need to minimize the risk of such errors. One way to do this is to have a group of people investigate and analyze the problem, share information and perspectives, and make recommendations.

Group problem solving has many advantages. When people from different cultures share their various ways of seeing a problem, they enrich our understanding.[1] We begin to see the world through the eyes of others. This may help us see the blind spots in our own thinking—the biases and misconceptions with which we may be burdened. Listening to different points of view can stimulate creative thinking about the problems that surround us.

In well-run problem-solving groups, people on all sides of an issue have a chance to discuss the similarities and differences of their perspectives. Through discussion, they may discover some areas of agreement that can become the basis for resolving differences. Additionally, people are usually willing to examine their differences in small group meetings where they feel free to explore compromises or new options for action. For these reasons, organizations often use a small group approach to problem solving and decision making. In fact, it is estimated that approximately twenty million meetings take place each day in the United States.[2]

People who are physically close may not constitute a group. To be considered a group, the people must interact over time to reach a goal.

Although working in groups has many advantages, there are also some common problems that can make groups ineffective. **Cultural gridlock** can stand in the way of effective group deliberations. Cultural gridlock may occur in groups whose members have different racial or ethnic backgrounds or come from different professional backgrounds. For example, in an organization, people in marketing and lab-cloistered scientists may bring different expectations to a meeting. In addition, culturally diverse participants may bring different perspectives on a problem, different agendas, different priorities, different procedures, different ways of communicating, and different standards of protocol to meetings. These differences may cause tension and sidetrack constructive discussions.

Dealing with cultural gridlock is never easy, but there are some things you can do to minimize its impact:

- Allow time for people to get acquainted before getting down to the business of the meeting.
- Provide a comfortable environment. Keep in mind that there are cultural differences in personal space requirements. Be sure you have enough room so that people don't feel crowded.
- Distribute an agenda for the meeting that lets people know what to expect.
- Be aware of language problems. Summarize discussions. Post key points on a chalkboard, a markerboard, or a flip chart. Avoid slang or jargon that some participants may not understand.
- Be sensitive to cultural differences, especially differences of protocol and nonverbal communication. Learn as much as you can about such factors before the meeting.[3]

Another problem inherent in group problem solving is the potential for **groupthink**, or the development of a one-track, uncritical frame of mind that leads to poor decisions.[4] Groupthink is most likely to occur when groups value strong positive interpersonal relationships more than they value the ability to perform effectively.[5] Members of a group may try to avoid any semblance of conflict in the group, which can lead to poor decision making. Other major factors that contribute to the development of groupthink include a strong leader preference for a certain decision and the lack of a clear method or set of procedures for conducting deliberations. Groupthink is dangerous because outsiders may assume that a problem-solving group has deliberated carefully and responsibly when in fact it has not.

Dealing with groupthink can be difficult, but there are some steps that can be taken to guard against it. First, groups need to be aware that groupthink is a potential problem that can impede their effectiveness. This awareness should include knowing the major symptoms of groupthink:

- Putting pressure on those who argue against what most of the group believe
- Censoring one's own thoughts when they differ from group beliefs
- Maintaining an illusion of the group's invulnerability
- Reinforcing an unquestioned belief in the group's moral rightness
- Attempting as a group to rationalize behaviors and decisions

The problems in decision making that accompany groupthink include (1) incomplete consideration of objectives, (2) poor information retrieval and analysis, and (3) an incomplete consideration of alternative solutions.[6]

Once the group becomes aware that it has a potential groupthink problem, members can initiate actions to minimize its negative effects. First, they should set standards for "vigilant search and appraisal that counter collective uncritical thinking and premature consensus."[7] This suggests that they must have a systematic way to approach the problem.

Group leaders can also initiate actions to help counter groupthink. Such actions might include:

- Reminding participants to *critically evaluate* the deliberations and recommendations of the group.
- Holding off voicing their own opinions until others have expressed their views.
- Assigning different members the role of the "devil's advocate," who must ask tough, critical questions about all proposals and ideas.
- Bringing in outsiders to listen and talk with the group about the issues under consideration.
- Encouraging creative conflict in which the group attacks ideas and issues, but not people.

Without good leadership, groups can become aimless and unproductive. Ineffective leadership may be one reason why executives often complain that their meetings take too long and accomplish too little.[8] Leaders must remember that their task is to *lead* a group meeting, not to *run* it. We consider effective group leadership in greater detail later in this chapter.

> ● TRY THIS
>
> Think of a time when you were working in a group that became infected with groupthink. What kinds of problems did this cause? Was anything done to correct it? What would you do differently now? Share your insights with a classmate and discuss the similarities and differences between the situations you each related.

GROUP PROBLEM-SOLVING TECHNIQUES

Group deliberations that are orderly, systematic, and thorough help people reach high-quality decisions.[9] Problem-solving groups can use a variety of methods to achieve their goals.[10] To be effective, groups must decide how they will proceed to assure maximum fairness and efficiency.[11] As we noted earlier, a systematic approach to problem solving can also help forestall a group's tendency toward groupthink.

REFLECTIVE THINKING AND PROBLEM SOLVING

The approach we recommend for most problem-solving groups is a modification of the **reflective-thinking** technique first proposed by John Dewey in 1910.[12] This systematic approach has five steps: (1) defining the problem, (2) generating potential solutions, (3) evaluating solution options, (4) developing a plan of action, and (5) evaluating the results. The amount of time devoted to each of these steps depends on the depth and complexity of the problem.

Step 1: Defining the Problem. Groups often mistakenly assume that the problem assigned to them is the *real* problem. However, sometimes the assigned problem is only a symptom or just one aspect of the actual problem. Therefore, even if a problem seems obvious, the group needs to define it carefully before looking for solutions. Groups can consider the following questions to help define the actual problem:

1. What exactly is the nature of the problem? (Describe the problem as concretely and specifically as possible.)

2. Why has the problem occurred? (Explore all possible causes of the problem.)

3. What is the history of the problem?

4. Who is affected by the problem, and how serious are these effects?

5. If the problem is solved, will things automatically be better? Could things possibly become worse?

6. Do we have the information we need to understand the problem completely? If not, how and where can we get this information? (Do not go any further until this information is in hand.)

7. Have we defined and stated the problem so that everyone understands what the group will work on? (Do not go any further until such understanding is reached.)

Step 2: Generating Solution Options.   Once a group has determined the nature and extent of the problem, members can begin generating solutions. **Brainstorming** is a technique that encourages all members to contribute freely to the range of options. This technique can help stimulate ideas.[13] Brainstorming aims at producing a large number of potential solutions. It works best when there are twelve or fewer group members.[14] At this stage in the problem-solving process, members should not attempt to evaluate the options or to come to a decision on what option to follow.

The following rules of brainstorming should be communicated to group members: First, give free voice to any ideas that you have, no matter how outrageous they may seem. Even something that sounds absolutely outlandish may contain the germ of a great idea. Second, go for quantity—the more ideas generated for the group to consider, the better the results. Third, no one is allowed to criticize any suggestion during this idea-generating phase. Finally, combine different ideas to come up with additional options.

Brainstorming usually involves a six-step process:

1. The leader asks each member in turn to contribute an idea. If the member whose turn it is does not have an idea, that member passes.

Work groups often generate problem solutions by brainstorming options.

2. A group member writes down all the ideas on a flip chart, markerboard, or chalkboard so that everyone can see them.

3. Brainstorming continues until all members have offered all their ideas.

4. The list of ideas is reviewed. At this time, participants may ask for clarification, add new options, or combine ideas into other alternatives.

5. The participants go back over the list to identify the most useful ideas.

6. The group leader designates a person to receive additional ideas that members may come up with after the official meeting. These ideas may be added to the list for consideration during the next phase of the problem-solving process.

There are many variations of brainstorming that may be helpful for generating ideas.[15] When time for meetings is in short supply or when status differences in the group may stifle ideas, one alternative may be to engage in **electronic brainstorming** in which participants generate their ideas in real-time chat groups or through E-mail on computers before meeting face to face.[16]

Step 3: Evaluating Solution Options. If at all possible, the group should take a break between generating solution options and evaluating them. During that time, group members can gather information about the feasibility of each option and determine whether and how it has been used elsewhere. When the group meets again, it should discuss options, using the following questions as a guide:

1. How costly will this option be?
2. How likely is this option to be successful?
3. How difficult will it be to enact this option?
4. When could this option take effect?
5. Would this option solve the problem completely?
6. What additional benefits might this option produce?
7. What additional problems might this option cause?

Groups often use a flip-chart sheet to summarize the answers to these questions for each option. They then post these summaries so that members can refer to them as they compare options. As options are evaluated, some of them will seem weak and will be dropped. Other options may be strengthened and refined.

The group also may combine options to generate new alternatives. For example, if the group is caught between option A, which promises improved efficiency, and option B, which promises lower cost, it may be possible to generate hybrid option C, which combines the best features of both. This approach is similar to the SIL (Successive Integration of Problem Elements) method developed at the Battelle Memorial Institute, a nonprofit research and development think tank. The SIL method is a six-step process:

1. A group of four to seven people independently generate solution options.
2. Two of the members successively read one of their ideas to the group.
3. The group discusses ways to integrate the two ideas into one solution.
4. A third member reads an idea, and the group attempts to integrate this idea with solution generated in step 3.
5. The "add-an-idea" cycle continues until all of the participants' ideas have been read aloud and the group has tried to integrate them.
6. The process is complete when the group reaches a consensus on a solution.[17]

After each alternative has been thoroughly considered, participants should rank the solutions in terms of their acceptability. The option receiving the highest overall rank becomes the proposed solution.

During evaluation, the leader must focus the discussion on the ideas that have been put forth and not on participants. It is not unusual for group members to become personally caught up with their own solutions. Resist this impulse in yourself and be tactfully aware of it in others. Discussing the strengths of an option before talking about its weaknesses can take some of the heat out of the process. Accept differences of opinion and conflict as a natural and necessary part of problem solving.

Step 4: Developing a Plan of Action. Once the group has selected a solution, it must determine the steps needed to implement it and the order in which these steps must be taken. For example, to improve company morale, a group might recommend a three-step plan: (1) better in-house training programs to increase employees' upward mobility, (2) a pay structure that rewards success in the training programs, and (3) increased participation in decision making as employees move into more responsible positions. As the group develops this plan, it should consider what might help or hinder it, the resources needed to enact it, and a timetable for its completion.

If the group cannot develop an action plan for the solution, or if insurmountable obstacles appear, the group should return to step 3 and reconsider its options.

Step 5: Evaluating Results. Not only must a problem-solving group plan how to implement a solution, it must also set up a system for evaluating the results of the plan after it is enacted. To do this, the group must establish criteria for evaluation, concentrating on these three questions:

1. What will we consider a successful outcome?

2. When can we expect this to happen?

3. What will we do if the plan doesn't work as expected?

The first two questions require the group to specify the desired outcomes and indicate how these outcomes can be recognized once the solution goes into effect. To monitor the ongoing success of a solution, such as the three-part plan to improve company morale presented in step 4, the group should decide on a reasonable set of expectations for each stage in the process. That way, the company can detect and correct problems as they occur, before they damage the plan as a whole. Having a scheduled sequence of expectations also provides a way to determine results while the plan is being enacted, rather than having to wait for the entire project to be completed. Positive results along the way can encourage group members by showing them they are on the right track. The third question indicates the importance of contingency plans: what to do if things don't go as expected.

OTHER APPROACHES TO GROUP PROBLEM SOLVING

While the systematic process described above works well in many situations, there are times when a different approach may be called for. When a problem requires the concerted efforts of people from different and separate areas of the public or private sectors, a **collaborative problem-solving** approach may be called for.[18] For example, in many urban areas, coalitions of business executives and educational professionals have come together to try to develop plans to prepare people for future jobs in the community. In such situations, the problems to be addressed are usually important and the resources are limited. Because there is no established authority structure and because the participants may have different expectations and goals, these coalitions often have difficulty accomplishing anything. To be most effective, the participants need to spend considerable time defining the problem and exploring one another's perspectives on the situation. This may allow them to recognize and admit their *interdependence,* at which point they can really begin to work together. The participants must come to see themselves not as members of group A (the executives) or group B (the educators), but as members of group C (the coalition). Leadership is especially difficult in such groups.

One approach that may be useful in such situations is the idea of **dialogue groups**. According to William Isaacs, director of the Dialogue Project at the Massachusetts Institute of Technology's Center for Organizational Learning, "Dialogue is a discipline of collective thinking and inquiry, a process for transforming the quality of conversation, and, in particular, the thinking that lies beneath it."[19] Such groups focus initially not on solving problems, but on understanding the problems in terms of the assumptions and embodied meanings that the participants bring to the interaction. The purpose of such groups is to establish a conversation between the participants from which shared meaning based on common ground and mutual trust can emerge.[20]

The role of the group leader or facilitator is critical in dialogue groups. According to Edgar Schein of the MIT Center, the group leader must:

- Organize the physical space so that it is as nearly a circle as possible. Whether or not people are seated at a table or tables is not as important as the sense of equality that comes from sitting in a circle.
- Introduce the general concept, then ask everyone to think of an experience she or he had in which such a dialogue led to "good communication."
- Ask people to share what the experience was and think about the characteristics of that experience. This works because people are relating concrete experiences, not abstract concepts.
- Ask group members to share what it was in such past experiences that led to good communication and write these characteristics on a flip chart.
- Ask the group to reflect on these characteristics by having each person in turn talk about his or her reactions.
- Let the conversation flow naturally once everyone has commented. This may require one and a half to two hours or more.
- Intervene as necessary to clarify, using concepts that focus on communication problems.
- Conclude the session by asking all members to comment in whatever way they choose.[21]

The dialogue method is not a substitute for other problem-solving techniques, such as the rational-thinking process presented earlier. Instead, it may be used as a precursor because discussion and debate usually work well only when members know and understand one another well enough to be "talking the same language."[22] A similar approach may be found in the Kettering Foundation's National Issues Forums.[23]

> ●**TRY THIS**
>
> Have you ever found yourself part of a group in which there were factions that did not trust one another? How effective was the group at solving problems or reaching its goals? How did you feel about being a member of the group? Share your perceptions with a classmate and come up with ideas of what you personally could have done to change the situation.

PARTICIPATING IN SMALL GROUPS

To be an effective group member, you must understand your responsibilities to the group. First, *you should come to meetings prepared to contribute.* You should have read the background materials and performed any tasks assigned to you by the group leader.

Second, *you should be open-minded*—willing to listen to and learn from others. You should be concerned with contributing to the overall effort rather than with dominating the discussion. Although you may have a well-defined point of view, don't be afraid

	Need to Do Less	Doing Fine	Need to Do More
1. I make my points concisely.	_____	_____	_____
2. I speak with confidence.	_____	_____	_____
3. I provide specific examples and details.	_____	_____	_____
4. I try to integrate ideas that are expressed.	_____	_____	_____
5. I let others know when I do not understand them.	_____	_____	_____
6. I let others know when I agree with them.	_____	_____	_____
7. I let others know tactfully when I disagree with them.	_____	_____	_____
8. I express my opinions.	_____	_____	_____
9. I suggest solutions to problems.	_____	_____	_____
10. I listen to understand.	_____	_____	_____
11. I try to understand before agreeing or disagreeing.	_____	_____	_____
12. I ask questions to get more information.	_____	_____	_____
13. I ask others for their opinions.	_____	_____	_____
14. I check for group agreement.	_____	_____	_____
15. I try to minimize tension.	_____	_____	_____
16. I accept help from others.	_____	_____	_____
17. I offer help to others.	_____	_____	_____
18. I let others have their say.	_____	_____	_____
19. I stand up for myself.	_____	_____	_____
20. I urge others to speak up.	_____	_____	_____

FIGURE 8.1
Group Communication Skills Self-Analysis Form

to admit you are wrong and don't become defensive when you are challenged. Willingness to change your views is not a sign of weakness, nor is obstinacy a strength.

Third, *be a constructive listener.* Speak only when you need information or can help to clarify an issue. Allow others to complete their points without interruption. Don't be afraid to object if you feel consensus is forming too quickly. You might save the meeting from groupthink. In short, each participant should strive to make a positive contribution to group effectiveness.

Analyzing your group communication skills can help you become a more effective group communicator. Use the self-analysis form in Figure 8.1 to steer you toward more constructive group-communication behaviors.

As you participate in groups, you should also keep in mind the following questions:

1. What is happening now in the group?

2. What should be happening in the group?

3. What can I do to make this come about?[24]

If you notice a difference between what the group is doing and what it *should be* doing to reach its goals, you have the opportunity to assume group leadership.

What does it mean to be a leader? Interest in leadership is very practical: *leaders help get the job done.* For over thirty-five years, social scientists have been studying leadership by analyzing group communication patterns.[25] This research suggests that two basic types of leadership behaviors emerge in most groups. The first is **task leadership** behavior, which directs the activity of the group toward a specified goal. The second is **social leadership** behavior, which helps build and maintain positive relationships among group members.

Task leaders initiate goal-related communication, including both giving and seeking information, opinions, and suggestions. A task leader might say, "We need more information on just how widespread sexual harassment is on campus. Let me tell you what Dean Johnson told me last Friday . . . " Or the task leader might ask, "Gwen, tell us what you found out from the Affirmative Action Office."

Social leaders initiate positive social communication behaviors, such as expressing agreement, helping the group release tension, or behaving in a generally friendly and supportive manner toward others. The social leader looks for chances to bestow compliments: "I think Gwen has made a very important point. You have really helped us by finding that out." The supportive effect of sincere compliments helps keep members from becoming defensive and helps maintain a constructive communication atmosphere. In a healthy communication climate, the two kinds of leadership behavior support each other and work to keep the group moving toward its goal in a positive way. When one person combines both styles of leadership, that person is likely to be highly effective.

Leadership has also been discussed in terms of how the leader performs the task and maintenance functions. An **autocratic leader** makes decisions without consultation, issues orders or gives direction, and controls the members of the group through the use of rewards or punishments. A **participative leader** functions in a more democratic fashion, seeking input from group members and giving them an active role in the decision-making process. A **free-rein leader** functions more as a group member than as a leader, leaving members free to decide what to do, how to do it, and when to do it. If you were working in an organization, you would probably say you worked *for* an autocratic leader, worked *with* a participative leader, and worked *in spite of* a free-rein leader. The questionnaire in Figure 8.2 on the next page will allow you to determine what type of leadership style you might tend to use.

As we move into the twenty-first century, a new way of looking at leadership style is emerging. Instead of classifying leaders as task-oriented and social-oriented or as autocratic, participative, or free-rein, it suggests that leadership styles are either transactional or transformational. **Transactional leadership** prevails in an environment based on power relationships and relies on reward and punishment to accomplish its ends. **Transformational leadership** appeals to "people's higher levels of motivation to contribute to a cause and add to the quality of life on the planet."[26] Transformational leadership may be the most effective way to bring about cooperation among diverse factions in a group and may help initiate

Even relatively informal groups develop leaders who may serve either task or social functions, or both.

YES	NO	1.	Do you enjoy "running the show?"
YES	NO	2.	Do you think it's worth the effort to explain the reasons for a decision before putting it into effect?
YES	NO	3.	Do you prefer the administrative leadership jobs—planning, paperwork, etc.—to working with people?
YES	NO	4.	A stranger comes into your department, and you know she's the new employee hired by one of your assistants. On approaching her, would you first ask her name or introduce yourself?
YES	NO	5.	Do you keep the people working for you up-to-date on developments affecting the group?
YES	NO	6.	When you give out assignments, do you state the goals and leave the methods up to subordinates?
YES	NO	7.	Do you think that it is a good idea to keep aloof from subordinates because familiarity reduces respect?
YES	NO	8.	In deciding the time for a group outing you heard that most prefer to have it on Wednesday, but you are certain that Thursday would be a better time. Would you put the matter to a vote?
YES	NO	9.	If you had your way would you reduce personal contacts and communication with employees?
YES	NO	10.	Do you find it fairly easy to fire someone?
YES	NO	11.	Do you feel the friendlier you are with your people, the better you will be able to lead them?
YES	NO	12.	After a lot of work time you figure out the answer to a problem. You relay the solution to an assistant who pokes it full of holes. Will you be annoyed that the problem is still unsolved rather than angry with the assistant?
YES	NO	13.	Do you agree that one of the best ways to avoid discipline problems is to provide adequate punishments for violations of rules?
YES	NO	14.	The way you handled a situation has been criticized. Would you try to sell your position to your group rather than make it clear that you are the boss and your decisions are final?
YES	NO	15.	Do you generally leave it up to subordinates to contact you for informal day-to-day communications?
YES	NO	16.	Do you feel that all subordinates should have a certain amount of personal loyalty to you?
YES	NO	17.	Do you favor appointing committees to resolve problems rather than deciding what to do by yourself?
YES	NO	18.	Do you believe that differences of opinion in a work group are healthy?

FIGURE **8 . 2**
What Kind of Leader Are You?

Source: Adapted from Mastery of Management *by Auren Uris, © 1968. Reprinted by permission of Putnam Berkeley, a division of Penguin Putnam, Inc. Scoring and interpretation may be found in the In Summary section of this chapter.*

dialogues that lead to intercultural understanding. It carries overtones of stewardship rather than management. Transformational leaders have the following qualities:

- They have a rich vision of what needs to be done.
- They are empathetic, so that people feel safe working with them.
- They are trusted because their words and actions are consistent.
- They give credit where credit is due.
- They help others develop.
- They share power.
- They are willing to take risks, experiment, and learn.
- They have a passion for their mission.

In short, transformational leaders lead with both their hearts and their heads. According to John Schuster, a management consultant who specializes in transformational leadership training, ". . . the heart is more difficult to develop. It's easier to get smarter than to become more caring."[27]

Are only a favored few of us destined to be leaders? Can you be a leader? To us, the "favored few" theory is primarily an ego trip for those who think they belong to this elite group. Most of us have leadership potential that can emerge in certain situations. To understand this potential, we need to consider the major components of **ethos**: competence, trustworthiness, likability, and forcefulness. An effective leader is *competent*. This means that the leader not only understands the problem that is being addressed, but also knows how to steer a group through the problem-solving process. An effective leader is *trustworthy*. This means that the leader is honest, is concerned about the good of the group, and places reaching the goal above his or her own personal ego concerns. An effective leader is *likable*. This means that he or she is friendly and can interact easily with others. To be truly likable, a person must truly like others. Likability is contagious. Finally, an effective leader is *forceful*. Sometimes forcefulness is interpreted as exercising power over others, but it also includes being enthusiastic and energetic. If the people in a group like the leader, believe that he or she knows what is going on, and trust him or her to have their best interests at heart, then power in its traditional sense is often unnecessary.

An effective leader should
✓ Have experience, knowledge, and insight into the group's problem
✓ Help define problems, set goals, initiate action, and follow through
✓ Be sensitive to the needs of participants
✓ Help resolve conflicts that arise during deliberations
✓ Give voice to group consensus as it emerges
✓ Adapt to changing circumstances
✓ Be able to represent the group to others

Don't be intimidated by this ideal portrait of an effective leader. Most of us have many of these qualities in varying degrees and can use them as the need for leadership arises. To be an effective leader, remember these simple goals: Help others to be effective and to get the job done. Cultivate an open leadership style that encourages all sides to air their views. Much of the training you receive in this course will help you become a successful leader. You may even find that you enjoy the experience.

PLANNING MEETINGS

In many situations, meetings seem to be time wasters. This may be because the people in charge of them do not know when to call meetings or how to plan and run them.[28] Meetings should be called when members need to

- Share information and discuss its meaning face to face.
- Decide on a common course of action.
- Establish a plan of action.
- Report on the progress of a plan, evaluate its effectiveness, and revise it if needed.

In addition to just knowing when to call meetings, you need to know how to plan and prepare for them. The following guidelines should help you plan more effective meetings:

1. *Have a specific purpose for holding a meeting.* Unnecessary meetings waste time. If your goal is simply to increase interaction, plan a social event rather than a meeting.

2. *Prepare an agenda* and distribute it to participants several days before the meeting. Having a list of topics to be covered gives members time to prepare and assemble information or materials that they might need. Be sure to solicit agenda items from participants.

3. *Keep meetings short and to the point.* After about an hour, groups usually grow weary and the law of diminishing returns sets in. Don't try to cover too much ground in a single meeting.

4. *Keep groups small in size.* You get more participation and interaction in smaller groups. In larger groups, people may be reluctant to ask questions or contribute ideas.

5. *Assemble groups that invite open discussions.* In business settings, the presence of someone's supervisor may inhibit honest interaction. You will get better participation if group members come from the same or nearly the same working level in the organization.

6. *Plan the site of the meeting.* Arrange for privacy and freedom from interruptions. A circular table or seating arrangement encourages participation because there is no power position in the arrangement. A rectangular table or a lectern and classroom arrangement may inhibit interaction.

7. *Prepare in advance for the meeting.* Have a short form of the agenda available at the meeting. Be certain that you have all of the necessary supplies, such as chalk, a flip chart, markers, note pads, and pencils. If you are planning to use audiovisual equipment, check in advance to be sure it is in working order.

CONDUCTING AN EFFECTIVE MEETING

Group leaders have more responsibilities than other members. Leaders must understand the problem-solving process the group will use so that deliberations can proceed in an orderly, constructive way. Leaders also should be well informed on the issues involved so that they can answer questions and keep the group moving toward its objective. The following list should be helpful in guiding your behavior as a group leader.

- Start and end the meeting on time.
- Present background information concisely and objectively.
- Lead but don't run the meeting.
- Be enthusiastic.
- Encourage differences of opinions. Get conflict out in the open so that it can be dealt with directly.
- Urge all members to participate. If group members are reticent, you may have to ask them directly to contribute.
- Keep discussion centered on the issue.
- At the close of a meeting, summarize what the group has accomplished.

As a group leader, you may need to present the group's recommendations to others. In this task, you function mainly as an informative speaker (for more on informative speaking, see Chapter 14). You should present the recommendations offered by the group, along with the major reasons for these recommendations. You should also mention any reasons against these recommendations or any reservations that may have surfaced during group deliberations. Your job in making this report is not to advocate, but to educate. Later, you may join in any discussion that follows with persuasive remarks that express your convictions on the subject.

GUIDELINES FOR FORMAL MEETINGS

The larger a group is, the more it may need formal procedures if it is to conduct a meeting successfully. Also, if a meeting involves a controversial subject, it is often wise to have a set of rules for conducting group business. Having clear-cut guidelines helps keep meetings from becoming chaotic and helps to assure fair treatment for all participants. In such situations, many groups operate by **parliamentary procedure.**[29]

Parliamentary procedure establishes an order of business for a meeting and lays out the way the group initiates discussions and reaches decisions. Under parliamentary procedure, a formal meeting proceeds as follows:

1. The chair calls the meeting to order.
2. The secretary reads the minutes of the previous meeting, which are corrected, if necessary, and approved.
3. Reports from group officers and committees are presented.
4. Unfinished business from the previous meeting is considered.
5. New business is introduced.
6. Announcements are made.
7. The meeting is formally adjourned.

All business in formal meetings goes forward by means of **motions**, which are proposals set before the group. Consider the following scenario. The chair of a group asks, "Is there any new business?" A member responds, "I move that we allot $100 to build a Homecoming float." This member has offered a **main motion**, a proposal that commits the group to some action. Before the group can discuss the motion, it must be seconded. If no one volunteers a second, the chair may ask, "Is there a second to this motion?"

Typically, another member will respond, "I second the motion." The purpose of a **second** is to ensure that more than one person wants to see the motion considered. Once a main motion has been made and seconded, it is open for discussion. It must be passed by majority vote, defeated, or otherwise resolved before the group can move on to other business. With the exception of a few technical motions (such as "I move we take a fifteen-minute recess" or "Point of personal privilege—can we do anything about the heat in this room?"), the main motion remains at the center of group attention until it is resolved.

Let us assume that as the group discusses the main motion in our example, some members believe that the amount of money proposed is insufficient. At this point, another member may say, "I move to amend the motion to provide $150 for the float." The **motion to amend** gives the group a chance to modify a main motion. It also must be seconded and, after discussion, must be resolved by majority vote before discussion goes forward. If the motion to amend passes, then the amended main motion must be considered further.

How does a group make a decision on a motion? There usually comes a time when discussion has pretty well played itself out. At this point the chair might say, "Do I hear a call for the question?" A **motion to call the question** ends the discussion; it requires a two-thirds vote for approval. Once the group votes to end discussion, it must then vote to accept or reject the motion. No further discussion can take place until the original or amended original motion has been voted upon.

Sometimes the discussion of a motion may reveal that the group is quite confused or sharply divided about an issue. At this point a member may make a **motion to table** the motion or "to lay [the motion] on the table," as it is technically called. This can be a backdoor way to dispose of a troublesome or defective motion without the pain of further divisive or confused discussion. At other times, the discussion of a motion may reveal that the group lacks important information that it needs in order to make an intelligent decision. At that point, we might hear from yet another member: "In light of our uncertainty on the cost issue, I move that we postpone further consideration of this motion until next week's meeting." The **motion to postpone consideration,** if approved, gives the chair a chance to appoint a committee to gather the information needed.

These are just some of the important motions and procedures that can help assure that formal group communication remains fair and constructive (see Figure 8.3). For more information on formal group communication procedures, consult the authoritative **Robert's Rules of Order.**

IN SUMMARY   Much important communication takes place in small group settings. A group is an accumulation of people interacting together over a period of time in order to reach specified goals.

Groups may be effective at handling problems because they give us more than just a single perception of an issue or situation. Groups may experience problems as a function of cultural gridlock, which may occur when people from different backgrounds work together. Groupthink may become a problem if the group values harmonious social relations more than solving the problem or reaching the goal.

Several methods may be used to solve problems in groups. The reflective-thinking method involves defining the problem, generating and evaluating solutions, develop-

Action	Requires Second	Can Be Debated	Can Be Amended	Vote Required	Function
Main motion	Yes	Yes	Yes	Majority	Commits group to a specific action or position.
Second	No	No	No	None	Assures that more than one group member wishes to see idea considered.
Move to amend	Yes	Yes	Yes	Majority	Allows group to modify and improve an existing motion.
Call question	Yes	No	No	Two-thirds	Brings discussion to an end and moves to a vote on the motion in question.
Table motion	Yes	No	No	Majority	Stops immediate consideration of the motion until a later unspecified time.
Postpone consideration	Yes	Yes	Yes	Majority	Stops immediate discussion and allows time for the group to obtain more information on the problem.
Move to adjourn	Yes	No	No	Majority	Formally ends meeting.

FIGURE **8.3**
Guide to Parliamentary Procedure

ing a plan of action, and evaluating the results. Brainstorming is an effective way of generating solutions. Electronic brainstorming may be conducted using computers. A collaborative problem-solving approach is helpful when a group consists of people with diverse and possibly incompatible backgrounds. Dialogue groups help uncover the differences that underlie thinking about a problem.

In groups, both group members and leaders share responsibility. Group members should come to meetings prepared to participate, be willing to listen to and learn from others, and be constructive listeners. Group leaders must see that the job gets done while maintaining positive social relationships in the group. Leaders may demonstrate an autocratic, participative, or free-rein style of leadership. Transactional leadership is based on power relationships, whereas transformational leadership appeals to people's higher levels of motivation. An effective leader must be competent, trustworthy, likable, and dynamic.

Meetings should have a specific purpose, follow a prepared agenda, and be kept as short as possible. Formal meetings may function best when they follow parliamentary procedure.

"WHAT KIND OF LEADER ARE YOU?" SCORING AND INTERPRETATION

To compute your score, mark the questions that you answered "yes." Then compare your answers with the groupings below:

A   1, 4, 7, 10, 13, 16
B   2, 5, 8, 11, 14, 17
C   3, 6, 9, 12, 15, 18

If most of your "yes" answers were in group A, you tend to be an autocratic leader; if most were in group B, you tend to be a participative leader; if most were in group C, you tend to be a free-rein leader.

TERMS TO KNOW

cultural gridlock	transactional leadership
groupthink	transformational leadership
reflective-thinking	ethos
brainstorming	parliamentary procedure
electronic brainstorming	motions
collaborative problem solving	main motion
dialogue groups	second
task leadership	motion to amend
social leadership	motion to call the question
autocratic leader	motion to table
participative leader	motion to postpone consideration
free-rein leader	Robert's Rules of Order

NOTES

1. Marc Hequet, "The Fine Art of Multicultural Meetings," *Training*, July 1993, 29(5), Compuserve, *Business Database Plus*, on-line, January 1996; William N. Isaacs, "Taking Flight: Dialogue, Collective Thinking, and Organizational Learning," *Organizational Dynamics*, Autumn 1993, 24(16), Compuserve, *Business Database Plus*, on-line, January 1996; Edgar H. Schein, "On Dialogue, Culture, and Organizational Learning," *Organizational Dynamics*, Autumn 1993, 40(12), Compuserve, *Business Database Plus*, on-line, January 1996.

2. Scot Ober, *Contemporary Business Communication* (Boston: Houghton Mifflin, 1995), 498.

3. Adapted from Hequet, "The Fine Art of Multicultural Meetings."

4. Paul R. Bernthal and Chester A. Insko, "Cohesiveness Without Groupthink: The Interactive Effects of Social and Task Cohesion," *Group and Organization Management*, March 1993, 66(22), Compuserve, *Business Database Plus*, on-line, January 1996; Christopher P. Neck and Charles C. Manz, "From Groupthink to Teamthink: Toward the Creation of Constructive Thought Patterns in Self-Managed Work Teams," *Human Relations*, August 1994, 929(24), Compuserve, *Business Database Plus*, on-line, January 1996.

5. Bernthal and Insko, "Cohesiveness Without Groupthink."

6. Neck and Manz, "From Groupthink to Teamthink."

7. I. L. Janis, *Groupthink: Psychological Studies of Policy Decisions and Fiascoes* (Boston: Houghton Mifflin, 1982), 245–246.

8. Gerald M. Goldhaber, *Organizational Communication* (Dubuque, Iowa: Brown, 1983), 263.

9. Harold Guetzow and John Gyr, "An Analysis of Conflict in Decision-Making Groups," *Human Behavior* (1954): 367–382; Norman R. F. Maier and Richard

A. Maier, "An Experimental Test of the Effects of 'Developmental' vs. 'Free' Discussion on the Quality of Group Decisions," *Journal of Applied Psychology* (1957): 320–323.

10. For an overview of other methods, see Patricia Hayes Andrews and Richard T. Herschel, *Organizational Communication: Empowerment in a Technological Society.* (Boston: Houghton Mifflin, 1996), 213–218.

11. Donelson R. Forsyth, *Group Dynamics,* 2nd ed. (Pacific Grove, Calif.: Brooks/Cole, 1990), 286–287.

12. The problem-solving process described here is adapted from William C. Morris and Marshall Sashkin. "Phases of Integrated Problem Solving (PIPS)," *The 1978 Annual Handbook for Group Facilitators,* ed. J. William Pfeiffer and John E. Jones, (La Jolla, Calif.: University Associates, 1978), 109–116.

13. Floyd Hurt, "Better Brainstorming," *Training and Development,* November 1944, 57(3), Compuserve, *Business Database Plus,* on-line, January 1996.

14. Ron Zemke, "In Search of Good Ideas," *Training,* January 1993, 46(6), Compuserve, *Business Database Plus,* on-line, January 1996.

15. Sivasailam Thiagarajan, "Take Five for Better Brainstorming," *Training and Development Journal,* February 1992, 37(6), Compuserve, *Business Database Plus,* on-line, January 1996; Hurt, "Better Brainstorming"; Zemke, "In Search of Good Ideas."

16. Srikumar S. Rao, "Meetings Go Better Electronically: Do Hard-Nosed Bosses Stifle Discussion? Try Conferencing Software," *Financial World,* 14 March 1995, 72(2), Compuserve, *Business Database Plus,* on-line, January 1996; Gail Kay, "Effective Meetings Through Electronic Brainstorming," *Management Quarterly,* Winter 1994, 15(12), Compuserve, *Business Database Plus,* on-line, January 1996; Milam Aiken, Mahesh Vanjami, and James Krosp, "Group Decision Support Systems," *Review of Business,* Spring 1995, 38(5), Compuserve, *Business Database Plus,* on-line, January 1996; and Michael C. Kettelhut, "How to Avoid Misusing Electronic Meeting Support," *Planning Review,* July–August 1994, 34(5), Compuserve, *Business Database Plus,* on-line, January 1996.

17. Zemke, "In Search of Good Ideas."

18. Jacqueline N. Hood, Jeanne M. Logsdon, and Judith Kenner Thompson, "Collaboration for Social Problem Solving: A Process Model;" *Business and Society,* Spring 1993, 1(17), Compuserve, *Business Database Plus,* on-line, January 1996.

19. Isaacs, "Taking Flight."

20. Schein, "On Dialogue, Culture, and Organizational Learning."

21. Ibid.

22. Ibid.

23. Michael Osborn and Suzanne Osborn, *Alliance for a Better Public Voice: The Communication Discipline and the National Issues Forums* (Dayton, Ohio: National Issues Forums Institute, 1991).

24. Adapted from David G. Smith, "D-I-D: A Three-Dimensional Model for Understanding Group Communication," *The 1977 Annual Handbook for Group*

Facilitators, ed. John E. Jones and J. William Pfeiffer (La Jolla, Calif.: University Associates, 1977), 106.

25. Robert F. Bales, *Interaction Process Analysis: A Method for the Study of Small Groups* (Cambridge, Mass.: Addison-Wesley, 1950); Robert F. Bales, *Personality and Interpersonal Behavior* (New York: Holt, Rinehart and Winston, 1970).

26. John P. Schuster, "Transforming Your Leadership Style," *Association Management,* January 1994, 39(5), Compuserve, *Business Database Plus,* on-line, January 1996.

27. Ibid.

28. Much of the material in this section is adapted from Robert D. Ramsey, "Making Meetings Work for You," *Supervision,* February 1994, 14(3), Compuserve, *Business Database Plus,* on-line, January 1996; Becky Jones, Midge Wilker, and Judy Stoner, "A Meeting Primer," *Management Review,* January 1995, 30(3), Compuserve, *Business Database Plus,* on-line, January 1996.

29. Darwin Patnode, *Robert's Rules of Order: Modern Edition* (Nashville, Tenn.: Thomas Nelson, 1989).

PUBLIC
SETTINGS

CHAPTER NINE

PRINCIPLES OF PUBLIC COMMUNICATION

THIS CHAPTER
will help you

- Understand how public communication relates to other types of communication

- Understand the benefits of public communication

- Understand the relationship between rhetoric and public communication

- Understand how the media affect public communication

WHEN THE **VOICES** OF democracy
ARE **SILENCED, FREEDOM**
BECOMES A **HOLLOW** concept.

—*A. H. Neuharth, Chairman, The Freedom Forum*

*P*ublic communication! Doesn't that mean I have to stand up in front of the class and give a speech? I don't think I like that very much. I'm not very good at getting up in front of people. It makes me nervous. Besides, I'm not going to be a politician. I'll never get up and give speeches outside the classroom. Why do I have to learn this stuff, anyhow?

Although you may think you will never have to make any public presentations outside of this classroom, you may be surprised at how often you will use the skills you learn here. Consider these examples:

- In your social issues class, you must make an oral presentation on your research project. You will be expected to answer questions and defend your results. This oral report counts as 15 percent of your project grade.

- You have been asked to coordinate your fraternity's community involvement project. You have to convince members to volunteer three hours a week of their time to act as "big brothers" for disadvantaged grade school students.

- You are going to San Francisco next week for a job interview with Software Products, Inc. Ms. Rodrigez, Software's personnel recruiter, has just called to tell you that you should be prepared to make a short presentation to Software's managers on the marketing research project you mentioned in your résumé.

- The local school board has been asked to remove *The Catcher in the Rye, To Kill a Mockingbird,* and *Of Mice and Men* from the high school library. A public hearing has been set for the next school board meeting. Someone must speak against this censorship. Because you feel strongly about the issue, you want to express your opinion.

Public communication consists of prepared messages that are presented to an audience. It is an inescapable part of our day-to-day lives. One major form of public communication is the public speech. In the remaining chapters of this book, we provide in-depth treatment of public speaking as a skill that you can develop in this class. Public communication principles can also make you a more critical and astute consumer of public messages. They will help you sort through and make sense of the barrage of informative and persuasive messages that bombards you on a daily basis, and they will alert you to the ways in which messages can be distorted or disguised.[1]

Public communication occurs in educational, civic, political, and organizational settings. Learning to prepare and make effective public presentations can equip you to handle some of the more important moments in your life—times when a grade may be decided, when a public problem you care about needs action, or when the chance for a job you want hangs in the balance. At such vital moments, family, spiritual, and material values may all depend on your ability to speak effectively. As you become more confident and skilled in public speaking, you may notice that you also improve in small group and interpersonal communication situations. As we develop in one dimension of oral communication, we develop in others as well.

In this chapter we will explore how public communication relates to other types of communication and how it builds on language, listening, and critical thinking skills.

● TRY THIS

Write down an example of a time when you were taken in by deceptive advertising. Working with several of your classmates, look for similarities among the incidences you each selected. Were there any cues that something was amiss? What can you do to avoid being taken in in the future?

We will consider the importance of public communication in terms of its personal and societal benefits. We also will analyze the relationships between rhetoric and public communication and the ways in which these are affected by the media.

HOW PUBLIC COMMUNICATION RELATES TO OTHER TYPES OF COMMUNICATION

Public communication differs in many ways from the other types of communication covered earlier in this book. Interpersonal communication takes place in a more private setting and typically involves two or three people who interact equally and directly with one another. The interactions tend to be unstructured, and the major focus is on the communication transaction, the immediate give and take of the participants. The roles of speaker and listener are frequently exchanged. Feedback is immediate and direct and includes both verbal and nonverbal behaviors.

Small group communication involves three or more people who interact in order to achieve a common goal. The setting is typically less private than that of interpersonal communication, but more private than that of public communication. The larger the group, the more structure is needed if it is to function efficiently. Once group size reaches about ten people, groups often decide to operate with a formal structure that governs interactions, such as parliamentary procedure. Consequently, groups almost always have leaders. The leaders may emerge from the interactions of the participants, or they may be formally appointed. In small group communication, the focus is on goal-directed interactions such as problem solving. There is usually an equal sharing of ideas, and the roles of speaker and listener are frequently exchanged. Feedback is immediate and direct and involves both verbal and nonverbal behaviors.

Public communication takes place in an open rather than a private setting and consists of a speaker communicating with an audience of listeners. The roles of speaker and listener are distinct and clearly defined. Speakers prepare messages and present them to the audience. The audience listens and responds to the messages. The roles of speaker and listener are seldom exchanged unless the presentation includes a question-and-answer session. The audience for public communication may be immediately present, as when a personnel manager speaks with a group of new employees during an orientation session. Or the audience may be removed from the speaker in time and/or place, as when a message is taped for presentation through electronic transmission. An immediate audience can provide direct feedback to a speaker. This feedback is most often nonverbal, including looks of interest or disinterest, nods of agreement, or frowns of disapproval. Verbal feedback tends to be limited. The audience for an electronically mediated presentation cannot provide immediate feedback to a speaker.

THE BENEFITS OF PUBLIC COMMUNICATION

Our opening examples described some of the immediately practical applications of public speaking skills. Beyond these, training in public communication provides additional personal and societal benefits.

PUBLIC SPEAKING BENEFITS INDIVIDUALS

Effective public speaking benefits speakers in many ways. During the preparation of a speech, you learn more about yourself. To select a meaningful topic, you must explore your own interests and positions on issues. To prepare a substantive message, you must expand your base of knowledge on your topic. Preparing an effective speech may be a positive growth experience, for it involves self-discovery and creative self-expression as you combine ideas and information in new ways.

During the preparation for your speech, you also learn about others. To tailor your message to your audience, you must be sensitive to their needs and interests. We hear a lot these days about "multiculturalism" and "cultural diversity." A major focus of these discussions centers on whether we should emphasize the commonality of our American identity or focus instead on the differences that define us as individuals.[2] Although this identity crisis seems quite recent, it reaches far back into the history of our country. Like many abstract and complex issues, it is often discussed in terms of the commonplace metaphors that structure the way we think and believe.[3]

One metaphor for American identity has been "the melting pot," which suggests that as various groups come to this country, they are melted down into an alloy. This metaphor was popular during the early twentieth century and was patterned on the steel mills of that period. The melting-pot metaphor suggested that immigrants would lose their ethnic identity as they became "Americanized." It is a highly ethnocentric metaphor, based on the assumption that "American" is best. Indeed, it even assumes that "America" refers only to the United States. It left little room for Asians, Hispanics, African Americans, Native Americans, or other ethnic groups that could not be or did not wish to be amalgamated.

A different metaphor for the American cultural experience can be found in the conclusion of Abraham Lincoln's first inaugural address, presented on the eve of the Civil War:

> *The mystic chords of memory, stretching from every battlefield, and patriot grave, to every living heart and hearthstone, all over this broad land, will yet swell the chorus of the Union, when again touched, as surely they will be, by the better angels of our nature.*[4]

Lincoln's image of the United States as a harmonious chorus suggests that individual voices can survive in our culture and that each voice makes a unique contribution. It also implies that the individual voices, when joined together, can create music that is more powerful and more beautiful than the voices when heard alone. It holds out the promise of a nation in which individualism and the common good not only survive, but enhance each other.[5]

In your classroom and in this book, you will hear many diverse voices. The importance of public communication for multiculturalism is that it allows us to listen to one another directly, to experience and savor that which makes each of us distinct and valuable, and to develop tolerance and appreciation for the various ways in which people live. Your experiences in this class should bring you closer to meeting one of the major goals of higher education: "to expand the mind and heart beyond fear of the unknown, opening them to the whole range of human experience."[6]

PUBLIC SPEAKING BENEFITS SOCIETIES

The political system of the United States is built on faith in public communication. Without open and responsible communication, there could be no freedom of choice, no informed decision making, no representative lawmaking by elected legislators. Our

Public communication is a necessary component of social change. If the change threatens a government, free speech may be suppressed.

nation's founders realized the crucial importance of freedom of speech when they wrote the First Amendment to the Constitution:

> Congress shall make no law respecting an establishment of religion, or prohibiting the free exercise thereof; or abridging the freedom of speech, or of the press; or the right of people peaceably to assemble, and to petition the government for a redress of grievances.

Although we often think of freedom of speech as an American right, it did not originate with the Bill of Rights. The idea of freedom of speech goes back at least to the golden age of Greece, when Pericles noted that the Athenians, "unlike any other nation . . . instead of looking on discussion as a stumbling-block in the way of action . . . think it an indispensable preliminary to any wise action at all."[7] Why was Athens so rare among the nations of that time? Why do we think our freedom of speech is unique? The answer is simple: to submit public decisions to open discussion is to distribute power. Those in power often don't like to give it up.

Public communication is the driving force for social change in most societies. The power of public communication is most obvious in totalitarian nations where communication channels are government-controlled. In such situations, public communication may take the form of an underground press, radio or television broadcasts originating outside the country, audio- or videotapes that are surreptitiously distributed, or Internet communications.

During World War II, the Voice of America began broadcasting news to an international audience. Later, Radio Free Europe and Radio Liberty were established to provide uncensored local news to Eastern Europe and the republics of the Soviet Union during the cold war. Their broadcasts were remarkably successful. For example, the Voice of America was instrumental in the liberation of Czechoslovakia. After being elected president of Czechoslovakia, Vaclav Haval visited the VOA's broadcasting service to express his appreciation for the role it played in the revolution: "You have informed us truthfully of events around the world and in our country as well, and in this way you helped to bring about the peaceful revolution which has at long last taken place."[8] Today Radio Martí and TV Martí beam programs to Cuba, and satellite transmissions of commercial television from the United States and Mexico are intercepted there by people with homemade receivers.[9] These public communication services provide access to information in places where freedom of speech remains a hollow concept.

RHETORIC AND PUBLIC COMMUNICATION

When you hear the word **rhetoric**, what comes to mind? A lot of meaningless hot air? Empty political promises? Purple prose designed more to befuddle the mind than to enlighten the listener? As it is generally used, the word *rhetoric* carries many negative connotations. Actually, the word has an honorable historical tradition.

Most communication scholars define *rhetoric* in the Aristotelian tradition as the study of public communication, or the "ability in each [particular] case, to see the available means of persuasion."[10] Donald C. Bryant, a contemporary rhetorical theorist, extended the definition to encompass "the adjustment of ideas to people and of people to ideas."[11] Bryant's broader definition allows the inclusion of informative as well as persuasive discourse in the study of rhetoric.

CLASSICAL BACKGROUND OF RHETORIC

The study of rhetoric as we know it today had its origins in ancient Greek academies, where the curriculum included mathematics, music, gymnastics, and rhetoric.[12] The most important contribution of the Greeks to the study of communication was Aristotle's treatise *On Rhetoric*. During the golden age of Greek civilization, approximately 350 years B.C., Aristotle was teaching the art of rhetoric to the citizens of Athens. Rhetoric was especially important in the Athenian democracy because there were no professional lawyers or judges. Cases going into litigation were decided by juries made up of over 200 citizens, and the contending parties had to speak for themselves. Rhetorical skills also were needed because all citizens were expected to participate in the assembly that established the laws of the land. Finally, rhetorical skills were an important component of ritual ceremonies in the Hellenic culture.

Aristotle organized and systematized the study of rhetoric. He described three major forms of discourse: **deliberative discourse**, used in lawmaking; **forensic discourse**, used in the courts; and **epideictic discourse**, used during ceremonies or rituals. He discussed three major types of appeals: **logos**, or appeals based on logical demonstrations; **pathos**, or appeals based on emotional arousal; and **ethos**, or appeals based on the character of the speaker. Aristotle stressed the importance of using examples and narratives to establish arguments. He further suggested that all speeches should have an introduction that gains attention, predisposes hearers positively toward the speaker, and makes clear the purpose of the speech; a body composed of propositions and proofs; and a conclusion that amplifies the subject and reminds the audience of the main points of the message.

Aristotle's *Rhetoric* laid the groundwork for later Roman rhetoricians. For example, Cicero described rhetoric as "an art made up of five great arts." He identified these arts as (1) **invention**, the discovery and selection of ideas, themes, and lines of argument for a speech; (2) **arrangement**, placing these ideas in an appropriate order; (3) **style**, expressing these ideas in the most effective language; (4) **memory**, storing these ideas in the mind so that they can readily be recalled; and (5) **delivery**, presenting the ideas to the audience. Quintilian later elaborated on the five great arts and stressed the importance of ethics, defining an ideal orator as a "good person speaking well."

Many of the topics covered in this text are based on the work of these classical theorists. For example, in Chapter 11 we discuss the importance of examples and narratives as supporting materials. Like both Aristotle and Cicero, we discuss the three major parts of a speech (the introduction, body, and conclusion) in Chapter 12, where we consider structuring messages, and in Chapters 14 and 15, where we present appropriate designs for informative and persuasive speaking. In our chapter on persuasive speaking (Chapter 15), we consider the three types of appeals proposed by Aristotle (*logos, pathos,* and *ethos*) and add to them appeals based on cultural traditions, or *mythos*. We also present material relevant to rhetoric's five great arts. The art of invention is covered in Chapter 10, where we provide a system for selecting and focusing a topic; in Chapter 11, where we discuss the selection of supporting materials; and in Chapter 15, where we cover developing arguments. The art of style and delivery is considered in Chapter 13.

Leni Reifenstahl thought of her World War II German propaganda film, *Triumph of the Will,* as an informative documentary. She still denies any propagandistic intent.

Finally, like Quintilian, we stress the ethical imperatives of public communication. We treat ethics in communication in this chapter, where we cover ethics as one of the criteria for determining what makes an effective public speech, and in Chapter 15, where we consider the ethical imperatives of persuasive speaking. Although more than 2,000 years have passed and the media of public communication have changed dramatically, much of what these classical theorists said still holds true today.

FUNCTIONS OF PUBLIC COMMUNICATION

Public communication serves five major functions: it can be used to inform, to persuade, to celebrate, to entertain, or to express feelings. Often these functions overlap within a single message, yet one will dominate. For example, the dominant function of advertisements is to persuade, but effective ads may also inform or entertain. Print advertisements, especially those for pharmaceutical products, are likely to have a strong informative component. On the other hand, television ads may have a strong entertainment component to keep audiences from "zapping" their messages with a remote control.[13]

The Informative Function.   The first major function of public communication is to provide information to an audience. **Informative discourse** can take many different forms. It may be written in books, periodicals, advertisements, or on-line computerized communication. Informative public communication may also be presented orally in public speeches or lectures, radio or television newscasts, and television or film documentaries in which the major purpose is to expand the listener's knowledge and understanding of a subject. Many informative public communications also contain a visual component. Books, articles, and advertisements often contain pictures as well as words. Televised newscasts and documentaries rely strongly on visuals to augment their messages. Speakers frequently use visual aids in lectures and speeches. We cover informative public communication in more detail in Chapter 14.

Public discourse that purports to be informative may have a persuasive **hidden agenda.** For example, in 1936 a classic German propaganda film, *Triumph of the Will,* was released. This film, directed by Leni Riefenstahl, was described as a documentary covering the 1934 Nazi Party rally in Nuremberg. Produced shortly after Hitler came to power, it led the audience to see Hitler in a positive light. *Triumph of the Will* is now considered one of the most masterful propaganda pieces ever produced, but to this day Riefenstahl still contends that it was a purely informative documentary.[14] Similarly, during World War II, the United States government issued a series of "information films" explaining America's involvement in the war. Released as part of the *Why We Fight* series, these films were produced by Frank Capra, the award-winning Hollywood director best known for his entertainment films such as *It's a Wonderful Life* and *Mr. Smith Goes to Washington.* Propaganda films were used for military indoctrination and were also shown in public theaters. Unlike Riefenstahl, Capra acknowledged the persuasive intent of his films, but he still cringed at their being labeled propaganda.[15]

The Persuasive Function.   The second major function of public communication is to persuade an audience to change their beliefs, attitudes, or behaviors. **Persuasive dis-**

course may also take many different forms. Like informative communications, persuasive communications can be written or presented orally and visually. Advertisements are the most common form of persuasive public communication. They call forth the entire arsenal of persuasive techniques and appeals.

Persuasive discourse also may have a hidden agenda. For example, although advertisements are designed to sell a specific product or service, they may serve other, less obvious persuasive purposes as well. Many advertisements rely on celebrity endorsements. So not only is the ad selling the product, it is also selling the lifestyle and values of the celebrity.[16] Although most people are aware that celebrities are paid for their endorsements, they seldom question the values of the celebrity who is featured or what this endorsement can mean to impressionable children and adolescents. Persuasive public communication is treated in greater detail in Chapter 15.

The Ceremonial Function. The third major function of public communication is to celebrate through ceremony and ritual. **Ceremonial discourse** commemorates an occasion, event, person, or group identity. This type of discourse also may take many forms—written or presented orally and visually, magazine articles, speeches, or television or film presentations. Awards shows offer speeches or videos that are tributes to sports and entertainment personalities. At their national conventions, the major political parties present films that celebrate their heroes. Organizations convey awards for achievement or longevity. Almost everyone is eulogized in a funeral service. Ceremonial discourse's hidden agenda is to extol the values of the culture or group, either as they do exist or as it is thought they should exist. Pericles' *Funeral Oration,* considered by many to epitomize this type of discourse, was presented at a ceremony honoring the Athenian soldiers who died during the Peloponnesian War. It extols the values and virtues of ancient Athens as much as, if not more than, the values and virtues of the deceased soldiers.

The Entertainment Function. The fourth function of public communication is to entertain. In the strictest sense, **entertainment discourse** is designed to amuse the audience. This type of communication may take many different forms, including novels, poetry, comic strips and books, after-dinner speeches, presentations by standup comics, cartoons, plays, movies, and television shows.[17] Like the other types of public discourse, entertainment discourse also may advance a hidden persuasive agenda.

Let's examine how this hidden agenda can function in television comedy. One media theorist refers to television as "America's court jester," which assumes the guise of an idiot while actually amassing power and authority.[18] During the socially turbulent era of the 1960s, television comedy was dominated by innocuous sitcoms such as *The Beverly Hillbillies, Leave It to Beaver,* and *Father Knows Best.* The comedies of the period portrayed an all-white middle-class United States with no divorces, no working women, no unplanned pregnancies, no drug or alcohol problems, no Jim Crow racism, and no antiwar protests—just the peaceful, prosperous suburban life of a stable nuclear family with two kids and a dog. The 1970s marked the beginnings of socially relevant comedies on television. *The Mary Tyler Moore Show,* featuring a young female journalist, marked the beginnings of a prime-time feminist consciousness. *M*A*S*H,* an implicit analogy between the Korean and Vietnam Wars, demonstrated the inanity of warfare. *All in the Family* and its spinoffs *Maude* and *The Jeffersons* took on sensitive topics such as racism and abortion. African American stars began to find a place in the lily-white world of television.

Television comedies may have a large persuasive effect for several reasons. First, comedy shows have a large audience. Thus, any effect they have, no matter how slight it may seem on the surface, may reverberate throughout the culture. Second, the persuasion is indirect, so the audience's guard is low. Viewers do not anticipate being persuaded, and so they are vulnerable because they are not prepared. Third, the degree of commitment to a position asked and the risk involved in watching is low, because "After all, this is not *real;* this is television." Because "it's only a story," sensitive subjects can be introduced to the public. This gives the audience time to contemplate the subject under relatively relaxed conditions. It legitimizes the subject and places it in the public agenda, perhaps preparing the way for later, more traditional public deliberations. The way the subject is presented may contribute to the public's acceptance or rejection when such deliberations eventually occur.

The Expressive Function. The final function of public communication is to express personal feelings about a subject. In the past, **expressive discourse** has generally been treated only as a form of interpersonal communication. However, in contemporary American society, expressive public discourse has come to play a prominent role in our daily lives through radio and television talk shows that deal with current political issues. Shows of this nature are not a recent phenomenon. Before World War II, the airwaves crackled with the voices of Father Coughlin and Gerald L. K. Smith prophesying doom and gloom and intensifying the distrust and disillusionment of their audiences.[19] What is new, however, is the interactive nature of these shows, which allows the disenchanted to rouse one another into an emotional frenzy.

Marvin Kalb, a former CBS reporter and now a professor at George Washington University, believes that talk shows fill an important void: "If we still gathered at town meetings, if your churches were still community centers, we wouldn't need talk radio. People feel increasingly disconnected, and talk radio gives them a sense of connection."[20] Current estimates suggest that there are over 3,200 radio talk shows nationwide, and that half of these are devoted to public policy issues.[21] The hosts of talk shows seldom present both sides of an issue; instead they create a black-and-white world in which everything is either good or bad.[22] They rely strongly on name calling and

Functions of Public Communication
✓   To inform and increase understanding
✓   To persuade and change attitudes and actions
✓   To celebrate and enhance values
✓   To entertain and amuse the audience
✓   To express feelings and provide a sense of connection

How Public Communication Works

✓   Public communication influences how we see things

✓   Public communication influences how we feel about things

✓   Public communication influences how we behave

✓   Public communication influences our group identities

incendiary language, such as "long-haired, maggot-infested, dope-smoking peace pansies," to provoke audience response. Although most of the hosts insist that their shows are purely "entertainment," the messages they advance may affect attitudes. For example, a recent *U.S. News & World Report* survey demonstrated that Rush Limbaugh's view "that Americans' life styles will not seriously harm the environment" raised voters' assessment of their own benign impact on the environment by more than 20 points.[23] In a recent poll by the Times Mirror Center for the People and the Press, 44 percent of U.S. listeners named talk radio as their chief source of political information.[24]

HOW PUBLIC COMMUNICATION WORKS

Public communication works through the use of strategic verbal or visual pictures.[25] These pictures are not simply a reflection of "what is out there," but a conglomerate of information, ideas, and feelings. The way something is introduced and presented may influence how we see it, how we feel about it, and how we act in relation to it. Public communication also can help establish and sustain our identity as members of a group.

Public Communication Influences the Way We See Things.   The first information or even misinformation we get on a subject may have a lasting impact on the way we see that subject. For example, when HIV was first introduced by the press, it was described as a disease affecting homosexual males, illegal IV drug users, and Haitian immigrants.[26] To the general public, the disease hardly seemed a cause for alarm. As the number of reported cases in the United States grew, an increase in the number of cases transmitted through heterosexual contact was noted; however, most of these cases were found among the inner-city poor.[27] Again, to the general population, there seemed to be no cause for alarm. When Magic Johnson announced that he was retiring from the NBA because he was HIV-positive, the general public began to be concerned. Johnson announced that he had contracted HIV through heterosexual encounters with multiple partners. One sympathetic sports reporter noted that the HIV death toll was "taking on Black Plague proportions."[28] Another warned that HIV could happen to anybody.[29] However, less than a month after Johnson's announcement, an article in a weekly newsmagazine suggested that public compassion was misplaced, that the HIV epidemic

Arthur Ashe announced at a press conference that he had AIDS. His candor, along with that of Eleanor Glaser and Mary Fisher who spoke at the Democratic and Republican conventions, helped to change the way HIV was depicted in the press.

represented a decay of "traditional morality," and that the good, moral, heterosexual citizens of this country had no reason for fear.[30]

It wasn't until Arthur Ashe announced that he had AIDS that the press's depiction of this illness began to change.[31] Ashe was forced to make his revelation after calls from a reporter and editor of *USA Today,* who were about to break the story.[32] Ashe was a prominent sports figure (the only African American male to win Wimbledon and the U.S. Open), an eminently respectable family man who had contracted HIV from a blood transfusion during heart surgery, a successful businessperson who had spoken out against apartheid and in favor of civil rights and the education of athletes, and a very private person who was reluctant to come out with news of his ailment.[33] Although Ashe's character was above reproach, the press still took pains to reassure the public that the chances of contracting the disease from blood transfusions were minimal.[34] If you were not homosexual or bisexual, did not use IV illegal drugs, were not sexually promiscuous, and were not an inner-city Black or Hispanic, you didn't really have anything to worry about.

Not long after Ashe's announcement, two well-to-do white women with AIDS addressed the Democratic and Republican National Conventions. Elizabeth Glaser, who addressed the Democrats, had contracted HIV from blood transfusions following the birth of her first child, who also died from AIDS. Mary Fisher, who addressed the Republicans, had contracted the HIV virus from her former husband, an IV drug user.[35] The testimony of these "respectable" victims helped to alter the way that HIV was depicted. HIV was no longer a topic that the general public could ignore because it could never happen to them.

Public Communication Influences the Way We Feel About Things. The way HIV was initially presented set the stage for indifference and negative feelings. Consequently, when Elizabeth Glaser and Mary Fisher made their presentations, they faced considerable persuasive challenges. They wanted to overcome indifference and arouse understanding and compassion. Elizabeth Glaser's message was direct and to the point. The beginning of her speech was a call for attention:

> *This is not about being a Republican or an Independent or a Democrat. It it about the future of each and every one of us . . . [I am] a strange spokesperson for such a group—a well-to-do white woman. But I have learned my lesson the hard way and I know that America has lost her path and is at risk of losing her soul. America, wake up! We are all in a struggle between life and death. . . . When I tell most people about HIV, in hopes that they will help and care, I see the look in their eyes— "It's not my problem," they are thinking. Well, it's everyone's problem.[36]*

She used personal examples based on her family's experience with the disease to arouse compassion. She closed with the following personal narrative:

> *My daughter lived seven years and in her last year, when she couldn't walk or talk, her wisdom shone through. She taught me to love when all I wanted to do was hate. She*

taught me to help others when all I wanted to do was help myself. She taught me to be brave, when all I felt was fear. My daughter and I loved each other with simplicity. America, we can do the same. This was the country that offered hope. This was the place where dreams could come true—not just economic dreams but dreams of freedom, justice and equality. We all need to hope that our dreams can come true. I challenge you to make it happen, because all our lives, not just mine, depend on it.[37]

Like Elizabeth Glaser, Mary Fisher attacked the problem directly:

Less than three months ago, at Platform Hearings in Salt Lake City, I asked the Republican party to lift the shroud of silence which has been draped over the issue of HIV and AIDS. I have come tonight to bring our silence to an end. . . . I ask you, here in this great hall, or listening in the quiet of your home to recognize that the AIDS virus is not a political creature. It does not care whether you are Democrat or Republican. It does not ask whether you are black or white, male or female, gay or straight, young or old. . . . We have killed each other—with our ignorance, our prejudice, and our silence. We may take refuge in our stereotypes, but we cannot hide there long. Because HIV asks only one thing of those it attacks: Are you human?[38]

Like Elizabeth Glaser, Mary Fisher also used personal examples involving her children to arouse compassion and tolerance:

I want my children to know that their mother was not a victim. She was a messenger. I do not want them to think, as I once did, that courage is the absence of fear. I want them to know that courage is the strength to act wisely when most we are afraid. . . . I will not hurry to leave you, my children. But when I go, I pray that you will not suffer shame on my account. To all within the sound of my voice, I appeal: Learn with me the lessons of history and of grace, so my children will not be afraid to say the word AIDS when I am gone. Then their children, and yours may not need to whisper it at all.[39]

Public Communication May Affect the Way We Behave. It is one thing to influence how people see or feel about a subject, but quite another to get them to act in relation to it. It often takes strong verbal or visual pictures coupled with an explicit call for action to get people moving. The call for action must let people know what they should do and how they should do it.

The most powerful verbal pictures take the form of examples or stories that illustrate either the negative consequences of inaction or the positive consequences of action. As the novelist John Steinbeck once observed, "It means very little to know that a million Chinese are starving unless you know one Chinese who is starving."[40] This is why speakers like Elizabeth Glaser and Mary Fisher used moving examples and narratives in their speeches. Such appeals are also used in advertising by groups like Save the Children, who tell you about a single child who needs your help, rather than overwhelming you with the numbers of starving children in Third World nations. When a problem is so vast, the little that one person can do hardly seems worth the effort. But if you tell us about little Maria, who lives in a barrio outside of Mexico City and for whom twenty dollars a month will provide food, shelter, clothing, and a opportunity to attend school, we can relate to this desperate child. We can help *her*. The depiction brings the problem into clear and compelling focus. It usually takes repeated efforts to transform even intense feelings into overt behavior. The challenge of moving an audience to action is extremely important. There are a variety of other techniques that can also be used to overcome it. These are covered in detail in Chapter 15.

Public Communication Influences Our Identity as Members of a Group. Bringing about effective resolutions of most significant problems requires group efforts. This is especially true when major social or political change is involved. Every four years the political parties in the United States conduct national conventions whose purpose is as much to revitalize and activate the parties' constituents as to nominate their candidates.

The influence of public communication on group identity is most evident in the development of social or political movements. Movements occur when a group works toward specific goals and remains active for an extended period of time. They arise when a large number of people feel disillusioned, discouraged, or disenfranchised. **Radical movements** seek to replace existing institutions with new ones based on different sets of fundatmental values. Radical movements encourage extreme positions on issues and arouse strong opposition. The American Revolution and the civil rights movement of the 1960s are examples of radical movements. **Innovational movements** also seek institutional change, but the changes do "not disturb the symbols and constraints of existing values or modify the social hierarchy."[41] The participants in innovational movements come from the mainstream of their culture. In contrast to radical movements, innovational movements are subject to less opposition because their values, members, and methods are traditional. Ross Perot's United We Stand America is an example of an innovational movement.

To develop and function effectively, a movement must have a strong leader who can bring people together and create a sense of group identity. The leader must be able to give voice to the disillusionment of the members and make them see that others share their feelings. The creation of a group of like-minded people provides a sense of social sanction and respectability for these feelings. Individuals may feel ineffective and helpless in relation to the giant social or political systems that impinge upon their lives, but as group members they often believe that they can act together to bring about reform. If and when a movement falters, public communication can help sustain group identity and revitalize group feelings and resolve.

Let's look at how United We Stand America used communication to establish and revitalize a political movement. United We Stand America became a force to be reckoned with during the 1992 presidential election campaign. At that time, more than 80 percent of Americans believed that the country was "on the wrong track" and that the "government was run for the benefit of a few big interests."[42] Such massive disillusionment sets the stage for the emergence of "savior politics"—politics under the control of a very strong leader who promises redemption.[43] Enter a person who seemed to epitomize many American myths—Horatio Alger, *Mr. Smith Goes to Washington,* Old Hickory, Daddy Warbucks, and Davy Crockett all rolled up into one—Ross Perot.[44]

Many people saw in Perot the strong leader they were seeking—the self-made man who was willing to go over, around, or through the system to get things done. Perot's outspoken manner, simple-sounding solutions to complex problems, populist sentiments, and pithy comments won him many followers from both the Democratic and Republican camps. He told people what they wanted to hear in language they could understand. On NBC's *Today* show, he commented that the reason President Bush didn't act on domestic issues "is the same reason I won't do brain surgery. I don't know how to do brain surgery. He doesn't understand domestic issues."[45] On what he saw as the administration's failure to act on the nation's economic problems, he quipped, "Maybe it was voodoo economics. Whatever it was, we are now in deep voodoo, I'll tell you that."

Perot offered no detailed position papers during his campaign. He felt that his supporters were not interested in his positions, they were interested in his principles.[46] His rallying cry was "Do it yesterday, damnit!"[47] Third-party candidates rarely get elected. They do, however, serve a valuable function by taking on the establishment. They can stimulate debate, force issues into the public agenda, and provide catharsis for their followers.[48] Although many of Perot's supporters were disillusioned by his "off-again on-again" campaign, he garnered 19 percent of the popular vote in the 1992 election. When asked after the election if he would run again in 1996, Perot said he "would rather undergo major surgery without anesthesia than become a candidate."[49]

The period immediately following the 1992 election was a time of relative inactivity for United We Stand. During the summer of 1995, however, Perot served as a "national powerbroker" at a convention of the faithful attended by some 3,000 to 6,000 delegates who paid their own way.[50] The social and political disillusionment of 1992 was still evident.[51] The delegates shared that disillusionment. They were characterized as "the radical middle"—"the 20 to 30 percent of the electorate at the center of the spectrum, disdainful of the two traditional parties and their special interests, ready to think about trying something new . . . the crucial swing vote in every major election."[52] The delegates assembled to hear thirty-six political speakers talk with them for eleven hours on Friday and ten hours on Saturday.[53]

The speakers at the convention represented a broad range of political positions—a virtual "all-you-can-eat political buffet."[54] Speakers included all of the major Republican presidential hopefuls and a diverse mix of Democrats, all speaking out in favor of fiscal responsibility, stronger ethics in government, and reform of entitlements.[55] This second coming of the Perotites illustrates the power of public communication to sustain group identity. The delegates were revitalized by their experiences and found "mutual reinforcement in telling each other that the political system is failing them."[56] Although as one delegate put it, they are a diverse group who "would have trouble ordering pizza together," they know what they "want from government—accountability, responsibility and vision."[57] Perot's power as a leader lay in his ability to bring together these "groups that would never come together around anyone else."[58] He saw his role very clearly: "I'm just one person. I'm a grain of sand, if you will. But grains of sand can do interesting things, because the grain of sand can irritate the oyster and make the pearl."[59]

● T R Y   T H I S

Select a social or political movement that you personally believe is important. Find out what prompted its development and who its leaders were. Share your findings with a classmate and determine how the movements you each investigated were similar and how they were different. Discuss how each movement was similar to the United We Stand movement, discussed here.

Earlier in this chapter, we discussed the importance of the mass media as a means of disseminating information aimed at social or political change and how entertainment presentations in the media can affect attitudes and values. The mass media have also profoundly affected the public discourse of politics. Changes in media technologies have been accompanied by changes in the way political campaigns in the United States are conducted.

PUBLIC COMMUNICATION AND THE MASS MEDIA

From the beginning of our country until the advent of radio in the late 1920s, almost all political campaigning was done either through printed materials or face to face at political rallies. Campaign workers distributed pamphlets and handbills urging voters to support their candidates. Candidates traveled from town to town, meeting voters and discussing their ideas on the issues of the day. The contact between candidates and voters was limited in terms of the numbers who actually heard a candidate, but it was also direct. Through the last half of the nineteenth century, voter turnout was high—up to 85 percent in some presidential elections. And although we often think of image building, negative advertising, pseudo-events (e.g., photo ops), and slogans as modern-day afflictions of our political system, they have a long, albeit inglorious history in American politics.[60]

THE ADVENT OF RADIO

By the late 1920s, radio broadcasting was replacing stump speaking as the primary means of political campaigning. The use of this new medium brought about many changes in political communication. It allowed a candidate to reach more people than ever before. Radio provided a diverse national audience. City slickers and country folk, Northerners and Southerners, the rich and the poor could all hear the same message at the same time.

The type of communication called for changed from formal orations to more conversational speaking. Politicians had to learn how to communicate through this new medium; those who couldn't or wouldn't fell by the wayside. In the 1924 presidential election (Republican Calvin Coolidge versus Democratic John Davis), the Republicans spent three times as much on radio coverage as the Democrats.[61] The results were decisive: Coolidge's popular vote was nearly double that of Davis, and his electoral vote nearly triple.[62]

Radio was a more intimate medium because the politicians were addressing small groups in the privacy of their homes. At the same time, it was also more remote. The politicians were physically distanced from the people. Radio was a medium of one-way communication that denied speakers access to immediate feedback from the audience. This led to the rise of political polling so that candidates could anticipate the reactions from the audience and structure their messages accordingly. Because listeners were free to change stations (the early version of channel surfing), speeches also had to be shorter and to the point to sustain attention.

THE ADVENT OF TELEVISION

During the 1952 presidential election, television was still in its infancy. About 15 million homes had television sets (compared to over 94 million in 1996).[63] *I Love Lucy* was the top-rated TV show.[64] Dwight D. Eisenhower was the first presidential candidate to fully use television in a presidential campaign.[65] He aired a series of forty talking-head commercials, "Eisenhower Answers America." His opponent, Adlai Stevenson, didn't like television and "refused to appear in campaign commercials, declaring, 'I think the American people will be shocked by such contempt for their intelligence; this isn't Ivory soap versus Palmolive.'"[66] Guess who won!

Since then, television has been the major link between the voters and the candidates in U.S. politics. Voters rarely meet the candidates face to face, except for the very small segment of the public that provides the immediate audience for their speeches, town meetings, or debates. Even then, the messages presented to a live audience are planned for the larger media audience that will be watching from their homes.

Any political campaign consists of three major elements: the candidates, the media, and the voters. Ideally, candidates would use the media to explain their positions on issues, present their voting records, show the differences between themselves and other candidates, and demonstrate their ability to make judgments under pressure. Similarly, the media would be a vehicle for contact between the candidates and the voters, avoid judgments of candidates' positions, and compare candidates' records with their promises. The public would seek out information on the candidates and issues from as many different sources as possible, avoid making decisions based on superficial factors, and demand interaction between candidates so that they could see how well the politicians can think on their feet and defend their positions when challenged.

Such an ideal system would generate the information and understanding voters need if they are to make informed and intelligent political decisions. Unfortunately, that is not the way the system functions. Although candidates may try to present their positions on issues, they often end up substituting image for substance. The candidates may be forced into this by the media, who focus attention on images, electability, and strategies rather than on positions, issues, or ideology.[67] Finally, the voters find themselves becoming apathetic and passive. In a survey conducted shortly before the 1996 campaigns, 66 percent of the people wanted more attention paid to issues, yet during the 1996 primaries only 15 percent of television news coverage dealt with the candidates' positions on policy issues.[68] An uninformed electorate can easily become an unconcerned electorate. Being unable to make an informed decision, they may decide not to make any decision at all. In the 1996 presidential election, less than 54 percent of eligible voters turned out at the polls, down from approximately 69 percent in the 1964 presidential election. In nonpresidential elections the turnout is even lower, averaging only about 46 percent over the past twenty years.[69]

In recent years a fourth factor in the political communication equation has emerged: the political consultants or spin doctors of Madison Avenue. Although presidential candidates have used media advisers since 1948, these advisers emerged as a truly potent force in the 1980s.[70] Advertisements and public appearances are tailored to convey the proper image—the one that best sells the candidate to the voters. Political conventions have become theatrical spectacles that have been described as "political infomercials," "high-tech sales pitches," and "televised pep rallies."[71] The work of the spin doctors is especially evident in political advertising. Political advertising is the principal way in which candidates communicate with voters.[72] In recent years, much of this advertising has been negative—a trend that many voters find disturbing.[73] Indeed, during the 1996 presidential election, approximately 70 percent of Dole's campaign spots were negative.[74] It has been suggested that negative advertising "demobilizes" the electorate, making it less likely that they will get out and vote.[75] The decline in voter turnout over the past three decades may support this conclusion.[76]

Television also has brought about other changes in political communication. Television sets a fast pace, so people become accustomed to listening to short bits of information.

● TRY THIS

Select an advertisement from a recent political campaign. (If you have trouble remembering an ad, go to "Dissect an Ad" at http://www.pbs.org/pov/totk/dissect.html.) Ask yourself the following questions about this advertisement: (1) Is it a positive or a negative ad? (2) Does it provide information about issues? (3) What type of image does it try to convey? (4) Do you think the ad is ethical? Share your insights with a classmate.

The language of political discourse has been tailored to provide eight- to ten-second "sound bites" that will make it into the evening news. Can you imagine how Lincoln's Emancipation Proclamation might have sounded had it been given in the age of TV? "Read my lips. No more slaves."

The visual images that dominate television bring speakers "up close and personal." Television is an even more intimate medium than radio. Everything that speakers do is magnified. The focus moves from the verbal to the visual aspects of a message. Television is more than just radio with pictures, but until the Nixon-Kennedy debates in 1960, few candidates recognized this. These debates, the first of their kind ever broadcast on television, provided the candidates with an opportunity to establish their images in the minds of the voters. The results of the first debate were a disaster for Nixon.[77]

During the two weeks before the first debate, Kennedy had been campaigning and vacationing in California. He looked tanned, energetic, and vigorous. On the other hand, Nixon had just spent two weeks in the hospital with an ulcerated infection in his leg. His natural paleness had been intensified by his illness, and he had lost so much weight that his shirt collar was loose. On the way into the studio, Nixon hit his sore leg with the corner of his car door. Not only was Nixon under physical stress at the time of the first debate, he was under psychological stress as well. On the Saturday before the debate, President Eisenhower was asked to give an example of a major idea of Vice President Nixon's that he had adopted. Ike replied, "If you give me a week, I might think of one."[78]

Immediately before the debate, the producer asked the candidates if they wanted makeup. Kennedy immediately replied, "No." Nixon also declined, but allowed his advisers to apply powder to cover his five-o'clock shadow. During the debate, the cameras zoomed in for reaction shots of the candidates listening to each other. In these reaction shots, Kennedy seemed poised and comfortable, while Nixon looked haggard and uncomfortable. Perspiration streaked his powdered face. He licked his lips repeatedly and frequently looked away from the speaker. In short, Nixon looked desperate and untrustworthy. These powerful visual messages magnified by the television camera probably played a major role in influencing people's voting behavior.

PUBLIC COMMUNICATION IN YOUR LIFE

Throughout your life, you will be a constant consumer and producer of public communication. In the remainder of this book, we hope to provide you with the tools you will need to fulfill these roles. As we focus on teaching you how to prepare messages for public presentation, you also will be learning how to analyze and evaluate the messages you receive.

In Chapter 10 we show you how to analyze your audience and select and focus a topic that will be meaningful to them. Chapter 11 shows you how to research your topic to gain responsible knowledge and introduces you to the major types of supporting materials you will need in order to add substance to your message. In Chapter 12, we teach you how to organize your ideas and information in a way that makes them easy for the audience to follow and understand. Chapter 13 focuses on language and presentation skills. It also provides suggestions for dealing with communication apprehension. Chapter 14 covers informative speaking. It explains the different types of informative speeches and provides the formats for frequently used designs. In Chapter 15 we discuss persuasive speaking, with a special emphasis on the ethics of persuasion.

Public communication consists of prepared messages that are presented to an audience. It occurs in educational, civic, political, and organizational settings. Public communication has both personal and societal benefits. Public speaking can provide a positive growth experience for speakers. Good speakers get to know themselves and their audiences better. The public speaking classroom can be a laboratory for multicultural interaction. Our political system is based on faith in public communication. The value of freedom of speech is most evident in countries where it is denied. People in such countries must often rely on outside sources such as the Voice of America to provide them with information on what is going on in the world.

Rhetoric involves the ability to see and use all available means of persuasion. It is the adjustment of ideas to people and people to ideas. The study of rhetoric as we know it today originated in ancient Greece. In his treatise *On Rhetoric,* Aristotle described the major forms of discourse and appeals and how a speech should be organized and presented to an audience. The Roman rhetoricians identifed the five great arts of rhetoric as invention, arrangement, style, memory, and delivery.

Public communication serves five major functions: to inform, persuade, celebrate, entertain, or express feelings. Informative discourse expands an audience's understanding of a subject. Persuasive discourse urges listeners to change their beliefs, attitudes, or behaviors. Ceremonial discourse commemorates an occasion, event, person, or group. The purpose of entertainment discourse is to amuse an audience. Expressive discourse conveys personal feelings about a subject. Each of these forms of discourse may be subject to a hidden agenda; for example, persuasive discourse may be put forth as purely informative in nature.

The development of mass media technologies has had a profound effect on public communication, especially in the area of politics. Through the 1920s, most political communication in the United States took place either face to face or in printed form. With the introduction of radio, political communication entered an new era. Radio communication increased the number of people that could be reached by a message and provided a diverse audience. It called for a more intimate presentation style because the audience was listening in the privacy of their homes. To sustain attention, political communication became shorter and more direct. The introduction of television brought additional changes to public communication. Since the early 1950s, television has been the major link between voters and candidates. Its focus on the visual aspects of a message gave rise to the emergence of the media consultants that work with most politicians today.

TERMS TO KNOW

public communication	memory
rhetoric	delivery
deliberative discourse	informative discourse
forensic discourse	hidden agenda
epideictic discourse	persuasive discourse
logos	ceremonial discourse
pathos	entertainment discourse
ethos	expressive discourse
invention	radical movements
arrangement	innovational movements
style	

NOTES

1.   For an especially good treatment of distorted messages, see Cynthia Crossen, *Tainted Truth: The Manipulation of Fact in America* (New York: Simon & Schuster, 1994).

2.   Arthur M. Schlesinger, *The Disuniting of America: Reflections on a Multicultural Society* (New York: Norton, 1992).

3.   George Lakoff and Mark Johnson, *Metaphors We Live By* (Chicago: The University of Chicago Press, 1980).

4.   T. Harry Williams, ed., *Abraham Lincoln: Selected Speeches, Messages, and Letters* (New York: Holt, Rinehart and Winston, 1964), 148.

5.   Although the struggle between conflicting metaphors describing the "American experience" began over a century ago, it persists to this day. See, for example, Michael Lind, "A Tossed Salad, Not a Melting Pot," *Washington Post National Weekly Edition,* 10–16 July 1995, 36.

6.   Arati R. Korwar, *War of Words: Speech Codes at Public Colleges and Universities* (Nashville, Tenn.: The Freedom Forum First Amendment Center at Vanderbilt University, 1994).

7.   From Pericles, "Funeral Oration," in Thucydides, *The History of the Peloponnesian War,* trans. Richard Crawley, rev. R. Feetham, *Great Books of the Western World,* Vol. 6 (Chicago: Britannica, 1990), 397.

8.   Jonas Bernstein, "Uncle Sam's Message Found Audiences That Listen Hard," *Insight,* 26 March 1990, 28.

9.   Tom Carter, "Dateline: Havana: Martí's Jammed but Pirated Cable a Hit," *The Washington Times,* 10 December 1993, A1.

10.   Aristotle, *On Rhetoric,* trans. George A. Kennedy (New York: Oxford, 1991), 36.

11.   Donald C. Bryant, "Rhetoric: Its Functions and Scope," *Quarterly Journal of Speech* (1953): 401–424.

12.   Patricia Bizzell and Bruce Herzberg, *The Rhetorical Tradition: Readings from Classical Times to the Present* (Boston: St. Martin's Press, 1990), 1–8.

13.   Some television advertisements actually parody popular entertainment. See Jessica Shaw, "Bench Marks," *Entertainment Weekly,* 4 November 1994, 11.

14.   Ray Muller, *The Wonderful, Horrible Life of Leni Riefenstahl* (Kino International, 1994). Aired on PBS, 5 July 1995.

15.   Bill Moyers, "The Propaganda Battle," *A Walk Through the Twentieth Century,* PBS, 1982.

16.   Jeffrey A. Trachtenberg, "Beyond the Hidden Persuaders: Psychological Aspects of Marketing," *Forbes,* 23 March 1987, 134–137; Clay Latimer, "Barkley's Peers Now Only Shrug at His Larger-than-Life Image," *Washington Times,* 25 December 1993, C4; "Michael Jordan's Magical Powers," *The Economist,* 1 June 1991, A28; "Saying No to Sneakers and Yes to Rice," *U.S. News & World Report,* 26 June 1995, 19.

17.   Some examples of rhetorical analysis of these genres include Barry Brummet, *Rhetorical Dimensions of Popular Culture* (Tuscaloosa: University of Alabama Press, 1991); Kathleen J. Turner, "Comic Strips: A Rhetorical Perspective," *Central States Speech Journal,* Vol. 28 (Spring 1977): 24–35; Caren J. Deming, "*Hill Street Blues* as

Narrative," *Critical Studies in Mass Communication,* Vol. 2 (March 1985): 1–22; Ethel S. Goodstein, "Southern Belles and Southern Buildings: The Built Environment as Text and Context in *Designing Women," Critical Studies in Mass Communication,* Vol. 9 (June 1992): 170–185.

18. David Marc, "Understanding Television," *Atlantic,* August 1984, 33–44.

19. For an excellent treatment of the shows of this period, see Leo Lowenthal and Norbert Guterman, *Prophets of Deceit* (Palo Alto, Calif.: Pacific Books, 1970).

20. Reported in Richard Corliss, "Look Who's Talking," *Time,* 23 January 1995, 23.

21. Leslie Phillips, "Airwaves Crackle with Criticism of Clinton Intimation," *USA Today,* 26 April 1995, 9A.

22. Lewis Grossberger, "The Rush Hours," *New York Times Magazine,* 16 December 1990, 58–59, 92, 94–95, 98–99.

23. Steven V. Roberts, "What a Rush!" *U.S. News & World Report,* 16 August 1993, 29.

24. Corliss, "Look Who's Talking."

25. This discussion of how public communication works is based on Michael Osborn, "Rhetorical Depiction," in *Form, Genre, and the Study of Political Discourse,* ed. Herbert W. Simons and Aram A. Aghazarian (Columbia: University of South Carolina Press, 1986), 79–107.

26. Claudia Wallis, "The Deadly Spread of Aids," Time, 6 September 1982, from *Time Almanac CDRom* (Washington: Compact Publishing, 1994).

27. Claudia Wallis, "You Haven't Heard Anything Yet," Time, 16 February 1987, from *Time Almanac CDRom* (Washington: Compact Publishing, 1994); Richard Stengel, "The Changing Face of Aids," *Time,* 17 August 1987, from *Time Almanac CDRom* (Washington: Compact Publishing, 1994).

28. Dan Daly, "A Sports Deity Proves Mortal," *Washington Times,* 8 November 1991, D1.

29. Pico Iyer, "It Can Happen to Anybody. Even Magic Johnson," *Time,* 18 November 1991, 26.

30. Woody West, "The AIDS Story Needs a Moral," *Insight,* 2 December 1991, 40.

31. Thom Loverro, "Ashe Reveals He Has AIDS," *Washington Times,* 9 April 1992, A1; Dan Daly, "Going Public with Tragedy," *Washington Times,* 9 April 1992, D1; "Ashe's Sad, Stunning AIDS Announcement," *Time,* 20 April 1992, 33.

32. Lance Morrow, "Fair Game?" *Time,* 20 April 1992, 74.

33. Daly, "Going Public with Tragedy."

34. Loverro, "Ashe Reveals He Has AIDS"; "Ashe's Sad, Stunning AIDS Announcement."

35. Martha Sherrill, "The Positive Side of HIV: Mary Fisher, Playing the Hand She Was Dealt," *Washington Post,* 31 May 1995, B1.

36. "Remarks by Elizabeth Glaser, July 14 Madison Square Garden, New York City," *Washington Post,* 25 August 1992, Z6.

37. Ibid.

38. "Remarks on AIDS at the 1992 Republican National Convention [from 3ed, *Public Speaking* credits]" reprinted by permission of the Republican National Committee.

39. Ibid.

40. John Steinbeck, preface to *The Forgotten Village,* as cited in Peter Lisca, *"The Grapes of Wrath* as Fiction," in *The Grapes of Wrath: Text and Criticism* (New York: Viking, 1977), 736.

41. Ralph R. Smith and Russel R. Windes, "The Innovational Movement: A Rhetorical Theory," *Quarterly Journal of Speech,* April 1975, 143.

42. Michael Kramer, "Ross Perot as Old Hickory," *Time,* 15 June 1992, 34.

43. Garry Wills, "The Power of the Savior," *Time,* 22 June 1992, 41–42. For additional insights into the nature of "savior politics," see Erich Fromm, *Escape from Freedom* (New York: Holt, Rinehart and Winston, 1941); Eric Hoffer, *The True Believer* (New York: Harper, 1951); T. W. Adorno, E. Frenkel-Brunswik, D. J. Levinson, and R. N. Standford, *The Authoritarian Personality* (New York: Harper, 1950); Milton Rokeach, *The Open and Closed Mind* (New York: Basic Books, 1960).

44. Joyce Price, "Could Horatio Alger Dream This?" *Washington Times,* 29 March 1992, A8; Walter Shapiro, "1-800-Pound Gorillas," *Time,* 6 April 1992, 16; George F. Will, "The Barefoot Billionaire," *Newsweek,* 1 June 1992, 78; David Gergen, Harrison Rainie, and Jerry Buckley, "Perot on Perot," *U.S. News & World Report,* 29 June 1992, 24–32; Jerry Buckley, "Righteous Ross," *U.S. News & World Report,* 1 June 1992, 29–31; George Church, "The Other Side of Ross," *Time,* 29 June 1992, 38–48; John Mintz, "Who Is Ross Perot?" *Washington Post National Weekly Edition,* 4–10 May 1992, 6–8; Tom Morganthau, "The Wild Card," *Newsweek,* 27 April 1992, 21–25.

45. Marsha Mercer, "Bid from a Billionaire?" *Washington Times,* 19 March 1992, A5.

46. Henry Muller and Richard Woodbury, "Working Folks say . . . 'We're Not Interested in Your Damn Position, Perot, We're Interested in Your Principles,' " *Time,* 25 May 1992, 36–43.

47. George F. Will, "That Man on Horseback," *Newsweek,* 20 April 1992, 86.

48. Ibid.

49. Laurence I. Barrett, "Heckler in Chief," *Time,* 29 March 1993, 27.

50. Scott Pendleton, "Pols Flock to Perot Conclave in Bid to Woo Swing Voters," *Christian Science Monitor,* 10 August 1995, 3; David S. Broder, "The Perot People," *Washington Post,* 15 August 1995, A17; David S. Broder, "Radical Middle Feels the Squeeze: Perot's Disaffected Decry Special Interests on Both Sides," *Washington Post,* 14 August 1995, A1; Robert D. Novak, "Perotites Watching, Waiting," *The Commercial Appeal,* 16 August 1995, A6.

51. Scott Pendleton, "Perot Army Seeks Change, Double Time," *Christian Science Monitor,* 14 August 1995, 4; Joe Klein, "Who Are These People: Perot's Odd Fawn-athon Highlights the Growing Anger of the Radical Middle," *Newsweek,* 21 August 1995, 31.

52. Klein, "Who Are These People"; Broder, "The Perot People"; Broder, "Radical Middle Feels the Squeeze."

53. Broder, "Radical Middle Feels the Squeeze."

54. Pendleton, "Pols Flock to Perot Conclave."

55. "Perot's Resonance [An Editorial]," *Christian Science Monitor,* 14 August 1995, 20.

56. Broder, "Radical Middle Feels the Squeeze."

57. Ibid.

58. E. J. Dionne, Jr., "And Pandering Pols," *Washington Post,* 15 August 1995, A17.

59. Cynthia Hanson, Abraham McLaughlin, and Peter Nordahl, "The News in Brief," *Christian Science Monitor,* 7 August 1995, 2.

60. Kathleen Hall Jamieson, *Packaging the Presidency* (New York: Oxford, 1984), 3–38.

61. Ibid.

62. *The 1994 Information Please Almanac* (Boston: Houghton Mifflin, 1993), 641.

63. Arthur Shulman and Roger Youman, *The Television Years* (New York: Popular Library, 1973), 72; Nielsen Media Research, 1996.

64. Craig T. Norback and Peter G. Norback, *TV Guide Almanac* (New York: Ballantine, 1980), 548.

65. Elizabeth Kolbert, "Candidates Sold Like Soap or Slung Like Dirt," *New York Times,* 17 July 1992, B1.

66. Ibid.

67. The Markle Foundation, "The Markle Presidential Election Watch Aims to Keep Public Informed on Issues, Media and Voters," 1996, http://www.markle.org/ewback.html.

68. The Markle Foundation, "The Markle Presidential Election Watch"; The Markle Foundation, "Report Card #2: Markle Presidential Election Watch Finds More Bite than Meat in TV Election News," 1996, http://www.markle.org/markwatc1.html.

69. Center for the American Woman and Politics, "Sex Differences in Voter Turnout," Eagleton Institute of Politics, Rutgers University, http://www-rci.rutgers.edu/~cawp/sexdiff.html; posted December 1997.

70. Walter Shapiro, "It's the Year of the Handlers," *Time,* 3 October 1988, from *Time Almanac CDRom* (Washington: Compact Publishing, 1994); Donald Devine, "Political Voodoo Practitioners," *Washington Times,* 2 September 1997, A11, http://www.townhall.com/conservative/columnists/Devine090297.html.

71. "Convention of Future: All Spin, All the Time," *USA Today,* 15 October 1996, http://www.usatoday.com/elect/ec/edc/edc100.htm.

72. Daniel Slocum Hinerfeld, "How Political Ads Subtract: It's Not the Negative Ads That Are Perverting Democracy. It's the Deceptive Ones," *Washington Monthly,* May 1990, 12–20.

73. The Markle Foundation,"The Markle Presidential Election Watch"; and Jac W. Germond Jules Witcover, "Everybody Deplores Negative Advertising—They Only Do It Because It Works," *Baltimore Sun,* 26 November 1996, http://www.sunspot.net/columnists/data/germond/0216germond.html.

74. Ken Goldstein, "Political Advertising and Political Persuasion in the 1996 Presidential Campaign," undated, http://www.asu.edu/clas/polisci/goldstein.html.

75. Stephen Ansolabehere and Shanto Iyengar, *Going Negative: How Political Ads Shrink and Polarize the Electorate* (New York: The Free Press, 1995).

76. Center for the American Woman and Politics, "Sex Differences in Voter Turnout."

77. Erik Barnouw, *Tube of Plenty: The Evolution of American Television,* rev. ed. (New York: Oxford, 1982); Sidney Kraus, ed., *The Great Debates: Kennedy vs. Nixon, 1960* (Bloomington: Indiana University Press, 1977); Garry Wills, *Nixon Agonistes: The Crisis of the Self-Made Man* (Boston: Houghton Mifflin, 1970); Jamieson, *Packaging the Presidency.*

78. Jamieson, *Packaging the Presidency,* 146.

MESSaGE PrEPARATION

A **JOURNEY** OF A THOUSAND MILES
BEGINS with a **SINGLE STEP.**

—*Chinese Proverb*

*C*an *you give me a topic for my speech? I just don't know what to talk about. I'm afraid I'll bore everyone in the class to death. I just can't seem to get started. I don't even know where to begin. If you'd just assign me a subject, maybe then I could get going.*

Preparing to speak before an audience can seem overwhelming, especially to beginning students. Simply getting started may be the most difficult part of speech preparation. If the task before you seems overwhelming, take it in small steps, advises Robert J. Kriegel, a performance psychologist who has counseled many professional athletes. While working as a ski instructor, Kriegel found that beginners would look all the way down to the bottom of a slope. The hill would seem too steep, and the challenge too difficult, and the novice skiers would back away. However, if he told them to think only of making the first turn, this would change their focus from something they thought they could not do to something they knew they could do.[1] Beginning speakers can also benefit from this advice. Look at the preparation of a speech as a series of steps leading to a goal. The flow chart in Figure 10.1 shows the major steps in the preparation of a speech and the order in which the steps should be taken.

Speech preparation begins with analyses of the speaking situation and the audience. These help you select an appropriate topic and hone in on those aspects of the subject that will be most meaningful for your listeners. They also can direct you toward a specific purpose and guide your research efficiently. As you can see from the arrows in Figure 10.1, you will work back and forth between these four steps in the first phase of your speech preparation.

The second phase of speech preparation has two steps: developing a preliminary outline and checking the adequacy of your preparation. In your preliminary outline, you should indicate the main points you will make in your presentation and the order in which you will make them. Your preliminary outline should also include the major subpoints and notations on supporting materials such as facts and figures, testimony, examples, narratives, or visual aids. It allows you to check the adequacy of your work to this point. For example, you may discover that you are trying to cover too much ground in a short presentation, which suggests that you may need to go back and rethink your purpose or topic. Or, you may discover that you don't have good supporting materials for one of your main points. That would suggest that you might need to do more research or redesign your speech. The final phase of speech preparation includes composing a formal outline and practicing your presentation. Three phases, eight steps, and you should be ready to approach the podium with confidence.

In this chapter we focus on the speaking situation and audience analysis. From there we move on to selecting and focusing a topic. Finally, we consider how you can determine your general and specific purposes and acquire responsible knowledge of your topic. Keep in mind that although these steps are discussed separately, in practice they overlap, and you will be constantly moving among them as you prepare a speech.

ANALYZING THE SPEAKING SITUATION

Every speaking situation has unique characteristics, and the techniques that make one speech successful may be inappropriate for another. The time, place, occasion, size of audience, and context in which a speech will be presented need to be taken into account as you plan and prepare your speech. For class-

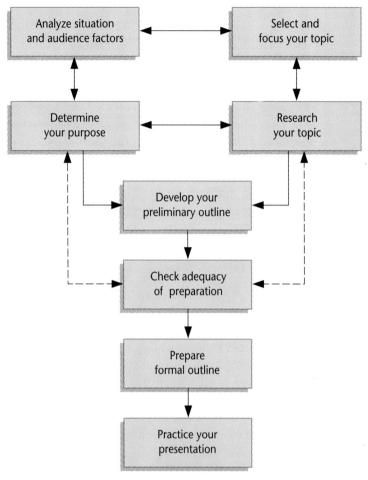

FIGURE **10.1**
Major Steps in the Preparation of a Speech

room presentations, all of the speaking situation factors except context are stable. For presentations outside of the classroom, it is easy to acquire such information by questioning the person who invited you to speak.

TIME

The time of day, day of the week, and amount of time allotted for speaking may call for different speech strategies. Early morning presentations require a more forceful presentation to awaken your audience. Speeches presented after a meal need a lively style to command attention. Monday speeches may call for vivid examples to jar people out of the relaxation of the weekend. Friday speeches need to be direct and to the point to maintain attention.

With regard to the amount of time allotted for your presentation, keep in mind that *the shorter your speaking time, the longer your preparation time.* For short speeches, you must focus tightly on your main points, support these with your most relevant and memorable facts and figures, testimony, examples, and narratives; and structure your message efficiently for maximum impact.

It is important to get a feel for where you will be speaking. A large room suggests that a more formal style would be appropriate.

PLACE

Find out as much as you can about the location where you will be speaking so that you can plan any adjustments that may be needed. You should find out such things as whether you will have a lectern, whether you can use visual aids or electronic equipment, and how good the acoustics will be. The place where you present your speech also may contain distractions that will require you to adjust your message or presentation. Speeches given outdoors need to be dramatic enough to overcome interference. Even in a classroom or office building, distractions may occur. If you can anticipate problems in advance, you can plan a strategy to handle them.

OCCASION

If the audience has been required to attend your speech, as in a mandatory employee meeting, you may have to work hard to interest them in your message. With a voluntary audience, you can assume that they already are interested in you or your subject. Even so, you must work to sustain their attention and satisfy their expectations. Audiences have rather definite ideas about what is appropriate for a given speaking situation. If they gather for what they believe will be an informative lecture and are bombarded with a sales pitch, their expectations will be violated and they may respond negatively.

SIZE OF THE AUDIENCE

Knowing the size of your audience can help you determine appropriate appeals, types of visual aids, language choice, and manner of presentation. Large audiences (over twenty people) are often diverse, so appeals and language may need to be more general or you may have to target specific subgroups. For example, a classroom audience composed of students from the business school might include marketing, accounting, finance, and computer science majors. If you were describing a new computer graphics program to such a diverse group, your language should be general enough for everyone to understand. You also might wish to direct specific comments to some of the subgroups within the audience—the marketing majors might be most concerned about how to use the program to create advertising copy, the finance majors might like to know how to use it for displaying statistical data, and the computer science majors might be most interested in ways to customize the program.

Large audiences require a more formal style of presentation because casualness may be interpreted as a lack of preparation or seriousness. Small audiences call for more informal presentations. You can make eye contact with listeners and modify your remarks as needed. In smaller groups you also can ask questions and solicit responses. Smaller groups may label as "stuffy" a more formal style in which you plant yourself behind a podium and read a manuscript.

CONTEXT

Speeches are presented within a context of recent events. In the classroom, speeches presented before yours will have a **preliminary tuning effect** that affects the mood of the audience. You need to be ready to adjust your message so that the tuning effect does not work against you. For example, if the speaker immediately before you spoke on a light topic and you want the audience to be in a more serious frame of mind for your speech, you may need to alter your introduction to change their mood:

> *Well, we've all enjoyed Elaine's humorous descriptions of the horrors of Halloween, but I'd like to talk with you today about a more serious horror—the horror of children killing children. Last year in our city, . . .*

Recent events outside the classroom will also affect the way the audience receives your speech. It is important that you stay abreast of news about your subject so that you can make changes if necessary. Suppose you have prepared a speech advocating a ban on semiautomatic weapons. The day before your presentation, a crazed gunman with a semiautomatic rifle kills fourteen people at a fast-food restaurant. It would be wise to include at least a reference to this event somewhere in your speech. Most of your listeners will know about the tragedy, and not mentioning it could damage your credibility.

Situational factors can be difficult to deal with, but it is important that you look upon them as challenges and try to make them work for you rather than against you. During graduation at Loyola Marymount University, the institution's president fell off the platform immediately before the commencement address. The speaker, Peter Ueberroth, organizer of the 1984 Los Angeles summer Olympic Games, recaptured the audience's attention and brought down the house by awarding the president a 4.5 in gymnastics.[2]

ANALYZING THE AUDIENCE

The more you know about your audience, the better your speech will be. Begin by defining your **primary audience**—those listeners you really hope to reach with your message. Designating a primary audience is particularly important when your topic is one on which the range of opinions may be diverse or opinions may be polarized. For example, your primary audience for a "don't drink and drive" speech might be those listeners who drink and have driven "under the influence" and those who might be tempted to do so, because these are the people you hope to convince. Your message might reinforce the beliefs of nondrinkers, but they would not be the primary audience for your message because they already agree with you.

AUDIENCE DEMOGRAPHICS

An effective audience analysis starts with information about **audience demographics**—age, gender, education, group affiliations, and sociocultural background. Politicians and advertisers rely heavily on such data for campaigns because they are easy to obtain and provide much valuable information. In making generalizations and predictions from demographics, however, you need to be careful to avoid stereotyping. Stereotypes are rigid depictions of a group that often suggest inferiority. For example, the elderly may be stereotyped as needy or athletes as unintelligent. Stereotyping suggests either that you lack information about a group or that you are inconsiderate,

Questions to Consider for Audience Analysis

✓ Who is the primary audience for my speech?

✓ How can I make listeners care about my topic?

✓ What aspects of my topic will be most relevant for my audience?

✓ What does my audience know about my topic?

✓ How does my audience feel about my topic?

✓ What values, beliefs, or attitudes do I share with my audience?

intolerant, or disrespectful. You can guard against stereotyping by combining information about a variety of demographic factors rather than relying too much on any one factor. Also keep in mind that factors will not all be equally important for all topics. For example, if you were preparing a speech on saving endangered species of wildlife, information about education level, group affiliations, and sociocultural background probably would be more important than age, race, or gender.

Knowledge of demographic factors can help guide a speaker in selecting and focusing a topic, developing a research strategy, and determining general and specific purposes. *When considering the demographic data available about your audience, always keep in mind that the most important thing is to show respect for your audience, regardless of its age, gender, education level, group affiliations, or sociocultural background.*

Age. People of different ages often are concerned about different aspects of a topic. For example, a speech on social security benefits to a young audience might best focus on disability protection and survivor's benefits. With an older audience, retirement planning and cost-of-living increases might be more appropriate. Age may also affect the way in which an audience responds to persuasive messages. As a general rule, younger listeners are flexible and open to new ideas; older listeners are more set in their ways.[3] Consequently, younger audiences are more susceptible to persuasive efforts.[4]

Gender. Attitudes about "appropriate" gender roles have changed dramatically over the past twenty-five years. Making generalizations based on traditional male and female roles can lead you into **sexual stereotyping.** Such stereotyping may be not only offensive to your audience, but also grossly inaccurate. For example, it may be based on unwarranted assumptions, such as "women don't understand or aren't interested in investments," when statistics show that 57 percent of all first-time New York Stock Exchange investors are women.[5] Although there are differences between men and women, let information about other demographic factors, such as education or group affiliations, temper generalizations based on gender.

You also should be careful not to use **sexist language,** which can be as subtle as the use of masculine pronouns when gender is unknown or irrelevant, or as blatant as referring to adult females as "girls." It may also include **marking** or adding a gender reference where none is needed, such as referring to "the female doctor." The use of sexist language can brand you as insensitive, intolerant, and inconsiderate.

Education. Information about the educational background of your audience suggests their knowledge and interests. Better-educated audiences are typically well informed about current affairs and have a broad range of interests. They tend to be more open-minded and to accept change more readily than less well-educated audiences. However, this does not mean that they are more easily persuaded. Better-educated audiences will be more critical in evaluating your evidence and arguments, so when you prepare a speech for such listeners, you should be especially thorough in your research and acknowledge all viable options for solving problems.[6]

Group Affiliations. The groups people belong to are tied in to their interests, knowledge, and attitudes. Knowing the occupations or career aspirations of your listeners can help you determine what they know about your subject, suggest the type of examples you should use, and help you select appropriate authorities to cite. Political affiliations provide insights into attitudes. As a general rule, Democrats are more concerned with social and domestic programs than Republicans, who focus on business interests and individual initiative. Social group membership is closely related to a person's interests. It can help you infer an audience's attitudes toward your topic and let you focus on the aspects of your subject that are most meaningful to them. For example, the focus of a speech on attracting industry to an area might be different for an audience of Jaycees, who would be most interested in the impact on the local economy, and for members of the Sierra Club, whose main concern might be its impact on the environment.

Sociocultural Background. As we noted in Chapter 1, people from different sociocultural backgrounds often have different experiences, interests, and ways of looking at things. Consider, for example, the different perspectives on gun control that urban and rural audiences may have. Urban audiences may associate guns with crime and violence. Rural audiences may associate them with hunting. Listeners with different ethnic or racial heritages may perceive problems differently because of the way they are affected by these problems. As with gender differences, it is important to avoid ethnic stereotypes and racist language or marking.

To reach listeners whose backgrounds differ radically from yours, you must find a common ground that can serve as a basis for identification. You should use supporting materials that demonstrate shared experiences or values. Personal narratives may help bring you and the audience closer together. You also must make culturally diverse audiences aware that they share a common stake in a problem.

AUDIENCE DYNAMICS

As useful as demographic information may be, it is just a starting point. A thorough audience analysis also includes **audience dynamics**—the beliefs, attitudes, values, and motivations of listeners.[7] Once you have gathered demographic data, you can begin to make inferences about these other factors.

● TRY THIS

Explain how you would tailor a speech on local environmental problems to an audience of (1) a group of fifteen Girl Scouts ages eleven to thirteen, (2) twenty residents of the Sunshine Home for Seniors, (3) a meeting of eight vegans (a vegetarian group), and (4) forty-five members of your school's Young Republicans Club.

Beliefs.   A **belief** is something we know, or think we know, about a subject. Information about your audience's beliefs is an important clue to what your listeners already think and can suggest additional information that you need to provide (or what misinformation you need to correct). Beliefs are acquired through experience and education. Some beliefs may be learned through direct experience; for example, "Asian students at our college study more than their peers." Other beliefs may be acquired indirectly from family, friends, and authority figures as we grow up; for example, "The Republican Party favors the wealthy." Some beliefs are **facts** that are verifiable, such as "The price of personal computers has dropped dramatically over the past five years." Other beliefs are **opinions** that may or may not be verifiable; for instance, "Japanese cars are better than American cars." A cluster of beliefs about a subject forms the basis of a person's attitude toward that subject.

Attitudes.   An **attitude** is a combination of beliefs about a subject, feelings toward it, and any predisposition to act toward it. Most attitudes have a strong judgmental component, meaning that you think the subject is either *good* or *bad*. The audience's attitude toward your topic can affect the way it receives your message. For example, if your audience has a negative attitude toward affirmative action, it may summarily reject any message advocating affirmative action programs without even listening to what you have to say. The reluctant audience poses special problems for the persuasive speaker. This subject is covered in greater detail in Chapter 15.

The audience also has an attitude toward you as a speaker. It may have an image of you as being either more or less competent, honest, attractive, or powerful. The way you are initially perceived as a speaker will be based on what the audience knows about you as you enter the speaking situation. You can increase the positive aspects of your image in the introduction to your speech by establishing identification with the audience and demonstrating your competence to speak on the subject. You also can enhance your image by including information and opinions from sources the audience respects and organizing your message clearly and succinctly.

The audience's attitude toward you will also be influenced by your attitude toward the audience. It goes without saying that you should be honest, sincere, and concerned with the well-being of your listeners. *Respect for the audience is extremely important.* You can show respect through careful preparation, which indicates that you take your topic and your audience seriously. It is also important for you to be appropriately dressed and neatly groomed for your presentation, as research indicates that attractive communicators are more effective.[8] You can also show respect by accepting differences of opinion—recognizing that those who disagree with you are not necessarily stupid or evil-minded. It is always wise to avoid opinionated language such as, "Only *baby killers* support a woman's freedom of choice." The use of such emotionally weighted language degrades you and can precipitate a **boomerang effect**, with the audience rejecting both you and your message.[9]

Values.   **Values** are abstract ideals that determine how we think we should behave and what we regard as the "right way" to live. Values may include such ideals as honesty, equality, peace, freedom, and salvation. Our personal, social, religious, and political values guide much of our thinking and behavior. They are the foundation for our most important beliefs and attitudes, providing us with standards for evaluation. Values are central to a person's self-concept and consequently are quite resistant to change. Information that clashes with a listener's values is likely to be rejected without much thought. References to shared values, however, can increase identification between speaker and audience and can enhance the persuasive impact of a speech.[10]

Motivation. **Motivation** is the psychological force that moves people to action and directs behavior toward specific goals. Our motivations include our needs, wants, and aspirations. The use of motivational appeals is central to all forms of public communication because these appeals are the most effective way to arouse and sustain interest in a message. Making people aware of a need and then showing them how to satisfy it is a major persuasive speech strategy.[11] Motivational appeals also are frequently used in advertising.[12]

Although all people share certain needs, the importance and intensity of any specific need may vary across situations. For example, if someone broke into your room and stole your computer, your need for safety would grow stronger. You would be receptive to speeches on campus security, especially if they offered a means of protecting your property. Needs may also vary with changing social conditions. Between 1957 and 1976, women developed increased needs for achievement and autonomy that were consistent with the increasing feminist consciousness in our culture.[13] Figure 10.2 describes some motivational appeals you may wish to consider in your audience analysis.[14]

1. **Comfort:** having enough to eat and drink, keeping warm when it is cool and cool when it is hot, being free from pain.

2. **Safety:** feeling secure in your surroundings, being protected from crime, surviving accidents and natural disasters, having an environment free of pollutants.

3. **Friendship:** establishing warm relations with others, being a member of a group or organization, being accepted by others, having someone to love and be loved by.

4. **Recognition:** being treated as valuable and important, having your achievements praised by others, receiving trophies or awards, being the center of attention.

5. **Variety:** longing for adventure, visiting new and unusual places, trying different things, changing jobs, moving to a new town, meeting new people.

6. **Control:** having a hand in your own destiny, planning for the future, fixing things and people, influencing or directing others, controlling your environment.

7. **Independence:** being able to stand on your own, being self-sufficient, making your own decisions, being your own person.

8. **Curiosity:** understanding the world around you, understanding yourself, understanding other people, questioning why things happen or why people act as they do, finding out about the unusual.

9. **Tradition:** having a sense of roots, having a feeling of continuity with the past, doing things as they have always been done, honoring your forebearers.

10. **Success:** accomplishing something of significance, overcoming obstacles to achieve your goals, doing better than expected, reaching the pinnacle of your profession.

11. **Nurturance:** taking care of others, comforting those in distress, aiding the helpless, caring for animals, giving to charitable organizations, providing volunteer service.

12. **Enjoyment:** doing something just for the fun of it, taking a vacation, pampering yourself, pursuing a hobby.

FIGURE **10.2**
Twelve Needs to Consider as Motivational Appeals

GATHERING AUDIENCE INFORMATION

You can get a great deal of information for audience analysis through observation. For classroom speeches, your instructor may administer an audience analysis questionnaire, such as the one in Figure 10.3, and distribute the results to the class. For presentations outside the classroom, you can often get useful information by questioning the person who asked you to speak.

Information about audience dynamics often must be inferred from other data. There are many published sources of information that help tie together audience demographics and audience dynamics. For example, each January the Higher Education Research Institute at UCLA releases the results of an annual survey of college freshmen. These results are usually reported in *USA Today* and are available

TRY THIS

Look over the list of needs in Figure 10.2 (on the previous page) and decide which ones relate to speeches with the following titles: "Champagne Living on a Beer Budget," "Divorce: The Rampant Disease of Our Time," "How to Succeed in College Without Killing Yourself," and "The Wisdom of Folk Medicine." Share your list with a classmate.

Sex: M F Age _____ Academic Year: FR SO JR SR GPA _____ Race _____

Marital status. _____ Religious preference _____

Major _____ State lived in longest _____

Current job: (full- or part-time) _____ Hours per week _____

Career aspirations: _____

Persons I admire most: (Male) _____ (Female) _____

Political preferences: [liberal, conservative, moderate]   [Democrat, Republican, other]
                              (circle one)   (circle one)

Group memberships (occupational, political, religious, or social)_____

_____

_____

Father's occupation _____ Mother's occupation _____

Place of birth _____ Places lived _____

Travel (in USA) _____

Travel (outside USA) _____

Hobbies _____

_____

Positive "trigger words" _____

Negative "trigger words" _____

The most important thing in my life right now is _____

_____

Topics on which I would like to hear an informative speech (name 3) _____

_____

Topics on which I would like to hear a persuasive speech (name 3) _____

_____

FIGURE 10.3
Audience Analysis Questionnaire

VALS:	http://future.sri.com/vals/survey.html
Equifax:	http://www.ends.com/low/lifequiz.html
PEW Political Ideology:	http://www.people-press.org/fit.htm
National Opinion Research Center:	http://www.icpsr.umich.edu/gss/about/gss/gssintro.htm
Gallup Organization:	http://www.gallup.com
American Demographics:	http://www.demographics.com/
Cyberpages Polls:	http://www.cyberpages.com/poll
University of North Carolina IRSS:	http://www.unc.edu/deps/irss/
Princeton Survey Research Center:	http://www.princeton.edu/~abelson/index.html
Cornell Survey Research Center:	http://www.ciser.cornell.edu/Welcome.html#pubs
Roper Center for Public Opinion Research:	http://www.lib.uconn.edu/RoperCenter

FIGURE **10.4**
Audience Analysis Web Sites

on-line at http://www.gse.ucla.edu/heri/heri.html. During major political campaigns, pollsters survey attitudes, beliefs, and values and report them in almost unbelievable detail.[15] The results of attitude surveys on many social and political issues are published in *American Demographics. USA Today* provides tidbits of poll results on a daily basis. *Harper's* magazine publishes a column of odd and assorted statistics ("Harper's Index") that often contains information related to attitudes, beliefs, values, and motivations. Market research specialists provide information on lifestyles and values related to demographic data. Much of this information is now available on the Internet. A sampling of relevant Web sites may be found in Figure 10.4.

If knowledge of your audience's attitude is critical to your presentation, you may wish to gather more specific information about your audience's interest in the topic, their knowledge about it, their attitude toward it, and the way they might evaluate sources of information you could cite in your speech. Figure 10.5 (on the following page) is a sample attitude questionnaire. Classroom surveys will not be as reliable as those conducted by professional pollsters, but they can yield useful results if you use the following guidelines for preparing your questionnaire:

- Plan your questions carefully to get the most useful information.
- Use language that is concrete, simple, clear, and unambiguous.
- Keep your questions short and to the point.
- Provide room for comments.
- Keep the questionnaire brief.

The more information you have about the speaking situation and the audience, the better job of preparing and presenting a speech you can do. Once you have thoroughly considered these factors, you can move on to selecting and focusing your topic.

If you are asked to make a speech outside the classroom setting, your topic may be part of the invitation. In speech classes, topic selection is usually left up to you. A good speech topic is appropriate to both the speaking situation and the audience. It should be meaningful, substantive, and interesting both to the

SELECTING AND FOCUSING YOUR TOPIC

For each question, please circle the number that most clearly represents your position.

1. How interested are you in the topic of capital punishment?

Very Interested			Unconcerned			Not Interested
7	6	5	4	3	2	1

2. How important do you think the issue of capital punishment is?

Very Important			No Opinion			Very Unimportant
7	6	5	4	3	2	1

3. How much do you know about capital punishment?

Very Little			Average Amount			Very Much
7	6	5	4	3	2	1

4. How would you describe your attitude toward capital punishment?

Total Opposition			Undecided			Total Support
7	6	5	4	3	2	1

5. Please place a check beside the sources of information on capital punishment that you would find the most acceptable.

_____ Attorney General's office

_____ FBI

_____ Local police department

_____ Criminal justice department of the university

_____ American Civil Liberties Union

_____ Local religious leaders

_____ Conference of Christians and Jews

_____ NAACP

_____ Other (please specify) _____

Comments:

FIGURE 10.5
Sample Attitude Questionnaire

audience and to you personally. If you do not really care about the topic, you will find it difficult to invest the time and effort necessary to prepare an effective speech. A good speech topic is also one about which you already know something. Personal involvement increases your credibility and makes the acquisition of responsible knowledge easier. Finally, a good speech topic is one that can be handled in the time allotted. This means that you must focus on a manageable aspect of the subject. For example, the topic "wildlife conservation" would be too broad for a short classroom presentation. It would be much better to focus on local efforts to save the manatee. That topic would be both more manageable and more meaningful to your audience.

CHARTING INTERESTS

One way to begin topic selection is to make a list of places, people, activities, events, things, goals, problems, and campus concerns that have personal importance for you; the list in Figure 10.6 is an example. Try to include at least four entries in each category. If you have problems thinking of entries, scan the popular press for ideas. Look through newspapers and magazines. What headlines or titles grab your attention? Keep in mind that the media can direct you to ideas for speeches, but they do not provide the speeches

It is sometimes difficult to communicate with a diverse audience. Look for common needs or values as a basis of communication.

for you. *Your speech must be designed to appeal to your audience.* You should always bring something new to your topic. After charting your interests, make a similar chart of apparent audience interests. From your classroom discussions and audience analysis, you should have some idea of your listeners' interests and concerns. Study the two charts together to pinpoint your best topic possibilities.

If you have a topic in mind, but you are not sure your audience will share your enthusiasm, then you must generate interest early in your speech. Motivate your audience to listen to your speech. Review the list of needs in Figure 10.2 and decide which ones you can most easily relate to your topic and your audience. Consider how you might use these appeals to show your listeners how the topic affects them personally or what they stand to gain from your message.

PLACES	PEOPLE	ACTIVITIES	EVENTS
Manatee Springs	Aunt Jimmie	canoeing	Pioneer Days festival
Antietam battlefield	Paul Newman	drying flowers	Civil War
Zuni pueblo	Maria Tallchief	traveling US	World War II
Yellowstone Park	Paula Jones	television	Mardi Gras
Buffalo Bill Museum	Sojourner Truth	junqueing	birthday parties
THINGS	GOALS	PROBLEMS	CAMPUS CONCERNS
Quilts	get degree	greenhouse effect	off-campus housing
Kachina dolls	get good job	wildlife extinction	date rape
Hurricanes	have family	alcohol abuse	crime on campus
Cartoon	visit Hawaii	sexual harassment	hazing
Grizzly bears	get grades up	homophobia	part-time work

FIGURE 10.6
Personal Interest Inventory

FOCUSING YOUR TOPIC

As you look over your interest inventory, you may find that most of your entries are too broad to use as topics for a short presentation. Now you must focus in on some manageable aspect of the subject that you can handle in the time allotted. One way to approach this task is to analyze your topic by asking *who, what, when, where, why,* and *how.* Let's apply these probes to the topic "Yellowstone Park" and see what ideas they can generate:

- *Who* uses Yellowstone Park? Who abuses the park? Who works at the park? Who decides on policy for the park?
- *What* are the major attractions at Yellowstone Park? What are some of the lesser-known attractions? What ecological damage was done by forest fires in the park? What can be done to forestall problems of overcrowding?
- *When* was Yellowstone established as a national park? When do most tourists visit the park? When is the park least crowded? When are roads impassable?
- *Where* can you go to get away from crowds in the park? Where do most of the grizzly bears live in the park? Where is it safe to backpack?
- *Why* are tourists warned not to feed the wildlife in the park? Why was the recent forest fire allowed to burn? Why are only hard-sided campers allowed in some areas? Why must all trout caught in the park be released?
- *How* can you find out more about the attractions in Yellowstone Park? How many tourists use the park each summer? How can you get a summer job at the park? How can you store food so that bears won't get it?

As you look over these probes, you will notice that certain themes emerge: some entries center on the history of the park, some on park attractions, and others on wildlife and ecological concerns. What would be the best topic for your speech on Yellowstone Park? That depends on your audience. If you live near Yellowstone, a speech on the major attractions would offer listeners little in terms of new information or ideas. Such an audience, however, might be interested in the history of the park or current ecological problems. On the other hand, if you live far from Yellowstone, a speech on major attractions could be appropriate. College students might be especially interested in how they could get a summer job at the park.

Criteria for a Good Speech Topic
- ✓   It is substantive and important
- ✓   It is interesting to me
- ✓   It can be made relevant and interesting to my audience
- ✓   I can learn enough about it to speak responsibly
- ✓   It is focused so that I can handle it in the time allotted
- ✓   It is appropriate for the time, place, and occasion of the speech

Your analysis of your general speech topic will probably yield several specific speech topics you could develop. Before you proceed further in your planning and preparation, you need to consider your purpose for speaking.

DETERMINING YOUR PURPOSE

You cannot prepare an effective speech unless you understand your purpose for speaking. *You must understand why you want to give this speech on this topic for this audience.* Thinking through your general and specific purposes will help you focus your research efforts most efficiently.

GENERAL PURPOSE

The **general purpose** of your speech is your overall reason for speaking. It will generally be either *to inform* or *to persuade*. For classroom speeches, the general purpose is usually part of the assignment. When your general purpose is to inform, your goal is to share knowledge with your audience, to enhance their understanding, to provide them with new information or fresh ideas about your topic. When your general purpose is to persuade, your aim is to influence the thinking and behavior of your listeners.

SPECIFIC PURPOSE

Your **specific purpose** indicates what you want your audience to understand, believe, or do as a result of hearing your speech. It should focus on those aspects of your topic that would be most relevant to your audience. Let's look at how a specific-purpose statement focuses the intent and topic of a speech:

Topic: Yellowstone Park
General Purpose: To inform
Specific Purpose: To inform my audience about major attractions in Yellowstone Park

Topic: Greenhouse effect
General Purpose: To persuade
Specific Purpose: To persuade my audience to take action to delay the onset of the greenhouse effect

ACQUIRING RESPONSIBLE KNOWLEDGE

Once you have your specific purpose in mind, you can begin a quest for responsible knowledge. **Responsible knowledge** is the most comprehensive understanding of your topic that you can acquire in the time you have available for preparation. When you ask an audience for their time and attention, you must give them something of value in return. Having responsible knowledge earns you the right to speak to your audience. In addition, whenever you speak to a group, you put your mind and character on display. If you haven't made an effort to acquire responsible knowledge, you might as well be saying, "Well, I'm not really prepared and have nothing much to say, but I really don't care."[16] Having responsible knowledge of your topic should enhance your perceived ethos in terms of both competence and character.[17]

Your search for responsible knowledge should lead you to substantive, reliable information about the major issues concerning your topic, what respected authorities have to say about it, recent developments on the subject, and any local applications that would be especially relevant for your audience. Your quest will lead you to facts and figures, testimony, examples, and narratives that can be used to substantiate your ideas. As you investigate your topic, you may also find materials that can be adapted for use as visual aids. We will cover these forms of supporting materials in detail in Chapter 11.

Because your preparation time will be limited, you should begin by developing a research strategy. Having such a strategy will help you make more efficient use of your time and enable you to locate and evaluate the materials you need. Start by assessing your personal knowledge and experiences to determine what additional information you might need to make a responsible presentation. Next, develop a strategy for obtaining this information using library resources, the Internet, and/or interviewing for information and opinions. Finally, conduct your research and make note cards to use as you organize your speech.

PERSONAL KNOWLEDGE AND EXPERIENCE

Personal knowledge and experience add credibility, authenticity, and interest to a speech. Describing how a problem feels will gain and hold the audience's attention and may make the audience more receptive. Personal anecdotes are most effective when you are not an acknowledged authority on a subject.[18] They help you seem better informed and more personable, making it easier for the audience to identify with you.

As valuable as it is, your experience will rarely be sufficient to provide all the information, facts and figures, and testimony that you will need for your speech. Your personal knowledge may be limited, the sources from which you learned may have been biased, or your experiences may not have been typical. Even people who are acknowledged authorities on a subject look to other experts to give credence to their messages. President Woodrow Wilson once suggested, "I use not only all the brains I have, but all I can borrow." Use your personal knowledge and experience as a starting point and expand it through research. Prepare a personal knowledge and experience summary sheet similar to the one shown in Figure 10.7. Include on your summary sheet what you know (or think you know) about the topic, where or how you learned it, and what additional information you might need to find. Also jot down any examples or narratives based on your experience so that you can remember them as you put your speech together. Use your summary sheet to give direction to your research.

THE INTERNET AS A RESEARCH TOOL

The Internet can be a very useful research tool in the preparation of speeches. It contains a wealth of information that is easily accessible through a personal computer that is hooked up via modem to an Internet service provider. Most colleges and universities make this on-line access available to their students either through their own personal computers or through the library.

It is beyond the scope of this book to teach you how to use the Internet. If you have never used it before and do not have on-line access, the following books might be helpful:

- John R. Levine and Carol Baroudi, *The Internet for Dummies,* IDG Books: Foster City, CA. (Look for the most recent edition.)
- Wayne Ause and Scott Arpajian, *How to Use the World Wide Web,* Ziff-Davis Press: Emeryville, CA, 1996.

What I Know (or Think I Know)	Where/How I Learned It	What I Need to Find Out
Not many grizzly bears in the park.	Worked there 2 summers; heard rangers talk about it; only saw 1 and I was looking.	Approximately how many bears are in the park?
Go to back country to see the grizzlies.	Same as above; personal experience.	Where in park are they most likely to be seen; specify trails and areas.
Grizzly attacks are rare.	Same as above.	When was first attack recorded? Last? Note number of attacks relative to number of tourists; relative to other types of injuries.
Camping precautions taken.	See above; see brochure; personal experience.	Information probably sufficient.

Examples/Narratives I might use in speech:

For the past two summers I've worked waiting tables at Mammoth Springs Lodge in Yellowstone Park. We got two days a week off and I spent nearly all my free time hiking and camping in the back country, far away from the tourists and crowds in the park. I counted up the number of hours I spent that way and discovered that I had logged in more than 350 hours in these remote locations—in the grizzly bear habitat of the park—hoping to see a bear. Only once in all those hours did I see a grizzly bear, and that was from a distance of about half a mile. If I hadn't been sitting quietly with my binoculars focused on a watering area, I probably would have missed seeing that one!

FIGURE **10.7**
Personal Knowledge Summary

- Joe Kraynak et al. *The Big Basics Book of the Internet,* Que Corp.: Indianapolis, IN, 1996.
- Mary Micco and Therese D. O'Neil, *Using the Internet,* Houghton Mifflin: Boston, MA 1996.
- Gary Gach, *The Pocket Guide to the Internet,* Simon & Schuster Pocket Books, New York, NY, 1996.

If you are on-line, you might check "Understanding and Using the Internet" (http://www.pbs.org/uti/) or "An Internet Tutorial" (http://www.msn.com/tutorial/default.html). These guides may be most useful because the Internet changes from day to day; therefore, anything written about it may be obsolete before the ink dries.

It has been said, and it is certainly true, that anyone can put anything on the Internet. This being the case, how can you be sure that the information you find fits our definition of responsible knowledge? One way to approach this problem is to apply the critical thinking skills discussed in Chapter 4. In addition to using these basic skills, you should consider the following guidelines that are applicable to Internet materials.

Begin by evaluating the source of the material:

- Is the document signed by an author?
- Is a URL or E-mail address provided?
- Is the source an authority on the subject?
  - Are the credentials of the source specified?
  - Does he or she list professional affiliation? occupation? educational background?

Personal computers and the Internet have made access to information easy to obtain.

- Can I verify the credentials of the source?
  - Check home page of Web site (delete all information in URL after server name).
  - Run a search with author's name in quotation marks.
- Check organizations/associations via Scholarly Societies Project (http://www.lib.uwaterloo.ca/society/overview.html).
- Run a search with name of organization/association in quotation marks.
- Use anonymous sources only for illustrative examples or lay testimony. Cite as an anonymous Internet document.

Next, evaluate the information provided:

- Is the source of statistical information identified?
- Is the information recent?
- Are the dates of information within the document provided?
- When was the document last updated?
- Is information in the text linked to other sources? Can you check these?
- Is a bibliography provided?
- How does this compare with other information in the field?
- Does the information seem objective and balanced?
- Are differing points of view presented?
- Is there more sizzle than substance in the document?
- Are spelling and grammar correct?
- Is the writing clear or unnecessarily obscure?

If the material checks out well using these questions as a guide, it probably falls within the realm of responsible knowledge. You can find a list of useful Web sites in Appendix A, "A Guide to Library and Internet Resources."

USING LIBRARY AND INTERNET RESOURCES

The major resources available for speakers include (1) sources of background information, (2) sources of access to information, (3) sources of in-depth information, (4) sources of current information, and (5) sources of local information. You should use all of these resources to acquire responsible knowledge of your subject. In this section we shall explore the types of resources available and show you how to prepare a research strategy that will help you use your time efficiently.

TRY THIS

Using the Internet, compile a list of ten web sites for almanacs, atlases, biographies, or quotations. Print out a copy of the list and bring it to share with your classmates.

Sources of Background Information. Even if you feel you know almost everything you need to know about your topic, you should begin by reading an authoritative review of the subject. This allows you to check the thoroughness and accuracy of your personal information. You may encounter new information or discover aspects of the topic you hadn't considered. The review also can help you focus your topic by pointing out the most important ideas. Review articles are found mainly in encyclopedias and specialized dictionaries housed in the reference section of the library. On the Internet, go to The Page Site (http://www.thepagesite.com/encycl_p.htm) for links to most of the encyclopedias on-line. General encyclopedias, such as *Encyclopaedia Britannica* (http://www.eb.com/), contain background information, specify key words to use in your search for in-depth information, and often list references for additional research. The articles are brief and written in lay language. Specialized encyclopedias, such as the *International Encyclopedia of the Social Sciences,* cover specific topics in greater detail. Specialized dictionaries, available on diverse subjects ranging from American slang to zoology, provide more than definitions and pronunciations. For example, *The Oxford English Dictionary* presents the origin, meaning, and history of English words. A directory of dictionaries on the Internet may be found at http://www.thepagesite.com/ dict_p.htm.

Sources of Access to Information. Since your preparation time for speeches is limited, you must know how to find information quickly. The major sources of access to information in the library include periodical indexes, newspaper indexes, and the card catalog. Some of the periodical indexes, such as the *Reader's Guide to Periodical Literature,* cover publications of general interest. Others, such as the *Business Periodicals Index,* are particular to a subject area. Many indexes are now available on computers, which saves research time. To access information from an index, you must identify key terms related to your topic. As noted above, most encyclopedia entries list relevant key terms. You can also identify key terms from the *Library of Congress Subject Headings,* which are used in the card catalog, or from a list of key terms provided with the resource.

On the Internet, the major sources of access to information are the search engines. Your service provider will probably provide links to a variety of search engines. Many of these tools are described and rated in Magellan (http://www.mckinley.com/) and the Encyclopedia Britannica Internet Guide (http://www.ebig.com/). The following search engines may be useful in the preparation of your speeches:

- Yahoo (http://www.yahoo.com/): contains subject guides.
- Excite (http://www.excite.com/): searches by concepts.
- Northern Light (http://www.nlsearch.com/): groups results for better focus.
- The Mining Company (http://www.miningco.com/): has mini-sites designed by humans.
- Inference Find (http://www.inference.com/infind/): a superfast search engine that clusters results.

> ● **TRY THIS**
>
> Check the periodicals catalog in your library and make a list of all the periodicals available that relate to a topic that interests you. Check those periodicals that you did not know were published. Locate the most recent copy of one of these unfamiliar periodicals and skim the table of contents. Read one of the articles and prepare source and idea cards. (See p. 221). Working in small groups in class, discuss what you learned about your library holdings and what you learned about your topic of interest.

Sources of In-Depth Information. Most of the facts and figures, testimony, examples, ideas for narratives, and materials for visual aids will come from in-depth sources of information such as periodicals and books. Appendix A contains an annotated list of periodicals that are especially useful in speech preparation. As you research your speech, try to use a variety of sources with different perspectives on your topic. Keep in mind that periodicals have a reputation of their own. Some periodicals, such as the *Wall Street Journal,* will be perceived as highly credible and objective, while other periodicals may be less acceptable to your audience. Even highly credible sources may be tinged with bias on certain topics. For example, the American Cancer Society might be an excellent source of information about the relationship between cancer and smoking, but biased on the question of government funding for medical research because of self-interest. As you read your in-depth material, you may discover that one book is frequently mentioned. If time permits, you should try to read this book. At the very least, you should check the *Book Review Index* to find and read the reviews of the book.

When you need facts and figures, consult an almanac, yearbook, or atlas. Almanacs and yearbooks provide accurate, up-to-date information on a wide range of topics. Such materials go beyond simple lists to include short articles and graphics that you can adapt for visual aids. Atlases are useful when your topic calls for geographic information. They often include data on population density or industrial production and are a good source of materials for visual aids. Biographical resources can provide information to qualify the experts you might cite in a speech. Quotations are useful for introductions and conclusions for speeches. Most books of quotations are indexed by topic and author, making it easy for you to find what someone important had to say about your subject. Most of the above resources are available on the Internet as well as in the library.

A word of caution: As we noted earlier in this chapter, *articles do not provide you with a speech,* rather they give you ideas, information, opinions, examples, and narratives for use in the speech that you prepare for your particular audience. If you simply summarize an article and present it as though it were your own, you are committing **plagiarism.** At most colleges and universities, plagiarism is punishable by grade reduction or suspension. You can avoid plagiarism by following these simple guidelines:

- *Do not summarize a single article for a speech.* Get information and ideas from a variety of sources and blend them into a unique approach to your topic.
- *Introduce the sources of quotations in your speech,* for example, "The late comedian George Jessel once noted, 'The mind is a wonderful organ. It begins working at birth and doesn't quit until you stand up to make a speech.'"
- *Identify your sources of information,* for example, "According to *The 1998 World Almanac,* you are almost twice as likely to be disabled by an accident in the home as by a car or work accident."
- *Give credit to the originators of ideas* that you use, for example, "Maria Martinez, director of student counseling services, suggests that there are two techniques that test-anxious students can use to get through final exams."

Sources of Current Information.   For topics that change rapidly, such as computer technology, the timeliness of information is important. Also, if you are not aware of current happenings related to your topic, your credibility may suffer. The best source of timely information is the Internet. By logging on to local newspapers and television stations throughout the world, you can keep abreast of happenings during crisis situations. Ecola Newsstand (http://www.ecola.com/) lists newspapers on-line in the United States and around the world. One of the best library sources for current information is *Facts on File,* a weekly publication that reports on current events by topics. Additional sources of current information include the most recent issues of newspaper and periodical indexes. To be on the safe side, you should also scan the latest weekly news magazines on the current periodicals shelves of your library.

Sources of Local Applications. To involve your audience with your subject, you should show them how it relates to them and their community. For example, if you were presenting a speech on problems of hazardous waste, it would be better to talk about that problem in your own area than in some place halfway across the country. Many libraries maintain a vertical file that contains newspaper clippings, pamphlets, and other materials about important local people or issues. These materials may contain the names of people you could interview for additional information or opinions. Your library may also have an index of your local newspaper and subscribe to regional magazines. Your local newspaper may also have archives that you can search through the Internet. For a list of searchable newspaper archives, check the Ecola Newsstand at http://www.ecola.com/archive/press/.

Developing a Research Strategy. The research strategy worksheet shown in Figure 10.8 on the following page should help you plan your research efficiently. Begin by having your topic and specific purpose clearly in mind. Use Appendix A or the Internet to identify a source of general information to start your search. Read that background material, take notes, and write down the key terms you will use to access in-depth information. Using library indexes and abstracts or an Internet search engine, build a bibliography on your topic. From your bibliography, identify the three or four articles or books that seem most relevant to your specific purpose. If timeliness is important for your topic, find one or two current references. Finally, check for local applications.

INTERVIEWING FOR INFORMATION

Personal interviews can be an excellent source of facts, examples, and testimony for your speeches. Material from interviews adds credibility to your speech. If you can say, "Randall Parrish, the director of research and development at Richards Electronics, told me . . . ," your audience will sit up and listen. But like personal experience, interviewing also poses problems. You may tend to accept your expert's opinions without evaluating them for accuracy and objectivity. Still, it is usually worth the effort to interview someone for additional supporting material.

If you plan to use an interview to obtain information for a speech, you must find the right person to interview, determine how to conduct the interview, establish contact, prepare for the interview, and record what you learn so that it is readily accessible for speech preparation.

Find the Right Person to Interview. Use your library's local resource file or the Internet archives of your local newspaper to identify an expert on your subject who is qualified by education, training, or experience. Don't overlook the most obvious source available to you—your own campus. Every college and university has faculty members who have expertise on a wide array of topics, and they are typically willing to take the time to talk to students in their offices.

Determine How to Conduct the Interview. It is usually preferable to conduct an interview face to face, but sometimes that is not practical. Telephone interviews can be used to verify information, acquire a brief quotation, or discover a person's opinion.[19] You can also interview a person via e-mail on the Internet. When preparing a speech on the effect of a recent NCAA regulation on college athletics, one University of Memphis student phoned the athletic directors of her own school and the Universities of

TOPIC _____

SPECIFIC PURPOSE _____

GENERAL INFORMATION SOURCES: (List source of general information applicable to your topic)

_____

KEY TERMS AND ACCESS TO INFORMATION SOURCES: (List the key terms you will use and two sources of access to information you will use to identify specific and/or in-depth references)

Key Terms   1._____   2._____

Access   1._____   2._____

SPECIFIC AND/OR IN-DEPTH INFORMATION REFERENCES: (List three or four references to specific and/or in-depth information applicable to your topic, of which at least two must be from periodicals or books.)

1. _____
   _____

2. _____
   _____

3. _____
   _____

4. _____
   _____

CURRENT INFORMATION REFERENCES: (List one or two sources of current information, if applicable to your topic.)

1. _____
   _____

2. _____
   _____

LOCAL APPLICATIONS SOURCES: (List one or two sources for local applications material, if applicable to your topic.)

1. _____
   _____

2. _____
   _____

FIGURE 10.8
Research Strategy Worksheet

Tennessee, Mississippi, and Arkansas for their opinions. All of the athletic directors were willing to talk with her, and she was able to quote them in her speech. That material appreciably enhanced her credibility on the subject.

Establish Contact. It is best to initiate contact with a letter that gives your expert an opportunity to prepare for the interview. You might include a list of the questions you wish to discuss. A well-written request can help establish your credibility. Follow up the letter with a phone call to schedule the interview. If time is short, however, you will probably initiate contact through a telephone call or e-mail either directly to the person you wish to interview or to that person's secretary. Tell him or her why you wish to conduct the interview and what kind of questions you want to ask. Don't be shy. A request for an interview is a compliment because it suggests that you value that person's opinion.

Prepare for the Interview. Complete your research before you conduct an interview so that you know what questions to ask and can interact intelligently on the subject. Write out your interview questions so that the responses will be relevant to your specific purpose. Keep your list of questions short—your expert is probably a busy person whose time is valuable.

Record What You Learn. It is better to take notes during an interview than to try to tape-record it because many people do not like to be taped. Tell your expert that you will be taking notes so that you can quote him or her correctly in your speech. If you are not certain you wrote down a response correctly, read it back to the person for confirmation. After you have completed the interview, find a quiet place to go over your notes and write out the answers to important questions while your expert's wording is still fresh in your mind.

TAKING NOTES ON YOUR RESEARCH

The best research in the world will not do you any good unless you take notes that will help you prepare your speech. Take notes on anything you read or hear that *might* be usable in your speech. It is better to have too much material to work with than too little. Many researchers prefer to make notes on index cards because they are easy to handle and sort into categories. You will need to prepare both source and idea cards for each article or book you might use.

Your **source cards** should contain standard bibliographical information: the author's name, the title of the article or book, the title of the periodical for an article, the place and date of publication for a book, the date of publication for an article, and the page references. You also may wish to include a short summary of the material, information about the author's qualifications, and any comments on or reactions to the material that you may have. Use **idea cards** to record facts and figures, examples, or quotations. Use a different card for each item of information you think you might use. Each idea card should have a heading that describes the information on the card, the source from which the material was taken, and the information itself.

IN SUMMARY

Speech planning and preparation should begin with analyses of the speaking situation and the audience. Situational factors you should consider include time, place, nature and purpose of the occasion, size of audience, and context. Your audience analysis should encompass both demographics and dynamics. Important demographic factors include age, gender, education level, group affiliations, and sociocultural background. Your analysis of audience dynamics should consider beliefs, attitudes, values, and motivations.

The information you gather about your audience will help you select and focus your topic. A good topic is one that is interesting to both you and the audience. It is substantive and meaningful, offering the audience something of value in exchange for the time they spend listening. It should be focused so that you can handle it in the time allotted for your presentation. Begin your search for a speech topic by charting your interests and your audience's interests, then look for areas of overlap. Analyze your topic area by asking who, what, when, where, why, and how. Further focus your topic by determining your general and specific purposes.

Once you have selected and focused your topic and determined your specific purpose for speaking, you can begin to acquire responsible knowledge of your topic. Responsible knowledge earns you the right to speak before an audience. The starting point in acquiring responsible knowledge is assessing what you already know about your topic. Next, develop a research strategy to find general information, sources of access, specific information, recent developments, and local applications. You may wish to supplement your research with information gleaned from interviews. Take notes on your research so that you can incorporate the material you find into your speech.

TERMS TO KNOW

preliminary tuning effect
primary audience
audience demographics
sexual stereotyping
sexist language
marking
audience dynamics
belief
facts
opinions

attitude
boomerang effect
values
motivation
general purpose
specific purpose
responsible knowledge
plagiarism
source cards
idea cards

NOTES

1. Robert J. Kriegel, *If It Ain't Broke . . . Break It!* (New York: Warner, 1991), 167–168.

2. Reported in *Time,* 17 June 1985, 68.

3. Milton Rokeach, *The Open and Closed Mind* (New York, Basic Books, 1960).

4. William J. McGuire, "Attitudes and Attitude Change," in *The Handbook of Social Psychology,* ed. Gardner Lindzey and Elliot Aronson (New York: Random House, 1985), 2:287– 288.

5. Anthony M. Casale and Philip Lerman, *USA Today: Tracking Tomorrow's Trends* (Kansas City, Mo.: Andrews, McMeel & Parker, 1986), 47.

6. McGuire, *Attitudes and Attitude Change,*: 271–272.

7. This discussion of beliefs, attitudes, and values is based on the works of Milton Rokeach. See especially *Beliefs, Attitudes, and Values: A Theory of Organization and Change* (San Francisco: Jossey-Bass, 1970); *The Nature of Human Values* (New York: Free Press, 1973); and *Understanding Human Values: Individual and Societal* (New York: Free Press, 1979).

8. J. Mills and E. Aronson, "Opinion Change as a Function of the Communicator's Attractiveness and Desire to Influence," *Journal of Personality and Social Psychology,* 1 (1965): 173–177.

9. R. S. Mahrley and J. C. McCroskey, "Opinionated Statements and Attitude Intensity as Predictors of Attitude Change and Source Credibility," *Speech Monographs* 37 (1970): 47–52.

10. Henry Z. Scheele, "Ronald Reagan's 1980 Acceptance Address: A Focus on American Values," *Western Speech Communication Journal* 48 (1984): 51–61.

11. The motivated sequence persuasive strategy was introduced in Alan Monroe's *Principles and Types of Speech* (New York: Scott, Foresman, 1935) and has been refined in later editions.

12. Jib Fowles, "Advertising's Fifteen Basic Appeals," *Et cetera* 39 (1982); reprinted in Robert Atwan, Barry Orton, and William Vesterman, *American Mass Media: Industries and Issues,* 3rd ed. (New York: Random House, 1986), 43–54.

13. J. Veroff et al., "Comparison of American Motives: 1957 versus 1976," *Journal of Personality and Social Psychology* 39 (1980): 1249–1262.

14. This list of needs is based on the classic work of Henry A. Murray, *Explorations in Personality* (New York: Oxford University Press, 1938). A contemporary measuring instrument based on these needs is the "Edwards Personal Preference Schedule" (New York: The Psychological Corporation).

15. Scott C. Ratzan, "The Real Agenda Setters: Pollsters in the 1988 Presidential Campaign," *American Behavioral Scientist* 32 (March–April 1989): 451–463.

16. William Norwood Brigance, in his classic public speaking text, *Speech: Its Techniques and Disciplines in a Free Society* (New York: Appleton-Century-Crofts, 1952), entitled his chapter on researching a speech "Earning the Right to Speak."

17. James C. McCroskey, *An Introduction to Rhetorical Communication,* 5th ed. (Englewood Cliffs, N.J.: Prentice-Hall, 1986), 72.

18. Study by J. Berger and R. Vartabedian, *Journal of Applied Social Psychology* 15(2), cited in Jeff Meer, "Political Intimacies: Better Left Unsaid," *Psychology Today,* January 1986, 19–20.

19. Michael Schumacher, "The Interview and Its Uses," in *1992 Writer's Market,* ed. Mark Kissling and Roseann Shaughnessy (Cincinnati: F & W Publications, 1991), 9.

CHAPTER ELEVEN

SUPPORTING MATERIALS

THIS CHAPTER will help you

- Use facts and figures to substantiate ideas

- Use definitions, explanations, and descriptions to clarify concepts

- Use expert, prestige, and lay testimony as appropriate

- Use examples to bring your speech to life and to clarify ideas

- Use narratives to involve your audience and illustrate abstract ideas

- Use comparison, contrast, or analogy to make ideas more understandable

- Develop and use presentation aids to enhance your message

THE **UNIVERSE** IS MADE OF **STORIES**, not atoms.

—M. Rukeyser

*S*o far, so good! I've analyzed my speaking situation and my audience, selected and focused my topic, determined my general and specific purposes, and conducted my research. Now I've got a whole stack of source and idea cards. Where do I go from here? What should I do next?

The next step in the development of your speech should be to go back through your research materials to identify supporting materials that you can use in your speech. **Supporting materials** include facts, statistics, definitions, explanations, descriptions, testimony, examples, narratives, comparisons, contrasts, analogies, and presentation aids. These materials are the basic building blocks of a speech. They help illustrate the meaning of topics, show the relevance of ideas, make material more memorable, and verify controversial statements or claims. You should look for impressive facts and figures that your audience will remember, and for information and opinions from authoritative sources that you can quote to further substantiate your ideas. Additionally, you should find or develop at least one example or narrative for each main point. Finally, you should go back through your research notes and look for material that you can adapt for presentation aids. In this section we will discuss the major types of supporting materials, how they should be used, and how to evaluate them in terms of practical and ethical considerations.

FACTS AND STATISTICS

Facts and statistics are the most objective and authoritative types of supporting material. They add substance to your ideas. Facts and figures are especially important when the ideas you wish to advance are unfamiliar to your audience or the point you want to make is controversial. If you are not an acknowledged expert on your topic, you must have this kind of "hard" data to support your ideas and claims.

FACTS

Facts are verifiable units of information that independent observers see and report consistently. Facts carry with them a presumption of truth. Listeners will evaluate information that you present in terms of its source, so it is important that you specify where you got your information. As we noted in Chapter 10, different sources of information have different reputations. For example, most audiences will regard information reported in the *Wall Street Journal* more highly than information reported in the *National Enquirer.*

Speakers rarely present facts without interpreting them. As we noted in Chapter 4, facts should not be confused with opinions. It is very easy for interpretations to move from fact to opinion with the addition of just a single ill-considered word. Consider the following examples:

Fact	*Opinion*
HIV is a communicable disease.	HIV is a *shameful* communicable disease.
Most State U. students complete their studies in four years	Most *hard-working* State U. students complete their studies in four years.
Television ads often rely on emotional appeals.	Television ads often rely on *unethical* emotional appeals.

STATISTICS

Statistics are numerical facts. They can be used to describe something in terms of its size or to make predictions, report trends, or show relationships. Statistics that are presented orally are difficult for people to understand, so you should tie numbers to something the audience can relate to easily. A brief explanation, an example, or a presentation aid can make numerical information more understandable. The following excerpt from a student speech urging listeners not to buy canned tuna demonstrates the use of an example to interpret statistics:

> *The National Marine Fisheries Service estimates that up to 130,000 dolphins are killed each year by being trapped in tuna nets. This means that from the time we entered this classroom until the time we leave it today, fifteen dolphins will be killed by commercial fishermen.*

Using Statistics
- ✓ Use the most recent and reliable statistics
- ✓ Use statistics from unbiased sources
- ✓ Do not stretch or twist the meaning of statistics
- ✓ Round off numbers whenever possible
- ✓ Amplify statistics with examples
- ✓ Don't use too many numbers

EVALUATING FACTS AND STATISTICS

In the course of your research, you will find a wide array of facts and figures. Before you make a definite decision to use certain information, evaluate it. Be sure that the material you have selected is relevant to your specific purpose and comes from a credible, objective source. Try to use the most recent facts and figures. Look for information that is confirmed by more than one source. Make certain that your facts and figures are truly representative rather than exceptions to the rule. Finally, be careful not to present opinions as facts.

DEFINITIONS, EXPLANATIONS, AND DESCRIPTIONS

Speakers typically weave facts into a speech by using definitions, explanations, or descriptions that clarify and expand the meaning of concepts and ideas.

DEFINITIONS

A **definition** is a simple, concise statement of meaning. Definitions help assure that the audience understands what you are talking about. You should provide definitions for any terms or ideas that are unfamiliar to your audience or that you may be using in some unusual way. A definition may relate to either the denotative or the connotative meaning of a word. **Denotative meaning** conveys the word's generally agreed-upon objective usage. On the other hand, **connotative meaning** conveys the feelings and attitudes associated with the word. Both types of definitions may be useful in speeches, depending on the circumstances and the message you wish to communicate.

For technical terms, a denotative definition, as provided by any standard dictionary but translated into easily understandable language, will usually suffice. For example, you might define *osteoporosis* as "a disease common in older women that is characterized by brittle bones and curvature of the spine." The more unfamiliar or abstract an idea is, the more important it is to define it. Definitions of abstract ideas often carry connotative overtones that are important to a message. In a speech on domestic violence against women, Donna Shalala, U.S. Secretary of Health and Human Services, provided the following connotative definition of domestic violence: "Domestic violence is terrorism. Terrorism in the home. And that is what we should call it."[1]

EXPLANATIONS

An **explanation** is longer and more detailed than a definition and clarifies what something is or how it works. Explanations are important when ideas are unfamiliar or complex. They tell the audience what they need to know in language they can understand. The following explanation of "old growth" could be used effectively in a speech on forest preservation:

> *From a traditional forester's view,* old-growth *forests are those in which wood production has reached its peak. . . . Old-growth forests contain many large, live, old trees. They are forests that have never been harvested. The Wilderness Society defines "classic" old growth as "containing at least eight big trees per acre exceeding 300 years in age or measuring more than 40 inches in diameter at breast height."*[2]

DESCRIPTIONS

Descriptions are "word pictures" that help an audience visualize what you are talking about. The best descriptions implant vivid images in the minds of the audience. Such images may establish a mood that sets the stage for persuasion. Note how the following description of the "monument" at Wounded Knee both paints a picture and establishes a mood:

> *Two red brick columns topped with a wrought iron arch and a small metal cross form the entrance to the grave site. The column to the right is in bad shape: cinder blocks from the base are missing; the brickwork near the top has deteriorated and tumbled to the ground; graffiti on the columns proclaim an attitude we found repeatedly expressed about the Bureau of Indian Affairs, "The BIA sucks!" Crumbling concrete steps lead you to the mass grave. The top of the grave is covered with gravel, punctuated by unruly patches of chickweed and crabgrass.*[3]

A description also may depict something the audience has never seen before or provide a new perspective on a familiar subject. The University of Memphis student audience for Stephen Huff's speech on earthquake preparedness was

Speakers who paint vivid word pictures can take the audience to the scene of the action. The speaker's description of the gravesite at Wounded Knee is clear and compelling.

familiar with the Mississippi River. They could easily visualize the river as it flows past their town. Stephen's vivid description of the river and surrounding area during the 1811–1812 New Madrid earthquakes helped them see it in a new way:

> *The Indians tell of the night that lasted for a week and the way the "Father of Waters"—the Mississippi River—ran backwards. Waterfalls were formed on the river. Islands disappeared. Land that was once in Arkansas—on the west bank of the river—ended up in Tennessee—on the east bank of the river. . . . Cracks up to ten feet wide opened and closed in the earth. Geysers squirted sand fifteen feet into the air. Whole forests sank into the earth as the land turned to quicksand.*[4]

TRY THIS

Share a brief description of the main street of your hometown with a classmate, then listen to his or her description. Could you see the place that was being described? Did the description arouse any positive or negative feelings? Discuss with your classmate how you each might have improved your description to make it more effective.

EVALUATING DEFINITIONS, EXPLANATIONS, AND DESCRIPTIONS

As you consider using definitions, explanations, or descriptions in your speech, ask yourself the following kinds of questions. Is the audience familiar with this concept? If so, these supporting materials are unnecessary and might even insult their intelligence. Is the audience familiar with the way I am using this concept? If not, a definition or explanation could help assure that they understand what you are saying. Can my audience "see" what I am talking about? If they can't, and if this is important to your message, a description may be called for. Finally, do I want to set a particular mood or establish an attitude toward my subject? If so, a description rich in vivid imagery can help you reach this goal.

TESTIMONY

Testimony supports an idea by showing what others have written or said about it. It can provide information or opinions on an issue or insight into the issue. Testimony is typically interwoven into a speech through quotations. You may choose to cite your source's exact words, quoting them **verbatim**, when the quotation is short, when the exact wording is important, or when the wording is especially eloquent. If the testimony comes from a composite of information, you may decide to **paraphrase** it, or restate in your own words the essence of what was said. There are three types of testimony that you can use: expert testimony from highly qualified authorities on your topic, lay testimony from ordinary citizens, and prestige testimony from respected or admired, but not necessarily expert, sources.

EXPERT TESTIMONY

Expert testimony comes from people who are qualified by training or experience to serve as authorities on a subject. For example, if you were preparing a speech in favor of handgun controls, you could use expert testimony from law enforcement officials or criminologists. Such testimony might include statements of information or opinion. Expert testimony can be used to establish the validity of ideas and is especially important if your topic is unfamiliar, technical, or controversial. As you look for expert testimony, keep in mind that an expert's competence is area-specific—in other words, statements can be used as *expert testimony* only when they fall within the area in which your expert is qualified. For example, law enforcement officials who could provide expert testimony on gun control might not qualify as experts on educational reform.

As you introduce expert testimony in your speeches, be certain that the audience is familiar with the qualifications of your authorities. If the person you are quoting is not well known, specify his or her credentials as you lead into your quotation or paraphrase:

> *Dr. Lee Takayama, chair of our Criminal Justice Department and former member of the Governor's Task Force on Inner-City Violence, said that licensing handguns would . . .*

LAY TESTIMONY

Lay testimony represents the voice of the people and is highly regarded in America. Newspapers bombard us with the latest statistics on what "the people" think about everything from abortion to zoo doo. In fact, *USA Today* features lay testimony along with the opinions of experts on its editorial page.[5] Lay testimony cannot be used to establish the truth of ideas; however, if listeners can identify with your sources because "they are just like us," they may be more willing to accept your ideas. Lay testimony also adds authenticity and compassion to ideas. Expert testimony deals primarily with facts and appeals to the intellect; lay testimony deals with feelings and appeals to emotions. Such testimony can be extremely powerful if the source has had direct experience with the issue under consideration. During the recent debates on gun control legislation, James Brady, the presidential press secretary who was shot during an assassination attempt on President Reagan, testified before the U.S. Senate Judiciary Subcommittee. Speaking from his wheelchair, he said:

> *There was a day when I walked the halls of this Senate and worked closely with many of you and your staffs. There was a wonderful day when I was fortunate enough to serve the President of the United States in a capacity I had dreamed of all my life. And for a time, I felt that people looked up to me. Today, I can tell you how hard it is to have people speaking down to me. But nothing has been harder than losing the independence and control we all so value in life. I need help getting out of bed, help taking a shower, and help getting dressed.*

> *There are some who oppose a simple seven-day waiting period for handgun purchases because it would inconvenience gun buyers. Well, I guess I am paying for their convenience. And I am one of the lucky ones. I survived being shot through the head. Other shooting victims are not as fortunate.[6]*

PRESTIGE TESTIMONY

The source of **prestige testimony** usually is a well-known and respected public figure, and its power is based on the person's good reputation. Prestige testimony may be used for the insight it provides into a topic. Celebrity endorsements are also a form of prestige testimony. The use of prestige testimony enhances the general credibility of a speech, but this testimony cannot be used to demonstrate the accuracy of information. Prestige testimony frequently takes the form of quotations used in the introduction or conclusion of a speech.

Celebrity endorsements are a form of prestige testimony. No one expects the celebrity to be an expert on the product.

One student speaker opened a speech opposing rating systems for television shows with the following quotation attributed to Clare Boothe Luce, writer, editor, former congresswoman, and first female American ambassador to a major country: "Censorship, like charity, should begin at home; but, unlike charity, it should end there."

EVALUATING TESTIMONY

It is important that you evaluate the testimony you plan to use in your speeches. You should assess the relevance and recency of the testimony and determine the credibility of your sources. Be certain that they are qualified to serve as expert witnesses for your position and will be acceptable to your audience. You also must be sure that the testimony you use is truly representative of your source's position. It is unethical to twist the meaning of what people say by quoting them out of context. For example, during a political campaign in Illinois, one state representative sent out a fund-raising letter that claimed that *Chicago* Magazine had singled him out for "special recognition." Indeed it had! He had been cited as "one of the state's ten worst legislators."[7] Finally, consider the type of testimony you have in terms of its intended use. Only expert testimony can be used to validate ideas. You can use lay testimony to increase authenticity, create identification, and appeal to compassion. You can use prestige testimony to enhance the overall credibility of your speech.

TRY THIS

Share with a classmate your reactions to a current television advertisement based on prestige celebrity testimony. What characteristics of the celebrity was the sponsor promoting? How effective do you think the ad was? What drawbacks are there to this type of advertising?

Using Testimony
✓ Select sources your audience will respect
✓ Point out the qualifications of sources as you cite them
✓ Be careful to quote or paraphrase material accurately
✓ Use only expert testimony to validate information
✓ Use lay testimony for identification and authenticity
✓ Use prestige testimony to enhance general credibility

EXAMPLES

Examples are verbal illustrations that function in speeches the same way that pictures do in a book. A speech without examples is boring and hard to follow. Examples help bring speeches to life and attract and sustain attention. Moreover, examples help clarify a message by showing concrete applications of abstract or technical ideas. Personalized examples, which use names and places, involve the audience with your message and create bonds of identification. Examples help listeners *experience* the meaning of your ideas, rather than simply *understanding* them. When you use an example to illustrate an idea, you are pointing out that what you have just said is important enough to bear repeating. Examples also give your listeners time to digest what you have told them before you move on to another idea. The examples that you use in your speeches may be brief or extended, factual or hypothetical.

BRIEF EXAMPLES

Brief examples are specific instances mentioned to support a point. Brief examples clustered together can help drive home a point. Harvey Jacobs, editor of the *Indianapolis News*, used the following brief examples to support his contention that readers were an endangered species:

> *Take a turn through the houses of today. How many new houses . . . have proper illumination for easy reading? How many new houses have bookcases? Take the average hotel or motel room. Can you find a spot in the room where you can sit down and be able to see to read a newspaper or a book?*[8]

EXTENDED EXAMPLES

Extended examples contain more details and allow you to dwell more fully on a single instance. They make it easier to convey a feeling about a topic than do brief examples. The speaker cited above also used the following extended example in his speech:

> *I have two sons, both relatively successful in the professional world. Both have college degrees—one a Ph.D.—-and both were reared in a newspaper home, with never less than two and sometimes three or four daily papers. Eight of their growing up years were in Chicago. The* Sun Times, *the* Tribune *and the* Daily News *were delivered to our home every day. Yet, these young men—yuppies, you might call them—do not subscribe to a daily newspaper. They tell me that a newspaper is not essential to their daily supply of information. I'm sorry that they feel this way, but they may be more typical of their age group than we are willing to admit.*[9]

FACTUAL EXAMPLES

Factual examples involve real people or events. They provide strong support for ideas because they are grounded in reality. When you actually know the people, factual examples are even stronger. If the examples you will use could be embarrassing, you can change the names of the people involved to protect their identity. The following factual example was used in a speech on the state of our culture:

> *In* New York Magazine, *only weeks ago, a veteran TV anchorman is reported to lament . . . about the declining caliber of TV reporters. He cites as an example the newsbreak that the terrorists who sabotaged the* Achille Lauro *were to be tried in absentia, which caused one reporter to run through the newsroom asking, "Where is Absentia?"*[10]

HYPOTHETICAL EXAMPLES

Hypothetical examples are composites of actual people, situations, or events. They may be drawn from experience or from reading on a topic. To be effective, hypothetical examples must represent reality and seem plausible to the audience. Hypothetical examples are often introduced with a phrase such as, "Imagine yourself in the following situation." The following hypothetical example could be used to illustrate the meaning of "cabin fever":

> *Picture the following: You're in a room with five other people—four of them under ten years old, brimming with energy. It's been raining for six days—a cold, heavy rain. No one can go outside. The kids run in circles and fight with one another. The other adult nags at you when awake and snores when asleep. What kind of mood would you be in?*

EVALUATING EXAMPLES

Evaluate examples in terms of their relevance, representativeness, and believability. You should also consider whether your examples are appropriate for your listeners. What works well with one audience may bomb with another. Finally, you should consider matters of taste and propriety. You can do yourself and your topic untold harm if you select an example that offends the sensibilities of your audience.

Using Examples

✓ Use examples to emphasize major points
✓ Use examples to gain attention and clarify ideas
✓ Name the people and places in your examples
✓ Use factual examples whenever possible
✓ Use examples that are believable and representative
✓ Keep examples brief and to the point
✓ Save examples for points of major importance

NARRATIVES

Narratives are stories that illustrate ideas. Narratives work well in speeches because people enjoy listening to stories. Humans are story-telling animals. Most children are brought up on narratives—stories that entertain, fables that warn of dangers, and parables that teach virtues. Narratives are especially effective in speeches because they involve listeners in creating meaning, so that the message becomes *their* discovery, *their* truth.

In speeches, narratives serve many of the same functions as examples: they make a speech livelier and help sustain attention, they clarify abstract or technical ideas, they help the audience experience the message, and they amplify a point. The memory of facts and figures fades with time, but narratives leave the audience with something to remember.

Because they so quickly involve listeners with the subject, narratives are often used in the introductions of speeches. Narratives that contain a light touch of humor also help make the audience comfortable.[11] One student, speaking on the importance of "selective disobedience," opened his speech with the following narrative:

> *Once when I was in high school, our football team had a slim lead near the end of a big game. We had just taken possession of the ball on our own 10-yard line with no time-outs left. The coach told the quarterback, "Run play 14 twice, then punt, no matter what happens!" The quarterback called play 14, and we gained 45 yards. He called it again, and we gained 40 more yards. By now the ball was on our opponent's 5-yard line, but the quarterback followed instructions and called for a punt. When our team came off the field as the ball changed hands, the coach grabbed the quarterback and yelled at him, "Why did you do that? What were you thinking about?" The quarterback replied, "I was thinking—we really do have a dumb coach!" Today I'd like to talk with you about the importance of practicing "selective disobedience"—about knowing when and how to break the rules.*

Because narratives can reinforce the essence of a message and are easily remembered, they also are frequently used as conclusions. Senator Dan Coats of Indiana used the following touching narrative as the conclusion of a speech entitled "The Virtue of Tolerance":

> *I recently came across a story about tolerance that affected me—not because it is rare, but because it is more common than you would imagine. It is about a young . . . woman who began, on her own, to visit terminally ill AIDS patients in the hospital. These men had no families and no visitors. So this woman brought them books and cookies and postage stamps, and a willingness to sit and listen and pray. She explained, "They are socially unacceptable because of their lifestyle, and medically unacceptable because of their diseases. They are scared. They are dying."*
>
> *. . . She offered a touch to the untouchable. She brought her attentiveness to men waiting for death. She accepted the humanity of the ostracized. She saw God's image in a shrunken and wasted body. This is tolerance humanized by . . . compassion. And this is really our goal. . . . Our society needs nothing more from you than this: . . . be tolerant of people of deep conviction.[12]*

There is an art to creating a good story and telling it well. Every story must have a beginning, a middle, and an end. The story must create suspense as it builds to its conclusion. You should set the story off from the rest of your speech with pauses. Your language should be colorful and active. If the story evokes laughter, wait for the laughter to subside before going on. Since storytelling is an intimate form of communication, you should reduce the distance between you and the audience—either physically by moving toward them or psychologically by being less formal. Finally, you should practice telling your story to get the wording and timing right. Corral your roommate or some friends and try it out to see if you can bring it off.

Be careful when you use humor in a speech. Don't tell a funny story just for the sake of amusing the audience. The use of humor in a speech requires considerable thought, planning, and caution if it is to be effective. Be certain that it is appropriate to your subject and furthers your specific purpose. Also be aware of the sensitivities of your audience. For example, religious, ethnic, racist, or sexist humor—however well intended—usually reflects poorly on a speaker. It can evoke such negative reactions from an audience that they don't even hear the rest of the speech. Avoid stories that are funny at the expense of others. If you poke fun at anyone, let it be yourself. Speakers who tell amusing stories about themselves sometimes rise in the esteem of listeners. When this technique is effective, the stories that seem to be putting the speakers down are actually building up their ethos.[13] Note how former President Jimmy Carter used this type of humor as he acknowledged his introduction as a speaker at commencement exercises at Rice University:

> *I didn't know what Charles [the person who introduced him] was going to say. For those who have been in politics and who are introduced, you never know what to expect. There was a time when I was introduced very simply. "Ladies and gentlemen, the President of the United States," period. But then when I left office I was quite often invited by lowly Democrats who were in charge of a program at an event. Then when I got there with two or three TV cameras, the leaders of the organization—almost invariably Republicans—would take over the introduction of me, and quite often the introduction would be a very negative one derived primarily from President Reagan's campaign notes. I had to do something to heal my relationship with the audience before I could speak, so I always would tell them after that, "Ladies and gentlemen, of all the introductions I've ever had in my life, that is the most recent."*[14]

Using Humor

✓ Use humor to put the audience at ease

✓ Be certain humor is relevant to your topic

✓ Remember the humor you use reflects on your character

✓ Don't be funny at the expense of others

✓ Don't overdo the use of humor

✓ Use humor only if you are good at telling stories

EVALUATING NARRATIVES

The guidelines for evaluating narratives are similar to those for evaluating examples. You must be certain that the narrative is relevant, plausible, representative, and appropriate for your particular audience. Use only narratives that are in good taste. Steer clear of sexist and ethnic stories. To be sure that your narrative will work with your audience, try it out first on some similar people. If they don't get the point, don't use it. Finally, your narratives should be fresh and interesting. If you discovered it in last month's *Reader's Digest*, chances are that many in the audience will have seen it as well.

TRY THIS

Tell a story or joke (keep it clean!) to a classmate, then listen to one in return. How easy was this for you? How comfortable are you communicating this way? What might you do to improve your storytelling ability?

Comparisons, contrasts, and analogies can be used in conjunction with facts and figures, definitions, explanations, descriptions, testimony, examples, and narratives to make them more understandable and memorable.

COMPARISON, CONTRAST, AND ANALOGY

COMPARISON

A **comparison** makes an unfamiliar idea more understandable or acceptable by relating it to something with which the audience is already familiar. Comparisons point out the similarities between things, as in the following example:

The proposal before us for licensing handguns is much like licensing drivers. You would have to take a written test to demonstrate that you know and understand the principles of handgun safety and regulations, just as you now have to take a written test to demonstrate your mastery of driving safety and regulations. You would have to take a "hands-on" test to demonstrate your skill in using a handgun, just as you have to demonstrate your ability to drive a car. And finally, you would be subjected to a background check to determine your suitability to be licensed to have a handgun, just as your application for a driver's license is checked for DUIs and moving traffic violations.

CONTRAST

A **contrast** points out the differences between things. Just as a red cross stands out more vividly against a white background than it does against an orange one, contrasts make things stand out by juxtaposing differences. Note how the remarks of Senator Daniel Patrick Moynihan use contrast to make statistics more striking and more memorable as he talks about New York City at the time of his graduation in 1943 and New York City in 1992:

In 1943 there were exactly 44 homicides by gunshot in the City of New York. Last year there were 1,499. In 1943 the illegitimacy rate in New York City was 3 percent. Last year it was 45 percent.[15]

Of course, if Senator Moynihan were making a similar statement about New York City in 1998, the contrast in numbers would be less dramatic.

ANALOGY

An **analogy** points out the similarities between things or concepts that are essentially dissimilar. In a **literal analogy**, the subjects come from the same realm of experience, such as football and soccer. In a **figurative analogy**, the subjects come from different realms of experience, such as business and sports. Analogies make concepts or ideas that are remote or poorly understood more immediate and comprehensible. They focus attention on qualities that might otherwise go unnoticed.[16] Note the use of both literal and figurative analogies in the following excerpt from a speech entitled "Succeeding in Japan":

I think of doing business in Japan as being like a game of football. But first, you need to know which game of football it is you are playing. Is it the American gridiron sport—or what the rest of the world calls football and what we call soccer?

American football is a bruising battle. The players are huge and strong. They have nicknames like "Refrigerator." And the game is played in short bursts of intense energy. In soccer-football, the players are smaller, but faster. Play is continuous. And a soccer fullback weighs less than lunch for a gridiron fullback.

In a nutshell, gridiron football is trench warfare: soccer football is the cavalry. Likewise, when it comes to business, the Japanese play a different game than we do.[17]

EVALUATING COMPARISONS, CONTRASTS, AND ANALOGIES

Before using comparisons or analogies, ask yourself the following questions: Are there enough similarities between the concepts or ideas? Are the similarities relevant to the idea I wish to support? Are the similarities significant, or are they superficial? Are any dissimilarities nonessential, or do they render the comparison or analogy invalid? To evaluate contrasts, you would ask yourself similar questions: Are there enough differences? Are the differences relevant to my purpose? Are the differences practical and meaningful? Are there any important similarities that would render the contrast invalid?

PRESENTATION AIDS

Presentation aids give the audience direct sensory contact with your message. They enhance understanding, especially with material that is difficult to communicate orally. Presentation aids also add authenticity and increase a message's credibility. People believe what they see more than they believe what they hear. Presentation aids add variety, which helps to sustain attention. Finally, presentation aids help a speech have a lasting impact because pictures are often more memorable than words. As valuable as presentation aids can be for a speech, however, they should never be used just for the sake of having a presentation aid. Use them only when they add something important to your message. Figure 11.1 lists some of the benefits of presentation aids.

There are many types of presentation aids that can be used in speeches. Each kind has certain advantages and disadvantages. You may choose people, objects and models, line drawings, graphs, or pictures. Your medium of presentation might be the chalkboard or markerboard, a flip chart, posterboard, handouts, slides or transparencies, or videotapes. Most personal computers are capable of generating professional-looking

1. Presentation aids can aid understanding and add authenticity to a message.
2. Presentation aids can make statistical information easier to comprehend.
3. Presentation aids can enhance your ethos.
4. Presentation aids can add variety to your speech.
5. Presentation aids can improve presentation skills.
6. Presentation aids can make a presentation more persuasive.

FIGURE **11.1**
Benefits of Using Presentation Aids

presentation aids. You may also make computerized multimedia presentations. Select the kind of presentation aid that most enhances your message.

PEOPLE

Whenever you speak, your appearance, gestures, and facial expressions add a nonverbal component to your message. You become a presentation aid in the speech. Be sure that the way you look complements rather than contradicts what you say. Additionally, certain activities, such as a proper golf swing or racing dive stance, can most easily be demonstrated using people. You can demonstrate these activities yourself or recruit someone to help you. If you use another person, be sure to get that person's permission and coach him or her in advance.

OBJECTS OR MODELS

Objects or models are often used to illustrate speeches of demonstration. Any objects you use must be large enough for everyone in the audience to see without straining, yet small enough to handle easily. If an object is too large, too small, too rare, or simply unavailable, a scale model may be used as a presentation aid. Inanimate objects make better presentation aids than living things, such as puppies, because they are easier to control. Avoid using objects that will make a mess and distract from your message. For example, if you want to demonstrate how to carve a pumpkin, make the initial cuts and clean out the seeds in advance.

You should keep objects out of sight until you are ready to talk about them. Don't clutter up a speech with too many presentation aids. One student brought six objects to illustrate materials used in the Montessori method of preschool education. She lined them up on the desk before beginning her speech. Listeners were so curious about what the objects were that they paid more attention to the objects than they did to the speaker. Don't let yourself be upstaged by a presentation aid.

LINE DRAWINGS

Line drawings, such as sketches or maps, may be drawn by hand or generated on a computer, and may be displayed on posters, on the chalkboard or markerboard, on a flip chart, in handouts, or in slides or transparencies. Sketches offer simplified representations of what you are describing. They should highlight the essential aspects of the subject. Commercially prepared maps contain too much detail to function well as presentation aids. If you want to use a map, draw one on posterboard and include only necessary information. Do not try to display drawings from books because they will be too small and difficult to handle. Instead, trace them, then enlarge them on posterboards or prepare slides or overhead projections from the tracings.

GRAPHS

Masses of numbers in a speech can overwhelm an audience. A well-designed graph can make statistics easier to understand and remember. The three most commonly used types of graphs are the pie graph, the bar graph, and the line graph. A **pie graph** is a

Murder/Victim Relationships

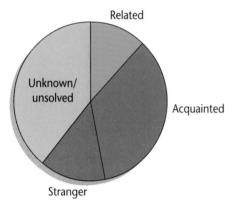

Information Please Almanac, 1995

FIGURE **11.2**
Sample Pie Chart

circle divided into segments that illustrate the size of parts in relation to the whole. The most effective pie graphs have five or fewer divisions (see Figure 11.2). A **bar graph** uses adjacent vertical or horizontal bars to show comparisons between two or more items or groups. The bars should be clearly distinguished by either color or pattern (see Figure 11.3). A **line graph** connects points on a grid to demonstrate changes across time and is useful for showing growth or decline. You should limit the number of lines on a graph to three or less to avoid confusion (see Figure 11.4).

PICTURES

Pictures add authenticity to a message, but they are difficult to use as presentation aids unless they are large enough to be seen by everyone in the audience. Additionally, pictures often contain unnecessary detail that distracts from the message. Despite these disadvantages, pictures can work well if they are carefully selected, controlled, and enlarged. Most copy centers can make colored enlargements that can be mounted on posterboards for use in a speech. Never pass around photographs while you are speaking.

CHALKBOARD OR MARKERBOARD

The chalkboard or markerboard (used with broad-tipped felt markers) works well when you want to offer a step-by-step demonstration, emphasize certain words or ideas, or clear up something the audience doesn't understand by creating a spontaneous presentation aid. However, these media also have some serious disadvantages. If you are not careful, your presentation aids may look sloppy, and the audience may not be able to decipher what you have written or drawn. Additionally, once you start using the board, you may overuse it. You should not use the board for anything that takes more than a few seconds to write or draw, and you should be careful not to talk to the board instead of the audience.

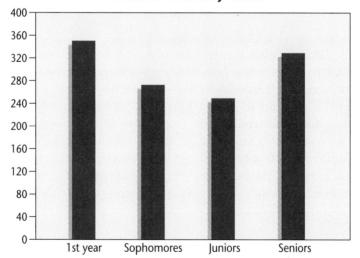

Student Affairs Office, 1996

FIGURE **11.3**
Sample Bar Graph

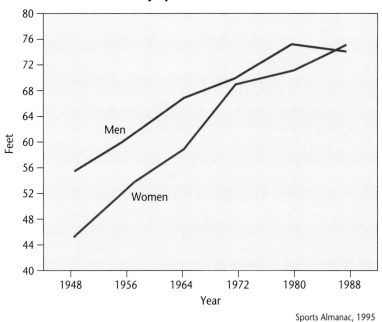

Olympic Shot Put Distances

Men

Women

Sports Almanac, 1995

FIGURE **11.4**
Sample Line Graph

FLIP CHART

A flip chart is a large, unlined tablet of newsprint measuring about two feet wide and three feet high. Flip charts offer many of the same advantages as the chalkboard and markerboard, but minimize the disadvantages. Because flip charts are portable, you can prepare your presentation aids before your speech, yet still have them available for on-the-spot adaptations. Flip charts are especially good when you want to use a series of presentation aids in a speech. They are frequently used in business presentations.

POSTERBOARD

The use of posterboard allows you to prepare a professional-looking presentation aid with a minimum investment. Writing looks best if it is done with press-on letters or a stencil. Posterboards may be used to display graphs, line drawings, or pictures. Posterboard displays should be simple and neat. Print should be large enough for everyone to read; titles should be approximately three inches high and other text not smaller than one and one-half inches high. You should leave space at the top and bottom of the board as well as side margins. Colors should be vivid and should contrast with the background for maximum effectiveness.

HANDOUTS

Handouts can be useful when your material is complex or when you want the audience to have a lasting reminder of your message. Their major disadvantage is that they can be a distraction. The audience may choose to read rather than listen. Never distribute a handout while you are speaking. If listeners need to refer to the material during your speech, distribute it ahead of time. If you use a handout to help listeners remember, distribute it after the presentation.

SLIDES OR TRANSPARENCIES

Slides shown with a traditional carousel projector are difficult to handle in public speeches because the room must be darkened, and unless you have remote-controlled equipment, you may need to speak from the rear of the room. Both of these problems divert attention from your speech. Transparency projections are easier to use than slides, and they can be made inexpensively at most copying centers. Moreover, you can add material to a transparency during your presentation, allowing for spontaneous adaptation.

Both slides and transparencies are often used in business presentations, so it would behoove you to know how to handle them. Be sure you know how to operate the equipment before you make your presentation, and that it is in proper working order. Have an extra light bulb just in case. Arrange your slides in the carousel in the proper order, and check to see that none of them are upside down. Unless you have remote-controlled equipment, plan to have someone else change the slides on cue. Rehearse coordinating your presentation with the showing of the slides or transparencies.

COMPUTER-ASSISTED PRESENTATIONS

The world of tomorrow has already pushed the world of today into the past. Your speech classroom may not be equipped for **multimedia presentations**, but when you move from college into the business world, you will encounter more and more sophisticated equipment for use in presentations. Over 65 percent of all corporations use some form of multimedia for presentations.[18] Moreover, the current generation is growing up in a multimedia environment. Grade school and middle school students across the country use computers, videos, and digitizers to produce daily news shows.[19] Your classroom audience, and the audiences you can expect to address in later business presentations, may expect you to use multimedia tools. Some of these tools are listed in Figure 11.5.

Adobe Acrobat	http://www.adobe.com/prodindex/acrobat/main.html
Adobe Acrobat Reader	http://www.adobe.com/prodindex/acrobat/readstep.html
Adobe Photoshop	http://www.adobe.com
ASAP Wordpower:	http://www.spco.com
Astound	http://www.astoundinc.com
Corel Presentations	http://www.corel.com/products/wordperfect/cp8/indes.htm
Harvard Graphics	http://www.spco.com/PRODUCTS/HARVMAIN.HTM
Lotus Freelance	http://www2.lotus.com/freelance.nsf
Macromedia Action	http://www.macromedia.com
PowerPoint (PC)	http://www.microsoft.com/products/prodref/127_ov.htm
PowerPoint (MAC)	http://www.microsoft.com/products/prodref/422_ov.htm

FIGURE 11.5
Multimedia Tools

It is one thing to note this trend in the style of presentation aids and quite another to offer useful advice about it. Technology is changing so rapidly that any specific advice we give concerning multimedia presentations will in all likelihood be obsolete by the time you read these words. Because computers are central to such presentations, however, we can offer some helpful general guidelines. Regularly updated information may be found on the Houghton Mifflin Company's College Division Web site at http://www.hmco.com/hmco/college. Other useful sites for updates on computer technology include TECHWEB (http://techweb. cmp. com/current/), ZDNET http://www.zdnet.com/), and C/NET (http://www.cnet.com/).

Computer-assisted presentations are often used in the work environment.

Most personal computers can generate a wide variety of presentation aids. They can develop sketches, maps, graphs, charts, and textual graphics for handouts, transparencies, and slides. More sophisticated computers can also reproduce pictures, add animation, and edit videotapes. The materials produced on computers are usually much neater and more accurate than those drawn by hand. Unless you have access to a blueprint-size printer, copier, or enlarger, computer graphics are less appropriate for posters.

To make presentation aids on a computer, you will need access to spreadsheet, word processing, graphics, and/or presentation software such as PowerPoint (http://www.microsoft.com/powerpoint) or Harvard Graphics (http:// www.spco.com/). Word processing, spreadsheet, and graphics programs will enable you to produce visuals for use as presentation aids. If you have access to appropriate software and an LCD projector or a PC-to-TV converter, the presentation programs allow you to both prepare your materials and present them to listeners.[20]

Computer-assisted presentations can bring together texts, numbers, pictures, and artwork made into slides, videos, animations, and audio materials. Many multimedia presentation programs are readily available. The most frequently used multimedia tool, Microsoft's PowerPoint, is bundled with the Microsoft Office package, which is included on many PCs when they are purchased.[21] Your campus computer lab may have training programs to help you learn how to access and use these materials. Several on-line tutorials are also available, including "How to Prepare and Deliver PowerPoint Presentations" (http://www.microsoft.com/mspowerpoint/productinfo/experttools/ present.HTM); "PowerPoint Guide" (http://www.emporia.edu/s/www/slim/resource/ ppoint/ppointguide.htm); and "PowerPoint Skills for the MAC" (http://cmetwww.cc. flinders.edu.au/courses/powerpoint_4.0/power.html). Materials such as graphs and charts that are generated with the computer can be changed at any time, even during a presentation. The programs come with a variety of templates that allow you to concentrate on your message rather than worrying about the design and development of your presentation aids.[22] The templates can be adapted to suit your particular needs.

As you use this new technology to develop presentation aids for your speeches, be careful not to get so caught up with the glitz and glitter that you lose sight of the fact that *it is your message that is most important.*[23] Using sophisticated technology in your presentation does not excuse you from the usual requirements for speaking.[24] As was noted recently in the *New York Times,* "Just remember that it is simply a tool, and it's the carpenter that builds the house."[25] In fact, if your presentation aids draw more attention than your ideas, they may be more of a hindrance than a help. Be especially careful not to get caught up in flashy transitions. It is better to be subtle than sensational. Even when you are preparing computer-generated materials or developing computer-assisted presentations, follow the customary guidelines for developing and using presentation aids put forth in this chapter. Don't use new technology just because it is there!

VIDEOTAPES

Videotapes should be used sparingly in short presentations because they can easily upstage the speaker. Moving images attract more attention than a speaking voice. Additionally, to be used effectively in speeches, a videotape segment must be carefully cued so that it begins and ends precisely where you want it to and should be artistically edited so that splices blend smoothly into one another without annoying jumps or auditory static. If properly prepared, however, videos can be used effectively. One speaker, a volunteer firefighter and student at Northwest Mississippi Community College, presented an effective informative speech on fire safety using a soundless videotape showing fire hazards around the home. He had shot the material himself and was able to show long shots of a room and then zoom in on the fire hazards.[26]

EVALUATING PRESENTATION AIDS

As with any type of supporting material, you should evaluate presentation aids in terms of their relevance. Never use a presentation aid just for the sake of using one. Be sure it adds something of value to your message. Additionally, you must be certain that your presentation aid is truly representative. Graphs and charts are especially vulnerable to problems of misrepresentation. For example, the bar graph in Figure 11.6 shows the

Women Partners in Accounting Firms

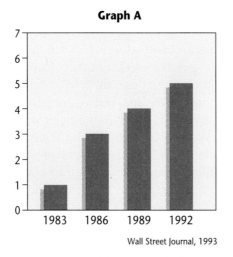

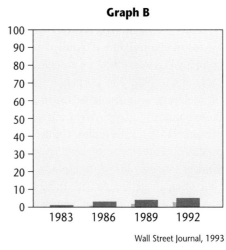

FIGURE **11.6**
Misleading Bar Graph and the Same Material Presented Clearly

percentage of women partners in major accounting firms across several years. Bar graph A could be misleading because it makes nothing look like something—the advances have gone from the pitiful to the sorry. Bar graph B in the same figure shows the whole picture and puts the gains into a proper perspective.[27]

ETHICAL CONSIDERATIONS IN USING PRESENTATION AIDS

Presentation aids are powerful, but they can also be deceptive. They can raise challenging ethical questions. For example, the most famous photographer of the Civil War, Matthew Brady, rearranged bodies on the battlefield to enhance the impact of his pictures. Eighty years later, another American war photographer carefully staged the now celebrated photograph of marines planting the flag at Iwo Jima.[28] Fifty years after that, *Time* magazine electronically manipulated a cover photograph of O. J. Simpson to "darken it and achieve a brooding, menacing quality."[29] On one hand, these famous images may be considered fabrications: They pretend to be what they are not. On the other hand, they may bring home the reality they represent more forcefully. In other words, the form of the photos is a lie, but the lie may work to reveal a deeper truth. So are these photographs unethical, or are they simply artistic?

Perhaps we can agree that with today's technology, the potential for abuse looms quite large. Video editing easily produces the illusion of reality. Consider how a recent movie depicts Forrest Gump shaking hands with Presidents Kennedy, Johnson, and Nixon. Or picture the Statue of Liberty putting down her torch to pick up and examine an American-made car, then smiling over its quality. In movies and television ads, such distortions can be amusing. In real life, they can be dangerous. Major television networks and newspapers have "staged" crashes and other visuals to make their stories more dramatic.[30]

All these practices may relate to the ancient adage "seeing is believing." Even though we know that the camera can lie, we don't want to believe that it does.[31] We are vulnerable to the "reality" revealed by our eyes. Our position on these ethical issues is the following:

- As a speaker, whenever you manipulate images so that they reveal your message more forcefully, you should alert your listeners to the illusion.
- You should be prepared to defend the illusion you create as a "better representation" of some underlying truth.
- As a listener, you should cultivate a healthy skepticism concerning visual images: for you, seeing should no longer be the same as believing.
- Whenever important claims are made and visual images are offered in support of them, you should ask for further confirmation and for additional evidence.

SELECTING AND USING SUPPORTING MATERIALS

There are no hard and fast rules for selecting supporting materials; however, the following general guidelines should help you choose wisely:

1. If an idea is *controversial,* you should rely primarily on facts, statistics, factual examples, or expert testimony from sources the audience will respect and accept.

2. If an idea or concept is *abstract,* you should use explanations, examples, narratives, or analogies to make it more meaningful for your audience.

3. If an idea or topic is highly *technical,* you should supplement facts and figures with expert testimony, definitions, explanations, examples, comparisons, contrasts, or analogies.

4. If you need to *arouse emotions,* you should use lay testimony, examples, comparisons, contrasts, analogies, or narratives.

5. If you need to *defuse emotions,* you should use facts, statistics, definitions, explanations, or expert testimony.

6. If your topic is *distant* from the lives of your listeners, you should use definitions, descriptions, explanations, comparisons, contrasts, analogies, examples, or narratives with which they can identify.

Although the need for certain types of supporting material may vary with different topics and different audiences, a good rule of thumb is that every main point should be supported with the most important and relevant facts and statistics available, with definitions, explanations, or descriptions provided if needed. You should also use the most appropriate type of testimony and at least one interesting example, narrative, or analogy. To make your presentation more dramatic or memorable, use comparisons or contrasts. The worksheet in Figure 11.7 may be used to help you work through supporting a point.

The following example illustrates how this worksheet can be used:

Statement	Suntans are not as "good" *for* you as they look *on* you.
Transition	Let's examine some of the evidence.
Facts and figures	According to a report of the American Cancer Society, prolonged exposure without protection is responsible for about 90 percent of all skin cancers.
Transition	Moreover, exposure to radiation accelerates the aging process.
Expert testimony	According to Dr. John M. Knox, head of dermatology at Baylor Medical School, "If you do biopsies on the buttocks of people ages seventy-five and thirty-five, you won't see any differences under the microscope . . . protected skin stays youthful much longer."
Transition	Let's look at one person who suffered the effects of overexposure.
Extended example	Jane was a fair-skinned blonde who as a child and teenager loved the sun. She would sunburn often, but she didn't think there would be any effects other than the short-term pain from the sunburn. Lying in the sun seemed so healthy and appealing, she didn't dream it could harm her. Now, at forty-five, she knows better. She couldn't believe her ears when her doctor said she had skin cancer. She felt she took good care of her body. Now she cannot go out into the sun, even for a few minutes, without using a sunscreen and wearing a hat, a long-sleeved shirt, and long pants.
Transition	What does all this mean?
Restatement	A suntan may make you *look* healthy, but it is *not healthy.* Overexposure to the sun causes cancer and premature aging. Are you willing to take that chance just to look good?

Statement _____

_____

Transition into facts or figures _____

    Factual information or statistics to support statement _____

    _____

    _____

Transition into testimony _____

    Expert, lay, or prestige testimony to support statement _____

    _____

    _____

Transition into example or narrative _____

    Example or narrative to support statement _____

    _____

    _____

Transition into restatement _____

Restatement of original assertion _____

_____

Bibliography:

FIGURE 11.7
Worksheet for Supporting a Point

IN SUMMARY

Direct your research toward finding supporting material for your speech. Look first for general information—facts and statistics that are relevant to your specific purpose and the major points you will want to make in your speech. Use this material to introduce your topic and to define, explain, or describe the major ideas or concepts. Keep your eyes open for testimony or quotations that you might use: expert testimony from qualified authorities, lay testimony from ordinary citizens who have experienced or are concerned with the issue, and prestige testimony that might enhance the general credibility of your message. Remember that examples and narratives are an important part of any speech. Use them to arouse and sustain attention, clarify abstract topics, develop audience-topic identification, and emphasize important points. Make your ideas more understandable through comparisons or analogies. Make them stand out by showing contrasts.

As you conduct your research, also be alert for material that can be adapted for use as presentation aids that will make your message easier to understand and remember. You may choose from people, objects or models, line drawings, graphs, or pictures and display them on chalkboards or markerboards, flip charts, or posterboards or in handouts, slides or transparencies, or videotapes. You may also make multimedia presentations if you have access to the proper equipment.

Evaluate any supporting materials you might use in your speech in terms of their relevance, reliability, and representativeness. Keep in mind that the reputations of your sources are important. Look for the most objective and unbiased information and testimony available. Use the latest information you can find on your topic. Be sure that examples and narratives are fresh, interesting, plausible, and appropriate to your audience.

Always start out with more supporting material than you will need so that you can select the very best for use in your presentation. Support each main point with facts or statistics, use the most appropriate testimony available, and include an example or narrative to drive your message home.

TERMS TO KNOW

supporting materials	extended examples
facts	factual examples
statistics	hypothetical examples
definition	narratives
denotative meaning	comparison
connotative meaning	contrast
explanation	analogy
descriptions	literal analogy
testimony	figurative analogy
verbatim	presentation aids
paraphrase	pie graph
expert testimony	bar graph
lay testimony	line graph
prestige testimony	multimedia presentations
examples	computer-assisted presentations
brief examples	

NOTES

1. Donna E. Shalala, "Domestic Terrorism: An Unacknowledged Epidemic," in VITAL SPEECHES OF THE DAY, 15 May 1994, 451.

2. Adapted from *The 1992 Information Please Environmental Almanac* (Boston: Houghton Mifflin, 1992), 144.

3. Cecile Larson, "The 'Monument' at Wounded Knee," in Michael and Suzanne Osborn, *Public Speaking,* 3rd ed. (Boston: Houghton Mifflin, 1994), B7.

4. Stephen Huff, "The New Madrid Earthquake Area," *Public Speaking,* 3rd ed. (Boston: Houghton Mifflin, 1994), 350–351.

5. For a detailed analysis of the power of lay testimony, see Michael Calvin McGee, "In Search of the People: A Rhetorical Alternative," *Quarterly Journal of Speech* 61 (1975): 235–249.

6. James S. Brady of Handgun Control, Inc.

7. "On the Campaign Trail," *Reader's Digest,* March 1992, 116.

8. Harvey Jacobs, former Editor at the *Indianapolis News* and Distinguished Editor-in-Residence at Franklin College, "Readers—An Endangered Species?" VITAL SPEECHES OF THE DAY, May 1985, pp. 446–447.

9. Ibid., 446–447.

10. Excerpted from *The State of the Culture: Approach the Year Three-Thousand*, a speech delivered at Hillsdale College, Hillsdale, Michigan on October 4, 1992, by Alexandra York and reprinted in VITAL SPEECHES OF THE DAY on 1 May 1993.

11. Roger Ailes, *You Are the Message* (New York: Doubleday, 1988), 70–74.

12. Dan Coats, "The Virtue of Tolerance," VITAL SPEECHES OF THE DAY, 15 August 1993, p. 648. Reprinted by permission.

13. Christie McGuffee Smith and Larry Powell, "The Use of Disparaging Humor by Group Leaders," *Southern Speech Communication Journal* 53 (1988): 279–292; and Charles R. Gruner, "Advice to the Beginning Speaker on Using Humor—What the Research Tells Us," *Communication Education* 34 (1985): 142–147.

14. Jimmy Carter, "Excellence Comes from a Repository That Doesn't Change: The True Meaning of Success," VITAL SPEECHES OF THE DAY, 1 July 1993, 546.

15. Daniel Patrick Moynihan, "Toward a New Intolerance," cited in William T. Quillen, "Freedom Day II: Reclaiming America," in *Vital Speeches of the Day,* 15 July 1993, 596.

16. Barbara Warnick and Edward S. Inch, *Critical Thinking and Communication: The Use of Reason in Argument* (New York: Macmillan, 1989), 105.

17. M. George Allen, "Succeeding in Japan: One Company's Perspective," in VITAL SPEECHES OF THE DAY, 1 May 1994, p. 430. Reprinted by permission.

18. Jan Ozer, "Presentations Come to Life," *Home Office Computing,* Compuserve, *Magazine Database Plus,* on-line, December 1994.

19. A multimedia presentation on NASA designed by third-grade students at St. John's Day School in Marlin, Texas, can be viewed at http://macserver.esc12tenet.edu/stjohns/Students.html.

20. Stephen C. Miller, "Presentation Programs-Part II: Hardware Hassles," *New York Times* on-line (http:www.nytimes.com/library/cyber/travel-log/), 4 November 1997.

21. Stephen C. Miller, "Presentation Programs Can Give Public Speakers a Leg Up," *New York Times* on-line (http:www.nytimes.com/library/cyber/travel-log/), 21 October, 1997.

22. Ripley Hatch, "Making the Best Presentations," *Nation's Business,* Compuserve, *Magazine Database Plus* on-line, August 1992.

23. Tom Bunzel, "Content—Not Technology—Is What Counts," *Computer Pictures,* Compuserve, *Magazine Database Plus* on-line, May–June, 1993.

24. John T. Phillips Jr., "Professional Presentations," *Records Management Quarterly,* Compuserve, *Magazine Database Plus* on-line, October 1994.

25. Miller, "Presentation Programs Can Give Public Speakers a Leg Up."

26. Example supplied by Mary Katherine McHenry, Northwest Mississippi Community College, Senatobia, Miss., 2 March 1994.

27. Lee Berton, "Deloitte Wants More Women for Top Posts in Accounting," *Wall Street Journal,* 28 February 1993, B1.

28. Cornelia Brunner, "Teaching Visual Literacy," *Electronic Learning,* Compuserve, *Magazine Database Plus,* on-line November–December 1994.

29. Arthur Goldsmith, "Digitally Altered Photography: The New Image Makers," *Britannica Book of the Year: 1995* (Chicago: Encyclopaedia Britannica, 1995), 135.

30. Gloria Borger, "The Story the Pictures Didn't Tell," *U.S. News & World Report,* 22 February 1993, 6–7; and John Leo, "Lapse or TV News Preview?" *Washington Times,* 3 March 1993, G3.

31. Kenneth Brower, "Photography in the Age of Falsification," *Atlantic Monthly,* May 1998, 95.

CHAPTER TWELVE

ORGANIZING AND OUTLINING YOUR SPEECH

THIS CHAPTER

will help you

- Appreciate the importance of organizing your message

- Determine the main points of your speech

- Arrange your main points in a simple, orderly, and balanced design

- Compose a working outline to check on the adequacy of your preparation

- Prepare an appealing introduction for your message

- Develop a memorable conclusion for your message

- Compose a final-draft outline so that you can see the flow of your speech

- Prepare a key-word outline to use during the presentation of your speech

EVERY **DISCOURSE** ought to be a **LIVING** CREATURE; having a body of its own AND HEAD AND FEET; THERE SHOULD BE A **MIDDLE, BEGINNING,** and **END,** adapted to one another and to the **WHOLE.**

—*Plato*

Why do I have to turn in an outline for my speech? This isn't a composition class! I'm supposed to learn how to give talks in this class, not how to write! Besides, I never can do an outline until I've written out in full what I want to say. Outlining is just a waste of time!

While outlining may seem like busy work, it is necessary for a well-organized speech. Just as you wouldn't start to build a house without a blueprint, you shouldn't try to prepare a speech without an outline. An outline helps you organize your ideas and see how the material you discovered in your research can best be used. It helps you plan a speech with a simple, orderly, balanced design. As we noted in Chapter 4, a well-organized speech also can help your audience listen better and retain information.

In this chapter we discuss the importance of organizing your message, show you how to determine and arrange the main points of your speech, lead you through the process of outlining your message, and help you develop effective introductions and conclusions for your speeches.

THE IMPORTANCE OF A WELL-ORGANIZED MESSAGE

Outlining your speech allows you to find problems and correct them before you make your presentation. As you prepare your outline, you will be able to see if your speech is complete. Have you covered all the main points? Have you left out anything important? Your outline also helps you check the relevance of your main points. Does each main point relate directly to your specific purpose? Does each reflect your thesis statement? Outlining also lets you see if supporting materials relate directly to the main points above them. Finally, your outline will help you assess the adequacy of your preparation. Do you have enough supporting material for each main point? Do you need to do more research to fill in the empty spaces?

How well your speech is organized will also affect how competent the audience thinks you are.[1] If your listeners believe that you are competent, they will be more receptive to your ideas. A poorly organized speech may leave the audience feeling that you have a muddled mind or that you didn't care enough about your topic or about them to prepare carefully. Either of these alternatives can impair your effectiveness as a speaker.

A well-organized message is easier for listeners to understand and remember. Suppose you must take an introductory physics course next semester and you get the following information on the instructors from Students for Better Teaching:

> **TRY THIS**
>
> Analyze the structure of your favorite television advertisement. How does it gain attention and establish credibility? What type of design does it follow? Does the conclusion tie in to the introduction? Do you think it would have been more effective if it had been designed differently?

Professor Johnson is very entertaining. He tells a lot of funny stories and puts on demonstrations that seem like a "magic show." It's hard to take notes in his classes, though, so when it's time for examinations, you may not know what to study because he doesn't explain difficult material in any systematic fashion.

Professor Martinez is very businesslike. She starts each lecture by reviewing the material covered in the last session and asks if anyone has questions. Her lectures are easy to follow and well organized. She points out what is important and uses clear examples that make difficult ideas easier to understand and apply.

Which instructor would you prefer and why? Given such a choice, most students would select the second instructor because a well-organized message is easier for people to follow, understand, and remember.[2]

DEVELOPING THE BODY OF YOUR SPEECH

The process of organizing and outlining your message begins with structuring the body of your speech. The body of your speech contains the substance of what you want to say. It is where you pursue your purposes and develop your major ideas. Only after you have developed the body of your speech can you prepare an introduction and conclusion that work well with your message. There are three steps involved in developing the body of your speech:

1. You must determine your main points.
2. You must arrange your main points effectively.
3. You must select supporting material to substantiate your main points.

DETERMINING YOUR MAIN POINTS

The process of organizing and outlining your message begins with the selection of the main points of your speech. Your **main points** are the key ideas in your message. They should help you fulfill your specific purpose. To select your main points, prepare a **research overview** that lists the main ideas from each source. Figure 12.1 presents a research overview for a speech on the greenhouse effect. With such an overview, you can identify repeated ideas. These should represent the most important aspects of your subject. Next, consider how these ideas fit in with your specific purpose. Use only ideas that are directly related to what you want to accomplish. Finally, review the main ideas again to see how they relate to what your audience needs to know. In this example, these major themes occur:

- The greenhouse effect is a gradual warming of the earth's atmosphere.
- The greenhouse effect is caused by too much carbon dioxide in the atmosphere.

Sierra Club Factsheet

1. melting icecaps and rise in sea level
2. increased carbon dioxide from burning fossil fuels
3. rise in global temperatures in 1980s and 1990s
4. deforestation problem

Envirolink

1. Problem:
   a. carbon dioxide too high
   b. hole in ozone layer
   c. climate changes
   d. health problems
2. Causes:
   a. loss of woodlands
   b. industrial pollution
   c. energy consumption

Gallup

1. fossil fuels blamed for warming
2. Americans oppose treaty
3. not seen as immediate threat
4. public uninformed

Easterbrook (12/1/97)

1. CO_2 up 1/3 since the Indust. Rev. on way to doubling
2. anti-smog car devices work
3. new hybrid engines get 66 mpg
4. vegetable fuel possible
5. need price incentives
6. carbon taxes might work
7. international cooperation needed

FIGURE **12.1**
Sample Research Overview

- Excessive carbon dioxide comes from burning of fossil fuels, industrial emissions, CFCs, methane, nitrous oxide, and loss of forestlands.
- The greenhouse effect may cause serious climate and health problems.

Once you have identified the major themes, you can see how these relate to your specific purpose, which in this example is "to inform my audience of the causes of the greenhouse effect." You should also consider what your audience may already know and what else they need to know. As you look at your overview, you realize that you must begin with a definition of the greenhouse effect and some consideration of the problems it can provoke before you get into its causes. With this in mind, you select the following main points:

- The loss of forests, which convert carbon dioxide to oxygen, contributes to the greenhouse effect.
- The greenhouse effect is a gradual warming of the earth due to human activity.
- Increased energy consumption contributes to the greenhouse effect.
- Industrial emissions contribute to the growth of the greenhouse effect.

ARRANGING YOUR MAIN POINTS

You should arrange your main points so that they make sense to your audience, are easy to follow, fit your material, and help you fulfill your specific purpose. A speech works best when it is arranged in the way people organize and store material in their minds.[3] We rarely store information as individual bits; instead, we cluster material into chunks that can be recalled in their entirety. For example, we store telephone numbers in two or three chunks, such as 813 - 847 - 2070, not as ten discrete digits 8 - 1 - 3 - 8 - 4 - 7 - 2 - 0 - 7 - 0. Drawing on our experience, we develop mental templates into which we fit incoming material. Such templates help us process new information efficiently. These mental templates are based on the principles of similarity, proximity, and closure.

Using the **principle of similarity**, we group together things that seem somehow alike. This principle underlies the *categorical design* for organizing a speech. Speakers are using categories when they present "the three major causes of the greenhouse effect" or "the four basic components of a computer system." Categories may be based on actual divisions of a subject or on customary ways of thinking.

The **principle of proximity** suggests that things that have a natural pattern in time or space should be presented in that manner. For example, a "how-to" speech should have a *sequential design* that presents the steps in the order in which they should be taken. To discuss events leading up to a current problem, you should use a *historical design* that presents the events in an orderly chronological sequence. If your research shows that major events occurred in 1955, 1970, and 1987, and you present them in this order, your speech will be easy to follow. However, if you jump around, going from 1970 to 1955 to 1987, your audience may find it hard to keep up with your message. For a speech describing a physical area, such as Yellowstone Park, you should use a *spatial design* in which you select a starting point and a direction to move in, and then take your audience on an orderly journey. This design gives listeners a verbal map that should be easy to follow.

The **principle of closure** is based on our natural tendency to seek completion. If you've ever started to read a magazine story in a waiting room, then discovered that the last page is missing, you'll understand how this principle works. Once you have established a pattern, you should follow it through to the end. Keep in mind the old childhood ditty, "Once a thing you have begun, never leave it 'til it's done." If you leave out an important category, your listeners may notice its absence. If you omit a step in a process, the audience may get confused. Two designs for which closure is essential are the *causation* and *problem-solution* designs. A causation design may explain a present problem and then discuss its causes, as in our example of the greenhouse effect. It may also look at an existing situation as a cause of future effects, predicting what will happen if the problem continues. The problem-solution design focuses the audience's attention on a problem and then provides a solution for it.

To further demonstrate how mental templates work, let us look at an example. Suppose you were asked to memorize the following list of twenty words:

red, apple, two, glove, foot, hat, banana, six, hand, yellow, shoe, blue, finger, four, grape, shirt, green, eight, lemon, toe

This looks rather difficult. However, if these same words are organized into groups based on similarity, the task becomes easier:

colors:	red, yellow, blue, green
fruits:	apple, banana, grape, lemon
numbers:	two, six, four, eight
apparel:	glove, hat, shoe, shirt
body parts:	foot, hand, finger, toe

This grouping applies the principle of similarity to form categories. You can make the task even easier if you arrange the items within the groups according to their proximity (hand, finger, foot, toe), or to provide closure (two, four, six, eight). If you keep these principles in mind as you organize your speech, your audience will be more likely to understand and remember what you have said.

BEGINNING YOUR WORKING OUTLINE

Your **working outline** is a *tentative* plan of your speech. It helps you organize and arrange the body of your message. Your working outline can show you how your ideas are developing and whether they fit together. It can also suggest what you may need to learn in order to speak more responsibly on your topic. You may make and modify several working outlines as you develop your speech. Figure 12.2 is a template for developing a working outline.

Begin your working outline by listing your topic, your general and specific purposes, and your thesis statement on a sheet of paper. Keep these clearly in mind as you develop your working outline.

Topic:	The greenhouse effect
General purpose:	To inform
Specific purpose:	To inform my audience of the causes of the greenhouse effect
Thesis statement:	The three major causes of the greenhouse effect are loss of forest-lands, industrial emissions, and increased energy consumption caused by population growth.

Next, look at the main points in your research overview and determine how to arrange them. In our continuing example of the greenhouse effect speech, the thesis

Topic:
Specific purpose:
Thesis statement:

Introduction

Attention-arousing material:
Establish credibility:
Thesis statement/preview:

[Transition to body of speech]

Body

Main point I
        Subpoints (List A, B, C, etc.)
                Sub-subpoints (List 1, 2, 3, etc.)
                        [Transition to second main point]
Main point *N*
        Subpoints (List A, B, C, etc.)
                Sub-subpoints (List 1, 2, 3, etc.)
                        [Transition to conclusion]

Conclusion
Summary statement:
Concluding remarks:

FIGURE **12.2**
Template for a Working Outline

statement suggests a causation design in which you explain the situation and then discuss its causes.

Main point I: The greenhouse effect is a gradual warming of the earth due to human activity.

Main point II: The loss of forestlands, which convert carbon dioxide to oxygen, contributes to the greenhouse effect.

Main point III: Industrial emissions contribute to the growth of the greenhouse effect.

Main point IV: Increased energy consumption contributes to the greenhouse effect.

Once you've listed and arranged your main points, you can break out these main points and add supporting materials to your working outline. Each main point of your speech should be divided into two or more **subpoints** that develop and clarify that main point. As a rule, your main points will be general statements and the subpoints under them will be more specific. Each subpoint must be directly related to the main point it follows and should make that point more understandable, more believable, or more compelling.[4]

As you select material for subpoints, ask yourself the following questions: How can this main point be broken down? What must I demonstrate before listeners will accept this main point? What supporting materials will work best in this case? As you develop your working outline, you might list the following subpoints for your first main point:

Main point I: The greenhouse effect is a gradual warming of the earth due to human activity.

Subpoints A. It comes from a high concentration of carbon dioxide in the atmosphere.

B. It is producing a hole in the ozone layer.

C. It makes the earth warmer.

D. It lets ultraviolet radiation come through.

E. It can cause climate problems.

F. It can cause health problems.

Once you have come this far, you should examine your subpoints. See how they relate to one another, if you can collapse two or more of them into one subpoint, if you need to break out the material into more specific and detailed **sub-subpoints**, and how you might best arrange these subpoints. In this phase of developing your working outline, you should also make notes on the supporting materials you will use. For example, the first main point in the working outline for the greenhouse effect speech might be broken out as follows:

Main point I: The greenhouse effect is a gradual warming of the earth due to human activity.

Subpoint A It comes from a high concentration of carbon dioxide (CO_2) in the atmosphere.

Sub-subpoints **1.** Five tons of carbon per person per year in U.S.

2. 1987 CO_2 at record high *(provide temperature data).*

Subpoint B It is producing a hole in the ozone layer.

Sub-subpoints **1.** Chlorofluorocarbons (CFCs) destroy the ozone shield.

2. More ultraviolet radiation comes through.

Subpoint C The greenhouse effect can cause serious problems.

Sub-subpoints **1.** It can cause climate problems *(cite possibilities).*

2. It can cause health problems *(describe potential problems).*

Follow this same procedure for each main point in your outline. Keep your audience at the center of your thinking. Remember the advice given to beginning journalists: *Never overestimate your audience's information, and never underestimate its intelligence!* Ask yourself the following questions:

● Will this information be clear and convincing?
● Will this example be effective with this audience?

- Does this material come from a source my listeners respect?
- Will my listeners be able to identify with this story?

Review the outline of the body of your speech to make sure that you have not left out anything important. Check the relevance of each of your main points to your thesis statement. Be sure your ideas are arranged in an orderly manner that is easy to follow. Be certain that each subpoint relates to the main point above it. Be sure you have enough supporting material to flesh out your presentation. If you are lacking in any of these areas, now is the time to correct the problem.

Determining and Arranging Your Main Points
- ✓ Prepare a research overview to identify repeated ideas
- ✓ Select points that are relevant and appropriate
- ✓ Limit the number of main points to five or less
- ✓ Use the principle of similarity to develop categories
- ✓ Use the principle of proximity for sequential or spatial designs
- ✓ Use the closure for causation and problem-solution designs

PREPARING AN INTRODUCTION AND CONCLUSION

Once you are satisfied with the way you have organized the body of your speech, you can move on to preparing the introduction and conclusion. These parts of a speech are especially important because listeners are most affected by what they hear at the beginning and end of a message.[5] The introduction allows you to make a good first impression and sets the stage for how your audience will respond. The conclusion provides you with one final opportunity to make a lasting impression on your audience.

PREPARING AN EFFECTIVE INTRODUCTION

The audience should be at the forefront of your thinking as you begin to prepare your introduction. As you begin your speech, the audience will have two basic questions in mind: "Why should I listen to this speech?" and "Why should I listen to this speaker?" These questions relate to two of the basic functions of an introduction. First, your introduction should capture your audience's attention and interest so that they *want* to listen carefully. Second, it should help establish you as a competent, trustworthy, and likable person. Finally, your introduction should preview your message to make it easier for the audience to follow.

Capturing Attention and Interest. All too often, beginning speakers open their presentations with, "Good afternoon. Today, I'm going to tell you about . . . ," then barrel right on into the meat of their message. Needless to say, this is not an effective introduction. It does not make your audience *want* to listen to your message. There are several good ways to attract, build, and hold the interest of your audience. These include (1) involving the audience, (2) relating your subject to personal experience, (3) asking rhetorical questions, (4) creating suspense, (5) opening with a narrative, (6) using a quotation, and (7) startling the audience.

Involving the Audience—One of the most frequently used involvement techniques is to compliment the audience. You can speak highly of the group, the location, or a person in the audience whom you know. This type of introduction can help establish common ground and build bonds of identification between the speaker and the audience. It is frequently used as an entree to formal speeches when custom requires a speaker to make some initial acknowledgments before moving into the speech itself. Bernard Shaw, CNN news anchor, used this technique to open an Alfred M. Landon Lecture on Public Issues at Kansas State University:

A well-organized presentation makes it easy for listeners to understand and remember a message. It also enhances the credibility of the speaker.

> *Ladies and gentlemen: I come to you at the invitation of one of the finest universities to grace this land. I come to you as a fellow midwesterner—just two states away—an Illinoisian who is fond of simplicity and directness, two of many characteristics Kansans appreciate. I come to you as a fellow American—proud that our nation, once again, has changed Presidential leadership without one mortar shot fired in the process—and relieved that a numbingly too-long campaign is over!*[6]

A less formal and often more effective way to involve your listeners is to relate your topic directly to their lives. This is especially important if your topic seems distant from their immediate concerns or experience. Beth Duncan wanted to address her classroom audience on Alzheimer's disease, a subject that her young audience might not be too concerned about. Beth helped her listeners relate to her speech with the following opening, in which she read the letter directly from a piece of folded stationery:[7]

> *I'd like to share with you a letter my roommate got from her grandmother, an educated and cultured woman. I watched her weep as she read it, and after she showed it to me, I understood why.*
>
> > *Dear Sally, I am finally around to answer your last. You have to look over me. ha. I am so sorry to when you called last Sunday why didn't you remind me. Steph had us all so upset leaving and not telling no she was going back but we have a good snow ha and Kathy can't drive on ice so I never get a pretty card but they have a thing to see through an envelope. I haven't got any in the bank until I get my homestead check so I'm just sending this. ha. When you was talking on the phone Cathy had Ben and got my groceries and I had to unlock the door. I forgot to say hold and I don't have Claudette's number so forgive me for being to silly. ha. Nara said to tell you she isn't doing no good well one is pretty good and my eves. Love, Nanny.*
>
> *Sally's grandmother has Alzheimer's disease. Over 2.5 million older people in the United States are afflicted with it. It could strike someone in our families—a grandparent, an aunt or uncle, or even our mother or father.*

When Beth had finished this introduction, her listeners were deeply involved with her topic. Moreover, realizing that this disease could affect their own families made them want to hear the rest of Beth's speech. You also can involve your listeners by relating your topic to your audience's motivations or attitudes and by using inclusive words such as *we* and *our*.

Relating Your Subject to Personal Experience—People are interested first in themselves, next in other people, then in things, and finally in ideas. This may explain why relating a topic to personal experience heightens audience interest. When speakers have been involved with a topic, they also gain credibility. We are almost always more willing to listen to others and take their advice if we know that they have traveled the road themselves. Relating the subject to personal experience can also help create common ground between speakers and listeners. This can be very important when the speaker faces a reluctant audience. Brock Adams, vice president for national issues of the National Audubon Society, recently addressed the Seattle Rotary Club on the Endangered Species Act. Because this speech was presented amid the ongoing controversy concerning logging restrictions in the spotted owl habitat, the introduction to this speech was especially critical. Adams combined the techniques of involving the audience and relating the topic to personal experience in this introduction:

> *It is always a distinct honor to be invited to speak before a prestigious group like the Rotary Club of Seattle. I thank you for inviting me to be here today, and not just because of the opportunity to share a few thoughts about this very important subject. Those of you who know me know that my roots here run very deep. It was 30 years ago that I moved here from the Midwest, because I wanted to live in what I thought then—and still do now—was the most beautiful part of the country.*
>
> *And those of you who know me know that my passion for this special Northwest land, its unique blend of mountain and forest and sea, goes even deeper . . . for it caused me to leave a law practice here, in order to devote my life to fight to help keep our way of life, keep the Northwest the special place it is. It has now become a life's work that has taken me many places, first all across the Northwest, and finally into "exile" as I now believe—in the nation's capital—that other Washington, where for better or worse, so many of the great issues of our time are finally resolved.*[8]

Asking Rhetorical Questions—When you ask a question, you generally expect an immediate and direct answer. When you use a **rhetorical question** to open a speech, however, you usually don't expect the audience to respond with an answer or information. What you want them to do is to think about the question. Rhetorical questions are used to arouse curiosity and to focus attention on your subject. Annette Berrington opened her classroom speech on safety belts by asking the audience:

> *How would you like to have your name in the paper? I can tell you a good way to get it there. Don't wear your seat belt while you're riding in a car. Yesterday I called Nashville and talked to Ben Dailey at the state Department of Safety. What he told me really blew my mind. Of the 997 people killed in automobile accidents in our state last year, 772 were not using a seat belt at the time of the crash! How do you like those odds? You have a much greater chance of being killed in an auto accident if you don't buckle up!*

The audience's first reaction to the opening question was to think that they would like to have their names in the paper—we all enjoy recognition. However, this soon changed when they realized the circumstances under which their names would appear. This introduction was adept at attracting and sustaining attention.

Creating Suspense—People love a sense of suspense, so long as they are not personally involved in the outcome. You can attract and sustain your listeners' attention by arousing their curiosity and then making them wait before you satisfy it. The following introduction creates curiosity and anticipation:

> *Getting knocked down is no disgrace. Champions are made by getting up just one more time than the opponent! The results are a matter of record about a man who suffered many defeats: Lost his job in 1832, defeated for legislature in 1832, failed in business in 1833, defeated for legislature in 1834, sweetheart died in 1835, had nervous breakdown in 1836, defeated for nomination for Congress in 1843, elected to Congress in 1846, lost renomination in 1848, rejected for land officer in 1849, defeated for Senate in 1854, defeated for nomination for Vice-President in 1856, defeated for Senate in 1858. In 1860 Abraham Lincoln was elected President of the United States. Lincoln proved that a big shot is just a little shot who keeps shooting. The greatest failures in the world are those who fail by not doing anything.*[9]

People enjoy hearing stories, so opening narratives are an effective way to arouse the audience's attention.

Opening with a Narrative—Humans began their love affair with stories around the campfires of ancient times. It is through stories that we remember the past and pass on our heritage to future generations. Stories may also be used to entertain or educate us—they depict abstract problems in human terms. In a speech delivered at Hillsdale College, Alexandra York used the following introductory narrative to illustrate the decline of "culture" in America:

> *A few years ago while recovering from a tennis injury, I worked out regularly with a personal trainer. At that time, the new Broadway musical casually named "Les Miz" had reawakened an interest in Victor Hugo's immortal book "Les Miserables" on which the play was based. New Yorkers were reading or re-reading the book with fervor—on subways and buses, on bank lines, in doctor's offices and even on exercise bikes. One day at my "very upscale" gym, the woman next to me warmed up on her bike reading a paperback of that great, classic novel which she had propped up on the handle bars while she cycled. A trainer wandered by—a male in his midthirties—and noted her reading material with visible surprise. He stopped short and asked in wonderment, "They made a book of it already?" So may we ask in wonderment, "What is the state of a culture where such a question can be asked by a college graduate?"*[10]

Leading with Humor—Humorous anecdotes are also often used in introductions. A touch of light humor can put an audience in a receptive mood for your message. To be most effective, humor must be fresh and directly relevant to your topic. It can sometimes help to "warm up" a reluctant audience, especially when the speaker is the object of the humor. Takakazu Kuriyama, Japanese ambassador to the United States, opened a speech at George Washington University with the following anecdote:

> *Thank you. I'm delighted to be part of your Ambassador Lecture Series. I think it's very brave of you to invite ambassadors to speak. We are not especially known for*

our oratory or clarity. Someone once noted that a diplomat is a person who thinks twice before saying nothing. Someone else said that if a diplomat says yes, he means perhaps; if he says perhaps, he means no; and if he says no, he's no diplomat.[11]

Using a Quotation—Opening your speech with a striking quotation from a well-known person both arouses interest and gives you some borrowed ethos. The most effective opening quotations are brief and to the point. If a quotation contains important information or the language is especially eloquent, you will want to cite the exact words. Susie Smith used the following quotation, attributed to the novelist William Faulkner, to introduce a classroom speech on work satisfaction:

You can't eat for eight hours a day, nor drink for eight hours a day, nor make love for eight hours a day—all you can do for eight hours is work. Which is the reason why man makes himself and everybody else so miserable.

Most books of quotations are indexed by key words and subjects as well as by authors. Collections of quotations are also available on the Internet (see Chapter 10 and Appendix A). These collections are an excellent source of striking statements that you might use to introduce your topic.

Startling the Audience—Anything that is truly unusual arouses attention and curiosity. Consider the headlines from the sensationalist tabloids: "Bigfoot Spotted in Northwest Arkansas!" "Woman Predicts Earthquake with Her Toes!" "Why I Went from Hero to Heroine: Ex-GI Tells All!" Here's how one student opened an informative speech by startling her audience:

If the statistics hold true, more than half of us in this room have risked our lives in the past year. Indeed, millions of college students have willingly exposed themselves to a life-threatening disease in the past year. That disease is cancer. Do you think these numbers exaggerate? Do you believe you're not at risk? Let's see.

Capturing Attention

✓ Show listeners how the topic applies to them
✓ Call on your personal experience with the topic
✓ Ask rhetorical questions to make the audience think
✓ Create an aura of suspense and anticipation
✓ Open with a narrative that is related to your topic
✓ Use a quotation from a well-known person
✓ Startle the audience with something unusual

> *How many of you smoke or use some form of tobacco? Raise your hands. Okay, that's six. Now, how many of you eat a lot of fatty fast food—hamburgers, french fries, pizza? Come on, raise your hands. Well, that's fourteen. Now, in the past year, how many of you took a sunbath—or went to a tanning parlor—or worked outside without using a sunscreen oil or lotion? That's seventeen! I guess my numbers were a little bit off, but I actually understated the probability. Today I want to tell you how you can lower your risk and avoid becoming a statistic in someone else's speech.*

When you use this technique, you must be sure not to go beyond the bounds of propriety. You want to startle your listeners into attention, not offend them.

Establishing Your Ethos as a Speaker. The second major function of an effective introduction is to establish you as a competent, trustworthy, and likable person. First impressions count.[12] You enter a speaking situation with some initial ethos based on the audience's previous experience with you. You must strengthen this initial ethos in the introduction of your speech.

You can seem competent only if you know what you are talking about. People listen more respectfully to those who speak from both knowledge and personal experience. The perception of competence can be strengthened if you select a topic that you already know something about and do research to qualify yourself as a responsible speaker. It will also help if your speech is well organized, if you use language correctly, and if you have practiced your presentation. Demonstrating self-confidence may also enhance it. There is, however, a delicate balance between seeming competent and seeming conceited. Be careful. If you keep your focus on your commitment to your topic and on sharing a message with your audience, you should be able to create the proper balance.

To create a perception of trustworthiness, you should be ethical, honest, and dependable. Listeners are more receptive when speakers are straightforward, sincere, and concerned with the consequences of their words. You can enhance your listeners' perceptions of your trustworthiness by demonstrating respect for those who may hold differing opinions while still maintaining your personal commitment to a position. It should be clear to your audience that you will not ask more of them than you ask of yourself. If you demonstrate consideration, understanding, tolerance, and respect, the audience should have a positive impression of your trustworthiness.

Finally, speakers who are perceived as likable are pleasant, friendly, and tactful. They treat listeners as friends, which inspires affection in return. Audiences are more willing to accept ideas and suggestions from speakers they like. A smile and direct eye contact signals listeners that you want to communicate. Likable speakers share their feelings as well as their thoughts. They are able to laugh at themselves.

When you establish positive ethos, you create the basis for one of the most powerful effects of communication: *identification* between you and your listeners.[13] Identification occurs when people break through the personal and cultural walls that separate them and share thoughts and feelings. When you seem competent, trustworthy, and likable, your listeners will *want* to identify with you, and your effectiveness as a speaker will be magnified.

● **TRY THIS**

Pair off with a classmate and discuss what you might do to improve your ethos during the introduction to your next presentation. After you have reached some consensus on things you might do, share your insights with the class.

Previewing Your Message. The final function of an introduction is to preview what is to follow in the body of your speech. The **preview** foreshadows the main points you will cover and offers your audience an overview of your speech. It makes it easier for your listeners to follow and understand your message. The preview usually comes near the end of the introduction and may serve as a transition into the body of your speech.

Martha Radner used the following preview in a speech on campus security problems:

> *We could be a lot safer if we adopted a bold new plan for campus security. First, I want to show you how dangerous our situation has become. Second, I'll explore why our current security is ineffective. And finally, I'll present my plan for a safer campus.*

By informing her listeners of her intentions and her speech design, Martha helped them listen more intelligently.

Selecting and Using Introductory Techniques. There are no hard-and-fast rules for determining exactly how you should open a speech. Review your research notes for materials that would make an effective introduction. Keep the following advice in mind:

* Consider your audience in relation to your topic. Use your introduction to tie *your* topic to *their* needs, interests, or well-being.
* Consider the mood you want to establish. Certain topics call for a light touch; others require more solemnity.
* Consider the time constraints. If you are to speak for seven minutes, you can't get bogged down in a five-minute introduction.
* Consider what you do best. Some people are effective storytellers, and others are better using striking statistics or eloquent quotations. Go with your strength.

Follow the format for an introduction provided in Figure 12.2, "Template for a Working Outline:" get the audience's attention, establish your credibility, then preview the essence of your message. When an introduction violates this order, it is usually less effective. Consider the following example from a speech presented at an honor society recognition conference.

> *Today I'm going to talk about the technology of the future. The theme for your conference is "Preparing for the 21st Century," and getting a grip on the technological changes ahead of us is the best way to prepare for the next century. I'll also tell you a little about Battelle [the speaker's company], and I'll make a few predictions about what our world will be like over the next 10 to 50 years. That has me a little nervous, because any time you start making predictions, you hope no one nearby has a tape recorder.*
>
> *Here's an example of what I mean. At the Chicago World's Fair way back in 1893, a group of 74 social commentators got together to look 100 years into the future—at the world of 1993. Here are some of their predictions. Many people will live to be 150. The government will have grown more simple, as true greatness tends always toward simplicity. Prisons will decline and divorce will be considered unnecessary. The Nicaraguan canal is as sure to be built as tides are to ebb and flow and the seasons to change.[14]*

How would you revise and reorganize this material to make it more effective?[15]

To get your speech off to a good start, you should write out your introduction word for word. When you are satisfied with what you have prepared, insert it into your working outline.

DEVELOPING AN EFFECTIVE CONCLUSION

Beginning speakers often seem awkward when they come to the end of their presentation. "That's all, folks!" may be an effective ending for a cartoon, but not for a speech. Saying, "That's it, I guess" or "Well, I'm done" with a sigh of relief suggests that you have not planned your speech very carefully. The final words of your speech should stay with your listeners, remind them of your message, provide a sense of closure, and, if appropriate, move them to action.

What works in cartoons doesn't work well in speeches. Always plan a conclusion for your presentation. Never end with "That's all."

Summarizing Your Message. Your conclusion should begin with a summary of the main points you made in your speech. This summary can function as a transition between the body of the speech and your final remarks. It signals the audience that you are about to finish and helps provide a sense of closure. The conclusion to the "greenhouse effect" speech that we have been tracking through this chapter might contain the following summary statement:

> *The greenhouse effect represents a clear and present danger to our world. If current conditions continue, we may face drastic climate changes and serious health problems. The major causes of the greenhouse effect are the loss of forestland, industrial emissions, and increased energy consumption.*

Concluding Remarks. Although the summary statement can itself offer a sense of closure, to seal that effect you need to provide some concluding remarks that will stay with your listeners. Many of the techniques that can be used to gain attention in an introduction can also be used to create a memorable conclusion. Using the same technique to close the speech as you used to open it can make your speech seem balanced and elegant.

Involving the Audience—At the beginning of a speech, you involve the audience by showing them how your message relates to their lives. At the conclusion of your speech, you may want to reemphasize this relationship. To conclude her speech on Alzheimer's disease, Beth Duncan reminded her audience of the importance of the topic. She concluded with these remarks:

> *Hopefully, none of you have a relative with Alzheimer's disease in your family. And hopefully, none of you will ever have to face this problem. But if you do, I hope I've provided you with enough information about the disease to help you realize the pain and anguish these people and their caretakers must endure.*

In some persuasive speeches, involving the audience may consist of a call to action. Anna Aley concluded a speech on substandard off-campus housing with a call to action. The complete text of this speech may be found in Appendix D.

> *Kansas State students have been putting up with substandard living conditions for too long. It's time we finally got together to do something about this problem. Join*

the Off-Campus Association. Sign my petition. Let's send a message to these slum-lords that we're not going to put up with this any more. We don't have to live in slums!

Asking Rhetorical Questions—When used in an introduction, questions arouse attention and curiosity. When used in a conclusion, questions give your audience something to think about after you have finished. Annette Berrington opened her speech on the use of seat belts with a rhetorical question, "How would you like to have your name in the paper?" Her final words were, "Are you really sure you'd like to have your name in the paper?" This final question echoed the beginning and served as a haunting reminder to buckle up when you get in the car. Had she closed with, "Remember, seat belts save lives," the effect would not have been as dramatic or as memorable.

Ending with a Narrative—Stories are remembered long after facts and figures are forgotten. A concluding narrative can help your audience experience the essence of your message. To conclude a speech on domestic terrorism, Donna E. Shalala, secretary of health and human services, used the following narrative:

> *Let me conclude by telling you about a child psychologist named Sandra Graham-Berman who took responsibility for doing even more [about the problem of domestic abuse]. Several years ago she became aware of a support group for battered women. But she heard that there was no professional support for their children. On her own time and with her own money she began a support group for the children of these battered women. She began to see the girls and boys act out, talk out, and draw out their fears and their frustrations. She helped them learn they are not alone in their pain. And she taught them that when mommy is in trouble—when she is being hurt by daddy—it's possible to get help by dialing 9-1-1.*
>
> *A few years later, a shy 8-year-old girl walked in on a fight. Her father—if you can believe it, a child psychiatrist—was beating her mother on the head with a hammer. Try to imagine that. Try to imagine what you would do. Well, that little girl knew what to do. She remembered the lesson taught to her by a caring adult. And so she went to that phone, picked it up, pressed 9-1-1 and saved her mother's life. The father is in prison now and the family's trying its best to build a new life. If that little girl can have the courage to pick up the telephone, surely we can have the courage to prevent such stories from happening.*[16]

Closing with a Quotation—A brief quotation that captures the essence of your message can make an effective conclusion. If one literary quotation is used to open a speech, another on the same theme can provide an elegant sense of closure. Susie Smith opened her speech on work satisfaction with a quotation from Faulkner that linked work with unhappiness. She closed the speech with a more positive quotation from Joseph Conrad that summed up the meaning of satisfying work:

> *I like what is in work—the chance to find yourself. Your own reality—for yourself, not for others—what no other person can ever know.*

The conclusion of your speech should satisfy the audience that what the speech promised has been delivered. Write out your summary statement and concluding remarks, just as you did with your introduction. This will help you avoid dwindling off into nothing at the end of your speech. When you are satisfied with your conclusion, insert it into your working outline.

COMPLETING YOUR WORKING OUTLINE

At this point, your working outline is almost complete. You should review it one more time to be sure that your introduction and conclusion fit well with the body of your speech and that your main points and supporting materials are arranged for maximum effectiveness. Once you are satisfied that your working outline is adequate, you can move on to the final step of this phase of your work: adding transitions to make your speech flow smoothly.

Using Transitions. **Transitions** serve as signposts that guide your listeners through your speech. They help listeners focus on the meaning of your ideas and prepare them for new material. They tie your speech together by showing how your points relate to one another. You should plan transitions (1) to connect the introduction to the body of your speech, (2) to connect each main point of your speech to the next main point you will present, and (3) to connect the body of the speech to the conclusion. Figure 12.3 gives some common transitions.

Some transitions are short phrases, such as "There is another important point we must consider. . . ." Or, transitions may be worded as phrases that link ideas, such as, "Now that you understand what the greenhouse effect is and why it is important, let's examine its major causes." This type of transition sums up what you have just said and directs your audience to your next point.

To indicate	Use
Time changes	until, now, since, previously, later, earlier, in the past, in the future, meanwhile, five years ago, just last month, tomorrow, following, before, at present, eventually
Additions	moreover, in addition, furthermore, besides
Comparison	compared with, both are, likewise, in comparison, similarly, of equal importance, another type of, like, alike, just as
Contrast	but, yet, however, on the other hand, conversely, still, otherwise, in contrast, unfortunately, despite, rather than, on the contrary
Cause-effect	therefore, consequently, thus, accordingly, so, as a result, hence, since, because of, due to, for this reason
Numerical order	first, second, third, in the first place, to begin with, initially, next, eventually, finally
Spatial relations	to the north, alongside, to the left, above, moving eastward, in front of, in back of, behind, next to, below, nearby, in the distance
Explanation	to illustrate, for example, for instance, case in point, in other words, to simplify, to clarify
Importance	most importantly, above all, keep this in mind, remember, listen carefully, take note of, indeed
The speech is ending	in short, finally, in conclusion, to summarize

FIGURE **12.3**
Common Transitions

A variety of stock words or phrases can be used to signal changes in a speech. For example, *until now, last month,* and *in the future* can be used to point out time changes. Words and phrases such as *furthermore, moreover,* and *in addition* show that you are expanding an idea. The use of the word *similarly* indicates that a comparison will follow. Phrases and words such as *on the other hand, unfortunately,* or *however* signal that a contrast is likely. *As a result* and *consequently* signal causal relationships. Introductory phrases like *as we step inside* or *as we move north* indicate spatial relationships.

The lack of planned transitions is apparent when speakers overuse the words *well, you know,* or *okay* as transitions. Write out the transitions you need in order to make your speech flow smoothly and insert them into your working outline.

One Final Review. By now you have completed all the work on your working outline. Read through it one more time and evaluate it again. Once you have finished this, you can move on to preparing your formal outline.

PREPARING A FORMAL OUTLINE

A **formal outline** follows the established protocols of outlining. Several of these protocols have been satisfied in the working outline. To turn your working outline into a formal outline, you need to select a title for your speech, use an accepted form of enumeration, write your main points and subpoints, and prepare a bibliography of major references. A sample formal outline for the speech on the "greenhouse effect" may be found in Figure 12.4.

SELECTING A TITLE FOR YOUR SPEECH

Titles are often optional for classroom speeches (check with your instructor). In situations outside the classroom, titles are useful for advertising speeches and attracting audiences. A title should prepare your audience for your speech. It should arouse curiosity and make people want to come and listen. A title should not promise too much or deceive the audience, lest the speech disappoint or frustrate listeners. Overblown titles can damage the speaker's ethos.

NUMBERING YOUR OUTLINE

Figure 12.4 illustrates a numbering system that follows the principles of coordination and subordination. It shows how to use numbers, letters, and indentation in an outline. The actual number of main points, subpoints, and sub-subpoints may vary, but the basic format remains the same.

The principle of **coordination** requires that all statements at any given level (main points, subpoints, etc.) be equally important. The principle of **subordination** requires that material descend in importance from the more general main points to the more specific subpoints and sub-subpoints. The more important a statement, the farther to the left it is positioned in the outline. This arrangement uses a standard set of symbols: Roman numerals, capital letters, Arabic numbers, and lowercase letters.

more important	**I.** Main point	**general**
	A. Subpoint	
	1. Sub-subpoint	
less important	a. Sub-sub-subpoint	**specific**

The Greenhouse Effect

Topic: The Greenhouse Effect
Specific purpose: To educate my audience on the causes of the greenhouse effect.
Thesis statement: The three major causes of the greenhouse effect are loss of forestlands, industrial emissions, and increased energy consumption.

INTRODUCTION

   I. Attention material: When Mark Twain was in London in 1897, a rumor of his death reached the editor of the *New York Journal* who wired its London correspondent, "HEAR MARK TWAIN DIED, SEND 1000 WORDS." The correspondent showed the telegram to Twain who wired back this message, "REPORT OF MY DEATH GREATLY EXAGGERATED." This answer applies equally well to the greenhouse effect. The reports of its death have been greatly exaggerated. More than twenty years ago, environmentalists urged scientists to look to Antarctica for signs of the greenhouse effect. In 1994 a giant iceberg—twenty-three miles wide and forty-eight miles long—almost as large as the state of Rhode Island broke off from the Larsen Ice Shelf in the Antarctic Peninsula. In 1997 new large crevasses were found. This suggests that the rest of the shelf is about to go. Do these signal the arrival of a full-fledged greenhouse effect? They may. And because of that possibility they simply cannot be ignored. The potential problems are simply too important to overlook.

  II. Credibility Material: Concern for the environment has always been a special interest of mine. I grew up in a rural area and learned to enjoy activities like hiking, camping, and fishing at an early age. I want the environment to be as nice and as safe for my children and grandchildren as it has been for me. I think when more people understand the environmental problems the world faces, we will have taken the first step toward solving them.

 III. Preview: The greenhouse effect is still with us. It did not die a premature death no matter how hard some people tried to bury it. Today I want to share with you what the greenhouse effect is and to explain its three major causes: the loss of forestlands, industrial pollution, and increased energy consumption.

[Transition: Let's begin with an explanation of what the greenhouse effect is.]

BODY

   I. The greenhouse effect is a gradual warming of the Earth due to human activity.
     A. It is characterized by a high concentration of carbon dioxide in the atmosphere.
       1. Each year five tons of carbon are pumped into the atmosphere for each man, woman, and child in the United States.
       2. In 1987 the level of carbon dioxide soared to a record high level.
       3. The three warmest years in this century all occurred in the 1990s.
     B. Carbon pollutants are producing a hole in the ozone layer.
       1. Chlorofluorocarbons act like an atmospheric Pac-Man.
       2. The hole in the ozone layer reduces the Earth's ability to protect us from ultraviolet radiation.
     C. If this problem is not corrected, we may see disastrous results.
       1. There could be dramatic climate changes.
         a. There could be widespread drought in the middle of continents.
         b. There could be increases in the frequency and severity of storms.
         c. There could be rising sea levels that might destroy coastal areas.
       2. There could be serious health problems.
         a. There could be an increase in skin cancer.
         b. There could be an increase in cataracts.
         c. There could be epidemics of malaria and encephalitis.

[Transition: Now that you understand what the greenhouse effect is and why it is important, let's examine its major causes.]

  II. One cause of the greenhouse effect is the loss of forestlands that convert carbon dioxide into oxygen.
     A. One football field sized area of forest is lost every second to cutting or burning.
     B. Burning forests add more carbon dioxide because smoke is produced.

[Transition: Now let's turn to the second major cause of the greenhouse effect.]

(continued)

FIGURE **12.4**
Sample Formal Outline

III. Industrial emissions also contribute to the growth of the greenhouse effect.
   A. Industrial contaminants account for more than twenty percent of our air pollution.
   B. Carbon dioxide is released when wood, coal, and oil are burned.
   C. Chlorofluorocarbons come from refrigeration and air conditioners.
   D. Nitrogen oxides are spewed out of vehicle exhausts and smokestacks.

[Transition: The last major cause of the greenhouse effect may be the most important.]

IV. Increased energy consumption contributes to ozone depletion.
   A. People consume oxygen and emit carbon dioxide.
   B. The more people there are, the more energy is consumed.
   C. Energy consumption is the single largest cause of the greenhouse effect.
      1. Fossil fuel use has more than doubled since 1950.
      2. Fossil fuels account for ninety percent of America's energy consumption.
      3. Transportation-related energy use accounts for approximately half of all air pollution.

[Transition to conclusion: The summary statement serves as an adequate transition.]

CONCLUSION

   I. Summary: The greenhouse effect represents a clear and present danger to our world. If current conditions continue, we may face drastic climate changes and serious health problems. Its major causes are the loss of forestlands, industrial emissions, and increased energy consumption.

   II. Concluding remarks: Vice-President Al Gore used the following story to illustrate how this problem can sneak up on us. In an address to the National Academy of Sciences, he said, "If dropped into a pot of boiling water, a frog will quickly jump out. But if the same frog is put into a pot and the water is slowly heated, the frog will stay put until boiled alive. So it is with pollution. . . . If we do not wake up to the slow heating of our environment, we may jump too late." The more we know about this problem, and the better we understand it, the less likely we are to be like the frog who gets boiled alive.

WORKS CITED

Adams, Kathleen et.al. "It Hasn't Been This Sizzling in Centuries," *Time,* Notebook Planet Watch Online, May 4, 1998, Accessed May 4, 1998, http://www.pathfinder.com/time/magazine/1998/dom/980504/notebook/planet_watch.it37.html.

Easterbrook, Gregg "Greenhouse Common Sense," *U.S. News,* December 1, 1997, Online December 1, 1997, Accessed May 4, 1998, http://www.usnews.com/usnews/issue/971201/1glob.htm.

Easterbrook, Gregg "Hot Air Treaty," *U.S. News,* December 22, 1997, Online December 22, 1997, Accessed May 4, 1998, http://www.usnews.com/usnews/issue/971222/trea.htm.

Envirolink, "Greenhouse Effect," Online 1997, Accessed May 2, 1998, http://www.envirolink.org/orgs/edf/planetvision.html.

Gallup, Alec and Lydia Saad, "Public Concerned, Not Alarmed About Global Warming," Online December 2, 1997, Accessed May 4, 1998, http://www.gallup.com/POLL_ARCHIVES/971202.htm.

Gore, Albert, Jr. *Earth in the Balance: Ecology and the Human Spirit,* Houghton Mifflin: Boston, 1992.

Gore, Albert, Jr. "The Global Environment: A National Security Issue." Keynote Address to the National Academy of Science Forum on Global Climate Change, Washington, D.C., May 1, 1989.

"Key Issues Get the Warming Conference's Cold Shoulder," *U.S. News,* December 15, 1997. Online December 15, 1997, Accessed May 4, 1998, http://www.usnews.com/usnews/issue/971215/15kyot.htm.

Monastersky, Richard, "Consensus Reached on Climate Change Causes," *Science News,* September 24, 1994, p. 198.

"Ozone Mystery Solved," *National Wildlife,* April/May 1995, p. 6.

Pew Foundation, "Americans Support Action on Global Warming," Online, November 1997, Accessed May 3, 1998, http://www.people-press.org/nov97rpt.htm.

Schneider, David, "Global Warming is Still a Hot Topic," *Scientific American,* February 1995, pp. 13–14.

Sierra Club, "Global Warming Fact Sheet," Online, Undated, Accessed May 4, 1998, http://www.sierraclub.org/global-warming/factsheets/basfact.htm.

FIGURE **12.4** (continued)

WORDING YOUR OUTLINE

Each main point and subpoint in your outline should be worded as a simple, independent sentence. If your points keep sprouting dependent clauses, you may need to reexamine and simplify the structure of your speech. Look for opportunities to use **parallel construction** when wording your main points. For example, if you were preparing a speech on the need for election financing reforms, you might word your main points as follows:

Main point I.   We need reform at the national level.

Main point II.   We need reform at the state level.

Main point III.   We need reform at the local level.

Main point IV.   But first, we need to reform ourselves.

Parallel construction makes a speech easier to understand and helps the main points stand out from the supporting materials. Not all material lends itself easily to parallel construction, but look for opportunities to use it when you can.

PREPARING A BIBLIOGRAPHY

The final item in your formal outline will be a bibliography of works you consulted in preparing your speech. If you conducted an interview, you should cite that information as well. Check with your instructor to see if he or she has a preferred format for citing references. The following guidelines will help you prepare a bibliography.

Books. All references to books should be arranged alphabetically by the last name of the author(s). List the author's name (last name first), followed by the title and publication information (city of publication: publisher, date). For example:

Beifuss, Joan T. *At the River I Stand: Memphis, the 1968 Strike, and Martin Luther King,* (Memphis: B & W Books, 1985).

Articles. References to articles should be arranged alphabetically by the last name of the author, or by the title if the author is not specified. List the author's name (last name first), followed by the title of the article, the name of the periodical, volume number (if not a magazine), date of publication, and page numbers. For example:

McKibben, Bill. "An Explosion of Green." the *Atlantic Monthly,* April 1995, 61–83.

"Ozone Mystery Solved." *National Wildlife,* April/May 1995, 6.

Miscellaneous References. Your bibliography may also include references to interviews, telephone calls, or other sources of information you used in preparing your speech. Sample formats are as follows:

Cox, Robert. Interview. *All Things Considered.* National Public Radio. WNYC, New York, 18 May 1996.

Internet Citations. If you use the Internet as a source of information for your speech, you must be certain that your citation is specific enough to enable another person to find the information easily. Internet citations should include the name of the author, the title of the work, publication information for any print version of the material, the name of the database or home page, the date of electronic publication, the date the researcher accessed the information, and the electronic address of the site. Both the American Psychological Association and the Modern Language Association have Web sites detailing their specific citation formats.[17] Check these Web sites for updated information on citation formats.

Checklist for a Formal Outline

✓ My topic, general purpose, specific purpose, and thesis statement are clearly stated

✓ My introduction contains attention-getting material, establishes my credibility, and previews my message

✓ My main points represent the most important ideas on my topic

✓ My main points are worded as full, declarative sentences

✓ My subpoints are divisions of the main points they follow

✓ My subpoints are more specific than the main points they follow

✓ All the points in my speech are supported by facts and figures, testimony, examples, or narratives

✓ My conclusion contains a summary and concluding remarks that reflect on the meaning and significance of my speech

✓ I have provided transitions where needed to make the speech flow smoothly

✓ I have compiled a bibliography of the works I consulted in preparation for my speech

PREPARING A KEY-WORD OUTLINE

You should not use your formal outline to present your speech. If you try to speak from a full-sentence outline, you will end up reading it. Instead, use an abbreviated **key-word outline**, which reduces your formal outline to a few words that trace the sequence of your ideas.

Attention: GREENHOUSE EFFECT NOT DEAD
Credibility: MY CONCERN FOR THE ENVIRONMENT
Preview: DEFINE AND EXPLAIN THREE MAJOR CAUSES

BODY

I. GRADUAL WARMING
   A. HIGH CO_2 IN ATMOSPHERE
   B. HOLE IN OZONE LAYER
   C. SERIOUS CONSEQUENCES
      1. CLIMATE CHANGES
      2. HEALTH PROBLEMS

II. LOSS OF FORESTLANDS THAT CONVERT CO_2 TO O_2
   A. CUTTING
   B. BURNING

III. INDUSTRIAL EMISSIONS
   A. TWENTY PERCENT OF AIR POLLUTION
   B. BURNING WOOD, COAL, AND OIL
   C. CFCs FROM REFRIGERATION AND AIR CONDITIONING
   D. NITROUS OXIDE FROM VEHICLES AND SMOKESTACKS

IV. INCREASED ENERGY CONSUMPTION
   A. PEOPLE CONSUME O_2 AND EMIT CO_2
   B. LARGEST SINGLE CAUSE OF GREENHOUSE EFFECT
      1. NIF: FOSSIL FUEL USE DOUBLED SINCE 1950
      2. NINETY PERCENT OF U S ENERGY CONSUMPTION
      3. TRANSPORTATION = HALF ALL AIR POLLUTION

CONCLUSION

Summary: PROBLEM AND CAUSES
Final Remarks: GORE STORY: FROG

FIGURE **12.5**
Sample Key-Word Outline

You may use your key-word outline as a prompt during your presentation. It should fit on a single piece of paper or on two or three index cards. The outline should be printed in large letters so that you can see it easily should you need to refer to it. A key-word outline for the speech on the "greenhouse effect" is shown in Figure 12.5.

IN SUMMARY

A speech that is carefully structured helps the audience understand the message and enhances the ethos of the speaker. Outlining a speech gives you an opportunity to find and correct problems with your work.

You should structure the body of your speech first so that you can develop an introduction and conclusion that fit well with the body of the speech. In planning the body of your speech, you must determine your main points, arrange them in an effective order, and select supporting materials to substantiate your ideas.

Your main points are the most important things you have to say about your topic. Prepare a research overview to look for repeated ideas to serve as main points. Check to see how these relate to your specific purpose. Arrange your main points so that they make sense to your audience and are easy to follow. Order these points using the principles of similarity, proximity, and closure.

A working outline is a tentative plan of your speech that can show you how your ideas are developing and whether they fit together. You may make and amend several working outlines as you develop your speech. Begin your working outline by listing your main points in the order in which you want to present them. Break out your main points into more specific subpoints and make notes of supporting materials that you will use. As you develop your working outline, keep your audience at the center of your thinking.

Once you are satisfied that you have appropriately organized the body of your speech, you can work on your introduction and conclusion. Your introduction should capture attention, build your credibility, and preview your message. Seven techniques can be used in your introduction to gain attention: (1) involve the audience, (2) relate personal experiences, (3) ask rhetorical questions, (4) create suspense, (5) tell a story, (6) use a quotation, and (7) startle your audience.

The conclusion of your speech should summarize the meaning of your message, provide a sense of closure, and leave the audience with something to remember. Many of the techniques that are used to gain attention in introductions may also be used in concluding remarks.

To complete your working outline, you should add transitions to make your speech flow smoothly and point out the relationships between your ideas. Transitions are needed between the introduction and the body of your speech, between your main points, and between the body and the conclusion of your speech.

A formal outline follows a number of conventions. These include dividing the speech into its three major parts, indicating coordination and subordination through an accepted form of enumeration, properly wording your main points and subpoints, and preparing a bibliography. You may also decide to select a title for your speech. After you have completed your formal outline, you should prepare a key-word outline for use as a "memory jogger" during your presentation.

TERMS TO KNOW

main points	rhetorical question
research overview	preview
principle of similarity	transitions
principle of proximity	formal outline
principle of closure	coordination
working outline	subordination
subpoints	parallel construction
sub-subpoints	key-word outline

NOTES

1. J. C. McCroskey and R. S. Mehrley, "The Effects of Disorganization and Nonfluency on Attitude Change and Source Credibility," *Communication Monographs* 36 (1969): 13–21.

2. Most of the research on the effects of structure was conducted in the 1960s and 1970s. Notable among these studies are Christopher Spicer and Ronald E. Bassett, "The Effect of Organization on Learning from an Informative Message," *Southern Speech Communication Journal* 41 (1976): 290–299 and Ernest Thompson, "Some Effects of Message Structure on Listener's Comprehension," *Speech Monographs* 34 (1967): 51–57.

3. Margaret Fitch Hauser, "Message Structure, Inference Making, and Recall," in *Communication Yearbook 8,* ed. Robert N. Bostrom and Bruce Westley (Beverly Hills, Calif.: Sage, 1984), 378–392.

4. Robert T. Oliver, Harold P. Zelko, and Paul D. Holtzman, *Communicative Speaking and Listening* (New York: Holt, 1968), 125.

5. Norman Miller and Donald T. Campbell, "Recency and Primacy in Persuasion as a Function of the Timing of Speeches and Measurements," *Journal of Abnormal and Social Psychology* 59 (1959): 1–9.

6. Bernard Shaw, "Our Attitude About Women: Democracy Is Not a Smooth Sauce" in VITAL SPEECHES OF THE DAY, February 1, 1993, p. 245. Reprinted by permission.

7. Reprinted by permission.

8. Brock Adams, "The Endangered Species Act: Implications for the Future"(address presented before the Rotary Club of Seattle, Washington, 13 January 1993).

9. Bob Lannom, "Patience, Persistence, and Perspiration," Parsons, Tenn. *News Leader,* 20 September 1989, 9.

10. Excerpted from *The State of the Culture: Approach the Year Three-Thousand,* a speech delivered at Hillsdale College, Hillsdale, Michigan on October 4, 1992, by Alexandra York and reprinted in VITAL SPEECHES OF THE DAY on May 1, 1993.

11. Takakzu Kuriyama, "Trade Relations: Japan Has Barriers as Does the U.S.," *Vital Speeches of the Day,* 1 May 1994, 421–422.

12. N. H. Anderson and A. A. Barrios, "Primary Effects in Personality Impression Formation," *Journal of Abnormal and Social Psychology* 63 (1961): 346–350.

13. Kenneth Burke, *A Rhetoric of Motives* (Berkeley and Los Angeles: University of California Press, 1969), 20–23.

14. Will Kopp, "Inventing the Future: Battelle's Vision of Tomorrow's Technology," VITAL SPEECHES OF THE DAY, February 1, 1994, p. 244.

15. A more effective version of this introduction would begin with the anecdote to gain attention, then move to establishing credibility by highlighting what the company does and what role the speaker has in this (unless such information was presented when the speaker himself was introduced), and finally conclude with the preview of the message.

16. Donna E. Shalala, "Domestic Terrorism: An Unacknowledged Epidemic," VITAL SPEECHES OF THE DAY, 15 May 1994, 453.

17. Modern Language Association, "Citing Sources from the World Wide Web," undated, accessed 4 May 1988, http://www.mla.org/main_stl.htm#sources and American Psychological Association, "How to Cite Information from the Internet and the World Wide Web," undated, accessed 4 May 1998, http://www.apa.org/journals/webref.html.

PRESENTING YOUR SPEECH

THIS CHAPTER will help you

- Know what makes an effective presentation
- Use language effectively in presentations
- Understand the different types of presentations
- Use audience feedback to make on-the-spot adjustments
- Handle questions and answers
- Prepare for video presentations
- Communicate with your voice and body
- Practice presenting your speech
- Cope with communication apprehension

WHOSOEVER HATH A GOOD **PRESENCE** and a GOOD **FASHION** CARRIES CONTINUAL letters of **RECOMMENDATION.**

—F. Bacon

Well, I suppose I'm about ready. I've selected a topic I truly care about. I've done more than enough research, so I feel that I really understand what I'm going to say. I've found a wealth of good information, exciting examples, interesting stories to tell, and testimony from people my audience respects. And I've worked up a really nice outline. Still, I'm worried about how my speech will go over. I'm just not very good at speaking before a group. I don't want to mess up all this hard work by blowing my presentation! Help!

Successful public speaking involves both *what* you say and *how* you say it. In this chapter, we cover what makes an effective presentation, differences between oral and written language, the types of presentation, using your voice and body to communicate effectively, practicing your presentation, using feedback to make on-the-spot adjustments, and controlling your nervousness.

WHAT MAKES AN EFFECTIVE PRESENTATION?

An effective presentation allows you to share your message with your audience. The words *community* and *communication* both stem from the Latin word for *common.* Effective presentations begin with your attitude. You must be committed to your subject and want to share this commitment with your audience. You must want to enlighten your listeners, change the way they think about your topic, or move them to action. The best-prepared speech will fall flat if it is not presented with enthusiasm. Enthusiasm gives a speech energy and forcefulness. It tells your audience that you really care about your topic and about them.

An effective presentation does not call attention to itself or distract the audience from the essence of your message. You want your listeners to focus on what you have to say, not the way you are saying it. Consequently, you should avoid an overblown elocutionary style, complete with pompous-sounding language, eloquent vocal patterns, and dramatic gestures. On the other hand, you must take care not to mumble or talk to your chest. Your presentation should be readily intelligible and loud enough to be heard in all parts of the room.

Finally, an effective presentation sounds natural and conversational—as though you were talking *with* your audience, not *at* them. Talking *with* people brings the audience and speaker closer together. In this day and age, when we are bombarded with media presentations that bring a speaker up close and personal, as audiences we have grown to expect, and even demand, a more intimate style. Television has changed the rules of the game.[1]

Communication scholars call the closeness between a speaker and an audience **immediacy.**[2] Immediacy increases the willingness of listeners to be influenced by a speaker.[3] It is closely akin to the concept of identification, which we discussed in Chapter 12. Speakers can foster immediacy in their presentations. They can reduce psychological distance by actually reducing the physical distance and removing physical barriers between themselves and the audience. For example, they can move out from behind the lectern or step closer to the audience. Other presentation techniques that help promote immediacy include smiling at the audience, maintaining eye contact, using gestures, demonstrating vocal variety, and having a relaxed posture.

Let us caution you that being natural and sounding conversational does not give you a license to be lax. Your goal should be *improved conversation* in which you are a *little* more formal and more careful than when you are talking casually with friends. While your speech should sound spontaneous, as though your words and ideas were coming together for the first time, it takes a lot of effort and practice to sound natural. One way to accomplish this goal is to master the use of oral language.

THE LANGUAGE OF SPEECHES

No one can tell you exactly how you should use language in a speech. The particular way you choose and arrange the words in a speech will vary according to the topic, audience, and situation. For example, language acceptable for a celebrity roast would be inappropriate for a memorial service. The language you use in a speech on the importance of saving endangered species would be different from the language you might use in a speech warning students of the dangers of "power shopping." There are, however, some clear-cut guidelines for language use in speeches. First, any effective speech must be presented in oral language. You should also observe the six C's of effective language use: clearness, concreteness, conciseness, correctness, colorfulness, and consideration.

ORAL COMMUNICATION STYLE

As James A. Winans, one of the founders of the speech communication discipline once said, "A speech is not an essay standing on its hind legs."[4] Good **oral language** differs from written language.[5] Oral language is more personal than written language. It contains more personal pronouns and self-references. Oral language is also more spontaneous and less formal than its written counterpart. The words are shorter and more familiar. Colloquial words help foster immediacy and identification. There is greater use of contractions and interjections. *Honest!* Oral language is more colorful than written language. Emotional words help move people to action. Absolutes such as *none, all, every, never,* and *always* are frequent.

The way words are arranged in oral communication differs from the way they are put together in written communication. Oral communication uses short, direct, conversational sentence patterns. Sentence fragments are acceptable. Repetition and

Differences Between Oral and Written Communication Styles
- ✓ Oral language is less formal
- ✓ Oral language is more colorful
- ✓ Oral language uses shorter, simpler sentences
- ✓ Oral language is more repetitive
- ✓ Oral language uses more examples and narratives
- ✓ Oral language rounds off numbers and statistics

rephrasing are frequent because listeners cannot go back and reread material they don't understand. Pauses and vocal variations add emphasis and clarify meaning. Even the use of supporting materials is different in oral communication. There are more direct quotations. Numbers and statistics are rounded off or replaced with words like *more, many, few,* or *some.* Examples and narratives are used more frequently to sustain audience interest. Conclusions are often guarded by qualifiers such as *unless* or *except.*

THE SIX C's OF EFFECTIVE LANGUAGE USE

Your presentation will be more effective if the language you use is clear, concrete, concise, correct, colorful, and considerate. These standards for language use can make your message easier to understand, more interesting, and more likely to be well received.

Clearness. **Clearness** helps your audience understand your message. Beginning speakers often fall into the **"thesaurus syndrome"**: they look for three-syllable words, believing that this will make them sound more intelligent. In reality, they may just sound obscure. If you want your message to be understood, stay with simple, familiar words. If you use a thesaurus, use it to find a shorter alternative.

The major enemy of clearness is the use of **jargon**. Every discipline has a language of its own—one that is not shared with the general public. When jargon is used, the results often are unpredictable. For example:

> *Back in the 1930s, during the early years of media communication, the novice editor of a small-town newspaper in Colorado wanted to get the final results of the Indianapolis 500 race for his next edition. Unfortunately, his paper's AP wire would close before the race was over. So the editor asked the AP to send him the results by some other means.*
>
> *The AP immediately wired back this reply "WILL OVERHEAD WINNER INDIANAPOLIS RACE." This meant that they would "overhead," or send the result by Western Union. The editor, however, wasn't familiar with the word "overhead" in that technical context. He assumed that the race had been completed and a driver named Will Overhead had won. His headline read, "OVERHEAD WINS INDIANAPOLIS RACE!"*

Speakers may also use jargon to befuddle an audience when they really want to hide what is going on. Public television commentator Bill Moyers warned of the dangers of this misuse of language:

> *If you would . . . serve democracy well, you must first save the language. Save it from the jargon of insiders who talk of the current budget debate in Washington as "megapolicy choices between freeze-feasible base lines." (Sounds more like a baseball game played in the Arctic Circle.) Save it from the smokescreen artists, who speak of "revenue enhancement" and "tax-base erosion control" when they really mean a tax increase.[6]*

When you speak to a lay audience, translate technical words into lay language and carefully define any unfamiliar terms that you must use.

Finally, **artful repetition** can make your messages clearer. Artful repetition involves previewing ideas, rephrasing information, enlightening with examples, and reviewing what you have said. Such repetition gives your listeners time to process the information you have given them before you move on to another idea. It is wise to follow this age-less advice: tell them what you are going to tell them, tell them, and then tell them what you have told them.

Concreteness.   **Concrete words** convey specific information. If your language is too ab-stract, your listeners may lose interest. Abstractness invites misunderstanding. Concrete language creates vivid pictures that help your audience visualize what you are talking about. These word pictures make it easier for listeners to remember your message. Consider the following levels of abstraction:

most abstract	my pet
	my dog
	my puppy
	my black puppy
most concrete	my black Labrador puppy

As you work on the wording of your speech, plan to use the most concrete words your subject permits.

Conciseness.   **Conciseness** means that you should use no more words than are necessary to express an idea. As Thomas Jefferson once said, "The most valuable of all talents is that of never using two words when one will do." Achieving conciseness in speeches is no easy matter.[7] As you may recall, we just suggested that artful repetition was an important component of clearness. How can you use repetition and still be concise?

One way to achieve conciseness is to focus attention on your main ideas. This means that you should limit the number of main points and keep the structure of your speech simple. The more complex your material, the less you should try to cover in a short speech. A second way to achieve conciseness is to avoid going off on tangents with "that reminds me of . . ." examples. A third way to achieve conciseness is to use **maxims**, those compact sayings that compress ideas into brief, memorable phrases. Historic max-ims include Winston Churchill's "I have nothing to offer but blood, toil, tears, and sweat," and John F. Kennedy's "Ask not what your country can do for you, ask what you can do for your country."

The brevity of maxims makes them ideally suited to the time constraints of televi-sion news. When used in contemporary speeches, maxims are usually called **sound bites.** Peggy Noonan, who coined the term, was a speechwriter for Presidents Reagan and Bush and, before that, a writer for CBS news. She once told Reagan's advisors, "Only eight seconds of the President's speech is going to wind up on the air. I know, because my job was to cut them for Dan Rather."[8] One problem with using maxims or sound bites is that you may be tempted to substitute them for well-supported arguments. Even Noonan cautions against their overuse; "writing a speech as a series of catch phrases," she said, "is a 'debasement of the art.'"[9] Develop a substantive speech first, then con-sider how you might use sound bites to make your message more memorable. Use them sparingly for maximum effect.

Correctness.   **Correctness** refers to the proper selection of words. Nothing damages your ethos more than a glaring misuse of language. Mistakes in word selection lead lis-teners to question your competence. They may feel that anyone who misuses language is not likely to provide good information or offer good advice.

One frequent mistake in word selection is confusing words that sound similar. Such confusions are called **malapropisms**, after Mrs. Malaprop, a character in an eighteenth-century play. She would say things like, "He is the very *pineapple* of politeness," when she meant *pinnacle*. Malapropisms can be used *purposely* as a source of humor. When used inadvertently, the effect is not really funny, and it reflects poorly on the competence of the speaker. For example, one U.S. senator declared that he would vigorously oppose any effort to build a "nuclear waste *suppository*" in his state.[10] Another senator, discussing a proposed constitutional amendment to balance the budget, said, "We're finally going to wrassle to the ground this gigantic *orgasm* that is just out of control."[11] The lesson here is clear: to avoid being *unintentionally* humorous, check out the meaning of any words you are uncertain about.

Colorfulness. **Colorfulness** refers to the vividness of language. Colorful language is animated, conveying the speaker's involvement and feelings. It uses the fragments and rhythms and colloquialisms of everyday conversation. Southerners are especially known for their "gift of gab," according to William Ferris, director of the Center for the Study of Southern Culture at the University of Mississippi. Ferris thinks Clinton is at his best when he "mixes indigenous Southern language and linguistic patterns with a command of the English language."[12] President Clinton is more likely to use colorful language in news conferences when his remarks are not scripted. For example, when talking about emergency room care, he didn't say, "It's expensive." He said, "It costs out the wazoo!"[13] Colorfulness also comes from repetition, overstatement, and understatement. When several of these techniques are combined, the results are often striking. Ann Richards, former governor of Texas, was well known for turning a fine phrase. In her keynote address at the 1988 Democratic National Convention, she took her own party to task for not involving women more directly:

> *Twelve years ago Barbara Jordan, another Texas woman, made the keynote address to the convention, and two women in 160 years is about par for the course. . . . But if you give us a chance, we can perform. After all, Ginger Rogers did everything that Fred Astaire did. She just did it backwards in high heels.*[14]

Look for opportunities to use colorful language in your speeches. Just be sure the language you use is appropriate to the occasion, your audience, and your topic.

Consideration. **Consideration** requires that you keep the sensitivities of your audience in mind as you select your words. It relates directly to two major elements of ethical public speaking: respect for the audience and concern for the consequences of your message.

As we noted in Chapter 10, you should avoid the use of sexist language. The use of such language can set off an intense emotional response in some listeners. For example, if you refer to adult females as "girls," or if all of the authority figures in your examples are males, listeners may feel that you are insensitive. Their emotional reactions can affect the way they respond to the heart of your message. Sexist language is not the only thing you must think about as you try to demonstrate consideration in your language use. It is quite likely that your classroom audience will include people from a number of different cultures. Recent census data show that almost 25 percent of Americans are of African, Asian, Hispanic, or Native

● TRY THIS

Think about the most and least effective instructors you have had. How did their use of language measure up on the criteria of clearness, concreteness, correctness, colorfulness, conciseness, and consideration? What does this tell you about the importance of these factors? Share your observations with a classmate.

American ancestry.[15] If you live in New Mexico, California, Hawaii, New York, or the District of Columbia, there is a greater than 50 percent chance that any two individuals you encounter will differ ethnically or racially.[16] In addition to gender, ethnic, and racial differences, your classmates may have diverse religious affiliations, lifestyles, and geographic identifications and come from different socioeconomic levels. As listeners, they may be very sensitive to any negative allusions you may inadvertently use.

A lack of consideration for the sensitivities of your audience almost always has negative consequences. At best, your listeners may be mildly offended; at worst, they may be angry enough to reject both you and your message. Be attuned to the diversity of your audience, be appreciative of the differences between cultural groups, and be careful of the words you choose when referring to those who may be different from you.

Avoiding Racist and Sexist Language

✓ Avoid slang terms for racial, ethnic, or religious groups

✓ Avoid generic he and gender-specific titles

✓ Avoid "markers" that introduce irrelevant allusions to race, gender, or ethnicity

✓ Avoid identifying people in terms of their partner's accomplishments

✓ Avoid sexist, racist, ethnic, or religious humor

METHODS OF PRESENTATION

There are four major methods of speech presentation: impromptu speaking, memorized text presentations, reading from a manuscript, and extemporaneous speaking. In addition to describing these methods and advising you when each is most appropriate, we shall offer suggestions on responding to feedback from your audience, handling questions and answers, and making video presentations.

IMPROMPTU SPEAKING

Impromptu speaking is done with little or no advance preparation. You must rely on your previous knowledge and experience to fashion a message. At work, you might find yourself being asked to make a presentation "in about fifteen minutes." In meetings, you may want to "say a few words" about something. You may also find impromptu speaking helpful in the classroom when you need to answer a question.

To prepare an impromptu presentation, focus on your purpose. What is it most important that the audience know? In light of your purpose, determine your main points. Don't try to cover very much. Limit yourself to one or two or three points. If you have access to any writing material, jot down a memory-jogging word for each idea, either in the order of the ideas' importance or as they seem to flow naturally. This skeletal outline

Type	Use	Advantages	Disadvantages
Impromptu	When you have no time for preparation or practice.	Spontaneity, ability to meet demands of the situation, open to feedback.	Less polished, less use of supporting material, less well researched, less well organized.
Memorized	For brief remarks such as a toast or award acceptance; when the wording of your introduction or conclusion is important.	Eloquent wording can be planned, can sound well polished.	Focusing on remembering can make you forget to communicate, speech must be written out in advance, style can sound sing-songy.
Manuscript	When exact wording is important, time constraints are strict, or your speech will be televised.	Precise wording can be planned in advance, timing can be down to seconds.	Most people don't read well; inhibits responding to feedback and adapting speech accordingly, may not practice enough.
Extemporaneous	Recommended for most speaking situations.	Spontaneity, ability to respond to audience feedback, encourages focusing on the essence of your message.	Requires considerable time for preparation and practice, excellence comes through experience.

FIGURE 13.1
Types of Presentations

will keep you from rambling or leaving out something important. Enumerate your main points: "My first point is. . . . Second, it is important to. . . ." Illustrate each point with information, an example, or a story. Use the **PRER formula:** state a *P*oint, give a *R*eason or *E*xample, then *R*estate the point. Keep your presentation short and focused. End with a summary of your remarks.

MEMORIZED TEXT PRESENTATIONS

Memorized text presentations are written out, committed to memory, and delivered word for word. Memorized text presentations are not recommended for most public speaking situations because they have many serious problems. Speakers who try to memorize their presentations often get so caught up with "remembering" that they forget about communicating. The result becomes more a soliloquy than a public speech and usually sounds stilted. Speaking from memory also binds you to a text and inhibits you from adapting to audience feedback. It can keep you from clarifying ideas that the audience doesn't understand. Finally, most people have problems writing in an oral style.

If you must memorize a speech, write it using good oral style. Commit the speech so thoroughly to memory that you can concentrate on communicating with your audience. If you experience a "mental block," *keep talking*. Restate or rephrase your last point to get your mind back on track.

READING FROM A MANUSCRIPT

In a **manuscript presentation**, a text is read to an audience. Manuscript presentations share many of the problems of memorized presentations. Speakers are bound to a text, which inhibits adapting to the audience. This problem is even more pronounced with

A manuscript presentation must be well-rehearsed, so the speaker does not lose contact with the audience. Modern TelePrompTers are unobtrusive.

manuscript presentations because speakers must keep their eyes on the script and often lose eye contact with listeners.

There are some additional problems that are exclusive to manuscript presentations. Most people do not read aloud well. When speakers plan to read a speech, they may not think that practice is important. When they don't practice enough, they end up glued to the manuscript and lose contact with the audience. Other problems may arise if manuscript pages get out of order, if a page gets lost, if the type is too small, or if perchance you grab the wrong paper or TelePrompTer material on your way to a presentation. Although this last predicament may sound improbable, it can happen—as it did when President Clinton was presenting his health care address to Congress in September of 1993.

Clinton had just finished revising his manuscript on the ride to the Capitol. The final changes were entered onto computer disks immediately before the speech. Here is a report of what happened:

> No one realized that a White House communications aide had already accidentally merged the new speech with an old file of the February 17 speech to Congress. . . . When Clinton took the podium minutes later, he was understandably alarmed to see a seven-month-old speech on the TelePrompTer's display screens. Clinton told the news to Gore. . . .Gore summoned Stephanopoulos, who scrambled to fix the mistake, eventually downloading the correct version. . . . But for seven minutes, Clinton vamped with just notes.[17]

During the first seven minutes of his presentation, the president was forced into an extemporaneous style—the method of presentation most communication instructors prefer. The speech was received with high acclaim:

> For a man reading the wrong speech off his TelePrompTer, Bill Clinton spoke with persuasive passion as he addressed Congress and the nation about health care last week. Gone was the Slick Willie. . . . Suddenly Clinton looked the leader millions of Americans hoped they were voting for: decisive, forceful, even visionary.[18]

Manuscript presentations are useful when accurate wording is important or time constraints are severe, as in legal announcements or media presentations that must be timed within seconds. Extemporaneous presentations may include quotations or technical information that should be read to ensure accuracy. Because you may need to make a manuscript presentation at some time, we include here some suggestions that should help you with this presentation style.

To make an effective manuscript presentation, write your speech using a good oral style. Use a word processor set at a 24-point or larger font to prepare your script so that you can read it without straining. Double- or triple-space the manuscript. Mark pauses.

Highlight material you want to emphasize. Practice your speech from the manuscript so that you are familiar enough with it to maintain eye contact with your audience.

Record yourself as you rehearse, using videotape if possible, then review your tape to evaluate your presentation. Do you sound as though you are *talking with* someone, or as if you are *reading?* Did you maintain *eye contact* with the imaginary audience? If you stumbled over phrasing or mispronounced certain words, revise your manuscript to make your presentation flow more smoothly. Strive for a conversational style of presentation.

EXTEMPORANEOUS SPEAKING

Extemporaneous speaking is *prepared and practiced, but not written out or memorized.* For extemporaneous speaking you prepare an outline, as we discussed in Chapter 12. You rehearse your speech using a key-word outline to jog your memory. Each time you practice, the wording will differ, and so your speech should sound spontaneous because it is. An extemporaneous presentation allows you to maintain eye contact with your listeners so that you can use feedback to adjust your message as needed.

Because extemporaneous speaking involves more preparation, it is more polished than impromptu speaking. This preparation shows up in the more careful organization of material, the greater support for your ideas, and the greater ease with which you present your speech. Most instructors prefer that you use the extemporaneous method of presentation for classroom speeches. Much of our advice in this book is offered with this method in mind.

RESPONDING TO FEEDBACK FROM YOUR AUDIENCE

Feedback is the immediate response of the audience to your speech. It is most often conveyed nonverbally through facial expressions, nods, or restless movements. At times, however, feedback may be verbal, such as "Amen!" or "No way!" Other feedback cues may come from physical actions, such as moving to the front of the room to hear better or leaving in disagreement.

Regardless of your method of presentation, you should maintain eye contact with your audience so that you can receive feedback. Use this feedback to determine whether your listeners understand you, whether they are interested in your message, and whether they agree with what you have said. Because positive feedback in these areas rarely causes problems, we are concentrating here on using negative feedback to make on-the-spot adjustments in your presentation.

You can usually tell if listeners don't understand by their dumbfounded expressions. If you see wide-eyed stares and mouths agape, you can be pretty certain that your listeners have gotten lost. If this happens, there are several things you can do. You can define or redefine an unfamiliar word. You can try rephrasing an idea to make it more intelligible. You can add another example to make an abstract concept more concrete. You can compare or contrast an unfamiliar idea with something the audience already knows. Or, you can ask a direct (not rhetorical) question, such as, "You didn't understand that, did you?" or "Do you know what CFCs are?"

It's easy to tell when an audience is bored. Listeners may yawn, wiggle in their seats, drum their fingers, read a newspaper, or even fall asleep. To regain their interest, you can use any of the techniques for gaining attention that we discussed in Chapter 12 when

Audience feedback during a presentation should be used to make on-the-spot adjustments to a message.

we considered your introduction. Remind them that this is important. Provide a personal example. Ask questions. Ask for examples. Call for a show of hands. Tell a story that brings your idea to life, maybe even injecting some light humor if that is appropriate to your topic. Startle the audience with an unusual statement. Show more enthusiasm yourself. Enthusiasm is contagious. Make your voice and gestures more animated. Move closer to the audience. Get out from behind the lectern. If none of these techniques work, stick with your message, stress your main points, and get yourself out of the situation as quickly and gracefully as possible.

Signs of disagreement can range from frowns and scowls to throwing rotten tomatoes to leaving in disgust. Few things can discombobulate a novice speaker as much as negative audience feedback! Fortunately, there are several techniques you can use to try to get your listeners to be more accepting of your message. If you anticipate resistance, work hard to establish your ethos in the introduction of your speech. It is vitally important that the audience see you as a competent, trustworthy, and likable person who has their best interests at heart. Although we covered this material in some detail in Chapter 12, it is important enough to merit reviewing here.

To be perceived as competent, you must *be* competent. Never try to present a speech on something you don't understand. Be overprepared for your speech—arm yourself with a surplus of information, examples, and testimony from sources that your audience respects. Organize your material very carefully. Practice your presentation until it is polished. Not only must you *be* competent, you must also *sound* competent. Demonstrate your trustworthiness by being straightforward, honest, and sincere. Show respect, tolerance, and understanding for positions different from yours. To seem likable, you must be pleasant, friendly, and tactful.

Try to establish common ground with your audience. It may be that although you differ on how things should be done, you agree on the ultimate goal. Point out areas of agreement. Stress the values that you share with the audience. Appeal to their sense of fair play and their respect for freedom of speech, for example: "I know you won't agree with all of this, but I'm sure you will be willing to hear me out." Avoid using inflammatory language that can fan the fires of disagreement. No matter what happens, don't blow your cool.

HANDLING QUESTIONS AND ANSWERS

After any presentation, you may need to respond to questions from the audience. If you prepared well for your speech, you will be well prepared to answer questions on your topic. Because you won't know exactly what questions will be asked, your responses will have to be impromptu. The following suggestions should make handling questions and answers easier for you.[19]

First, *prepare for questions in advance.* Be thorough enough in your research to be confident of your ability to answer any rational question. Anticipate questions that listeners might ask and think about how to answer them. Practice your speech before some friends and have them ask questions.

Second, *repeat the question.* This is especially important if the question was long or complicated. This tactic serves several purposes. Paraphrasing ensures that everyone in the audience hears the question, it gives you time to think of your answer, and it helps you be sure you understood the question.

Third, *maintain eye contact with the audience as you answer.* Note that we said with the *audience,* not just with the questioner. Look first at the questioner, then make eye contact with other audience members, returning your gaze to the questioner as you finish your answer. The purpose of a question-and-answer period should be to increase the audience's understanding, not to carry on a private conversation with one person.

Fourth, *defuse hostile questions.* Reword emotional questions in objective language so that you do not get caught up emotionally yourself. Suppose you are asked, "Why do you want to throw away our money on people who are too lazy to work?" You might respond with, "I understand your frustration, and I think what you really want to know is, 'Why aren't our current programs helping people break out of the chains of unemployment?'"

Simply saying "I don't know" can also help to defuse a hostile questioner. Roger Ailes, a political media advisor for three U.S. presidents, described how former New York City mayor Ed Koch once used this technique. Koch had spent three hundred thousand dollars putting bike lanes in Manhattan. However, cars were driving in the bike lanes. Cyclists were running over pedestrians. The money seemed to have been wasted. Soon thereafter, when Koch was running for reelection, he appeared on a "meet-the-press" type show. This is how the questioning went:

> One reporter led off with "Mayor Koch, in light of the financial difficulties in New York City, how could you possibly justify wasting three hundred thousand dollars on bike lanes?" Koch smiled and he said, "You're right. It was a terrible idea." He went on. "I thought it would work. It didn't. It was one of the worst mistakes I ever made." And he stopped. Now nobody knew what to do. They had another twenty-six minutes of the program left. They all had prepared questions about the bike lanes, and so the next person feebly asked, "But, Mayor Koch, how could you do this?" And Mayor Koch said, "I already told you, it was stupid. I did a dumb thing. It didn't work." And he stopped again. Now there were twenty-five minutes left and nothing to ask him. It was brilliant.[20]

Fifth, *keep your answers short and to the point.* Don't use a question-and-answer session to give another speech.

Sixth, *handle nonquestions politely.* If someone starts to give a speech rather than ask a question, wait until he or she pauses for breath and then cut in with something like, "Thank you for your comment," or "That's an interesting perspective. Next question." Don't get caught up in a shouting match. Stay in command of the situation.

Finally, *bring the question-and-answer session to a close.* Call for a final question and summarize the essence of your message to refocus the audience on the major points of your presentation.

MAKING VIDEO PRESENTATIONS

In this media-intense world, it is very likely that you will have to make video presentations. You may find yourself speaking live on closed-circuit television, videotaping materials at work, or appearing on commercial television. With minor adaptations, the training you receive in this class should serve you well in such situations.[21]

Television brings a speaker close to viewers. It magnifies every visual aspect of you and your message. Therefore, you should dress conservatively, avoiding shiny fabrics, glittery jewelry, and flashy prints that might "swim" on the screen. You also should not wear white or very light pastels because they reflect glare. Ask in advance about the color of the studio backdrop. If you have light hair or if the backdrop will be light, wear dark clothing for contrast. Both men and women will need makeup in order to look natural on television. Have powder available to reduce skin shine or hide a five-o'clock shadow. Women should use makeup lightly because the camera will intensify it. Avoid glasses with tinted lenses; they will appear even darker on the screen.

Television requires a conversational mode of presentation. Your audience may be individuals or very small groups assembled in their homes. Imagine yourself talking with someone in an informal setting. Since you will have no immediate feedback, your meaning must be instantly clear. Use language that is colorful and concrete so that your audience will remember your message. Use previews and internal summaries to keep viewers on track. If you plan to use presentation aids, talk with studio personnel to be sure your materials will work in that setting.

Vocal variety and facial expressions will be your most important forms of body language. Television will magnify your movements and vocal changes. Slight head movements and underplayed facial expressions should be enough to reinforce your ideas. Avoid abrupt changes in loudness as a means of vocal emphasis. Rely instead on subtle changes in tempo, pitch, and inflection, and on brief pauses to emphasize your ideas.

For most televised presentations, timing is crucial. Five minutes of air time means five minutes, not five minutes and ten seconds. If you run overtime, you may be cut off in midsentence. For this reason, television favors manuscript presentations read from a TelePrompTer. The TelePrompTer controls timing, and also preserves the illusion of direct eye contact between speakers and listeners. Ask studio production personnel how to use the TelePrompTer equipment.

If at all possible, rehearse your presentation in the studio with the help of production personnel. Try to develop a positive relationship with the studio workers. Your success partly depends on how well they do their jobs. Provide them with a manuscript that has been marked to show when you will move around or use a visual aid. Practice speaking from the TelePrompTer, striving to sound spontaneous and direct.

Use the microphone correctly. Don't blow into it to see if it's working. Don't fiddle with the mike while you are presenting your speech. Remember, it will pick up *all* sounds, including shuffling papers or tapping on a lectern. If you use a stand or hand-held microphone, position it below your mouth about ten inches away. The closer the microphone is to your mouth, the more it will pick up unwanted noises like whistled *s* sounds. If you use a lavaliere microphone, production personnel will clip it to your clothing. Microphones with cords will restrict your movements. If you plan to move about, know where the cord is so that you don't trip over it.

Don't be put off by distractions in the studio as you practice and present your speech. Studio workers may need to confer with one another while you are speaking. This is a necessary part of their business. They are not being rude. Even though they are in the room with you, they are not your audience. Keep your mind on your ideas and your eyes on the camera. The camera may seem strange at first, but think of it as a friendly, receptive face waiting to hear what you have to say. Your eye contact with the camera becomes your eye contact with your audience.

Be prepared for lighting and voice checks before the actual taping begins. Take advantage of this time to run through your introduction. Before you begin your speech and after you finish, always assume that any microphone or camera near you is "live." Don't say or do anything you wouldn't want your audience to hear or see.

Even though the situation is strange, try to relax. If you are standing, stand at ease. If you are sitting, lean slightly forward as you would if you were talking to someone in the chair next to you. The floor director will give you a countdown before the camera starts to roll. Clear your throat and be ready to start on cue. Begin with a smile, if this is appropriate for your topic, as you make eye contact with the camera. If several cameras are trained on you, a red light will tell you which camera is on. During your presentation, studio personnel may communicate with you using special sign language. The director will tell you what cues they will use.[22]

The TelePrompTer script will appear directly below or on the lens of the camera. Practice your speech ahead of time until you almost have it memorized so that you can glance at the script as a whole. If you have to read it word by word, your eyes may be continually shifting (which makes you look suspicious). If you make a mistake, keep going. Do not stop unless the director says "cut." If appropriate, for your topic, smile when you finish and continue looking at the camera to allow time for a fade-out.

USING YOUR VOICE AND BODY TO COMMUNICATE EFFECTIVELY

Your voice and your body are your major communication tools. They determine the first impression your audience has of you. Although we cannot turn you into something you are not, we can offer suggestions for making your voice and body work better to enhance your presentations.

USING YOUR VOICE TO COMMUNICATE EFFECTIVELY

If you doubt that your voice has an important effect on the meaning listeners attach to words, consider the following simple sentences: "I don't believe it." "You did that." "Give me a break." How many different meanings can you create just by varying your pace, emphasis, and inflections?

A good speaking voice conveys your ideas clearly and enhances your ethos. It must carry not only the meaning, but also the feeling of your message. Additionally, all aspects of the way you speak affect your ethos. If you mispronounce words, your credibility may suffer. If you mumble, people may think you are trying to hide something. If you are overly loud and strident, listeners may not find you very likable.

The first step in developing a more effective speaking voice is to evaluate the way you usually talk. Tape-record yourself speaking spontaneously and then reading material from a text. Listen to the tape and ask yourself the following questions: (1) Does my voice convey the meaning I intend? (2) Would I want to listen to this voice if I were in the audience? and (3) Does my voice present me at my best? If you answered no to any of these questions, you may need to work on your loudness, tempo, pitch, variety, or diction.

The proper **loudness** is important for effective presentations. No speech can be effective if the audience can't hear it. When you speak before a group, you should speak slightly louder than you do when talking with friends. The size of the room, the presence or absence of a microphone, and background noise may call for adjustments in the volume of your voice. Take your cues from audience feedback. If you are not loud enough, you may see listeners leaning forward, straining to hear you.

Variations in loudness can express emotion. The more excited or angrier we are, the louder we speak. Be careful not to let yourself get caught in the trap of having only two options: loud and louder. Reducing volume can also express emotion effectively. Listen to your tape to determine if you were speaking loud enough to be heard and if your variations in loudness were sufficient to convey your meaning. If your answer in either case is no, tape-record some material in which you exaggerate loudness changes to see how it sounds.

The **tempo** at which you speak should vary with the type of material you are presenting. Tempo contributes to the mood of your speech. Serious, complex topics call for a slower rate; a faster pace is best for lighter topics. Beginning speakers often have difficulty controlling the speed of their speaking. Often they speak so fast that their listeners cannot keep up with them. This rapid rate communicates their desire to get through the speech as quickly as possible and sit down! Others may speak so slowly that they sound as if they are drugged. Speakers who talk too fast can lose the audience because the listeners cannot keep up. Speakers who talk too slowly can lull an audience to sleep. Neither extreme lends itself to effective communication. Pauses are oral punctuation marks. They are one of the most effective but least used ways to emphasize meaning. A pause before or after a word or phrase highlights its importance. Pauses give listeners time to ponder what you have said. They clarify the relationships among ideas, phrases, and sentences.

Review your tape to determine if you are using tempo effectively. Are you speaking too quickly or too slowly? Do you vary your speed to fit your material? Are you using pauses effectively? If the answer to any of these questions is no, try taping some more material and work to improve your use of tempo and pauses.

Your **pitch** can range from low and deep to high and squeaky. Pitch has many subtle meanings associated with it. People typically think that a low pitch sounds adult and authoritative, whereas a high pitch sounds childish or tentative. Most people can change their speaking pitch, just as they can change their singing pitch. Listen to your tape to determine if you are satisfied with the pitch of your voice. Do you sound mature and strong? If not, try making another recording, this time concentrating on adjusting your pitch so that you sound more commanding.

In addition to your usual speaking pitch, you also use **inflections,** or variations in pitch, to express meaning. Inflection patterns provide the melody of speech. Just recite any limerick and you'll understand what we mean. Inflections signal differences between questions and statements, show whether you are being sincere or sarcastic, and convey moods. A lack of inflection makes for a monotonous presentation that listeners will find boring. On the other hand, overdone or repetitious inflection patterns can be grotesque. Such inflection patterns typically occur when a speaker has memorized a script, but has no real commitment to its meaning. You can almost always recognize a telephone sales pitch by the inflection pattern the speaker uses.

When you speak before a group, don't be surprised if your pitch seems higher than usual. Your voice is sensitive to emotions and generally goes up in pitch when you feel you are under stress. Listen again to your tape and see if you are satisfied with your overall pitch level and use of inflection. If you are not, tape yourself again, trying to use a lower pitch and more or less inflection as necessary.

We have already mentioned the need for variety in our discussions of loudness, tempo, and pitch. Vocal variety adds color to a speech. It gives your message a sense of vitality. It energizes the audience. Even the best-prepared speech can be ruined by a poor presentation. The level of variety called for in a speech depends on two factors: your personality and the mood that is appropriate to your topic. Make a tape of yourself practicing your next speech and check to be sure that the variety level is appropriate. If it is not, keep practicing and taping until your speech sounds the way you want it to.

We use the term **diction** to describe the way you articulate individual speech sounds, the way you enunciate words in context, and the way you pronounce individual words. Diction also includes variations in dialects. All of these factors can affect your ethos and influence how well your speech is received by the audience.

Problems in **articulation** occur when speakers have difficulty making certain speech sounds. For example, a speaker may substitute an *f* for a *th*, saying "wif us" instead of "with us." Minor variations in articulation usually do not disrupt communication. However, if the audience cannot understand the speaker or if the variations are associated with low social or economic status, they need attention. Such problems are best handled by a speech pathologist, who helps a person produce the sounds correctly. If you have such problems, contact the speech clinic on your campus.

Problems of **enunciation** involve the way you pronounce words in context. In casual conversations, speakers often slur their words—for example, saying "Swatuh thought" for "That's what I thought." This type of lazy enunciation is not acceptable in public communication. Be careful not to run words together as you speak. Remember, your goal is an *improved* conversational pattern. On the other hand, avoid meticulously overenunciating each and every syllable; this sounds pompous and pretentious. Check your tape recording for enunciation problems and practice correcting them as necessary.

Pronunciation includes both the use of correct sounds and the proper accent on syllables in words. If you are uncertain of how to pronounce a word, consult a dictionary. The most damaging pronunciation problems are those involving the mispronunciation of common words. For example, how do you pronounce the following words?

government	library
February	picture
nuclear	secretary
ask	just

Unless you are careful, you may find yourself slipping into these common mispronunciations:

goverment	liberry
Febuary	pitcher
nuculer	sekerterry
axe	jist

Mispronouncing common words damages your ethos. Most of us are aware of the words we habitually mispronounce and can say them properly when we think about it. When you are presenting your speech is the time to think about it.

A **dialect** is a speech pattern typical of a geographic area or ethnic group. There is no such thing as a right or wrong, superior or inferior dialect. However, there may be times

TRY THIS ●

Make a list of the words you most often mispronounce. Practice saying these words correctly every day for a week. See if you can carry these changes over into social conversations and speech presentations.

when having a distinct dialect is a disadvantage. Listeners may have stereotypical ideas about people who speak with certain dialects. For example, those raised in the South often find a New England dialect abrasive, and midwesterners may associate a southern dialect with mental slowness. You should strive to develop a dialect pattern that represents the best standards of the *educated* people of your area or group.

Vocal distracters are repeated sounds, words, or phrases that interfere with effective communication. Some speakers use too many "ers" and "ums," "wells" and "okays," or "you knows" without realizing that they are doing it. You may be using vocal distracters to fill in time while you think about what to say next. Or, the distracters may be a sign of nervousness. Listen to your tape to see if you inject such distracters into your spontaneous speech. Simply becoming aware that you are using them is often enough to help you control them. If you had a lot of distracters in your spontaneous speech, tape yourself again trying to talk without them. Also, don't use "okay" or "well" to substitute for planned transitions.

USING YOUR BODY TO COMMUNICATE EFFECTIVELY

You begin to communicate with an audience before you utter a single word. Your personal appearance, facial expressions, and movements form the **body language** of your speech. What you communicate with your body should be consistent with your words.

Your clothing and grooming affect how you are perceived. They are an important part of the first impression you make on people. Your dress and grooming may also affect how you see yourself and how you behave. A police officer may not act as authoritatively out of uniform as when dressed in blue. You may even have a special "good luck" outfit that raises your confidence. When you are scheduled to speak, dress in a way that makes you feel good about yourself. Giving a speech is a *special occasion,* so you should dress more formally than you normally do for classes to emphasize to yourself and your audience that your speech is important. When you are speaking outside the classroom, try to conform to the dress standards of your audience. When in doubt, err on the side of dressing conservatively.

Posture is also an important factor in appearance. When you stand for a presentation, stand up straight, but "at ease" rather than at "military attention." If you are using a lectern, don't lean on it. Avoid grabbing the sides of the lectern and hanging on as though it were going to sprout wings and fly away. Keep your arms at your side and your hands free to gesture when necessary.

Most of us believe that we can judge character, determine people's feelings, and tell if people are honest from their facial expressions. If there is any conflict between what we see and what we hear, we will usually believe our eyes rather than our ears. In our American culture, eye contact suggests honesty, openness, and respect. Therefore, making eye contact with an audience is very important. Not only is eye contact your most direct channel for feedback, but a lack of eye contact may suggest to listeners that you do not care about them, that you are trying to put something over on them, or that you are afraid of them. When you reach the place where you are going to speak, pause and look at your audience for a few seconds without saying anything. During your speech, try to make eye contact with all sections of your audience. Don't just stare at one or two people. It may make them uncomfortable. Start your speech with a smile unless this is inappropriate to your message. Let your face reflect and reinforce the meanings of your words. An expressionless face suggests indifference. If you have selected a topic that you truly care about and you concentrate on sharing your ideas and feelings about it, the proper facial expressions should come naturally.

Gestures should seem natural, even when planned and practiced.

Movement and gestures are important components of body language. Movement calls attention to itself; therefore, you want to be sure that your words and gestures work in harmony. You should avoid random movements such as rocking from side to side, bouncing up and down, or pacing back and forth. The gestures and movements you use in a public speech should seem as natural and spontaneous as the ones you use in casual conversation. Let your ideas and feelings prompt your gestures. Contrived gestures look artificial. Probably every speech instructor has encountered students like the one who stood with his arms making a circle above him as he said, "We need to get *around* this problem." That's carrying body language too far. Don't point to your head every time you say "think," or spread your arms wide every time you say "big." Such gestures do not look natural.

If you are to gesture effectively during a speech, your hands and body should be positioned so that they do not inhibit action. For example, if your hands are jammed into your pockets and you feel an urge to gesture, you may look like a chicken flapping its wings. Keep your arms and hands in a relaxed position at your sides or in front of you, where they are free to move when the impulse hits. Once you begin a gesture, let it move naturally and fully. Don't raise your hand halfway, then stop with your arm awkwardly frozen in midair. When you have completed a gesture, let your arms and hands return to your sides, so that you will be able to use them again when you need to.

In addition to gesturing with your arms and hands, you may want to add other movement to your speech. As we noted in our discussion of immediacy, getting out from behind a lectern and moving closer to your audience are invitations to identification. President Clinton used this technique effectively in the televised debates of the 1992 campaign. At one point, Clinton actually rose from his seat and approached the audience as he fielded a question. This behavior signaled that he felt a special closeness to that problem and to his listeners. His body language enhanced his identification with the audience.

PRACTICING YOUR PRESENTATION

Practice may not make perfect, but it certainly improves your chances of presenting an effective speech. Silently reading through your outline is not the same thing as practicing your speech. You must *actually speak the speech*. To present an effective speech, you should rehearse your presentation until you feel that the speech is part of you. As you practice, you can try out the words and techniques you have been considering. Something that seemed like a good idea may not work particularly well when you actually try it. It is better to discover this during rehearsal than during your presentation.

Try to practice your presentation under the same kinds of conditions in which you will be presenting your speech. Stand up while you practice. Imagine your listeners in front of you. Picture them responding positively to your words. If possible, practice in your classroom or in another room where the speaking arrangements are similar. Begin your practice using your full-sentence outline. Once you are comfortable with the flow of ideas, switch to your key-word outline and practice until the outline transfers from the paper to your head. Keep material you must read at a minimum. Type or print each quotation on a single index card. Practice reading your quotations until you can present them naturally, glancing down only occasionally at your notes. If you will be using a lectern, place your key-word outline or quotation cards so that you can maintain eye contact with the audience while reading. If you are not using a lectern, hold your cards in your hand and raise them when it is time to read. If you will be using presentation aids, practice handling them until they are smoothly integrated into your presentation. Check the timing of your speech.

If possible, tape yourself as you rehearse your speech. If video equipment is available, you can both hear and see yourself. Use the tape to evaluate your presentation. Try to be a tough, but constructive critic. Look for specific points where you need improvement. Practice your speech at least once before a friend or friends. Their outside opinions may be more objective than your self-evaluation, and practicing in front of them will give you a feel for speaking to real people. Seek constructive feedback from your friends by asking them specific questions: Was it easy for them to follow you? Could they identify your main points? Were your ideas clear and well supported? Did they learn something from your message? Were they convinced by your arguments? Did you seem to be in command? Did you have any mannerisms that distracted them? Were you speaking loudly and slowly enough?

Practicing Your Presentation
✓ Practice standing up and speaking aloud
✓ Practice from your full-sentence outline, then switch to your key-word outline
✓ Work on maintaining eye contact with an imaginary audience
✓ Practice integrating presentation aids into your message
✓ Check the timing of your speech, and add or cut if necessary
✓ Continue practicing until you feel comfortable and confident

On the day you are assigned to speak, get to class early enough to look over your outline one last time so that it is fresh in your mind. If you have devoted sufficient time and energy to your preparation and practice, you should feel confident about communicating with your audience.

When you give speeches, it is natural to have **communication apprehension**, characterized by butterflies in your stomach and sweat on the palms of your hands. In fact, there would be something wrong with you if you didn't have such feelings (see Appendix D). The absence of any nervousness could suggest that you don't care about your audience or your message. Almost everyone who faces a public audience experiences problems of this kind—even seasoned performers. The late Edward R. Murrow, prize-winning radio and television commentator, had to learn to handle such fears: "The best speakers know enough to be scared. . . . The only difference between the pros and the novices is that the pros have trained the butterflies to fly in formation." You are not alone.

There are many reasons why speaking in public can be frightening. A recent study suggested that one-third of those surveyed reported experiencing excessive anxiety when speaking before a large audience.[23] Figure 13.2 lists the types of fears reported in the study. As a beginning speaker, you may believe that your presentation has to be perfect if it is to be effective. No presentation is ever perfect. Even former president Ronald Reagan, who was known as "the great communicator," bumbled some lines and repeated himself in his presentations. It's all right if you make a mistake, and besides, your listeners probably won't even notice it unless you tell them. You also may fear that the audience is lying in wait, ready to pounce on any little mistake you might make. In reality, most audiences—especially classroom audiences—want speakers to succeed. You may worry that everyone will know how scared you are. Actually, most listeners won't know this unless you tell them. You may believe that as soon as you stand up, something dreadful is going to happen to you—you'll throw up or pass out. This seldom happens. As you can see, many fears about public speaking are based on irrational thinking.

There are, however, some rational reasons why people are not comfortable speaking in public. Addressing a large group of people is not an everyday occurrence for most people, and people tend to be ill at ease in unfamiliar situations. Moreover, you usually will have to speak in public only on *important* occasions, when much depends on how well you express your ideas. This element of risk, combined with the feeling of strangeness, can make you feel realistically apprehensive. The most important thing to remember is, *don't be too anxious about your anxiety.* Accept these feelings as natural and

COPING WITH COMMUNICATION APPREHENSION

Specific fear	Percent reporting
Trembling or shaking	80%
Mind going blank	74%
Doing or saying something embarrassing	64%
Unable to continue talking	63%
Not making sense	59%
Sounding foolish	59%

FIGURE **13.2**
Public Speaking Fears

Source: Adapted from Stein, Walker and Forde, 1996

use the energy they generate to make your presentation more dynamic. Train your butterflies to fly in formation.

What can you do to put this nervous energy to work for you? If you find yourself building up a high level of anxiety before a speech, practice relaxation exercises. While breathing deeply and slowly, concentrate on tensing and relaxing your muscles, starting from your neck and working down to your feet. This will help control the physical symptoms of apprehension.[24] Identify irrational negative messages that you are sending yourself and replace them with positive, constructive messages. Instead of saying, "I'm going to sound stupid," say, "I've prepared thoroughly and I know what I'm talking about."[25] Picture yourself succeeding as a speaker, and practice with that image in mind.[26] Don't think of your presentation as a performance; think of it as an act of two-way communication in which you are sharing ideas.[27]

There are some other things you can do to line up those butterflies. Select a topic that excites you, so that you will get so involved with your message that there is little room left in your mind for worrying about yourself. Choose a topic that you already know something about, so that you will be more confident.[28] Build on that foundation of personal knowledge. Research your topic carefully. Outline your presentation. *Practice! Practice! Practice!* The better prepared you are, the more confident you will be. Memorize your introduction so that you can get off to a good start. You may find that once you get the ball rolling, your nervousness disappears. Keep your focus on your message and your audience, not on yourself. Remember, your major purpose is to share your ideas, not to display your oratorical brilliance.

Finally, *act* confident, even if you don't *feel* confident. Don't discuss your anxiety with classmates before you speak. When it is your turn, walk briskly to the front of the room, look at your audience, and smile if it is appropriate to your topic. Whatever happens during your speech, remember that listeners cannot see and hear inside you. They know only what you show them. Show them a controlled speaker communicating well-researched and carefully prepared ideas. Don't say anything like, "Gee, am I scared!" It

---

TRY THIS ●

Identify two or three negative messages you send yourself about speaking in public. Share these with a classmate and ask her or him how you might make these messages more constructive.

Controlling Communication Apprehension

✓ Prepare and practice thoroughly to develop confidence

✓ Focus on communicating with your audience

✓ Use relaxation exercises to control physical tension

✓ Replace negative messages with constructive ones

✓ Visualize yourself being successful

✓ Select a topic that excites you

✓ Develop responsible knowledge of your topic

✓ Practice, practice, practice, then practice some more

✓ Act confident, even if you don't feel that way

may make your audience uncomfortable as well. If you can put your listeners at ease by acting confident yourself, they can relax and give you the positive feedback that will make you a more assured and better speaker.

IN SUMMARY

An effective presentation allows you to share your message with your audience. It demonstrates your commitment and enthusiasm and fosters immediacy and identification. Effective presentations do not call attention to themselves; they sound natural and conversational.

Oral language is more personal and spontaneous than written language. The words are shorter, and colloquial words are acceptable. Contractions, interjections, and sentence fragments are often used. Repetition and rephrasing are necessary because listeners cannot reread something they don't understand. Effective oral communication uses language that is clear, concrete, concise, correct, colorful, and considerate.

There are four major methods of speech presentation. Impromptu speaking relies on previous knowledge or experience and is used when one has little or no time for preparation. Memorized text presentations are written out in advance and committed to memory. They are not recommended for most public speaking situations; however, you may wish to memorize the introductions and conclusions of your speeches. Manuscript presentations in which a written script is read to an audience are used mainly when accurate wording is important or time constraints are severe. Extemporaneous speaking is prepared and practiced, but not written out or memorized. It gives the speaker an opportunity to obtain immediate feedback from the audience.

Effective speakers use feedback from the audience during their presentations to make on-the-spot adjustments to their speeches. Feedback can provide information on whether the audience understands you, is interested in your message, and agrees with your suggestions.

If you anticipate questions and answers following a presentation, you should prepare for this in advance. When responding to a questioner, always repeat the question. Maintain eye contact with the audience, not just the questioner, as you answer. Defuse hostile questions by rewording them more objectively. Don't lose your cool. Keep answers short and to the point, handle nonquestions politely, stay in control of the situation, and bring the session to a close by calling for a final question or summarizing your ideas.

Only minor adaptations are necessary for video presentations. Pay special attention to your appearance because it will be magnified on the screen. Strive for a conversational presentation, and use subtle vocal variety and changes in facial expressions for emphasis. Familiarize yourself with the studio setting and practice using the TelePrompTer.

Your voice and body are the major tools you use to communicate with others. Vocal characteristics you should pay attention to include loudness, tempo, pitch, inflections, variety, and diction. You should speak loudly enough to be heard, maintain a tempo that is appropriate to your material, use variety of pitch and inflections to demonstrate meaning, and use acceptable diction. Avoid using vocal distracters. Don't let problems in these areas mar a well-prepared presentation.

Your body language during a presentation should complement your message. Take care with your personal appearance and grooming when you are to present a speech. Stand straight but relaxed. Make eye contact with your audience, and let your face reflect and reinforce the meaning of your words. Use movements and gestures that are natural and spontaneous.

The final step in speech preparation is practice. You should practice aloud in surroundings similar to those in which you will actually present your speech. Begin by practicing from your full-sentence outline; then move to your key-word outline when you are comfortable with your material. Check the timing of your speech. Tape-record yourself and evaluate your presentation.

It is only natural to have some fear of speaking in public. You can keep communication apprehension from being disabling by practicing relaxation exercises, sending yourself positive messages, visualizing yourself being successful, and thinking of your presentation as sharing, not performing. You should also select a topic that excites you and that you already know something about, research and prepare your message adequately, and practice your performance until you are comfortable with it.

TERMS TO KNOW

immediacy	memorized text presentations
oral language	manuscript presentation
clearness	extemporaneous speaking
thesaurus syndrome	feedback
jargon	loudness
artful repetition	tempo
concrete words	pitch
conciseness	inflections
maxims	diction
sound bites	articulation
correctness	enunciation
malapropisms	pronunciation
colorfulness	dialect
consideration	vocal distracters
impromptu speaking	body language
PRER formula	communication apprehension

NOTES

1. Roger Ailes, *You Are the Message: Getting What You Want by Being Who You Are* (New York: Doubleday, 1988), 15–19.

2. James C. McCroskey, *An Introduction to Rhetorical Communication*, 6th ed. (Englewood Cliffs, N.J.: Prentice-Hall, 1993), 263–264.

3. Virginia P. Richmond, James C. McCroskey, and S. K. Payne, *Nonverbal Behavior in Interpersonal Relations*, 2nd ed. (Englewood Cliffs, N.J.: Prentice-Hall, 1991), 208–228.

4. Cited in John F. Wilson and Carroll C. Arnold, *Public Speaking as a Liberal Art*, 3rd ed. (Boston: Allyn and Bacon, 1974), 225.

5. Lois Einhorn, "Oral and Written Style: An Examination of Differences," *Southern States Communication Journal* 43 (Spring 1978), 302–311; McCroskey, *An Introduction to Rhetorical Communication,* 215; Wilson and Arnold, *Public Speaking as a Liberal Art,* 225–228.

6. From Bill Moyers, "Commencement Address," University of Texas; cited in *Time,* 19 June 1985, 68.

7. Milo O. Frank, *How to Get Your Point Across in 30 Seconds or Less* (New York: Simon & Schuster, 1986). Frank, who has for many years conducted communication skills seminars for executives and politicians, has devoted an entire book to the subject of conciseness.

8. Sheila Weller, "Queen of the Sound Bites: Peggy Noonan, George Bush's Write Arm," *Ms.* December 1988, 84.

9. Ibid.

10. Richard Lacayo,"Picking Lemons for the Plums?" *Time,* 31 July 1989, 17.

11. "Overheard," *Newsweek,* 25 May 1992, 21.

12. "Southern-speak: Clinton Uses It Well," *Norfolk Virginian-Pilot and Ledger-Star,* 10 April 1994, A6.

13. Ibid.

14. Ann Richards, "Keynote Address," VITAL SPEECHES OF THE DAY, August 15, 1988, p. 647.

15. Felicity Barringer, "Census Shows Profound Change in Racial Makeup of the Nation," *New York Times,* 11 March 1991, A1.

16. "Measuring Diversity: How Does Your State Rate?" *National Education Association Today,* September 1992, 8.

17. Michael Duffy, "Picture of Health," Time, 4 October 1993, 28 ff, from *Time Almanac Reference Ed. CD-ROM* (Washington: Compact Publishing, 1994).

18. "A Letter to Our Readers," *Newsweek,* 4 October 1993, 29.

19. The guidelines for handling questions and answers represent a compendium of ideas from the following sources: Stephen D. Body, "Nine Steps to a Successful Question-and-Answer Session," *Management Solutions,* May 1988, 16–17; J. Donald Ragsdale and Alan L. Mikels, "Effects of Question Periods on a Speaker's Credibility with a Television Audience," *Southern States Communication Journal* (Spring 1975), 302–312; Dorothy Sarnoff, *Never Be Nervous Again* (New York: Ballantine, 1987); Laurie Schloff and Marcia Yudkin, *Smart Speaking: Sixty-Second Strategies* (New York: Holt, 1991); and Alan Zaremba, "Q and A: The Other Part of Your Presentation," *Management World,* January–February 1989, 8–10.

20. Ailes, *You Are the Message,* 170.

21. The authors are indebted to Professor Roxanne Gee of the television and film area in the Department of Communication Studies at the University of Memphis for her assistance and suggestions in putting together this advice.

22. Illustrations of major video hand signals may be found in Stewart W. Hyde, *Television and Radio Announcing,* 6th ed. (Boston: Houghton Mifflin, 1991), 80–85.

23. M. B. Stein, J. R. Walker, and D. R. Forde, "Public Speaking Fears in a Community Sample: Prevalence, Impact on Functioning, and Diagnostic Classification," *Archives of General Psychiatry,* February 1996, 169–174, *Thrive Online Health Library,* accessed July 1997, http://www.thriveonline.com/@14vdSwUA@G5s2ojN/ thrive/health/Library/CAD/abstract25252.html.

24. Gustav Friedrich and Blaine Goss, "Systematic Desensitization," in *Avoiding Communication: Shyness, Reticence, and Communication Apprehension,* ed. John A. Daly and James C. McCroskey (Beverly Hills, Calif.: Sage, 1984), 173–188.

25. William J. Fremouw and Michael D. Scott, "Cognitive Restructuring: An Alternative Method for the Treatment of Communication Apprehension," *Communication Education* 28 (May 1979): 129–133.

26.   Tim Hopf and Joe Ayers, "Coping with Public Speaking Anxiety: An Examination of Various Combinations of Systematic Desensitization, Skills Training, and Visualization," *Journal of Applied Communication Research* 20 (1992), 183–198.

27.   Michael T. Motley, *Overcoming Your Fear of Public Speaking* (Boston: Houghton Mifflin, 1997).

28.   John A. Daly, Anita L. Vangelisti, Heather L. Neel, and P. Daniel Cavanaugh, "Pre-Performance Concerns Associated with Public Speaking Anxiety," *Communication Quarterly* 37 (1989): 39–53.

INFORMATIVE SPEAKING

THIS CHAPTER
will help you

○ Understand the basic functions of informative speaking

○ Apply principles of motivation and attention to help listeners learn from your message

○ Become familiar with the different types of informative speeches and the designs most appropriate to each

○ Prepare and present effective informative speeches

THE IMPROVEMENT OF **UNDERSTANDING** IS FOR TWO ENDS: first our own **INCREASE** OF KNOWLEDGE; SECONDLY, TO ENABLE US TO **DELIVER** THAT knowledge to **OTHERS.**

—J. Locke

Our next assignment is to prepare an informative speech. Right? Well, what exactly do you mean by informative? Am I supposed to "show-and-tell"? Is this like giving a book report? I've done that before. And we've already covered visual aids, organizing, and outlining. What more is there to learn about informative speaking that I don't already know? Why is informative speaking important?

Without the sharing of information, there would be no civilization. *Sharing knowledge is the essence of informative speaking.* Shared information can be vital to survival. Alarm systems warn us of impending hurricanes and tornadoes. News of medical breakthroughs and lifestyle information can help us live longer when it is communicated in a way that we can understand. Beyond simply enabling us to live, information helps us live better. We can learn how to work smarter, not harder. We can learn how to do things for ourselves that we might have to pay someone else to do. How many learning experiences have you had in which informative communication did not play a major role?

Information is also a valuable commodity in and of itself. Information is power. Companies raid other companies for employees with know-how and creativity. Graduate schools look for students who have the background knowledge necessary for success. Countries and companies engage in espionage activities to learn what their friends and enemies are doing. An incompetent manager who feels that he or she is losing power may even try to withhold information in an effort to maintain control (a strategy that usually backfires).

Throughout our lives, we are constantly exchanging information with others. The better you can do this, the more successful you will be in life. In this chapter we look at the major functions of informative communication, suggest ways to make it easier for listeners to learn from your messages, describe the major types of informative speeches, and present some speech designs that are appropriate to these types.

THE FUNCTIONS OF INFORMATIVE SPEAKING

Informative speaking serves three basic functions. First, informative speaking empowers listeners by sharing information and ideas. Second, informative speaking shapes listeners' perceptions. Finally, informative speaking helps set an agenda for public awareness and concern.

SHARING INFORMATION AND IDEAS

An informative speech *gives* something to listeners. It asks listeners only to attend to the message and learn from it, not to change their beliefs or behaviors. For example, one student gave an informative speech that revealed the dangers of prolonged exposure to ultraviolet radiation but did not ask her audience to boycott tanning salons. Although informative speaking makes modest demands on listeners, the demands on speakers are high. Good informative speakers must have a thorough understanding of their subject. It is one thing to know something well enough to satisfy yourself. It is quite another to know something well enough to communicate it effectively to others.

In informative speaking, the speaker functions basically as a teacher. Sharing information reduces ignorance. It can clarify options for action by helping us to better understand a topic so that we can make more informed decisions. An effective informative speech doesn't simply tell listeners things they already know. The **informative value** of a speech is measured by how much new and important information or understanding it gives the audience. The informative value of a speech begins with audience analysis and topic selection. For your message to be truly informative, it must add to your audience's knowledge or provide a fresh perspective.

As you prepare your informative speech, ask yourself the following questions: "Is my topic significant enough to merit an informative speech?" "What do my listeners already know about my topic, and what more do they need to know?" and "Do I have sufficient understanding of my topic to help others understand it better?" The answers to these questions should help you present a speech with high informative value.

SHAPING AUDIENCE PERCEPTIONS

When speakers share information with audiences, they also share their perspectives or points of view. Speakers are always selective with regard to what information they communicate, highlighting ideas and material that they believe best represent their subject. It is virtually impossible to cover everything there is to know about any important or significant subject in a short message. Consequently, informative speaking involves interpretations of information. When we hear an informative speech on a new topic, the message can establish how we feel about about that topic, as well as what we know about it. That can influence the way we respond to later communications on the subject. We call this the **prepersuasive function** of informative communication.

For example, suppose you heard *one* of two speeches on teaching as a career choice. One speech, presented by an enthusiastic teacher, described the personal rewards the speaker obtained from teaching and stressed the joys of helping children learn. The other, presented by a teacher suffering from burnout, focused on classroom discipline problems and administrative red tape. Neither speaker suggested that you should or should not become a teacher. Each provided what he or she believed was an accurate picture of teaching as a profession. Each of these speeches provided a different predisposition to behave. If you heard only the first speaker, you might be more inclined to consider a message urging you to become a teacher than if you heard only the second speaker.

If you have strong feelings about your subject, you must keep in mind that your message has the power to shape perceptions. Be careful not to present a distorted perspective. If listeners feel that you are massaging the truth or presenting a biased perspective, they may dismiss your message and question your trustworthiness.

SETTING THE AGENDA

The amount of information reaching people today is at an all-time high. Special news networks broadcast twenty-four hours a day. News service wires can be accessed on the Internet. Talk shows fill the airways. This inundation of information from the mass media serves an **agenda-setting function.**[1] As the media present the "news," they also tell us what we *should* be thinking about. By allotting a certain amount of coverage to a topic, the media establish the importance of that topic in the public mind.

Informative speaking also performs an agenda-setting function. As it directs our attention to different topics and shapes our perception of them, it influences what we feel is important. The informative speech "The Monument at Wounded Knee" (the text may be found in Appendix E) demonstrates this agenda-setting function as it shapes perceptions about our country's policy toward Native Americans. Hearing such a message could predispose listeners to favor better treatment for this group. As you prepare an informative speech, remember the power you have to establish the importance of your topic in the minds of your audience. Consider the ethical consequences of your words.

HELPING YOUR AUDIENCE LEARN

The success of an informative message can be measured by the answer to one simple question: "Does the listener learn from the speech?" To help your listeners learn from and remember your message, you should motivate them by establishing its relevance, hold their attention throughout your message, and structure your message so that it is clear and readily understood.

ESTABLISHING RELEVANCE

If you want listeners to remember your message, you must tell them why and how your message relates to their needs. In Chapter 10 we discussed motivation as a factor in audience analysis and provided you with a list of twelve needs that are often used as motivational appeals. Go back to this list on p. 207 and decide which of these needs are most relevant to your topic and your audience. Then, tie your message to these needs, either through direct statements or indirectly through the use of examples or narratives. For example, in a speech describing how to interview for a job, you might begin by talking about the problem of finding a good job in today's marketplace, then provide an example that illustrates how a good interview can make the difference in who gets hired. In the preview part of the introduction of your speech, you might say:

> Today I'm going to describe three factors that can determine whether or not you get the job of your dreams. First, . . .

This gives your audience a reason to want to listen to the rest of your speech. You have begun the learning process by motivating your listeners.

SUSTAINING ATTENTION

Once you have established the relevance of your message to your listeners, you must sustain their attention throughout your speech. In Chapter 12 we discussed the importance of gaining the audience's attention with your introduction. The same techniques that are used to attract attention can also be used to sustain attention throughout your presentation. Remind your listeners that your message is important. Call on authorities they know and respect to bolster your position. Demonstrate the importance of your message through examples they can relate to. Use narratives to clarify abstract concepts and get your listeners caught up with your message. Startle your listeners with contrasts. Use artful repetition. Ask rhetorical questions to engage the audience in a mental dialogue. Use striking words or phrases that will stick in their minds. Strive for variety in both content and presentation style. Use presentation aids so that they both see and hear what you are talking about.

Finally, as we also noted in Chapter 12, you can help your listeners learn by providing previews and summaries

TRY THIS

Consider the best and worst instructors you have had in college. What techniques did the good instructors use to motivate you to learn? What did the poor instructors do that turned you off? Share your insights with your classmates.

and by organizing your ideas in an orderly fashion. In the remainder of this chapter, we will look at the major types of informative speeches and the design formats that are most often used to structure informative messages.

Helping Listeners Learn

✓ Tailor your presentation to the needs of your audience

✓ Tell your listeners how they can benefit from your presentation

✓ Sustain attention with variety of content and style

✓ Use presentation aids so that listeners can see as well as hear

✓ Organize your points so that they are easy to follow

✓ Provide previews and summaries to aid retention

TYPES OF INFORMATIVE SPEECHES

As we mentioned earlier, the major purpose of an informative speech is to share knowledge in order to expand your listeners' understanding or competence. To achieve this, an informative speech will typically describe, demonstrate, or explain its subject. We shall cover each of these types, and we also include a discussion of briefings, an important subtype of informative speaking.

SPEECHES OF DESCRIPTION

A **speech of description** should give your listeners a clear picture of your subject, be it an activity, object, person, or place. The sample speech "The Monument at Wounded Knee" in Appendix E provides a vivid picture of the grave site and monument. An effective speech of description relies heavily on the artful use of language. The words must be clear, concrete, and colorful because they must carry both the substance and the feeling of your message. Thus, in the "Monument" speech, the landscape is not simply desolate; it is characterized as "flat, sun-baked fields and an occasional eroded gully." The speaker goes on to describe the monument:

> The "monument" itself rests on a concrete slab to the right of the grave. It's a typical, large, old-fashioned granite cemetery marker, a pillar about six feet high topped with an urn—the kind of gravestone you might see in any cemetery with graves from the turn of the century. The inscription tells us that it was erected by the families of those who were killed at Wounded Knee. Weeds grow through the cracks in the concrete at its base.

The topic, purpose, and materials selected for a descriptive speech should suggest the appropriate design. The "Monument" speech follows a spatial pattern. Other designs that may be used for speeches of description are the sequential, categorical, and comparative designs, which are discussed later in this chapter.

SPEECHES OF DEMONSTRATION

A **speech of demonstration** shows the audience how to do something or how something works. Dance instructors teach us how to do the "Texas two-step." Others may tell us how to do research on the Internet or how to prepare for the Graduate Record Examination. The tip-off to a speech of demonstration is the phrase "how to." These speeches basically lay out a process.

The goal of a speech of demonstration may be either *understanding* or *application*: the speech may show listeners how something is done or instruct them so that they can do it themselves. If understanding is your goal, you can usually demonstrate more complex processes in a short speech than you can if your goal is application. For example, you might be able to present a seven-minute speech on how grades are collected, recorded, and distributed on your campus, but you could not expect your audience to be able to apply this knowledge and set up a grade-processing system after hearing your presentation. However, in a short presentation you should be able to teach your classmates a practical skill that they can *apply* in their lives, such as how to read a textbook more efficiently.

The lesson here is clear: adjust your purpose (to understand or to apply) to suit the complexity of your subject and the time allotted for your presentation. Regardless of which purpose you choose, most speeches of demonstration follow the sequential design, discussed in detail later in this chapter. One final consideration: most speeches of demonstration are helped by the use of presentation aids. These aids can range from you modeling the activity, to objects used in the process you are demonstrating, to an overhead projection, flip chart, or poster listing the steps in order. If you are preparing a speech of demonstration, review the material on presentation aids in Chapter 11 to determine which of these you could use to help your audience better understand your message. Show-and-tell is usually much more effective than just telling.

SPEECHES OF EXPLANATION

A **speech of explanation** informs listeners about a subject that is more abstract or more complex than the subjects dealt with through speeches of description or demonstration. Speeches of explanation are challenging because abstract subjects are difficult to understand. To meet this challenge, Katherine Rowan, a communication scholar at Purdue University, suggests that speakers should do the following:

1. Clearly define the subject in terms of its critical features.

2. Compare an example with a nonexample (an instance one thinks might be an example but is not).

3. Provide additional examples to reinforce what listeners have learned.[2]

Note how Stephen Lee uses this technique in his speech of explanation "The Trouble with Statistics." (The complete text of this speech may be found in Appendix E.) In this section, Stephen is talking about the results of a change in the way unemployment figures are computed. When military personnel were added to the computations, the unemployment rate *apparently* went down. But did it actually go down? Here is how Stephen handled this:

> *Look at what happened to the number. It changed. Look at what happened to the way the number was computed. It changed, too. But what happened to the very real*

problem of civilian unemployment, which we all assumed this number to represent? It had not changed at all. It all goes back to what Lester T. Thurow said in his basic theory of economics, "A difference is only a difference if it truly makes a difference." Many times a difference in a number does not represent a difference in the real world.

Speeches of explanation present quite a challenge to beginning speakers. They demand clear, concrete, correct language and a heavy reliance on examples to amplify and clarify abstract ideas. Speeches of explanation may use any of the designs described later in this chapter.

BRIEFINGS

A **briefing** is a short informative presentation, typically presented in an organizational setting. It will usually be either a speech of description or a speech of explanation. Briefings often take place during meetings, as when you are called upon to give a status report or an update on a project on which you have been working. Briefings also take place in one-on-one situations, as when you report to your supervisor at work. Occupational, military, governmental, social, and religious organizations all use oral briefings as an important mode of communication.

Press conferences often take the form of a briefing that is followed by questions and answers.

Briefings are best presented extemporaneously, which means that you will have prepared and practiced your presentation. At times, however, you may be called on to "just say a few words" with little or no time for preparation and practice, which means you must make an impromptu presentation. Your success in such communication situations can mean the difference between advancing in an organization and staying in a dead-end job. The skills that you learn in this class can, with minor adaptations, prepare you to make effective briefings.

Because the stakes are usually high when you make a briefing in an occupational setting, most of our suggestions concern how to make effective briefings at work. Most "how-to" books on communicating in organizations stress the importance of brevity, clarity, and directness.[3] When executives in eighteen organizations were asked, "What makes a poor presentation?" they responded with the following factors:

- Confusing organization
- Poor delivery
- Too much technical jargon
- Too long
- No examples or comparisons[4]

These observations suggest some clear guidelines as you prepare to make a briefing.

First, a briefing should be what its name suggests—brief. This means you must cut out extraneous material that is not related directly to your main points. Keep your introduction and conclusions short. Begin with a preview and end with a summary.

Second, organize your ideas before you open your mouth. How can you possibly be organized when you are suddenly called upon in a meeting to "tell us about your project"? The answer is simple: prepare in advance. (Also, see our guidelines for making an impromptu presentation in Chapter 13.) *Never go into a meeting in which there is even the slightest possibility that you might be asked to report without a skeleton outline of a presentation.* Select a simple design and make a key-word outline of points you should cover and the order in which you should cover them. Put this outline on a note card and carry it with you. Your supervisors and colleagues will be impressed with your foresight.

Third, rely heavily on carefully verified facts and figures, expert testimony, and short examples for supporting materials. Don't drift off into long stories. Use comparison and contrast to make your points clearly and directly.

Fourth, adapt your language to your audience. If you are an engineer reporting on a project to a group of nonengineer managers, use the language of management, not the language of engineering. Tell them what they need to know in language they can understand.

Fifth, present your message with confidence. Be sure everyone can see and hear you. Stand up, if necessary. Look listeners in the eye. Speak firmly, with an air of assurance. After all, the project is yours, and you are the expert on it.

Finally, be prepared to deal with questions, especially the tough ones. Deal with tough questions forthrightly and honestly. No one likes bad news, but worse news comes when you don't deliver the bad news to those who need to know it *when* they need to know it. Review our suggestions for handling question-and-answer sessions in Chapter 13.

Preparing for a Briefing

✓ Keep your remarks short and to the point

✓ Always be prepared to make a presentation in a meeting

✓ Organize your main points in the simplest design possible

✓ Start with a preview; conclude with a summary

✓ Use facts and figures, expert testimony, brief examples, comparisons, and/or contrasts to support your points

✓ Avoid technical jargon

✓ Present your message with confidence

INFORMATIVE SPEECH DESIGNS

There are five major design formats that are appropriate for most informative speeches: spatial, categorical, comparative, sequential, and causation. These designs may also be used in persuasive speeches.

SPATIAL DESIGN

A **spatial design** is appropriate for speeches that describe places or that locate subjects within a physical arrangement. Suppose someone were to ask you to name the time zones in the United States. If you live in Washington, D.C., you would probably reply,

"Eastern, Central, Mountain, and Pacific." If you live in California, you might answer, "Pacific, Mountain, Central, and Eastern."[5] If you answered either way, you would have been using a spatial design organized on the principle of proximity discussed in Chapter 12.

A spatial design takes listeners on an *orderly* imaginary journey from one place to another. It provides listeners with a verbal map. To develop a spatial design, select a starting point, determine a direction, and then move systematically from one place to the next in terms of nearness. For example, if you wanted to take listeners on a tour of the Napa Valley wine country, you might start with Domaine Chandon at the south end and move progressively to the Couvason Vineyards at the north end of the valley. Once you begin a pattern of movement, you should stay with it through your entire speech. If you change directions in the middle, your listeners may get lost. If possible, make the most interesting site your final destination.

The body of a speech using a spatial design might have the following format:

THESIS STATEMENT: When you visit Yellowstone, stop first at the South Entrance Visitor's Center, then drive northwest to Old Faithful, north to Mammoth Hot Springs, and southeast to the Grand Canyon of the Yellowstone.

I. Your first stop should be at the South Entrance Visitor's Center.
   A. Talk with a park ranger to help plan your trip.
   B. Attend a lecture or film to orient yourself to the park.
   C. Pick up materials and maps to make your tour more meaningful.

II. Drive northwest through the Geyser Valley to Old Faithful.
   A. Hike the boardwalks in the Upper-Geyser Basin.
   B. Join the crowds waiting for Old Faithful to erupt.
   C. Have lunch at Old Faithful Inn.

III. Continue north to Mammoth Hot Springs.
   A. Plan to spend the night at the lodge or in one of the cabins.
   B. Attend the evening lectures or films on the history of the park.

IV. Drive southeast to the Grand Canyon of the Yellowstone.
   A. Take in the view from Inspiration Point.
   B. Hike down the trail for a better view of the waterfalls.

CATEGORICAL DESIGN

The **categorical design** is based on the principle of similarity discussed in Chapter 12, and is useful for subjects that have natural or customary divisions. Natural divisions may exist within the subject itself, such as red, white, and blended wines. Customary divisions are typical but artificial ways of thinking about a subject, such as the four food groups that are essential to a healthy diet. Categories are the mind's way of ordering our world. They help us sort out incoming information so that it does not overwhelm us.

When you prepare speeches using a categorical design, each category becomes a main point for development. For a short presentation, you should limit yourself to no more than four categories. Any subject that breaks down into five or more categories may be too complex for oral presentation. You may need to collapse some of the categories into subpoints or consider a different approach to your topic. Categorical designs are most effective when you begin and end the body of the speech with the most important categories because the first point gains attention and the final point gives the speech a sense of climax.

A categorical speech on the elements of a healthy diet might take the following format:

THESIS STATEMENT: A healthy diet is high in complex carbohydrates, fruits, and vegetables, and low in dairy products, meats and eggs, and fats.

I. You should eat six to eleven servings of whole-grain breads, cereals, rice, or pasta each day.

   A. They are a major source of fiber necessary for good digestion.

   B. They provide the complex carbohydrates needed for energy.

   C. They can help keep you from feeling hungry.

II. You should eat five to nine helpings of vegetables and fruits each day.

   A. They help fill you up without filling you out.

   B. They are a major source of vitamins and minerals.

   C. They may help prevent diseases such as scurvy and cancer.

III. You should limit dairy products, meats, and eggs to four to six servings a day.

   A. They are too prevalent in American diets.

   B. They are high in cholesterol, which is related to heart disease.

   C. You should choose carefully from this group.

      1. Opt for low-fat milk, frozen desserts, and cheeses.

      2. Choose chicken and fish over beef and pork.

      3. Use egg substitutes or limit eggs to three or four a week.

IV. You should restrict fat intake to less than 30 percent of your daily calories.

   A. Fats make you fat.

   B. Saturated fats increase cholesterol in the body.

   C. Fat intake can be controlled and limited easily.

      1. Olive oil and canola oil are low in saturated fats.

      2. Fat-free salad dressings and mayonnaise are readily available.

      3. You can use butter-flavored sprays for cooking and flavoring.

      4. You can cut back on "fast foods" and "junk foods" because they are high in fat and limited in nutritional value.

COMPARATIVE DESIGN

A **comparative design** is useful when your topic is new to your audience, abstract, highly technical, or simply difficult to understand. It may also be used when you wish to describe dramatic changes in a subject or discuss the right or wrong ways of doing something. Comparative designs aid comprehension by relating the topic to something the audience already knows and understands.

There are three basic variations of the comparative design. It may be based on (1) a literal analogy, (2) a figurative analogy, or (3) a comparison and contrast format. In a **literal analogy**, the subjects compared are drawn from the same field of experience. For example, a student in one of our classes described the game of rugger as played in his native Sri Lanka by comparing it with the American game of football. In a **figurative analogy**, the subjects compared are drawn from totally different realms of experience—for example, a speaker might relate the body's struggle against infection to a military campaign. A **comparison and contrast** design points out both similarities and differences between subjects or ideas. Comparative designs are especially useful in speeches of description, speeches of explanation, and briefings because they make subjects more understandable. They may also be used in speeches of demonstration to contrast the right and wrong ways of doing something.

It is important to keep the audience in mind as you prepare an informative lecture.

In a speech using any of the comparative designs, each similarity or difference becomes a main point. In the interest of simplicity, you should limit yourself to four or fewer points of similarity in a short presentation. In addition, you must be sure that any things you compare are essentially similar, or that any things you contrast are essentially different. This is especially true in the case of figurative analogies. If you stretch the comparison too far, the design will seem strained or contrived. It could backfire and damage your credibility.

The following example illustrates the use of a comparison and contrast design:

THESIS STATEMENT: Over two decades—from the 1960s to the 1990s—the women we saw in advertisements began to change.

I. The products women were used to advertise changed.

  A. In the 1960s, 75 percent of females shown were in ads for products used in the kitchen or bath.

  B. By the 1990s, only 45 percent of females shown were in ads for products used in the kitchen or bath.

  C. By the 1990s, females were appearing in more ads for high-ticket products.

II. Women in advertisements began to appear in different roles.

  A. There were changes in the numbers of women shown in domestic (wife/mother) roles.

    1. In the 1960s, two-thirds of women in ads were shown in domestic (wife, mother) roles.

    2. By the 1990s, less than half of the women in ads were shown in domestic roles.

  B. There were changes in the occupational roles of women in advertisements.

    1. In the 1960s, only 9 percent of the females in ads had an identifiable occupation.

    2. By the 1990s, 18 percent of the females in ads had an identifiable occupation.

3. In the 1960s, working females in ads were restricted to low-paying, traditionally female occupations.

4. By the 1990s, the majority of females shown in occupation roles were depicted in nontraditional jobs.

III. There have been changes in the apparent ages of women in ads.

A. In the 1960s, almost 80 percent of the women in ads appeared to be under thirty years of age.

B. By the 1990s, only about half of the women in ads appeared to be under thirty years of age.

IV. The overall attitude toward women in ads appears to have changed.

A. In the 1960s, most women were portrayed in demeaning ways, as dumb and dependent sex objects.

B. By the 1990s, more women were portrayed as intelligent, achieving, and independent individuals.

SEQUENTIAL DESIGN

A **sequential design** follows a chronological time pattern. It may be used to provide a historical perspective on a situation in a speech of explanation, or to present the steps in a process in a speech of demonstration.

When you use a sequential design to provide a historical perspective, you may start with the beginning of an idea or issue and trace it up to the present. For example, a speech on the evolution of the T-shirt from undergarment to bearer of messages to high-fashion apparel would follow such a pattern. Or, you may start with the present and trace an issue or situation back to its origins. If you were talking about the Orlando Magic NBA team's rapid rise to the championship finals in the 1994/1995 season, you might note that

1. The year they made it to the finals, they acquired Horace Grant from the Chicago Bulls.

2. The year before that, they drafted Penny Hardaway from the University of Memphis.

3. The year before that—only three years into their franchise—they picked up Shaquille O'Neal as their first-round draft choice.

Because of time limitations, you must be careful to narrow your topic to manageable proportions. You must be selective, choosing landmark events that are relevant to your purpose. As you telescope time this way, be sure the events you select are representative of the situation and not based on personal biases. These landmark events become the main points in your message. Arrange them as they occur in time. Do not present them in a random order, or your speech will be hard for the audience to follow.

A sequential design for a speech of demonstration is effective because it allows you to take the audience step by step through a process as you talk with them about it. You begin by determining the necessary steps in the process and then decide the order in which they must take place. These steps become the main points of your speech. In a short presentation, you should have no more than five steps as main points. If you have more, try to cluster some of them, making them subpoints. It is also helpful to enumerate the steps as you make your presentation.

The following outline of main points illustrates a sequential design for a speech of demonstration.

THESIS STATEMENT: The five steps in efficient textbook reading are: (1) skimming, (2) reading, (3) rereading, (4) reciting, and (5) reviewing.

I. First, skim through the chapter to get the "big picture."

   A. Identify the major ideas that will be covered from large-print section headings.

   B. Find and read any summary statements.

   C. Find and read any boxed materials.

   D. Begin a key-word skeleton outline of major topics that will be covered.

II. Second, read the chapter a section at a time.

   A. Make notes to yourself in the margins.

      1. Write questions about material you do not understand.

      2. Write a brief summary of ideas you do understand.

      3. Make numbered lists of any materials presented in series.

   B. Look up the definitions of unfamiliar words in the book's glossary or a dictionary.

   C. Go back and highlight the section you have just read.

      1. Highlight only the major ideas.

      2. Highlight no more than 10 percent of the text.

III. Third, reread the chapter.

   A. Fill in your skeleton outline with more details.

   B. Try to answer the questions you wrote in the margin.

   C. Write out questions to ask your instructor on anything that is still not clear.

IV. Fourth, recite what you have read.

   A. Use your skeleton outline to make an oral presentation to yourself on the chapter.

   B. Talk about what you have read with someone else.

      1. Ask your roommate, a classmate, or a significant other to listen.

      2. See if you can explain the material so that the other person understands it.

V. Finally, review the material within twenty-four hours.

   A. Review your skeleton outline.

   B. Reread the highlighted material.

   C. See if you can answer any more of your questions now that you have had time to digest the material.

Presenting the steps in this orderly manner helps you "walk and talk" your listeners through the process. They should now understand how to begin and what to do in the proper order.

CAUSATION DESIGN

A **causation design** explains a situation, condition, or event in terms of the causes that led up to it. This design is often used in speeches of explanation that try to make the world understandable. When you use a causation design, you may begin with a description of an existing condition, then probe for its causes. The description of the existing condition becomes the first main point in the body of the speech, with the causes being subsequent main points. The causation design may also be used to predict events or conditions in the future. In that case, the present condition is the first main point in the body of the speech, and the predictions become the subsequent main points. The causes or predictions may be grouped into categories, with these categories arranged in order of their importance. They may also be presented sequentially.

Speeches of causation are subject to one very serious problem: the tendency to oversimplify. Any complex situation that is worth talking about will generally have many underlying causes. And, any given set of conditions may lead to many different future effects with only minimal changes. Be wary of overly simple explanations and overly ambitious predictions.

A speech of causation explaining the greenhouse effect might have the following basic structure of main ideas:

THESIS STATEMENT: The three major causes of the greenhouse effect are loss of forestlands, industrial emissions, and increased energy consumption related to population growth.

I. One cause of the greenhouse effect is the loss of forestlands, which convert carbon dioxide into oxygen.

   A. One football-field-sized area of forest is lost every second from cutting or burning.

   B. Burning off woodlands increases the amount of carbon dioxide in the atmosphere through the smoke that is produced.

II. Industrial emissions also contribute to the growth of the greenhouse effect.

   A. Industrial contaminants account for more than 20 percent of our air pollution.

   B. Carbon dioxide is released in large quantities when wood, coal, and oil are burned.

   C. Chlorofluorocarbons come from refrigeration and air conditioners.

   D. Nitrogen oxides are spewed out of vehicle exhausts and smokestacks.

III. Increased energy consumption contributes to ozone depletion.

   A. People consume oxygen and emit carbon dioxide into the atmosphere.

   B. The more people there are, especially in industrialized countries, the more energy is consumed.

   C. Energy consumption is the single largest cause of the greenhouse effect.

      1. Fossil fuel use has more than doubled since 1950.

      2. Fossil fuels account for 90 percent of America's energy consumption.

      3. Transportation-related energy use accounts for half of all air pollution.

Figure 14.1 summarizes the use of each of these designs.

Design	Use when
Spatial	Your topic involves places or objects located within a physical environment. It allows you to take your audience on an orderly *oral tour* of your topic from place to place.
Categorical	Your topic has natural or customary divisions. Each category becomes a main point for development. Useful when you need to organize large amounts of material.
Comparative	Your topic is new to your audience, abstract, technical, or simply difficult to comprehend. Helps make material more meaningful by comparing or contrasting it with something the audience already knows and understands.
Sequential	Your topic can be arranged chronologically. It is useful for describing a process as a series of steps or explaining a subject as a sequence of historical landmark developments.
Causation	Your topic involves a situation, condition, or event that is best understood in terms of its underlying causes. May also be used to predict the future from existing conditions. The causes may be grouped by categories or presented chronologically.

FIGURE 14.1
What Designs to Use When

IN SUMMARY

Sharing knowledge is the essence of informative speaking. It enables us to live better and work smarter. In short, information is power.

Informative speaking performs three basic functions: sharing of information and ideas, shaping listener perceptions, and setting an agenda of public concerns.

From your listeners' perspective, an informative speech is a learning experience. To make it easier for the audience to learn from your message, show them how your subject relates to their needs. Once you have established the relevance of your message and motivated your audience to listen and hear, you must sustain their attention throughout your presentation. Help them remember your message by organizing your material in an orderly fashion and providing previews and summaries.

Informative speeches may be classified as speeches of description, demonstration, or explanation. Speeches of description provide listeners with a clear picture of your subject. Speeches of demonstration show the audience how something is done. Speeches of explanation inform listeners about abstract and complex subjects. Briefings are an important subtype of informative speeches that are presented mainly in organizational settings.

The designs most frequently employed in informative speeches are the spatial, categorical, comparative, sequential, and causation designs. A spatial design orders the main points as they occur in physical space. It is useful for describing objects or places. A categorical design uses actual divisions of a subject or traditional ways of thinking about it. Categories help listeners sort out incoming information so that it does not overwhelm them. There are three subtypes of comparative speech designs: literal analogies, figurative analogies, and comparison and contrast. They are useful when a subject is unfamiliar, abstract, highly technical, or otherwise difficult to understand.

Comparative designs may also be used to describe changes in a subject or to demonstrate the right and wrong ways of doing something. A sequential design follows a chronological time pattern and may be used to provide a historical perspective on a situation or to present the steps in a process in a speech of demonstration. A causation design explains how one condition generates or is generated by another. The causation design is subject to oversimplification.

TERMS TO KNOW

informative value
prepersuasive function
agenda-setting function
speech of description
speech of demonstration
speech of explanation
briefing
spatial design

categorical design
comparative design
literal analogy
figurative analogy
comparison and contrast
sequential design
causation design

NOTES

1. Melvin L. DeFleur and Everette E. Dennis, *Understanding Mass Communication: A Liberal Arts Perspective* (Boston: Houghton Mifflin, 1994), 506–507. This concept originated from a study by Maxwell E. McCombs and Donald Shaw, "The Agenda-Setting Function of the Mass Media," *Public Opinion Quarterly,* 1972, 176–187.

2. Katherine E. Rowan, "Goals, Obstacles, and Strategies in Risk Commu-nication: A Problem-Solving Approach to Improving Communication About Risks," *Journal of Applied Communication Research* 19 (1991): 314.

3. Notable among such books are Milo O. Frank, *How to Get Your Point Across in 30 Seconds or Less* (New York: Simon & Schuster, 1986); William Parkhurst, *The Eloquent Executive: How to Sound Your Best: High-Impact Speaking in Meetings Large and Small* (New York: Avon, 1988); Joan Detz, *Can You Say a Few Words? How to Prepare and Deliver* (New York: St. Martin's Press, 1991); Sunja Hamlin, *How to Talk So People Listen* (New York: Harper & Row, 1988); Burton Kaplan, *The Manager's Complete Guide to Speech Writing* (New York: Free Press, 1988); Dorothy Leeds, *PowerSpeak* (New York: Berkeley Books, 1991); Lilly Walters, *Secrets of Successful Speakers: How You Can Motivate, Captivate and Persuade* (New York: McGraw-Hill, 1993); Laurie Schloff and Marcia Yudkin, *Smart Speaking: Sixty-Second Strategies* (New York: Holt, 1991); and Jeff Scott Cook, *The Elements of Speech Writing and Public Speaking* (New York: Macmillan, 1989).

4. J. E. Hollingsworth, "Oral Briefings," *Management Review,* August 1968, 2–10.

5. Adapted from material supplied by Randy Scott, Department of Communication, Weber State University, Ogden, Utah.

Sample Informative SPEECH

WARMING OUR WORLD AND CHILLING OUR FUTURE

When Mark Twain was in London in 1897, a rumor reached the editor of the *New York Journal*, who immediately wired his London correspondent: "HEAR MARK TWAIN DIED, SEND 1000 WORDS." The correspondent showed the telegram to Twain, who sent back this message: "REPORT OF MY DEATH GREATLY EXAGGERATED." This response applies to my speech topic today. Despite the efforts of some to write its obituary, and to erase it from the public's agenda, the greenhouse effect is a growing, not a declining, problem. The reports of its death have been greatly exaggerated.

Almost twenty years ago, environmentalists urged scientists to look to Antarctica for signs of what they called the "greenhouse effect"—the gradual warming of the earth because of human activity. During the winter of 1995, *Time* magazine reported that a gigantic iceberg—23 miles wide and 48 miles long, almost as large as the state of Rhode Island— broke off the Larsen Ice Shelf in the Antarctic Peninsula. During the winter of 1997, new large crevasses were found in the shelf. These suggest that the rest of the shelf is ready to break loose. Do these things signal the arrival of full-scale global warming? They may. Is the greenhouse effect catching up with us? It may be. And because of this possibility, these reports simply cannot be ignored. Combined with other recently reported evidence from NASA's Upper Atmosphere Research Satellite, which proves—according to *National Wildlife* magazine—that "chemicals generated by human activity cause the ozone hole . . . over the Antarctic," they are ominous signs for our future. The potential problems this can cause us are simply too important to overlook.

Now, I'm an outdoor person. I love hiking, camping, and fishing, so it's not hard for me to have a great deal of concern for the environment. But even if you are not an outdoor person, you probably still like to breathe clean air and drink safe water, and not have to worry about being out in the sun too long. All of us have a lot at stake here. Today I want to share with you what I've learned about the greenhouse effect and its causes. Recent polls conducted by the Gallup Organization and the Pew Foundation indicate that while most Americans are somewhat concerned about global warming, we are not concerned enough to sanction programs that will cost us money. They also indicate that we don't really understand what is going on or what is at stake. We need to be concerned, first, about the loss of woodlands, second, about industrial emissions, and third, about overall spectacular increases in world energy consumption.

Let's begin by understanding more about the greenhouse effect. According to the Sierra Club Fact Sheet of 1997, it is characterized by a high concentration of carbon dioxide in the atmosphere. Each year five tons of carbon are pumped into the atmosphere for each man, woman, and child in the United States. You heard that right! That's five tons for each of us! This overabundance of carbon in the atmosphere is heating things up. The three hottest years since the Industrial Revolution all occurred during the 1990s. In fact, the *nine warmest years in this century have all occurred since 1980!* This is carrying "toasty" a bit too far.

Note how source citations become oral footnotes woven into the text of the message. These oral footnotes make the speech authoritative and strengthen the speaker's credibility.

Note that the speaker mentions the name of the periodical and the source of the surveys, rather than the authors of the reports. The speaker correctly assumes that the name of the periodical or survey group will be more meaningful than the name of the report's author.

Note how the speech emphasizes documentation in citing the NASA project director. A controversial speech calls for a great deal of documentation to support the validity of information. To keep the speech from being too technical, the speaker ties it to familiar symbols, such as "mother earth."

According to Anne Douglas, project director of NASA, this warming comes from carbon pollutants, which are punching a hole in the ozone layer. Carbon pollutants, such as chlorofluorocarbons—or CFCs—act like an atmospheric Pac-Man devouring the ozone shield. The ozone hole reduces our protection from ultraviolet radiation. If this problem is not corrected, mother earth won't seem quite so motherly.

For instance: There could be dramatic climate changes, causing widespread drought in areas that are not used to it. There could be dangerous and costly increases in the frequency and severity of storms. There could be floods from rising sea levels that could destroy coastal cities and small islands. If even a tenth of Antarctica's ice melts, sea levels would rise 12 to 30 feet. Folks, think twice before you invest in real estate at the seashore.

The speaker's appeal here to listeners' concern for themselves and their offspring might have greater impact if it used an example or narrative and cited the sources of the information.

Beyond these spectacular effects on the environment, there could be serious health problems. These are up-close-and-personal problems for you, more so for your children, even more so for your grandchildren. Skin cancers could increase as much as 26 percent if ozone levels drop by 10 percent. There could be a dramatic increase in the number of cataracts. Even our immune systems could be damaged, creating new problems that could dwarf the AIDS epidemic. If we don't change the trajectory we're on, if we don't intervene to modify the causes of the greenhouse effect, then all these health problems will result from the increased exposure to ultraviolet radiation.

Okay, so there is a problem. Well, what are the causes? Let's examine them, one by one. The first is the loss of woodlands, which convert carbon dioxide into oxygen. Without trees to make this conversion, the carbon pollutants escape into the ozone layer. We are literally putting the heat on Mother Nature to make more room for humans and their activities. One football-field-sized area of forest is lost every second through cutting or burning. The burning of forests further increases the amount of carbon dioxide in the atmosphere because of the smoke that is produced. Forest loss occurs in the rain forests in Central and South America, where teak and mahogany are logged for furniture and houses. It also occurs in the national forests in the United States that are logged by timber companies. Much of this American wood is shipped overseas. Forest loss also comes when land is cleared for development.

The use of colorful phrases like "putting the heat on Mother Nature" gains attention, and the comparison to a football field helps bring the size of the problem into focus.

An even greater cause of the greenhouse effect is industrial emissions. Here the picture is dramatic—and not very encouraging. The burning of wood, coal, and oil releases large amounts of carbon dioxide into the atmosphere. Industrial refrigeration and air conditioning units add their foul contribution. Nitrogen oxides are spewed out of industrial smokestacks. These contaminants account for more than 20 percent of our air pollution. And this kind of pollution continues to grow! Every day, more and more Third World nations become more and more industrialized, and use more and more fuel. But, guess what! We Americans are the worst offenders. We have only 5 percent of the world's population, but we use 26 percent of the world's oil, release 26 percent of the world's nitrogen oxide, and produce 22 percent of the world's carbon dioxide emissions. It's time to do something about it!

Active verbs like *spew* create ugly pictures in listeners' minds.

All of this leads us to the last major cause of the greenhouse effect, which is also the most important. *Personal energy consumption is the single largest cause of the greenhouse effect.* It's as though each of us were a smokestack, fouling the air. We consume oxygen and emit carbon dioxide into the atmosphere. The more of us there are, especially in industrialized countries, the more energy we consume. And here's another point: as living standards rise around the world, people develop greater expectations—they all want to live the good life. This means they all want to use more energy. If you multiply more

The struggle to bring this technical subject to life for listeners makes this speech particularly interesting in its use of language. Note the dramatic image that compares people to smokestacks, and the analogy to the movie Fatal Attraction.

people times rising expectations, you can see what this means for energy consumption—and for the greenhouse effect!

According to the Sierra Club Fact Sheet, fossil fuel use doubled from 1950 to 1990, and 90 percent of America's energy consumption comes from fossil fuels. Fossil fuels, such as gas and oil and electricity generated from power plants, heat and cool our homes and provide our transportation. Transportation-related energy use accounts for approximately half of all air pollution in our country. The amount of fuel we use for transportation is growing day by day as more and more people buy trucks and sport utility vehicles. In 1950 there were 40 million cars in the United States. Today there are more than 140 million cars in America. The great American love affair with the car continues, even though this is a "fatal attraction." The American Lung Association has estimated that we spend about $40 billion a year in health care costs related to air pollution. Environmental damage from air pollution costs us another $60 to $100 billion a year. In short, we have to pay through the nose for the problems we create by driving gas guzzlers and keeping our houses too hot in the winter and too cold in the summer.

In conclusion, if you want to know why we have a greenhouse effect, listen for the falling trees, watch the industrial smokestacks darkening the sky, and smell the exhaust fumes we are pumping into the air. The greenhouse effect is a monster we all are creating. And if we don't stop, we, and our children, and our children's children will face even more drastic climate changes and serious health problems.

Vice President Al Gore used the following story to illustrate how the greenhouse effect can sneak up on us. In an address to the National Academy of Sciences, he said, "If dropped into a pot of boiling water, a frog will quickly jump out. But if the same frog is put into a pot and the water is slowly heated, the frog will stay put until boiled alive. So it is with pollution. . . . If we do not wake up to the slow heating of our environment, we may jump too late." The more we know about this problem, and the better we understand it, the more likely we are to jump and the less likely we are to be boiled alive.

REFERENCES

Adams, Kathleen, et al. "It Hasn't Been This Sizzling in Centuries." *Time,* Notebook Planet Watch on-line, 4 May 1998, accessed 4 May 1998, http://www.pathfinder.com/time/magazine/1998/dom/980504/notebook/planet_watch.it37.html.

Easterbrook, Gregg. "Greenhouse Common Sense." *U.S. News,* 1 December 1997, on-line 1 December 1997, accessed 4 May 1998, http://www.usnews.com/usnews/issue/971201/1glob.htm.

———"Hot Air Treaty." *U.S. News,* 22 December 1997, on-line 22 December 1997, accessed 4 May 1998, http://www.usnews.com/usnews/issue/971222/trea.htm.

Envirolink. "Greenhouse Effect." on-line 1997, accessed 2 May 1998, http://www.envirolink.org/orgs/edf/planetvision.html.

Gallup, Alec, and Lydia Saad. "Public Concerned, Not Alarmed About Global Warming" on-line 2 December 1997, accessed 4 May 1998, http://www.gallup.com/POLL_ARCHIVES/971202.htm.

Gore, Albert, Jr. *Earth in the Balance: Ecology and the Human Spirit.* Boston: Houghton Mifflin: 1992.

———"The Global Environment: A National Security Issue." Keynote Address to the National Academy of Science Forum on Global Climate Change, Washington, D.C., 1 May 1989.

"Key Issues Get the Warming Conference's Cold Shoulder." *U.S. News,* 15 December 1997, on-line 15 December 1997, accessed 4 May 1998, http://www.usnews.com/usnews/issue/971215/15kyot.htm.

Monastersky, Richard. "Consensus Reached on Climate Change Causes." *Science News,* 24 September 1994, 198.

"Ozone Mystery Solved." *National Wildlife,* April/May 1995, 6.

Pew Foundation. "Americans Support Action on Global Warming." on-line November 1997, accessed 3 May 1998, http://www.people-press.org/nov 97rpt.htm.

Sierra Club. "Global Warming Fact Sheet." on-line, undated, accessed 4 May 1998, http://www.sierraclub.org/global-warming/factsheets/basfact.htm.

CHAPTER FIFTEEN

PErSuASIVE SpEAKING

THIS CHAPTER

will help you

- Realize the importance of persuasion in our culture

- Understand the steps in the persuasive process

- Cope with major challenges of persuasive speaking

- Develop arguments using evidence, proofs, and reasoning

- Avoid defective persuasion

- Understand the different types of persuasive speeches and their appropriate designs

- Prepare and present effective persuasive speeches

WE ARE **GOVERNED** NOT BY armies and police BUT BY IDEAS.

—M. Caird

M *ake a persuasive speech? Gee, I don't know. I've got this thing about not wanting to force my ideas on anyone. You know—freedom of speech and thought and all that. Besides, I don't like anyone telling me what I ought to do or how I ought to think about things. I'm not really into propagandizing or selling. Why do I have to do this?*

Many students have misgivings about the persuasive speech assignment. This is understandable. You are surrounded by a constant barrage of persuasive messages from the time you awake to the commercials that spew from your clock radio until the time you nod off amidst the ads on late-night TV. You may feel so bombarded by persuasive messages in your day-to-day life that you want nothing to do with constructing such messages yourself. You also may equate persuasion with coercion or propaganda, and be put off by the mere mention of the term. Or, you may believe that any attempt at persuading others is an infringement on personal freedom. Finally, you may not realize the vital role that persuasion should and must play in maintaining our political system and our way of life.

Persuasion is part of the ongoing public argument in our culture. Ethical persuasion involves **deliberation**—those public discussions in which people on all sides of an issue are encouraged to have their say before a decision is made. Public deliberation on important issues takes place in newspapers and magazines, on television, and in open meetings sponsored by civic and social organizations. Our political system is based on the belief that persuasion is more ethical and more practical than force. Public deliberation is what makes democracy work.

Persuasion may be best defined in terms of its function. *The function of persuasive speaking is to change the beliefs, attitudes, or actions of others.* Persuasive speaking urges listeners to make choices from among options. This always involves an element of risk for the listener. Consequently, persuasive speakers have an ethical obligation that goes beyond that of informative speakers. They must be willing to assume responsibility for the consequences of their words.

Because persuasion is inescapable, it is important that you understand it, so that you control it rather than having it control you. In this chapter we examine the process of persuasion so that we can better understand how persuasion works. This understanding should make us better at persuading others and less vulnerable to their attempts to persuade us. We next consider some of the major challenges that persuasive speakers must meet: facing a reluctant audience, gaining commitment from listeners, overcoming audience inertia, and maintaining high ethical standards. We also explore the process of constructing arguments with good reasons and sound reasoning, including the use of evidence, the development of appeals, the application of reasoning, and the avoidance of defective persuasion. Finally, we present the three basic types of persuasive speeches and the organizational designs that are most appropriate for them.

TRY THIS

For the next twenty-four hours, keep a log of the times when you either encountered or practiced persuasion. Note when you were most and least persuaded and when you were most and least persuasive. See if you can determine why. Share your insights with the class.

THE PROCESS OF PERSUASION

Our starting point for understanding persuasion is an exploration of how the process works. Persuasion is not an all-or-nothing phenomenon, it progresses in phases.[1] These phases include awareness, understanding, agreement, and enactment. A persuasive message may be considered successful if it simply moves people along through the process.

AWARENESS

Persuasion begins with **awareness.** Before any changes can take place, listeners must know about a problem, pay attention to it, and understand how it relates to their lives. This phase is popularly called **consciousness-raising.** As we noted in the last chapter, informative speaking often fulfills this function. It paves the way for later persuasive messages. All social movements begin with the development of an awareness of a problem.[2] For example, before they could hope for changes in the way in which females were depicted in children's books, feminists had to make people aware that there was a problem with always depicting boys in active roles and girls in passive roles.[3] They had to show that this could inhibit personal growth, self-esteem, and ambition in young females. In her speech "We Don't Have to Live in Slums" (complete text in Appendix D), Anna Aley had to draw people's attention to the problem of substandard student housing before she could expect them to take action to correct it.[4] The speech on environmental stewardship that is included at the end of this chapter assumes that people are already aware of the problem of pollution and simply reinforces that awareness before presenting a solution. Persuasive speakers must be sure the audience is aware of the problem before moving on to the next phase in the persuasive process.

UNDERSTANDING

The second phase in the persuasive process is **understanding.** This includes both understanding the reasons supporting a position and understanding how to carry out the actions proposed. Understanding is critical when listeners are aware of a problem, but don't know how to resolve it. Understanding is enhanced by the presentation of sound arguments supported by evidence, as we will discuss in detail later in this chapter. *Understanding actually empowers listeners by providing them with clear guidelines so that they know how to put proposals into effect.* The sample persuasive speech at the end of this chapter gives listeners specific suggestions on how they can reduce, refuse, and reuse to foster environmental stewardship.

AGREEMENT

The third phase in the persuasive process is **agreement.** You can raise your listeners' awareness of a problem, explain why it is important, and show them how to correct it, but they must agree with your arguments and recommendations before persuasion can occur. Agreement can range from small concessions to total commitment. Lesser degrees of agreement can represent success in situations in which listeners must change their attitudes or risk a great deal by accepting your ideas. Agreement usually results from providing good reasons and sound reasoning.

ENACTMENT

The final stage in the persuasive process is **enactment.** It involves moving the audience from agreement, to action. If you can get listeners to sign a petition, raise their hands, or voice agreement, you have begun the process of enactment. Moving audiences from acceptance to action is one of the major challenges for persuasive speakers that we cover in more detail later in this chapter. It is difficult to get listeners to act because they often must change other beliefs to make them consistent with their new attitudes and behaviors. They may lose friends or social status because of the changes. During the civil rights movement of the 1960s, we heard many courageous students present speeches advocating peaceful integration. Their success could be measured only as a matter of degree. Massive changes in attitudes or actions are rarely achieved through a single message. Widespread changes may require a campaign of persuasive messages carried out over an extended period of time, in which any single speech plays a small but vital role.

In summary, persuasion is a complicated process. Any single persuasive effort must focus on the phase in which it can make the most effective contribution: raising awareness, building understanding, seeking agreement, or promoting action. To develop a successful persuasive speech, you must carefully analyze your audience and adapt your message to the specific challenge of the persuasive situation that you anticipate.

THE CHALLENGES OF PERSUASIVE SPEAKING

Persuasive speaking is more challenging than informative speaking. The major challenges facing persuasive speakers include enticing a reluctant audience to listen, overcoming audience inertia, and satisfying the criteria for ethical persuasion.

THE CHALLENGE OF THE RELUCTANT AUDIENCE

Attitudes and beliefs that are important to your listeners are especially difficult to change. If you face an audience that opposes your position, small achievements may represent success. Fortunately, there are some time-proven strategies to use when you find yourself in such a situation.[5] The following five techniques may be helpful when you find yourself speaking to a reluctant audience:

1. *Establish good will early in the speech.* Here you can use many of the suggestions we made concerning the development of your ethos in the introduction to your speech (see Chapter 12). Point out any beliefs, attitudes, and values that you share with the audience. Let your listeners know that you start from common ground.

2. *Begin with areas of agreement before you take on areas of disagreement.* Starting out with areas of agreement puts listeners in a receptive state of mind. Starting out with areas of disagreement may make them defensive. Instead of attending to what you have to say, they may concentrate on refuting your ideas. If the audience is hostile to your ideas, you may need to take an indirect approach in which you present your evidence and reasoning before you announce your purpose.

3. *Cite experts who your audience will respect and accept.* Determine what authorities your audience respects, and then bolster your case with "borrowed ethos." For example, if your listeners are politically conservative, they would be more influenced by testimony from Newt Gingrich or William F. Buckley Jr. than by testimony from Al Gore or Edward Kennedy.

4. *Set modest goals for change.* If you anticipate considerable opposition, you might ask only for a fair hearing for your message, hoping for a consciousness-raising effect. If you ask for too much change, you may create a **boomerang effect** in which the audience reacts by opposing your position even more strongly.[6]

5. *Make a multisided presentation* in which you first acknowledge and then refute major opposing arguments. This helps your credibility in two important ways. First, it enhances your perceived trustworthiness by showing your respect for the opposition. You suggest that their position merits consideration, even though you have a better option. Second, you enhance your perceived competence by showing your knowledge of the opposing position and your understanding of the reasons why people accept it.

Speaking to a reluctant audience is never easy. But you can't predict what new thoughts your ideas may stimulate or what delayed positive reactions to your message there might be. Even if it only keeps alive the democratic tradition of dissent, your speech will have served a valuable function. It may cause listeners to reevaluate their positions and understand their own convictions better.[7]

THE CHALLENGE OF OVERCOMING INERTIA

It is one thing to agree with a speaker and quite another to accept the inconvenience, cost, and risk that moving from agreement to action may require. It is always easier for people to do nothing than to do something. Your audience may not be willing to act because even though they agree with your position, they are not fully committed to it. Again, there are some time-proven strategies to use when you find yourself in this position. The following six strategies may help you move listeners to action:

1. *Provide the information your listeners need if they are to make a commitment.* Often a single missing fact or unanswered question can hold an audience back. Work such material into your presentation. For example, you might say, "I know that many of you agree with me, but are wondering, 'How much will this cost?'" Anticipating reservations and providing the information needed to overcome them can help move audiences to commitment.

2. *Strengthen your position with borrowed ethos.* Earlier we suggested this as a strategy for persuading a reluctant audience to listen. It is equally applicable with an uncommitted audience that is not quite ready to take action. Listeners may be hesitant because they question your credibility. They may think, "Well, he's just another student like me. Who is he to tell me what to do?" In such cases, you can borrow ethos in the form of expert testimony from sources your audience trusts and respects.

3. *Affirm and apply common values.* Persuasive speeches that threaten your audience's values are usually not effective. You must show them that what you propose is consistent with what they believe and hold dear. For example, suppose your listeners are resisting your educational program for the disadvantaged because they think that people ought to take care of themselves. If you can show them that your plan represents "a hand up, not a handout," they may be more receptive to your proposal.

4. *Revitalize shared beliefs.* When speakers and audiences celebrate shared beliefs, the result is often a renewed sense of commitment. The sharing of beliefs may involve retelling cultural myths and resurrecting heroes. At political conventions, Washington, Jefferson, and Lincoln are often called forth in stories and films. These references invoke a common heritage and relate it to the present.[8] They can be used to break down the barriers of diversity in an audience and bring differing factions together to pursue the same goal.

5. *Demonstrate the importance of involvement.* Unless people believe that a problem affects them directly, they may be reluctant to act. Show your listeners how the quality of their lives depends on their action. Describe the satisfactions they will receive as a result of their actions. Envision the future as Martin Luther King Jr. did in his final speech, when he said, "I may not get there with you, but I can see the Promised Land." King's vision of that Promised Land helped his audience of sanitation workers recommit to their strike against the city of Memphis.

6. *Present a clear plan of action that makes it easy for the audience to comply.* Before people can act, they must know what to do. Be specific in your instructions. Tell them what needs to be done, who needs to do it, and how to proceed. Make it easy for them to get started. Instead of merely urging listeners to write their congressional representatives, provide them with addresses and phone numbers, a petition to sign, or preprinted and addressed postcards to send. Once you get listeners to take the first critical step, further actions come easier.

Moving an audience from agreement to action is not an easy task. But if you can provide information and expert support, affirm and revitalize shared beliefs and values, impress listeners with the necessity for action, and get them to take the first step, the results can be very satisfying.

THE CHALLENGE OF ETHICAL PERSUASION

We are exposed to unethical persuasion almost every day. Persuasive messages are passed off as information in the "infomercials" on cable television. Ads for everything from cars to cosmetics promise that the products being advertised will make us sexier or richer, or will improve our social lives. But, it is not only advertising that causes us to question the ethics of persuasion. Politicians often tell "read-my-lips" whoppers, inundate us with suspicious statistics, make dubious denials, and dance around questions they don't want to answer directly.[9] Major television networks and newspapers "stage" visuals to make their stories more dramatic.[10] Talk show hosts sometimes play fast and loose with facts and use inflammatory language.[11] Our government has fed us more than one public "disinformation" campaign.[12] Historical, political, social, academic, and literary leaders have had their ethics questioned and found wanting.[13] It's little wonder that people have lost trust in major institutions. As a consumer of persuasive messages, you can at least partially protect yourself by applying the critical thinking skills we discussed in Chapter 4. As a producer of persuasive messages, you must guard against both intentional and inadvertent ethical violations.

As we noted earlier, persuasive speakers have a serious ethical obligation because they are asking listeners to change their beliefs, attitudes, or behaviors. As you begin preparing your persuasive speech, ask yourself these three questions:[14]

Political speeches may end with a call for action. Jesse Jackson often registered voters at the conclusion of his speeches.

- What is my ethical responsibility to this audience?
- Could I publicly defend the ethics of my message?
- What does this message say about my character?

Your responses to these questions should help you keep ethics in mind throughout your preparation and presentation.

It is also important to understand what constitutes an ethical speech. Although communication scholars have proposed many different lists of ethical standards, they agree on the basic principles of ethical communication.[15] *An ethical speech is based on respect for the audience, responsible knowledge of the topic, and concern for the consequences of your words.*

Because people have different backgrounds, experiences, and interests, their opinions on important issues may vary widely. Ethical speakers are sensitive to such differences. *Ethical speakers value freedom of choice and trust listeners to respond rationally.* Consider two speakers: One conveys the attitude, "I know the truth and anyone who disagrees is stupid." The other approaches the audience with the attitude, "You have a right to a different opinion, but I have some ideas I would like you to consider." Which speaker do you think would be more effective?

As we noted earlier (see Chapter 13), consideration is one of the six C's of effective language use. It is also one of the ethical mandates of persuasive communication. Consideration for others means, at the very least, that you should avoid name-calling, a particularly vicious form of character attack. Obviously, racial, sexist, religious, and ethnic epithets should be avoided. You should also avoid using trigger words to set off emotional responses. For example, southerners resent being called "bubbas," Hispanics do not like being called "spics," and fundamentalists take offense when they are called "Bible thumpers." Name-calling is especially prevalent during political campaigns. During the 1992 elections, George Bush called Al Gore "the Ozone Man," which annoyed environmentalists. Name-calling reflects poorly on the character of the speaker. When you must go on the attack, *attack issues and ideas, not people.* Never substitute emotional arousal for objective evidence and sound reasoning.

Respect for the audience also means that you should not conceal your motives for speaking. If you have a personal interest in the outcome, your listeners need to know this so that they can factor it into their response. Hiding your motives can backfire on you. For example, if you heard a speech promoting annuities for retirement, then discovered that the speaker was selling annuities, you would probably feel that you had been manipulated. However, if the speaker was an independent financial counselor who was not selling anything, you would feel that you had been advised.

Ethical persuaders acknowledge opposing arguments even as they argue for their own position and explain why they prefer it. This is not only ethical, but also practical. Research has shown that multisided presentations usually have a more lasting influence than messages that reveal only the speaker's side of the issue.[16]

Finally, respect for the audience means that you must not adapt your message too much. As we noted in Chapter 10, it is important for you to tailor your message to fit your audience. However, this does not mean that you should waffle, taking one position with one group of listeners and a different position with another group. Such tactics always get persuasive speakers in trouble and tarnish their reputations. It is ethical to adapt your message in terms of language choices, supporting materials (especially the authorities you cite as experts), and the organizational patterns you select. It is unethical to adapt it to such an extent that you compromise your convictions.

Responsible knowledge is vital to ethical persuasion. Having responsible knowledge earns you the right to speak to your audience. It provides the audience with an opportunity to make a rational choice grounded in evidence and reason. As we noted in Chapter 10, responsible knowledge is the most comprehensive understanding of your topic that you can acquire. To acquire responsible knowledge, you must be thorough in your quest for information. And you must not suppress material that does not support your position. If you discover such information, you must figure out some way to refute it. If you are unable to rationally refute contradictions, you may need to rethink or modify your position.

Honesty is the very heart and soul of responsible knowledge. You must never fabricate evidence. Always check your information, especially if it falls into the realm of things that "everybody knows." What *everybody knows* may not be the same as what *actually is.* Avoid plagiarism. (Review the guidelines for avoiding plagiarism in Chapter 10.) Identify your sources, especially when presenting unusual facts, statistics, or expert testimony. Assess the accuracy and objectivity of sources, being alert to the possibility of bias. A biased source is one that has such a strong self-interest in an issue that it cannot be expected to be entirely objective. For example, the American Cancer Society might be an excellent source of information on the relationship between cancer and smoking. However, on the issue of government funding for medical research, the same group may be biased because of self-interest. Don't quote authorities out of context, distorting the meaning of their words and misrepresenting their positions.

Guard against your own biases by seeking out information that represents a variety of perspectives on a problem. Don't look just for information that will support your position. Appendix A contains a list of periodicals that represent diverse political and social perspectives. Always read at least one article that will offer a different perspective on the situation. It will enhance your own understanding of the problem and provide you with the information you need to make a multisided presentation.

TRY THIS

Think of a topic with which you may be too personally involved or on which you may be too biased to make an objective persuasive situation. Read one article from a reputable periodical that takes an opposing position. How did reading this material affect you? Share your insights with the class.

Responsible knowledge makes clear distinctions among facts, opinions, and inferences. For example, the statement that "drug testing of college athletes is widespread" is a fact that can be documented with the numbers and names of schools doing such testing. The assertion that "drug testing of student athletes is unconstitutional" is an opinion that should be documented with testimony from legal experts. The claim that "drug testing is intended to protect the reputations of institutions more than the health of athletes" is an inference that must be supported with an even wider array of evidence to substantiate its validity. It is unethical to present opinions as facts or to base conclusions on undocumented inferences.

Finally, responsible knowledge precludes oversimplifying a problem. Most issues that are worth speaking about are complex and should not be reduced to polarized extremes. Oversimplification often leads to exaggerated claims. An ethical persuader avoids absolute statements like, "We must never reopen trade with Cuba," but qualifies such statements to fit the situation. For example, an ethical speaker might say, *"As long as conditions do not change,* we should not reopen trade with Cuba." If you overstate your case, your position will seem less credible and your personal ethos will suffer.

An ethical speech is one that listeners are better for having heard. The effects of your speech should be beneficial. Long-range, lasting solutions are preferable to a quick fix. Concern for consequences must cover not only the ultimate objective of your persuasive message, but also the means you employ to reach that objective. Be sure that what you advocate is in the best interest of your audience and that your strategies follow the ethical principles described earlier.

Having concern for the consequences of persuasion also means recognizing the power of language to affect the reputations and fate of others. It can make people see a situation from a particular perspective, arouse strong feelings about an issue, bring people together or divide them, and move them to action.[17] For example, during wars, the enemy are often depicted as animals. Once we start thinking of people as animals, it becomes easier to destroy them without our typical abhorrence for taking human life. In extreme cases, such depictions have even been used to justify the "extermination" of large populations. The infamous World War II German propaganda film *The Eternal Jew* referred to the Jewish people as vermin while showing pictures of rats crawling out of sewer gratings. Speakers who use strong language must realize how powerful words can be. Whoever started the saying, "Sticks and stones can break my bones, but words can never hurt me!" was surely one of the great fools of all time. Words can hurt. The greater the possible consequences, the more speakers must assess the potential effects of their language.

Guidelines for Ethical Persuasion

✓   Avoid name-calling; attack ideas, not people

✓   Be open about what you stand to gain from your proposal

✓   Don't adapt to the point of compromising convictions

✓   Argue from responsible knowledge

✓   Don't fabricate data, distort information, or exaggerate

✓   Acknowledge sources of information and ideas

✓   Don't try to pass off opinions as facts

✓   Don't use pathos, mythos, or ethos to hide a lack of evidence

✓   Be sure what you propose is in the best interest of your audience

GOOD REASONS AND SOUND REASONING

Good reasons and sound reasoning are necessary for persuasion to be effective. **Good reasons** develop from a combination of evidence and appeals. **Evidence** is the name given to supporting materials used in persuasive messages. **Appeals** are the strategies used to reach the audience. Carefully constructed **arguments** arrange evidence and appeals to demonstrate the legitimacy of ideas and suggestions. Arguments are needed to persuade undecided or reluctant listeners. They also may be used to reinforce the views of those who already support the speaker's position. Together, these elements form an integrated system—from the simplest bit of evidence to the most complex array of arguments—that drives the persuasive process. They constitute the good reasons and sound reasoning of persuasion.

GOOD REASONS

Listeners usually demand good reasons before they will change their beliefs, attitudes, or behaviors.[18] Good reasons are based on the values and principles of social behavior that make civilized life possible. They show that something is *admirable, obligatory,* or

All ethical persuasive speeches must be based on sound evidence. Graphic demonstrations can make statistics more memorable.

desirable. Admirable good reasons are based on such values as fairness, conscientiousness, honesty, or courage. They suggest that "we ought to do this because it is the right thing to do." Obligatory good reasons are based on the principles that underlie our social and moral responsibilities. They are the things that "we ought to do because it is our duty to do so." Desirable good reasons are based on self-interest. They are the things that "we ought to do because the results will be beneficial, pleasant, or worthwhile." Both evidence and appeals contribute to the development of good reasons.

Evidence. Evidence is the most basic component of persuasion. It is the supporting material—facts and figures, testimony, examples, and narratives—that substantiates assertions. Evidence adds strength, authority, and objectivity to a speech. It makes people take your message seriously by elevating it above the realm of personal opinion. As you do your research, look for evidence that is relevant, recent, and derived from sources your audience will respect and accept.

Facts and Figures—All ethical persuasion must be grounded in information. The more you ask of listeners, the more facts and figures you must have to justify your recommendations for change. Note how facts and figures are used to describe the problem of pollution in the sample speech at the end of this chapter. The speaker provides specific facts and figures—the amount of garbage collected on beaches, the amount of solid waste each citizen produces, the extent of water pollution in streams and rivers. Moreover, the speaker cites the sources of this information, sources that the audience can be expected to respect and accept: *U.S. News & World Report, Time,* the Environmental Protection Agency, *The Environmental Almanac*, and the *Information Please Almanac.* This same pattern of presenting specific information from reputable sources continues throughout the speech. It prepares the audience for the recommendations the speaker will make later in the presentation.

Testimony—When you use testimony in a persuasive speech, you are calling on witnesses to confirm your position and recommendations. Introduce these witnesses carefully, citing their credentials. Rely primarily on expert testimony from qualified authorities. In her persuasive speech (see text in Appendix E), Gina Norman cites former U.S. surgeon general C. Everett Koop on the dangers of secondhand smoke. Use lay testimony and prestige testimony sparingly to aid identification or to provide insight into your topic.

Examples—In persuasive speeches, examples not only illustrate ideas, they help move listeners by exciting emotions such as sympathy, fear, or anger. Whenever possible, use factual examples based on real people and events. Hypothetical examples are less powerful because they did not actually happen. Note how Anna Aley uses the factual example of what happened to another student living in her apartment building to reinforce the seriousness of the problem of substandard off campus housing:

> *One day last November, Jack was at home when a fuse blew—as usual. And, as usual, he went to the fuse box to flip the switch back on. When he touched the switch, it delivered such a shock that it literally threw this guy the size of a football player backwards and down a flight of stairs. He lay there at the bottom, unable to move, for a full hour before his roommate came home and called an ambulance.*

Narratives—In persuasive speeches a narrative may be used to carry listeners to the scene of a problem and involve them in the drama it creates. Narratives are frequently used in the introduction or conclusion of persuasive speeches. Elizabeth Glaser used a narrative introduction in a speech presented at the 1992 Democratic National Convention urging listeners to support HIV research:

> *I'm Elizabeth Glaser. Eleven years ago, while giving birth to my first child I hemorrhaged and was transfused with seven pints of blood. Four years later I found out that I had been infected with the AIDS virus and had unknowingly passed it to my daughter, Ariel, through my breast milk and my son, Jake, in utero. Twenty years ago, I wanted to be at the Democratic Convention because it was a way to participate in my country. Today I am here because it is a matter of life and death. Exactly four years ago my daughter died of AIDS. She did not survive the Reagan administration. I am here because my son and I may not survive four more years of leaders who say they care but do nothing. I am in a race with the clock.*[19]

Using Evidence

✓ Have enough facts and figures to justify your arguments
✓ Use the most recent facts and figures available
✓ Describe the credentials of your sources
✓ Rely primarily on factual examples to add authenticity
✓ Use examples and narratives to humanize problems
✓ Use a variety of sources and types of evidence

Appeals. Appeals are applications of evidence that act as means of persuasion.[20] They interpret evidence to provide good reasons for accepting a speaker's recommendations. Classical rhetoric suggested that there were three types of appeals: (1) **logos**, or appeals based on rational evidence, (2) **ethos**, or appeals based on the character of the speaker or sources cited, and (3) **pathos**, or appeals based on emotional arousal. Contemporary rhetorical theorists suggest a fourth type of appeal, **mythos**, or appeals based on cultural traditions.[21] Each type of appeal brings its own special strength to a persuasive message.

Each type of appeal is ethically acceptable when used appropriately. Effective persuasive speeches use a variety of appeals.

Facts and figures, factual examples, and expert testimony are the major forms of rational evidence (logos) used in persuasive speeches. They demonstrate that a situation is real, not simply something invented by the speaker. Facts and figures are rarely presented in isolation, but are usually followed by a factual example or expert testimony to make them more understandable and more credible. For example, the sample persuasive speech on environmental stewardship first gives the number of disposable cups used by college students, then follows it with a factual example citing instances of programs that have solved this problem:

> *Did you know that the average American college student goes through 500 disposable cups every year? Carry a mug in your backpack and you can cut that number down to nothing. Other students do it. The University of North Carolina, the University of Vermont, UCLA, James Madison, and the University of Illinois all have successful "use your own mug" programs.*

The use of rational appeals demonstrates the speaker's faith in the audience's intelligence. It implies that if people are provided with facts and shown how to interpret them, they will come to the proper conclusion.

Ethos appeals assume that listeners are persuaded by the credibility of message sources. The sources in persuasive speeches are the speakers themselves and the sources of their evidence. In Chapters 12 and 13 we offered suggestions on how to enhance your ethos in the introduction of your speech and through your manner of presentation. Here we concentrate on the ethos of the sources of the facts, figures, and testimony you use as evidence in your speeches. Listeners will evaluate these sources of information and opinions in terms of their competence, trustworthiness, and likableness. If these evaluations are positive, listeners are more likely to be influenced by your message.

Let's examine how one student speaker used such appeals to change attitudes about suntanning:

> *The 1997 edition of* The Family Doctor *tells us that 32,000 new cases of malignant melanoma were reported in 1996, that at least one in every seven Americans will develop some form of skin cancer, and that a person with more than six serious sunburns in a lifetime is two and a half times more likely to develop these cancers. In a FDA report, Wendell Scarberry, a skin cancer patient who has had over a hundred surgeries, urges us to be careful: "You can't cure skin cancer by just whacking it off."*

This combination of expert and lay testimony makes it difficult for listeners to ignore the speaker's recommendations. Appeals based on the testimony of competent and trustworthy sources are extremely important in persuasive speaking. Identify your sources and point out why they are qualified to speak on your subject.

People act on feelings as well as on knowledge. They usually respond strongly when their emotions are aroused. Appeals to emotions can help change attitudes and behavior. Examples and narratives are the types of evidence most often used to develop emotional appeals. Let's look at how one student speaker used pathos in a speech on living wills[22]:

> *Harry Smith was a cranky, obstinate old farmer. He loved bowling, Glenn Miller music, and Monday night football. He was also dying from lung cancer. Harry*

didn't like doctors, and he didn't like hospitals, and he didn't like modern medicine. Harry didn't want to live in pain, and he hated being dependent on anyone, yet like so many others, Harry never told this to his family or signed a living will. When his cancer got so bad that he could no longer speak for himself, Harry's children stepped in to make decisions about his health care. Out of a sense of guilt over the things they hadn't done and the love they hadn't expressed, they refused to let Harry die. He was subjected to ventilators, artificial feedings, and all the wizardry modern medicine offers. Harry finally did die, but only after months of agony with no hope of recovery. Because Harry had not signed a living will, his doctor had no choice but to subject him to senseless torture that he didn't want.

Emotional appeals are often the only way to convince people of the human aspects of a problem or the need for immediate action. They should, however, be used with caution. If emotional appeals seem contrived, listeners may feel that they are being manipulated. Appeals to negative emotions such as fear and guilt are especially tricky, since they can boomerang, discrediting both the speaker and the subject. When you use emotional appeals, be sure you back up what you say with information, factual examples, and expert testimony. Understate rather than overstate emotional appeals.

Mythos appeals are based on a group's traditions. Transmitted through stories and sayings that evoke a sense of cultural pride, these traditions express the social character of a people. Mythos appeals are frequently based on political or religious narratives. The Bible and the Koran provide a rich storehouse of parables, often used in political as well as religious discourse.[23] Americans have been raised on narratives such as those that stress the hardship of Washington's winter at Valley Forge or tell of the Underground Railroad. Such stories impress on us the meaning and value of freedom. We often use "frontier" myths to explain the American character.[24] In his speech accepting the Democratic presidential nomination in 1960, John F. Kennedy called on the myth of the American frontier to move Americans to action:

> *The New Frontier of which I speak is not a set of promises—it is a set of challenges. It sums up not what I intend to offer the American people, but what I intend to ask of them.*[25]

Bill Clinton's use of "the New Covenant" as a campaign slogan and in his speech accepting the Democratic presidential nomination in 1992 echoed Kennedy's "New Frontier" and added biblical connotations as well.[26]

The unique contribution of mythos is to help listeners understand how a speaker's recommendations fit with the beliefs and values of the group. Like pathos, mythos must be used with caution. Do not use mythos to cover up a lack of basic information or sound reasoning in a speech.

SOUND REASONING

Sound reasoning occurs when speakers arrange evidence and appeals into carefully constructed arguments to support their position. There are three major forms of reasoning: inductive, deductive, and analogical.

● TRY THIS

Find a print advertisement that demonstrates each of the four types of appeals. Determine if the appeals used are relevant to the service or product being advertised. Do these ads meet the criteria for ethical communication? Do you think they are effective? Share your insights with the class.

Inductive reasoning begins with the accumulation of specific instances or pieces of evidence and then draws general conclusions based on that information. For example, in the sample speech at the end of this chapter, the statement of the problem is based on an accumulation of brief examples that demonstrate its scope and severity. As you can see, inductive reasoning builds a powerful sense of need by accumulating evidence until any reasonable listener can no longer deny the urgency of the situation.

In inductive reasoning, appeals are based on facts and figures, expert testimony, and factual examples. These are the most powerful forms of evidence because they emphasize the reality of a problem. Pathos and mythos are usually secondary appeals that can be used to bring home the human aspects of a problem. For inductive reasoning to work well, you must possess responsible knowledge of your topic so that you can present sufficient information to justify conclusions. Your observations must be recent and relevant. They must be representative of the situation as it usually exists, not exceptions to the rule. The conclusions you draw must be directly related to the information you present.

Deductive reasoning begins with a generally accepted principle, then relates a specific situation to that principle in order to reach a conclusion. Deductive reasoning may take the form of a **syllogism**, with a major premise, minor premise, and conclusion. The **major premise** is the generally accepted principle on which the reasoning is based. Major premises may be based on traditionally accepted beliefs or developed through inductive reasoning. For example, in the speech at the end of this chapter, the major premise, "polluting is wrong," is based on a generally accepted principle that is further bolstered by the inductive reasoning used in the statement of the problem.

The **minor premise** of a syllogism directs attention to the specific issue at hand. In our sample persuasive speech, the minor premise is "overconsumption is causing land, water, and air pollution." The minor premise must relate directly to the major premise and should be established by presenting evidence that demonstrates that relationship. Once the minor premise has been established, deductive reasoning moves on to the **conclusion** that tells us what we should believe or do. In this example, the conclusion is, "We should become environmental stewards by reducing, refusing, and reusing." If the audience accepts the major and minor premises, then the reasoning leads them to accept the conclusion.

To use deductive reasoning effectively in persuasive speeches, you must be certain that the audience will accept your major premise. Never take this for granted. Remind listeners of the problem. Review the facts. Use examples or narratives to amplify its importance. Once your major premise is established, concentrate on demonstrating the relationship of the specific issue to the major premise. Provide evidence that supports the connection. Finally, be certain that your conclusion follows directly from the major and minor premises and provides a clear direction for your listeners.

Analogical reasoning is useful when you must provide a special perspective on an unfamiliar or complex problem by relating it to something that is familiar and easily understood. It is reasoning based on a comparison. In Chapter 11 we discussed using analogies as supporting material to make ideas more memorable or easier to understand. In persuasive speeches, analogical reasoning serves these two purposes and may also help change attitudes through association. The speaker hopes that the audience's attitude toward the familiar idea will be transferred to the problematic situation. Therefore, it is important that the audience's attitude toward the familiar idea advanced is positive.

An example of analogical reasoning may be found in the ongoing debate over our nation's drug policy. Those who favor legalizing "recreational" drugs frequently base their arguments on an analogy to Prohibition. They argue that Prohibition caused more problems than it solved, that outlawing recreational drugs has had the same effect, and that it is impossible to legislate away a human desire. They further contend that legalizing drugs would put dealers out of business, just as the repeal of Prohibition brought about the downfall of the gangsters of the 1930s. As this example shows, analogical reasoning emphasizes strategic points of comparison between similar situations. People on both sides of an issue will focus on these points, using evidence to attack or defend them. Opponents of legalizing drugs claim that there are important differences between drugs and alcohol, and that alcohol is not as addictive as heroin or cocaine.

A major weakness of analogical reasoning is that it usually concentrates on one similar situation rather than ranging across many situations. So, although analogical reasoning may seem more concrete and more interesting than inductive or deductive reasoning, it may also be less reliable. Before you decide to use analogical reasoning, be certain that the important similarities between the situations outweigh the dissimilarities. If you must strain to make the analogy fit, try a different approach.

AVOIDING DEFECTIVE PERSUASION

It takes hard work to develop a persuasive speech. Do not waste all this work by committing the errors in persuasion called **fallacies**. Fallacies can contaminate the evidence you use, the appeals you develop, or the reasoning you employ. Recognizing common fallacies will help you guard against them, both as a consumer and as a producer of persuasive messages.

Three common fallacies involving evidence are the slippery slope fallacy, the red herring fallacy, and the myth of the mean. The **slippery slope** fallacy occurs when a speaker assumes that once anything bad happens, it will establish an irreversible trend leading to disaster. It typically involves oversimplification and outlandish exaggeration. For example, a prominent religious leader recently suggested that feminism was "a socialist, anti-family political movement that encourages women to leave their husbands, kill their children, practice witchcraft, destroy capitalism, and become lesbians."[27] The **red herring** fallacy occurs when irrelevant material is injected into an argument to divert attention from the real issue. In the current abortion controversy, some pro-choice advocates try to discredit their opponents by suggesting that they are terrorists, thereby associating the entire pro-life movement with those few who have been convicted of bombing clinics. In return, some pro-life advocates try to discredit their opponents by arguing that many abortion clinics are underwritten by "Mafia money." Such charges divert attention from the central issues of the controversy. The **myth of the mean** creates an illusion that an average actually exists. A speaker could tell you not to worry about poverty in Tunica County because the average income there is well above the poverty level. This average could be misleading if a few very wealthy families skew it.

Two common fallacies in the use of appeals are the ad hominem fallacy and begging the question. The **ad hominem** fallacy is an attack on the proponents of a position rather than on the issues. It is name-calling at its worst because it is usually used when one side in a controversy finds that it cannot logically attack the opposing position. Once started, it degenerates into a childish game in which both sides hurl invectives at the other. In environmental controversies, conservationists are often called "tree huggers" and their opponents "rapists of the land." **Begging the question** is another diversionary tactic that involves using appeals inappropriately. All ethical persuasion must be grounded in information. In begging the question, emotional appeals replace information rather than supplement it. These appeals use such colorful language and are presented with such conviction that the speakers *appear* to have established a conclusion when, in fact, they have not. They have simply substituted strong emotions for good reasons and sound reasoning.

Reasoning fallacies take many forms. Among the most common are the post hoc fallacy, the non sequitur fallacy, and the fallacy of hasty generalization. The **post hoc** fallacy confuses association with causation by assuming that if one event follows another, the second was obviously caused by the first. It is the basis of many superstitions. It also is one of the worst forms of oversimplification. For example, a speaker might argue that the divorce rate has been going up because more women are getting college degrees, so we ought to discourage women from attending college. The **non sequitur** fallacy occurs when the conclusion of an argument does not follow from the premises or evidence.

The fallacy of **hasty generalization** is an error of inductive reasoning that results from insufficient observations. For example, a speaker might reason, "My big sister in Alpha Chi got a D from Professor Osborn. The guy who sits next to me in history got an F from her. I'm struggling to make a C in her class. Therefore Professor Osborn is a tough grader." To avoid hasty generalization, you would need to know what Professor Osborn's grade distribution looks like over an extended period of time and across courses, plus how her grades compare with those given by other professors teaching the same courses.

Persuasion is constantly threatened by flaws and deception. In a world of competing views, we often see human nature revealed in its petty as well as its finer moments. As you plan and present your persuasive speeches and listen to those presented by others, be on guard against fallacies.

TRY THIS

See if you can identify the non sequiturs and other fallacies in the following excerpt from a speech against gun control legislation:

> *Back when the country was founded—if you look back that far into history you'll find that they needed guns. And they defeated an outfit that was trying to disarm them. And, as a result of our having guns and being able to use them, we won. That was the start of the United States of America. We won a war. And of course, ever since that time we've been involved, and there've been people that would like to take us over. If you've read Marx and Lenin you know that one of their great ambitions is to disarm a nation. And so here you have a reason to be armed: to see to it that no one is going to disarm us.*[28]

TYPES OF PERSUASIVE SPEECHES

There are three major types of persuasive speeches: those that address attitudes, those that urge action, and those that contend with opposition. Although a single speech may perform all three of these functions, most of the time one of them will dominate.

SPEECHES ADDRESSING ATTITUDES

The purpose of **speeches addressing attitudes** is to form, change, or reinforce the way listeners feel about something. As we noted in Chapter 10, a person's beliefs, attitudes, and values are integral parts of her or his personality. Changes in attitudes may force listeners to reorganize their entire belief systems to keep things in balance. Consequently, attitudes are difficult to change. Obviously, the greater the change you ask for, the more difficult it will be to achieve your goal. With short presentations, you should be content to seek minor changes. Asking too much of listeners may cause them to reject the speaker and cling more stubbornly to their initial attitudes. Changing attitudes, however, is often easier than changing behavior. For that reason, speeches addressing attitudes are often used to pave the way for speeches urging action.

Gina Norman's persuasive speech on secondhand smoke (see Appendix E) is an example of a persuasive speech addressing attitudes. Note that this speech does not contain a plan of action. She doesn't urge listeners to lobby for regulations prohibiting smoking in public places. She doesn't ask them to confront smokers who light up around them. All she asks is a fair hearing for her position and a possible change in the way they feel about secondhand smoke.

SPEECHES URGING ACTION

Speeches urging action encourage listeners to take action either as individuals or as members of a group. The sample persuasive speech at the end of this chapter asks listeners to make individual changes to make the environment better for everybody. Speeches advocating group action must develop a group identity for the audience. Anna Aley's speech on the problem of substandard housing (see Appendix E) contained this effective appeal to group identity:

> *What can one student do to change the practices of numerous Manhattan landlords? Nothing, if that student is alone. But just think of what we could accomplish if we got all 13,600 off-campus students involved in this issue! Think what we could accomplish if we got even a fraction of those students involved!*

Speeches urging action usually involve risk. Therefore, speakers must present compelling reasons to overcome the audience's natural caution. The consequences of acting and not acting must be clearly spelled out. The plan presented must be practical and reasonable. The suggestions for overcoming audience inertia presented earlier in this chapter should be applied in this type of persuasive speech.

SPEECHES OF CONTENTION

In **speeches of contention,** you directly refute opposing arguments to clear the way for the attitudes or actions you are proposing. Speeches of contention are most appropriate for controversial issues on which your audience may have divided sentiments or when your audience opposes your position. Speeches of contention force you to make a two-sided or multisided presentation. Before you can hope for a change in the way your audience feels or acts, you must weaken the structure of opposing arguments.

Speeches of contention are always risky. When people's attitudes, beliefs, or values are challenged, they often become defensive and more difficult to persuade. Why then would you choose to give such a speech? Speeches of contention are called for when immediate danger threatens and milder forms of persuasion may take too long to be

Civic meetings, such as those of governing bodies or a school board, often include a series of short persuasive messages.

effective. To secure immediate action, you may have to refute beliefs directly and discredit the arguments that support them with indisputable facts, figures, and expert testimony. Speeches of contention may also be the best strategy when your topic is extremely important to you for personal or moral reasons. You may feel that your listeners' opposition is so strong that your only hope is to shock them with a direct, frontal attack that shows them why they are wrong. Or you may even decide that your chances for persuasion are small, but that your position deserves to be heard with all the power, reason, and conviction you can muster. You can have your say and feel better for it.

PERSUASIVE SPEECH DESIGNS

As you consider the type of persuasive speech you will develop, you must also decide how to structure your speech. Many of the designs suggested for informative speeches can be adapted for use with persuasive speeches. In this section, we will show you how to adapt these designs, then present three designs that are used exclusively in persuasive speeches: the problem-solution design, the motivated sequence design, and the refutative design.

ADAPTED INFORMATIVE DESIGNS

Categorical Design. The categorical design is easily adapted to persuasive speaking. It can be modified into a **statement of reasons design**, in which each reason becomes a main point for development. Statement of reasons designs are most useful for speeches addressing changes in attitudes or behavior. The suggestions we advanced for using the categorical design in informative speeches also apply to this design. Limit the number of reasons you present to no more than four. Begin and end with your most important reasons. The outline format for the statement of reasons design would be the same as that used for an informative categorical design.

Comparative Design. The comparative design may be adapted into a **comparative advantages design** for use in persuasive speeches. The comparative advantages design is most useful in speeches urging a change in action or policy. For example, you might wish to present a speech urging the audience to consider the advantages of a flat income tax as opposed to the graduated income tax we now have. In this case, the comparative advantages design would begin with an explanation of the proposed change. Each main point of the body of the speech would show how the new program is superior to the old one in terms of the advantages it would bring. Each main point should be supported with facts and figures, expert testimony, or factual examples to show that your proposal is best. As in all comparative designs, you should limit yourself to four or fewer points in a short presentation. The outline format for a comparative advantages design would be the same as that used for an informative comparative design.

Sequential Design. In persuasive speeches, the sequential design is used most often at the subpoint level to present a plan of action. It allows you to take the audience through the plan step by step so that they know what has to be done when and by whom. When the steps are presented sequentially, your listeners get a feel for how the plan will work. You should limit the number of steps you propose and enumerate them as you present them. The outline format would be the same as that used for a process speech, except that the steps in the plan would be subpoints rather than main points.

PROBLEM-SOLUTION DESIGN

The **problem-solution design** first convinces listeners that they have a problem, then shows them how to deal with it. It is especially useful for speeches urging action. It may also be used in speeches addressing attitudes. In a problem-solution design, be careful not to overwhelm your listeners with too much detail. Cover the most important features of the problem, then show the audience how your solution will work. The first main point in the body of a problem-solution speech presents the problem. Subpoints under it may describe the problem, show its importance, and demonstrate the consequences of inaction. The second main point presents the solution to the problem, with subpoints demonstrating how the solution addresses the problem and specifying a plan of action. The sample persuasive speech at the end of this chapter has the following design:

THESIS STATEMENT: We can reduce environmental pollution by reducing the amount of energy we use, refusing to buy products that are environmentally unsound or to shop at stores that aren't environmentally friendly, and reusing things we already have while recycling what we cannot reuse.

I. Environmental pollution is a serious problem.
   A. Our land is polluted with excessive garbage.
   B. Our rivers and streams are polluted.
   C. The air we breathe is polluted.

II. We can be stewards of the environment.
   A. We can reduce the amount of energy we consume.
   B. We can "just say no" to things that are environmentally unsound.
   C. We can reuse and recycle.

MOTIVATED SEQUENCE DESIGN

The **motivated sequence design** is a five-step variation of the problem-solution design.[29] It is most appropriate for speeches urging action. The steps in the motivated sequence are (1) arouse attention, (2) demonstrate a need for change, (3) satisfy the need with a solution, (4) visualize the results of the change, and (5) present a call for action. The outline format for a motivated sequence design includes material presented in the introduction and conclusion as well as in the body of the speech. Step 1, arouse attention, would be part of the introduction. Step 5, present a call for action, would be part of the conclusion. Steps 2, 3, and 4 would be the main points in the body of the speech.

   Let's look at how this design might work in a speech urging students to volunteer for community service:

THESIS STATEMENT: Our community needs volunteers, and it is easy for students to become involved.

1. Arouse attention [introduction]	How pressed are you for time? How many hours each day do you spend in class? Four? Five? Maybe six if you have a lab. How much time do you spend each day studying? Two hours? Three? This does leave a little bit of time left over. Time you might waste drinking coffee in the union or just fritter

away doing nothing. Well, there is something useful you could be doing. You could work as a student volunteer for an organization that needs your help.

2. Demonstrate need [body]

I. Many organizations in our community rely on volunteers.

   A. Funding for these organizations is insufficient.
   B. The number of volunteers has decreased in the past two years.
   C. Without volunteers, groups may have to cut services or close completely.

3. Satisfy need [body]

II. It is easy to get involved.

   A. The student affairs office has a community service coordinator.
   B. United Way has a volunteer coordinator.
   C. These coordinators help match volunteers and organizations.
      1. They have a monthly listing of groups that need workers.
      2. They screen volunteers before referring them to groups.

4. Visualize results [body]

III. Volunteering benefits both the volunteer and the community.

   A. The personal rewards are great.
      1. It gives you a sense of accomplishment.
      2. It makes you feel that you are needed.
   B. The community rewards are great.
      1. Volunteers help feed the homeless.
      2. Volunteer big brothers and sisters work with children who need help and attention.

5. Call for action [conclusion]

Go to the student affairs office and talk to Patsy Vesta, the community service coordinator. Go by the United Way office in City Hall and talk with Bruce Tsou, the volunteer coordinator. Either one will be glad to get you started. Join with me to make our community a better place to live. Do something for others. Do something for yourself. Be a volunteer. Act today.

REFUTATIVE DESIGN

The **refutative design** is used primarily in speeches of contention. In the refutative design, speakers try to raise doubts about an opposing position by revealing its inconsistencies and deficiencies. To make a refutative design work effectively, you must be familiar with the opposition's arguments and evidence. Each main point in the body of the speech refutes an opposing point or argument. It is usually wise to take on the opposition's weakest point first. Address issues, arguments, and evidence with your refutations. Avoid personal attacks unless credibility issues are relevant and unavoidable.

There are five steps in developing an effective refutation. These steps should be followed in sequence for each point you plan to refute.

1. State the point you are going to refute and explain why it is important.
2. Tell listeners how you are going to refute this point.
3. Provide evidence to refute the point.
4. Spell out the conclusion for the audience.
5. Explain the significance of your refutation.

For example, you might try to refute the argument that CFCs do not contribute to the greenhouse effect in the following manner:

State the point you will refute	Back in 1993, when the backlash against environmentalism got into full swing, the loudest opponents attacked the very idea of a greenhouse effect. One of their most outspoken advocates, Rush Limbaugh, said that anyone who claims that CFCs destroy ozone is a "dunderhead alarmist," and that the ozone hole develops from volcanic eruptions and sea spray, not CFCs.
Tell how you will refute this point	I want to share with you today some well-documented evidence that demonstrates that CFCs are a major cause of the ozone depletion that causes the greenhouse effect.
Present evidence from credible sources	According to a 1995 NASA study, three years of satellite observations show that both hydrogen fluoride and CFCs are present before an ozone hole develops. Hydrogen fluoride *is not present* in volcanic emissions or sea spray. It cannot be produced by volcanic emissions or sea spray. It is produced by the breakdown of CFCs from refrigeration and air-conditioning coolants and Styrofoam wastes. Dr. Ralph Cicerone of the University of California at Irvine has noted, "This is about as good a case as you will find in this field of science. It's only a controversy in the media."
State your conclusion	This evidence demonstrates that the anti-environmentalists are wrong. The ozone hole is not a natural phenomenon, it is the result of human pollution.

Design	Use when
Categorical (Statement of Reasons)	Your main ideas are reasons for change. Each reason becomes a main point for development.
Comparative (Comparative Advantages)	You want to demonstrate why your proposal is superior to another option. Each advantage becomes a main point for development.
Sequential	Your speech presents a plan of action that should be carried out in a specific order. The sequential design will be used primarily at the subpoint level of development.
Problem-solution	Your topic involves a problem that needs to be solved and a solution that corrects the problem. Your first main point describes the problem. Your second main point details the solution.
Motivated sequence	Your topic involves a problem that needs to be solved. Your introduction gains attention. The body of your speech consists of three main points that (1) establish need, (2) satisfy that need, and (3) picture the results. Your conclusion contains a call for action.
Refutative	Your topic involves an issue that has strong opposition that you must refute in order to establish your position. Each opposing claim or argument becomes a main point for development.

FIGURE **15.1**
What Designs to Use When

Explain the significance of your refutation

That's typical of the attacks on environmentalists. A lot of sound and fury, name-calling, and dubious information that is not grounded in sound scientific research. Most of these opponents' so-called data come from studies funded by industrial coalitions that have a vested interest in the results.

In an actual speech using a refutative design, you would present far more evidence than we have provided in our simplified example. Since it takes a considerable amount of time to refute each point, you should limit the number of points you will refute to three in a short presentation.

Figure 15.1 summarizes when each of these designs should be used.

IN SUMMARY   Persuasive communication is inescapable. Persuasion is also vital to our political system, which is based on the principle of rule by *deliberation* and choice, not coercion or force. The function of persuasive speaking is to change beliefs, attitudes, or behaviors. It urges listeners to make a choice from among options.

Persuasion is a process that progresses in phases. These phases include awareness, understanding, agreement, and enactment. The awareness phase of persuasion serves a consciousness-raising function. Understanding involves both realizing why a problem is important and knowing what needs to be done to correct it. Agreement can range from small concessions to total commitment. The enactment phase moves the audience from agreement to action. Major changes in beliefs, attitudes, or behaviors may require a campaign of persuasive messages in which any single speech plays a small but vital role.

Persuasive speakers must meet many challenges. They may need to entice a reluctant audience to listen or overcome audience inertia. The major challenge in persuasive speaking involves ethical considerations. An ethical persuasive speech is based on respect for the audience, responsible knowledge of the topic, and concern for the consequences of the message.

Good reasons and sound reasoning are necessary for persuasion to be effective. Good reasons develop from a combination of evidence and appeals. Evidence is supporting material used in persuasive discourse. All persuasive speeches should be supported with facts and figures, expert testimony, or factual examples. Hypothetical examples and narratives may be used to humanize a problem. Appeals are the strategies used to reach the audience. Four types of appeals may be used in persuasive speeches. *Logos* appeals are based on rational evidence. *Ethos* appeals are based on speaker credibility and the reputation of sources of evidence. *Pathos* appeals call for emotional responses. *Mythos* appeals evoke the cultural heritage of a group.

Sound reasoning involves arranging evidence and appeals into carefully constructed arguments. Inductive reasoning works from specific instances to general conclusions about them. Deductive reasoning works from the general to the specific. It can take the form of a syllogism, with a major premise, a minor premise, and a conclusion. Analogical reasoning creates a special perspective on a subject by relating it to something similar.

Fallacies are common in persuasive communications. They can contaminate the evidence you present, the appeals you develop, or the reasoning you employ. Common fallacies affecting evidence include the slippery slope fallacy, the red herring fallacy, and the myth of the mean. Common fallacies affecting appeals are ad hominem attacks and begging the question. Common fallacies of reasoning include the post hoc fallacy, the non sequitur fallacy, and the fallacy of hasty generalization.

The three major types of persuasive speeches address attitudes, urge action, and contend with opposition. Speeches addressing attitudes may aim for small changes or radical conversions. The latter type of change is difficult and runs the risk of a boomerang effect. Speeches urging action call on listeners to become agents of change, either individually or as part of a group. Speeches of contention confront the opposition directly by refuting their major arguments.

Many of the designs used for informative speeches can be adapted for use in persuasive speeches. The categorical design can be adapted into a statement of reasons design. The comparative design may be adapted into a comparative advantages design. The sequential design may be used at the subpoint level to spell out the steps in a plan of action. There are three designs that are used exclusively in persuasive speaking. The problem-solution design convinces listeners that they have a problem, then shows them how to deal with it. The motivated sequence design has five steps: arousing attention, demonstrating need, satisfying the need, visualizing the results, and calling for action. The refutative design systematically attacks the evidence and arguments of the opposition by stating the point you will refute, telling how you will refute it, presenting your evidence, stating your conclusion, and explaining the significance of the refutation.

TERMS TO KNOW

deliberation	conclusion
awareness	analogical reasoning
consciousness-raising	fallacies
understanding	slippery slope
agreement	red herring
enactment	myth of the mean
boomerang effect	ad hominem
good reasons	begging the question
evidence	post hoc
appeals	non sequitur
arguments	hasty generalization
logos	speeches addressing attitudes
ethos	speeches urging action
pathos	speeches of contention
mythos	statement of reasons design
inductive reasoning	comparative advantages design
deductive reasoning	problem-solution design
syllogism	motivated sequence design
major premise	refutative design
minor premise	

NOTES

1. William J. McGuire, "Attitudes and Attitude Change," in *The Handbook of Social Psychology, Vol. 1*, ed. Gardner Lindzey and Elliot Aronson (New York: Random House, 1985), 258–261.

2. Roger Brown, *Social Psychology* (New York, Free Press, 1965), 709–763.

3. Gloria Steinem, *Revolution from Within: A Book of Self-Esteem* (New York, Little, Brown, 1992), 120.

4. Anna Aley, "We Don't Have to Live in Slums." Ms. Aley, a student at Kansas State University, gave this persuasive speech as a class assignment. It was later presented in a campus forum and reprinted in the local newspaper, *The Manhattan Mercury,* which followed up with investigative reports and a sympathetic editorial. Brought to the attention of the mayor and city commission, her speech inspired reforms in the city's rental housing code. Used with permission.

5. The suggestions advanced in this section are a modification of the co-active approach described by Herbert W. Simons, *Persuasion: Understanding, Practice, and Analysis,* 2nd ed. (New York: Random House, 1986), 153.

6. N. H. Anderson, "Integration Theory and Attitude Change," *Psychology Review* 78 (1971): 171–206.

7. Additional support for the value of minority opinions may be found in Charlene Jeanne Nemeth, "Differential Contributions of Majority and Minority Influence," *Psychology Review* 93 (1986): 23–32.

8. Michael Osborn, "Rhetorical Depiction," in *Form, Genre, and the Study of Political Discourse,* ed. Herbert W. Simons and Aram A. Aghazarian (Columbia: University of South Carolina Press, 1986), 79–107.

9. Walter Shapiro, "Lies, Lies, Lies: How to Tell if a Politician Is Lying," *Time*, 5 October 1992, 38.

10. Gloria Borger, "The Story the Pictures Didn't Tell," *U.S. News & World Report*, 22 February 1993, 6–7 and John Leo, "Lapse or TV News Preview?" *Washington Times*, 3 March 1993, G3.

11. Robin DeRosa, "Clinton Hits Airwave 'Hatred,'" *USA Today*, 5 April 1995, A1 Joshua Shenk, "The Master Fact-Twister," *Commercial Appeal*, 10 May 1994, A7 (originally published in *New Republic*).

12. Michael Elliott, "America's Nuclear Secrets," *Newsweek*, 27 December 1993, 14–19; Evan Thomas, "Sins of a Paranoid Age," *Newsweek*, 27 December 1993, 20; Stephen Budiansky, "Playing Patriot Games," *U.S. News & World Report*, 22 November 1993, 16; Richard Corliss, "Look Who's Talking: The Explosion of Radio Call-In Shows Has Created a New Form of Electronic Populism and Demagoguery," *Time*, 23 January 1995, 22–25. For up-to-date, detailed analyses of disinformation campaigns, see the Internet site Disinform at http://www.disinfo.com/disInfo/PROP/media/PROP_media.htm.

13. Richard Shenkman, *Legends, Lies, and Cherished Myths of American History* (New York: Morrow, 1988); Gary Wills, "Dishonest Abe," *Time*, 5 October 1992; "Scholars Confirm Plagiarism in King Thesis," *Washington Times*, 11 October 1991, A3; Paul Gray, "The Purloined Letters," *Time*, 26 April 1993, 59; "Scholars Access Roots of 'Roots,'" *Washington Times*, 25 February 1993, E4; "Boston U. Dean Resigns Amid Plagiarism Dispute," *Washington Times*, 15 July 1991, B10.

14. Adapted from Richard L. Johannensen, *Ethics in Communication*, 3rd ed. (Prospect Heights, Ill.: Waveland, 1990), 17–20.

15. In addition to the Johannensen text cited above, see Karen Greenwood, ed., *Conversations on Communication Ethics* (Norwood, N.J.: Ablex, 1991) and James A. Jaska and Michael S. Pritchard, *Communication Ethics: Methods of Analysis*, 2nd ed. (Belmont, Calif.: Wadsworth, 1994).

16. Mike Allen et al., "Testing a Model of Message Sidedness: Three Replications," *Communication Monographs* 57 (1990): 275–290.

17. Osborn, "Rhetorical Depiction."

18. Karl R. Wallace, "The Substance of Rhetoric: Good Reasons," *Quarterly Journal of Speech* (1963): 239–249 and Walter R. Fisher, "Toward a Logic of Good Reasons," *Quarterly Journal of Speech* (1978): 376–384.

19. "AIDS: A Personal Story," by Elizabeth Glaser, Co-founder, Pediatric AIDS Foundation. Speech delivered at the Democratic National Convention.

20. George A. Kennedy, *Aristotle on Rhetoric: A Theory of Civic Discourse* (New York: Oxford, 1991), 36–47.

21. For a representative sampling of such scholarship, see Janice Hocker Rushing, "The Rhetoric of the American Western Myth," *Communication Monographs* (1983): 14–32; Martha Solomon, "The 'Positive Woman's' Journey: A Mythic Analysis of the Rhetoric of STOP ERA," *Quarterly Journal of Speech* (1979): 262–274; and papers presented at a symposium on mythic analysis, *Communication Studies* (1990): 101–160.

22. Reprinted by permission.

23. Roderick P. Hart, *The Political Pulpit* (West Lafayette, Ind.: Purdue University Press, 1977) and Morris M. Womack, *Learning to Live from the Parables* (Joplin, Mo.: College Press, 1995).

24.   Janice Hocker Rushing, pp. 14–32 and Ronald H. Carpenter, "America's Tragic Metaphor: Our Twentieth Century Combatants as Frontiersmen," *Quarterly Journal of Speech* (1990): 1–22.

25.   John Fitzgerald Kennedy, "Acceptance Address, 1960," in *The Great Society: A Sourcebook of Speeches,* ed. Glenn R. Capp (Belmont, Calif.: Dickenson, 1969), 14.

26.   Laurence I. Barrett, "Pulpit Politics," *Time,* 31 August 1992, 34 and Bill Clinton, "Acceptance Address," presented at the Democratic National Convention, 16 July 1992, text reprinted in *Vital Speeches of the Day,* 15 August 1992, 642–645.

27.   Gilbert Cranberg, "Even Sensible Iowa Bows to the Religious Right," *Los Angeles Times,* 17 August 1992, B5.

28.   Joe Foss, "The Right to Bear Arms" (speech presented to the National Press Club, Washington, D.C., 14 March 1989, from C-Span transcript of speech).

29.   The motivated sequence design was introduced in Alan Monroe, *Principles and Types of Speech* (Chicago: Scott, Foresman, 1935) and has been refined in later editions.

Sample Persuasive SPEECH

REDUCE, REFUSE, REUSE

"It isn't easy being green." Recognize this line? Kermit, the frog, right? One of the Muppets? You got it! Those of us raised on *Sesame Street* know that Kermit's song was all about what it's like to be different—what it's like to be green in a world that isn't. But I want to apply this line in a different context—a context in which it's equally applicable. I want to tell you how "it isn't easy being green" in an ecological sense.

The environment is very important to me. I like camping and hiking and fishing. To me, being outside and enjoying nature is the ultimate high. But sometimes, being outside has its downside. Have you ever walked through the woods, thinking you'd gotten away from it all—and then tripped over a beer can? Have you ever found the beauty of a river spoiled by an old used tire gathering moss? Have you ever gone to the beach and found you couldn't swim because the water was polluted? Have you ever had trouble seeing the mountains because of the smog? Or, even worse, had trouble breathing the air? Well, I have. And it's things like this that have turned me into a budding environmentalist.

For me at first, it wasn't "easy being green." I had to break some bad habits because I was part of the problem myself. Once I broke through, it got easier, and now it's almost become second nature. Today I want to share with you why pollution is such a big problem and what you can do to help solve it. I want to introduce you to what I call "the three R's of environmental stewardship: *reduce . . . refuse . . . reuse. Reduce* the amount of energy you use. *Refuse* to buy products that are environmentally unsound or to shop at stores that aren't environmentally friendly. And *reuse* by finding new uses for things you might otherwise throw away and recycling all that you can.

I don't think many of us would deny that pollution is a problem. We've already heard a speech that pointed out the dangers of the greenhouse effect. Let me add some fuel to the fire. According to *U.S. News & World Report,* in 1991 667 pounds of garbage was collected for every mile of beach in the United States. There are more than 28,000 miles of beach in the United States, so that's almost 19 million pounds of garbage. Just from beaches alone! And that's just the tip of the wasteberg. Figures released by the Environmental Protection Agency as reported in the *Environmental Almanac* show that the average U.S. citizen produces more than one-half ton of solid waste each year. With a population of almost 260 million people, that's over 130 million tons of waste per year. Can you picture how much trash that is? The writing paper alone that we throw out each year is enough to build a twelve-foot-high wall from Los Angeles to New York.

The situation with water isn't much better. According to the *Information Please Almanac,* nearly half of our rivers are too polluted to support their intended uses for drinking water, recreation, or fisheries. And how about the air we breathe? The almanac tells us that this too is getting worse, with cars accounting for over half of all air pollution in the country. Furthermore, *Time* magazine warns us that air pollution can reduce life spans as much as two years, even in areas that meet current federal air quality standards.

"Enough already," I hear you thinking. "So we have a problem. What can we do?" Let's look at these "three R's" one at a time—*reduce, refuse, reuse.* The first *R* stands for *reduce.* And I'm not talking about weight. I'm talking about the amount of energy you use by driving too much and by using too much gas and electricity in your home.

This introduction gains attention and creates identification by referring to a shared cultural experience. The speaker establishes personal credibility and invites listeners to confirm from their own experience the urgency of environmental problems. The unstated major premise is, "We have a responsibility to protect the environment in which we live from serious pollution."

As the speaker presents his thesis statement and previews his speech, the simple formula—reduce, refuse, reuse—is easy to remember.

This speech uses inductive argument to confirm the minor premise, "Pollution has reached a serious level." The speaker reminds listeners of evidence from a previous speech, and adds other facts, statistics, and testimony. Vivid images help dramatize the problem.

The speaker begins by defining terms and reminds listeners of their habits that need correcting. The speech offers excellent advice on how to "reduce," but might benefit from analogical argument to show how similar programs have reduced energy consumption.

Driving. Need something from a store four blocks away? What do you do? You drive. Drive to campus. Drive to work. Drive on dates. Drive home. Drive just for the fun of it. Drive, drive, drive! It's our national passion. What are the options? Take the bus to school and you won't have to worry about parking. Carpool. Ride a bike. Walk anyplace that's closer than a mile. Exercise is good for you. You can also reduce the amount of energy you use by keeping your car in good shape. And, when you're lucky enough to get a new car, get one that's energy-efficient.

"Well, all right," you may be thinking, "I know I can drive less, but what about my utilities? I don't want to be uncomfortable." You don't have to be. Here are some easy things to do to save energy and save money. Set your thermostat below 68 in the winter and above 78 in the summer, then dress for comfort. When you go to bed or leave your apartment for any length of time—even just for the day—adjust your thermostat. It will heat back up or cool back down quickly.

Buy a fan. Ceiling fans are good because they move the warm air down in the winter and keep you cooler in the summer. You can buy one for less than $30.00 and install it yourself. Some other things you can do. Turn down the thermostat on your hot water heater to 130 degrees. Water heaters are the second largest energy user in the home. Use your microwave for more than just reheating coffee. It's more energy-efficient than your stove. Buy fluorescent light bulbs. These may sound like little things, but little things can add up to big savings.

Now, let's move on to the second *R: refuse.* Do you remember back in grade school being told, "Just say no!" Well, do it! Just say no to products that are environmentally unsound! Just say no to merchants that don't demonstrate an environmental consciousness! Just say no! Money talks.

For starters, learn to recognize the recycling logo [shows small poster with logo] and buy products that carry this symbol. Buy paper products made from recycled paper. They're not much more expensive. For example, this notebook [shows notebook] made of recycled paper costs just ten cents more than one not made with recycled paper. Think of that dime as a gift to the environment. Learn what companies support environmental causes and choose their products. For example, did you know that Kelloggs has packaged its cornflakes in boxes made from recycled paper since 1906? Buy products with the least amount of packaging.

The speaker "names names" of stores that are committed to saving the environment.

Be selective about where you shop. Find stores that encourage recycling. Anderton's will give you three cents for every used grocery bag you return and reuse. That'll make up for that dime you lost on the notebook! Some stores have recycling facilities. Some offer information on consumer and environmental concerns.

So much for groceries, now on to fast foods places. Watch out for Styrofoam! It isn't biodegradable. Go where they use paper instead of plastic. And let manufacturers and merchants know your feelings. Money talks. Hit them where it hurts—hit them in the pocketbook.

The speech seems most successful in the "reuse" part of the proposal. Listing colleges that have successful "use your own mug" programs lays the groundwork for an analogical argument. It would have been better had the speaker provided more detail on the success of these programs.

Now, the third *R—reuse.* Stick with products that are reusable or recyclable. Did you know that the average college student goes through 500 disposable cups every year? Carry a mug in your backpack and you can cut that number down to nothing. Other students do it. The University of North Carolina, the University of Vermont, UCLA, and the University of Illinois all have successful "use your own mug" programs. Maintain and repair what you already have rather than replacing it. Rinse out plastic bags and reuse them.

Find innovative ways to reuse. Use both sides of computer paper for your rough drafts. Then save what is left for recycling. Every ton of recycled paper saves 380 gallons of gas. Read the newspaper at the library. Swap magazines with friends. Donate anything usable that you no longer need to a thrift shop. If you want even more ideas on ways to use things, you can find over 30 pages of them on the Rainforest Web site. The URL is on the list of environmental Web sites I'll distribute after my speech.

Finally, recycle. According to the *Washington Times,* more than 40 percent of landfill material comes from paper, so recycling paper is the single most effective thing we can do to reduce waste. Each ton of recycled paper saves 3.3 cubic yards of space at the local dump. Recycling paper also saves trees. Wastepaper represents the largest untapped forest in the world. Recycled paper gets reused as newsprint, stationery products, boxes, and insulation. Recycled bottles and cans are redeemable for cash. Recycled plastics show up in cars, carpets, and clothes. Even used tires can be recycled into asphalt for highway construction or mixed with soil for athletic fields.

There are some people who say that our faith in recycling is misplaced. That recycling costs us more than it saves. One so-called specialist went so far as to say that "Americans could put all the trash generated over the next thousand years into a landfill 100 yards high and 35 miles square." I just can't buy that! I wonder if he's driven by our landfill out Murphy Road lately?

> At this point the speaker takes a stab at acknowledging counterarguments, but doesn't carry it far enough to be effective.

In closing, let me urge you to do your part in the battle against pollution. *Reduce, refuse,* and *reuse.* It isn't always easy being green. It may be a little inconvenient, but it will be worth it in the long run. Let me close by sharing with you a poem I clipped out of the paper several years ago. The poem was written by Ed Stein of the *Rocky Mountain News* (with apologies to William Shakespeare):

> The conclusion repeats the three R's and ties the ending to the beginning. The poetic conclusion of the speech—Stein's parody of the witches' speech from *Macbeth*—is quite effective.

> *Double, double toil and trouble, fire burn and cauldron bubble.*
> *Toxic waste and PCBs, bring on suffering and disease.*
> *Acid rain and nuclear spills, infect all with assorted ills.*
> *Leach into the lake and river, poison both the lung and liver.*
> *Spread this waste upon the land, into the flesh of child and man.*
> *By the damage man has done, something wicked this way comes.*

REFERENCES

Browning-Ferris Industries and Earthwatch 3. "One Hundred Things You Can Do for Our Planet." Undated brochure.

"Database." *U.S. News & World Report,* 15 June 1992, 10.

Information Please Almanac. Boston: Houghton Mifflin, 1996.

Innerst, Carol. "Students Try Cupfuls of Concern." *Washington Times,* 12 August 1991, A5.

Miller, Karen L. "The Greening of the Web: Reduce, Reuse, Recycle, Research, React—and Buy." *New York Times,* 23 January 1988, on-line, accessed 4 May 1988, http://www.nytimes.com/library/cyber/week/.

Pisik, Betsy. "Concern for the Environment a Top-Shelf Item for Grocers." *Washington Times,* 23 March 1993, C3.

Rainforest. "Reuse Your Trash." Posted 11 April 1998, accessed 6 May 1998, http://www.geocities.com/Rainforest/5002/index.html.

Sierra Club. "Green Tips." Undated, accessed 6 May, 1988, http://www.sierraclub.org/chapters/ny/longisland/green.htm.

APPENDIX A:
A GUIDE TO LIBRARY AND INTERNET RESOURCES

LIBRARY RESOURCES

GENERAL INFORMATION AND BACKGROUND

General Encyclopedias and Dictionaries

American Heritage Dictionary
Collier's Encyclopedia
Encyclopedia Americana
Encyclopaedia Brittannica
Oxford English Dictionary

Specialized Encyclopedias and Dictionaries

Black's Law Dictionary
Dictionary of American History
Dictionary of Americanisms
Dictionary of the History of Ideas
Dictionary of Psychology
Dictionary of Science
Dictionary of Word and Phrase Origins
Encyclopedia of Associations
Encyclopedia of Education
Encyclopedia of Philosophy
Encyclopedia of Religion and Ethics
Encyclopedia of Science and Technology
Encyclopedia of World Art
Harper's Bible Dictionary
International Encyclopedia of the Social Sciences
Safire's Political Dictionary
Scientific Encyclopedia
Webster's New World Dictionary of Business Terms

SOURCES FOR ACCESS TO INFORMATION

Periodical Indexes and Abstracts

American Statistics Index: a master guide to government statistical publications.
Art Index: covers photography, films, architecture, fine arts, graphic arts, and design.
Biography Index: lists current articles and books containing biographical information.
Business Index: covers business and industry periodicals.
Business Periodicals Index: covers business, economics, computers, advertising, etc.
Congressional Information Service: Index and Abstracts: 2 volumes covering working papers of Congress, hearings, reports, and special publications of congressional committees.
Education Index: covers articles relating to children and/or education.
Engineering Index: covers international journals and special technical reports.
Environment: Index and Abstract: covers articles relating to environmental issues.
Federal Index: covers *Congressional Record, Weekly Compilation of Presidential Documents, Federal Register, Code of Federal Regulations, United States Code,* etc.

General Science Index: covers fields such as astronomy, botany, genetics, mathematics, physics, and oceanography.

Humanities Index: covers fields such as archaeology, folklore, history, language and literature, performing arts, and philosophy.

Index Medicus: covers journal articles, editorials, and biographies related to medicine.

MLA International Bibliography: covers modern languages, literatures, and linguistics.

Music Index: covers popular music, dance, jazz, and classical music.

Psychology Abstracts: covers articles in psychology and related journals.

Reader's Guide to Periodical Literature: covers popular periodicals.

Social Sciences Index: covers anthropology, psychology, sociology, and related areas.

United Nations Document Index (UNDEX): covers publications of the United Nations.

Women's Studies Abstracts: covers books, pamphlets, and periodicals on topics relevant to women.

Newspaper Indexes

New York Times Index

Christian Science Monitor Index

Wall Street Journal Index

The Newspaper Index (1972): includes a variety of regional and major market newspapers.

Computerized and CD-ROM Indexes

General Periodicals Index: 1,100 general, business, and academic publications since 1987.

Reader's Guide to Periodical Literature: going back to 1983.

Magazine Index: covers 350 popular magazines going back to the 1940s.

Infotrac: covers general periodicals and government documents from 1985 to present.

Educational Resources Information Center (ERIC): covers all aspects of education.

Business Index: covers business periodicals, books, the *New York Times* financial section, and the *Wall Street Journal.*

National Newspaper Index: covers the *New York Times, Christian Science Monitor, Wall Street Journal, Washington Post,* and *Los Angeles Times.*

SOURCES FOR SPECIFIC AND/OR IN-DEPTH INFORMATION

Almanacs, Yearbooks, etc.

Annual Register of World Events

Book of Lists

Canadian Almanac and Directory

Economic Almanac

Information Please Almanac

Information Please Environmental Almanac

Old Farmer's Almanac

Statistical Abstract of the United States

World Almanac and Book of Facts

Whitaker's Almanack: Great Britain

Atlases

The Times Atlas of the World
Rand McNally World Atlas
Township Atlas of the United States
Webster's New Geographic Dictionary

Biographical Information

Who's Who: published since 1849; mainly Britons
Who's Who in America: biannually since 1899
Who's Who of American Women: since 1958
International Who's Who: since 1935
Notable American Women
The Dictionary of Canadian Biography
The Dictionary of American Biography: deceased Americans
The Directory of American Scholars
American Men and Women of Science
Current Biography

Quotations

Bartlett's Familiar Quotations
Oxford Dictionary of Quotations
Peter's Quotations: Ideas for Our Time
Simpson's Contemporary Quotations
The Quotable Woman
Beyond Bartlett: Quotations By and About Women

Selected Periodicals[1]

American Demographics: focuses on demographic trends and changing demographics.
American Heritage: an interesting history magazine.
Americana: contemporary approach to American history focusing on preservation.
Business Week: concentrates on business news, patterned after weekly newsmagazines.
Changing Times: Kiplinger's monthly report on personal finance.
Columbia Journalism Review: critical analysis of media issues.
Consumer Reports: a good source of information on consumer goods and services.
Discover: popular science magazine.
Ebony: articles for and about Black readers.
Equinox: in-depth profiles of Canadian people, places, and wildlife.
Foreign Affairs: establishment quarterly, very influential in government circles.
Gray's Sporting Journal: upscale outdoor magazine.
Harper's: high-quality general issue magazine.
Harvard Business Review: upscale articles on business and management.
Harvard Medical School Health Letter: source of reliable, up-to-date medical information
    written so that the lay reader can understand it.
Inquiry: libertarian publication (pro-free enterprise, anti-big government).
Modern Maturity: publication of the American Association of Retired Persons.
Money: covers personal finance and consumer issues.
Mother Jones: radical left-wing publication; occasionally has good exposés.

Nation (The): liberal perspective on contemporary political issues.

National Parks: publication of the National Parks and Conservation Association.

National Review: conservative perspective on contemporary issues.

Natural History: published by the American Museum of Natural History.

New Republic (The): liberal perspective on contemporary issues.

Newsletter on Intellectual Freedom: published by the American Library Association, contains lists of censored books.

Nucleus: quarterly report of the Union of Concerned Scientists.

Omni: science for nonscientists.

Quarterly Review of Doublespeak: excellent exposé on the uses of language to con the public.

Science News: good weekly on what's new in science.

Scientific American: good science monthly; difficult reading for lay audience.

Sierra: emphasizes conservation and environmental politics.

Smithsonian: articles cover popular culture and the fine arts, history, and natural science.

Soviet Life: slick Soviet monthly patterned after *Life.*

Today's Health: published by the American Medical Association.

Village Voice: left-wing; good political exposés.

Wilderness: quarterly publication of the Wilderness Society, a nonprofit organization devoted to conservation and preservation.

Wilson Quarterly: summaries of articles in other magazines plus original articles on many contemporary subjects.

SOURCES FOR CURRENT INFORMATION

Facts on File: A Weekly Digest of World Events with Cumulative Index
Recent issues of periodicals, especially newsweeklies
Recent issues of newspapers

SOURCES FOR LOCAL INFORMATION

Vertical File Index
Index to major local or area newspapers
City or state magazines from your area

WEB BROWSERS AND SEARCH TOOLS

INTERNET
RESOURCES

BrowserWatch (up-to-date news on browser downloads): http://www.browserwatch.com/

Netguide Live (search tool and more): http://www.netguide.com

Lexis-Nexis: http://www.lexis-nexis.com

ERIC: http://ericir.syr.edu/.

Research It: http://www.itools.com/research-it/research-it.html

One Look: http://www.onelook.com/browse.shtml

MISCELLANEOUS PAGES WITH RELEVANT WEB-SITE LINKS

Scoop: http://scoop.evansville.net
Carnegie Mellon English Server: http://english-www.hss.cmu.edu/
University of Iowa Communication Studies: www.uiowa.edu/~commstud/index.html
Libraries Online: http://library.usask.ca/hytelnet/usa/usall.html
Internet Public Library: http://www.ipl.org/
Virtual Library: http://www.w3.org/vl/
Research It: http://www.itools.com/research-it/research-it.html
New York Times Navigator:
     http://www.nytimes.com/library/tech/reference/cynavi.html

MULTIMEDIA RESOURCES

Multimedia Links: http://www.cdmi.com/Lunch/multimedia.html
Index to Multimedia Information Sources: http://viswiz.gmd.de/MulitmediaInfol.
Interactive Multimedia Association: http://www.ima.org/

HEALTH ISSUES

Prevention: http://www.prevention.com/
Centers for Disease Control and Prevention: http://www.cdc.gov
Medline: http://www.healthgate.com
National Library of Medicine: http://www.nlm.nih.gov/
Merck Manual (guide to diseases): http://www.merck.com/
World Health Organization: http://www.who.ch
Hardin Library for the Health Sciences: http://www.arcade.uiowa.edu/
     hardin-www/md.html
Medline: http://www.ncbi.nlm.nih.gov/PubMed/
RxList: The Internet Drug List: http://www.rxlist.com/

MUSEUMS AND ART GALLERIES

Guide to Museums and Cultural Resources: http://www.lam.mus.ca.us/webmuseums/
Museum Online Resource Review: http://www.okc.com/morr/
National Museum of the American Indian: http://www.si.edu/nmai
National Civil Rights Museum: http://www.mecca.org/~crights/ncrm.html
American Museum of Natural History: http://www.amnh.org
The Louvre: http:// www.paris.org/Musees/Louvre
National Museum of American Art: http://www.nmaa.si.edu:80
Smithsonian: http://www.si.edu/i+d

ENVIRONMENTAL CONCERNS

EnviroLink: http://www.envirolink.org/
Greenpeace: http://www.greenpeace.org/greenpeace.htm
Sierra Club: http://www.sierraclub.org/

Environmental Ethics: http:// www.cep.unt.edu/

National Environmental Information Service: http://www.neis.com/neis.html

National Parks and Conservation Association: http://www.npca.org/

National Recycling Coalition: http://www.recycle.net/recycle/Associations/
rs000145.html

WOMEN'S RESOURCES

The Web for Women (directory of sites for women):
http://www.dogpatch.org/women.html

WWWomen: http://www.wwwomen.com/

Women Leaders Online: http://www.wlo.org/

National Organization of Women: http://now.org/now/

BOOKS AND LITERATURE

Project Gutenberg: http://jg.cso.uiuc.edu/PG/welcome.html

Shakespeare: http://the-tech.mit.edu/Shakespeare/works.html

The Bible (in seven languages): http:// www.gospelcom.net/bible

Alex (electronic texts catalog): http://www.lib.ncsu.edu/staff/morgan/alex/
alex-index.html

Electronic Books and Text Sites: http://www.awa.com/library/omnimedia/links.html

Online Books Page: http://www.cs.cmu.edu/Web/books.html

Online Literature Library: http:// www.literature.org/Works/

NEWS

Vanderbilt University TV News Archive: http://tvnews.vanderbilt.edu/

Newslink: http://www.newslink.org

Ecola Newstand: http://www.ecola.com/news/

Campus Newspapers on the Internet: http://beacon-asa.utk.edu/
resources/papers.html

Pathfinder (Time Warner publications): http://www.pathfinder.com

New York Times: http://www.nytimes.com

USA Today: http://www.usatoday.com

CNN Interactive: http://www.cnn.com

AP Wire Service: http://www.trib.com/NEWS/APwire.html.

U.S. News & World Report: http://www.usnews.com

Washington Post: http://www.washingtonpost.com/

Los Angeles Times: http://www.latimes.com/

Times of London: http://www.the-times.co.uk/

COMMUNICATION—GENERAL

American Communication Association:
http://www.uark.edu/depts/comminfo/www/ACA.html

Archives of American Public Address: http://douglass.speech.nwu.edu/

Historical Speeches Archive: http://www.webcorp.com/sounds/index.htm

National Communication Association: http://www.natcom.org
Gifts of Speech (speeches by women):
   http://ripley.wo.sbc.edu/departmental/library/gos/

SCIENCE—GENERAL

Scientific American: http://www.sciam.com/
Discovery: http://www.discovery.com
Science Frontiers: http://www.knowledge.co.uk/frontiers/

HUMANITIES—GENERAL

HNet: http://h-net2.msu.edu/
History Net: http://www.thehistorynet.com/
World Lecture Hall: http://www.utexas.edu/world/lecture/com/
Humanities Hub: http:// www.gu.edu.au/gwis/hub/hub.culture.html
Biography Find: http://www.biography.com/find.html
Edsitement: http://edsitement.neh.fed.us

PHILANTHROPIES AND CHARITIES

Better Business Bureau Philanthropy Advisory Service: http://
   www.igc.apc.org/cbbb/pas.html
Philanthropy Journal Online (links to charities):
   http://www.philanthropy~journal.org
Select Nonprofit organizations on Internet: http://www.fiu.edu/~time4chg/
   non-profit.html
CHARITIESUSA: http://www.charitiesusa.com
International Service Agencies: http://www.charity.org
United Way: http:// www.unitedway.org

DIVERSITY CONCERNS

American Demographics: http://www.demographics.com
Diversity University: http://www.du.org/places/du/
Diversity Links: http://www.latino.sscnet.ucla.edu/diversity/html#AA
NAACP: http://www.bin.com/assocorg/naacp/naacp.htm
Latino Web: http://www.catalog.com/favision/latnoweb.htm
Native American Information: http://www.freenet.ufl.edu/~native
Asian American Network: http://www.aaa.net rk
Jewish Family & Life: http://www.jewishfamily.com
Anti-Defamation League: http://www.adl.org/
B'nai B'rith: http://bnaibrith.org/ijm/

MEDIA LITERACY

Disinform: http:// www.disinform.com/disInfo/PROP/media/PROP_media.htm.
Center for Media Literacy: http://websites.earthlink.net/~cml

University of Oregon Media Literacy Project:
  http://interact.uoregon.edu/MediaLit/HomePage
Visual Literacy: http://www.pomona.edu/visual-lit/intro/html
New Mexico Media Literacy Project: http://www.aa.edu
Freedom of Information Center: http://www.missouri.edu/~foiwww

GOVERNMENT AND POLITICS

Great American Web Site (citizen's guide to government sites):
  http://www.uncle-sam.com
Central Intelligence Agency (World Fact Book): http://www.odci.gov/cia
Department of Justice (includes FBI): http://www.usdoj.gov/
Library of Congress (more than 70 million documents): http://www.loc.gov
United Nations: http://www.un.org
FedWorld Information Network: http://www.fedworld.gov/
U.S. Historical Documents: http://wiretap.spies.com/Gopher/Gov/us-history
U.S. Census Bureau: http://www.census.gov
White House: http://www.whitehouse.gov
U.S. House of Representatives: http://www.house.gov
Political Scientists Guide to the Internet:
  http://www.trincoll.edu/~pols/guide/home.html
First Amendment Center: http://www.freedomforum.org/first/welcome.
Political Commercials Archive: http://www.ou.edu/pcarchiv/
U.S. Senate: http://www.senate.gov
U.S. Department of Education: http://www.ed.gov
C-Span: http://www.c-span.org
Political Education for Everyday Life: http://english-www.cmu.edu/bs/

BUSINESS AND COMMERCE

Business Connections: http://www.nytimes.com/library/cyber/reference/buscom.html
Global Interactive Business Directory: http://www.pronett.com
Consumer Information Catalog: http://www.gsa.gov/staff/pa/cic/cic.htm
Netsearch Business Web Pages: http://www.netmail.com/
Business Netiquette International: http:// www.wp.com/fredfish/Netiq.html
Business Women's Network: http://www.tpag.com/bwn.html
Minority/Women's Business Connection: http://www.mwbe.com/mwbe/default.htm
Business Week: http://www.businessweek.com

LANGUAGE

American Slanguage: http:// www.slanguage.com
StreetSpeak: http://www.jayi.com/jayi/Fishnet/StreetSpeak
Quotations: http://www.cc.columbia.edu/aci/bartleby/bartlett
Roget's Thesaurus: http://humanities.uchicago.edu/forms_unrest/ROGET.html
Jack Lynch's Grammar Notes: http://www.english.upenn.edu/~jlynch/grammar.html
ERIC Clearinghouse on Reading, English, and Communication:
http://www.indiana.edu/~eric_rec/

LEGAL CONCERNS

Findlaw: http://www.findlaw.com
LawInfo: http:// www.lawinfo.com/
Internet Legal Resource Guide: http://uts.cc.utexas.edu/~juris/
Law Journal Extra!: http://www.ljx.com/
West's Legal Directory: http://www.wld.com/
Decisions of U.S. Supreme Court: http://www.law.cornell.edu/supct/supct.table.html

RELIGION

The Bible Browser: http://goon.stg.brown.edu/bible_browser/pbeasy.shtml
Comparative Religion: http://weber.u.washington.edu/~madin
First Church of Cyberspace: http://execpc.com/~chender
The Vatican: http://www.vatican.va
Episcopal Church Home Page: http://www.ai.mit.edu/people/mib/anglican/
    anglican.html
United Methodist Information: http://www.umc.org
Society of Friends: http://www.misc.org/geeks/bnorum/quaker
Unitarian Universalist Association: http://www.una.org

NOTES 1.   This list of periodicals includes some of the less familiar magazines and journals that may be useful for speech preparation. Check your library's periodicals catalog for other possibilities.

APPENDIX B:
INTERVIEWING

You suddenly discover that your checkbook balance is low—you need more money to live on while you're in school. Summer vacation is coming up, and you want to do something with your time that is constructive, not to mention making some money to help defray next year's expenses. You've just filled out your "Intent to Graduate Form" when it suddenly dawns on you, "Now, I've got to find a job." Any of these situations sound familiar? If so, you may soon find yourself being interviewed for a job.

Applying for almost any position will involve a job interview. Your ability to conduct yourself well in a selection interview will play a large role in determining whether or not you are offered a position. Indeed, given almost equal qualifications in terms of training and experience, the job interview is the single most important factor in selection decisions.[1] In Chapter 10, we discussed interviewing from the perspective of how to plan and conduct an interview to gain responsible knowledge of a topic. In this appendix, we change the focus from you as the interviewer to you as the person being interviewed.

Many of the skills you are learning in this course should help improve your interviewing abilities. The interview situation combines aspects of both interpersonal and public communication. For example, the material on self-awareness in Chapter 5 should help you take stock of your personal strengths and weaknesses. The discussion in Chapter 7 on the distinction between tactful and tactless communication should help you phrase your responses more acceptably in interview interactions. Similarly, the material on audience analysis and research in Chapter 10 should help you devise an interview strategy that presents you in the best possible light. In Chapter 11 you learned how to develop examples to use in a speech. In interviews you may be asked for behavioral examples to demonstrate that you can handle a variety of work situations. These are just some of the ways in which the material from this text can be adapted to meet your needs in an interview.

Although much of the material in this appendix may sound like just plain old common sense, it is amazing what dumb or unthinking things some people do in job interviews.[2] For example, during an interview one candidate wore a Walkman, saying "I can listen to you and the music at the same time!" Perhaps the applicant believed that this showed versatility. Another candidate, who had missed lunch, ate a hamburger and french fries during the interview. One claimed that he would demonstrate corporate loyalty by having the company logo tattooed on his arm, and another asked to use the phone to call her counselor for advice on how to answer a specific interview question.

Let's look first at what selection interviews are and the various types of selection interviewing situations you might encounter. A selection interview can involve a person from outside the organization who is seeking employment or a current employee who is looking to change jobs or gain a promotion.

Selecting a person for a position typically begins with a short *screening interview,* which may be conducted in a college placement setting, on-site at the organization where the opening exists, or, in our high-tech age, on the Internet or via E-mail. A screening interview may run anywhere from fifteen minutes to half an hour in length; the questions will be very general. It will probably be conducted by a trained human resource specialist who works for the organization. The screening interview is used to weed out unqualified candidates, so as a job seeker you must take this very seriously. As one human resource specialist put it, "It is not enough just to 'show up' for the interviews and hope that someone will miraculously offer you a job. You have to perform at your peak to gain any mileage from on-campus interviewing."[3] Don't give the interviewer a reason to disqualify you. Figure B.1 lists some of the things that turn interviewers off on job candidates.[4]

If you make it through a screening interview, you may expect to move on to a full-fledged *employment interview,* which is typically conducted on-site by a departmental manager. Depending on the level of the position and the personnel policies of the organization, you may be interviewed one-on-one by a manager, sequentially by several managers, or in a *panel interview* where you respond to questions from several interviewers at the same time. If the job you are applying for involves a high degree of stress, such as a position as a customer service representative or emergency service worker, you may be subjected to a *stress interview* to determine how well you can function when the going gets rough.

When I (Osborn) was working in the human resources department of a large metropolitan city government, the standing joke about the Fire Department's interview format was that the chief would ask a candidate three questions: (1) Why do you want to be a fireman? (2) Who are you kin to in the department? and (3) Who did you vote for in the last election? Fortunately, those days are gone forever. Most companies now train any management personnel who may be conducting employment interviews to perform what are called behavioral interviews. In a *behavioral interview,* the interviewer asks the candidate to supply specific examples that demonstrate that he or she has specific skills, abilities, or personality characteristics that are considered relevant to the position for which the person has applied. Oftentimes these skills, abilities, or characteristics have been identified through a job analysis based on what organizational psychologists call a critical incidents technique. Later in this chapter we will supply you with a list of the types of characteristics that may be looked for in behavioral interviews and some typical questions that might be asked.

1. Has a cocky, arrogant attitude
2. Exaggerates accomplishments
3. Doesn't listen or respond to feedback
4. Interrupts the interviewer
5. Isn't courteous
6. Seems bored
7. Shows up late for the interview
8. Speaks poorly of others
9. Lacks confidence
10. Knows nothing about the company
11. Evades questions
12. Gives canned answers
13. Drones on when a simple answer would do
14. Doesn't ask questions
15. Uses improper grammar or mispronounces words
16. Is inappropriately dressed or groomed
17. Seems artificially animated
18. Avoids eye-contact with the interviewer
19. Has a limp or overly strong handshake
20. Has poor table manners

FIGURE **B.1**
Interview Turn-offs

SO YOU'RE GOING TO AN INTERVIEW

In Chapter 10 we presented a flow chart of the steps involved in the preparation of a speech and the order in which these steps should be taken. Here, we will apply this same technique to preparing yourself for an interview. In preparing for an interview, the first phase of this model is most applicable. Although you will not be outlining a presentation, you can anticipate the type of questions you might be asked in an interview and practice responding to them.

The first steps in interview preparation include taking stock of those aspects of your training and experience that are most relevant to the job, setting your objectives for the interview, analyzing the situation and audience, and conducting research to acquire responsible knowledge about the organization and the job.

TAKING STOCK OF YOUR ASSETS

In most employment interviews, you will be asked a variety of questions centering on your interests, skills, and abilities; your strengths and weaknesses; your accomplishments; and your career aspirations. You may be asked such questions as:

- Why did you choose this college?
- How did you decide on your major?
- Why do you want to work for us?
- What are your strengths?
- What are your weaknesses?
- What have you done that you are most proud of?
- What do you want to be doing ten years from now?
- What is the greatest challenge you have faced? How did you handle this?

You will respond to such questions more effectively if you sit down and take stock of yourself beforehand. Prepare a Self-analysis Worksheet like the one shown in Figure B.2. Under each heading, try to come up with at least four responses. Use your résumé to stimulate your thinking. Take into account the courses you've had, your extracurricular activities, and any paid work, internships, or volunteer activities that might be relevant to a job. Once you have made your lists, think of an example that will illustrate each item. Interviewers do not want one-word responses to their questions. As we noted earlier, they want concrete examples based on things you have done.

STRENGTHS	WEAKNESSES	SKILLS
Planning and organizing	Easily angered	Writing ability
Stay with things til done	One-track mind	Computer-competent
Quick learner	Do too much myself	Piano playing
Loyal to friends	Too loyal to friends?	Track athlete
ACCOMPLISHMENTS	**INTERESTS**	**CAREER GOALS**
Valedictorian, high school	Music (concerts)	Write corporate newsletters
Editor, campus newspaper	Reading	Director of Corporate Communications
3.5 GPA	Work with children	
H.S. all-state track team		

FIGURE B.2
Self-Analysis Worksheet

A note of caution: *Do not memorize these examples!* Looking at Figure B.1, we see that interviewers do not like "canned" or obviously pre-prepared and memorized answers. Additionally, an example that you have written out and memorized may not exactly fit an interviewer's question, so it can sound either irrelevant or as though you are evading the question. You must also be careful as you develop possible responses to questions about your weaknesses. In discussing a weakness or past mistake, try to mention only something that is not directly relevant to the job in question, then phrase it as a challenge or growth opportunity. Tailor examples to show you overcame the problem or learned a valuable lesson from the experience.

DETERMINING YOUR OBJECTIVES

During selection interviews, the interviewer and the job candidate have different, but complementary, objectives. The interviewer's objectives are (1) to describe the company and job in such a way that the candidate will want to work in that job for the company, and (2) to evaluate the candidate to determine if she or he is qualified and if the company would like to have that person as an employee. The candidate must (1) convince the interviewer that his or her credentials qualify him or her for the position, and (2) evaluate the job and the company to see if he or she would like to work there. In short, the interview is basically a "sales meeting, and the product you are pushing is yourself."[5]

Another way of looking at the first of these candidate objectives is to think about how you can put your best foot forward in an interview. Remember, you only have one chance to make a first impression, so make it a good one. It may be helpful to review the concept of ethos that we developed earlier in this book. People tend to consider four basic factors as they evaluate others: (1) their competence, (2) their integrity, (3) their likableness, and (4) their dynamism. Let's look at how you might optimize these in an employment interview situation.

Competence. Interviewers will look at a variety of different things in assessing your competence. They will consider such things as your background experience and training as revealed on your résumé.[6] They will also look at how well your résumé is prepared. Think of your résumé as a presentation aid (see Chapter 11). Does it look neat? Is it well organized? Is it printed on high-quality paper? Is it free from glaring errors of spelling and grammar? Don't be like one hapless applicant who wrote, "I have lurnt Word Perfect 6.0, computor and spreadsheat progroms."[7] Run the grammar and spelling checker on your computer before you prepare your final draft. Be sure you have enough white space: Leave adequate margins on both sides and at the top and bottom of the page. If you need help preparing your résumé, contact your campus placement center.

Interviewers will also assess your competence in terms of how you look—how well you are groomed and the way you are dressed.[8] Although final hiring decisions are rarely determined by these factors, they weigh strongly in the first impression that you make. An employment interview is a special occasion, and you should treat it as such. Be sure you are impeccably groomed. It should go without saying that you should be clean. You can't go straight from a PE class to a campus interview without taking a shower. Your hair should be neat and businesslike. Be careful about hairstyles that fall down over your eyes. Continually brushing them away can be an unnecessary distraction. Your nails should be clean and neatly trimmed. Women should avoid bright or dark nail polish. Makeup should be subtle and understated. You should avoid strong perfumes or aftershave.

You should dress conservatively for the occasion—a suit or sports jacket, dress shirt, and tie for men and a skirted suit or tailored dress for women. Your clothes should be clean, neatly pressed, and well fitting. Both men and women should wear dress shoes— no sneakers, sandals, or boat shoes. Men should wear socks and women should wear hose regardless of how hot it is. Jewelry should be kept to a minimum. If you have any question about the proper dress for an interview with a company, ask someone in your campus placement service for advice or call the human resources office at the company and ask them about the standard work attire in their company. Dressing appropriately is a sign of respect—respect for yourself, for the situation, and for the interviewer. Take advantage of this opportunity to present yourself in a positive light.

Initial impressions of competence are also based on how well you talk. Is your voice pleasant to listen to? Do you pronounce words correctly? Do you use the right words to say what you mean? Do you sound conversational as you answer questions? In short, do you sound like a literate, educated person? As in a public speech, in an interview you want to speak a little more formally than you would in casual conversation. You should be careful about words you sometimes mispronounce, avoid slang, and not try out new polysyllabic words of which you are not sure of the meaning.

Answer all questions to the best of your ability. If a question seems complicated, rephrase it and play it back to the interviewer before you answer. For example, you might say something like, "You want to know how my experience as a camp counselor might relate to my ability to handle the diverse customers I'd have to deal with?" Let your inflection pattern pose this as a question rather than a statement, then look for feedback (a nod or an uh-huh) before you proceed with an answer. Don't just pull out some response that you've worked out in advance that is somehow tangentially related to the question. It may sound as though you are evading the question or you are coming out of left field. Keep your answers simple and to the point. Follow part of our formula for impromptu speaking: Make a statement and support it with an example or reason. Don't drone on and on until you put the interviewer to sleep.

Last, but not least, you should know what you are talking about. Never apply for a job for which you know you are not qualified. If you don't understand a question, ask for clarification. If you are asked a question that you cannot handle, admit it—but let the interviewer know that you are willing to learn. Finally, it is vital that you know something about the company and the job for which you are applying. We cover this area in greater detail in our discussion of audience analysis and the search for responsible knowledge.

Integrity. It is very important to be honest in a job interview. In addition to the fact that lying is unethical, there is another very good reason for being scrupulously honest about your credentials: If you get a job through misrepresentation of either your credentials or your motivations, there is a strong likelihood that you will be misplaced. You may end up in a job that you hate and/or one in which you perform poorly—a lose-lose situation to be avoided at all costs.[9] Also, if you start out with "stretched" credentials, you will have to maintain this fiction consistently throughout the interview. Most job applicants, especially those who feel they must make themselves look more qualified than they actually are, cannot carry this off very well. Inconsistencies in interview information generally result in the applicant's being disqualified.

Don't misrepresent your credentials. Be sure that everything that you put in your résumé or job application or say in an interview will hold up under scrutiny. Employers do check references. They may ask for a transcript to determine the applicability of your education. Companies also contact previous employers to verify the positions you held and the length of time you worked for a company. If any discrepancies arise between what you claim and what the employer finds out, you will probably be disqualified. If the discrepancy is discovered after you have been hired, you will probably be fired.

Another thing to avoid is exaggerating your experience or your contributions in past jobs. Note in Figure B.1 that exaggerating accomplishments is one of the interviewer turnoffs. This also can make you seem cocky and arrogant—another turnoff, which gives this tactic a double whammy! At best you will seem slightly ridiculous. Human resource specialists call the tendency to exaggerate the *coffee-machine syndrome:* "the affliction of a junior clerk who claimed success for an Apollo space mission based on his relationships with certain scientists, established at the coffee machine."[10] Don't make yourself the butt of interviewers' jokes!

One of the major nonverbal behaviors associated with integrity in our country is eye contact. As we noted in both Chapters 3 and 13, failure to make or sustain eye contact can suggest disinterest or emotional discomfort. It may also indicate that you are trying to hide something. On the other hand, too much uninterrupted eye contact (staring) can make the recipient uncomfortable. Our best advice is that the amount of eye contact you have with an interviewer should be similar to the amount of eye contact you have with an audience in public speaking. Eye contact is most important when you are talking to someone. You can look away or avert your eyes when you are concentrating or thinking of an answer.

Likableness. To win a job, it is not enough just to seem competent and honest. You must also seem likable. Likable people are positive and optimistic. They manifest many of the characteristics of immediacy that we discussed in Chapter 13. They smile a lot, maintain appropriate eye contact, talk and gesture naturally, and seem generally relaxed with others. Likable people may be self-confident, but they don't act superior or snobbish. Let your confidence show through in the poise with which you answer questions, but don't brag about yourself.

Likable people also are not given to complaining about or being highly critical of others. One question most interviewers will ask is, "How well did you get along with your boss?" Even if you worked for an absolutely impossible person, never tell an interviewer that. Remember the advice your mother gave you: "If you can't say something nice about someone, don't say anything at all." Think of the nicest thing possible about your boss and base your answer on that. Never volunteer negative information about other people, about past jobs, or about yourself.

Courtesy and good manners weigh heavily in determining whether you are labeled likable. The first act of courtesy you can perform is arriving for your interview on time. This will also affect your perceived competence in terms of how well you can find your way around and how responsible you are. If you are being interviewed on-site at a company, be sure you know how to get there, whether or not public transportation is available, and, if you will be driving, where you will park. If possible, make a "dry run" ahead of time so that you know how much time to allot. Always plan to arrive at the site *at least* fifteen minutes before your scheduled interview. This will give you time to go to the rest room to freshen up. Bring some serious reading material in case you are kept waiting. (Do not bring that trashy novel you may be reading or copies of *Playgirl* or *Soldier of Fortune.*) If you run into an emergency that might delay you, like a wreck that has traffic tied up, find some way to get to a phone and let people know that you will be late, why this is the case, and when they can expect you.

You can also demonstrate courtesy by learning the interviewer's name and using it during the interview. To help remember that name, use it as soon as you hear it. Unless you are told otherwise, do not call the interviewer by his or her first name.

Everybody likes a good listener. Listening attentively is also a sign of courtesy. Listen to a question all the way through before you try to answer it. Whatever you do, don't interrupt the interviewer. Be certain you understand the question before you frame your answer. Review our suggestions for handling questions and answers in Chapter 13 and use what is applicable to the employment interview situation. Maintain eye contact while the interviewer is talking to you and use what you see, as well as what you hear, as feedback. Refer back to the material on adapting to audience feedback in Chapter 13 for more specific suggestions in this area.

If you are being interviewed sequentially by several people in a company, you may be taken out for lunch or dinner. Consider this part of the interview. Do not assume that because everyone is eating, you are no longer being evaluated. Be very careful about your table manners. This is not the time to pig out, even if you are taken to an all-you-can-eat buffet. Order lightly. Select food that is easily digestible, and stay away from things like spaghetti (should you twirl it, cut it with your fork, or slurp it into your mouth?) or fried chicken (which you might be tempted to eat with your fingers).

Dynamism. The amount of enthusiasm you show during an interview is very important. Companies like to hire people who obviously want to work for them and who are energetic enough to tackle tough jobs.[11] The interviewer's evaluation of your dynamism will probably begin with your initial handshake. It should be firm and businesslike. Your hand should not seem limp and lifeless like a dead fish, nor should the receiver of your handshake feel as though he or she needs an orthopedic specialist to repair the damaged bones and muscles. Practice your handshake with a friend until it feels comfortable.

A second factor that affects the perception of your dynamism is how energetic you seem. Perhaps you're not a morning person—you're the type who needs four cups of coffee to get you going, and you're really not at your best until after 11:00 A.M.—yet you find yourself scheduled for an 8:00 A.M. onsite interview. You know it will take you at least thirty minutes to get to the site—make that forty-five minutes to allow for rush hour traffic. This means you have to be ready to go by 7:15 in the morning! How can you possibly handle this? Try to change your sleeping and waking habits several days before the scheduled interview. For example, if you usually go to bed at two o'clock and get up at ten o'clock, move your bedtime back to one and set the alarm for nine the first night, then drag yourself out of the sack no matter how traumatic it seems. Keep changing your timetable until you have worked back to an eleven-to-six schedule for a couple of nights. Even though you may still feel a little sleepy when you get up, the adrenaline from the excitement of an interview should give you an extra boost.

It will be difficult for you to seem enthusiastic about a job you don't want. As we noted earlier, commitment to a subject is important in public speaking. You have to feel some personal enthusiasm if you are to be effective. The same holds true in an employment interview. Don't schedule an interview for a job that you know you really don't want or that you know you really are not qualified for. If you do this, you probably will *be* bored, and you will *sound* bored. You will just be wasting your time and the interviewer's time as well.

Enthusiasm is also conveyed through the way you use your voice and body to communicate. Are your vocal patterns varied, or are you speaking in a monotone? Do you gesture naturally, or are you sitting on your hands? Does your posture tell the interviewer that you are alert and interested? How does this fit in with the turnoff in Figure B.1, "Seems artificially animated"? Our best advice is, aim for improved conversation.

You want to sound natural, but not quite as animated as you might be in an exuberant conversation with your friends. Tone things down just a little and you will probably strike the right note.

ANALYZING THE AUDIENCE AND GAINING RESPONSIBLE KNOWLEDGE

These two components of interview preparation go hand-in-hand. The more you know about the job for which you are applying and the company in which the job is located, the better your chances for landing the job.[12] Surprisingly, only about 5 percent of job applicants take the time to do any research on a company before an interview.[13] Preparing yourself in this way can help you stand out from the crowd. Additionally, researching the position and the company in advance can help you anticipate many of the questions you may be asked in an interview.[14] It can also help you frame questions you might wish to ask the interviewer.

As you do research on a company, you should try to learn about the company's history, its products or services, its market position, its top executives, its major competitors, and its plans for growth. Look through the company's annual report if one is available. Gaining responsible knowledge of the position and the company is worth all the time it will take you to do this. So how should you begin?

If you are scheduling a campus interview, check first with your campus placement service. It may well have copies of the job descriptions for the positions it is listing and a variety of brochures or other materials about the company. This should be your starting point.

A second source of timely and reliable information on companies is the Internet. You can run a search using the company's name. This may yield the company's URL or sites with recent information about the company. To get an outside perspective on current company news, run the search engine for the business pages of the *New York Times Online* (http://www.nytimes.com) or the *Wall Street Journal Online* (http://www.wsj.com). If the company is a small regional or local company, check the archives of newspapers in the city or state where the company is located (find links to these newspapers on line at Ecola Newsstand at http://www.ecola.com). Lists of corporate Web sites as well as information on specific companies may be found at the following locations:

Internic Whois	http://www.internic.net/wp/whois.html
Hoover Online	http://www.hoovers.com
U.S. S.E.C.	http://www.sec.gov
Edgar Online	http://www.edgar-online.com
BizWeb	http://www.bizweb.com
Companies Online	http://www.companiesOnline.com
Inc. magazine	http://www.inc.com
Fortune	http://www.pathfinder.com
NetPartners	http://www.netpart.com/resource/search.html

These sites may contain lists of employment opportunities within the company, complete with thumbnail job descriptions of available positions. You may also find useful information on new and fast-breaking developments in the field as well as in the company.

You can also find information on companies in your campus library. Some library resources that might be helpful include the latest editions of the following:

The Information Please Business Almanac and Sourcebook
The Business One Irwin Business and Investment Almanac
Business Rankings and Salary Index
Dun's Directory of Service Companies
Louis Rukeyser's Business Almanac
Moody's Industrial Manual
Standard and Poor's Register of Corporations, Directors, and Executives
The Job Vault: The One-Stop Job Search Resource

Prepare for an interview as thoroughly and conscientiously as you would for a speech. It will pay off in the end.

ANTICIPATING INTERVIEW QUESTIONS

Well, now, we know you're thinking, "I've taken stock of myself, determined my objectives, and acquired at least a fair amount of responsible knowledge about the job and the company, but how on earth will I know what kind of questions I will be asked?" Earlier in this appendix, we mentioned several stock questions you can expect to be asked in a screening interview. Is there anything else you should prepare for? Yes.

For starters, the interviewer may begin by looking over your résumé or job application and asking questions based on the information you provide. Look over your own résumé and see what questions you might want answered if you were considering hiring this person for a job. Are there any gaps in employment? What were you doing at that time? Were there any interruptions in education? Why did these occur? Does this GPA reflect your true ability? Once you feel you can adequately answer questions like these, take a look at the job description for the position you seek. What skills, abilities, experience, education, or personal characteristics might be relevant to success in this job? The answer to this last question will help you to anticipate the types of questions you might be asked in a behavioral interview. The ten general job-related interview dimensions in the following list are indicative of the factors and questions that might be considered.

1. *Achievement motivation:* the desire to be successful, accomplish something of significance, and set high standards for one's own performance.

   Everyone has a "secret ambition," something he or she would like to be if there were no constraints such as money, time, or talent. Tell me about your secret ambition.

   How do you define success? How do you know when you have done a good job?

2. *Flexibility:* the ability to adapt to changing situations and different people.

   Have you ever worked in a job that did not match well with your abilities, likes, or interests? Tell me how you handled this.

   Have you ever been described as "hard-headed"? By whom? Why? Do you agree with this description?

3. *Organization and planning skills:* the ability to establish a course of action that leads to a specific goal.

   How do you schedule your time on an average work or school day?

   When you have a great deal to do, how do you keep track of things that require your attention?

4. *Leadership potential:* the ability to take charge, directing the activities of others toward a goal.

   Tell me about a situation in which you had to step in and take charge during a problem. What did you do? How did others react? How did things turn out?

   Why do you think you would be an effective leader?

5. *Integrity:* the ability to maintain social, ethical, and organizational standards.

   Tell me about a time when you were pressured by colleagues or friends to disclose confidential information. How did you react? How did you feel?

   Almost everyone has told a "white lie" from time to time and gotten caught in this. Tell me about a time when this has happened to you.

6. *Decisiveness:* the ability to make decisions and take action when necessary.

   Tell me about a situation in which you had to stand up for a decision you made, even though it made you unpopular. How did you react? How did you feel?

   You made a decision that you thought was right, even though it was unpopular. A week later some evidence surfaced that made you question your original position, and you now think it was wrong. What would you do?

7. *Dependability:* the willingness to stay with a job until it is completed and to conform to acceptable standards of attendance and punctuality.

   Tell me about a time when you had to put in extra hours or go beyond what was normally called for to complete a project or job. How did you feel about this?

   What do you think are legitimate reasons for missing work or classes? How many times were you absent from work or classes last year? What were the reasons?

8. *Energy:* the stamina and ability to maintain a high activity level.

   Tell me about your most physically demanding job or leisure activity. How often do you do this? How much do you like it?

   If you knew this job would require you to work fifty hours per week for the next four months, would you still be interested in it? Why or why not?

9. *Initiative:* the willingness to originate action and act independently within the scope of assigned accountability.

   What obstacles have you had to overcome to get where you are today? How did you do this?

   Do you consider yourself to be a "self-starter," or are you better at implementing the ideas of others?

10. *Interpersonal skills:* the ability to work well with others in different and varying situations.

    Some people are easier than others to work with or work for. Tell me about the kind of person you like to work with and the kind you like to work for.

In addition to such general behavioral questions, you can anticipate additional questions related to specific disciplines or a specific job. An excellent resource for familiarizing yourself with such material is *Adams Job Interview Almanac and CD-ROM* (Adams Media Corporation, 1997). This book lists specific questions for you to consider that are related to seventy-five different jobs in fourteen different work areas. The almanac is sold with a CD-ROM to allow interactive practice in answering these questions.

Finally, you must practice for your interview. Make out a list of potential questions and then ask your roommate or a friend to run you through a mock interview. Be sure to have this person follow up your answers with probes for more information. This type of interview preparation should help you perform better in those situations where much is at stake.

NOTES

1. Joanne M. Coletta-Levine, "Job Seekers Must Walk Fine Line in Interviews," Career Resources, Townonline, 28 July, 1996, downloaded 13 May, 1998; http://www.tononline.com/working/careerres/jc072896.html.

2. For additional funny and not-so-funny examples, see, "Job Interview Shenanigans," http://www.oberlin.edu/~consult/jeremy/text/hob.html.

3. "On-Campus Interview Success," College Grad Job Hunter, Copyright Quantum Leap Publishing 1998, downloaded 6 May, 1998, http://www.collegegrad.com/book/17-0.html.

4. These characteristics are a compilation of those gleaned from personal experience as a human relations specialist in business and from the following sources: Coletta-Levine, "Job Seekers Must Walk Fine Line in Interviews"; "The Ten Most Common Mistakes People Make During Their Interviews," Careercity, copyright 1996, 1997, Adams Media Corporation, downloaded 13 May, 1998, http://www.careercity.com/hot/experts/artrose/artten.asp; "MBAs Who Tell Stories Get a Jump on the Job Search," JobWeb, copyright 1996 National Association of Colleges and Employers, downloaded 16 May, 1998, http://www.jobweb.org/Pubs/Pr/1025N2.HTM; and "Interview Training," Vanderbilt University Career Center, undated, downloaded 16 May, 1998, http://www.vanderbilt.edu/career/inttr.htm.

5. Sabra Chartrand, "The Art of Selling Yourself in an Interview," *New York Times Online*, Job Market, 1 September, 1996, downloaded 15 May, 1998, http://www.nytimes.com/library/jobmarket/0901sabra.html.

6. "Selling Yourself: Write a Winning Resume," Monumental General Insurance Group Getting Past Go; 21 July, 1997, downloaded 13 May, 1998, http://www.mongen.com/getgo/sell.html.

7. Anne Fisher, "Stupid Resume Tricks: How to Avoid Getting Hired," Smart Managing, *Fortune Online*, 21 July, 1997, downloaded 15 May, 1998, http://www.pathfinder.com/fortune/1997/970721/ask2.html.

8. Barbara Mulligan, "Dressing the Part," Job Choices on Line, JobWeb, undated, downloaded 16 May, 1998, http://www.jobweb.org/JCOnline/features/newinterview/dresh.shtml; Manchester Partners International, "Dress

for Success and Other Interview Do's," Career Resources, Townonline, posted 26 May, 1996, downloaded 7 May, 1998, http://www.townonline.com/working/careerres/js052696.html; and "Dressing for Success," CareerCity, copyright 1996, 1997, Adams Media Corporation, downloaded 13 May, 1998, http://www.careercity.com/hot/getjob/prep/dres2.asp.

9. "Landing the Job You Want Reveals Interview Techniques Learned from Experts," Career Resources, Townonline, 23 February, 1997, downloaded 7 May, 1998, http://www.townonline.com/working/careerres/022397p4a.htm.

10. "Ten Interview Questions," Careercity, copyright 1996, 1997, Adams Media Corporation, downloaded 13 May, 1998, http://www.careercity.com/hot/getjob/intervie/tenquest.asp.

11. Wendy S. Enelow, "Job Interviews," Catapult JobWeb, copyright 1995 National Association of Colleges and Employers, downloaded 13 May, 1998, http://www.jobweb.org/catapult/enelow-i.html; and Coletta-Levine, "Job Seekers Must Walk Fine Line in Interviews."

12. "Landing the Job You Want Reveals Interview Techniques Learned from Experts," Career Resources, Townonline, 23 February, 1997, downloaded 7 May, 1998, http://www.townonline.com/working/careerres/022397p4a.htm.

13. Manchester Partners International, "Dress for Success and Other Interview Do's."

14. Joyce Lain Kennedy, "Women, Display Confidence in Job Interviews," Career Resources, Townonline, 11 December, 1997, downloaded 7 May, 1998, http://www.townonline.com/working/careerres/121197p1.html.

APPENDIX C:
PROFILES OF THE 16 MYERS-BRIGGS TYPES[1]

A s stated in the text, the descriptions given in Chapter 5 may or may not be sufficient to allow you to identify your type. Thus, care must be taken when consulting a particular profile for insights to the self—you may or may not be consulting the correct profile. For a more valid indicator of your own type, various questionnaires are available.

The primary reason for presenting these profiles is not to provide you with individual analysis, but rather to point out the range of "normal differences" among individuals of all types. Browse through all of the profiles to see how all sixteen types have particular strengths, tendencies, and idiosyncrasies; both communication-related and otherwise.

ISTJ

Percentage of population. About 6%.

General traits. ISTJ types have a strong sense of responsibility. They are generally quiet, private, and reserved. They are diligent, thorough, and dependable. They are also organized, practical, and self-reliant, having the ability to get things done without being distracted. They do their work without drawing attention to themselves, so their efforts and contributions sometimes go unappreciated.

Communication strengths. ISTJs often have excellent interpersonal skills.

Potential communication difficulties. ISTJs often expect a bottom-line, no-nonsense response from others, and some communication partners will have difficulty with this. They distrust ostentatiousness and may not be as receptive as they should be to those whose tastes are not as practical as their own.

ISTP

Percentage of population. About 6%.

General traits. ISTP types are quiet, reserved, and objective. They can be very loyal to "their own," and can be quite insubordinate to others, preferring to "do their own thing" rather than to play by others' rules. They are interested in cause and effect, may be mechanically inclined, and often enjoy participating in sports and thrill-seeking activities such as skiing and skydiving. They are keenly observant and analytical and like to organize facts logically.

Communication strengths. ISTPs have a quiet sense of humor that others find endearing.

Potential communication difficulties. ISTPs often are less developed than others in verbal skills, preferring instead to "communicate" through action.

ISFJ

Percentage of population. About 6%.

General traits. ISFJ types are usually very concerned about the feelings of others, and they do everything in their power to help others. They are good with details, facts, and figures and have a strong sense of duty. They have perseverance and are very responsible, meticulous, and conscientious. ISFJs dislike arrogance, putting on of airs, and other façades regarding social or economic station.

Communication strengths. ISFJs are loyal friends. They relate especially well when people are in need of help.

Potential communication difficulties. ISFJs are sometimes attracted to irresponsible mates (for example those with alcohol or other dependency problems), believing their motive to be one of rescue when it is really one of reform, and thus may experience corresponding relational difficulties.

ISFP

Percentage of population. About 5%.

General traits. ISFP types are tolerant unless one of their inner values is compromised. They thrive on harmony. They care about others deeply, but they usually show their feelings by their actions, not their words. They tend to avoid being leaders, but they are loyal followers, usually rather modest about their achievements. They enjoy starting many projects. They are quiet but friendly. They get what needs to be done accomplished but do not like to be rushed.

Communication strengths. The ISFP is the kindest of all the types, and the kindness is unconditional. The ISFP is especially sensitive to the pain and suffering of others, and has sympathy beyond that of any of the other types.

Potential communication difficulties. The ISFP is probably the most misunderstood of all the types. This comes in part from the ISFP's tendency not to express him/herself directly. ISFPs shun disagreements, hesitate to force their opinions on others, and tend to give up rather easily on efforts at verbal expression.

INFJ

Percentage of population. About 1%.

General traits. INFJ types are quietly efficient and are great problem solvers. They enjoy being creative and tend to generate many new ideas. They value harmony and seek the approval of others. They have very strong convictions based on their personal values. They put effort into what they do and feel a need to serve humanity in a useful, orderly way. The future and plans for the future are more important than the present.

Communication strengths. INFJs have strong empathy for others' emotions or intentions. They listen well, and are cooperative with others. They handle people empathetically and sympathetically, and tend to ignore unpleasant or unflattering facts about those with whom they are dealing. They can be elegant in their communication, having a talent for using language with a personalized style.

Potential communication difficulties. Since INFJs are private and tend not to disclose except with those they especially trust, others find it hard to get to know them. INFJs find conflict especially unpleasant and difficult. They are easily hurt by criticism, and may become despondent if subjected to frequent criticism.

INFP

Percentage of population. About 1%.

General traits. INFP types are idealistic and true to their personal convictions. They prefer working alone, and although they are friendly, being sociable is not very important to them. They have a tendency to take on more than they can reasonably accomplish. They are more concerned with helping others than with collecting possessions or controlling their surroundings. Once they accept you as a friend, you are a friend for life. They are flexible and enjoy doing things on the spur of the moment.

Communication strengths. Despite INFPs' tendency to maintain their psychological distance, they are well aware of others, aware of others' feelings, and relate well.

Potential communication difficulties. INFPs may have difficulty in expressing affection directly. They communicate interest and affection indirectly, but need to ensure that their indirect messages are indeed received and understood.

INTJ

Percentage of population. About 1%.

General traits. INTJs are the most individualistic, self-confident, and independent of all the types. They are also the least impressed by authority, rank, or title. They value knowledge and competence. They are introspective, analytical, and often skeptical. They look for ways to improve practically everything and can be very determined. They are quiet, forceful leaders. Their daring intuition and their insights make them see the big picture.

Communication strengths. INTJs are very logical, able to see the "big picture" as well as the connections of subparts that have constructed it; and when they remember that the logic is not always so obvious to others, they can explain it well.

Potential communication difficulties. INTJs often trivialize interpersonal rituals designed to put partners at ease. For example, they often view small talk as wasted time, unknowingly signaling a sense of being anxious to terminate the interaction. Psychological distance is sometimes created in INTJs' relationships because others feel that the INTJ can see right through them, and also feel that they are not up to the high standards the INTJ tends to demand of him/herself and others.

INTP

Percentage of population. About 1%.

General traits. INTP types are more interested in ideas than in people. They have a thirst for knowledge for its own sake rather than for practical uses or human concerns.

They tend to be quiet people who dislike large parties and small talk. They are introspective and like using logic and analysis to solve problems. They often do well in theoretical or scientific areas. They are flexible and open-minded concerning new ideas and possibilities.

Communication strengths. INTPs are cooperative, compliant, and easy to get along with. Their logic and analytical ability can be valuable in relevant contexts.

Potential communication difficulties. INTPs' messages are often difficult for others to understand because they are stated in a way that is too complicated to follow. Often INTPs could benefit by simplifying their statements. Often INTPs find it difficult to express their emotions, at least verbally. They may need to attempt such expression nevertheless, to prevent the mate or partner from feeling that he or she is being taken for granted.

ESTP

Percentage of population. About 13%.

General traits. ESTP types live for the moment. They do not worry, do not hurry, but simply enjoy whatever comes along. They are action-oriented people who want to be moving and doing instead of pondering and planning. They like hands-on tasks and would rather assemble a project on their own than read the directions or listen to explanations. When faced with problems, they work quickly to solve them. Socially, they have many friends and are openly accepting of others and themselves. For many ESTPs, deep commitments are hard to come by. Unknowingly, perhaps, ESTPs often base their friendships upon what there is to gain from them.

Communication strengths. ESTPs are sensitive to others' nonverbal cues, and quick to infer others' motives (although sometimes inaccurately). The typical ESTP is attentive to his/her mate in public, and is smooth and charming in social situations.

Potential communication difficulties. ESTPs often have a low tolerance for, and are poor listeners to, others' long explanations geared toward complete understanding of a problem or situation. They tend to tune in only to information that can be used for the ends they have in mind.

ESTJ

Percentage of population. About 13%.

General traits. ESTJ types are realistic as well as practical. They have a high regard for organization, efficiency, scheduling, projects, data, and decision making. They are determined and tough-minded. They frequently rise to positions of responsibility. They make good administrators and leaders as long as they can remember that their way is not necessarily the only way, and to value others' views and feelings.

Communication strengths. ESTJs generally are loyal to their country, institution, and friends. As such, they tend to be faithful mates and parents. They do not shirk their duties, even if this means sacrifice on their part.

Potential communication difficulties. ESTJs are sometimes nonresponsive to others' points of view. They jump to conclusions too quickly at times. They often are unwilling to listen patiently to opposing views, especially when they are in positions of authority.

ESFP

Percentage of population. About 14%.

General traits. ESFP types are flamboyant, fun-loving people who savor the present. They have many, many friends and will go out of their way to help them. Because they like people and physical movement, they love attending parties and participating in sports and/or exercising. They would rather work with facts than with theories. While scholastic achievement usually is not their strong suit, they provide strength and support in practical situations because of their common-sense approach. ESFPs have a low tolerance for anxiety, and try to avoid it by ignoring the unpleasant side of situations—which is not always realistic.

Communication strengths. ESFPs are smooth and charming, and radiate warmth and optimism. They are fun to be around and are probably the most generous of the types. Often they are excellent conversationalists.

Potential communication difficulties. ESFPs can be unpredictable in relationships, and this can cause tension if their partner is among the quieter types. As communication receivers, ESFPs are vulnerable to psychological seduction (sales, advertising, persuasion), even physical seduction, often giving in easily to the requests of others.

ESFJ

Percentage of population. About 13%.

General traits. ESFJ types bring harmony to almost any situation or occasion and become upset by conflict. Because of their warmheartedness, sympathy, talkativeness, and caring ways, they make everyone feel at home and comfortable. They place others' needs before their own. They are popular people, and they work well with others and make good group members because of their dedication and their ability to organize and structure situations. They are the most sociable of all the types.

Communication strengths. See the general description above.

Potential communication difficulties. ESFJs can exhibit a leaning toward pessimism, and their prognostications of gloom and doom can cause discomfort in others. One solution is to keep their fears to themselves; perhaps better would be to gain a more optimistic or realistic perspective.

ENFP

Percentage of population. About 5%.

General traits. ENFPs have warm, outgoing personalities. They are very good at dealing with people or situations because of their enthusiasm and persuasiveness. They are people-oriented, striving for understanding without criticism. Often they attribute more power and status to authority figures than is warranted. They value people being authentic, but are often dissatisfied with their own efforts at authenticity. ENFPs are ingenious, imaginative, and perceptive. But they can make serious errors in judgment because they tend to focus only on information that supports their own opinions and biases.

Communication strengths. ENFPs are warm, enthusiastic, and personable. They often are excellent at getting people together, and very good at initiating (though not always good at the detailed planning of) meetings, conferences, and get-togethers.

Potential communication difficulties. ENFPs are keen observers of others. But they tend to go beyond what is observed, and interpret others' "hidden motives"—often negatively and often inaccurately. This can introduce unnecessary interference into their relationships.

ENFJ

Percentage of population. About 5%.

General traits. ENFJ types are often leaders. Their tact and fluency make them very persuasive. They are comfortable at leading group discussions and are acutely aware of others' feelings, needs, and contributions. They are innovative and future-oriented, with strong organizational skills. They encourage camaraderie among others and are usually popular and sociable.

Communication strengths. ENFJs are adept at relating to others with empathy. They feel true concern for others' needs, feelings, and beliefs. (This sometimes becomes counterproductive when they empathize to the point of taking on others' problems as if they were their own.) They handle others with charm and concern, and given that they are comfortable either as leaders or as followers, ENFJs typically are popular and enjoyable to be around.

Potential communication difficulties. ENFJs take communication for granted, casually assuming others' understanding and agreement. Thus, they will be occasionally surprised and/or hurt that their messages were misunderstood or that their opinions were not agreed with. Though ENFJs often have a gift for oral expression, they are often weak at expressing themselves in writing.

ENTP

Percentage of population. About 5%.

General traits. ENTP types tend to have many interests and abilities and to process information quickly. Because they speak knowledgeably about many subjects and are challenged by the logic of controversy, they will argue either side of an issue just for the sake of argument. They are excellent problem solvers, but dislike doing routine tasks. Their fascination with fresh ideas may constantly lead them in new directions, but they are adept at logically explaining these changes of focus. They are noticeable because they are energetic, enthusiastic, and animated.

Communication strengths. ENTPs tend to be fascinating conversationalists.

Potential communication difficulties. Acquaintances who do not understand the ENTP's enjoyment of arguing and debating just for the fun of it may see an ENTP as too argumentative. Moreover, the ENTP's tendency to employ debate tactics to the disadvantage of conversation partners—even valued friends—can rub others the wrong way.

ENTJ

Percentage of population. About 5%.

General traits. ENTJs prefer to be leaders because they like to be in control of themselves, others, and all situations. They have great confidence, persuasiveness, and enthusiasm, and they want their opinions known on any topic being discussed. Their vision of the future usually results in long range plans that include concrete organizational plans or products. ENTJs base their opinions on impersonal data and like to see the same objectivity in others. On the other hand, they sometimes make decisions too hastily, overlooking relevant facts and others' feelings. ENTJs tend to be quite demanding of their mates.

Communication strengths. ENTJs are good at reasoning and intelligent talk, and are often effective public speakers.

Potential communication difficulties. ENTJs often need to be more careful and more patient in their communication. Often they need to stop and listen to the other person's side, especially to those not in a position to talk back.

NOTES

1. These profiles are drawn especially from R. Hellyer, C. Robinson, & P. Sherwood, *Study Skills for Learning Power* (Boston: Houghton Mifflin, 1998); and also from D. Keirsey and M. Bates, *Please Understand Me* (Del Mar, Calif., Prometheus Nemesis, 1984), and I. B. Myers, *Introduction to Type* (Gainesville, Fla. Center for Applications of Psychological Type, 1976). See the two latter sources for more complete profiles.

APpEnDIX D:
DEALING WITH PUBLIC-SPEAKING ANXIETY

One of the primary concerns of many public speakers, in both classroom and "real-world" situations, is their anxiety, or "stage fright." Sometimes two or three turns in a public-speaking course is all that is needed to reduce the anxiety to a comfortable level. Sometimes, more than that is needed.

In cases where the anxiety is especially bothersome, it usually takes more than a chapter or an appendix in a textbook to adequately solve the problem. What we wish to do in the following discussion, therefore, is to allow you to assess and understand your anxiety, and to introduce solutions you may wish to pursue elsewhere if you decide your level of anxiety warrants the effort.

HOW BAD IS YOUR ANXIETY?

Suppose your instructor were to ask, after a round of classroom speeches, "As audience members, how many speakers did you notice who seemed to be experiencing anxiety?" Chances are, you probably would think of only one or two cases. But if the question were, "As speakers, how many of you who spoke today felt more anxiety than you would like?" practically all of the speakers would raise their hand. Other speakers' anxiety is not as apparent to us as our own is. Thus, it is natural for us to think that our own anxiety is more extreme than theirs, and that ours is more extreme than normal. This may not be the case, however.

One way to gauge your relative public-speaking anxiety is via the questionnaire in Figure D.1 (on p. 382). You may wish to take ten minutes to complete and score it now.

Chances are, you didn't score as high on the anxiety scale as you thought you would. Thus, you can take comfort in knowing that your anxiety, compared to others', is not as high as you may have thought. Still, your anxiety may be higher than you would like, whether others' is more severe or not. If you scored in the Moderately Low range, your classroom instruction and experience probably will be all that is needed for you to reach a comfortable state. If you scored in the Moderate range, our brief discussion here should be at least somewhat helpful. If you scored in the Moderately High or High range, it is possible that your classroom instruction and the following discussion will be helpful, but it may be advisable for you to pursue one of the more complete therapies mentioned below.

A second way to gauge your anxiety level is to compare your anxiety experience with descriptions of others'. Virtually everyone, regardless of their anxiety level, experiences three identifiable phases of public-speaking anxiety:

1. Just before the speech is to begin, there is a perceptible increase in anxiety. This *anticipation reaction* may be manifested by increased heart rate, sweaty palms, dry mouth, and so forth.

2. When the speaker faces the audience and begins the speech, there is a much greater surge of anxiety. This *confrontation reaction* is manifested by an even higher increase in heart rate, and often by a slight disorientation.

3. As the speech continues, the anxiety begins to subside. Once this *adaptation reaction* begins, it usually continues throughout the speech. In some cases, anxiety will subside to the prespeech level.

High-anxiety and low-anxiety speakers experience these three phases differently. For high-anxiety speakers, the anticipation reaction is bothersome and distracting. It is accompanied by self-doubt about preparedness and readiness to give the speech.

DIRECTIONS: Assume that you have to give a speech within the next few weeks. For each of the statements below, indicate the degree to which the statement applies to you, within the context of giving a future speech. Mark whether you strongly agree (SA), agree (A), are undecided (U), disagree (D), or strongly disagree (SD) with each statement. Circle the SA, A, U, D, or SD choices. Do not write in the blanks next to the questions. *Work quickly; just record your first impression.*

___ 1. While preparing for the speech, I would feel uncomfortably tense and nervous.	SA_5	A_4	U_3	D_2	SD_1
___ 2. I feel uncomfortably tense at the very thought of giving a speech in the near future.	SA_5	A_4	U_3	D_2	SD_1
___ 3. My thoughts would become confused and jumbled when I was giving a speech.	SA_5	A_4	U_3	D_2	SD_1
___ 4. Right after giving the speech I would feel that I'd had a pleasant experience.	SA_1	A_2	U_3	D_4	SD_5
___ 5. I would get anxious when thinking about the speech coming up.	SA_5	A_4	U_3	D_2	SD_1
___ 6. I would have no fear of giving the speech.	SA_1	A_2	U_3	D_4	SD_5
___ 7. Although I would be nervous just before starting the speech, after starting it I would soon settle down and feel calm and comfortable.	SA_1	A_2	U_3	D_4	SD_5
___ 8. I would look forward to giving the speech.	SA_1	A_2	U_3	D_4	SD_5
___ 9. As soon as I knew that I would have to give the speech, I would feel myself getting tense.	SA_5	A_4	U_3	D_2	SD_1
___ 10. My hands would tremble when I was giving the speech.	SA_5	A_4	U_3	D_2	SD_1
___ 11. I would feel relaxed while giving the speech.	SA_1	A_2	U_3	D_4	SD_5
___ 12. I would enjoy preparing for the speech.	SA_1	A_2	U_3	D_4	SD_5
___ 13. I would be in constant fear of forgetting what I had prepared to say.	SA_5	A_4	U_3	D_2	SD_1
___ 14. I would get uncomfortably anxious if someone asked me something that I did not know about my topic.	SA_5	A_4	U_3	D_2	SD_1
___ 15. I would face the prospect of giving the speech with confidence.	SA_1	A_2	U_3	D_4	SD_5
___ 16. I would feel that I was in complete possession of myself during the speech.	SA_1	A_2	U_3	D_4	SD_5
___ 17. My mind would be clear when giving the speech.	SA_1	A_2	U_3	D_4	SD_5
___ 18. I would not dread giving the speech.	SA_1	A_2	U_3	D_4	SD_5
___ 19. I would perspire too much just before starting the speech.	SA_5	A_4	U_3	D_2	SD_1
___ 20. I would be bothered by a very fast heart rate just as I started the speech.	SA_5	A_4	U_3	D_2	SD_1
___ 21. I would experience considerable anxiety at the speech site (room, auditorium, etc.) just before my speech was to start.	SA_5	A_4	U_3	D_2	SD_1

FIGURE **D.1**

A Gauge of Public-Speaking Anxiety

"A Gauge of Public Speaking Anxiety," adapted from "Personal Report of Public Speaking Anxiety," by James C. McCroskey. Appeared in McCroskey's "Measures of Communication-Bound Anxiety," Speech Monographs, vol. 37, no. 4, p. 276. Used by permission of the National Communication Association.

Moreover, once the anxiety is detected, it may build somewhat, both physically and psychologically. For low-anxiety speakers, the anticipation reaction is noticed, but it is mild and not particularly distracting. Often it is interpreted positively as a sign of being "charged up" or psychologically "ready," rather than negatively as being unprepared. It is worthwhile to take note of whether your own anticipation reaction is closer to that of more anxious or less anxious speakers.

___	22.	Certain parts of my body would feel very tense and rigid during the speech.	SA_5	A_4	U_3	D_2	SD_1
___	23.	Realizing that only a little time remained in the speech would make me very tense and anxious.	SA_5	A_4	U_3	D_2	SD_1
___	24.	While giving the speech I would know that I could control my feelings of tension and stress.	SA_1	A_2	U_3	D_4	SD_5
___	25.	I would breathe too fast just before starting the speech.	SA_5	A_4	U_3	D_2	SD_1
___	26.	I would feel comfortable and relaxed in the hour or so just before giving the speech.	SA_1	A_2	U_3	D_4	SD_5
___	27.	I would do poorly on the speech because I would be anxious.	SA_5	A_4	U_3	D_2	SD_1
___	28.	I would feel uncomfortably anxious when first scheduling the date of the speaking engagement.	SA_5	A_4	U_3	D_2	SD_1
___	29.	If I were to make a mistake while giving the speech, I would find it hard to concentrate on the parts that followed.	SA_5	A_4	U_3	D_2	SD_1
___	30.	During the speech I would experience a feeling of helplessness building up inside me.	SA_5	A_4	U_3	D_2	SD_1
___	31.	I would have trouble falling asleep the night before the speech.	SA_5	A_4	U_3	D_2	SD_1
___	32.	My heart would beat too fast while I presented the speech.	SA_5	A_4	U_3	D_2	SD_1
___	33.	I would feel uncomfortably anxious while waiting to give my speech.	SA_5	A_4	U_3	D_2	SD_1
___	34.	While giving the speech I would get so nervous that I would forget facts I really knew.	SA_5	A_4	U_3	D_2	SD_1

___ (TOTAL)

To determine your anxiety score:

1. Fill in the blank next to each "question" with the NUMBER accompanying the response you circled. BE CAREFUL to enter the CORRECT NUMBER. NOTICE that the numbers printed with the responses are not consistent for every question.

2. Add up the numbers you recorded for the 34 questions. The sum is your anxiety score. Interpret as follows:

	INTERPRETATION
Score	**Public-Speaking Anxiety Level**
34-84	Low
85-92	Moderately Low
93-110	Moderate
111-119	Moderately High
120-170	High

FIGURE **D.1** (continued)

And you may do likewise for the confrontation and adaptation reactions. For high-anxiety speakers, the confrontation reaction is truly huge. Heart rate soars to the 130s or higher (one's normal resting heart rate typically is in the low 70s), and the speaker feels disoriented and robotic. This lasts for about sixty seconds or more before the adaptation phase begins. And once the adaptation reaction begins, it is very gradual—so much so that some high-anxiety speakers do not consciously recognize their adaptation, but believe (mistakenly) that their confrontation level of anxiety persists throughout the speech. For low-anxiety speakers, the confrontation reaction is very noticeable also. But it is not nearly as severe (with heart rates in the 110s or so), it is taken in stride and is not psychologically bothersome, there is little or no disorientation, and the anxiety surge is very short-lived, lasting about ten seconds or so. Thus the adaptation reaction begins much sooner for low-anxiety speakers. And once it begins, it is rapid, with a very comfortable level of "nonanxiety" being reached by the end of the speech introduction or sooner.

This comparison is useful not only in helping you to identify your own relative anxiety level, but also in identifying reasonable *targets* for anxiety reduction. The higher-anxiety speaker should not aspire to a total elimination of anxiety, for this is simply unreasonable. (It has been said that the only way to have zero anxiety is to not care at all about the speech or the audience. This makes for anxiety-free speeches, but also makes for very poor speeches!) Rather, the target should be to move toward the pattern of the low-anxiety speaker: nondistracting though perceptible prespeech anxiety, an unpleasant but short-lived and clear-headed confrontation reaction, followed by a very rapid and complete adaptation.

COMPONENTS OF PUBLIC-SPEAKING ANXIETY

Virtually all situational anxiety involves at least three components: (1) The *situation is assessed* in a way that triggers the autonomic nervous system, the body's natural "fight or flight" response to certain kinds of emergency, (2) the body produces *physiological manifestations* of the assessment—increased heart rate, increased respiration, and so forth—and (3) the mind provides a *psychological explanation* of the physiological symptoms, usually with an emotion label and a rationale. For example, if you were taking a walk in the woods, were about to step over a fallen log, and heard the unmistakable buzz of a rattlesnake rattle, you might (1) sense danger, (2) feel physiological reactions, and (3) interpret the reactions as *fear,* justifying the fear with a recognition that the sound is that of a rattlesnake, and that rattlesnakes can be dangerous. On the other hand, someone else—someone who hunts rattlesnakes as a hobby, for example—might perceive the rattle in a way that does not even trigger the anxiety response.

With public-speaking anxiety, the phases presumably are the same: (1) The situation is perceived in a way that triggers the autonomic nervous system, (2) physiological responses are produced and perceived, and (3) these symptoms are interpreted. Usually, the interpretation is that the symptoms represent fear. According to some theories of public-speaking anxiety, an interesting phenomenon occurs at this point. In order to *justify* fear in a public-speaking situation, there must be *consequences* of which to be fearful. So the anxious speaker begins to invent consequences—I might embarrass myself, I might make a bad grade on the speech, I might make a fool of myself, and so forth. These assessments of the situation amplify the response to the original assessment, so that now there is a snowball effect, with increased physiological response, increased "fear," and even more certainty of the potential consequences.

THERAPIES AND SOLUTIONS

There are several approaches available for reducing public-speaking anxiety. We will describe three of the most popular and effective methods, two briefly and one in more detail.

Most therapies or programs target one of the three anxiety components we discussed earlier. Of those that target the physiological dimension, the most popular and effective is a program called *systematic desensitization* (SD). This approach trains the individual in techniques for muscle relaxation, and then requires the individual to remain relaxed while imagining him- or herself in various situations related to public speaking. Typically, the program begins with an image of something fairly remote from delivering a speech. For example, the first step might be to maintain relaxation while imagining oneself in the audience of someone else's speech. Once total relaxation can be attained with this image, the process is repeated with a slightly more stressful image. After about a dozen graduated steps, the final step is to maintain physical relaxation while imagining oneself giving a speech. In rare cases, systematic desensitization for public-speaking anxiety is available through college counseling centers. Most often it must be obtained off-campus through clinical psychologists or professional counselors.

Of the therapies that target the interpretation phase of public-speaking anxiety, the most popular is *rational emotive therapy* (RET). The idea is to get the anxious speaker to realize that many of his or her "fears" are irrational. The speaker attempts to articulate what he or she is afraid of in the speaking situation, then the counselor points out logical flaws in the reasoning that links fear to the imagined consequences. As a simple example, when I (Motley) ask anxious public-speaking students to tell me what they are afraid of, sometimes the answer is, "I'm afraid of getting a bad grade." But it is easy to prove that this is *not* the reason for the anxiety: I offer to allow the speech to remain ungraded, yet their anxiety remains. (We will see why in a moment.) In effect, RET involves "disproving" one after another of the speaker's supposed reasons for fear. Like SD, RET is available primarily through professional counselors and psychologists.

THE COM APPROACH

A new and especially promising approach to reducing public-speaking anxiety is *communication orientation modification*, or COM. It is considered to be about twice as effective as SD and RET. Moreover, it does not require visiting a professional psychologist or counselor. One very effective presentation of the COM program is available in booklet form, for example.[1]

We are going to examine the COM approach in a bit more detail than the other therapies we have mentioned. At the least, the discussion will provide additional information about public-speaking anxiety. It will also provide information that you may find useful for improving your speeches, independent of anxiety. It may even help a little bit with your anxiety. By no means will we be able to present enough of the program here to achieve major anxiety reductions, however. Speakers with high- or moderately high anxiety, and some with moderate anxiety should by all means pursue a more complete program—COM or otherwise—if substantial anxiety reduction is desired.

The Performance Orientation. Whereas SD targets the second anxiety phase (physical reactions) and RET targets the final phase (fear interpretations), COM targets the initial phase—the way the situation is perceived. Just as the ordinary individual and the seasoned snake hunter will perceive the rattle-in-the-woods situation differently, it appears that higher-anxiety and lower-anxiety speakers view the public-speaking situation differently. Higher-anxiety speakers almost always assume a *performance* orientation to public speaking, whereas lower-anxiety speakers more often have a *communication* orientation. Thus, the COM approach to anxiety reduction attempts to replace the performance orientation with a communication orientation.

More specifically, most anxious speakers view speeches as *performances*. They view the speaker's task as one of satisfying an audience of "critics"—critics who are set on evaluating the speaker's *behaviors,* such as eye contact, gestures, vocal variety, and so forth. Often the speaker cannot describe exactly what constitutes "good" communication behavior in the eyes of the supposed audience-critics, but there is a vague assumption that "proper" public-speaking behaviors should be different—somehow "better"—than ordinary communication behaviors. Performance-oriented speakers imagine the secret of good speaking to be a matter of following a list of fairly specific do's and don'ts, much as in performing as part of a music concert, or a play, or a dance recital.

A useful analogy is to say that the anxious speaker tends to view the speech much as one would view Olympic competitions in diving, ice skating, or gymnastics: Individual judges score the performance by rendering personal verdicts based on how skillfully various tiny parts of the performance were executed. Minor mistakes mean lost points, major mistakes can ruin the entire effort, and even a flawless performance may not be appreciated by a biased judge. The anxious speaker tends to view his or her situation in much the same way. The objective—as with any performer about to be critiqued—is to impress the critics. And as with most performances, this translates into showing off unusual special skills.

Another parallel between performances and the perspective of most anxious speakers is that both are preoccupied with the aesthetic dimensions of the task—the "artistic impression," to use the figure skating analogy again. Rather than thinking of gestures, eye contact, transitions, examples, and so forth as serving practical, communicative functions, the speaker will assume that the purpose of these devices is to make a polished impression. Just as there is a proper way to perform a skater's double axel or a gymnast's iron cross, anxious speakers will assume (incorrectly) that there is a single best way to stand, move, gesture, and so forth during a speech. And just as musical performances require that certain notes be played in a certain order, many speakers assume (again incorrectly) that the words spoken during their speeches should be spoken as rehearsed. This makes for mechanical, artificial speeches. And it makes for anxiety-ridden speakers.

To put it another way, the performance orientation has certain anxiety-arousing associations built in: Anxiety occurs in almost *any* situation in which we know or believe we are being *evaluated,* almost any situation in which we feel we are being "placed under a microscope" or *scrutinized,* and almost any situation calling for us to follow *formal rules* or procedures with which we do not feel familiar.

The Communication Orientation. The preferred alternative to the performance perspective is a communication orientation, Here, the goals and behaviors that make for an effective speech are assumed to be much more like those of ordinary, everyday communication encounters than like public performances. This view is entirely consistent with contemporary instruction in public speaking, by the way. Thus, a communication orientation serves the double function of improving one's public speaking *and* reducing anxiety.

As a simple example of this double function, notice that true performances—plays, musical recitals, and so forth—usually present memorized material. If you have ever experienced a memory lapse during a performance, you know why having a memorized routine increases one's anxiety. Performance-oriented speakers likewise tend to assume the need for a scripted speech, and their dependence on a script increases their anxiety. As audience members, however, we don't like hearing scripted speeches. They sound artificial and phony. Thus, when a communication-oriented speaker assumes the latitude of more natural spontaneity in a speech, the approach tends both to improve the speech *and* to reduce the anxiety.

Whereas the performance orientation induces anxiety by assuming that the audience is focusing on, and evaluating, performance skills, the communication orientation emphasizes practical goals (communication objectives) and more realistic audience responses. Before seeing how this works in the public-speaking context, notice how it worked in the following example of a true performance situation:

> *A jazz combo of which I am a member recently played its debut performance. As we assembled our instruments and equipment, the dominant topic of conversation was the stage fright being experienced by most of the members. But the anxiety was almost totally and immediately eliminated by suggesting that our real goal was not to get applause, but for the audience to have fun. And the audience would probably have fun if we had fun, so we should just stop worrying and have some fun playing our music. A nice fringe benefit was that this not only eliminated the anxiety, but in turn improved our music, I think. And it is a safe assumption that whatever "mistakes" we made were easily ignored or forgiven [probably not even noticed] by the audience because they were having fun with the music.[2]*

The analogy for public-speaking situations is that the communication orientation recognizes the objective of a speech as being to achieve the primary *communicative purpose*—usually, modifying attitudes or behaviors and/or providing worthwhile information. Thus, the goal of the speaker is to have the audience *understand* his or her information and point of view.

To contrast the performance and communication orientations, I am reminded of a high school commencement speech I heard a few years ago in which the valedictorian employed spectacular oratorical flair—fancy language, dramatic shifts in pace and volume, practiced gestures, and so forth. Afterward, I asked another audience member her thoughts on what the speaker had said. Her reply was, "I really didn't *understand* what he said, but it certainly was a good speech, wasn't it?" From a performance perspective the answer might be *yes,* but from a communication orientation the answer would be *no.*

From a communication perspective, *a good speech is one that achieves its communication objectives*—period. If it does so with minimal oratorical eloquence (or, for that matter, even with considerable awkwardness), it is still a good speech. And on the other hand, if the speech does not achieve its communicative purpose(s), then it is an unsuccessful speech regardless of the "quality" of eye contact, gestures, voice, and other features.

As one more contrast between the two orientations, imagine how, ideally, one would *evaluate* a speech from the two perspectives. With a performance perspective, you would want each member of the audience to fill out a score card evaluating various behavioral dimensions of your speech. The issue would be how impressed they were with *you as a speaker.* With a communication orientation, you would want to give your audience a quiz before the speech to discover their present knowledge and/or attitudes about your topic; then, a few days after the speech, give another quiz to discover whether they understood and remembered the main points of your speech (and/or changed their attitudes and behaviors in the desired direction). The issue would be *whether the message reached them.* In other words, the criterion would be the effect of the message, not their impression of the speaker. Obviously, neither evaluation method is available for real-world speeches. But the speaker has the option of deciding which evaluative criterion to employ as a personal target in his or her speeches. And the choice affects the anxiety level.

The Communication Orientation and Reduced Anxiety. One of the reasons that a communication orientation reduces anxiety is that it makes public speaking somewhat analogous to everyday communication. While we may not have confidence in our ability to meet a checklist of performance-oriented criteria, we should be confident in our ability to achieve communication-oriented criteria, because we do so every day in our serious conversations.

There are, after all, only three differences between a speech and a turn in a serious conversation, and all are *advantageous* from a communication perspective. First, for a speech (as compared to conversation), we prepare longer—research, organize, fine-tune, etc.—before we say what we want to say. In other words, we get to *think before we speak,* which is always advantageous in communication. Second, we get to speak longer before the communication "partner" gets a turn. Communicatively, it is advantageous to have a long, uninterrupted turn in which to explicate, develop, and exemplify our points. Third, we get to share our ideas with more people than in ordinary conversation. Assuming we have a message that we believe is worthwhile to share, the speech situation provides a rare opportunity for communicative efficiency. From a *performance* point of view, all of these are negatives. More time to prepare is interpreted as leading to a greater expectation of "perfection;" the longer the speaking turn, the more opportunity there is for "mistakes;" and the larger the audience, the more instances of evaluative scrutiny. But from a communication perspective, these public-speaking features are welcomed, for they increase the likelihood of effective and efficient communication.

Just as importantly, the communication orientation finds analogies to conversation in terms of the communicative *behaviors* appropriate to public speaking. For example, the COM approach emphasizes that the delivery behaviors of public speaking should be very much the same as those of one's natural conversation style—the same way of gesturing, the same vocal inflections, the same nonscripted word-choice spontaneity (from very brief notes rather than a script), the same eye contact (with minor modifications for public speaking), and so forth. A *natural, conversational* delivery style is preferred. Thus, the communication-oriented speaker can have confidence that he or she already knows how to deliver a speech, since it should be delivered in the same way as the conversation he or she delivers every day.

The COM Program. For most high-anxiety speakers, it is easy to accept the *logic* suggesting that the performance orientation should be more anxiety-ridden than the communication orientation. To actually abandon the performance orientation and replace it with a communication perspective is difficult for many high-anxiety speakers, however, because the performance orientation has been deeply ingrained. The COM program employs several stages and components to help the high-anxiety speaker to make the orientation shift.

We will mention a few of these components very briefly here—not to substitute for the more complete COM program (which is about ninety pages or so), but to provide food for thought to all public speakers and to preview the COM program for those who may wish to pursue it.

For example, when trying to abandon the performance orientation, it is worthwhile to consider its *origins*. Most likely, one of the origins is found in our early classroom experiences with speeches, which—unlike real-world speeches—really *were* much more a performance event than a communication event for most of us. Reciting the Gettysburg Address, the Preamble to the Constitution, and so forth for a group of classmates is hardly a communication effort, since the message is not the speaker's own, the audience (at least the teacher, if not the whole class) has already heard it, and so forth. The same is true of grade-school book reports, when we know darn well that the audience of classmates couldn't care less, when we assume that the only purpose is to prove to the teacher that we actually read the book, when we get critiqued by the teacher for things like not talking loudly enough, and when we get critiqued by classmates who counted the number of times we said "uh." The COM program emphasizes these and other early experiences in the context of explaining the source of the performance orientation. But even for nonanxious speakers, the artificiality of one's early "public-speaking" experiences is interesting to reflect upon and to contrast with more realistic public-speaking situations.

It is valuable also to consider one's own *mental processes as an audience member* for others' real-world (nonclassroom) speeches. How much of what the performance orientation assumes about audiences, and how much of what the communication orientation assumes, is true of *you* when you sit in the audience for someone else's speech? Do you keep a running mental tally of the speaker's mistakes, are you scrutinizing the speaker's every move, are you demanding oratorical eloquence, are you daring the speaker to prove that he or she can give a flawless performance, and so forth? Or, are you listening for what the speaker has to say, hoping that it will be worthwhile? The COM program "proves" that the assumptions of the communication orientation are more valid than those of the performance orientation by asking us to reflect upon our own experience as real-world audience members. Within the context of reducing anxiety, this serves to show that audiences are communication-oriented, and are, for all practical purposes, oblivious to "mistakes" when communication objectives are being met. Independent of anxiety reduction, however, it can be useful for almost any speaker to reflect upon his or her own experiences as an audience member for others' speeches.

Along similar lines, it is worthwhile to reflect on one's preferences as an audience member for speakers' *delivery styles*. Most audience members prefer natural, or *direct*, speakers—those who seem to be talking with us as they would in conversation, rather than orating at us in a more impersonal or formal mode. The COM program develops this notion for a wide range of delivery behaviors to drive home the point that public speakers *already have* the necessary repertoire of delivery tools, and that their experience as everyday interpersonal communicators is proof of this. For all speakers, in fact, regardless of their anxiety level, the admonition to "be natural" is worth remembering.

It is useful also to examine the anxious speaker's specific *fears* in detail, and to see how they are countered from a communication perspective. For some of these fears, you can probably guess the communication-orientation rebuttal from the discussion thus far. For example, "I'm afraid because public speaking is an unfamiliar situation" is countered by pointing out that, upon close inspection, hardly anything about public speaking delivery is different from everyday conversation, so that public speaking is not such a foreign situation after all. Or, "I'm afraid the audience will ridicule me if I make a mistake" is countered with evidence that audiences hardly notice, much less ridicule, mistakes, that audiences actually do not like flawless oratory, that professional speakers plant fake "mistakes" to make themselves appear more human, and so forth. The COM program works through nine of the most common fears of high-anxiety speakers in detail to show how the fears are unfounded.

REDUCTION OF PUBLIC-SPEAKING ANXIETY—A FINAL WORD

Almost any brief discussion of anxiety reduction warrants the familiar admonition that "a little knowledge can be a dangerous thing." It has not necessarily been the purpose of this discussion to achieve a reduction of your public-speaking anxiety. If, by chance, the discussion has generated a reaction of, "Wow, I never thought of it that way," and your anxiety has subsided somewhat as a result, then we are pleased, of course. But typically, reputable efforts to reduce public-speaking anxiety are much more involved than this discussion can be.

Thus, the danger of a brief discussion is that it can discourage high-anxiety speakers from seeking a more complete program that could indeed be helpful. For example, some people will hear a brief description of systematic desensitization or rational emotive therapy, decide to try it themselves without professional intervention, be unsuccessful (since the program was not administered properly), and conclude (incorrectly) that their anxiety cannot be treated. Or, you might read what we have said about the COM approach, notice that your anxiety is still present, and conclude (incorrectly) that the more complete program is no different and that public-speaking anxiety is something you will just have to live with.

It is important to recognize that anxiety usually cannot be reduced substantially through brief discussions. But it is also important to recognize that it *can* be reduced substantially through more complete programs. If your own anxiety is at a level that you find uncomfortable, take heart from the knowledge that various programs are available: SD or RET through professional counselors, COM through the book referenced here,[3] and maybe others that your campus counseling center or communication instructor would advise.

NOTES

1. From *Overcoming Your Fear of Public Speaking: A Proven Method* by Michael T. Motley, (Boston: Houghton Mifflin, 1997).

2. Ibid., p. 12.

3. Ibid.

APPENDIX E:
SAMPLE SPEECHES

Sample Informative SPEECHES

THE "MONUMENT" AT WOUNDED KNEE
CECILE LARSON

We Americans are big on monuments. We build monuments in memory of our heroes. Washington, Jefferson, and Lincoln live on in our nation's capital. We erect monuments to honor our martyrs. The Minute Man still stands guard at Concord. The flag is ever raised over Iwo Jima. Sometimes we even construct monuments to commemorate victims. In Ashburn Park downtown there is a monument to those who died in the yellow fever epidemics. However, there are some things in our history that we don't memorialize. Perhaps we would just as soon forget what happened. Last summer I visited such a place—the massacre site at Wounded Knee.

In case you have forgotten what happened at Wounded Knee, let me refresh your memory. On December 29, 1890, shortly after Sitting Bull had been murdered by the authorities, about 400 half-frozen, starving, and frightened Indians who had fled the nearby reservation were attacked by the Seventh Cavalry. When the fighting ended, between 200 and 300 Sioux had died—two-thirds of them women and children. Their remains are buried in a common grave at the site of the massacre.

Wounded Knee is located in the Pine Ridge Reservation in southwestern South Dakota—about a three-hour drive from where Presidents Washington, Jefferson, Theodore Roosevelt, and Lincoln are enshrined in the granite face of Mount Rushmore. The reservation is directly south of the Badlands National Park, a magnificently desolate area of wind-eroded buttes and multicolored spires.

We entered the reservation driving south from the Badlands Visitor's Center. The landscape of the Pine Ridge Reservation retains much of the desolation of the Badlands but lacks its magnificence. Flat, sun-baked fields and an occasional eroded gully stretch as far as the eye can see. There are no signs or highway markers to lead the curious tourist to Wounded Knee. Even the *Rand-McNally Atlas* doesn't help you find your way. We got lost three times and had to stop and ask directions.

When we finally arrived at Wounded Knee, there was no official historic marker to tell us what had happened there. Instead, there was a large, handmade wooden sign—crudely lettered in white on black. The sign first directed our attention to our left—to the gully where the massacre took place. The mass grave site was to our right—across the road and up a small hill.

Two red-brick columns topped with a wrought-iron arch and a small metal cross form the entrance to the grave site. The column to the right is in bad shape: Cinder blocks from the base are missing; the brickwork near the top has deteriorated and tumbled to the ground; graffiti on the columns proclaim an attitude we found repeatedly expressed about the Bureau of Indian Affairs—"The BIA sucks!"

Crumbling concrete steps lead you to the mass grave. The top of the grave is covered with gravel, punctuated by unruly patches of chickweed and crabgrass. These same weeds also grow along the base of the broken chain-link fence that surrounds the grave, the "monument," and a small cemetery.

The "monument" itself rests on a concrete slab to the right of the grave. It's a typical, large, old-fashioned granite cemetery marker, a pillar about six feet high topped with an urn—the kind of gravestone you might see in any cemetery with graves from the turn of the century. The inscription tells us that it was erected by the families of those who were killed at Wounded Knee. Weeds grow through the cracks in the concrete at its base.

There are no granite headstones in the adjacent cemetery, only simple white wooden crosses that tell a story of people who died young. There is no neatly manicured grass. There are no flowers. Only the unrelenting and unforgiving weeds.

Yes, Americans are big on monuments. We build them to memorialize our heroes, to honor our martyrs, and sometimes, even to commemorate victims. But only when it makes us feel good.

THE TROUBLE WITH NUMBERS[1]
STEPHEN LEE

Name, Bill Smith. Address, 103 Main Street, Smalltown, USA. Height, 5'11"; weight, 185 pounds. Who is this person? Why, he's the average American. Bill makes a comfortable $32,000 each year. His car gets 18.9 miles to the gallon. He reads 4.2 novels every year, each with 482.73 pages. He receives 9.7 gifts every Christmas, and he brushes his teeth 1.9 times every day. The average American.

Today it seems we hear a lot of this person. Someone who is supposedly like all of us and yet not like any of us. After all, how many men do you know with 2.7 children? No, Bill is by no means real. His composition is not one of flesh and blood. Instead Bill is the product of cold and heartless data. Born of a national almanac, Bill is nothing more than a statistic.

But the characteristics of Bill Smith and the way we interpret them are highly reflective of our society's misuse, abuse, and general overuse of statistics. As Darrell Huff tells us in his essay *How to Lie with Statistics,* "Americans use statistics like drunks use lamp posts, for support instead of illumination." He was referring to the unfailing dependence that we Americans put on statistics. He continues: "We prefer to record and measure ourselves with numbers and what we can't measure we assume not to exist at all." But what are these mystic symbols and figures? And more importantly, how do they affect us? Humorist Artemus Ward once said, "It ain't so much what we know that gets us in trouble. It's the things we know that ain't so."

Now such was the case in the government. Our government is faulted for many problems. Statistical misuse is perhaps one of the greatest. This was clearly demonstrated in March of 1983, when the computation of the unemployment rate was changed to encompass military personnel. Now this had a significant impact, as the number changed from 10.6 percent to 10.1 percent. Some people said this was a political ploy of President Reagan, trying to make himself look good in the public spectrum, while others claimed this was a highly justified move, since, after all, military personnel were employed. But I think there is a more important question that needs to be answered. Look at what happened to the number. It changed. Look at what happened to the way the number was computed. It changed, too. But what happened to the very real problem of civilian unemployment, which we all assumed this number to represent? It had not changed at all. It all goes back to what Lester T. Thurow said in his basic theory of economics, "A difference is only a difference if it truly makes a difference." Many times a difference in a number does not represent a difference in the real world. This was the case in the late 1970s when housing was taken out of the consumer price index. Now as contradictory as it might sound, while inflation continued to skyrocket, the inflation rate actually stagnated.

In our society we even misuse something as simple as a baseball statistic, denoting one player as good, batting .350, while another one is bad, batting .150. But what do these figures tell us about his moral character, his interaction with other players, his leadership abilities—any of which any coach will tell you is necessary for the well-rounded player? While numbers may be convincing, so much of what they imply, as Ward said, simply "ain't so." Perhaps we can all relate to standardized tests, where the quality of one's education is measured by the quantity of correct circles on a piece of paper. You may not be aware of how misleading statistics are on the university level, but look closer when a university advertises that 95 percent of its needy students receive financial aid. It sounds good, but the truth behind this claim is the fact that the university is the one who determines who is needy, and thereby allocates aid accordingly.

Perhaps the greatest inadequacy surrounding statistics lies not in what is wrong with these numbers, but instead with the way we use them. Numbers are only numbers. Many times we forget this. We forget that there are very real humans and very real human conditions behind these statistics. And yes, we are all affected by them. The only solution to our statistical dilemma is to better understand what a statistic is and what a statistic is not. We need to more adequately comprehend what a statistic can do, but what a number cannot do.

So when you go home today, read your paper. Eat your meal, watch TV. You don't have to go looking for statistics. They're all around us. But this time be aware of them. Train yourself not to passively sit by as seemingly innocent numbers are flashed before your eyes. Learn to question what hides behind those numbers. I think it's interesting, and indeed fascinating, that statistics have come to dominate our decision making in America today. But don't get me wrong. I am not saying that statistics are bad, but that statistics can be misleading. And without careful management they can do more harm than good. Carl Tucker summed it up best in his book, *The Data Game*. He wrote: "Statistics and lists are obviously useful tools. They, in their own way, can tell us what happened, but never why that mattered." And in the end that is the only question worth answering. So as you leave, remember: three-fourths of the people always comprise 75 percent of the population.

Sample Persuasive SPEECHES

WE DON'T HAVE TO LIVE IN SLUMS[2]
ANNA ALEY

Slumlords—you'd expect them in New York or Chicago, but in Manhattan, Kansas? You'd better believe there are slumlords in Manhattan, and they pose a direct threat to you if you ever plan to rent an off-campus apartment.

I know about slumlords; I rented a basement apartment from one last semester. I guess I first suspected something was wrong when I discovered dead roaches in the refrigerator. I definitely knew something was wrong when I discovered the leaks: The one in the bathroom that kept the bathroom carpet constantly soggy and molding and the one in the kitchen that allowed water from the upstairs neighbor's bathroom to seep into the kitchen cabinets and collect in my dishes.

Then there were the serious problems. The hot water heater and furnace were connected improperly and posed a fire hazard. They were situated next to the only exit. There was no smoke detector or fire extinguisher and no emergency way out—the windows were too small for escape. I was living in an accident waiting to happen—and paying for it.

The worst thing about my ordeal was that I was not an isolated instance; many Kansas State students are living in unsafe housing and paying for it, not only with their money, but their happiness, their grades, their health, and their safety.

We can't be sure how many students are living in substandard housing—housing that does not meet the code specifications required of rental property. We can be sure, however, that a large number of Kansas State students are at risk of being caught in the same situation I was. According to the registrar, approximately 17,800 students are attending Kansas State this semester. Housing claims that 4,200 live in the dorms. This means that approximately 13,600 students live off-campus. Some live in fraternities or sororities, some live at home, but most live in off-campus apartments, as I do.

Many of these 13,600 students share traits that make them likely to settle for substandard housing. For example, many students want to live close to campus. If you've ever driven through the surrounding neighborhoods, you know that much of the available housing is in older houses, houses that were never meant to be divided into separate rental units. Students are also often limited in the amount they can pay for rent; some landlords, such as mine, will use low rent as an excuse not to fix anything and to let the apartment deteriorate. Most importantly, many students are young and, consequently, naive when it comes to selecting an apartment. They don't know the housing codes; but even if they did, they don't know how to check to make sure the apartment is in compliance. Let's face it—how many of us know how to check a hot water heater to make sure it's connected properly?

Adding to the problem of the number of students willing to settle for substandard housing is the number of landlords willing to supply it. Currently, the Consumer Relations Board here at Kansas State has on file student complaints against approximately one hundred landlords. There are surely complaints against many more that have never been formally reported.

There are two main causes of the substandard student housing problem. The first—and most significant—is the simple fact that it is possible for a landlord to lease an apartment that does not meet housing code requirements. The Manhattan Housing Code Inspector will evaluate an apartment, but only after the tenant has given the landlord a written complaint and the landlord has had fourteen days to remedy the situation. In other words, the way things are now, the only way the Housing Code Inspector can evaluate an apartment to see if it's safe to be lived in is if someone has been living in it for at least two weeks!

A second cause of the problem is the fact that campus services designed to help students avoid substandard housing are not well known. The Consumer Relations Board here at Kansas State can help students inspect apartments for safety before they sign a lease, it can provide students with vital information on their rights as tenants, and it can mediate in landlord-tenant disputes. The problem is, many people don't know these services exist. The Consumer Relations Board is not listed in the university catalogue; it is not mentioned in any of the admissions literature. The only places it is mentioned are in alphabetically organized references such as the phone book, but you have to already know it exists to look it up! The Consumer Relations Board does receive money for advertising from the student senate, but it is only enough to run a little two-by-three-inch ad once every month. That is not large enough or frequent enough to be noticed by many who could use these services.

It's clear that we have a problem, but what may not seem so clear is what we can do about it. After all, what can one student do to change the practices of numerous Manhattan landlords? Nothing, if that student is alone. But just think of what we could accomplish if we got all 13,600 off-campus students involved in this issue! Think what we could accomplish if we got even a fraction of those students involved! This is what Wade Whitmer, director of the Consumer Relations Board, is attempting to do. He is reorganizing the Off-Campus Association in an effort to pass a city ordinance requiring landlords to have their apartments inspected for safety before those apartments can be rented out. The Manhattan code inspector has already tried to get just such an ordinance passed, but the only people who showed up at the public forums were known slumlords, who obviously weren't in favor of the proposed ordinance. No one showed up to argue in favor of the ordinance, so the city commissioners figured that no one wanted it and voted it down. If we can get the Off-Campus Association organized and involved, however, the commissioners will see that someone does want the ordinance, and they will be more likely to pass it the next time it is proposed. You can do a great service to your fellow students—and to yourself—by joining the Off-Campus Association.

A second thing you can do to help ensure that no more Kansas State students have to go through what I did is sign my petition asking the student senate to increase the Consumer Relations Board's advertising budget. Let's face it—a service cannot do anybody any good if no one knows about it. Consumer Relations Board's services are simply too valuable to let go to waste.

An important thing to remember about substandard housing is that it is not only distasteful, it is dangerous. In the end, I was lucky. I got out of my apartment with little more than bad memories. My upstairs neighbor was not so lucky. The main problem with his apartment was that the electrical wiring was done improperly; there were too many outlets for too few circuits, so the fuses were always blowing. One day last November, Jack was at home when a fuse blew—as usual. And, as usual, he went to the fuse box to flip the switch back on. When he touched the switch, it delivered such a shock that it literally threw this guy the size of a football player backwards and down a flight of stairs. He lay there at the bottom, unable to move, for a full hour before his roommate came home and called an ambulance.

Jack was lucky. His back was not broken. But he did rip many of the muscles in his back. Now he has to go to physical therapy, and he is not expected to fully recover.

Kansas State students have been putting up with substandard living conditions for too long. It's time we finally got together to do something about this problem. Join the Off-Campus Association. Sign my petition. Let's send a message to these slumlords that we're not going to put up with this any more. We don't have to live in slums!

SECONDHAND SMOKE[3]
GINA NORMAN

Have you ever breathed smoke from someone else's cigarette? Have you ever sat beside someone or behind someone, they light up a cigarette, they take one puff, and then they're either holding it out to the side or they set it in an ashtray? In my case I feel that I usually end up smoking more of that cigarette than the actual smoker does. As an involuntary smoker, a nonsmoker breathing smoke from others, you are at an increased risk for several diseases. According to former U.S. Surgeon General C. Everett Koop, it is now clear that disease risk due to the inhalation of tobacco smoke is not limited to the individual smoking. According to the American Cancer Society and our own *Fitness and Wellness* book here at Memphis State, undiluted sidestream smoke has higher concentrations of the toxic and carcinogenic compounds than are found in mainstream smoke.

For the reason of smokers not being able to control the excess smoke from their cigarettes, cigars, and pipes, I believe smoking should be banned in public places. I'd like to share with you today the reasons for my statement, which include personal experiences and some statistics that I've obtained. My first personal experience was when I was little. I suffered from chronic upper respiratory infections, inner ear infections, and colds. I was in and out of the doctor's office all the time. My father smoked two packs of cigarettes a day. When I moved out, when I got older, I didn't have this problem, although I didn't connect it to cigarette smoking at that time. My other personal experience is where I work. As of last year, our office became nonsmoking. The two years previous that I worked there it was a smoking office. Every month it seemed I was going to the doctor for upper respiratory or inner ear infections. Finally they referred me to an allergist. And the allergist, Dr. Philip Lieberman here in Memphis, said I was allergic to smoke. I told him that out office is huge and I sat on the far, far end in the nonsmoking section. He said that didn't matter. In an enclosed area, the air you're breathing is just recirculated. It's the same air that everybody breathes. The air conditioner heating ducts take the air in and then another duct pulls the air back out. So even though you may not be smelling the smoke, you're still breathing the compounds from it.

Our office, as I said, went nonsmoking January of '92. I think I've been maybe twice to the doctor for upper respiratory infections, so it's dropped significantly since our office became nonsmoking. These are just my personal experiences of how smoking aggravates my upper respiratory system, my inner ear, and my sinuses.

Now I'd like to share with you some statistics that I've obtained. According to the American Heart Association, environmental tobacco smoke, ETS, causes an estimated 53,000 deaths annually in the United States—two-thirds from heart disease and 4,000 from lung disease. The *Journal of the American Medical Association* concluded this January that heart disease is an important consequence to the exposure of environmental tobacco smoke. According again to the *Fitness and Wellness* book here at Memphis State, passive smoke aggravates and may precipitate angina. That's chest pain that is a result of diminished supply of blood to the heart. And it also states that secondhand smoke induces small airway dysfunctions in adults. According to the *American Journal of Public Health,* infants born to women who smoke during pregnancy are more likely to die from sudden infant death syndrome. The American Academy of Pediatrics estimates that nine million American children under the age of five may be exposed to environmental tobacco smoke. The American Cancer Society states that children exposed to secondhand smoke have increased risk of respiratory illnesses and infections, impaired development of lung function, and middle ear infections—which is exactly what I had when I was growing up. This is from *Cancer Facts and Figures* 1992. The Environmental Science Advisory Board, in reviewing evidence that environmental tobacco smoke causes excess lung cancer in adults and respiratory illnesses in children, has recommended that environmental tobacco smoke be classified as a Class A, which is a known human carcinogen.

Now this is taken from *Newsweek* 1992 [she refers to chart]. *Newsweek* got this from the Environmental Protection Agency. It's a draft they put out about the dangers of secondhand smoke. The Environmental Protection Agency is saying that secondhand smoke causes 3,000 lung cancer deaths a year; 35,000 heart disease deaths a year; contributes to 150,000 to 300,000 respiratory infections in babies, mainly bronchitis and pneumonia, resulting in 7,500 to 15,000 hospitalizations. It triggers 8,000 to 26,000 new cases of asthma in previously unaffected children and exacerbates symptoms in 400,000 to 1 million asthmatic children. In a study done by the *Journal of the American Medical Association* earlier this year, out of 663 nonsmokers who either lived with smokers or worked in a smoking environment, 91 percent had metabolic byproducts of nicotine in the urine, including 162 who reported no exposure to environmental tobacco smoke for four days.

Now I know that this sounds like I have no empathy for the smoker, but I do. Someone I am very close to smokes, my husband. He's tried to quit for me, but he's had a lot of problems. He has a lot of physical withdrawal with quitting smoking. The bottom line, too, is he likes it. He likes to smoke. It helps him to concentrate when he's working, it helps him relax, and it's social. A lot of his friends smoke, and when they get together for a game, they like to smoke. I respect his choice for smoking. I respect anybody who smokes; I respect their choice; they have that choice to smoke. However, it's not my choice. And when a smoker smokes in an enclosed area, that smoker takes away the choice for a nonsmoker. I feel that banning smoking in all public places is necessary to protect the health of people who do not smoke.

In closing I'd like to quote Julia Carol—she's with the Americans for Nonsmokers' Rights—when she was quoted in *Newsweek,* June 1992, that separate seating was a nice thought. But sitting in the nonsmoking section of a building is like swimming in the nonchlorinated section of a pool. The difference of course is that a little chlorine won't kill you. Other people's smoke may.

NOTES   1.   Reprinted by permission.

2.   Reprinted by permission.

3.   Reprinted by permission.

PHoTo CrEDITS

PART OPENERS **p. 1**, Mark Richards/PhotoEdit; **p. 87**, Myrleen Cate/Photo Network; **p. 175**, Chip Henderson, Tony Stone Images.

CHAPTER 1 **p. 3**, David Young-Wolff/PhotoEdit; **p. 4**, Siteman/Monkmeyer; **p. 14**, THE FAR SIDE © FARWORKS, Inc. Used by permission. All rights reserved.

CHAPTER 2 **p. 23**, THE FAR SIDE © FARWORKS, Inc. Used by permission. All rights reserved; **p. 27**, G. Brad Lewis/Tony Stone Images; **p. 27**, Peter Simon/Stock Boston.

CHAPTER 3 **p. 52**, R. Lord/The Image Works; **p. 56**, AP/Wide World; **p. 59**, Bill Gallery/Stock Boston.

CHAPTER 4 **p. 72**, Miro Vintoniv/Stock Boston; **p. 75**, AP/CNN, Greg Sailor/Wide World Photos; **p. 79**, Bob Daemmrich/Stock Boston.

CHAPTER 5 **p. 93**, © Copyright Paramount Pictures/Photofest; p. 94, Das/Monkmeyer Press; **p. 94**, Ben Osborne/Tony Stone Images.

CHAPTER 6 **p. 114**, THE FAR SIDE © FARWORKS, Inc. Used by permission. All rights reserved.

CHAPTER 7 **p. 134**, Gale Zucker/Stock Boston; **p. 134**, David Oliver/Tony Stone Images; **p. 142**, Paul Elledge/Outline.

CHAPTER 8 **p. 158**, Bachmann/The Image Works; **p. 160**, Tom McCarthy/PhotoEdit; **p. 165**, Rhoda Sidney/Stock Boston.

CHAPTER 9 **p. 180**, Moyer/Gamma-Liaison; **p. 186**, Novovitch/Gamma-Liaison.

CHAPTER 10 **p. 202**, Tom Campbell/Photo Network; **p. 211**, David Young-Wolff/PhotoEdit; **p. 216**, Ullmann/Monkmeyer Press.

CHAPTER 11 **p. 227**, Vince Streano/The Image Works; **p. 229**, Michael Newman/PhotoEdit; **p. 241**, Jim Commentucci/The Image Works.

CHAPTER 12 **p. 257**, © Copyright Stratford Studios; **p. 259**, Bob Daemmrich/Stock Boston; **p. 263**, Photofest.

CHAPTER 13 **p. 282**, Halstead/Liaison; **p. 284**, Gary Walts/The Image Works; **p. 291**, Dick Blume/The Image Works.

CHAPTER 14 **p. 305**, Kealy/Liaison; **p. 309**, Bob Daemmrich/The Image Works.

CHAPTER 15 **p. 324**, Bob Daemmrich/The Image Works; **p. 328**, Stephen Jaffe/The Image Works; **p. 335**, Bob Daemmrich/The Image Works.

INdEx

Absent dating, 29, 46
Absent indexing, 29, 46
Academics
    group projects, *see* Small group
        communication
    listening skills and, 73, 83
Accent gestures, 56, 68
Acoustics of speech location, 202
Action, speeches urging, 335, 341, 342
Active verbs, 316
Adams, Brock, 258, 273n
Adaptation, contextual, 15
Adapted informative designs, 336
Adaptors, 56–57, 68
Addington, D.W., 69n
Ad hominem, 333, 342
Adler, Ronald B., 84n
Adorno, T.W., 196n
Advance preparation for impromptu speaking,
    280
Advertising
    celebrity endorsements, 229–230
    effective listening and, 73–74, 83
    motivational appeals in, 207
    persuasive discourse in, 182–183
    political campaigns and, 191
Affect display, 53, 68
After-dinner speeches, 183
After-meal speeches, 201
Age, and audience demographics, 204, 221
Agenda for meeting, 168
Agenda-setting function, 301–302, 314
Aggressiveness, 149, 154
Aghazarian, Aram A., 195n, 342n
Agreement
    areas of, 322
    in persuasive speaking, 321, 340–341,
        342
AIDS epidemic, effect of public communication,
    185–188
Aiken, Milam, 173n
Ailes, Roger, 247n, 296n
Aley, Anna, 342n
Allen, M. George, 247n
Allen, Mike, 343n
Almanacs, library resources for, 351
Altruistic mode, 92, 104
Ambiguity, 32–34, 46
    context and, 34
*American Heritage Dictionary of the English
    Language, The,* 46n
American Psychological Association, 273n
Analogical reasoning, 332–333, 341, 342,
    346
Analogy, 235–236, 246
    in informative speaking, 316

Analysis
    of audience, 203–209, 221, 367–368
    goals and subgoals, 15–16
    self-analysis, *see* Self-analysis
    of speaking situation, 200–203, 221
    topic analysis, 212–213, 221
Andersen, P.A., 19n, 69n
Anderson, N.H., 273n, 342n
Andrews, Patricia Hayes, 172n
Anecdotes, humorous, 259–260
Anger, control of, 99
Ansolabehere, Stephen, 197n
Anticipation of conflict situations, 142
Anxiety
    body position and, 57
    public speaking, *see* Public speaking anxiety
    situational communication anxiety, 101–102,
        104
Appeals, in persuasive speaking, 329–331,
    342
Appearance, *see* Physical appearance
Application, 304
Appreciative listening, 72, 83, 84
Appropriateness of language, 279
Arbitrariness of symbols, 46
Arguments
    counterarguments, 347
    inductive argument, 345
    opposing arguments, 325
    in persuasive speaking, 321, 325, 327, 342
    speeches of contention and, 335–336
Argyle, M., 69n
Aristotle, 181, 193, 194n
Arnold, Carroll C., 296n
Aronson, E., 222n
Aronson, Elliot, 342n
Arrangement, 181, 193
Artful repetition, 277–278, 296
Art galleries, Internet resources for, 354
Articulation, 289, 296
Artifacts, 64, 68
Arts of rhetoric, 181
Ashe, Arthur, 186
Ashworth, B.E., 85n
Assertiveness, 148–149, 154
    tact and, 153
Assimilation, 78, 84
Assistance, to friends, 108–109
Assumptions
    about conflict, 139–140
    closure, 36–37
    communicative intention of nonverbal
        behavior, 50
    of context, 34–35
    prediction, 37–38
Atlases, library resources for, 352

Attention
    capturing, 256–260
    sustaining, 302–303
Attention span, and effective listening, 79–80,
    83
Attitude(s), 206, 222
    of audience, 206
    effective listening and, 78–79
    in effective presentation, 275
    persuasive speaking and, 320, 334–335
Attitude questionnaire, 210 (fig.)
Attraction-criticism reversals, 121, 122 (fig.),
    129
Attractiveness of communicator, 206
Attribution theory, 92, 104
Atwan, Robert, 223n
Audience
    analysis of, 203, 221, 367–368
    boredom of, 283–284
    capturing attention of, 256–260
    complimenting, 257
    education of, 205, 221
    expectations of, 202
    gathering information about, 208–209
    group affiliations, 205, 221
    hostile questions from, 285, 295
    humor and, 259
    identification with speaker, 257, 261
    influence of speaker on, 275
    introduction, and, 256
    involvement of, 257, 263–264
    offending, 261
    primary audience, 203, 222
    in public communication, 178
    questions from, 284–285, 295
    receptive mood of, 259
    relating to lives of, 257–258
    relevance to, 302
    reluctant, 322–323
    size of, 202, 221
    sociocultural background of, 205, 221
    startling of, 260–261
    sustaining attention of, 302–303
    text read to, 281–283
    voluntary, 202
    see also Receiver
Audience demographics, 203–205, 221, 222
Audience dynamics, 205–207, 221, 222
Audience perceptions, 301
Auer, J. Jeffery, 85n
Authenticity, 236, 238
Authorities, 302
Autocratic leader, 165, 171
Awareness, in persuasive speaking, 321, 340, 342
Awkwardness, deception as remedy for, 145
Ayers, Joe, 298n

401